BUSINESS ETHICS

Ethical Decision Making and Cases

8TH EDITION

BUSINESS ETHICS

Ethical Decision Making and Cases

8TH EDITION

O. C. Ferrell
University of New Mexico

John Fraedrich
Southern Illinois University—Carbondale

Linda Ferrell
University of New Mexico

Australia • Brazil • Japan • Korea • Mexico • Singapore • Spain • United Kingdom • United States

Business Ethics: Ethical Decision Making & Cases, 8th Edition

O.C. Ferrell, John Fraedrich and Linda Ferrell

Vice President of Editorial, Business: Jack W. Calhoun

Acquisitions Editor: Michele Rhoades

Sr. Developmental Editor: Joanne Dauksewicz

Marketing Manager: Nathan Anderson

Marketing Communications Manager: Jim Overly

Content Project Manager: Corey Geissler

Media Editor: Rob Ellington

Sr. Manufacturing Coordinator: Kevin Kluck

Production Service: Integra

Sr. Art Director: Tippy McIntosh

Permission Editor Text: Mardell Glinski Schultz

Permission Editor Images: Deanna Ettinger

Internal Designer: Craig Ramsdell, Ramsdell Design

Cover Designer: Craig Ramsdell, Ramsdell Design

Cover Image: Daryl Benson, Photodisc/Getty Images

Library of Congress Control Number: 2009939854

ISBN-13: 978-1-4390-4223-6

ISBN-10: 1-4390-4223-3

South-Western Cengage Learning
5191 Natorp Boulevard
Mason, OH 45040
USA

Cengage Learning products are represented in Canada by Nelson Education, Ltd.

Printed in the United States of America
2 3 4 5 13 12 11 10

To Anita and Robert Chandler.

— O.C. Ferrell

To Brett Pierce Nafziger.

— Linda Ferrell

To my parents, Bernice and Gerhard and my grandchildren Emma, Matthew, and Hyrum.

— John Fraedrich

BRIEF CONTENTS

Daryl Benson

PREFACE

Twenty years ago, the first edition of *Business Ethics: Ethical Decision Making and Cases* became the first textbook to use a managerial framework to teach business ethics. The Eighth Edition builds on this record of success and provides an enhanced teaching package to help teach the fastest-growing business course in the last two decades. In all higher education institutions there are three times as many courses in business ethics than there were in 1990. This dramatic increase has occurred as a result of stakeholder concerns about ethical conduct and public policy to encourage corporate ethics programs. No longer is ethics considered merely an independent personal decision; rather, managers are held responsible both within and outside their company for building an ethical organizational culture. As the market leader with over 550 institutions using our book, we are working to keep you, the instructor, up to date on the ever-changing issues and research within business ethics.

The Eighth Edition continues to change the way business ethics is taught and reflects the issues, challenges, and opportunities students will face in managing ethics in any organization. While we base each chapter on ethical frameworks and research from the academic community, we also include knowledge and best practices from business and public policy decisions from governments and international entities. This real-world approach to business ethics helps prepare students to face ethical challenges in business, and develop an ability to make ethical decisions in our global economy.

The past decade has seen the demise of many corporations, and some industries, that failed to appropriately incorporate ethics into their decision making processes. In the first few years of the twenty-first century, we saw the failure of Enron, Worldcom, and many other firms that engaged in deception, fraud, and misconduct. The focus was on excessive risk-taking. Public policy in the form of the Sarbanes-Oxley Act and Federal Sentencing Guidelines for Organizations (FSGO) amendments was developed to prevent future misconduct. Only five years after these events, the financial industry pushed the global economy into the deepest recession in 80 years. It was discovered that excessive risk-taking, misconduct, and the failure to address stakeholders' interests were again to blame. These factors contributed to the downfall of many financial institutions, including Lehman Brothers, Bears Stearns, Countrywide Financial, Merrill Lynch, and Washington Mutual. Without a government rescue, many large banks would have failed. All these events increased regulations and laws encouraging organizations to develop programs that improve ethical conduct and prevent misconduct.

Using a managerial framework, we explain how ethics can be integrated into strategic business decisions. This framework provides an *overview of the concepts, processes, mandatory, core, and voluntary business practices* associated with successful business ethics programs. Some approaches to business ethics are excellent as exercises in intellectual reasoning, but they cannot deal with the many actual issues and considerations that people in business organizations face. Our approach prepares students for the real ethical issues and dilemmas that they will face in their business careers.

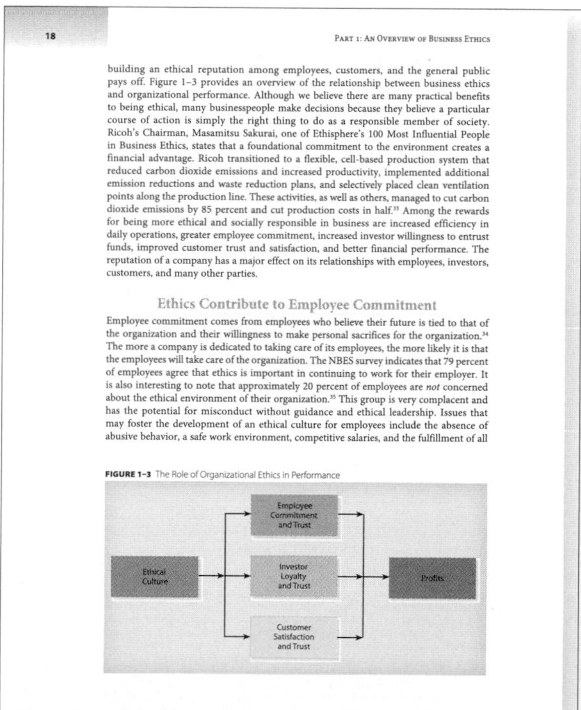

18 PART 1: AN OVERVIEW OF BUSINESS ETHICS

building an ethical reputation among employees, customers, and the general public pays off. Figure 1–3 provides an overview of the relationship between business ethics and organizational performance. Although we believe there are many practical benefits to being ethical, many businesspeople make decisions because they believe a particular course of action is simply the right thing to do as a responsible member of society. Ricoh's Chairman, Masamitsu Sakurai, one of Ethisphere's 100 Most Influential People in Business Ethics, states that a foundational commitment to the environment creates a financial advantage. Ricoh transitioned to a flexible, cell-based production system that reduced carbon dioxide emissions and increased productivity, implemented additional emission reductions and waste reduction plans, and selectively placed clean ventilation points along the production line. These activities, as well as others, managed to cut carbon dioxide emissions by 85 percent and cut production costs in half.[33] Among the rewards for being more ethical and socially responsible in business are increased efficiency in daily operations, greater employee commitment, increased investor willingness to entrust funds, improved customer trust and satisfaction, and better financial performance. The reputation of a company has a major effect on its relationships with employees, investors, customers, and many other parties.

Ethics Contribute to Employee Commitment

Employee commitment comes from employees who believe their future is tied to that of the organization and their willingness to make personal sacrifices for the organization.[34] The more a company is dedicated to taking care of its employees, the more likely it is that the employees will take care of the organization. The NBES survey indicates that 79 percent of employees agree that ethics is important in continuing to work for their employer. It is also interesting to note that approximately 20 percent of employees are *not* concerned about the ethical environment of their organization.[35] This group is very complacent and has the potential for misconduct without guidance and ethical leadership. Issues that may foster the development of an ethical culture for employees include the absence of abusive behavior, a safe work environment, competitive salaries, and the fulfillment of all

FIGURE 1–3 The Role of Organizational Ethics in Performance

We have been diligent in this revision to provide the most relevant examples of how the lack of business ethics has challenged our economic viability and entangled countries and companies around the world. This book remains the market leader because it *addresses the complex environment of ethical decision making in organizations and pragmatic, actual business concerns.* Every individual has unique personal principles and values, and every organization has its own set of values, rules, and organizational ethical culture. Business ethics must consider the organizational culture and interdependent relationships between the individual and other significant persons involved in organizational decision making. Without effective guidance, a businessperson cannot make ethical decisions while facing a short-term orientation, feeling organizational pressure to perform well and seeing rewards based on outcomes in a challenging competitive environment.

Employees cannot make the best, most ethical decisions in a vacuum devoid of the influence of organizational codes, policies, and culture. Most employees and all managers are responsible not only for their own ethical conduct, but for the conduct of coworkers and those who they supervise. Therefore, teaching business ethics as an exercise in independent and group decision making helps to acknowledge key influences upon (un)ethical conduct of coworkers and managers. Employees must be taught how to recognize and when to report and address ethical issues in the workplace. Students must also learn how to "fit in" the ethical culture of their organization and be responsible for their own decisions while upholding the ethical standards of the organization. In this edition we help readers understand that in an organizational environment, their values are weighted differently from actions taken outside the business world. Profit is one element that distinguishes business versus nonbusiness decisions.

By focusing on the issues and organizational environments, this book provides students the opportunity to see the roles and responsibilities they will face in business. The past decade has reinforced that business ethics is not a "fad" but a prevailing set of risks that organizations face on an ongoing basis, and organizations are now demanding better, more informed employees. Governments, universities, and colleges now understand that the ethical decision process must be taught.

Our primary goal has always been to enhance the awareness and the ethical decision making skills that students will need to make business ethics decisions that contribute to responsible business conduct. By focusing on these concerns and issues of today's challenging business environment, we demonstrate that the study of business ethics is imperative to the long-term well-being of not only businesses, but also our economic system.

PHILOSOPHY OF THIS TEXT

Business ethics in organizations requires principle-based leadership from top management and purposeful actions that include planning and implementation of standards of appropriate conduct, as well as openness and continuous effort to improve the organization's ethical performance. Although personal values are important in ethical decision making, they are just one of the components that guide the decisions, actions, and policies of organizations. The burden of ethical behavior relates to the organization's values and traditions, not just to the individuals who make the decisions and carry them out. A firm's ability to plan and implement ethical business standards depends in part on structuring resources and activities to achieve ethical objectives in an effective and efficient manner.

The purpose of this book is to help students improve their ability to make ethical decisions in business by providing them with a framework that they can use to identify, analyze, and resolve ethical issues in business decision making. Individual values and ethics are important in this process. By studying business ethics, students begin to understand how to cope with conflicts between their personal values and those of the organization.

CHAPTER 4: THE INSTITUTIONALIZATION OF BUSINESS ETHICS 95

FIGURE 4–1 Elements of an Ethical Culture

MANDATED REQUIREMENTS FOR LEGAL COMPLIANCE

Laws and regulations are established by governments to set minimum standards for responsible behavior—society's codification of what is right and wrong. Laws regulating business conduct are passed because certain stakeholders believe that business cannot be trusted to do what is right in certain areas, such as consumer safety and environmental protection. Because public policy is dynamic and often changes in response to business abuses and consumer demands for safety and equality, many laws have been passed to resolve specific problems and issues. But the opinions of society, as expressed in legislation, can change over time, and different courts or state legislatures may take diverging views. For example, the thrust of most business legislation can be summed up as follows: Any practice is permitted that does not substantially lessen or reduce competition or harm consumers or society. Courts differ, however, in their interpretations of what constitutes a "substantial" reduction of competition. Laws can help businesspeople determine what society believes at a certain time, but what is legally wrong today may be perceived as acceptable tomorrow, and vice versa. After generations of fame for its top-secret bank accounts, Swiss banks have been forced to disclose information about some of their clients. The rules are changing, however, and countries like Switzerland, Liechtenstein, and Luxembourg now must share information on potential tax dodgers with government agencies like the Internal Revenue Service. One bank alone, UBS, may harbor the secret bank accounts of 52,000 American tax dodgers.[2] However, personal views on legal and illegal activity in this area vary tremendously and explain why accounting firms struggle to advise.[3] Instructions to employees to "just obey the law" are meaningless without effective training and experience in dealing with specific legal risk areas.

Many ethical decisions in business are close calls. It often takes years of experience in a particular industry to know what is acceptable. We do not, in this book, provide ethical answers but instead attempt to prepare students to make informed ethical decisions. First, we do not moralize by indicating what to do in a specific situation. Second, although we provide an overview of moral philosophies and decision making processes, we do not prescribe any one philosophy or process as best or most ethical. Third, by itself, this book will not make students more ethical nor will it tell them how to judge the ethical behavior of others. Rather, its goal is to help students understand and use their current values and convictions in making business decisions and to encourage everyone to think about the effects of their decisions on business and society.

Many people believe that business ethics cannot be taught. Although we do not claim to teach ethics, we suggest that by studying business ethics a person can improve ethical decision making by identifying ethical issues and recognizing the approaches available to resolve them. An organization's reward system can reinforce appropriate behavior and help shape attitudes and beliefs about important issues. For example, the success of some campaigns to end racial or gender discrimination in the workplace provides evidence that attitudes and behavior can be changed with new information, awareness, and shared values.

CONTENT AND ORGANIZATION

In writing *Business Ethics*, Eighth Edition, we strived to be as informative, complete, accessible, and up to date as possible. Instead of focusing on one area of ethics, such as moral philosophy or social responsibility, we provide balanced coverage of all areas relevant to the current development and practice of ethical decision making. In short, we have tried to keep pace with new developments and current thinking in teaching and practices.

The first half of the text consists of ten chapters, which provide a framework to identify, analyze, and understand how businesspeople make ethical decisions and deal with ethical issues. Several enhancements have been made to chapter content for this edition. Some of the most important are listed in the next paragraphs.

Part One, "An Overview of Business Ethics," includes two chapters that help provide a broader context for the study of business ethics. Chapter 1, "The Importance of Business Ethics," has been revised with many new examples and survey results to describe issues and concerns important to business ethics. Chapter 2, "Stakeholder Relationships, Social Responsibility, and Corporate Governance," has been significantly reorganized and updated with new examples and issues. This chapter was reorganized and expanded to develop an overall framework for the text.

Part Two, "Ethical Issues and the Institutionalization of Business Ethics," consists of two chapters that provide the background that students need to identify ethical issues and understand how society, through the legal system, has attempted to hold organizations responsible for managing these issues. Chapter 3, "Emerging Business Ethics Issues," has been significantly reorganized and updated and provides expanded coverage of business ethics issues. Reviewers requested more detail on key issues that create ethical decisions. Within this edition, we have increased the depth of ethical issues and have updated the following new issues: abusive and intimidating behavior, lying, bribery, corporate intelligence, environmental issues, intellectual property rights, and privacy. Chapter 4, "The Institutionalization of Business Ethics" examines key elements of core or best practices in corporate America today along with legislation and regulation requirements that support business ethics initiatives. The chapter is divided into three main areas: voluntary, mandated, and core boundaries.

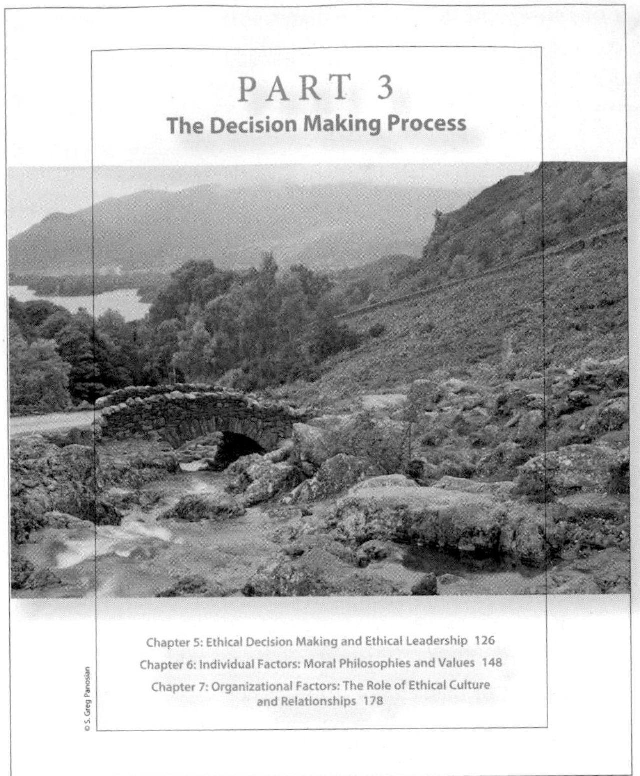

Part Three, "The Decision Making Process" consists of three chapters, which provide a framework to identify, analyze, and understand how businesspeople make ethical decisions and deal with ethical issues. Chapter 5, "Ethical Decision Making and Ethical Leadership," has been revised and updated to reflect current research and understanding of ethical decision making and contains a new section on ethical leadership. Chapter 6, "Individual Factors: Moral Philosophies and Values," has been updated and revised to explore the role of moral philosophies and moral development as individual factors in the ethical decision making process. This chapter now includes a new section on white-collar crime. Chapter 7, "Organizational Factors: The Role of Ethical Culture and Relationships," considers organizational influences on business decisions, such as role relationships, differential association, and other organizational pressures, as well as whistle-blowing.

Part Four, "Implementing Business Ethics in a Global Economy," looks at specific measures that companies can take to build an effective ethics program, as well as how these programs may be affected by global issues. Chapter 8, "Developing an Effective Ethics Program," has been refined and updated with corporate best practices for developing effective ethics programs. Chapter 9, "Implementing and Auditing Ethics Programs," offers a framework for auditing ethics initiatives as well as the importance of doing so. Such audits can help companies pinpoint problem areas, measure their progress in improving conduct, and even provide a "debriefing" opportunity after a crisis. Finally, Chapter 10, "Globalization of Ethical Decision Making" is completely revised to reflect the complex and dynamic events that almost caused a global depression. This chapter will help students understand the major issues involved in making decisions in a global environment.

Part Five consists of eighteen cases that bring reality into the learning process. Nine of these cases are new to the eighth edition, and the remaining nine have been revised and updated. The companies and situations portrayed in these cases are real; names and other facts are not disguised; and all cases include developments up to the end of 2009. By reading and analyzing these cases, students can gain insight into ethical decisions and the realities of making decisions in complex situations.

TEXT FEATURES

Many tools are available in this text to help both students and instructors in the quest to improve students' ability to make ethical business decisions.

- Each chapter opens with an outline and a list of learning objectives.
- Immediately following is "An Ethical Dilemma" that should provoke discussion about ethical issues related to the chapter. The short vignette describes a hypothetical incident involving an ethical conflict. Questions at the end of the "Ethical Dilemma" section focus discussion on how the dilemma could be resolved.
- At the end of each chapter are a chapter summary and an important terms list, both of which are handy tools for review. Also included at the end of each chapter is a "Resolving Ethical Business Challenges" section. The vignette describes a realistic drama that helps students experience the process of ethical decision making. The "Resolving Ethical Business Challenges" minicases presented in this text are hypothetical; any resemblance to real persons, companies, or situations is coincidental. Keep in mind that there are no right or wrong solutions to the minicases. The ethical dilemmas and real-life situations provide an opportunity for students to use concepts in the chapter to resolve ethical issues.
- Each chapter concludes with a series of questions that allow students to test their EQ (Ethics Quotient).
- Cases. In Part Five, following each real-world case are questions to guide students in recognizing and resolving ethical issues. For some cases, students can conduct additional research to determine recent developments because many ethical issues in companies take years to resolve.

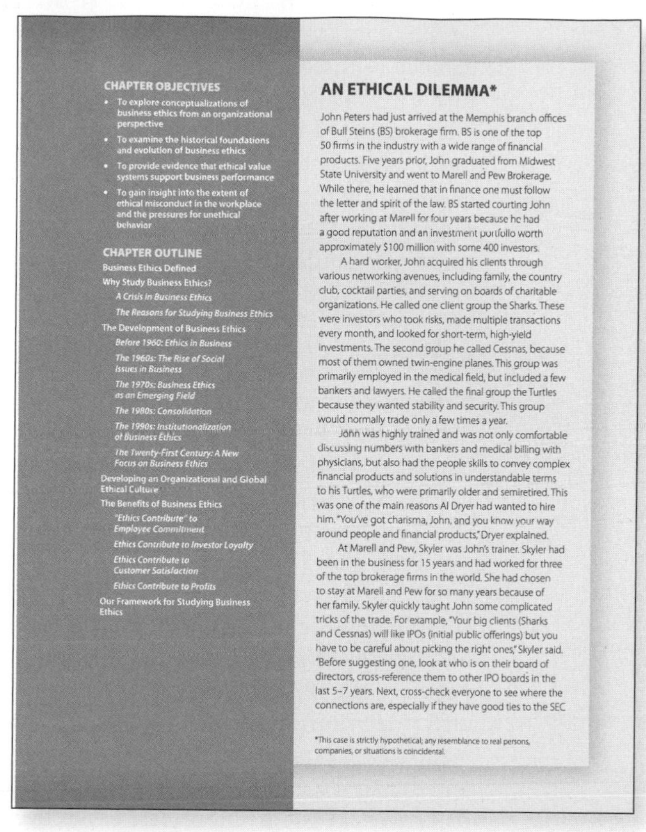

CHAPTER OBJECTIVES

- To explore conceptualizations of business ethics from an organizational perspective
- To examine the historical foundations and evolution of business ethics
- To provide evidence that ethical value systems support business performance
- To gain insight into the extent of ethical misconduct in the workplace and the pressures for unethical behavior

CHAPTER OUTLINE

AN ETHICAL DILEMMA*

John Peters had just arrived at the Memphis branch offices of Bull Steins (BS) brokerage firm. BS is one of the top 50 firms in the industry with a wide range of financial products. Five years prior, John graduated from Midwest State University and went to Marell and Pew Brokerage. While there, he learned that in finance one must follow the letter and spirit of the law. BS started courting John after working at Marell for four years because he had a good reputation and an investment portfolio worth approximately $100 million with some 400 investors.

A hard worker, John acquired his clients through various networking avenues, including family, the country club, cocktail parties, and serving on boards of charitable organizations. He called one client group the Sharks. These were investors who took risks, made multiple transactions every month, and looked for short-term, high-yield investments. The second group he called Cessnas, because most of them owned twin-engine planes. This group was primarily employed in the medical field, but included a few bankers and lawyers. He called the final group the Turtles because they wanted stability and security. This group would normally trade only a few times a year.

John was highly trained and was not only comfortable discussing numbers with bankers and medical billing with physicians, but also had the people skills to convey complex financial products and solutions in understandable terms to his Turtles, who were primarily older and semiretired. This was one of the main reasons Al Dryer had wanted to hire him. "You've got charisma, John, and you know your way around people and financial products," Dryer explained.

At Marell and Pew, Skyler was John's trainer. Skyler had been in the business for 15 years and had worked for three of the top brokerage firms in the world. She had chosen to stay at Marell and Pew for so many years because of her family. Skyler quickly taught John some complicated tricks of the trade. For example, "Your big clients (Sharks and Cessnas) will like IPOs (initial public offerings) but you have to be careful about picking the right ones," Skyler said. "Before suggesting one, look at who is on their board of directors, cross-reference them to other IPO boards in the last 5–7 years. Next, cross-check everyone to see where the connections are, especially if they have good ties to the SEC

*This case is strictly hypothetical; any resemblance to real persons, companies, or situations is coincidental.

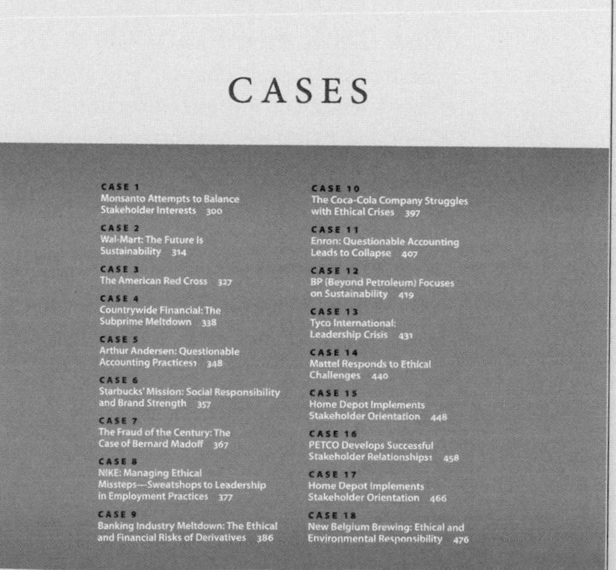

CASES

EFFECTIVE TOOLS FOR TEACHING AND LEARNING

Instructor's Resource Manual. The *Instructor's Resource Manual* contains a wealth of information. Teaching notes for every chapter include a brief chapter summary, detailed lecture outline, and notes for using the "Ethical Dilemma" and "Resolving Ethical Business Challenges" sections. Detailed case notes point out the key issues involved and offer suggested answers to the questions. A separate section provides guidelines for using case analysis in teaching business ethics. Detailed notes are provided to guide the instructor in analyzing or grading the cases. Simulation role-play cases, as well as implementation suggestions, are included. For others involved in attempting to simulate more of the actual constructs students will face in their business careers we suggest accessing **http://www.businessreality.org/.**

Role-Play Cases. The Eighth Edition provides six behavioral simulation role-play cases developed for use in the business ethics course. The role-play cases and implementation methods can be found in the *Instructor's Resource Manual* and on the website. Role-play cases may be used as a culminating experience to help students integrate concepts covered in the text. Alternatively, the cases may be used as an ongoing exercise to provide students with extensive opportunities for interacting and making ethical decisions.

Role-play cases simulate a complex, realistic, and timely business ethics situation. Students form teams and make decisions based on an assigned role. The role-play case complements and enhances traditional approaches to business learning experiences because it (1) gives students the opportunity to practice making decisions that have business ethics consequences; (2) re-creates the power, pressures, and information that affect decision making at various levels of management; (3) provides students with a team-based experience that enriches their skills and understanding of group processes and dynamics; and (4) uses a feedback period to allow for the exploration of complex and controversial issues in business ethics decision making. The role-play cases can be used with classes of any size.

Test Bank and Exam View. The *Test Bank* provides multiple-choice and essay questions for each chapter and includes a mix of objective and application questions. *ExamView*, a computerized version of the Test Bank, provides instructors with all the tools they need to create, author/edit, customize, and deliver multiple types of tests. Instructors can import questions directly from the test bank, create their own questions, or edit existing questions.

Instructor's Resource CD-ROM. This instructor's CD provides a variety of teaching resources in electronic format, allowing for easy customization to meet specific instructional needs. Files include Word files of the Test Bank, along with its computerized version, *ExamView;* Lecture PowerPoint® slides; and Word and PDF files from the Instructor's Resource Manual.

Videos. A DVD is also available to support the Eighth Edition. The seventeen segments can be used across several chapters, and the Video Guide (which appears at the end of the

Instructor Manual) contains a matrix intended to show the closest relationships between the videos and chapter topics. The Video Guide also includes summaries of each video as well as teaching guidelines and issues for discussion.

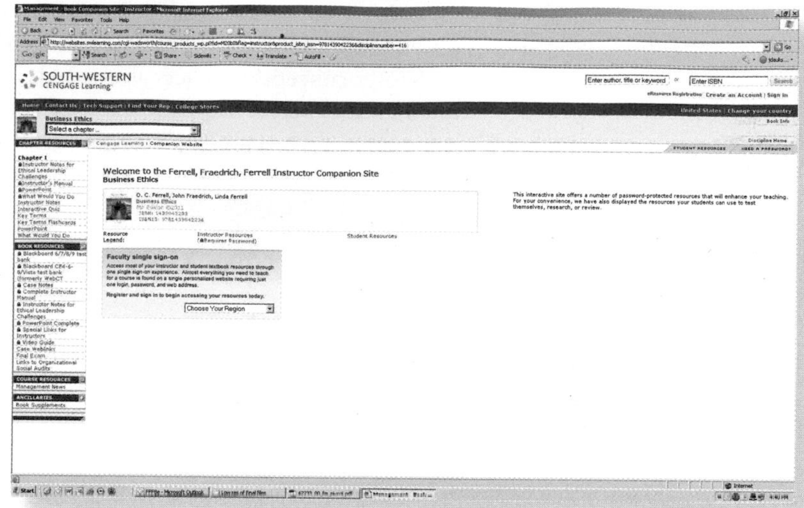

Instructor Companion Site. The Instructor Companion Site can be found at www.cengage.com/management/ferrell. It includes a complete Instructor Manual, Word files from both the Instructor Manual and Test Bank, and PowerPoint slides for easy downloading.

e-businessethics.com. Additional instructor resources can be found at www.e-businessethics.com. Also at e-businessethics.com, instructors can learn more about a teaching business ethics certificate program offered twice annually through the University of New Mexico. Instructors will find an opportunity to sign up for WSJ business ethics abstracts at www.professorjournal.com.

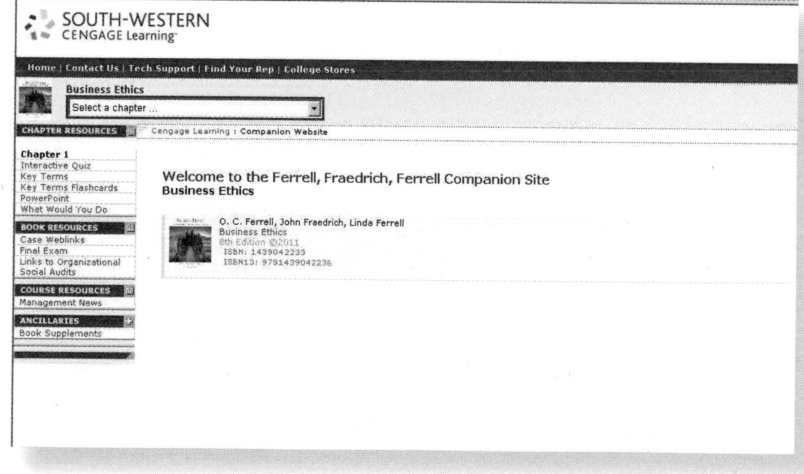

Student Companion Site. The Student Companion Site can also be found at www.cengage.com/management/ferrell. The website developed for the eighth edition provides up-to-date examples, issues, and interactive learning devices to assist students in improving their decision making skills. The student companion site has been created to take advantage of information available on the Internet while providing interactive skill-building exercises that can help students practice ethical decision making. The site contains links to companies and organizations highlighted in each chapter; case website links; links to social audits; interactive quizzes, which help students master chapter content through multiple-choice questions; and What Would You Do? exercises. Four Ethical Leadership Challenge scenarios are also available for each chapter. A premium website, **CourseMate**, is also available with a number of online study tools, including flashcards, additional interactive quizzes, student PowerPoint slides, crossword puzzles, and games. Lockheed Martin's Gray Matters ethics game is also available on the premium site.

WebTUTOR™

WebTutor ™. Whether you want to Web-enable your class or teach entirely online, WebTutor provides customizable text-specific content within your course system. This content-rich, web-based teaching and learning aid reinforces chapter concepts and acts as an electronic student study guide. WebTutor provides students with interactive chapter review quizzes, critical-thinking, writing-improvement exercises, flashcards, PowerPoints, and links to online videos.

ACKNOWLEDGMENTS

A number of individuals provided reviews and suggestions that helped to improve this text. We sincerely appreciate their time and effort.

Donald Acker
Brown Mackie College

Donna Allen
Northwest Nazarene University

Suzanne Allen
Walsh University

Carolyn Ashe
University of Houston–Downtown

Laura Barelman
Wayne State College

Russell Bedard
Eastern Nazarene College

B. Barbara Boerner
Brevard College

Judie Bucholz
Guilford College

Greg Buntz
University of the Pacific

Julie Campbell
Adams State College

April Chatham-Carpenter
University of Northern Iowa

Leslie Connell
University of Central Florida

Peggy Cunningham
Queen's University

Carla Dando
Idaho State University

James E. Donovan
Detroit College of Business

Douglas Dow
University of Texas at Dallas

A. Charles Drubel
Muskingum College

Philip F. Esler
University of St. Andrews

Joseph M. Foster
Indiana Vocational Technical College—Evansville

Terry Gable
Truman State University

Robert Giacalone
University of Richmond

Suresh Gopalan
West Texas A&M University

Mark Hammer
Northwest Nazarene University

Charles E. Harris, Jr.
Texas A&M University

Kenneth A. Heischmidt
Southeast Missouri State University

Neil Herndon
Educational Consultant

Walter Hill
Green River Community College

Jack Hires
Valparaiso University

David Jacobs
American University

R. J. Johansen
Montana State University–Bozeman

Edward Kimman
Vrije Universiteit

Janet Knight
Purdue North Central

Anita Leffel
University of Texas at San Antonio

Barbara Limbach
Chadron State College

Nick Lockard
Texas Lutheran College

Terry Loe
Kennesaw State University

Nick Maddox
Stetson University

Isabelle Maignan
Vrije Universiteit Amsterdam

Phylis Mansfield
Pennsylvania State University–Erie

Robert Markus
Babson College

Randy McLeod
Harding University

Francy Milner
University of Colorado

Ali Mir
William Paterson University

Debi P. Mishra
Binghamton University, State University of New York

Patrick E. Murphy
University of Notre Dame

Lester Myers
University of San Francisco

Cynthia Nicola
Carlow College

Carol Nielsen
Bemidji State University

Lee Richardson
University of Baltimore

William M. Sannwald
San Diego State University

Zachary Shank
Albuquerque Technical Vocational Institute

Cynthia A. M. Simerly
Lakeland Community College

Karen Smith
Columbia Southern University

Filiz Tabak
Towson University

Debbie Thorne
Texas State University–San Marcos

Wanda V. Turner
Ferris State College

Gina Vega
Salem State College

William C. Ward
Mid-Continent University

David Wasieleski
Duquesne University

Jim Weber
Duquesne University

Ed Weiss
National-Louis University

Joseph W. Weiss
Bentley University

Jan Zahrly
University of North Dakota

We wish to acknowledge the many people who assisted us in writing this book. We are deeply grateful to Jennifer Jackson for her work in organizing and managing the revision process. We would also like to thank Jennifer Sawayda and Jessica Talley for all their assistance in this edition. We are also indebted to Melanie Drever, Barbara Gilmer, and Gwyneth V. Walters for their contributions to previous editions of this text. Debbie Thorne, Texas State University–San Marcos, provided advice and guidance on the text and cases. Finally, we express appreciation to the administration and to our colleagues at the University of New Mexico and Southern Illinois University at Carbondale for their support.

We invite your comments, questions, or criticisms. We want to do our best to provide teaching materials that enhance the study of business ethics. Your suggestions will be sincerely appreciated.

O. C. Ferrell
John Fraedrich
Linda Ferrell

PART 1
An Overview of Business Ethics

CHAPTER 1

The Importance of Business Ethics

CHAPTER OBJECTIVES

- To explore conceptualizations of business ethics from an organizational perspective
- To examine the historical foundations and evolution of business ethics
- To provide evidence that ethical value systems support business performance
- To gain insight into the extent of ethical misconduct in the workplace and the pressures for unethical behavior

CHAPTER OUTLINE

Business Ethics Defined

Why Study Business Ethics?

- *A Crisis in Business Ethics*
- *The Reasons for Studying Business Ethics*

The Development of Business Ethics

- *Before 1960: Ethics in Business*
- *The 1960s: The Rise of Social Issues in Business*
- *The 1970s: Business Ethics as an Emerging Field*
- *The 1980s: Consolidation*
- *The 1990s: Institutionalization of Business Ethics*
- *The Twenty-First Century: A New Focus on Business Ethics*

Developing an Organizational and Global Ethical Culture

The Benefits of Business Ethics

- *"Ethics Contribute" to Employee Commitment*
- *Ethics Contribute to Investor Loyalty*
- *Ethics Contribute to Customer Satisfaction*
- *Ethics Contribute to Profits*

Our Framework for Studying Business Ethics

AN ETHICAL DILEMMA*

John Peters had just arrived at the Memphis branch offices of Bull Steins (BS) brokerage firm. BS is one of the top 50 firms in the industry with a wide range of financial products. Five years prior, John graduated from Midwest State University and went to Marell and Pew Brokerage. While there, he learned that in finance one must follow the letter and spirit of the law. BS started courting John after working at Marell for four years because he had a good reputation and an investment portfolio worth approximately $100 million with some 400 investors.

A hard worker, John acquired his clients through various networking avenues, including family, the country club, cocktail parties, and serving on boards of charitable organizations. He called one client group the Sharks. These were investors who took risks, made multiple transactions every month, and looked for short-term, high-yield investments. The second group he called Cessnas, because most of them owned twin-engine planes. This group was primarily employed in the medical field, but included a few bankers and lawyers. He called the final group the Turtles because they wanted stability and security. This group would normally trade only a few times a year.

John was highly trained and was not only comfortable discussing numbers with bankers and medical billing with physicians, but also had the people skills to convey complex financial products and solutions in understandable terms to his Turtles, who were primarily older and semiretired. This was one of the main reasons Al Dryer had wanted to hire him. "You've got charisma, John, and you know your way around people and financial products," Dryer explained.

At Marell and Pew, Skyler was John's trainer. Skyler had been in the business for 15 years and had worked for three of the top brokerage firms in the world. She had chosen to stay at Marell and Pew for so many years because of her family. Skyler quickly taught John some complicated tricks of the trade. For example, "Your big clients (Sharks and Cessnas) will like IPOs (initial public offerings) but you have to be careful about picking the right ones," Skyler said. "Before suggesting one, look at who is on their board of directors, cross-reference them to other IPO boards in the last 5–7 years. Next, cross-check everyone to see where the connections are, especially if they have good ties to the SEC

*This case is strictly hypothetical; any resemblance to real persons, companies, or situations is coincidental.

(Securities and Exchange Commission). Finally, you want to check these people and the companies they have been associated with. Check every IPO these people were involved in and what Moody's ratings were prior to the IPO. As you know, Moody's is one of two IPO rating companies in the United States and they're hurting for revenue because of the financial downturn. If you see a bias in how they rate because of personal relations to the IPO people, you've got a winner," Skyler smiled.

During his five years at the company, Skyler had taught John about shorting, naked shorting, and churning. She explained shorting by using an example. "If I own 1,000 shares at $100/share and you think the stock is going to tank (go down), you 'borrow' my shares at $100/share, sell them, and the next week the stock goes down to $80/share. You call your broker and buy back the 1,000 shares at $80 and give me my 1,000 shares at $80/share. Do you see what happened?" Skyler asked. "You borrowed my shares and sold them for $100,000. The following week, when the company stock fell to $80, you repurchased those 1,000 shares for $80,000 and gave them back to me. In the meantime, you pocketed the difference of $20,000." Skyler went on, "Naked short selling is the same as shorting but you don't pay any money for the stock," explained Skyler. "There is a three-day grace period between buying and selling. That means you have at least three days of FREE MONEY!"

Al Dryer instructed John to wait to resign until late on Friday so that BS could send out packets to each of his accounts about switching companies. John thought about this, but was told by others this was standard practice. "But what about the noncompete clause I signed? It says I can't do that," said John to a few brokers not associated with either firm. Their response was, "It's done all the time." On Friday John did what BS asked and nothing happened. Six months went by and John's portfolio had increased to $150 million. Other brokers began imitating John's strategy. For example, for his Sharks, John would buy and sell at BS and call some of his buddies to do the same thing using money from his SHARKS. Another tactic involved selling futures contracts without providing evidence that he held the shares sold (naked shorting). While much of what he was doing was risky, John had become so successful that he guaranteed his Turtles against any loss.

Several years later John was buying and selling derivatives, a form of futures contract that gets its value from assets such as commodities, equities (stocks), bonds, interest rates, exchange rates, or even an index of weather conditions. While his risk-taking Shark group had expanded threefold, John's Cessna pool had all but dried up. However, his Turtles had grown dramatically to an average worth of $500,000. The portfolio he managed had topped $750 million, a lot more than he had when he started at BS ($500 million in Sharks and $250 million for Turtles).

"This year is going to be better than last year," said John to some of the brokers at BS. But expenses had been rising fast. John's expense account included country club memberships, sports tickets, trips for clients, etc. Instead of charging the firm, John would always pay them from his own pocket. By indirectly letting his clients know it was his money he was spending on them, his clients were grateful for his largess and those who would have grumbled about delays in the delivery of securities purchased were less apt to do so. John saw a great opportunity to make his heavy hitters happy with him. Unbeknownst to them, he would buy and sell stocks for these clients and later surprise them with the profits.

By this time, John was training new hires at BS, which would have taken away a lot of his personal and professional time if he had done it right. But John had a lot of other things on his mind. He had decided to get married and adopt children. His soon-to-be wife, Leslie, quit her job to be a full-time mom and was designing their new 18,000-square-foot home. With all these activities going on at once, John was not paying attention to the four new brokers and their training. Because John was a senior partner, he had to sign off on every trade they made. It became so time consuming to manage everything that he spent an hour a day just signing the four other brokers' trades.

Then one Monday morning John received a call from the SEC asking about some trades made by the four new brokers. "It appears to us there may be some nonpublic information your brokers have concerning several IPOs," the agent said. "If they do have such information, this could be considered insider information. John, I'm calling you because we go way back to our college days, but I have to know," said the agent. John thanked him and went straight to the new brokers and asked them about the IPO. One of the new brokers replied, "John, you told us that in order to excel in this business, you need to be an expert on knowing exactly where things become legal and illegal. You said trust me, I've been doing this for 15 years, and I've never had a problem. We just did what you've taught us."

John knew that if they did have insider information, he'd probably be found partially responsible because he was supposed to be training them. At the very minimum, the SEC would start checking his trades over the past several years. He also knew that, when subjected to scrutiny, some of his past trades might be deemed questionable as well.

What should John do?

QUESTIONS • EXERCISES

1. What is/are John's ethical issues?
2. Are there any legal considerations for John?
3. Discuss the implications of each decision John has made and will make.

The ability to recognize and deal with complex business ethics issues has become a significant priority in twenty-first-century companies. In recent years, a number of well-publicized scandals resulted in public outrage about deception and fraud in business and a demand for improved business ethics and greater corporate responsibility. The publicity and debate surrounding highly visible legal and ethical lapses at a number of well-known firms, including AIG, Countrywide Financial, and Fannie Mae, highlight the need for businesses to integrate ethics and responsibility into all business decisions. The global financial crisis took a toll on consumer trust of financial services companies. A study of 650 U.S. consumers by Lightspeed Research and Cohn & Wolfe revealed that 66 percent of respondents did not feel that the financial services industry would help them to regain the wealth that they lost during the recession. Words used to describe this industry included greedy, impersonal, opportunistic, and distant. Table 1–1 summarizes the survey results.[1]

Largely in response to this crisis, business decisions and activities have come under greater scrutiny by many different constituents, including consumers, employees, investors, government regulators, and special interest groups. Additionally, new legislation and regulations designed to encourage higher ethical standards in business have been put in place.

The field of business ethics deals with questions about whether specific business practices are acceptable. For example, should a salesperson omit facts about a product's poor safety record in a sales presentation to a client? Should an accountant report inaccuracies that he or she discovered in an audit of a client, knowing the auditing company will probably be fired by the client for doing so? Should an automobile tire manufacturer intentionally conceal safety concerns to avoid a massive and costly tire recall? Regardless of their legality, others will certainly judge the actions taken in such situations as right or wrong, ethical or unethical. By its very nature, the field of business ethics is controversial, and there is no universally accepted approach for resolving its issues.

TABLE 1–1 American Distrust of the Financial Services Industry

Negative Responses Related to the Industry	%
Greedy	32
Impersonal	32
Opportunistic	26
Distant from me	22
Positive Responses Related to the Industry	**%**
Trustworthy	13
Honest	10
Ethical	5
Transparent	3
Sympathetic	3

Source: "New US Consumer Survey Shows High Distrust of Financial Services Companies," *Business Wire*, January 20, 2009, http://findarticles.com/p/articles/mi_m0EIN/is_2009_Jan_20/ai_n31202849/ (accessed May 27, 2009).

A Junior Achievement/Deloitte survey of teens showed that 71 percent feel prepared to make ethical decisions in the workplace. However, of those surveyed, 38 percent feel it is sometimes necessary to lie, cheat, plagiarize, or engage in violence to succeed. One-fourth think cheating on a test is acceptable and most can justify it saying that their desire to succeed is grounds for the behavior.[2] If today's students are tomorrow's leaders, there is likely to be a correlation between acceptable behavior today and tomorrow, adding to the argument that the leaders of today must be prepared for the ethical risks associated with this downward trend. According to another poll by Deloitte and Touche of teenagers aged 13 to 18 years old, when asked if people who practice good business ethics are more successful than those who don't, 69 percent of teenagers agreed.[3] On the other hand, another survey indicated that many students do not define copying answers from another student's paper or downloading copyrighted music or content for classroom work as cheating.[4]

Before we get started, it is important to state our philosophies regarding this book. First, we do not moralize by telling you what is right or wrong in a specific situation. Second, although we provide an overview of group and individual decision making processes, we do not prescribe any one philosophy or process as best or most ethical. Third, by itself, this book will not make you more ethical, nor will it tell you how to judge the ethical behavior of others. Rather, its goal is to help you understand and use your current values and convictions when making business decisions so that you think about the effects of those decisions on business and society. In addition, this book will help you understand what businesses are doing to improve their ethical conduct. To this end, we aim to help you learn to recognize and resolve ethical issues within business organizations. As a manager, you will be responsible for your decisions and the ethical conduct of the employees you supervise. The framework we develop in this book therefore focuses on how organizational ethical decisions are made and on ways companies can improve their ethical conduct.

In this chapter, we first develop a definition of business ethics and discuss why it has become an important topic in business education. We also discuss why studying business ethics can be beneficial. Next, we examine the evolution of business ethics in North America. Then we explore the performance benefits of ethical decision making for businesses. Finally, we provide a brief overview of the framework we use for examining business ethics in this text.

BUSINESS ETHICS DEFINED

The term *ethics* has many nuances. It has been defined as "inquiry into the nature and grounds of morality where the term morality is taken to mean moral judgments, standards and rules of conduct."[5] Ethics has also been called the study and philosophy of human conduct, with an emphasis on determining right and wrong. *The American Heritage Dictionary* offers these definitions of ethics: "The study of the general nature of morals and of specific moral choices; moral philosophy; and the rules or standards governing the conduct of the members of a profession."[6] One difference between an ordinary decision and an ethical one lies in "the point where the accepted rules no longer serve, and the decision maker is faced with the responsibility for weighing values and reaching a judgment in a situation which is not quite the same as any he or she has faced before."[7] Another difference relates to the amount of emphasis that decision makers place on their own values and accepted practices within their company. Consequently, values and judgments play a critical role when we make ethical decisions.

Building on these definitions, we can begin to develop a concept of business ethics. Most people would agree that high ethical standards require both businesses and individuals to conform to sound moral principles. However, some special aspects must be considered when applying ethics to business. First, to survive, businesses must earn a profit. If profits are realized through misconduct, however, the life of the organization may be shortened. Many firms, including Lehman Brothers and Enron, that made headlines due to wrongdoing and scandal ultimately went bankrupt or failed because of the legal and financial repercussions of their misconduct. Second, businesses must balance their desires for profits against the needs and desires of society. Maintaining this balance often requires compromises or trade-offs. To address these unique aspects of the business world, society has developed rules—both legal and implicit—to guide businesses in their efforts to earn profits in ways that do not harm individuals or society as a whole.

Most definitions of business ethics relate to rules, standards, and moral principles regarding what is right or wrong in specific situations. For our purposes, **business ethics** comprises the principles, values, and standards that guide behavior in the world of business. **Principles** are specific and pervasive boundaries for behavior that are universal and absolute. Principles often become the basis for rules. Some examples of principles include freedom of speech, fundamentals of justice, and equal rights to civil liberties. **Values** are used to develop norms that are socially enforced. Integrity, accountability, and trust are examples of values. Investors, employees, customers, interest groups, the legal system, and the community often determine whether a specific action is right or wrong, ethical or unethical. Although these groups are not necessarily "right," their judgments influence society's acceptance or rejection of a business and its activities.

WHY STUDY BUSINESS ETHICS?

A Crisis in Business Ethics

As we've already mentioned, ethical misconduct has become a major concern in business today. The Ethics Resource Center conducted the National Business Ethics Survey (NBES) of about 3,000 U.S. employees to gather reliable data on key ethics and compliance outcomes and to help identify and better understand the ethics issues that are important to employees. The NBES found that observed misconduct is higher in large organizations—those with more than 500 employees—than in smaller ones and that there are also differences in observed misconduct across employee levels. Reporting of misconduct is most likely to come from upper-level management, as compared to lower-level supervisors and nonmanagement employees. Employees in lower-level positions have more of a tendency to not understand misconduct or be complacent about what misconduct they observe. Figure 1–1 shows the percentage of respondents who say that they trust a variety of business categories. Notice that the levels of consumer trust in most industries is declining. Among senior managers, 77 percent of employees report observed misconduct, while among nonmanagement, only 48 percent of employees report observed misconduct.[8]

Specific Issues Abusive behavior, harassment, accounting fraud, conflicts of interest, defective products, bribery, and employee theft are all problems cited as evidence of declining ethical standards. For example, Satyam Computer Services, an outsourcing firm in India, worked with more than one-third of the Fortune 500 companies. The chairman of the company disclosed that $1.04 billion in cash and assets did not exist and that earnings and assets were inflated for years. The scandal was compared to Enron.[9] A survey by Harris Interactive shows that corporate reputation is at its lowest point in the past decade of their annual "Reputation Quotient" polls. Eighty-eight percent rated the reputation of corporate America today as "not good" or "terrible." Among the least admired companies

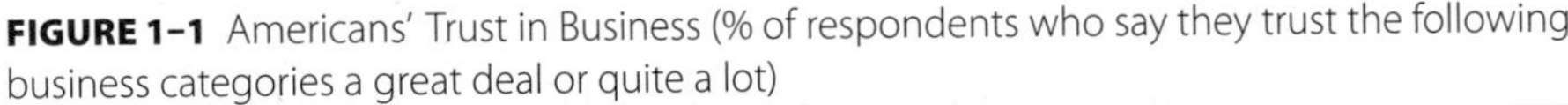

FIGURE 1–1 Americans' Trust in Business (% of respondents who say they trust the following business categories a great deal or quite a lot)

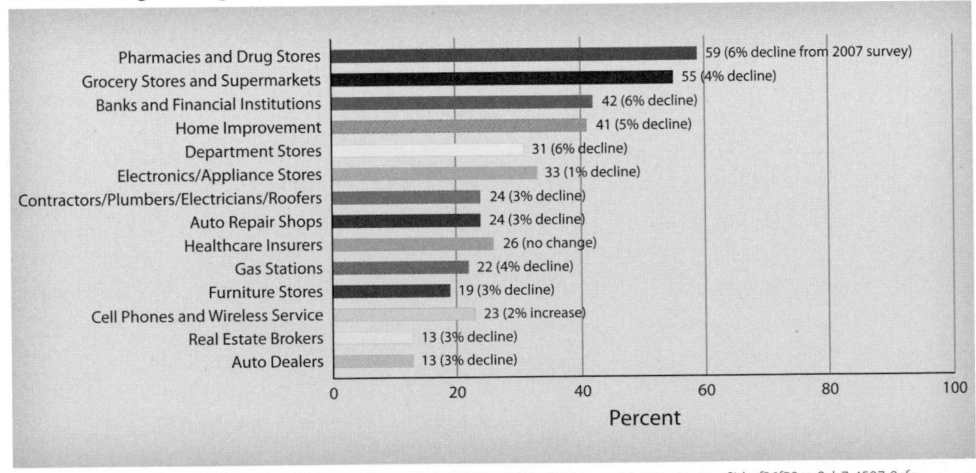

Source: Better Business Bureau/Gallup Trust in Business Index, April 2008, http://www.bbb.org/us/sitepage.aspx?id =f36f50cc-8cb7-4507-9cfc-2f2d7aa2c3fc (accessed January 13, 2009).

are AIG, Halliburton, General Motors, Chrysler, Washington Mutual, Citigroup, Merrill Lynch, ExxonMobil, and Ford Motor Company. There remain companies that are admired by respondents, including Johnson & Johnson, Google, Sony, Coca-Cola, Kraft Foods, Amazon.com, Microsoft, General Mills, 3M, and Toyota Motor. The economic lapses associated with the recession have damaged the "emotional appeal" of many companies, which is often the strongest driver of reputation.[10]

Insider trading remains a serious issue in business and in ethics. Eugene Plotkin, a former Goldman Sachs executive, was sentenced to almost five years in prison for a case of insider trading that yielded about $6.7 million. The Harvard graduate worked with a former Merrill Lynch analyst, a New Jersey postal worker, and two workers at a *Business Week* printing press. The former Merrill Lynch employee provided tips to Plotkin at Goldman on mergers and acquisitions. Another angle involved getting prepublication copies of *Business Week* and trading on that information. The third element involved working with a New Jersey postal worker who served on the Bristol-Myers Squibb grand jury investigation and shared inside information with Plotkin.[11]

Inflating earnings involves attempting to embellish or enhance a firm's profitability in a manner that is inconsistent with past practice, common regulatory guidelines, or industry practice. Many companies maintain a focus on making short-term profits and know that analysts and investors critique the company according to its ability to "make the numbers." PricewaterhouseCoopers (PWC) was forced to pay $97.5 million to settle a class action lawsuit for involvement with AIG in overstating their earnings. This settlement is a small part of a larger case against both AIG and its former CEO, Hank Greenberg. AIG's improper accounting for reinsurance and other dealings led to a restatement of earnings in the amount of $3.9 billion. The lawsuit normally proceeds against the company and personnel first, with the related firms (such as PWC) paying a percentage of that settlement.[12] Highly publicized cases such as this one strengthen the perception that ethical standards in business need to be raised.

Ethics play an important role in the public sector as well. In government, several politicians and some high-ranking officials have experienced significant negative publicity and some have had to resign in disgrace over ethical indiscretions. Alaskan Senator Ted Stevens was convicted of 7 felony counts of corruption weeks before the election of President Barack Obama. He was charged with hiding $250,000 in gifts he had allegedly received from oil companies. The U.S. Department of Justice filed a motion to have the case dismissed against Stevens due to mishandled evidence, and the case was officially dropped. However, the impact of the negative publicity on the senator was significant and most likely contributed to his losing his bid for reelection.[13]

Irv Lewis "Scooter" Libby, a White House advisor, was indicted on five counts of criminal charges: one count of obstruction of justice, two counts of perjury, and two counts of making false statements.[14] Each count carries a $250,000 fine and maximum prison term of 30 years.

Several scientists have been accused of falsifying research data, which could invalidate later research based on their data and jeopardize trust in all scientific research. Bell Labs, for example, fired a scientist for falsifying experiments on superconductivity and molecular electronics and for misrepresenting data in scientific publications. Jan Hendrik Schon's work on creating tiny, powerful microprocessors seemed poised to significantly advance microprocessor technology and potentially bring yet another Nobel Prize in physics to the award-winning laboratory, a subsidiary of Lucent Technologies.[15] Hwang Woo-Suk was found to have faked some of his famous stem cell research in which he claimed to have created 30 cloned human embryos and made stem cell lines from skin cells of 11 people, as well as producing the world's first cloned dog. He also apologized for using eggs from his own female researchers, which was in breach of guidelines, but still denies fabricating his research.[16]

Even sports can be subject to ethical lapses. Manny Ramirez was suspended for 50 games from the Los Angeles Dodgers for violating the league's drug policy. Ramirez tested positive for a female fertility drug that has been taken by steroid users to increase testosterone levels. The ban on playing cost Ramirez $7.7 million of his $25 million annual salary. Ramirez stated that he was under a doctor's care for a "personal health issue" and indicated that he thought the medication was allowed. Baseball players are encouraged to check a hotline that identifies legal and illegal substances and encourages players to seek "therapeutic use exemptions" for legitimate use of banned substances.[17]

Whether made in business, politics, science, or sports, most decisions are judged as either right or wrong, ethical or unethical. Regardless of what an individual believes about a particular action, if society judges it to be unethical or wrong, whether correctly or not, that judgment directly affects the organization's ability to achieve its business goals. For this reason alone, it is important to understand business ethics and recognize ethical issues.

> *Regardless of what an individual believes about a particular action, if society judges it to be unethical or wrong, whether correctly or not, that judgment directly affects the organization's ability to achieve its business goals.*

The Reasons for Studying Business Ethics

Studying business ethics is valuable for several reasons. Business ethics is not merely an extension of an individual's own personal ethics. Many people believe that if a company hires good people with strong ethical values, then it will be a "good citizen" organization. But as we show throughout this text, an individual's personal values and moral philosophies are only one factor in the ethical decision making process. True, moral rules can be applied to a variety of situations in life, and some people do not distinguish everyday ethical issues from business ones. Our concern, however, is with the application of principles and standards in the business context. Many important ethical issues do not arise very often in the business context, although they remain complex moral dilemmas in one's own personal life. For example, although abortion and the possibility of human cloning are moral issues in many people's lives, they are usually not an issue in most business organizations.

Professionals in any field, including business, must deal with individuals' personal moral dilemmas because these issues affect everyone's ability to function on the job. Normally, a business does not establish rules or policies on personal ethical issues such as sex or the use of alcohol outside the workplace; indeed, in some cases, such policies would be illegal. Only when a person's preferences or values influence his or her performance on the job do an individual's ethics play a major role in the evaluation of business decisions.

Just being a good person and, in your own view, having sound personal ethics may not be sufficient to enable you to handle the ethical issues that arise in a business organization. It is important to recognize the relationship between legal and ethical decisions. Although abstract virtues linked to the high moral ground of truthfulness, honesty, fairness, and openness are often assumed to be self-evident and accepted by all employees, business-strategy decisions involve complex and detailed discussions. For example, there is considerable debate over what constitutes antitrust, deceptive advertising, and violations of the Foreign Corrupt Practices Act. A high level of personal moral development may not prevent an individual from violating the law in a complicated organizational context where even experienced lawyers debate the exact meaning of the law. Some approaches to business ethics assume that ethics training is for people whose personal moral development is unacceptable, but that is not the case. Because organizations are culturally diverse and personal values must be respected, ensuring collective agreement on organizational ethics (that is, codes reasonably capable of preventing misconduct) is as vital as any other effort an organization's management may undertake.

Many people who have limited business experience suddenly find themselves making decisions about product quality, advertising, pricing, sales techniques, hiring practices, and pollution control. The values they learned from family, religion, and school may not provide specific guidelines for these complex business decisions. In other words, a person's experiences and decisions at home, in school, and in the community may be quite different from his or her experiences and decisions at work. Many business ethics decisions are close calls. In addition, managerial responsibility for the conduct of others requires knowledge of ethics and compliance processes and systems. Years of experience in a particular industry may be required to know what is acceptable. For example, Caraco Pharmaceutical Laboratories, a generic drug manufacturer, voluntarily recalled all tablets of its digoxin drug used by patients with heart failure and abnormal heart rhythms. The drug was recalled because of variation in sizing, which could impact the actual dosage received by a patient. The recall was designed to protect those who were using the drug and the company had to carefully assess the product and the potential harm it could cause in its more inconsistent form. Significant medical expertise and testing resulted in the recall.[18]

Studying business ethics will help you begin to identify ethical issues when they arise and recognize the approaches available for resolving them. You will also learn more about the ethical decision making process and about ways to promote ethical behavior within your organization. By studying business ethics, you may begin to understand how to cope with conflicts between your own personal values and those of the organization in which you work.

THE DEVELOPMENT OF BUSINESS ETHICS

The study of business ethics in North America has evolved through five distinct stages—(1) before 1960, (2) the 1960s, (3) the 1970s, (4) the 1980s, and (5) the 1990s—and continues to evolve in the twenty-first century (see Table 1–2).

Before 1960: Ethics in Business

Prior to 1960, the United States went through several agonizing phases of questioning the concept of capitalism. In the 1920s, the progressive movement attempted to provide citizens with a "living wage," defined as income sufficient for education, recreation, health, and retirement. Businesses were asked to check unwarranted price increases and any other practices that would hurt a family's "living wage." In the 1930s came the New Deal, which specifically blamed business for the country's economic woes. Business was asked to work more closely with the government to raise family income. By the 1950s, the New Deal had evolved into the Fair Deal by President Harry S. Truman; this program defined such matters as civil rights and environmental responsibility as ethical issues that businesses had to address.

Until 1960 ethical issues related to business were often discussed within the domain of theology or philosophy. Individual moral issues related to business were addressed in

TABLE 1–2 A Timeline of Ethical and Socially Responsible Concerns

1960s	1970s	1980s	1990s	2000s
Environmental issues	Employee militancy	Bribes and illegal contracting practices	Sweatshops and unsafe working conditions in third-world countries	Cybercrime
Civil rights issues	Human rights issues	Influence peddling	Rising corporate liability for personal damages (for example, cigarette companies)	Financial misconduct
Increased employee–employer tension	Covering up rather than correcting issues	Deceptive advertising	Financial mismanagement and fraud	Global issues, Chinese product safety
Changing work ethic	Disadvantaged consumer	Financial fraud (for example, savings and loan scandal)	Organizational ethical misconduct	Sustainability
Rising drug use		Transparency issues		Intellectual property theft

Source: Adapted from "Business Ethics Timeline," *Ethics Resource Center*, http://www.ethics.org/resources/business-ethics-timeline.asp (accessed May 27, 2009). Copyright © 2006, Ethics Resource Center (ERC). Used with permission of the ERC, 1747 Pennsylvania Ave., N.W., Suite 400, Washington, DC 2006, www.ethics.org.

churches, synagogues, and mosques. Religious leaders raised questions about fair wages, labor practices, and the morality of capitalism. For example, Catholic social ethics, which were expressed in a series of papal encyclicals, included concern for morality in business, workers' rights, and living wages; for humanistic values rather than materialistic ones; and for improving the conditions of the poor. Some Catholic colleges and universities began to offer courses in social ethics. Protestants also developed ethics courses in their seminaries and schools of theology and addressed issues concerning morality and ethics in business. The Protestant work ethic encouraged individuals to be frugal, work hard, and attain success in the capitalistic system. Such religious traditions provided a foundation for the future field of business ethics. Each religion applied its moral concepts not only to business but also to government, politics, the family, personal life, and all other aspects of life.

The 1960s: The Rise of Social Issues in Business

During the 1960s, American society turned to causes. An antibusiness attitude developed as many critics attacked the vested interests that controlled the economic and political sides of society—the so-called military-industrial complex. The 1960s saw the decay of inner cities and the growth of ecological problems such as pollution and the disposal of toxic and nuclear wastes. This period also witnessed the rise of consumerism—activities undertaken by independent individuals, groups, and organizations to protect their rights as consumers. In 1962 President John F. Kennedy delivered a "Special Message on Protecting the Consumer Interest" in which he outlined four basic consumer rights: the right to safety, the right to be informed, the right to choose, and the right to be heard. These came to be known as the **Consumers' Bill of Rights.**

The modern consumer movement is generally considered to have begun in 1965 with the publication of Ralph Nader's *Unsafe at Any Speed*, which criticized the auto industry as a whole, and General Motors Corporation (GM) in particular, for putting profit and style ahead of lives and safety. GM's Corvair was the main target of Nader's criticism. His consumer protection organization, popularly known as Nader's Raiders, fought successfully for legislation that required automobile makers to equip cars with safety belts, padded dashboards, stronger door latches, head restraints, shatterproof windshields, and collapsible steering columns. Consumer activists also helped secure passage of several consumer protection laws such as the Wholesome Meat Act of 1967, the Radiation Control for Health and Safety Act of 1968, the Clean Water Act of 1972, and the Toxic Substance Act of 1976.[19]

After Kennedy came President Lyndon B. Johnson and the Great Society, which extended national capitalism and told the business community that the U.S. government's responsibility was to provide the citizen with some degree of economic stability, equality, and social justice. Activities that could destabilize the economy or discriminate against any class of citizens began to be viewed as unethical and unlawful.

The 1970s: Business Ethics as an Emerging Field

Business ethics began to develop as a field of study in the 1970s. Theologians and philosophers had laid the groundwork by suggesting that certain principles could be applied to business activities. Using this foundation, business professors began to teach and write about corporate **social responsibility,** an organization's obligation to maximize its positive impact on stakeholders and to minimize its negative impact. Philosophers increased their involvement, applying ethical theory and philosophical analysis to structure the discipline of business ethics. Companies became more concerned with their public images, and as social demands grew, many businesses realized that they had to address ethical issues more directly. The Nixon administration's Watergate scandal focused public interest on the importance of ethics in government. Conferences were held to discuss the social responsibilities and ethical issues of business. Centers dealing with issues of business ethics were established. Interdisciplinary meetings brought business professors, theologians, philosophers, and businesspeople together. President Jimmy Carter attempted to focus on personal and administrative efforts to uphold ethical principles in government. The Foreign Corrupt Practices Act was passed during his administration, making it illegal for U.S. businesses to bribe government officials of other countries.

By the end of the 1970s, a number of major ethical issues had emerged, such as bribery, deceptive advertising, price collusion, product safety, and the environment. *Business ethics* became a common expression and was no longer considered an oxymoron. Academic researchers sought to identify ethical issues and describe how businesspeople might choose to act in particular situations. However, only limited efforts were made to describe how the ethical decision making process worked and to identify the many variables that influence this process in organizations.

The 1980s: Consolidation

In the 1980s, business academics and practitioners acknowledged business ethics as a field of study. A growing and varied group of institutions with diverse interests promoted its study. Business ethics organizations grew to include thousands of members. Five hundred courses in business ethics were offered at colleges across the country, with more than 40,000 students enrolled. Centers for business ethics provided publications, courses, conferences, and seminars. Business ethics was also a prominent concern within such leading companies as General Electric, Chase Manhattan, General Motors, Atlantic Richfield, Caterpillar, and S. C. Johnson & Son, Inc. Many of these firms established ethics and social policy committees to address ethical issues.

In the 1980s, the **Defense Industry Initiative on Business Ethics and Conduct** (DII) was developed to guide corporate support for ethical conduct. In 1986 eighteen defense contractors drafted principles for guiding business ethics and conduct.[20] The organization has since grown to nearly 50 members. This effort established a method for discussing best practices and working tactics to link organizational practice and policy to successful ethical compliance. The DII includes six principles. First, DII supports codes of conduct and their widespread distribution. These codes of conduct must be understandable and provide details on more substantive areas. Second, member companies are expected to provide ethics training for their employees as well as continuous support between training periods. Third, defense contractors must create an open atmosphere in which employees feel comfortable reporting violations without fear of retribution. Fourth, companies need to perform extensive internal audits and develop effective internal reporting and voluntary disclosure plans. Fifth, DII insists that member companies preserve the integrity of the defense industry. Finally, member companies must adopt a philosophy of public accountability.[21]

The 1980s ushered in the Reagan–Bush eras, with the accompanying belief that self-regulation, rather than regulation by government, was in the public's interest. Many tariffs and trade barriers were lifted, and businesses merged and divested within an increasingly global atmosphere. Thus, while business schools were offering courses in business ethics, the rules of business were changing at a phenomenal rate because of less regulation. Corporations that once were nationally based began operating internationally and found themselves mired in value structures where accepted rules of business behavior no longer applied.

The 1990s: Institutionalization of Business Ethics

The administration of President Bill Clinton continued to support self-regulation and free trade. However, it also took unprecedented government action to deal with health-related social issues such as teenage smoking. Its proposals included restricting cigarette advertising, banning vending machine sales, and ending the use of cigarette logos in connection with sports events.[22] Clinton also appointed Arthur Levitt as chairman of the Securities and Exchange Commission in 1993. Levitt unsuccessfully pushed for many reforms that could have prevented the accounting ethics scandals exemplified by Enron and WorldCom.[23]

The **Federal Sentencing Guidelines for Organizations** (FSGO), approved by Congress in November 1991, set the tone for organizational ethical compliance programs in the 1990s. The guidelines, which were based on the six principles of the DII,[24] broke new ground by codifying into law incentives to reward organizations for taking action to prevent misconduct such as developing effective internal legal and ethical compliance programs.[25] Provisions in the guidelines mitigate penalties for businesses that strive to root out misconduct and establish high ethical and legal standards.[26] On the other hand, under FSGO, if a company lacks an effective ethical compliance program and its employees violate the law, it can incur severe penalties. The guidelines focus on firms taking action to prevent and detect business misconduct in cooperation with government regulation. At the heart of the FSGO is the carrot-and-stick approach: By taking preventive action against misconduct, a company may avoid onerous penalties should a violation occur. A mechanical approach using legalistic logic will not suffice to avert serious penalties. The company must develop corporate values, enforce its own code of ethics, and strive to prevent misconduct.

The Twenty-First Century: A New Focus on Business Ethics

Although business ethics appeared to become more institutionalized in the 1990s, new evidence emerged in the early 2000s that more than a few business executives and managers had not fully embraced the public's desire for high ethical standards. For example, Bruce Bent, Sr. and his son Bruce Bent II were accused of engaging in fraud in misleading investors, ratings firms, and trustees when the assets of their Reserve Primary Fund fell. The accused reassured investors that the company had ample resources to support the broader declines in the financial market when, in fact, they did not. The Fund had $785 million in Lehman commercial paper, which ultimately became worthless.[27]

Arthur Andersen, a "Big Five" accounting firm, was convicted of obstructing justice after shredding documents related to its role as Enron's auditor.[28] The reputation of the once venerable accounting firm disappeared overnight, along with most of its clients, and the firm ultimately went out of business. Later the Supreme Court overruled the Arthur Andersen obstruction-of-justice conviction, but it was too late for the firm to recover. In addition to problems with its auditing of Enron, Arthur Andersen also faced questions surrounding its audits of other companies that were charged with employing questionable accounting practices, including Halliburton, WorldCom, Global Crossing, Dynegy, Qwest, and Sunbeam.[29] These accounting scandals made it evident that falsifying financial reports and reaping questionable benefits had become part of the culture of many companies. Firms outside the United States, such as Royal Ahold in the Netherlands and Parmalat in Italy, became major examples of accounting misconduct from a global perspective.

Such abuses increased public and political demands to improve ethical standards in business. In a survey of 20,000 people across 20 countries, trust in global companies had declined significantly.[30] To address the loss of confidence in financial reporting and corporate ethics, Congress in 2002 passed the **Sarbanes–Oxley Act,** the most far-reaching change in organizational control and accounting regulations since the Securities and Exchange Act of 1934. The new law made securities fraud a criminal offense and stiffened penalties for corporate fraud. It also created an accounting oversight board that requires corporations to establish codes of ethics for financial reporting and to develop greater transparency in financial reports to investors and other interested parties. Additionally, the law requires top executives to sign off on their firms' financial reports, and they risk fines and long prison sentences if they misrepresent their companies' financial position. The legislation further requires company executives to disclose stock sales immediately and prohibits companies from giving loans to top managers.[31]

> ***The company must develop corporate values, enforce its own code of ethics, and strive to prevent misconduct.***

The 2004 amendment to the FSGO requires that a business's governing authority be well informed about its ethics program with respect to content, implementation, and effectiveness. This places the responsibility squarely on the shoulders of the firm's leadership, usually the board of directors. The board is required to oversee the discovery of risks and to design, implement, and modify approaches to deal with those risks.

The Sarbanes–Oxley Act and the FSGO have institutionalized the need to discover and address ethical and legal risk. Top management and the board of directors of a corporation are accountable for discovering risk associated with ethical conduct. Such specific industries as the public sector, energy and chemicals, health care, insurance, and retail have to discover the unique risk associated with their operations and develop an ethics program to prevent ethical misconduct before it creates a crisis. Most firms are developing formal and informal mechanisms to have interactive communication and transparency about issues associated with the risk of misconduct. Business leaders should view that their greatest danger is not discovering serious misconduct or illegal activities somewhere in the organization. Unfortunately, most managers do not view the risk of an ethical disaster as important as the risk associated with fires, natural disasters, or technology failure. Ethical disasters can be significantly more damaging to a company's reputation than risks that are managed through insurance and other methods. The great investor Warren Buffett has stated that it is impossible to eradicate all wrongdoing in a large organization and that one can only hope that the misconduct is small and is caught in time. Buffett's fears came true in 2008 when the financial system collapsed because of pervasive, systemic use of instruments such as credit default swaps, risky debt such as subprime lending, and corruption in major corporations. The government was forced to step in and bail out many financial companies. Later, because of the weak financial system and reduced consumption, the government also had to step in to help major automotive companies GM and Chrysler. The U.S. government is now a majority shareholder in GM, an unprecedented move. Not since the Great Depression and President Franklin Delano Roosevelt has the United States seen such widespread government intervention and regulation—something that most deem necessary, but which is nevertheless worrisome to free market capitalists.

The basic assumptions of capitalism are under debate as countries around the world work to stabilize markets and question those that managed the money of individual corporations and nonprofits. The financial crisis caused many to question government institutions that provide oversight and regulation. As changes are made, there is a need to address issues related to law, ethics, and the required level of compliance necessary for government and business to serve the public interest.

In the KPMG Forensic Integrity Survey, employees were asked whether they had "personally seen" or had "firsthand knowledge of" misconduct within their organizations over the prior 12-month period. Roughly three-quarters of employees— 76 percent—reported that they had observed misconduct in the prior 12-month period.[32]

Figure 1–2 shows the results of misconduct by industry; there are generally high levels of observed misconduct across all industries. Employees in highly regulated financial industries, such as banking, finance, and insurance, reported relatively lower rates of misconduct within their organizations compared with others. While employees working in the public sector, which has not been subject to many of the new regulatory mandates placed on its private-sector counterparts, reported relatively higher rates of misconduct compared with others.

DEVELOPING AN ORGANIZATIONAL AND GLOBAL ETHICAL CULTURE

The current trend is away from legally based compliance initiatives in organizations to cultural initiatives that make ethics a part of core organizational values. To develop more ethical corporate cultures, many businesses are communicating core values to their employees by creating ethics programs and appointing ethics officers to oversee them. The ethical component of a corporate culture relates to the values, beliefs, and established and enforced patterns of conduct that employees use to identify and respond to ethical issues. The term **ethical culture** can be viewed as the character or decision making process that employees

FIGURE 1–2 Prevalence of Misconduct by Industry During the Prior 12 Months

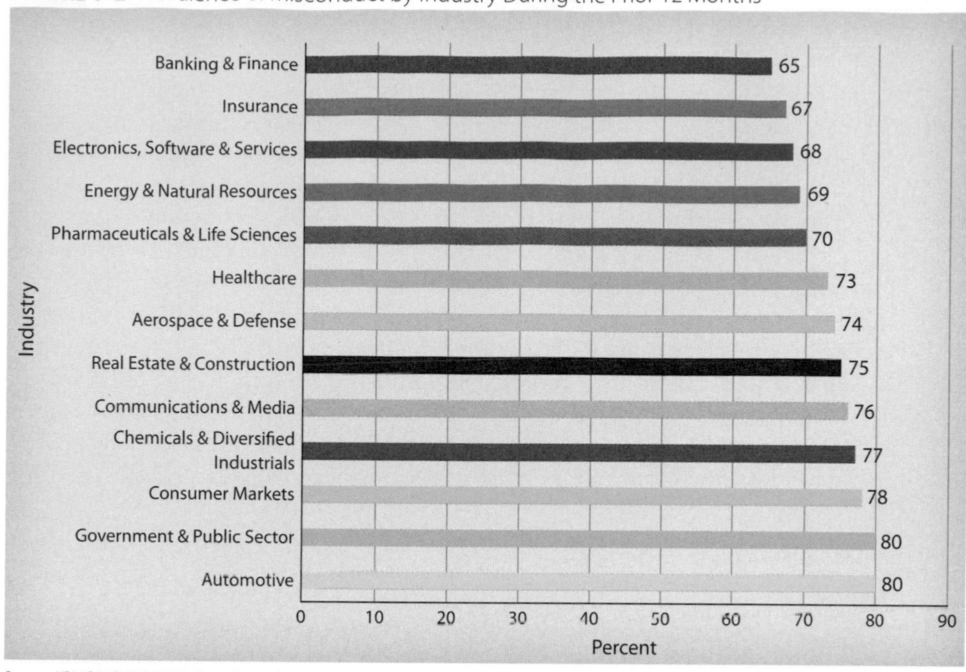

Source: KPMG LLP (U.S.) 2008, http://www.kpmg.com.br/publicacoes/forensic/Integrity_Survey_2008_2009.pdf (accessed August 4, 2009).

use to determine whether their responses to ethical issues are right or wrong. Ethical culture is used to describe the component of corporate culture that captures the values and norms that an organization defines as appropriate conduct. The goal of an ethical culture is to minimize the need for enforced compliance of rules and maximize the use of principles that contribute to ethical reasoning in difficult or new situations. An ethical culture creates shared values and support for ethical decisions and is driven by top management.

Globally, businesses are working more closely together to establish standards of acceptable behavior. We are already seeing collaborative efforts by a range of organizations to establish goals and mandate minimum levels of ethical behavior, from the European Union, the North American Free Trade Agreement (NAFTA), the Common Market of the Southern Cone (MERCOSUR), and the World Trade Organization (WTO) to, more recently, the Council on Economic Priorities' Social Accountability 8000 (SA 8000), the Ethical Trading Initiative, and the U.S. Apparel Industry Partnership. Some companies will not do business with organizations that do not support and abide by these standards. The development of global codes of ethics, such as the Caux Round Table, highlights common ethical concerns for global firms. The Caux Round Table (www.cauxroundtable.org) is a group of businesses, political leaders, and concerned interest groups that desire responsible behavior in the global community.

THE BENEFITS OF BUSINESS ETHICS

The field of business ethics continues to change rapidly as more firms recognize the benefits of improving ethical conduct and the link between business ethics and financial performance. Both research and examples from the business world demonstrate that building an ethical reputation among employees, customers, and the general public pays off. Figure 1–3 provides an overview of the relationship between business ethics and organizational performance. Although we believe there are many practical benefits to being ethical, many businesspeople make decisions because they believe a particular course of action is simply the right thing to do as a responsible member of society. Ricoh's Chairman, Masamitsu Sakurai, one of Ethisphere's 100 Most Influential People in Business Ethics, states that a foundational commitment to the environment creates a financial advantage. Ricoh transitioned to a flexible, cell-based production system that reduced carbon dioxide emissions and increased productivity, implemented additional emission reductions and waste reduction plans, and selectively placed clean ventilation points along the production line. These activities, as well as others, managed to cut carbon dioxide emissions by 85 percent and cut production costs in half.[33] Among the rewards for being more ethical and socially responsible in business are increased efficiency in daily operations, greater employee commitment, increased investor willingness to entrust funds, improved customer trust and satisfaction, and better financial performance. The reputation of a company has a major effect on its relationships with employees, investors, customers, and many other parties.

Ethics Contribute to Employee Commitment

Employee commitment comes from employees who believe their future is tied to that of the organization and their willingness to make personal sacrifices for the organization.[34] The more a company is dedicated to taking care of its employees, the more likely it is that the employees will take care of the organization. The NBES survey indicates that 79 percent of employees agree that ethics is important in continuing to work for their employer. It is also interesting to note that approximately 20 percent of employees are *not* concerned about the ethical environment of their organization.[35] This group is very complacent and has the potential for misconduct without guidance and ethical leadership. Issues that may foster the development of an ethical culture for employees include the absence of abusive behavior, a safe work environment, competitive salaries, and the fulfillment of all

FIGURE 1–3 The Role of Organizational Ethics in Performance

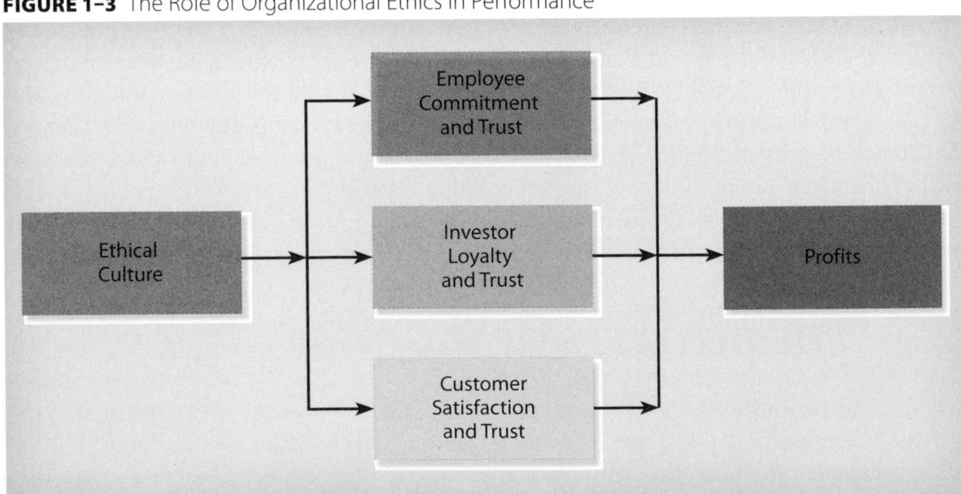

contractual obligations toward employees. An ethics and compliance program can support values and appropriate conduct. Social programs that may improve the ethical culture range from work–family programs and stock ownership plans to community service. Home Depot associates, for example, participate in disaster-relief efforts after hurricanes and tornadoes by rebuilding roofs, repairing water damage, planting trees, and clearing roads in their communities. Because employees spend a considerable amount of their waking time at work, a commitment by the organization to goodwill and respect for its employees usually increases the employees' loyalty to the organization and their support of its objectives. After years of bad publicity regarding environmental damage and its poor treatment of workers, Wal-Mart appears to have realized the importance of corporate social responsibility to a company's bottom line. Over 92 percent of Wal-Mart associates now have health insurance, and Wal-Mart has been working hard to improve diversity as well. In 2008 alone, Wal-Mart received 37 separate awards and distinctions for its diversity efforts. The company has taken strides toward being more sustainable as well—by doing everything from introducing low-emissions vehicles to its shipping fleet and installing solar panels on store rooftops. Wal-Mart has even stated a goal to be zero-waste.[36]

Employees' perception that their firm has an ethical culture leads to performance-enhancing outcomes within the organization.[37] For the sake of both productivity and teamwork, it is essential that employees both within and between departments throughout the organization share a common vision of trust. The influence of higher levels of trust is greatest on relationships within departments or work groups, but trust is a significant factor in relationships between departments as well. Consequently, programs that create a work environment that is trustworthy make individuals more willing to rely and act on the decisions and actions of their coworkers. In such a work environment, employees can reasonably expect to be treated with full respect and consideration by their coworkers and superiors. Trusting relationships between upper management and managers and their subordinates contribute to greater decision making efficiencies. One survey found that when employees see values such as honesty, respect, and trust applied frequently in the workplace, they feel less pressure to compromise ethical standards, observe less misconduct, are more satisfied with their organizations overall, and feel more valued as employees.[38]

The ethical culture of a company seems to matter to employees. According to a report on employee loyalty and work practices, companies viewed as highly ethical by their employees were six times more likely to keep their workers.[39] Also, employees who view their company as having a strong community involvement feel more loyal to their employers and feel positive about themselves.

Ethics Contribute to Investor Loyalty

Ethical conduct results in shareholder loyalty and can contribute to success that supports even broader social causes and concerns. Former Wal-Mart CEO Lee Scott has stated that "As businesses, we have a responsibility to society. We also have an extraordinary opportunity. Let me be clear about this point, there is no conflict between delivering value to shareholders and helping solve bigger societal problems. In fact, they can build upon each other when developed, aligned, and executed right."[40]

Investors today are increasingly concerned about the ethics, social responsibility, and reputation of companies in which they invest, and various socially responsible mutual funds and asset management firms can help investors purchase stock in ethical companies.

Investors are also recognizing that an ethical culture provides a foundation for efficiency, productivity, and profits. On the other hand, investors know too that negative publicity, lawsuits, and fines can lower stock prices, diminish customer loyalty, and threaten a company's long-term viability. Many companies accused of misconduct have experienced dramatic declines in the value of their stock when concerned investors divested their stocks and bonds. Warren Buffett and his company Berkshire Hathaway command significant respect from investors because of their track record of financial returns and the integrity of their organizations. Buffett says, "I want employees to ask themselves whether they are willing to have any contemplated act appear the next day on the front page of their local paper—to be read by their spouses, children and friends—with the reporting done by an informed and critical reporter." The high level of accountability and trust Buffett places in his employees translates into investor trust and confidence.[41]

TIAA-CREF investor participants were asked would they choose a financial services company with strong ethics or higher returns. Surprisingly, 92 percent of respondents said they would choose ethics while only 5 percent chose higher returns.[42]

"Customer satisfaction is one of the most important factors in successful business strategy."

Investors look at the bottom line for profits or the potential for increased stock prices or dividends. But they also look for any potential flaws in the company's performance, conduct, and financial reports. Therefore, gaining investors' trust and confidence is vital to sustaining the financial stability of the firm.

Ethics Contribute to Customer Satisfaction

It is generally accepted that customer satisfaction is one of the most important factors in successful business strategy. Although a company must continue to develop, alter, and adapt products to keep pace with customers' changing desires and preferences, it must also seek to develop long-term relationships with customers and its stakeholders. Patagonia, Inc. has engaged in a broad array of environmentally, socially responsible and ethical behaviors over many years to better connect with its target markets. The company has donated more than $31 million to over 1,000 environmentally oriented causes. Employees can volunteer for an environmental group and get up to two months pay. The entire clothing line was sourced using organic cotton in 1996. Targeting Generation Y, the company is selling "Vote the Environment" t-shirts and donates $5 from each to the League of Conservation Voters. In addition, the company is currently creating the Patagonia National Park to protect wildland ecosystems and biodiversity in Chile and Argentina. All new facilities are being built with LEED certification showing their commitment to green building and the environment.[43]

For most businesses, both repeat purchases and an enduring relationship of mutual respect and cooperation with their customers are essential for success. By focusing on customer satisfaction, a company continually deepens the customer's dependence on the company, and as the customer's confidence grows, the firm gains a better understanding of how to serve the customer so the relationship may endure. Successful businesses provide an opportunity for customer feedback, which can engage the customer in cooperative problem solving. As is often pointed out, a happy customer will come back, but a disgruntled customer will tell others about his or her dissatisfaction with a company and discourage friends from dealing with it.

The public's trust is essential to maintaining a good long-term relationship between a business and consumers. The Millennium Poll of 25,000 citizens in 23 countries found that almost 60 percent of people focus on social responsibility ahead of brand reputation or financial factors when forming impressions of companies.[44] As social responsibility becomes more important for companies, it has been suggested that corporate social responsibility is a sign of good management and that it may, according to one study, indicate good financial performance. However, another study indicates that the reverse may be true, that companies who have good financial performance are able to spend more money on social responsibility.[45] Google would be an example of such a company. Google shows extreme care for its employees at its Googleplex headquarters in Mountain View, CA. Investment in their employees satisfaction and retention involves providing bicycles for efficient travel between meetings, lava lamps, massage chairs, shared work cubicles to allow for intellectual stimulation and idea generation, laptops for every employee, foosball, pool tables, volleyball courts, assorted video games, pianos, ping pong tables, lap pools, gyms, yoga and dance classes, meditation classes, wine tasting groups, film clubs, salsa dancing clubs, healthy lunches for staff at a wide variety of cafes, outdoor seating for "brainstorming," and snack rooms packed with various snacks and drinks.[46]

When an organization has a strong ethical environment, it usually focuses on the core value of placing customers' interests first. Putting customers first does not mean that the interests of employees, investors, and local communities should be ignored, however. An ethical culture that focuses on customers incorporates the interests of all employees, suppliers, and other interested parties in decisions and actions. Employees working in an ethical environment support and contribute to the process of understanding customers' demands and concerns. Ethical conduct toward customers builds a strong competitive position that has been shown to affect business performance and product innovation positively.

Ethics Contribute to Profits

A company cannot nurture and develop an ethical culture unless it has achieved adequate financial performance in terms of profits. Businesses with greater resources—regardless of their staff size—have the means to practice social responsibility while serving their customers, valuing their employees, and establishing trust with the public. Ethical conduct toward customers builds a strong competitive position that has been shown to affect business performance and product innovation positively.[47] Green Mountain Coffee Company, which sells products under the Green Mountain, Newman's Own, and Keurig brands, has built a strong reputation on social responsibility. The company donates to local and coffee-growing communities, as well as buys carbon offsets. Also, 28 percent of its coffee purchases are Fair Trade certified. Its CSR activities have led to more business. Organizations such as Creighton University chose to purchase Green Mountain Coffee products because students and educators appreciate the company's environmentally friendly practices.[48] Every day, business newspapers and magazines offer new examples of the consequences of business misconduct. It is worth noting, however, that most of these companies have learned from their mistakes and recovered after they implemented programs to improve ethical and legal conduct.

Ample evidence shows that being ethical pays off with better performance. As indicated earlier, companies that are perceived by their employees as having a high degree of honesty and integrity have a much higher average total return to shareholders than do companies perceived as having a low degree of honesty and integrity.[49] A recent study demonstrates that, even using a variety of measurement methods, companies actively engaging in corporate social responsibility have higher pre-tax income than firms that are merely focused on financial performance; therefore ambition and performance are not in conflict with being ethical.[50] These results provide strong evidence that corporate concern for ethical conduct is becoming a part of strategic planning toward obtaining the outcome of higher profitability. Rather than being just a compliance program, ethics is becoming one of the management issues within the effort to achieve competitive advantage.

OUR FRAMEWORK FOR STUDYING BUSINESS ETHICS

We have developed a framework for this text to help you understand how people make ethical decisions and deal with ethical issues. Table 1–3 summarizes each element in the framework and describes where each topic is discussed in this book.

In Part One, we provide an overview of business ethics. Chapter 1 defines the term *business ethics* and explores the development and importance of this critical business area. In Chapter 2, we explore the role of various stakeholder groups in social responsibility and corporate governance.

Part Two focuses on ethical issues and the institutionalization of business ethics. In Chapter 3, we examine business issues that create ethical decision making in organizations. In Chapter 4, we look at the institutionalization of business ethics including both mandatory and voluntary societal concerns.

In Part Three, we delineate the ethical decision making process and then look at both individual factors and organizational factors that influence decisions. Chapter 5 describes the ethical decision making process from an organizational perspective. Chapter 6 explores individual factors that may influence ethical decisions in business, including moral philosophies and cognitive moral development. Chapter 7 focuses on the organizational dimensions including corporate culture, relationships, and conflicts.

In Part Four, we explore systems and processes associated with implementing business ethics into global strategic planning. Chapter 8 discusses the development of an effective ethics program. In Chapter 9, we examine issues related to implementing and auditing ethics programs. And finally, Chapter 10 considers ethical issues in a global context.

We hope that this framework will help you to develop a balanced understanding of the various perspectives and alternatives available to you when making ethical business decisions. Regardless of your own personal values, the more you know about how individuals make decisions, the better prepared you will be to cope with difficult ethical decisions. Such knowledge will help you improve and control the ethical decision making environment in which you work.

It is your job to make the final decision in an ethical situation that affects you. Sometimes that decision may be right; sometimes it may be wrong. It is always easy to look back with hindsight and know what one should have done in a particular situation. At the time, however, the choices might not have been so clear. To give you practice making ethical decisions, Part Five of this book contains a number of cases. In addition, each chapter begins with a vignette, "An Ethical Dilemma," and ends with a minicase, "Resolving Ethical Business Challenges," that involves ethical problems. We hope they will give you a better sense of the challenges of making ethical decisions in the real business world.

TABLE 1–3 Our Framework for Studying Business Ethics

Chapter	Highlights
1. The Importance of Business Ethics	• Definitions
	• Reasons for studying business ethics
	• History
	• Benefits of business ethics
2. Stakeholder Relationships, Social Responsibility, and Corporate Governance	• Stakeholder relationships
	• Stakeholder influences in social responsibility
	• Corporate governance
3. Emerging Business Ethics Issues	• Recognizing an ethical issue
	• Honesty, fairness, and integrity
	• Ethical issues and dilemmas in business: abusive and disruptive behavior, lying, conflicts of interest, bribery, corporate intelligence, discrimination, sexual harassment, environmental issues, fraud, insider trading, intellectual property rights, and privacy
	• Determining an ethical issue in business
4. The Institutionalization of Business Ethics	• Mandatory requirements
	• Voluntary requirements
	• Core practices
	• Federal Sentencing Guidelines for Organizations
	• Sarbanes–Oxley Act
5. Ethical Decision Making and Ethical Leadership	• Ethical issue intensity
	• Individual factors in decision making
	• Organizational factors in decision making
	• Opportunity in decision making
	• Business ethics evaluations and intentions
	• The role of leadership in a corporate culture
	• Leadership styles influence ethical decisions
	• Habits of strong ethical leaders

(continued)

TABLE 1–3 Our Framework for Studying Business Ethics *(continued)*

Chapter	Highlights
6. Individual Factors: Moral Philosophies and Values	• Moral philosophies, including teleological development philosophies; and cognitive moral deontological, relativist, virtue ethics, and justice philosophies
	• Stages of cognitive moral development
7. Organizational Factors: The Role of Ethical Culture and Relationships	• Corporate culture
	• Interpersonal relationships
	• Whistle-blowing
	• Opportunity and conflict
8. Developing an Effective Ethics Program	• Ethics programs
	• Codes of ethics
	• Program responsibility
	• Communication of ethical standards
	• Systems to monitor and enforce ethical standards
	• Continuous improvement of ethics programs
9. Implementing and Auditing Ethics Programs	• Implementation programs
	• Ethics audits
10. Business Ethics in a Global Economy	• Ethical perceptions economy
	• Culture and cultural relations
	• Multinational corporations
	• Universal ethics
	• Global ethics issues

SUMMARY

This chapter provides an overview of the field of business ethics and introduces the framework for the discussion of business ethics. Business ethics comprises principles and standards that guide behavior in the world of business. Investors, employees, customers, interest groups, the legal system, and the community often determine whether a specific action is right or wrong, ethical or unethical.

Studying business ethics is important for many reasons. Recent incidents of unethical activity in business underscore the widespread need for a better understanding of the factors that contribute to ethical and unethical decisions. Individuals' personal moral philosophies and decision making experience may not be sufficient to guide them in the business world. Studying business ethics will help you begin to identify ethical issues and recognize the approaches available to resolve them.

The study of business ethics evolved through five distinct stages. Before 1960, business ethics issues were discussed primarily from a religious perspective. The 1960s saw the emergence of many social issues involving business and the idea of social conscience as well as a rise in consumerism, which culminated with Kennedy's Consumers' Bill of Rights. Business ethics began to develop as an independent field of study in the 1970s, with academics and practitioners exploring ethical issues and attempting to understand how individuals and organizations make ethical decisions. These experts began to teach and write about the idea of corporate social responsibility, an organization's obligation to maximize its positive impact on stakeholders and to minimize its negative impact. In the 1980s, centers of business ethics provided publications, courses, conferences, and seminars, and many companies established ethics committees and social policy committees. The Defense Industry Initiative on Business Ethics and Conduct was developed to guide corporate support for ethical conduct; its principles had a major impact on corporate ethics.

However, less government regulation and an increase in businesses with international operations raised new ethical issues. In the 1990s, government continued to support self-regulation. The FSGO sets the tone for organizational ethics programs by providing incentives for companies to take action to prevent organizational misconduct. The twenty-first century ushered in a new set of ethics scandals, suggesting that many companies had not fully embraced the public's desire for higher ethical standards. The Sarbanes–Oxley Act therefore stiffened penalties for corporate fraud and established an accounting oversight board. The current trend is away from legally based ethical initiatives in organizations toward cultural initiatives that make ethics a part of core organizational values. The ethical component of a corporate culture relates to the values, beliefs, and established and enforced patterns of conduct that employees use to identify and respond to ethical issues. The term *ethical culture* describes the component of corporate culture that captures the rules and principles that an organization defines as appropriate conduct. It can be viewed as the character or decision making process that employees use to determine whether their responses to ethical issues are right or wrong.

Research and anecdotes demonstrate that building an ethical reputation among employees, customers, and the general public provides benefits that include increased efficiency in daily operations, greater employee commitment, increased investor willingness to entrust funds, improved customer trust and satisfaction, and better financial performance. The reputation of a company has a major effect on its relationships with employees, investors, customers, and many other parties and thus has the potential to affect its bottom line.

Finally, this text introduces a framework for studying business ethics. Each chapter addresses some aspect of business ethics and decision making within a business context. The major concerns are ethical issues in business, stakeholder relationships, social responsibility and corporate governance, emerging business ethics issues, the institutionalization of business ethics, understanding the ethical decision making process, moral philosophies and cognitive moral development, corporate culture, organizational relationships and conflicts, developing an effective ethics program, implementing and auditing the ethics program, and global business ethics.

IMPORTANT TERMS FOR REVIEW

business ethics

principles

values

Consumers' Bill of Rights

social responsibility

Defense Industry Initiative on Business Ethics and Conduct

Federal Sentencing Guidelines for Organizations

Sarbanes–Oxley Act

ethical culture

RESOLVING ETHICAL BUSINESS CHALLENGES*

Frank Garcia was just starting out as a salesperson with Acme Corporation. Acme's corporate culture was top-down, or hierarchical. Because of the competitive nature of the medical supplies industry, few mistakes were tolerated. Otis Hillman was a buyer for Thermocare, a national hospital chain. Frank's first meeting with Otis was a success, resulting in a $500,000 contract. This sale represented a significant increase for Acme and an additional $1,000 bonus for Frank.

Some months later, Frank called on Thermocare, seeking to increase the contract by $500,000. "Otis, I think you'll need the additional inventory. It looks as if you didn't have enough at the end of last quarter," said Frank.

"You may be right. Business has picked up. Maybe it's because of your product, but then again, maybe not. It's still not clear to me whether Acme is the best for us. Speaking of which, I heard that you have season tickets to the Cubs!" replied Otis.

Frank thought for a moment and said, "Otis, I know that part of your increases is due to our quality products. How about we discuss this over a ball game?"

"Well, OK," Otis agreed.

By the seventh-inning stretch, Frank had convinced Otis that the additional inventory was needed and offered to give Thermocare a pair of season tickets. When Frank's boss, Amber, heard of the sale, she was very pleased. "Frank, this is great. We've been trying to get Thermocare's business for a long time. You seem to have connected with their buyer." As a result of the Thermocare account, Frank received another large bonus check and a letter of achievement from the vice president of marketing.

Two quarters later, Frank had become one of the top producers in the division. At the beginning of the quarter, Frank had run the numbers on Thermocare's account and found that business was booming. The numbers showed that Otis's business could probably handle an additional $750,000 worth of goods without hurting return on assets. As Frank went over the figures with Otis, Otis's response was, "You know, Frank, I've really enjoyed the season tickets, but this is a big increase." As the conversation meandered, Frank soon found out that Otis and his wife had never been to Cancun, Mexico. Frank had never been in a situation like this before, so he excused himself to another room and called Amber about what he was thinking of doing.

"Are you kidding!" responded Amber. "Why are you even calling me on this? I'll find the money somewhere to pay for it."

"Is this OK with Acme?" asked Frank.

"You let me worry about that," Amber told him.

When Frank suggested that Otis and his wife be his guests in Cancun, the conversation seemed to go smoothly. In Cancun, Otis decided to purchase the additional goods, for which Frank received another bonus increase and another positive letter from headquarters.

Some time later, Amber announced to her division that they would be taking all of their best clients to Las Vegas for a thank-you party. One of those invited was Thermocare. When they arrived, Amber gave each person $500 and said, "I want you to know that Acme is very grateful for the business that you have provided us. As a result of your understanding the qualitative differences of our products, we have doubled our production facilities. This trip and everything that goes with it for the next few days is our small way of saying thank you. Every one of you has your salesperson here. If there is anything that you need, please let him or her know, and we'll try to accommodate you. Have a good time!"

That night Otis saw Frank at dinner and suggested to him that he was interested in attending an "adult entertainment" club. When Frank came to Amber about this, she said, "Is he asking you to go with him?"

"No, Amber, not me!"

"Well, then, if he's not asking you to go, I don't understand why you're talking to me. Didn't I say we'd take care of their needs?"

"But what will Acme say if this gets out?" asked Frank.

"Don't worry; it won't," said Amber.

QUESTIONS • EXERCISES

1. What are the potential ethical issues faced by Acme Corporation?
2. What should Acme do if there is a desire to make ethics a part of its core organizational values?
3. Identify the ethical issues of which Frank needs to be aware.
4. Discuss the advantages and disadvantages of each decision that Frank could make.

*This case is strictly hypothetical; any resemblance to real persons, companies, or situations is coincidental.

CHECK YOUR EQ

Check your EQ, or Ethics Quotient, by completing the following. Assess your performance to evaluate your overall understanding of the chapter material.

1.	Business ethics focuses mostly on personal ethical issues.	**Yes**	**No**
2.	Business ethics deals with right or wrong behavior within a particular organization.	**Yes**	**No**
3.	An ethical culture is based upon the norms and values of the company.	**Yes**	**No**
4.	Business ethics contributes to investor loyalty.	**Yes**	**No**
5.	The trend is away from cultural or ethically based initiatives to legal initiatives in organizations.	**Yes**	**No**
6.	Investments in business ethics do not support the bottom line.	**Yes**	**No**

ANSWERS: **1. No.** Business ethics focuses on organizational concerns (legal and ethical—employees, customers, suppliers, society). **2. Yes.** That stems from the basic definition. **3. Yes.** Norms and values help create an organizational culture and are key in supporting or not supporting ethical conduct. **4. Yes.** Many studies have shown that trust and ethical conduct contribute to investor loyalty. **5. No.** Many businesses are communicating their core values to their employees by creating ethics programs and appointing ethics officers to oversee them. **6. No.** Ethics initiatives cause consumer, employee, and shareholder loyalty and positive behavior that contributes to the bottom line.

CHAPTER 2

Stakeholder Relationships, Social Responsibility, and Corporate Governance

CHAPTER OBJECTIVES

- To identify stakeholders' roles in business ethics
- To define social responsibility
- To examine the relationship between stakeholder orientation and social responsibility
- To delineate a stakeholder orientation in creating corporate social responsibility
- To explore the role of corporate governance in structuring ethics and social responsibility in business
- To list the steps involved in implementing a stakeholder perspective in social responsibility and business ethics

CHAPTER OUTLINE

Stakeholders Define Ethical Issues in Business

Identifying Stakeholders

A Stakeholder Orientation

Social Responsibility and the Importance of a Stakeholder Orientation

Social Responsibility and Ethics

Corporate Governance Provides Formalized Responsibility to Stakeholders

Views of Corporate Governance

The Role of Boards of Directors

Implementing a Stakeholder Perspective

Step 1: Assessing the Corporate Culture

Step 2: Identifying Stakeholder Groups

Step 3: Identifying Stakeholder Issues

Step 4: Assessing Organizational Commitment to Social Responsibility

Step 5: Identifying Resources and Determining Urgency

Step 6: Gaining Stakeholder Feedback

AN ETHICAL DILEMMA*

Carla knew something was wrong when Jack got back to his desk. He had been with Aker & Aker Accounting (A&A) for 17 years, starting there right after graduation and progressing through the ranks. Jack was a strong supporter of the company, and that was why Carla had been assigned to him. Carla had been with A&A for two years. She had graduated in the top 10 percent of her class and passed the CPA exam on the first try. She had chosen A&A over one of the "Big Four" firms because A&A was the biggest and best firm in Smallville, Ohio, where her husband, Frank, managed a locally owned machine tools company. She and Frank had just purchased a new home when things started to turn strange with Jack, her boss.

"What's the matter, Jack?" Carla asked.

"Well, you'll hear about it sooner or later. I've been denied a partner's position. Can you imagine that? I have been working 60- and 70-hour weeks for the last 10 years, and all that management can say to me is 'not at this time,'" complained Jack.

Carla asked, "So what else did they say?"

Jack turned red and blurted out, "They said maybe in a few more years. I've done all that they've asked me to do. I've sacrificed a lot, and now they say a few more years. It's not fair."

"What are you going to do?" Carla asked.

"I don't know," Jack said. "I just don't know."

Six months later, Carla noticed that Jack was behaving oddly. He came in late and left early. One Sunday Carla went into the office for some files and found Jack copying some of the software that A&A used in auditing and consulting. A couple of weeks later, at a dinner party, Carla overheard a conversation about Jack doing consulting work for some small firms. Monday morning, she asked him if what she had heard was true.

Jack responded, "Yes, Carla, it's true. I have a few clients that I do work for on occasion."

"Don't you think there's a conflict of interest between you and A&A?" asked Carla.

"No," said Jack. "You see, these clients are not technically within the market area of A&A. Besides, I was counting on that promotion to help pay some extra bills. My oldest son decided to go to a private university, which is an extra $25,000 each year. Plus our medical plan at A&A doesn't

*This case is strictly hypothetical; any resemblance to real persons, companies, or situations is coincidental.

cover some of my medical problems. And you don't want to know the cost. The only way I can afford to pay for these things is to do some extra work on the side."

"But what if A&A finds out?" Carla asked. "Won't they terminate you?"

"I don't want to think about that. Besides, if they don't find out for another six months, I may be able to start my own company."

"How?" asked Carla.

"Don't be naive, Carla. You came in that Sunday. You know."

Carla realized that Jack had been using A&A software for his own gain. "That's stealing!" she said.

"Stealing?" Jack's voice grew calm. "Like when you use the office phones for personal long-distance calls? Like when you decided to volunteer to help out your church and copied all those things for them on the company machine? If I'm stealing, you're a thief as well. But let's not get into this discussion. I'm not hurting A&A and, who knows, maybe within the next year I'll become a partner and can quit my night job."

Carla backed off from the discussion and said nothing more. She couldn't afford to antagonize her boss and risk bad performance ratings. She and Frank had bills, too. She also knew that she wouldn't be able to get another job at the same pay if she quit. Moving to another town was not an option because of Frank's business. She had no physical evidence to take to the partners, which meant that it would be her word against Jack's, and he had 17 years of experience with the company.

QUESTIONS • EXERCISES

1. Identify the ethical issues in this case.
2. Assume you are Carla. Discuss your options and what the consequences of each option might be.
3. Assume you are Jack. Discuss your options.
4. Discuss any additional information you feel you might need before making your decision.

Business ethics issues, conflicts, and successes revolve around relationships. Building effective relationships is considered one of the more important areas of business today. A business exists because of relationships between employees, customers, shareholders or investors, suppliers, and managers who develop strategies to attain success. In addition, an organization usually has a governing authority often called a board of directors that provides oversight and direction to make sure that the organization stays focused on objectives in an ethical, legal, and socially acceptable manner. When unethical acts are discovered in organizations, it is often found that in most instances there is knowing cooperation or compliancy that facilitates the acceptance and perpetuation of unethical conduct.[1] Therefore, relationships are not only associated with organizational success but also with organizational misconduct.

A stakeholder framework helps identify the internal stakeholders such as employees, boards of directors, and managers and external stakeholders such as customers, special interest groups, regulators, and others who agree, collaborate, and have confrontations on ethical issues. Most ethical issues exist because of conflicts in values and belief patterns about right and wrong between and within stakeholder groups. This framework allows a firm to identify, monitor, and respond to the needs, values, and expectations of different stakeholder groups.

The formal system of accountability and control of ethical and socially responsible behavior is corporate governance. In theory, the board of directors provides oversight for all decisions and use of resources. Ethical issues relate to the role of the board of directors, shareholder relationship, internal control, risk management, and executive compensation. Ethical leadership is associated with appropriate corporate governance.

In this chapter, we first focus on the concept of stakeholders and examine how a stakeholder framework can help understand organizational ethics. Then we identify stakeholders and the importance of a stakeholder orientation. Using the stakeholder framework, social responsibility is explored, including the various dimensions of social responsibility. Next, corporate governance as a dimension of social responsibility and ethical decision making is covered to provide an understanding of the importance of oversight in responding to stakeholders. Finally, we provide the steps for implementing a stakeholder perspective in creating social responsibility and ethical decisions in business.

STAKEHOLDERS DEFINE ETHICAL ISSUES IN BUSINESS

In a business context, customers, investors and shareholders, employees, suppliers, government agencies, communities, and many others who have a "stake" or claim in some aspect of a company's products, operations, markets, industry, and outcomes are known as **stakeholders.** These groups are influenced by business, but they also have the ability to influence businesses; thus, the relationship between companies and their stakeholders is a two-way street.[2]

Sometimes activities and negative press generated by special interest groups can force a company to change its practices. For example, People for the Ethical Treatment of Animals (PETA) launched a campaign again McDonald's to try to force the company to halt inhumane treatment of chickens among its egg suppliers. McDonald's did change their policies, although they deny that PETA's actions had any direct effect. More recently, PETA has targeted McDonald's again—this time focusing on the ways that chickens are raised and slaughtered at the company's meat suppliers. Burger King, on the other hand, received an award from PETA in 2008 for its improvements in animal welfare.[3] Many firms experienced conflicts with key stakeholders, and consequently damaged their reputations and shareholder confidence during the 2008–2009 financial crisis. While many threats to reputation stem from uncontrollable events and the environment, ethical misconduct is more difficult to overcome than poor financial performance. Stakeholders who are most directly affected by negative events will have a corresponding shift in their perceptions of a firm's reputation. On the other hand, firms such as financial institutions that receive negative publicity for misconduct destroy trust and tarnish their reputations, which will make it more difficult to retain existing customers or attract new ones.[4]

Consider the decision made by Bear Stearns, at the time an investment bank, to allow managers to invest clients' money in high-risk, highly leveraged portfolio instruments, which were backed in part by subprime mortgages. While losing money is not a crime, Ralph Cioffi and Matthew Tannin, the founders and portfolio managers of two Bear Stearns hedge funds, are charged with making false statements in the months leading to the funds' demise. These Bear Stearns managers made reassuring public statements to investors ("we are very comfortable with exactly where we are") on April 25, 2007, although private e-mails days earlier stated "if we believe the internal report is anywhere close to accurate, I think we should close the funds now." The plaintiff's class action lawyers claimed that

Bear Stearns' problems were compounded two months later when Bear Stearns CEO James E. Cayne assured investors that "the balance sheet, capital base, and liquidity profile have never been stronger. Bear Stearns' risk exposures to high-profile sectors are moderate and well-controlled."[5] Several months later the company sought emergency funding from the government and was sold to JP Morgan Chase.[6] Of course it's impossible to know if CEO Cayne knew the true state of the financial situation at the time he made his comment, but the damage to the reputation of the company from these events was fatal. Once the credibility of a firm's statements has been destroyed, the reputation of the company and trust with stakeholders is almost impossible to recover. While prosecutors asked questions after the firm's collapse, at this time there is no active criminal inquiry into the CEO's statements. To maintain trust and confidence with stakeholders, CEOs and other top managers are expected to tell the truth to prevent customers and investors from being damaged by the failure to receive timely and accurate information. Providing untruthful or deceptive information to stakeholders, if not illegal, is unethical.

The financial crisis was based on a failure to consider the ramifications of unethical decision making affecting all stakeholders, including society and the economic system. The foundation of the crisis was subprime loans, involving lending money to people who could not possibly repay their loans. Many companies engaged in providing fictitious financial information. For example, in California a Mexican strawberry picker with an income of $14,000 who spoke no English was lent all the money he needed to buy a house for $720,000.[7] This reckless disregard for the impact on financial organizations that purchased the loan obligations, which could never be repaid, was at the heart of the 2008–2009 financial crisis.

Ethical misconduct and decisions that damage stakeholders will generally impact the company's reputation both from investor confidence and consumer confidence perspectives. As investor perceptions and decisions begin to take their toll, shareholder value will drop, exposing the company to consumer scrutiny that can increase the damage. Reputation is a factor in the consumers' perceptions of product attributes and corporate image features that lead to consumer willingness to purchase goods and services at profitable prices. Bailed-out bank Citigroup halted payments of some bonuses after public backlash became a problem. Public disgust and outrage over the payment of bonuses to executives in failing financial firms was high after AIG paid retention bonuses to its executives, even after the government had spent billions to rescue the firm. Citigroup determined that the issue was too politically sensitive, and made the ethically questionable decision to hold off on making the payments until the political climate cooled down.[8] Some scandals may lead to boycotts and aggressive campaigns to dampen sales and earnings. Nike experienced such a backlash from its use of offshore subcontractors to manufacture its shoes and clothing. When Nike claimed no responsibility for the subcontractors' poor working conditions and extremely low wages, some consumers demanded greater accountability and responsibility by engaging in boycotts, letter-writing campaigns, and public service announcements. Nike ultimately responded to the growing negative publicity by changing its practices and becoming a model company in managing offshore manufacturing.[9]

New reforms to improve corporate accountability and transparency also suggest that other stakeholders—including banks, attorneys, and public accounting firms—can play a major role in fostering responsible decision making.[10] Stakeholders apply their values and standards to many diverse issues—working conditions, consumer rights, environmental conservation, product safety, and proper information disclosure—that may or may not directly affect an individual stakeholder's own welfare. We can assess the level of social responsibility that an organization bears by scrutinizing its effects on the issues of concern to its stakeholders.[11]

Stakeholders provide resources that are more or less critical to a firm's long-term success. These resources may be both tangible and intangible. Shareholders, for example, supply capital; suppliers offer material resources or intangible knowledge; employees and managers grant expertise, leadership, and commitment; customers generate revenue and provide loyalty and positive word-of-mouth promotion; local communities provide infrastructure; and the media transmits positive corporate images. When individual stakeholders share similar expectations about desirable business conduct, they may choose to establish or join formal communities that are dedicated to better defining and advocating these values and expectations. Stakeholders' ability to withdraw—or to threaten to withdraw—these needed resources gives them power over businesses.[12]

Identifying Stakeholders

We can identify two different types of stakeholders. **Primary stakeholders** are those whose continued association is absolutely necessary for a firm's survival; these include employees, customers, investors, and shareholders, as well as the governments and communities that provide necessary infrastructure. Some firms take actions that can damage relationships with primary stakeholders. Figure 2-1 indicates that, after experiencing some declines in 2007, strong ethical corporate cultures are back on the rise, with strong cultures making

FIGURE 2–1 After Declining, Strength of Organizational Culture is on the Rise Again

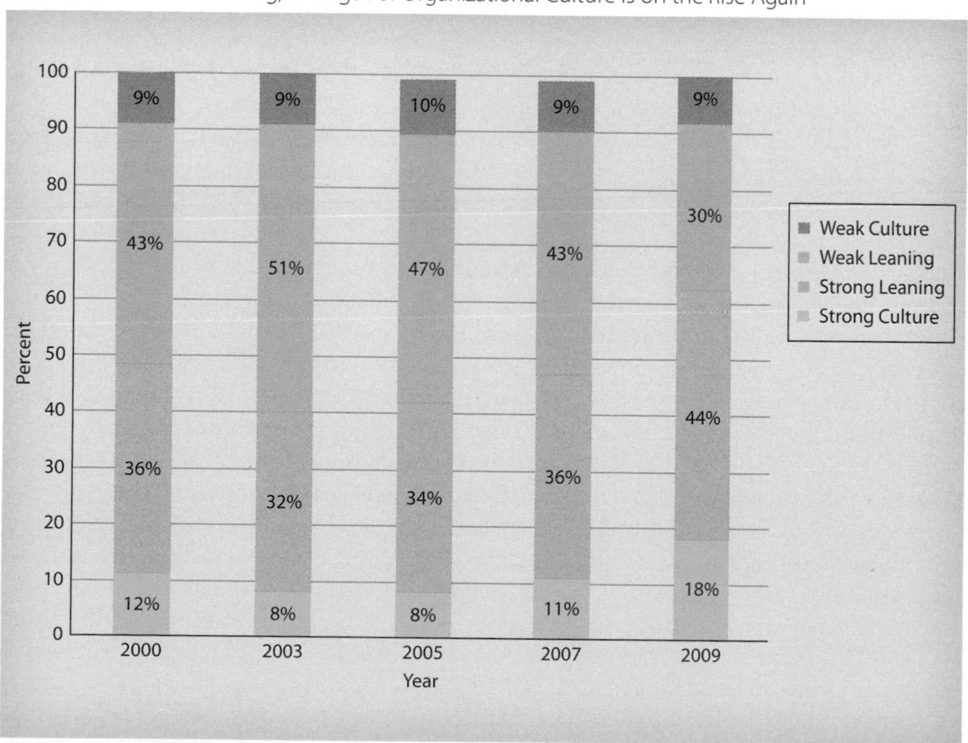

Note: Due to rounding, some totals do note equal 100 percent.

Source: "2009 National Business Ethics Survey: Ethics in the Recession," (Washington D.C.: Ethics Resource Center, 2009): p. 14.

a large 9% jump in 2009. Ethical corporate cultures are linked to positive relationships with stakeholders. Concern for stakeholders' needs and expectations is necessary to avoid ethical conflicts.

Secondary stakeholders do not typically engage in transactions with a company and thus are not essential for its survival; these include the media, trade associations, and special interest groups. The American Association of Retired People (AARP), a special interest group, works to support retirees' rights such as health care benefits. Both primary and secondary stakeholders embrace specific values and standards that dictate what constitutes acceptable or unacceptable corporate behaviors. It is important for managers to recognize that while primary groups may present more day-to-day concerns, secondary groups cannot be ignored or given less consideration in the ethical decision making process.[13] Table 2–1 shows a select list of issues important to various stakeholder groups and how corporations impact these issues.

Figure 2–2 offers a conceptualization of the relationship between businesses and stakeholders. In this **stakeholder interaction model,** there are two-way relationships between the firm and a host of stakeholders. In addition to the fundamental input of investors, employees, and suppliers, this approach recognizes other stakeholders and explicitly acknowledges the dialogue that exists between a firm's internal and external environments.

A Stakeholder Orientation

The degree to which a firm understands and addresses stakeholder demands can be referred to as a **stakeholder orientation.** This orientation comprises three sets of activities: (1) the organization-wide generation of data about stakeholder groups and assessment of the firm's effects on these groups, (2) the distribution of this information throughout the firm, and (3) the organization's responsiveness as a whole to this intelligence.[14]

Generating data about stakeholders begins with identifying the stakeholders that are relevant to the firm. Relevant stakeholder communities should be analyzed on the basis of the power that each enjoys as well as by the ties between them. Next, the firm should characterize the concerns about the business's conduct that each relevant stakeholder group shares. This information can be derived from formal research, including surveys, focus groups, internet searches, or press reviews. For example, Ford Motor Company obtains input on social and environmental responsibility issues from company representatives, suppliers, customers, and community leaders. Shell has an online discussion forum where website visitors are invited to express their opinions on the company's activities and their implications. Employees and managers can also generate this information informally as they carry out their daily activities. For example, purchasing managers know about suppliers' demands, public relations executives about the media, legal counselors about the regulatory environment, financial executives about investors, sales representatives about customers, and human resources advisers about employees. Finally, the company should evaluate its impact on the issues that are important to the various stakeholders it has identified.[15]

Given the variety of the employees involved in the generation of information about stakeholders, it is essential that this intelligence be circulated throughout the firm. This requires that the firm facilitate the communication of information about the nature of relevant stakeholder communities, stakeholder issues, and the current impact of the firm on these issues to all members of the organization. The dissemination of stakeholder

TABLE 2–1 Examples of Stakeholder Issues and Associated Measures of Corporate Impacts

Stakeholder Groups and Issues	Potential Indicators of Corporate Impact on These Issues
Employees	
1. Compensation and benefits	• Ratio of lowest wage to national legal minimum or to local cost of living
2. Training and development	• Changes in average years of training of employees
3. Employee diversity	• Percentages of employees from different genders and races
4. Occupational health and safety	• Standard injury rates and absentee rates
5. Communications with management	• Availability of open-door policies or ombudsmen
Customers	
1. Product safety and quality	• Number of product recalls over time
2. Management of customer complaints	• Number of customer complaints and availability of procedures to answer them
3. Services to disabled customers	• Availability and nature of measures taken to ensure services to disabled customers
Investors	
1. Transparency of shareholder communications	• Availability of procedures to inform shareholders about corporate activities
2. Shareholder rights	• Frequency and type of litigation involving violations of shareholder rights
Suppliers	
1. Encouraging suppliers in developing countries	• Prices offered to suppliers in developed countries in comparison to countries' other suppliers
2. Encouraging minority suppliers	• Percentage of minority suppliers
Community	
1. Public health and safety protection	• Availability of emergency response plan
2. Conservation of energy and materials	• Data on reduction of waste produced and comparison to industry
3. Donations and support of local organizations	• Annual employee time spent in community service
Environmental Groups	
1. Minimizing the use of energy	• Amount of electricity purchased; percentage of "green" electricity
2. Minimizing emissions and waste	• Type, amount, and designation of waste generated
3. Minimizing adverse environmental effects of goods and services	• Percentage of product weight reclaimed after use

FIGURE 2–2 Interactions between a Company and Its Primary and Secondary Stakeholders

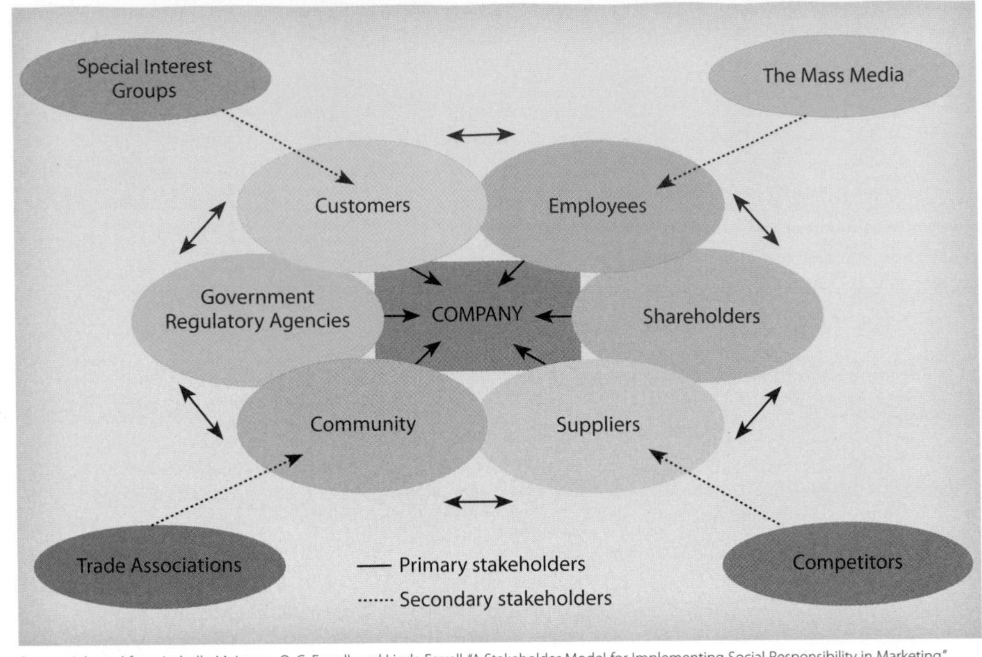

Source: Adapted from Isabelle Maignan, O. C. Ferrell, and Linda Ferrell, "A Stakeholder Model for Implementing Social Responsibility in Marketing," *European Journal of Marketing* 39 (2005): 956–977. Used with permission.

intelligence can be organized formally through activities such as newsletters and internal information forums.[16]

A stakeholder orientation is not complete unless it includes activities that address stakeholder issues. For example, many Chinese manufacturers and companies that use Chinese suppliers have been under attack in recent years over concern for product safety. From lead-tainted toys at Mattel, melamine-tainted dairy products, and potentially deadly generic drugs (which is a highly lucrative $75 billion a year business that employs over five million Chinese people)—China has faced serious allegations and criticisms over its lack of oversight and concern for consumer welfare.[17]

The responsiveness of the organization as a whole to stakeholder intelligence consists of the initiatives that the firm adopts to ensure that it abides by or exceeds stakeholder expectations and has a positive impact on stakeholder issues. Such activities are likely to be specific to a particular stakeholder group (for example, family-friendly work schedules) or to a particular stakeholder issue (for example, pollution reduction programs). These responsiveness processes typically involve the participation of the concerned stakeholder groups. Kraft, for example, includes special interest groups and university representatives in its programs to become sensitized to present and future ethical issues.

A stakeholder orientation can be viewed as a continuum in that firms are likely to adopt the concept to varying degrees. To gauge a given firm's stakeholder orientation, it is necessary to evaluate the extent to which the firm adopts behaviors that typify both the generation and dissemination of stakeholder intelligence and responsiveness to it. A given organization may generate and disseminate more intelligence about certain stakeholder communities than about others and, as a result, may respond to that intelligence differently.[18]

SOCIAL RESPONSIBILITY AND THE IMPORTANCE OF A STAKEHOLDER ORIENTATION

From the perspective of social responsibility, business ethics embodies values, norms, and expectations that reflect a concern of major stakeholders, including consumers, employees, shareholders, suppliers, competitors, and the community. In other words, these stakeholders have concerns about what is fair, just, or in keeping with respect for stakeholders' rights.

Many businesspeople and scholars have questioned the role of ethics and social responsibility in business. Legal and economic responsibilities are generally accepted as the most important determinants of performance: "If this is well done," say classical theorists, "profits are maximized more or less continuously and firms carry out their major responsibilities to society."[19] Some economists believe that if companies address economic and legal issues, they are satisfying the demands of society and that trying to anticipate and meet additional needs would be almost impossible. Milton Friedman has been quoted as saying that "the basic mission of business [is] thus to produce goods and services at a profit, and in doing this, business [is] making its maximum contribution to society and, in fact, being socially responsible."[20] Even with the business ethics scandals of the twenty-first century, Friedman suggests that although those individuals guilty of wrongdoing should be held accountable, the market is a better deterrent than new laws and regulations at deterring firms from wrongdoing.[21] Thus, Friedman would diminish the role of stakeholders such as the government and employees in requiring that businesses demonstrate responsible and ethical behavior.

This Darwinian form of capitalism has been exported to many developing countries, such as Russia, and is associated with a "Wild West" economy where anything goes in business. Friedman's capitalism is a far cry from Adam Smith's, one of the founders of capitalism. Smith created the concept of the invisible hand and spoke about self-interest; however, he went on to explain that "this common good is associated with six psychological motives and that each individual has to produce for the common good, with values such as Propriety, Prudence, Reason, Sentiment and promoting the happiness of mankind."[22] These values could be associated with the needs and concerns of stakeholders. Smith established normative expectations for motives and behaviors in his theories about the invisible hand.

In the twenty-first century, Friedman's form of capitalism is being replaced by Smith's original concept of capitalism (or what is now called enlightened capitalism), a notion of capitalism that reemphasizes stakeholder concerns and issues. This shift may be occurring faster in developed countries than in those still being developed. The recent involvement of the government in owning major interest in General Motors and AIG, and minority ownership of large banks such as Citigroup, changes the face of capitalism in the United States. The government's $819 billion stimulus package passed in 2009 increased its reach and provided funding to reshape energy, health care, and education policy. Theodore Levitt, a renowned business professor, once wrote that although profits are required for business just like eating is required for living, profit is not the purpose of business any more than eating is the purpose of life.[23] Norman Bowie, a well-known philosopher, extended Levitt's sentiment by noting that focusing on profit alone can create an unfavorable paradox that causes a firm to fail to achieve its objective. Bowie contends that when a business also cares about the well-being of stakeholders, it earns trust and cooperation that ultimately reduce costs and increase productivity.[24]

TABLE 2–2 *Fortune*'s Best and Worst Companies for Social Responsibility

Best Companies	Worst Companies
1. Anheuser-Busch	1. Circuit City Stores
2. Marriott International	2. Family Dollar Stores
3. Integrys Energy Group	3. Dillard's
4. Walt Disney	4. Sears Holding
5. Herman Miller	5. Tribune
6. Edison	6. Hon Hai Precision Industries
7. Starbucks	7. Fiat
8. Steelcase	8. PEMEX
9. Union Pacific	9. Surgutneftegas*
10. Fortune Brands	10. Huawei Technologies*

*tied

Source: From *Fortune*, "America's Most Admired Companies, Social Responsibility." Copyright © 2009 Time Inc. All rights reserved. March 16, 2009, http://money.cnn.com/magazines/fortune/mostadmired/2009/best_worst/best4.html (accessed August 4, 2009).

It should be obvious from this discussion that ethics and social responsibility cannot be just a reactive approach to issues as they arise. Only if firms make ethical concerns a part of their foundation and incorporate ethics in their business strategy can social responsibility as a concept be embedded in daily decision making. Herman Miller is an office furniture company that is known for its social responsibility initiatives. The company is one of a few office furniture producers in the world that are certified by the Business and Institutional Furniture Manufacturers Association to be exceptionally low-emissions.[25] A description of corporate social responsibility should include rights and duties, consequences and values—all of which refer to specific strategic decisions. The ethical component of business strategy should be capable of providing an assessment of top management, work group, and individual behavior as it relates to ethical decisions. Table 2–2 lists *Fortune*'s best and worst companies in terms of social responsibility.

SOCIAL RESPONSIBILITY AND ETHICS

The concepts of ethics and social responsibility are often used interchangeably, although each has a distinct meaning. In Chapter 1, we defined the term *social responsibility* as an organization's obligation to maximize its positive impact on stakeholders and to minimize its negative impact. PNC Financial Services Group, for example, contributes $28 million annually in grants and corporate sponsorships to arts, community improvement, and educational causes. The company also supports employees with flexible work schedules and backup and holiday daycare, as well as a free daycare center for new parents. For its operations and technology center in Pittsburgh, the company built the nation's largest "green building," conforming to environmental guidelines on site planning, energy efficiency, water conservation, material conservation, and indoor environmental quality. It also built several "green" bank branches in New Jersey.[26]

Another example of a company being green is Whole Foods, which installs solar panels on many of its stores and buys wind power credits to offset more than 100 percents of its non-renewable energy use.[27] General Electric also pledged to decrease pollution and double research and development spending on cleaner technologies.[28] Wal-Mart has also joined the growing ranks of green companies. It has a number of environmentally friendlier stores, which reduce energy consumption and pollution. Wal-Mart hopes to take what it learns from the stores and use it in all of the new stores that it builds.[29] Like Wal-Mart and General Electric, many businesses have tried to determine what relationships, obligations, and duties are appropriate between the organization and various stakeholders. Social responsibility can be viewed as a contract with society, whereas business ethics involves carefully thought-out rules or heuristics of business conduct that guide decision making.

If social responsibility is considered an important corporate concern, then it does need quantitative credibility. Employee satisfaction, consumer loyalty, and other stakeholder concerns can be quantified to some extent, but some of the values and other dimensions are more qualitative. The International Organization for Standardization (ISO) established ISO 26000, which is a corporate social responsibility regulation that cannot be used for certification purposes or audits but is meant as a guideline to encourage discussions on the role of social responsibility and the importance of stakeholders. ISO 1400 is an environmental regulation standard any business can adopt to help it reduce its carbon footprint, pollution, and waste.[30] Many U.S. firms are purchasing renewable energy, especially solar and wind power, to reduce their carbon footprints. The United States is the leading wind power generator in the world, producing around 21 percent of the world's supply.[31] Whereas corporate responsibility needs quantitative credibility, significant aspects are more qualitative in nature: employee satisfaction, customer motivations, company values, and ethical decision making processes, for instance. All to some extent can be broken down into quantitative data, but the essence of them cannot. However, they also shift constantly, which makes yesterday's survey an addition to today's recycle bin.[32]

There are four levels of social responsibility—economic, legal, ethical, and philanthropic—and they can be viewed as steps (see Figure 2–3).[33] At the most basic level, companies have an economic responsibility to be profitable so that they can provide a return on investment to their owners and investors, create jobs for the community, and contribute

FIGURE 2–3 Steps of Social Responsibility

Philanthropic: "giving back" to society

Ethical: following standards of acceptable behavior as judged by stakeholders

Economic: maximizing stakeholder wealth and/or value

Legal: abiding by all laws and government regulations

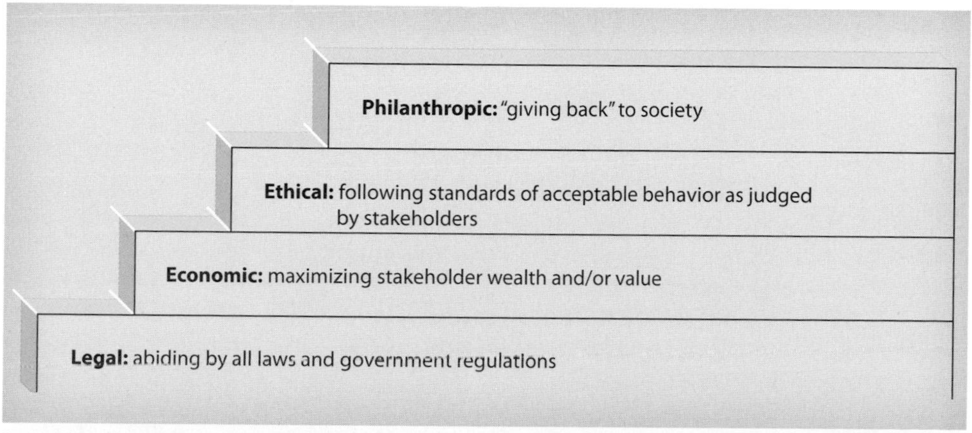

Source: Adapted from Archie B. Carroll, "The Pyramid of Corporate Social Responsibility: Toward the Moral Management of Organizational Stakeholders," *Business Horizons* (July–August 1991): 42, Figure 3.

goods and services to the economy. Of course, businesses are also expected to obey all laws and regulations. Business ethics, as previously defined, comprises principles and standards that guide behavior in the world of business. Finally, philanthropic responsibility refers to activities that are not required of businesses but promote human welfare or goodwill. Ethics, then, is one dimension of social responsibility.

The term **corporate citizenship** is often used to express the extent to which businesses strategically meet the economic, legal, ethical, and philanthropic responsibilities placed on them by their various stakeholders.[34] Corporate citizenship has four interrelated dimensions: strong sustained economic performance, rigorous compliance, ethical actions beyond what the law requires, and voluntary contributions that advance the reputation and stakeholder commitment of the organization. A firm's commitment to corporate citizenship indicates a strategic focus on fulfilling the social responsibilities that its stakeholders expect of it. Corporate citizenship involves acting on the firm's commitment to the corporate citizenship philosophy and measuring the extent to which it follows through by actually implementing citizenship initiatives. Table 2–3 lists some of the world's most ethical companies, all of which have demonstrated commitment to stakeholders.

Reputation is one of an organization's greatest intangible assets with tangible value. The value of a positive reputation is difficult to quantify, but it is very important. A single negative incident can influence perceptions of a corporation's image and reputation instantly and for years afterwards. Corporate reputation, image, and brands are more important than ever and are among the most critical aspects of sustaining relationships with constituents including investors, customers, financial analysts, media, and government watchdogs. It takes companies decades to build a great reputation, yet just one slip can cost a company dearly. Although an organization does not control its reputation in a direct sense, its actions, choices, behaviors, and consequences do influence the reputation that exists in perceptions of stakeholders. Companies such as Exxon Mobil, Chevron Corporation, and Royal Dutch Shell Plc. received low ratings from the public in a corporate reputation survey for what the public perceived as the "heartless" spike in prices at the pump while the companies were enjoying record profits. A recent Gallup survey found that more consumers than not feel negative toward industries. Over 55 percent of consumers view their mood as negative, with only 7 percent ranking it positive.[35]

TABLE 2–3 A Selection of the World's most Ethical Companies

Trader Joe's	Salesforce.com, Inc.
Xerox	Honeywell International
Nike	Texas Instruments, Inc.
T-Mobile	Unilever
Intel Corporation	Rockwell Automation
General Electric	Waste Management
PepsiCo	Zappos.com
AstraZeneca	Dell Inc.
Stonyfield Farm	Cisco Systems
General Mills	IKEA

Source: "2009 World's Most Ethics Companies," Ethisphere Institute, http://ethisphere.com/wme2009/ (accessed June 2, 2009).

CORPORATE GOVERNANCE PROVIDES FORMALIZED RESPONSIBILITY TO STAKEHOLDERS

Most businesses, and often courses taught in colleges of business, operate under the belief that the purpose of business is to maximize profits for shareholders. In 1919 the Michigan Supreme Court in the case of *Dodge v. Ford Motor Co.*[36] ruled that a business exists for the profit of shareholders and the board of directors should focus on that objective. On the other hand, the stakeholder model places the board of directors in the central position to balance the interests and conflicts of the various constituencies. External control of the corporation includes not only government regulation but also key stakeholders including employees, consumers, and communities to exert pressures to responsible conduct. Many of the obligations to balance stakeholder interests have been institutionalized in legislation that provides incentives for responsible conduct. Shareholders have been pushing for more power in the boardroom, as many feel their interests have not been well represented in issues such as executive compensation.

Today, the failure to balance stakeholder interests can result in a failure to maximize shareholders' wealth. Oftentimes, money managers fail to handle their clients' money as carefully as they handle their own. This can result in risky trades and even large losses, as many have seen in the extreme cases of the unethical conduct of people such as Allen Stanford or Bernard Madoff.[37] Most firms are moving more toward a balanced stakeholder model as they see that this approach will sustain the relationships necessary for long-run success.

Both directors and officers of corporations are fiduciaries for the shareholders. Fiduciaries are persons placed in positions of trust who use due care and loyalty in acting on behalf of the best interests of the organization. There is a duty of care, also called a *duty of diligence*, to make informed and prudent decisions.[38] Directors have a duty to avoid ethical misconduct in their director role and to provide leadership in decisions to prevent ethical misconduct in the organization.

Directors are not held responsible for negative outcomes if they are informed and diligent in their decision making. Questions arose when firms such as Countrywide Financial engaged in misconduct, such as granting subprime loans to customers who could not afford them. This means board members have an obligation to request information, research, use accountants and attorneys, and obtain the services of ethical compliance consultants. The National Association of Corporate Directors, which is a board of directors trade group, has helped to formulate a guide to boards to help them to do a better job of governing corporate America.[39]

The duty of loyalty means that all decisions should be in the interests of the corporation and its stakeholders. Conflicts of interest exist when a director uses the position to obtain personal gain, usually at the expense of the organization. For example, before the Sarbanes–Oxley Act in 2002, directors could give themselves and officers interest-free loans. Scandals at Tyco, Kmart, and WorldCom are all associated with officers receiving personal loans that damaged the corporation.

Officer compensation packages challenge directors, especially those on the board and not independent. Directors have an opportunity to vote for others' compensation in return for their own increased compensation. After the financial crisis began in late 2008, many top executives at failed firms received multimillion dollar bonuses in spite of the fact that their companies required huge government bailouts simply to stay afloat. AIG received a great deal of criticism after it paid out $165 million in bonuses to executives, even after the company received $180 billion in bailout money. Many feel that large executive bonuses point to a pervasive culture of greed and a sense of entitlement that has caused many of the problems on Wall Street in recent years.[40] Opportunities to know about the investments, business ventures, and stock market information create issues that could violate the duty of loyalty. Insider trading of a firm's stock has very specific rules, and violations can result in serious punishment. The obligations of directors and officers for legal and ethical responsibility interface and fit together based on their fiduciary relationships. Ethical values should guide decisions and buffer the possibility of illegal conduct. With increased pressure on directors to provide oversight for organizational ethics, there is a trend toward directors receiving training to increase their competency in ethics programs development, as well as other areas such as accounting. Automated systems to monitor and measure the occurrence of ethical issues within the organization are increasingly being used to assist in this oversight process.

To remove the opportunity for employees to make unethical decisions, most companies have developed formal systems of accountability, oversight, and control—known as **corporate governance.** *Accountability* refers to how closely workplace decisions are aligned with a firm's stated strategic direction and its compliance with ethical and legal considerations. *Oversight* provides a system of checks and balances that limit employees' and managers' opportunities to deviate from policies and strategies and that prevent unethical and illegal activities. *Control* is the process of auditing and improving organizational decisions and actions.

A clear delineation of accountability helps employees, customers, investors, government regulators, and other stakeholders understand why and how the organization chooses and achieves its goals. Corporate governance establishes fundamental systems and processes: for preventing and detecting misconduct, for investigating and disciplining, and for recovery and continuous improvement. Effective corporate governance creates a compliance and ethics culture so that employees feel that integrity is at the core of competitiveness.[41] Even if a company has adopted a consensus approach for decision making, there should be oversight and authority for delegating tasks, making difficult and sometimes controversial decisions, balancing power throughout the firm, and maintaining ethical compliance. Governance also provides mechanisms for identifying risks and for planning for recovery when mistakes or problems occur.

The development of stakeholder orientation should interface with the corporation's governance structure. Corporate governance is also part of a firm's corporate culture that establishes the integrity of all relationships. A governance system that does not provide checks and balances creates opportunities for top managers to put their own self-interests before those of important stakeholders. While many people lost their investments, some CEOs were able to profit off of the latest recession, even as their companies and shareholders fared poorly. Some directors even tweaked performance targets in order to make goals easier to achieve so that they could receive more bonus money. Bonuses have become a very contentious issue—as they are the part of an executive's pay most tied to performance. Many people are asking why executives continue to receive bonuses as their companies fail, but most of the time bonuses are tied to targets other than stock prices.[42] Concerns about the need for greater corporate governance are not limited to the United States. Reforms in governance structures and issues are occurring all over the world.[43] In many nations, companies are being pressured to implement stronger corporate governance mechanisms by international investors, by the process of becoming privatized after years of unaccountability as state companies, or by the desire to imitate successful governance movements in the United States, Japan, and the European Union.[44]

TABLE 2–4 Corporate Governance Issues

Executive compensation
Composition and structure of the board of directors
Auditing and control
Risk management
CEO selection and termination decisions
Integrity of financial reporting
Stakeholder participation and input into decisions
Compliance with corporate governance reform
Role of the CEO in board decisions
Organizational ethics programs

Table 2–4 lists examples of major corporate governance issues. These issues normally involve strategic-level decisions and actions taken by boards of directors, business owners, top executives, and other managers with high levels of authority and accountability. Although these people have often been relatively free from scrutiny, changes in technology, consumer activism, government attention, recent ethical scandals, and other factors have brought new attention to such issues as transparency, executive pay, risk and control, resource accountability, strategic direction, stockholder rights, and other decisions made for the organization.

Views of Corporate Governance

To better understand the role of corporate governance in business today, it is important to consider how it relates to fundamental beliefs about the purpose of business. Some organizations take the view that as long as they are maximizing shareholder wealth and profitability, they are fulfilling their core responsibilities. Other firms, however, believe that a business is an important member, even citizen, of society and therefore must assume broad responsibilities that include complying with social norms and expectations. From these assumptions, we can derive two major approaches to corporate governance: the shareholder model and the stakeholder model.[45]

The **shareholder model of corporate governance** is founded in classic economic precepts, including the goal of maximizing wealth for investors and owners. For publicly traded firms, corporate governance focuses on developing and improving the formal system for maintaining performance accountability between top management and the firms' shareholders.[46] Thus, a shareholder orientation should drive a firm's decisions toward serving the best interests of investors. Underlying these decisions is a classic agency problem, where ownership (that is, investors) and control (that is, managers) are separate. Managers act as agents for investors, whose primary goal is increasing the value of the stock they own. However, investors and managers are distinct parties with unique insights, goals, and values with respect to the business. Managers, for example, may have motivations beyond stockholder value, such as market share, personal compensation, or attachment to particular products and projects. Because of these potential differences, corporate governance mechanisms are needed to align investor and management interests. The shareholder model has been criticized for its somewhat singular purpose and focus because there are other ways of "investing" in a business. Suppliers, creditors, customers, employees, business partners, the community, and others also invest their resources into the success of the firm.[47]

The **stakeholder model of corporate governance** adopts a broader view of the purpose of business. Although a company has a responsibility for economic success and viability to satisfy its stockholders, it also must answer to other stakeholders, including employees, suppliers, government regulators, communities, and special interest groups with which it interacts. Due to limited resources, companies must determine which of their stakeholders are primary. Once the primary groups have been identified, managers must then implement the appropriate corporate governance mechanisms to promote the development of long-term relationships.[48] This approach entails creating governance systems that consider stakeholder welfare in tandem with corporate needs and interests.

Although these two approaches seem to represent the ends of a continuum, the reality is that the shareholder model is a more restrictive precursor to the stakeholder orientation. Many businesses have evolved into the stakeholder model as a result of government initiatives, consumer activism, industry activity, and other external forces.

The Role of Boards of Directors

For public corporations, boards of directors hold the ultimate responsibility for their firms' success or failure, as well as for the ethics of their actions. This governing authority is being held responsible by the 2004 and 2007 amendments to the Federal Sentencing Guidelines for Organizations (FSGO) for creating an ethical culture that provides leadership, values, and compliance. The members of a company's board of directors assume legal responsibility for the firm's resources and decisions, and they appoint its top executive officers. Board members have a fiduciary duty, meaning they have assumed a position of trust and confidence that entails certain responsibilities, including acting in the best interests of those they serve. Thus, board membership is not intended as a vehicle for personal financial gain; rather, it provides the intangible benefit of ensuring the success of both the organization and people involved in the fiduciary arrangement. The role and expectations of boards of directors assumed greater significance after the accounting scandals of the early 2000s and the 2008–2009 financial crisis motivated many shareholders and other stakeholders to demand greater accountability from boards.[49] The U.S. Treasury Secretary, Timothy Geithner, is trying to change how the government goes about overseeing risk-taking in financial markets. He is pushing for stricter rules on financial management and controls on hedge funds and money market mutual funds. He believes that the United States needs greater openness and transparency, greater oversight and enforcement, and clearer more common sense language in the financial system.[50]

The traditional approach to directorship assumed that board members managed the corporation's business. Research and practical observation have shown that boards of directors rarely, if ever, perform the management function.[51] Compensation of directors can be a difficult ethical area. When considering executive pay raises, directors may put their own self-interest above the interests of the shareholders.[52] First, boards meet only a few times a year, which precludes them from managing effectively. In addition, the complexity of modern organizations mandates full attention on a daily basis. Thus, boards of directors are concerned primarily with monitoring the decisions made by executives on behalf of the company. This includes choosing top executives, assessing their performance, helping set strategic direction, and ensuring that oversight, control, and accountability mechanisms are in place. In sum, board members assume ultimate authority for their organization's effectiveness and subsequent performance.

Many CEOs have lost their jobs because the board of directors was scared. Notable examples include Michael Eisner from Disney, Carly Fiorina from Hewlett-Packard, and Rick Wagoner of General Motors. The main reason for the CEO firings was that the boards feared financial losses stemming from shareholder lawsuits against the chairs of Enron and WorldCom over their roles in the collapse of those firms. Both settlements called for the directors to pay large sums from their own pockets.[53]

Greater Demands for Accountability and Transparency. Just as improved ethical decision making requires more of employees and executives, so too are boards of directors feeling greater demands for accountability and transparency. In the past, board members were often retired company executives or friends of current executives, but the trend today is toward "outside directors" who have little vested interest in the firm before assuming the director role. Inside directors are corporate officers, consultants, major shareholders, or others who benefit directly from the success of the organization. Directors today are increasingly chosen for their expertise, competence, and ability to bring diverse perspectives to strategic discussions. Outside directors are also thought to bring more independence to the monitoring function because they are not bound by past allegiances, friendships, a current role in the company, or some other issue that may create a conflict of interest.

> *Directors today are increasingly chosen for their expertise, competence, and ability to bring diverse perspectives to strategic discussions.*

Many of the corporate scandals uncovered in recent years might have been prevented if each of the companies' boards of directors had been better qualified, more knowledgeable, and less biased. Shareholder involvement in changing the makeup of boards has always run into difficulties. Most boards are not true democracies, with shareholders ultimately wielding little power over decisions.[54] A survey by *USA Today* found that corporate boards have considerable overlap. More than 1,000 corporate board members sit on four or more company boards, and of the nearly 2,000 boards of directors in the United States, more than 22,000 of their members are linked to boards of more than one company. For example, of the 1,000 largest companies, one-fifth share at least one board member with another top 1,000 firms. This overlap creates the opportunity for conflicts of interest in decision making and limits the independence of individual boards of directors. To counteract act this, luxury retailer Saks Inc. voted to hold annual board member elections, as opposed to every three years, and that directors must receive a majority of votes to win. The change is part of an effort to improve accountability at the company, which, along with many other retailers, suffered a serious decline in share prices over the course of 2008 and 2009.[55] In some cases, it seems that individuals earned placement on multiple boards of directors because they gained a reputation for going along with top management and never asking questions. This may foster a corporate culture that limits outside oversight of top managers' decisions.

Although labor and public pension fund activities have waged hundreds of proxy battles in recent years, they rarely have much effect on the target companies. Now shareholder activists are attacking the process by which directors themselves are elected. Shareholders at Saks are not the only ones to vote to change board election rules. Resolutions at hundreds of companies require directors to gain a majority of votes cast to join the board. It is hoped that this practice will make boards of directors more attentive and accountable.[56]

Executive Compensation. One of the biggest issues that corporate boards of directors face is **executive compensation.** In fact, most boards spend more time deciding how much to compensate top executives than they do ensuring the integrity of the company's financial reporting systems.[57] How executives are compensated for their leadership, organizational service, and performance has become a controversial topic. Indeed, 73 percent of respondents in a *BusinessWeek*/Harris poll indicated they believe that top officers of large U.S. companies receive too much compensation, while only 21 percent reported executive compensation as "just about the right amount."[58] U.S. lawmakers subpoenaed the names of American International Group (AIG) executives who received $165 million in bonuses after the company was bailed out by the government. The firm stated that it decided to make the publicly unpopular payments because many of them were contractually required. Nevertheless, the move seemed arrogant and out of touch to many lawmakers and stakeholders, and former AIG CEO Edward Liddy requested the executives return the bonuses.[59]

Many people believe that no executive is worth millions of dollars in annual salary and stock options, even if he or she has brought great financial return to investors. Their concerns often center on the relationship between the highest-paid executives and median employee wages in the company. If this ratio is perceived as too large, then critics believe that either employees are not being compensated fairly or high executive salaries represent an improper use of company resources. According to the AFL-CIO, average executive pay is $10.4 million. Executive bonuses alone are an average of $336,248—this is nine times what the average salaried worker receives in pay each year. Add to this that companies have received nearly a billion dollars in government bailout money—money that comes from taxpayers.[60] Understandably, many stakeholders are angry about this situation. Because of this enormous difference, the business press is now usually careful to support high levels of executive compensation only when it is directly linked to strong company performance.

Although the issue of executive compensation has received much attention in the media of late, some business owners have long recognized its potential ill effects. In the early twentieth century, for example, capitalist J. P. Morgan implemented a policy that limited the pay of top managers in businesses that he owned to no more than 20 times the pay of any other employee.[61]

Other people argue that because executives assume so much risk on behalf of the company, they deserve the rewards that follow from strong company performance. In addition, many executives' personal and professional lives meld to the point that they are "on call" 24 hours a day. Because not everyone has the skill, experience, and desire to become an executive, with the accompanying pressure and responsibility, market forces dictate a high level of compensation. When the pool of qualified individuals is limited, many corporate board members feel that offering large compensation packages is the only way to attract and retain top executives and so ensure that their firms are not left without strong leadership. In an era when top executives are increasingly willing to "jump ship" to other firms that offer higher pay, potentially lucrative stock options, bonuses, and other benefits, such thinking is not without merit.[62]

Executive compensation is a difficult but important issue for boards of directors and other stakeholders to consider because it receives much attention in the media, sparks shareholder concern, and is hotly debated in discussions of corporate governance. One area for board members to consider is the extent to which executive compensation is linked to company performance. Plans that base compensation on the achievement of several performance goals, including profits and revenues, are intended to align the interests of owners with management. Amid rising complaints about excessive executive compensation, an increasing number of corporate boards are imposing performance targets on the stock and stock options they include in their CEOs' pay package. The SEC proposed that companies disclose how they compensate lower-ranking employees, as well as top executives. This was part of a review of executive pay policies that addresses the belief that many financial corporations have historically taken on too much risk. The SEC believes that compensation may be linked to excessive risk-taking.[63] Another issue is whether performance-linked compensation encourages executives to focus on short-term performance at the expense of long-term growth.[64] Shareholders today, however, may be growing more concerned about transparency than short-term performance and executive compensation. One study determined that companies that divulge more details about their corporate governance practices generate higher shareholder returns than less transparent companies.[65]

IMPLEMENTING A STAKEHOLDER PERSPECTIVE

An organization that develops effective corporate governance and understands the importance of business ethics and social responsibility in achieving success should develop some processes for managing these important concerns. Although there are many different approaches, we provide some steps that have been found effective to utilize the stakeholder framework in managing responsibility and business ethics. The steps include (1) assessing the corporate culture, (2) identifying stakeholder groups, (3) identifying stakeholder issues, (4) assessing organizational commitment to social responsibility, (5) identifying resources and determining urgency, and (6) gaining stakeholder feedback. The importance of these steps is to include feedback from relevant stakeholders in formulating organizational strategy and implementation.

> *The SEC believes that compensation may be linked to excessive risk-taking.*

Step 1: Assessing the Corporate Culture

To enhance organizational fit, a social responsibility program must align with the corporate culture of the organization. The purpose of this first step is to identify the organizational mission, values, and norms that are likely to have implications for social responsibility. In particular, relevant existing values and norms are those that specify the stakeholder groups and stakeholder issues that are deemed most important by the organization. Very often, relevant organizational values and norms can be found in corporate documents such as the mission statement, annual reports, sales brochures, or websites. For example, Green Mountain Coffee is a pioneer in helping struggling coffee growers by paying them fair trade prices. The company also offers microloans to coffee-growing families, to underwrite business ventures that diversify agricultural economies. It was number one on the *Business Ethics* "100 Best Corporate Citizens" for several years.[66]

Step 2: Identifying Stakeholder Groups

In managing this stage, it is important to recognize stakeholder needs, wants, and desires. Many important issues gain visibility because key constituencies such as consumer groups, regulators, or the media express an interest. When agreement, collaboration, or even confrontations exist on an issue, there is a need for a decision making process. A model of collaboration to overcome the adversarial approaches to problem solving has been suggested. Managers can identify relevant stakeholders who may be affected by or may influence the development of organizational policy.

Stakeholders have some level of power over a business because they are in the position to withhold, or at least threaten to withhold, organizational resources. Stakeholders have the most power when their own survival is not really affected by the success of the organization and when they have access to vital organizational resources. For example, most consumers of shoes do not need to buy Nike shoes. Therefore, if they decide to boycott Nike, they have to endure only minor inconveniences. Nevertheless, their loyalty to Nike is vital to the continued success of the sport apparel giant. The proper assessment of the power held by a given stakeholder community also requires an evaluation of the extent to which that community can collaborate with others to pressure the firm.

Step 3: Identifying Stakeholder Issues

> *"Stakeholders have the most power when their own survival is not really affected by the success of the organization"*

Together, steps 1 and 2 lead to the identification of the stakeholders who are both the most powerful and legitimate. The level of power and legitimacy determines the degree of urgency in addressing their needs. Step 3 consists then in understanding the nature of the main issues of concern to these stakeholders. Conditions for collaboration exist when problems are so complex that multiple stakeholders are required to resolve the issue and the weaknesses of adversarial approaches are understood.

For example, obesity in children is becoming an issue across groups and stakeholders.[67] The United States is the most obese nation, with almost 40 percent of the population obese or overweight, and this has caused a huge rise in health problems.

While Americans have traditionally not supported government health care plans, increasing health care costs are causing some stakeholders to reconsider their stance. Currently, 6 out of 10 people put off going to the doctor because of the high cost, with a quarter saying that someone in their family has had trouble paying off medical bills. In fact, 59 percent of people believe that health care reform is a very high priority, and 67 percent believe that a public medical insurance plan should be available for people.[68] The current administration is working to create a national plan to address the health care crisis. As a result, stakeholder concerns have pushed the government into taking action on this important issue.

Step 4: Assessing Organizational Commitment to Social Responsibility

Steps 1 through 3 consist of generating information about social responsibility among a variety of influencers in and around the organization. Step 4 brings these three first stages together to arrive at an understanding of social responsibility that specifically matches the organization of interest. This general definition will then be used to evaluate current practices and to select concrete social responsibility initiatives. Firms such as Starbucks have selected activities that address stakeholder concerns. Starbucks has formalized its initiatives in official documents such as annual reports, web pages, and company brochures. Starbucks has a website devoted to social responsibility. Starbucks is concerned with the environment and integrates policies and programs throughout all aspects of operations to minimize their environmental impact. They also have many community-building programs that help them be good neighbors and contribute positively to the communities where their partners and customers live, work, and play.[69]

Step 5: Identifying Resources and Determining Urgency

The prioritization of stakeholders and issues, along with the assessment of past performance, provides for allocating resources. Two main criteria can be considered: First is the level of financial and organizational investments required by different actions; second is the urgency when prioritizing social responsibility challenges. When the challenge under consideration is viewed as significant and when stakeholder pressures on the issue could be expected, then the challenge can be considered as urgent. For example, Wal-Mart has been the focus of legislation in Maryland, which tried to make the retailer pay more for its employee health care. The legislation failed in its attempt to require employers with more than 10,000 workers to spend at least 8 percent of their payroll on employee health care.[70] Twenty-two other states are now considering this legislation. Wal-Mart has now offered to improve health care benefits for its employees as a direct result of the pressure.[71]

Step 6: Gaining Stakeholder Feedback

Stakeholder feedback can be generated through a variety of means. First, stakeholders' general assessment of the firm and its practices can be obtained through satisfaction or reputation surveys. Second, to gauge stakeholders' perceptions of the firm's contributions to specific issues, stakeholder-generated media such as blogs, websites, podcasts, and newsletters can be assessed. Third, more formal research may be conducted using focus groups, observation, and surveys. Many watchdog groups have utilized the web to inform consumers and to publicize their messages. For example, Consumer Watchdog, a California-based group that keeps an eye on everything from education to the oil industry, applauded Costco for breaking with oil industry norms and seeking to sell fairly priced fuel. Costco announced that it would adjust gas prices in hot months, when heat causes gas to expand, so that consumers get the same amount of energy out of every gallon they pump.[72]

SUMMARY

Business ethics, issues, and conflicts revolve around relationships. Customers, investors and shareholders, employees, suppliers, government agencies, communities, and many others who have a stake or claim in some aspect of a company's products, operations, markets, industry, and outcomes are known as stakeholders. They are both influenced by and have the ability to affect businesses. Stakeholders provide both tangible and intangible resources that are more or less critical to a firm's long-term success, and their ability to withdraw—or to threaten to withdraw—these resources gives them power. Stakeholders define significant ethical issues in business.

Primary stakeholders are those whose continued association is absolutely necessary for a firm's survival, whereas secondary stakeholders do not typically engage in transactions with a company and thus are not essential for its survival. The stakeholder interaction model suggests that there are two-way relationships between the firm and a host of stakeholders. The degree to which a firm understands and addresses stakeholder demands can be expressed as a stakeholder orientation, which includes three sets of activities: (1) the generation of data across the firm about its stakeholder groups and the assessment of the firm's effects on these groups, (2) the distribution of this information throughout the firm, and (3) the responsiveness of every level of the firm to this intelligence. A stakeholder orientation can be viewed as a continuum in that firms are likely to adopt the concept to varying degrees.

Although the concepts of business ethics and social responsibility are often used interchangeably, the two terms have distinct meanings. Social responsibility in business refers to an organization's obligation to maximize its positive impact and minimize its negative impact on society. There are four levels of social responsibility—economic, legal, ethical, and philanthropic—and they can be viewed as a pyramid. The term *corporate citizenship* is often used to communicate the extent to which businesses strategically meet the economic, legal, ethical, and philanthropic responsibilities placed on them by their various stakeholders.

From a social responsibility perspective, business ethics embodies standards, norms, and expectations that reflect a concern of major stakeholders including consumers, employees, shareholders, suppliers, competitors, and the community. Only if firms include ethical concerns in their foundational values and incorporate ethics in their business strategy can social responsibility as a value be embedded in daily decision making.

Most businesses operate under the assumption that the main purpose of business is to maximize profits for shareholders. The stakeholders model places the board of directors in the central position to balance the interests and conflicts of the various constituencies. Both directors and officers of corporations are fiduciaries for the shareholders. Fiduciaries are persons placed in positions of trust who use due care and loyalty in acting on behalf of the best interests of the organization. There is a duty of care (also called a duty of diligence) to make informed and prudent decisions. Directors have a duty to avoid ethical misconduct in their director role and to provide leadership in decisions to prevent ethical misconduct in the organization. To remove the opportunity for employees to make unethical decisions, most companies have developed formal systems of accountability, oversight, and control, known as corporate governance. Accountability refers to how closely workplace decisions are aligned with a firm's stated strategic direction and its compliance with ethical and legal considerations. Oversight provides a system of checks and balances that limit employees' and managers' opportunities to deviate from policies and strategies and that prevent unethical and illegal activities. Control is the process of auditing and improving organizational decisions and actions.

There are two perceptions of corporate governance, which can be viewed as a continuum. The shareholder model is founded in classic economic precepts, including the maximization of wealth for investors and owners. The stakeholder model adopts a broader view of the purpose of business that includes satisfying the concerns of other stakeholders, from employees, suppliers, and government regulators to communities and special interest groups.

Two major elements of corporate governance that relate to ethical decision making are the role of the board of directors and executive compensation. The members of a public corporation's board of directors assume legal responsibility for the firm's resources and decisions. Important issues related to corporate boards of directors include accountability, transparency, and independence. Boards of directors are also responsible for appointing and setting the compensation for top executive officers, a controversial topic. Concerns about executive pay may center on the often-disproportionate relationship between the highest-paid executives and median employee wages in the company.

IMPORTANT TERMS FOR REVIEW

stakeholder

primary stakeholder

secondary stakeholder

stakeholder interaction model

stakeholder orientation

corporate citizenship

reputation

corporate governance

shareholder model of corporate governance

stakeholder model of corporate governance

executive compensation

RESOLVING ETHICAL BUSINESS CHALLENGES*

Kent was getting pressure from his boss, parents, and wife about the marketing campaign for Broadway Corporation's new video game called "Lucky." He had been working for Broadway for about two years, and the Lucky game was his first big project. After Kent and his wife, Amy, graduated from college, they decided to go back to their hometown of Las Cruces, New Mexico, near the Mexican border. Kent's father knew the president of Broadway, which enabled Kent to get a job in its marketing department. Broadway is a medium-size company with about 500 employees, making it one of the largest employers in Las Cruces. Broadway develops, manufactures, and markets video arcade games.

Within the video arcade industry, competition is fierce. Games typically have a life cycle of only 18 to 24 months. One of the key strategies in the industry is providing unique, visually stimulating games by using color graphics technology, fast action, and participant interaction. The target markets for Broadway's video products are children aged 5 to 12 and teenagers aged 13 to 19. Males constitute 75 percent of the market.

When Kent first started with Broadway, his task was to conduct market research on the types of games that players desired. His research showed that the market wanted more action (violence), quicker graphics, multiple levels of difficulty, and sound. Further research showed that certain tones and types of sound were more pleasing than others. As part of his research, Kent also observed people in video arcades, where he found that many became hypnotized by a game and would quickly put in quarters when told to do so. Research suggested that many target consumers exhibited the same symptoms as compulsive gamblers. Kent's research results were well received by the company, which developed several new games using his information. The new games were instant hits with the market.

In his continuing research, Kent found that the consumer's level of intensity increased as the game's intensity level increased. Several reports later, Kent suggested that target consumers might be willing, at strategic periods in a video game, to insert multiple coins. For example, a player who wanted to move to a higher level of difficulty would have to insert two coins; to play the final level, three coins would have to be inserted. When the idea was tested, Kent found it did increase game productivity.

Kent also noticed that video games that gave positive reinforcements to the consumer, such as audio cues, were played much more frequently than others. He reported his findings to Brad, Broadway's president, who asked Kent to apply the information to the development of new games. Kent suggested having the machines give candy to the game players when they attained specific goals. For the teen market, the company modified the idea: The machines would give back coins at certain levels during the game. Players could then use the coins at strategic levels to play a "slot-type" chance opening of the next level. By inserting an element of chance, these games generated more coin input than output, and game productivity increased dramatically. These innovations were quite successful, giving Broadway a larger share of the market and Kent a promotion to product manager.

Kent's newest assignment was the Lucky game—a fast-action scenario in which the goal was to destroy the enemy before being destroyed. Kent expanded on the slot-type game for the older market, with two additions. First, the game employed virtual reality technology, which gives the player the sensation of actually being in the game. Second, keeping in mind that most of the teenage consumers were male, Kent incorporated a female character who, at each level, removed a piece of her clothing and taunted the player. A win at the highest level left her nude. Test market results suggested that the two additions increased profitability per game dramatically.

Several weeks later, Brad asked about the Lucky project. "I think we've got a real problem, Brad," Kent told him. "Maybe the nudity is a bad idea. Some people will be really upset about it." Brad was displeased with Kent's response.

Word got around fast that the Lucky project had stalled. During dinner with his parents, Kent mentioned the Lucky project, and his dad said something that affected Kent. "You know, son, the Lucky project will bring in a great deal of revenue for Broadway, and jobs are at stake. Some of your coworkers are upset with your stand on this project. I'm not telling you what to do, but there's more at stake here than just a video game."

The next day Kent had a meeting with Brad about Lucky. "Well," Brad asked, "what have you decided?"

Kent answered, "I don't think we should go with the nudity idea."

Brad answered, "You know, Kent, you're right. The U.S. market just isn't ready to see full nudity as well as graphic violence in arcades in their local malls. That's why I've contacted an Internet provider who will take our game and put it on the Internet as an adult product. I've also checked out the foreign markets and found that we can sell the machines to the Mexican market if we tone down the violence. The Taiwanese joint venture group has okayed the version we have now, but they would like you to develop something that is more graphic in both areas. You see, they already have similar versions of this type of game now, and their market is ready to go to the next level. I see the Internet market as secondary because we can't get the virtual reality equipment and software into an Internet mode. Maybe when PCs get faster, we'll be able to tap into it at that level, but not now. So, Kent, do you understand what you need to be doing on Lucky?"

QUESTIONS • EXERCISES

1. What are the ethical and legal issues?
2. What are Kent's options?
3. Discuss the acceptability and commercial use of sex, violence, and gambling in the United States.
4. Are marketing sex, violence, and gambling acceptable in other countries if they fit their culture?

*This case is strictly hypothetical; any resemblance to real persons, companies, or situations is coincidental.

CHECK YOUR EQ

Check your EQ, or Ethics Quotient, by completing the following. Assess your performance to evaluate your overall understanding of the chapter material.

1. Social responsibility in business refers to maximizing the visibility of social involvement. **Yes No**
2. Stakeholders provide resources that are more or less critical to a firm's long-term success. **Yes No**
3. Three primary stakeholders are customers, special interest groups, and the media. **Yes No**
4. The most significant influence on ethical behavior in the organization is the opportunity to engage in unethical behavior. **Yes No**
5. The stakeholder perspective is useful in managing social responsibility and business ethics. **Yes No**

ANSWERS **1. No.** Social responsibility refers to an organization's obligation to maximize its positive impact on society and minimize its negative impact. **2. Yes.** These resources are both tangible and intangible. **3. No.** Although customers are primary stakeholders, special interest groups and the media are usually considered secondary stakeholders. **4. No.** Other influences such as corporate culture have more impact on ethical decisions within the organization. **5. Yes.** The six steps to implement this approach were provided in this chapter.

PART 2
Ethical Issues and the Institutionalization of Business Ethics

CHAPTER 3

Emerging Business Ethics Issues

CHAPTER OBJECTIVES

- To define ethical issues in the context of organizational ethics
- To examine ethical issues as they relate to the basic values of honesty, fairness, and integrity
- To delineate abusive and intimidating behavior, lying, conflicts of interest, bribery, corporate intelligence, discrimination, sexual harassment, environmental issues, fraud, insider trading, intellectual property rights, and privacy as business ethics issues
- To examine the challenge of determining an ethical issue in business

CHAPTER OUTLINE

AN ETHICAL DILEMMA*

As Lavonda sat in the Ethics Office of the vice president of Emma-Action Pharmaceuticals (EAP), she was worried. Because she was new in the company and didn't know the unwritten rules, the chain-of-command philosophy, and the employees and associates around her very well, her time in the office was very uncomfortable. Given how well things had started, it was painful for her to remember how she had gotten here.

Lavonda had been lured away from her last company because of her expertise in the pharmaceutical industry and her early success in management. Out of college just three and a half years, she had gotten out of the gate remarkably quickly. She had helpful mentors, challenging tasks that she excelled in, and came in below budget on each assignment. Lavonda was typically described as effective and efficient; in fact, at the last company, they even started to call her "E."

But the lure of a six-figure salary, the encounter with Allen (her future boss at EAP), and the chance to be close to her elderly mother made it nearly impossible for Lavonda to say no. She loved her mother and, being an only child, felt responsible for her. Her mother once said that she would prefer to take her own life rather than move to a nursing home.

In the beginning, Lavonda's immediate supervisor, Allen, had been very charming and taught her about the company, its products, the salespeople, and the politics. She knew from experience that she would have to earn the respect of the salespeople she would manage, all of whom were 10 years her senior, and the fact that these men had never had a female boss was just another hurdle to overcome. Allen had helped her find a nice house in a good neighborhood, had assisted with the moving, and eventually had become more than her superior. The months slipped by, and their relationship had become "close," to the point where they began to discuss living arrangements. And then something strange happened—she heard a story about Allen and Karline.

Karline, who had come to EAP six months prior to Lavonda, worked in Human Resources, and in a few short months she had become head of the HR department at EAP amidst rumors of Allen "helping" her get the promotion. Six more months passed, and Lavonda learned that the rumors about Karline and Allen were probably true. She heard the same type of scenario that she had experienced for herself: friend, helping with housing, possible intimacy, and so on. The rumors became so intense that Lavonda confronted

Allen about them and discovered that they were true. Devastated, Lavonda ended the relationship with Allen in a heated confrontation, but it seemed as though Allen didn't understand that it was over.

Weeks went by with little contact between the two of them, and then one afternoon Allen stopped by her office. He apologized for his behavior, and Lavonda accepted his apology. But the next day he stopped by and began to touch and even grope Lavonda. She made a joke of it to defuse the situation, but several days later Allen repeated the same behavior, making several sexual remarks. He asked, "Honey, why can't it be like it was before?" and then whispered some graphic sexual language.

Lavonda's face reddened and she said, "Allen, you are a pig. How dare you say such things to me! You've crossed the line. I've never heard such filth. Don't you ever say such things to me again, or I'll report you to Human Resources!"

Several weeks went by, and Lavonda got a phone call from Allen in which he described even more sexually suggestive things. Every few days, Allen would stop by or call and remind her of some "private" experience they had together, using vulgar sexual language. He would taunt her by saying, "Lavonda, you know you want this from me." It became almost a daily ritual. Allen never wrote any of the things that he described to her, being sure not to leave tangible proof of his behavior, but occasionally he would grab or attempt to grab her sexually.

Eventually, Lavonda had had enough and went to the Human Resources department to complain formally about Allen, his sexual advances, and the hostile environment that they had created. The person she met at HR was Karline. As Lavonda described the situation in detail, she finally said, "Karline, I need you to help me. What Allen is doing to me is wrong and illegal. I can't get my work done. He's undermining my position with my sales staff, he's giving me poor evaluations, and he's suggesting that I could change all that if I wanted to!"

Karline's response was, "Lavonda, I've heard what you've said, but I also have had people come to me with some very disturbing reports about you as well. For example, you and Allen were supposedly sleeping together, and he is your direct supervisor. If this was the case, then it should have been reported immediately; but it wasn't. You have no tangible evidence except for your word. Even if I believed you, the allegation that you had been sexually active with Allen can be construed as making all of what you've said mutual or consensual. If that's the case, then I would have to fire you because of the superior–employee ethics code, and a letter would go into your permanent file that would probably haunt your career for years to come. From my perspective, we can call this an informal and confidential meeting that is not to be repeated, or you can continue this formally and take your chances. It's your call, Lavonda, but you should know that I am disinclined to support your accusations."

In shock, Lavonda mumbled a thank you to Karline and left her office. The next day Allen stopped by, smiled, waved his finger at her and said, "Your performance review is next week, and it doesn't look good. By the way, just so you know, the pharmaceutical industry is quite small, and I have friends at all the majors. Oh, I forgot to tell you how sorry I am for your mother and her cancer diagnosis. Chemo and the side effects are very draining. I'm glad that you're close by to help her through the ordeal. They say it takes months to fully recover. It would be horrible if you weren't here to help her and she had to go to a nursing home. Those places scare me."

Lavonda said, "Allen, why are you doing this to me? I'm not fond of you anymore. We have no future together. Doesn't that tell you something?"

Allen smiled and said, "It tells me that you're not interested in a permanent relationship, which is good, because neither am I. And you know that if you want to be promoted or go to another company with a good recommendation, it all starts with me. Lavonda, there might be another 'solution' to your perceived problem. You know that new sales rep you just hired out of school, Soo-Chin? Well, if you could have her assigned to me and maybe 'coax her in the right way,' I know of a position in the company that would be a promotion for you and you wouldn't be around me. But everything depends upon the success of your coaxing."

So now here Lavonda was, about to meet with the vice president of ethical affairs. As she got up from the chair, she pondered her alternatives and what had led her there. In school she had learned that each company had its own individual code of ethics, but she didn't know the reality of the code at EAP until it was too late.

QUESTIONS • EXERCISES

1. Keeping in mind the facts and timeline of this situation, discuss Lavonda's situation in terms of legal and ethical issues.
2. Discuss Lavonda's alternatives and possible professional and private outcomes for her.
3. Is Allen in violation of sexual harassment and/or sexual discrimination laws in the United States?
4. Certainly Allen has damaged Lavonda's performance level; however, discuss whether he has created a legally hostile work environment.

*This case is strictly hypothetical; any resemblance to real persons, companies, or situations is coincidental.

Stakeholders' ethical concerns determine whether specific business actions and decisions are perceived as ethical or unethical. In the case of the government, community, and society, what was merely an ethical issue can soon become a legal debate and eventually law. Most ethical conflicts in which there are perceived dangers turn into litigation. Additionally, stakeholders often raise ethical issues when they exert pressure on businesses to make decisions that serve their particular agendas. For example, corporate shareholders often demand that managers make decisions that boost short-term earnings, thus maintaining or increasing the value of the shares of stock they own in that firm. Atlanta-based home builder Beazer Homes was issued a cease and desist order by the SEC when it was discovered that the company had fraudulently manipulated funds to smooth earnings fluctuations. When the real estate market was booming in Atlanta, the company put portions of its earnings in "rainy day funds" that it planned to use later to smooth out reported income during slow times. The company clearly anticipated that the housing bubble would burst, and was trying to find a way to keep investors happy over the long term. However, its solution was deemed illegal.[1]

People make ethical decisions only after they recognize that a particular issue or situation has an ethical component; thus, a first step toward understanding business ethics is to develop ethical issue awareness. Ethical issues typically arise because of conflicts among individuals' personal moral philosophies and values, the values and culture of the organizations in which they work, and those of the society in which they live. The business environment presents many potential ethical conflicts. For example, a company's efforts to achieve its organizational objectives may collide with its employees' endeavors to fulfill their own personal goals. Similarly, consumers' desires for safe and quality products may conflict with a manufacturer's need to earn adequate profits. The ambition of top executives to secure sizable increases in compensation may conflict with the desires of shareholders to control costs and increase the value of the corporation. For example, for companies being helped by the government bailout, strict rules for executive pay have been established retroactively. For example, any firm receiving funds is restricted from paying top performers bonuses equal to more than one-third of their total annual compensation. The compensation rules will mostly apply to more than 350 banks. Bank of America CEO Kenneth D. Lewis was paid $16.4 million in 2007. Under the bailout plan his 2009 compensation would be limited to $2.25 million.[2] A manager's wish to hire specific employees that he or she likes may be at odds with the organization's intent to hire the best-qualified candidates, as well as with society's aim to offer equal opportunity to women and members of minority groups.

Characteristics of the job, the culture, and the organization of the society in which one does business can also create ethical issues. Gaining familiarity with the ethical issues that frequently arise in the business world will help you identify and resolve them when they occur.

In this chapter, we consider some of the ethical issues that are emerging in business today, including how these issues arise from the demands of specific stakeholder groups. In the first half of the chapter, we explain certain universal ethical concepts that pervade business ethics, such as honesty, fairness, and integrity. The second half of the chapter explores a number of emerging ethical issues, including abusive and intimidating behavior, lying, conflicts of interest, bribery, corporate intelligence, discrimination, sexual harassment, environmental issues, fraud, insider trading, intellectual property rights, and privacy. We also examine the challenge of determining an ethical issue in business. Because of the global financial meltdown, there are certain practices and products that have or will become issues and will either be defined as illegal or unethical in the coming years. It is important that you understand that what was once legal can become an ethical issue, resulting in well-known practices becoming illegal.

RECOGNIZING AN ETHICAL ISSUE

Although we have described a number of relationships and situations that may generate ethical issues, in practice it can be difficult to recognize specific ethical issues. Failure to acknowledge such ethical issues is a great danger in any organization, particularly if business is treated as a "game" in which ordinary rules of fairness do not apply. Sometimes people who take this view are willing to do things that are not only unethical but also illegal so that they can maximize their own position or boost the profits of their organization. Those involved in the marketplace have an additional set of values related to profit, increased revenue, earnings per share, sales, return on assets, and/or return on investment that must be addressed. All or part of these objectives come into play within business and impact what people will do and how they justify their actions. In one's home life, one does not have the profit motive with which to contend. To be clear, businesspeople do not have a unique set of values from others; rather, the values they have are weighted differently when doing business activities because of the additional responsibilities associated with the marketplace.

Business decisions, like personal decisions, involve an unsettled situation or dilemma. Just because an activity is considered an ethical issue does not mean the behavior is necessarily unethical. An ethical issue is simply a situation, a problem, or even an opportunity that requires thought, discussion, or investigation to make a decision. And because the business world is dynamic, new ethical issues are emerging all the time. Table 3–1 defines specific ethical issues identified by employees in the National Business Ethics Survey (NBES). Three types of misconduct make up 30 percent of the ethical problems within organizations. Putting one's own interests ahead of the organization, abusive behavior, and lying to employees are all personal in nature, but these activities are

TABLE 3-1 Specific Types of Observed Misconduct.

	2009	2007
Company Resource Abuse	23%	N/A
Abusive behavior	22%	21%
Lying to employees	19%	20%
Email or internet abuse	18%	18%
Conflicts of interest	16%	22%
Discrimination	14%	12%
Lying to stakeholders	12%	14%
Employee benefit violations	11%	N/A
Health or safety violations	11%	15%
Employee privacy breach	10%	N/A
Improper hiring practices	10%	10%
Falsifying time or expenses	10%	N/A
Poor product quality	9%	10%
Stealing	9%	12%
Sexual harassment	7%	10%
Substance abuse	7%	N/A
Document alteration	6%	6%
Misuse of company's confidential information	6%	6%
Customer privacy breach	6%	N/A
Environmental violations	4%	6%

Source: "2009 National Business Ethics Survey: Ethics in the Recession," (Washington D.C.: Ethics Resource Center, 2009): p. 32–33.

sometimes committed by individuals in the belief that they are furthering organizational goals. Misreporting hours worked, safety violations, and provision of low-quality goods and services are the top three issues that directly relate to the firm's agenda. Table 3–1 compares the percentage of employees who observed specific types of misconduct over the past two National Business Ethics Surveys.

Employees could select more than one form of misconduct; therefore, each type of misconduct represents the percentage of employees who saw that particular act. Although Table 3–1 documents many types of ethical issues that exist in organizations, it is impossible to list every conceivable ethical issue. Any type of manipulation, deceit, or even just the absence of transparency in decision making can create harm to others. For example, collusion is a secret agreement between two or more parties for a fraudulent, illegal, or deceitful purpose. "Deceitful purpose" is the relevant phrase in regard to business ethics, in that it suggests trickery, misrepresentation, or a strategy designed to lead others to believe one truth but not the entire truth.

Honesty

Honesty refers to truthfulness or trustworthiness. To be honest is to tell the truth to the best of your knowledge without hiding anything. Confucius defined several levels of honesty. The shallowest is called *Li*, and it relates to the superficial desires of a person. A key principle to *Li* is striving to convey feelings that outwardly are or appear to be honest but that are ultimately driven by self-interest. The second level is *Yi*, or righteousness, where a person does what is right based on reciprocity. The deepest level of honesty is called *Ren*, and it is based on an understanding of and empathy toward others. The Confucian version of Kant's Golden Rule is to treat your inferiors as you would want superiors to treat you. As a result, virtues such as familial honor and reputation for honesty become paramount.

Issues related to honesty also arise because business is sometimes regarded as a "game" governed by its own rules rather than by those of society. Author Eric Beversluis suggests that honesty is a problem because people often reason along these lines:

1. Business relationships are a subset of human relationships that are governed by their own rules, which, in a market society, involve competition, profit maximization, and personal advancement within the organization.
2. Business can therefore be considered a game people play, comparable in certain respects to competitive sports such as basketball or boxing.
3. Ordinary rules and morality do not hold in games like basketball or boxing. (What if a basketball player did unto others as he would have them do unto him? What if a boxer decided it was wrong to try to injure another person?)
4. Logically, then, if business is a game like basketball or boxing, ordinary ethical rules do not apply.[3]

This type of reasoning leads many people to conclude that anything is acceptable in business. Indeed, several books have compared business to warfare—for example, *The Guerrilla Marketing Handbook* and *Sun Tsu: The Art of War for Managers*. The common theme in these books is that surprise attacks, guerrilla warfare, and other warlike tactics are necessary to win the battle for consumers' dollars. An example of this mentality at work is Larry Ellison, the CEO of Oracle. Ellison's warlike mentality is demonstrated by his decision to sell PeopleSoft's technology and let most of its 8,000 employees go. PeopleSoft CEO Craig Conway stated that "Ellison has followed a page straight out of Genghis Khan." Ellison has frequently recited phrases of the thirteenth-century Mongol warlord such as "It's not enough that we win; everyone else must lose."[4] Ellison was ordered to donate $100 million to charity and pay another $22 million to the attorneys who sued him for alleged stock-trading abuses. Ellison argues that he acted in good faith and in the best interests of Oracle and Oracle's shareholders.[5]

This business-as-war mentality may foster the idea that honesty is unnecessary in business. In addition, an intensely competitive environment creates the potential for companies to engage in questionable conduct. For example, as competition in the market for beer intensified, Miller, Coors, and Anheuser-Busch increasingly created advertising and offered products that appealed to younger consumers, even though marketing to minors under the age of 21 is illegal.

Many argue, however, that business is not a game like basketball or boxing; because people are not economically self-sufficient, they cannot withdraw from the game of business. Therefore, business ethics must not only make clear what rules apply in the "game" of business but must also develop rules appropriate to the involuntary nature of participation in it.[6]

Because of the economic motive, many in business can become confused with the opposite of honesty—dishonesty. Dishonesty can be broadly defined as a lack of integrity, incomplete disclosure, and an unwillingness to tell the truth. Dishonesty is also synonymous with lying, cheating, and stealing. Lying, cheating, and stealing are the actions usually associated with dishonest conduct. The causes of dishonesty are complex and relate to both individual and organizational pressures. Many employees lie to help achieve performance objectives. For example, they may be asked to lie about when a customer will receive a purchase. Lying can be segmented into (1) causing damage or harm; (2) a "white lie," which doesn't cause damage but can be called an excuse or something told to benefit someone else; and (3) statements that are obviously meant to engage or entertain with no malice. These definitions will become important to the remainder of this chapter.

Fairness

Fairness is the quality of being just, equitable, and impartial. Fairness clearly overlaps with other commonly used terms such as justice, equity, equality, and morality. There are three fundamental elements that seem to motivate people to be fair: equality, reciprocity, and optimization. In business, **equality** is about how wealth or income is distributed between employees within a company, a country, or across the globe.

Reciprocity is an interchange of giving and receiving in social relationships. Reciprocity occurs when an action that has an effect upon another is reciprocated with an action that has an approximately equal effect upon the other. Reciprocity is the return of small favors that are approximately equal in value. For example, reciprocity implies that workers be compensated with wages that are approximately equal to their effort. An ethical issue about reciprocity for business is the amount CEOs and other executives are paid in relation to their employees. Is a 431 to 1 pay ratio an example of ethical reciprocity? That is the average wage distance between a CEO and a production worker in the United States.

> *Dishonesty can be broadly defined as a lack of integrity, incomplete disclosure, and an unwillingness to tell the truth.*

Optimization is the trade-off between equity (that is, equality or fairness) and efficiency (that is, maximum productivity). Discriminating on the basis of gender, race, or religion is generally considered to be unfair because these qualities have little bearing upon a person's ability to do a job. The optimal way is to choose the employee who is the most talented, most proficient, most educated, and most able. Ideas of fairness are sometimes shaped by vested interests. One or both parties in the relationship may view an action as unfair or unethical because the outcome was less beneficial than expected.

Integrity

Integrity is one of the most important and often-cited terms regarding virtue, and refers to being whole, sound, and in an unimpaired condition. In an organization, it means uncompromising adherence to ethical values. Integrity is connected to acting ethically; in other words, there are substantive or normative constraints on what it means to act with integrity. This usually rests on an organization's enduring values and unwillingness to deviate from standards of behavior.

At a minimum, businesses are expected to follow all applicable laws and regulations. In addition, organizations should not knowingly harm customers, clients, employees, or even other competitors through deception, misrepresentation, or coercion. Although businesspeople often act in their own economic self-interest, ethical business relations should be grounded on honesty, integrity, fairness, justice, and trust. Buyers should be able to trust sellers; lenders should be able to trust borrowers. Failure to live up to these expectations or to abide by laws and standards destroys trust and makes it difficult, if not impossible, to continue business exchanges.[7] These virtues become the glue that holds business relationships together, making everything else more effective and efficient.

ETHICAL ISSUES AND DILEMMAS IN BUSINESS

As mentioned earlier, stakeholders define a business's ethical issues. An **ethical issue** is a problem, situation, or opportunity that requires an individual, group, or organization to choose among several actions that must be evaluated as right or wrong, ethical or unethical. An **ethical dilemma** is a problem, situation, or opportunity that requires an individual, group, or organization to choose among several wrong or unethical actions. There is not simply one right or ethical choice in a dilemma, only less unethical or illegal choices as perceived by any and all stakeholders.

A constructive next step toward identifying and resolving ethical issues is to classify the issues that are relevant to most business organizations. In this section, we classify ethical issues in relation to abusive or intimidating behavior, lying, conflicts of interest, bribery, corporate intelligence, discrimination, sexual harassment, environmental issues, fraud, insider trading, intellectual property rights, and privacy issues. In addition, a short review of the financial industry, its problem products, and the Securities and Exchange Commission are given.

Figure 3–1 reflects the ethical issues that are most likely to have impact on shareholder value for companies over the next five years. It is interesting to note that executives feel that their companies' shareholder value will be significantly affected by job loss and offshoring jobs when outsourcing to improve efficiency. Surprisingly, the ability to exert political influence or political involvement is also a major issue.

Abusive or Intimidating Behavior

Abusive or **intimidating behavior** is the most common ethical problem for employees, but what does it mean to be abusive or intimidating? The concepts can mean anything—physical threats, false accusations, being annoying, profanity, insults, yelling, harshness, ignoring someone, and unreasonableness—and the meaning of these words can differ by person. It is important to understand that with each term there is a continuum. For example, what one person may define as yelling might be another's definition of normal speech. Civility in our society has been a concern, and the workplace is no exception. The productivity level of many organizations has been damaged by the time spent unraveling abusive relationships.

FIGURE 3-1 Issues the Affect Shareholder Value: What are the top issues likely to affect shareholder value?

Rank	Issue
1	Layoffs and offshoring
2	Political pressure from companies
3	Sustainability issues, global warming (tied)
4	Pension and retirement benefits (tied)
5	Privacy and data security
6	Employee benefits
7	Opposition to foreign investment and free trade
8	Healthier/safer product requirements (tied)
9	Affordability of products for poor consumers (tied)
10	Ethical standards for advertising and marketing

Adapted from "The McKinsey Global Survey of Business Executives: Business and Society," *The McKinsey Quarterly: The Online Journal of McKinsey & Co.*, January 2006, http://www.mckinseyquarterly.com/The_McKinsey_Global_Survey_of_Business_Executives__Business_and_Society_1741 (accessed March 8, 2006)

Is it abusive behavior to ask an employee to complete a project rather than be with a family member or relative in a crisis situation? What does it mean to speak profanely? Is profanity only related to specific words or terms that are common in today's business world? If you are using words that are normal in your language but others consider profanity, have you just insulted, abused, or disrespected them?

Within the concept of abusive behavior or intimidation, intent should be a consideration. If the employee was trying to convey a compliment, then it was probably a mistake. What if a male manager asks his female subordinate if she has a date for tonight because she is dressed so nice? Does the way (voice inflection) a word is said become important? Add to this the fact that we now live in a multicultural environment doing business and working with many different cultural groups and the businessperson soon realizes the depth of the ethical and legal issues that may arise. Finally, you have the problem of word meanings by age and within cultures. Is it okay to say "honey" to an employee, fellow employee, employee friend, and/or your superior, and does it depend on gender or location? For example, if you were to call a friend that worked with you "honey" in southern Illinois, Arkansas, or Kentucky, do you have the same acceptability factor in northern Illinois, Michigan, or Minnesota? Does abusive behavior vary by different genders? It is possible the term *honey* could be acceptable speech in some environments, and be construed as being abusive or intimidating in other situations?

Bullying is associated with a hostile workplace where someone (or a group) considered a target is threatened, harassed, belittled, or verbally abused or overly criticized. Bullying may create what some may call a hostile environment, but this term is generally associated with sexual harassment. Bullying can cause psychological damage that can result in health-endangering consequences to the target. As Table 3–2 indicates, bullying can use a

TABLE 3-2 Actions Associated with Bullies

1. Spreading rumors to damage others
2. Blocking others' communication in the workplace
3. Flaunting status or authority to take advantage of others
4. Discrediting others' ideas and opinions
5. Use of e-mails to demean others
6. Failing to communicate or return communication
7. Insults, yelling, and shouting
8. Using terminology to discriminate by gender, race, or age
9. Using eye or body language to hurt others or their reputation
10. Taking credit for others' work or ideas

Source: Cathi McMahan, "Are You A Bully?" *Inside Seven*, California Department of Transportation Newsletter, June 1999, page 6.

mix of verbal, nonverbal, and manipulative threatening expressions to damage workplace productivity. One may wonder why workers tolerate such activities; the problem is that 81 percent of workplace bullies are supervisors. Bullying happens more than people realize. For example, 37 percent (54 million) of American workers have been bullied at work and when witnesses are included it rises to 49 percent (71.5 million), and an estimated 72 percent of the perpetrators are employers.[8]

The concept of "bullying" in the workplace is now considered a legal issue. Some suggest that employers take the following steps to minimize workplace bullying:

- They should have policies in place that make it clear that bullying behaviors will not be tolerated.
- The employee handbook should emphasize that workers must treat each other with respect.
- Employers should encourage employees who feel bullied to report the conduct, much the same as discriminatory harassment complaints are handled.[9]

Bullying can also occur between companies that are in intense competition. Even respected companies such as Intel have been accused of monopolistic bullying. A competitor, Advanced Micro Devices (AMD), claimed in a lawsuit that 38 companies, including Dell and Sony, were strong-arming customers into buying Intel chips rather than those marketed by AMD. The AMD lawsuit seeks billions of dollars and will take years to litigate. In many cases, the alleged misconduct can have not only monetary and legal implications but also can threaten reputation, investor confidence, and customer loyalty. A front-cover *Forbes* headline stated "Intel to AMD: Drop Dead." An example of the intense competition and Intel's ability to use its large size won it the high-profile Apple account, displacing IBM and Freescale. ADM said it had no opportunity to bid because Intel offered to deploy 600 Indian engineers to help Apple software run more smoothly on Intel chips.[10] Intel's actions have landed it in trouble in the European Union, however, where courts found the company guilty of antitrust violations and anticompetitive behavior regarding competitor Advanced Micro Devices (AMD). AMD alleged that Intel was preventing the company from being competitive through such practices as paying computer makers rebates for using Intel chips and selling chips at below cost. The EU courts sided with AMD and Intel was fined a record $1.45 billion, which it continues to fight in courts. The EU is notoriously hard on antitrust cases. Microsoft too has been found guilty and has racked up $2 billion in fines over multiple years in the EU.[11]

Lying

Earlier in this chapter, we discussed the definitions of **lying** and how it relates to distorting the truth. We mentioned three types of lies, one of which is joking without malice. The other two can become very troublesome for businesses. For example, one can lie by commission or omission. *Commission lying* is creating a perception or belief by words that intentionally deceive the receiver of the message, for example, lying about being at work, expense reports, or carrying out work assignments. Commission lying also entails intentionally creating "noise" within the communication that knowingly confuses or deceives the receiver. *Noise* can be defined as technical explanations that the communicator knows the receiver does not understand. It can be the intentional use of communication forms that make it difficult for the receiver to actually hear the true message. Using legal terms or terms relating to unfamiliar processes and systems to explain what was done in a work situation facilitate this type of lie.

Lying by commission can involve complex forms, procedures, contracts, words that are spelled the same but have different meanings, or refuting the truth with a false statement. Forms of commission lying include puffery in advertising. For example, saying that a product is "homemade" when it is made in a factory is lying. "Made from scratch" in cooking technically means that all ingredients within the product were distinct and separate and were not combined prior to the beginning of the production process. One can lie by commission by showing a picture of the product that does not reflect the actual product. This happens frequently in business. For example, a national fast-food chain came out with a new product that had lettuce in it. There are many types of lettuce and the lettuce used in the national ad campaign both in print and TV used romaine lettuce. Yet this fast-food chain does not purchase that variety; it purchases iceberg lettuce. The obvious reason for using romaine in the ad is that it is prettier or more appealing than shredded iceberg lettuce. Another example is Schick's complaint against Gillette, alleging that the latter's claims for its Mach 3 Turbo Razor as "the world's best shave" and "the best a man can get" are false and misleading.

Omission lying is intentionally not informing the channel member of any differences, problems, safety warnings, or negative issues relating to the product, service, or company that significantly affects awareness, intention, or behavior. A classic example for decades was the tobacco manufacturers that did not allow negative research to appear on cigarettes and cigars. The drug Vioxx is being questioned because the manufacturer allegedly did not inform consumers as to the degree and occurrence of side effects, one of which is death. Finally, when lying damages others, it can be the focus of a lawsuit. For example, prosecutors and civil lawsuits often reduce misconduct to lying about a fact such as financial performance that has the potential to damage others. CEOs at AIG, Lehman Brothers, Fannie Mae, and Freddie Mac were scrutinized to see if they told the truth about the financial conditions of their companies.

When a lie becomes unethical in business, it is based on the context and intent to distort the truth. A lie becomes illegal if it is determined by the judgment of courts to damage others. Some businesspeople may believe that one must lie a little or that the occasional lie is sanctioned by the organization. The question you need to ask is whether lies are distorting openness and transparency and other values that are associated with ethical behavior.

Conflicts of Interest

A **conflict of interest** exists when an individual must choose whether to advance his or her own interests, those of the organization, or those of some other group. The medical industry has been faced with many accusations of conflicts of interest with doctors and medical schools regarding payments. For example, Harvard Medical School received an 'F' grade on its conflict of interest policies from the American Medical Student Association. One professor alone was forced to disclose 47 company affiliations from which he was receiving money.[12] To address the problem, a government panel has called for full disclosure of all payments made to doctors, researchers, and universities. The fear is that financial donations from medical and pharmaceutical companies could sway researchers' findings and what is taught in classrooms.[13]

"To avoid conflicts of interest, employees must be able to separate their private interests from their business dealings."

To avoid conflicts of interest, employees must be able to separate their private interests from their business dealings. Organizations must also avoid potential conflicts of interest when providing products.[14] The U.S. General Accounting Office has found conflicts of interest when the government has awarded bids on defense contracts. The conflicts of interest usually relate to hiring friends, relatives, or retired military officers to enhance the probability of getting the contract.[15]

Bribery

Bribery is the practice of offering something (usually money) in order to gain an illicit advantage. The key issue regarding whether or not something is considered bribery is determining whether the act is illicit or contrary to accepted morality or convention. Bribery therefore is defined as an unlawful act, but it can be a business ethics issue. The reason is that bribery can be defined differently in varying situations and cultural environments.

Bribery can be defined many ways. For example, there is something called active corruption or **active bribery,** meaning that the person who promises or gives the bribe commits the offense. **Passive bribery** is an offense committed by the official who receives the bribe. It is not an offense, however, if the advantage was permitted or required by the written law or regulation of the foreign public official's country, including case law.

Small **facilitation payments** made to obtain or retain business or other improper advantages do not constitute bribery payments. In some countries, such payments are made to induce public officials to perform their functions, such as issuing licenses or permits. However, criminalization by other countries does not seem a practical or effective complementary action. In many developed countries, it is generally recognized that employees should not accept bribes, personal payments, gifts, or special favors from people who hope to influence the outcome of a decision. However, bribery is an accepted way of doing business in many countries. Bribes have been associated with the downfall of many managers, legislators, and government officials. One source estimates that some $80 billion is paid out worldwide in the form of bribes or some other payoff every year.[16]

When a government official accepts a bribe, it is usually from a business that seeks some favor—perhaps a chance to influence legislation that affects it. Giving bribes to legislators or public officials, then, is a business ethics issue. The U.S. Department of Justice cracked down on cases of bribery involving hundreds of companies. Under these investigations Halliburton Company agreed to pay nearly $600 million after bribing officials in Nigeria in order to win oil contracts.[17]

Corporate Intelligence

Many issues related to corporate intelligence have surfaced in the last few years. Defined broadly, **corporate intelligence** is the collection and analysis of information on markets, technologies, customers, and competitors, as well as on socioeconomic and external political trends. There are three distinct types of intelligence models: a passive monitoring system for early warning, tactical field support, and support dedicated to top-management strategy. Today, theft of trade secrets is estimated at $100 billion. One explanation is the increase in people with intelligence-gathering competence and the proliferation of advanced technology.[18]

Corporate intelligence (CI) involves an in-depth discovery of information from corporate records, court documents, regulatory filings, and press releases, as well as any other background information that can be found about a company or its executives. Corporate intelligence is a legitimate inquiry into meaningful information that can be used in staying competitive. Corporate intelligence, like other areas in business, can be abused if due diligence is not taken to maintain legal and ethical methods of discovery. Computers, LANs (local-area networks), and the Internet have made the theft of trade secrets very easy. Proprietary information like secret formulas, manufacturing schematics, merger or acquisition plans, and marketing strategies all have tremendous value. NewRiver Inc. brought a suit against the investment research firm Morningstar Inc., accusing it of using Internet espionage to copy information off of a patented system for handling mutual fund prospectuses. Morningstar does not deny accessing the system, but claims it was only for "benchmarking purposes," and claims that it did not enter any password-protected areas of the site.[19] A lack of security and proper training allows one to use a variety of techniques to gain access to a company's vital information. Some techniques for accessing valuable corporate information include physically removing the hard drive and copying the information to another machine, hacking, dumpster diving, social engineering, bribery, and hiring away key employees.

Hacking is considered one of the top three methods for obtaining trade secrets. Currently, there are over 100,000 websites that offer free downloadable and customizable hacking tools that require no in-depth knowledge of protocols or Internet protocol addressing. Hacking has three categories: system, remote, and physical. **System hacking** assumes that the attacker already has access to a low-level, privileged-user account. **Remote hacking** involves attempting to remotely penetrate a system across the Internet. A remote hacker usually begins with no special privileges and tries to obtain higher level or administrative access. Several forms of this type of hacking include unexpected input, buffer overflows, default configurations, and poor system administrator practices. **Physical hacking** requires that the CI agent enter a facility personally. Once inside, he or she can find a vacant or unsecured workstation with an employee's login name and password. Next, the CI agent searches for memos or unused letterheads and inserts the documents into the corporate mail system. Or the CI agent could gain physical access to a server or telephone room, look for remote-access equipment, note any telephone numbers written on wall jacks, and place a protocol analyzer in a wiring closet to capture data, user names, and passwords.

Social engineering is another popular method of obtaining valuable corporate information. The basic goals are the same as hacking. **Social engineering** is the tricking of individuals into revealing their passwords or other valuable corporate information. Tactics include casual conversations with relatives of company executives and sending e-mail claiming to be a system administrator that asks for passwords under the guise of "important system administration work." Another common social engineering trick is **shoulder surfing,** in which someone simply looks over an employee's shoulder while he or she types in a password. **Password guessing** is another easy social engineering technique. If a person can find out personal things about someone, he or she might be able to use that information to guess a password. For example, a child's name, birthdays and anniversaries, and Social Security numbers are all common passwords and are easily guessed or figured out by someone trying to do so.

Dumpster diving is messy but very successful for acquiring trade secrets. Once trash is discarded onto a public street or alley, it is considered fair game. Trash can provide a rich source of information for any CI agent. Phone books can give a hacker names and numbers of people to target and impersonate. Organizational charts contain information about people who are in positions of authority within the organization. Memos provide small amounts of useful information and assist in the creation of authentic-looking fake memos.

Whacking is wireless hacking. To eavesdrop on wireless networks, all a CI agent needs is the right kind of radio and to be within range of a wireless transmission. Once tapped into a wireless network, an intruder can easily access anything on both the wired and wireless networks because the data sent over networks is usually unencrypted. If a company is not using wireless networking, an attacker can pose as a janitor and insert a rogue wireless access node into a supposedly secure hard-wired network.

Phone eavesdropping is yet another tool in the game of CI agent. A person with a digital recording device can monitor and record a fax line. By playing the recording back an intruder can reproduce an exact copy of a message without anyone's knowledge. Even without monitoring a fax line, a fax sent to a "communal" fax machine can be read or copied. By picking up an extension or by tapping a telephone, it is possible to record the tones that represent someone's account number and password using a tape recorder. The tape recording can then be replayed over the telephone to gain access to someone else's account.

Discrimination

Although a person's racial and sexual prejudices belong to the domain of individual ethics, racial and sexual discrimination in the workplace creates ethical issues within the business world. **Discrimination** on the basis of race, color, religion, sex, marital status, sexual orientation, public assistance status, disability, age, national origin, or veteran status is illegal in the United States. Additionally, discrimination on the basis of political opinions or affiliation with a union is defined as harassment.

A company in the United States can be sued if it (1) refuses to hire an individual, (2) maintains a system of employment that unreasonably excludes an individual from employment, (3) discharges an individual, or (4) discriminates against an individual with respect to hiring, employment terms, promotion, or privileges of employment as it relates to the definition of discrimination.

Race, gender, and age discrimination are a major source of ethical and legal debate in the workplace. Between 75,000 and 80,000 charges of discrimination are filed annually with the **Equal Employment Opportunity Commission** (EEOC).[20] Discrimination remains a significant ethical issue in business despite nearly 40 years of legislation attempting to outlaw it. For example, there are only two black chairs/CEOs of Fortune 500 companies: Richard D. Parsons of Dime Savings Bank of New York, and Ursula Burns of Xerox, who is also the first-ever African American woman to be CEO of a Fortune 500 company.

Once dominated by European American men, the U.S. workforce today includes significantly more women, African Americans, Hispanics, and other minorities, as well as disabled and older workers. Experts project that within the next 50 years, Hispanics will represent 24 percent of the population, and African Americans and Asian/Pacific Islanders will comprise 13 percent and 9 percent, respectively.[21] These groups have traditionally faced discrimination and higher unemployment rates and been denied opportunities to assume leadership roles in corporate America. Another form of discrimination involves discriminating against individuals on the basis of age. The **Age Discrimination in Employment Act** specifically outlaws hiring practices that discriminate against people between the ages of 49 and 69, as well as those that require employees to retire before the age of 70. Despite this legislation, charges of age discrimination persist in the workplace. For example, the EEOC has charged Sidley Austin Brown & Wood, a Chicago-based international law firm with over 1,500 lawyers, with age discrimination when it selected "partners" for expulsion from the firm on account of their age. The act prohibits employers with 20 or more employees from making employment decisions, including decisions regarding the termination of employment, on the basis of age or from requiring retirement after the age of 40. EEOC trial attorney Deborah Hamilton stated that "having the power to fire an employee does not mean that a law firm or any other covered employer can do so because of the employee's age, if the employee is over 40. That is a violation of the ADEA and that the making of unlawful age-based selections for termination is precisely what EEOC is targeting in this lawsuit."[22] For example, Lockheed Martin Global Telecommunications settled its age discrimination lawsuit filed by eight older employees for $773,000. Sprint Nextel settled its age discrimination lawsuit for $57 million. The settlement involves around 1,700 former Sprint employees. After legal fees ($21 million) each plaintiff will receive a settlement between $4,000 and $35,000, for an average of $20,000.[23]

> *"Race, gender, and age discrimination are a major source of ethical and legal debate in the workplace."*

A survey by the American Association for Retired Persons (AARP), an advocacy organization for people aged 50 years and older, highlighted how little most companies value older workers. When the AARP mailed invitations to 10,000 companies for a chance to compete for a listing in *Modern Maturity* magazine as one of the "best employers for workers over 50," it received just 14 applications. Given that nearly 20 percent of the nation's workers will be 55 years old or over by 2015, many companies need to change their approach toward older workers.[24]

To help build workforces that reflect their customer base, many companies have initiated **affirmative action programs,** which involve efforts to recruit, hire, train, and promote qualified individuals from groups that have traditionally been discriminated against on the basis of race, gender, or other characteristics. Such initiatives may be imposed by federal law on an employer that contracts or subcontracts for business with the federal government, as part of a settlement agreement with a state or federal agency, or by court order.[25] For example, Safeway, a chain of supermarkets, established a program to expand opportunities for women in middle- and upper-level management after settling a sex-discrimination lawsuit.[26] However, many companies voluntarily implement affirmative action plans in order to build a more diverse workforce.[27] For example, a Chicago real estate developer decided to help employers identify available female workers by launching the Female Employment Initiative, an outreach program designed to create opportunities for women in the construction industry through training programs, counseling and information services, and referral listings.[28]

Although many people believe that affirmative action requires that quotas be used to govern employment decisions, it is important to note that two decades of Supreme Court rulings have made it clear that affirmative action does not permit or require quotas, reverse discrimination, or favorable treatment of unqualified women or minorities. To ensure that affirmative action programs are fair, the Supreme Court has established a number of standards to guide their implementation: (1) There must be a strong reason for developing an affirmative action program; (2) affirmative action programs must apply only to qualified candidates; and (3) affirmative action programs must be limited and temporary and therefore cannot include "rigid and inflexible quotas."[29]

Discrimination can also be an ethical issue in business when companies use race or other personal factors to discriminate against specific groups of customers. Many companies have been accused of using race to deny service or charge higher prices to certain ethnic groups. For example, four airlines have settled lawsuits alleging discrimination against perceived Arab, Middle Eastern, or Southeast Asian descent passengers. United, American, Continental, and Delta have all denied any violations but agreed to spend as much as $1.5 million to train staff on respecting civil rights.[30]

Sexual Harassment

Sexual harassment is a form of sex discrimination that violates Title VII of the Civil Rights Act of 1964. Title VII applies to employers with 15 or more employees, including state and local governments. To understand the magnitude of this volatile issue, in one year the EEOC received 13,136 charges of sexual harassment, of which over 15 percent were filed by men. In another recent year, the EEOC resolved 13,786 sexual harassment charges and recovered $37.1 million in penalties.[31] **Sexual harassment** can be defined as any repeated, unwanted behavior of a sexual nature perpetrated upon one individual by another. It may be verbal, visual, written, or physical and can occur between people of different genders or those of the same sex. "Workplace display of sexually explicit material—photos, magazines, or posters—may constitute a hostile work environment harassment, even though the private possession, reading, and consensual sharing of such materials is protected under the Constitution."[32]

Even the United Nations, an organization whose mission is to protect human rights globally, has dealt with a series of sexual harassment cases. Many U.N. employees who have made or faced accusations claim that the system is poorly equipped to handle complaints, resulting in unfair, slow, and arbitrary rulings. For example, one employee who claimed she was harassed for years in Gaza saw her superior cleared by one of his colleagues.[33]

To establish sexual harassment, an employee must understand the definition of a **hostile work environment,** for which three criteria must be met: the conduct was unwelcome; the conduct was severe, pervasive, and regarded by the claimant as so hostile or offensive as to alter his or her conditions of employment; and the conduct was such that a reasonable person would find it hostile or offensive. To assert a hostile work environment, an employee need not prove that it seriously affected his or her psychological well-being nor caused an injury; the decisive issue is whether the conduct interfered with the claimant's work performance.[34]

Sexual harassment includes unwanted sexual approaches (including touching, feeling, groping) and/or repeated unpleasant, degrading, or sexist remarks directed toward an employee with the implied suggestion that the target's employment status, promotion, or favorable treatment depend on a positive response and/or cooperation. It can be regarded as a private nuisance, unfair labor practice, or, in some states, a civil wrong (tort) that may be the basis for a lawsuit against the individual who made the advances and against the employer who did not take steps to halt the harassment. The law is primarily concerned with the impact of the behavior and not the intent. An important facet of sexual harassment law is its focus on the victim's reasonable behaviors and expectations.[35] However the definition of reasonable varies from state to state, as does the concept of expectations. In addition, an argument used by some in defense of sexual harassment is the freedom of speech granted by the First Amendment.

> *An important facet of sexual harassment law is its focus on the victim's reasonable behaviors and expectations.*

The key ethical issue within sexual harassment is called dual relationships or unethically intimate relationships. A **dual relationship** is defined as a personal, loving, and/or sexual relationship with someone with whom you share professional responsibilities. Potentially, **unethical dual relationships** are those where the relationship causes either a direct or indirect conflict of interest or a risk of impairment to professional judgment.[36] Another important factor in these cases is intent. If the sexual advances in any form are considered mutual, then consent is created. The problem is that, unless the employee or employer gets something in writing before the romantic action, consent can always be questioned, and when it comes to sexual harassment, the alleged perpetrator must prove mutual consent.

For example, in a case in Illinois, a professor made advances to his office assistant, repeatedly asking her "Do you love me?" and "Would you ever marry a man like me?" He would also ask her for hugs, rub her shoulders, and tickle her. The assistant was troubled by these behaviors, and although she confided her distress to the proper authorities, nothing was done until she went to another institution and filed an official complaint. The university responded by directing the professor to undergo training in proper behavior toward female students and by placing a letter in his personnel file, outlining the actions to be taken and the method for evaluating their effectiveness. In this case, the university believed that there was no duality and the EEOC awarded no monetary damages to the assistant.

Three former female employees sued Florida-based Airguide Corporation and its parent company, Pioneer Metals, Inc., for sexual harassment. The courts awarded each of the three women $1 million, but the penalties for sexual harassment do not stop there. In addition, Airguide and Pioneer Metals must conduct annual training in 19 facilities in Florida and undergo monitoring by the EEOC for three years.[37]

To avoid sexual misconduct or harassment charges a company should, at the minimum, take the following steps:

1. *Establish a statement of policy* naming someone in the company as ultimately responsible for preventing harassment at the company.
2. *Establish a definition of sexual harassment* that includes unwelcome advances, requests for sexual favors, and any other verbal, visual, or physical conduct of a sexual nature; that provides examples of each; and that reminds employees that the list of examples is not all-inclusive.
3. *Establish a nonretaliation policy* that protects complainants and witnesses.
4. *Establish specific procedures for prevention* of such practices at early stages. However, if a company puts these procedures in writing, they are expected by law to train, measure, and ensure that the policies are being enforced.
5. *Establish, enforce, and encourage* victims of sexual harassment to report the behavior to authorized individuals.
6. *Establish a reporting procedure.*
7. *Make sure that the company has timely reporting requirements to the proper authorities.* Usually, there is a time limitation to file the complaint for a formal administrative sexual charge, ranging from six months to a year. However, the failure to meet a shorter complaint period (for example, 60 to 90 days) so that a "rapid response" and remediation may occur and to help to ensure a harassment-free environment could be a company's defense against the charge that it was negligent.

Once these steps have been taken, a training program should identify and describe forms of sexual harassment and give examples, outline the grievance procedure, explain how to use the procedures and discuss the importance of them, discuss the penalty for violation, and train employees for the essential need of a workplace that is free from harassment, offensive conduct, or intimidation. A corporation's training program should cover such items as how to spot sexual harassment; how to investigate complaints including proper documentation; what to do about observed sexual harassment, even when no complaint has been filed; how to keep the work environment as professional and non-hostile as possible; how to teach employees that the consequences can be dismissal; and how to train management to understand follow-up procedures on incidents.

Environmental Issues

Environmental issues are becoming the significant concerns within the business community. The **Kyoto Protocol,** one example of the world's growing concern about global warming, is an international treaty on climate change committed to reducing emissions of carbon dioxide and five other greenhouse gases and to engaging in emissions trading if member signatories maintain or increase emissions of these gases. The objective is to stabilize greenhouse gas concentrations in the atmosphere at a level that would prevent dangerous climate changes. Some current estimates indicate that, if these objectives are not successfully and completely implemented, the predicted global temperature increase could be between 1.4°C to 5.8°C. Possible massive tidal surges and extreme weather patterns are in store for our planet in the future if countries do not restrict specific gases emanating from business activities. The United States is one of the only countries not to sign the protocol.

Water pollution results from the dumping of raw sewage and toxic chemicals into rivers and oceans, from oil and gasoline spills, and from the burial of industrial wastes in the ground where they may filter into underground water supplies. Fertilizers and pesticides used in farming and grounds maintenance also drain into water supplies with each rainfall. When these chemicals reach the oceans, they encourage the growth of algae that use up all the nearby oxygen, thus killing the sea life. According to the Environmental Protection Agency (EPA), more than one-third of the nation's rivers, lakes, and coastal waters are not safe for swimming or fishing as a result of contaminated runoff.

Waste management has flourished in Europe, especially in Germany, and appears to be growing globally. One green issue is plastic; in the United States alone, 30 million plastic bottles are thrown away daily for a total of nearly 11 billion a year. Those that are recycled use large amounts of energy in the recycling process. An even bigger problem for the future is that, as the world becomes more capitalistic, more people will buy more things using plastics that are made from oil and that do not degrade easily. Consumers currently consider recycling to be the most important thing they can do to live "greener" lives, as Figure 3–2 demonstrates. However, more drastic measures will need to be made by businesses and consumers alike to cut back on energy consumption and waste.

Buildings are rarely considered major pollution sources. Yet 33 percent of major U.S. energy use, 33 percent of major greenhouse gas emissions, and 30 percent of raw material use are the result of buildings.[38] Currently, there are two competitive certification groups that authorize schools, houses, and commercial buildings as green. These two rival groups, Green Globes and Leadership in Energy and Environmental Design (LEED), are vying for leadership in government adoption of environmental rules that determine

FIGURE 3–2 Consumers' Favorite Green Practices

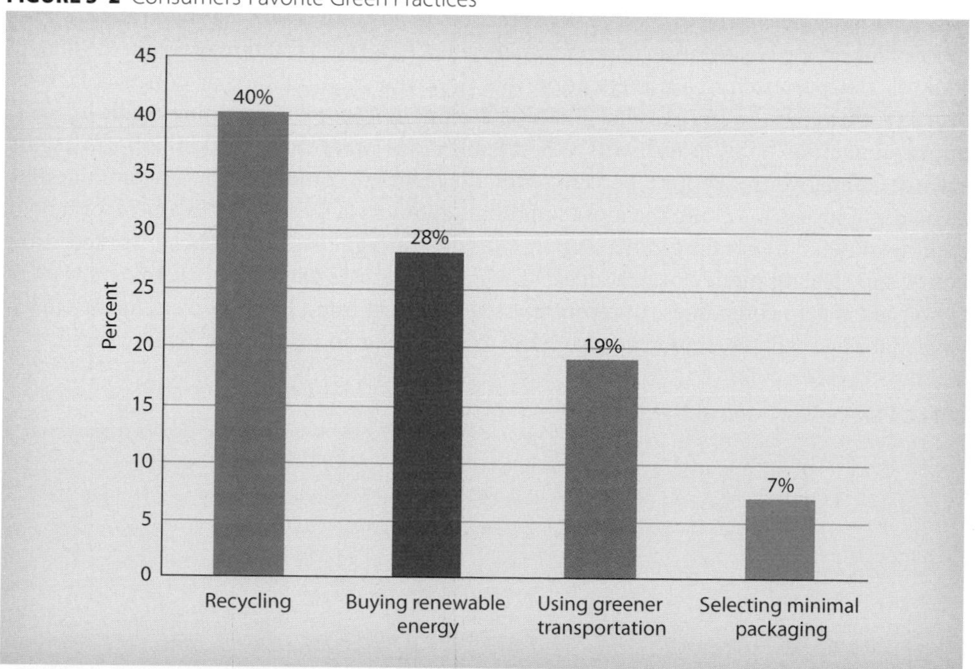

Source: "Environmentally Friendly Choices," *USA Today Snapshots*, March 3, 2009, from Green Seal and Enviromedia Social Marketing survey of 1,000 adults by Opinion Research Corp.

whether a building can be called green. There is concern about stakeholder relationships between the two groups. Green Globes is led by a former timber company executive and received much of its seed money from timber and wood products companies. LEED is a nonprofit organization with less ties to business interests. Already two states, Maryland and Arkansas, have adopted Green Globes as an alternative to LEED, giving officials an alternative for government-funded construction. The Clinton Presidential Library in Little Rock as well as the 7 World Trade Center, the first tower rebuilt near Ground Zero in New York, was certified by Green Globes.[39]

Green energy sources are often considered "green" because they are perceived to lower carbon emissions and create less pollution. They include natural energetic processes that can be harnessed with little pollution. Anaerobic digestion or biomass, geothermal, wind, small-scale hydropower, solar, and tidal power fall under this category. Some definitions may also include power derived from the incineration of waste. Some organizations have specifically classified nuclear power as green energy, but environmental organizations indicate the problems with nuclear waste and claim that this energy is neither efficient nor effective in cutting CO2 emissions, excluding it from clean energy. No power source is entirely impact-free. All energy sources require energy and give rise to some degree of pollution from manufacture of the technology.

Companies that do not recognize the profit potentials and ethical ramifications to brand and corporate reputation will pay later. For example, Exxon Mobil's CEO, Rex Tillerson, has encouraged the U.S. Congress to enact a tax on greenhouse gas emissions in order to fight global warming. "My greatest concern is that policy makers will attempt to mandate or ordain solutions that are doomed to fail," Mr. Tillerson said.[40]

Fraud

When an individual engages in deceptive practices to advance his or her own interests over those of his or her organization or some other group, charges of fraud may result. In general, **fraud** is any purposeful communication that deceives, manipulates, or conceals facts in order to create a false impression. Fraud is a crime and convictions may result in fines, imprisonment, or both. Fraud costs U.S. organizations more than $400 billion a year; the average company loses about 6 percent of total revenues to fraud and abuses committed by its own employees.[41] Among the most common fraudulent activities employees report about their coworkers are stealing office supplies or shoplifting, claiming to have worked extra hours, and stealing money or products.[42] Table 3–3 indicates what fraud examiners view as the biggest risk to companies. In recent years, accounting fraud has become a major ethical issue, but as we will see, fraud can also relate to marketing and consumer issues as well.

TABLE 3-3 Greatest Fraud Risk for Companies

Conflicts of interest	56%
Fraudulent financial statements	57%
Billing schemes	22%
Expense and reimbursement schemes	41%
Bribery/economic extortions	35%

Source: "The 2007 Oversight Systems Report on Corporate Fraud," Ethics World, http://www.ethicsworld.org/ethicsandemployees/PDF%20links/Oversight_2007_Fraud_Survey.pdf (accessed March 12, 2009).

Accounting fraud usually involves a corporation's financial reports in which companies provide important information on which investors and others base decisions that may involve millions of dollars. If the documents contain inaccurate information, whether intentionally or not, then lawsuits and criminal penalties may result. For example, trustees of New Century Financial Corporation sued its auditor, KPMG, for "reckless and grossly negligent audits" that hid the company's financial problems and sped its collapse. New Century was one of the early casualties of the subprime mortgage crisis, but was once one of the country's largest mortgage lenders to those with poor credit histories. After it disclosed accounting errors not discovered by KPMG the company collapsed.[43] Scrutiny of financial reporting increased dramatically in the wake of accounting scandals in the early twenty-first century. As a result of the negative publicity surrounding the allegations of accounting fraud at a number of companies, many firms were forced to take a second look at their financial documents. More than a few chose to restate their earnings to avoid being drawn into the scandal.[44] For example, WellCare Health Plans Inc. was forced to restate over three years of its earnings following a Florida Medicare fraud investigation that also led to changes in management and a loss of profits.[45]

The field of accounting has changed dramatically over the last decade. The profession used to have a club-type mentality: Those who became certified public accountants (CPAs) were not concerned about competition. Now CPAs advertise their skills and short-term results in an environment in which competition has increased and overall billable hours have significantly decreased because of technological innovations. Additionally, accountants are now permitted to charge performance-based fees rather than hourly rates, a rule change that encouraged some large accounting firms to promote tax-avoidance strategies for high-income individuals because the firms can charge 10 to 40 percent of the amount of taxes saved.[46]

Pressures on accountants today include time, reduced fees, client requests to alter opinions concerning financial conditions or lower tax payments, and increased competition. Other issues that accountants face daily involve compliance with complex rules and regulations, data overload, contingent fees, and commissions. An accountant's life is filled with rules and data that have to be interpreted correctly, and because of such pressures and the ethical predicaments they spawn, problems within the accounting industry are on the rise.

As a result, accountants must abide by a strict code of ethics that defines their responsibilities to their clients and the public interest. The code also discusses the concepts of integrity, objectivity, independence, and due care. Despite the standards the code provides, the accounting industry has been the source of numerous fraud investigations in recent years. Congress passed the Sarbanes–Oxley Act in 2002 to address many of the issues that could create conflicts of interest for accounting firms auditing public corporations. The law generally prohibits accounting firms from providing both auditing and consulting services to the same firm. Additionally, the law specifies that corporate boards of directors must include outside directors with financial knowledge on the company's audit committee.

Marketing fraud—the process of creating, distributing, promoting, and pricing products—is another business area that generates potential ethical issues. False or misleading marketing communications can destroy customers' trust in a company. Lying, a major ethical issue involving communications, is potentially a significant problem. In both external and internal communications, it causes ethical predicaments because it destroys trust. Misleading marketing can also cost consumers hard-earned money. A U.S. district court passed judgment on Ira Rubin and his company Global Marketing

Group. Rubin allegedly debited millions of dollars from U.S. consumers' bank accounts on behalf of many telemarketing scams dating back to 2003. The judgment involved a halt on all payment processing associated with the case.[47] False or deceptive advertising is a key issue in marketing communications. One set of laws that is common to many countries are laws concerning deceptive advertising—that is, advertisements that are not clearly labeled as advertisements. For example, in the United States, Section 5 of the Federal Trade Commission (FTC) Act addresses deceptive advertising. Abuses in advertising can range from exaggerated claims and concealed facts to outright lying, although improper categorization of advertising claims is the critical point. Courts place false or misleading advertisements into three categories: puffery, implied falsity, and literal falsity. **Puffery** can be defined as exaggerated advertising, blustering, and boasting upon which no reasonable buyer would rely and is not actionable under the Lanham Act. For example, in a Lanham Act suit between two shaving products companies, the defendant advertised that the moisturizing strip on its shaving razor was "six times smoother" than its competitors' strips, while showing a man rubbing his hand down his face. The court rejected the defendant's argument that "six times smoother" implied that only the moisturizing strip on the razor's head was smoother. Instead, the court found that the "six times smoother" advertising claim implied that the consumer would receive a smoother shave from the defendant's razor as a whole, a claim that was false.[48]

Implied falsity means that the message has a tendency to mislead, confuse, or deceive the public. The advertising claims that use implied falsity are those that are literally true but imply another message that is false. In most cases, this can be done only through a time-consuming and expensive consumer survey, whose results are often inconclusive.[49]

The characterization of an advertising claim as **literally false** can be divided into two subcategories: *tests prove* (*establishment claims*), in which the advertisement cites a study or test that establishes the claim; and *bald assertions* (*non-establishment claims*), in which the advertisement makes a claim that cannot be substantiated, as when a commercial states that a certain product is superior to any other on the market. For example, the FTC filed formal complaints against Stock Value 1 Inc. and Comstar Communications Inc. for making unsubstantiated claims that their radiation-protection patches block the electromagnetic energy emitted by cellular telephones. The FTC's complaint charged that the companies "made false statements that their products had been scientifically 'proven' and tested," when in fact that was not the case.[50]

Another form of advertising abuse involves making ambiguous statements in which the words are so weak or general that the viewer, reader, or listener must infer the advertiser's intended message. These "weasel words" are inherently vague and enable the advertiser to deny any intent to deceive. The verb *help* is a good example (as in expressions such as "helps prevent," "helps fight," "helps make you feel").[51] Consumers may view such advertisements as unethical because they fail to communicate all the information needed to make a good purchasing decision or because they deceive the consumer outright.

Labeling issues are even murkier. For example, Netgear Inc. agreed to settle a class action lawsuit that claimed it exaggerated the data-transfer speeds of its wireless equipment. As part of the settlement, the company must pay $700,000 in legal fees, give a 15 percent discount to members of the class action, donate $25,000 of product to charity, and include disclaimers about the data-transfer speed of its products.[52]

Slamming, or changing a customer's phone service without authorization, is an important issue involving labeling that is specific to the telephone industry. AT&T sued

Business Discount Plan (BDP), accusing it of using fraud and deception to routinely "slam" customers to its telecommunication service by suggesting that BDP was affiliated with AT&T. As part of the settlement, BDP had to send letters to consumers telling them that BDP was not affiliated with AT&T.[53] Such misleading behavior creates ethical issues because the communicated messages do not include all the information that consumers need to make good purchasing decisions, frustrating and angering customers who feel that they have been deceived. In addition, they damage the seller's credibility and reputation.

Advertising and direct sales communication can also mislead by concealing the facts within the message. For instance, a salesperson anxious to sell a medical insurance policy might list a large number of illnesses covered by the policy but fail to mention that it does not cover some commonly covered illnesses. Indeed, the fastest-growing area of fraudulent activity is in direct marketing, which employs the telephone and impersonal media to communicate information to customers, who then purchase products via mail, telephone, or the Internet.

Consumer Fraud

Consumer fraud is when consumers attempt to deceive businesses for their own gain. The FTC estimates that more than 25 million consumers annually engage in consumer fraud.[54] Shoplifting, for example, accounts for 35 percent of the losses at the largest U.S. retail chains, although this figure is still far outweighed by the nearly 44 percent of losses perpetrated by store employees, according to the National Retail Security Survey. Together with vendor fraud and administrative error, these losses cost U.S. retailers $36 billion annually and are on the rise. Retail shrinkage, or stealing from stores, accounts for losses averaging around 1.52 percent of total sales and 92 percent of retailers surveyed say that they have been a victim.[55]

"Consumer fraud involves intentional deception to derive an unfair economic advantage by an individual or group over an organization."

Consumers engage in many other forms of fraud against businesses, including price tag switching, item switching, lying to obtain age-related and other discounts, and taking advantage of generous return policies by returning used items, especially clothing that has been worn (with the price tags still attached). Such behavior by consumers affects retail stores as well as other consumers who, for example, may unwittingly purchase new clothing that has actually been worn.[56]

Consumer fraud involves intentional deception to derive an unfair economic advantage by an individual or group over an organization. Examples of fraudulent activities include shoplifting, collusion or duplicity, and guile. *Collusion* typically involves an employee who assists the consumer in fraud. For example, a cashier may not ring up all merchandise or may give an unwarranted discount. *Duplicity* may involve a consumer staging an accident in a grocery store and then seeking damages against the store for its lack of attention to safety. A consumer may purchase, wear, and then return an item of clothing for a full refund. In other situations, the consumer may ask for a refund by claiming a defect. *Guile* is associated with a person who is crafty or understands right/wrong behavior but uses tricks to obtain an unfair advantage. The advantage is unfair because the person has the intent to go against the right behavior or end. Although some of these acts warrant legal prosecution, they can be very difficult to prove, and many companies are reluctant to accuse patrons of a crime when there is no way to verify it. Businesses that operate with the "customer is always right" philosophy have found that some consumers will take advantage of this promise and have therefore modified return policies to curb unfair use.

Financial Misconduct

The failure to understand and manage ethical risks played a significant role in the financial crisis and recession of 2008–2009. While there is a difference between bad business decisions and business misconduct, there is also a thin line between the ethics of using only financial incentives to gauge performance and the use of holistic measures that include ethics, transparency, and responsibility to stakeholders. From CEOs to traders and brokers, lucrative financial incentives existed for performance in the financial industry.

The global recession was caused in part by a failure of the financial industry to take appropriate responsibility for its decision to utilize risky and complex financial instruments. Loopholes in regulations and the failures of regulators were exploited. Corporate cultures were built on rewards for taking risks rather than rewards for creating value for stakeholders. Ethical decisions were based more on what was legal rather than what was the right thing to do. Unfortunately, most stakeholders, including the public, regulators, and the mass media, do not always understand the nature of the financial risks taken on by banks and other institutions to generate profits. The intangible nature of financial products makes it difficult to understand complex financial transactions. Problems in the subprime mortgage markets sound the alarm for the most recent recession.

> *"The top executives or CEOs are ultimately responsible for the repercussions of their employees' decisions."*

Ethics issues emerged early in subprime lending, with loan officers receiving commissions on securing loans from borrowers with no consequences if the borrower defaulted on the loan. "Liar loans" were soon developed to create more sales and higher personal compensation for lenders. Lenders would encourage subprime borrowers to provide false information on their loan applications in order to qualify for and secure the loan. Some appraisers provided inflated home values in order to increase the loan amount. In other instances consumers were asked to falsify their incomes to make the loan more attractive to the lending institution. The opportunity for misconduct was widespread. Top managers, and even CEOs, were complacent about the wrongdoings as long as profits were good. Congress and President Clinton encouraged Fannie Mae and Freddie Mac to support home ownership among low-income people by giving out home mortgages. Throughout the early 2000s, in an economy with rapidly increasing home values, the culture of unethical behavior was not apparent to most people. When home values started to decline and individuals were "upside down" on their loans (owing more than the equity of the home), the failures and unethical behavior of lending and borrowing institutions became more obvious.

The top executives or CEOs are ultimately responsible for the repercussions of their employees' decisions. Top executives at Merrill Lynch awarded $3.6 billion in bonuses shortly before its merger with Bank of America in 2008. A combined $121 million went to four top executives. This was done in spite of the fact that Merrill Lynch had to be rescued by the government to save it from bankruptcy. Two ethics issues are at play. First, paying out the bonuses at all; and second, rushing their distribution in order to complete the job before Bank of America's takeover. Risk management in the financial industry is a key concern, including paying bonuses to executives who failed in their duties. Unfortunately, at the same time the industry was focused on its own bottom line, regulatory agencies and Congress were not proactive in investigating early cases of financial misconduct and the systemic issues that led to the crisis. The legal and regulatory systems were more focused on individual misconduct rather than systemic ethical failures.

Insider Trading

An insider is any officer, director, or owner of 10 percent or more of a class of a company's securities. There are two types of **insider trading:** illegal and legal. *Illegal insider trading* is the buying or selling of stocks by insiders who possess material that is still not public. The act, which puts insiders in breach of their fiduciary duty, can be committed by anyone who has access to nonpublic material, such as brokers, family, friends, and employees. In addition, someone caught "tipping" an outsider with material nonpublic information can also be found liable. The Securities and Exchange Commission brought a first-ever case alleging insider trading in credit default swaps in New York. The case centers on a small profit earned in the buyout of Dutch Media Company VNU NV. It alleges that a salesperson for Deutsche Bank AG passed on confidential information about VNU to a trader at Millennium Partners, who then allegedly used the information to earn a $1.2 million profit on credit default swaps tied to the value of the company's debt.[57] To determine if an insider gave a tip illegally, the SEC uses the *Dirks test,* which states that if a tipster breaches his or her trust with the company and understands that this was a breach, he or she is liable for insider trading.

Legal insider trading involves legally buying and selling stock in an insider's own company, but not all the time. Insiders are required to report their insider transactions within two business days of the date the transaction occurred. For example, if an insider sold 10,000 shares on Monday, June 12, he or she would have to report this change to the SEC by Wednesday, June 14. To deter insider trading, insiders are prevented from buying and selling their company stock within a six-month period; therefore, insiders buy stock when they feel the company will perform well over the long term.

A major player in the subprime mortgage crisis, Countrywide Financial's former CEO, Angelo Mozilo, was charged with fraud and insider trading. Mozilo was accused of fraudulently deliberately misleading investors about the risks being taken by the company. The SEC also alleges that Mozilo engaged in insider trading when he sold his Countrywide stock for $140 million in profits when he knew that the company's business was deteriorating.[58]

Intellectual Property Rights

Intellectual property rights involve the legal protection of intellectual properties such as music, books, and movies. Laws such as the Copyright Act of 1976, the Digital Millennium Copyright Act, and the Digital Theft Deterrence and Copyright Damages Improvement Act of 1999 were designed to protect the creators of intellectual property. However, with the advance of technology, ethical issues still abound for websites. For example, until it was sued for copyright infringement and subsequently changed its business model, Napster.com allowed individuals to download copyrighted music for personal use without providing compensation to the artists.

A decision by the Federal Copyright Office (FCO) helped lay the groundwork for intellectual property rules in a digital world. The FCO decided to make it illegal for Web users to hack through barriers that copyright holders erect around material released online, allowing only two exceptions. The first exception was for software that blocks users from finding obscene or controversial material on the Web, and the second was for people who want to bypass malfunctioning security features of software or other copyrighted goods they have purchased. This decision reflects the fact that copyright owners are typically being favored in digital copyright issues.[59] There have been many lawsuits related to this issue, and some have had costly results. MP3.com paid Universal Music Group $53.4 million to end its dispute with major record label over copyright infringement.[60]

As China has grown into an economic powerhouse, the market for pirated goods of all types ranging from DVDs to pharmaceuticals, and even cars, has grown into a multibillion dollar industry.[61] China's government has thus far proven weak in protecting intellectual property, and the underground market for such pirated goods—which are sold all over the world—has grown at a rapid pace. While intellectual property rights infringement always poses a threat from companies that risk losing profits and reputation, it can also threaten the health and well-being of consumers. For example, illegally produced medications, when consumed by unknowing consumers, can cause sickness and even death. Research on software piracy has shown that high levels of economic well-being and an advanced technology sector are effective in deterring software piracy.[62] Perhaps as China's economy moves forward piracy will become less of a problem, but in the meantime it poses a major threat.

> *"There are few legal protections of an employee's right to privacy,"*

Privacy Issues

Consumer advocates continue to warn consumers about new threats to their privacy, especially within the health care and Internet industries. As the number of people using the Internet increases, the areas of concern related to its use increase as well.[63] Some **privacy issues** that must be addressed by businesses include the monitoring of employees' use of available technology and consumer privacy. Current research suggests that, even if businesses use price discounts or personalized services, consumers remain suspicious. However, certain consumers are still willing to provide personal information, despite the potential risks.[64]

A challenge for companies today is meeting their business needs while protecting employees' desires for privacy. There are few legal protections of an employee's right to privacy, which allows businesses a great deal of flexibility in establishing policies regarding employees' privacy while they are on company property and using company equipment. The increased use of electronic communications in the workplace and technological advances that permit employee monitoring and surveillance have provided companies with new opportunities to obtain data about employees. From computer monitoring and telephone taping to video surveillance and GPS satellite tracking, employers are using technology to manage their productivity and protect their resources.

To motivate employee compliance, over 25 percent of 596 companies have fired workers for misusing the Internet, 6 percent have fired employees for misusing office telephones, 76 percent monitor their workers' website connections, and 65 percent use software to block connections to inappropriate websites. In addition, 36 percent of those employers track content, keystrokes, and time spent at keyboards and store the data in order to review it later. Employers are also notifying employees when they are being watched; of the organizations monitoring employees, 80 percent informed their workers.[65]

Because of the increased legal and regulatory investigations, employers have established policies governing personal e-mail use, personal Internet use, personal instant messenger use, personal blogs, and operation of personal websites on company time. Companies are also concerned about inappropriate telephone use, such as 1-900 lines or personal long-distance calls. Hence, some businesses routinely track phone numbers and, in selected job categories, record and review all employees' phone calls. More than half of the companies surveyed use video monitoring to counter theft, violence, and sabotage. The use of video surveillance to track employees' on-the-job performance has also increased, although companies that videotape workers usually notify them of the practice.

Concerns about employee privacy extend to Europe as well. In Finland an executive vice president and several employees of Sonera Corporation were arrested as part of an investigation into whether the wireless telecommunications company violated the privacy of its workers by monitoring their call records, a serious offense in Finland. The investigation was launched after a local newspaper reported that Sonera was tracing employees' phone calls in order to identify who may have leaked information about the company to the media. The company denied the accusation.[66]

Clearly conveying the organization's policy on workplace privacy should reduce the opportunity for employee lawsuits and the resulting costs of such actions. However, if a company fails to monitor employees' use of e-mail and the Internet, the costs can be huge. For example, Chevron Corporation agreed to pay $2.2 million to employees who claimed that unmonitored sexually harassing e-mail created a threatening environment for them.[67] Instituting practices that show respect for employee privacy but that do not abdicate the employer's responsibility should help create a climate of trust that promotes opportunities for resolving employee–employer disputes without lawsuits.

Electronic monitoring allows a company to determine whether productivity is being reduced because employees are spending too much time on personal Web activities. Knowing this can then enable the company to take steps to remedy the situation. Internet filtering companies such as Cyber Patrol, Surfcontrol, Surfwatch, and WebSense provide products that block employee access to websites deemed distracting or objectionable. WebSense launched AfterWork.com, a personal homepage for each employee at a company that allows employees to visit nonwork-related websites during breaks and lunch, as well as before and after work hours.[68] One survey about this subject found that 58 percent of employees considered using company resources for personal Web surfing to be an "extremely serious" or "very serious" business ethics violation.[69]

There are two dimensions to consumer privacy: consumer awareness of information collection and a growing lack of consumer control over how companies use the personal information that they collect. For example, many are not aware that Google Inc. reserves the right to track every time you click on a link from one of its searches.[70] Online purchases and even random Web surfing can be tracked without a consumer's knowledge. A survey by the Progress and Freedom Foundation found that 96 percent of popular commercial websites collect personally identifying information from visitors.[71]

For example, the FTC asked a federal judge to shut down Odysseus Marketing Inc. on the grounds that it secretly installed spyware that could not be removed by the consumers whose computers it infected. The company offered a free software package to make peer-to-peer file sharing anonymous, but consumers ended up downloading a program called Clientman, a spyware program that altered search results, disseminated pop-up ads, and installed third-party ads without notice to consumers. The company denies any wrongdoing.[72]

A U.S. Department of Commerce study on e-commerce and privacy found that 81 percent of Internet users and 79 percent of consumers who buy products and services over the Web were concerned about online threats to privacy.[73] Another survey found that 38 percent of respondents felt that it is never ethical to track customers' Web activities, and 64 percent said that they do not trust websites that do.[74] These concerns have led some companies to cut back on the amount of information they collect: Of the sites surveyed by the Progress and Freedom Foundation, 84 percent indicated that they are collecting less data than before.[75] However, many consumers have expressed a low level of confidence in their ability to avoid becoming a victim of credit or debit card fraud.

Companies are also working to find ways to improve consumers' trust in their websites. For example, an increasing number of websites display an online seal from BBBOnline, available only to sites that subscribe to certain standards. A similar seal is available through TRUSTe, a nonprofit global initiative that certifies those websites that adhere to its principles. (Visit http://e-businessethics.com for more on Internet privacy.)

THE CHALLENGE OF DETERMINING AN ETHICAL ISSUE IN BUSINESS

Most ethical issues will become visible through stakeholder concerns about an event, activity, or the results of a business decision. The mass media, special interest groups, and individuals, through the use of blogs, podcasts, or other individual-generated media, often generate discussion about the ethicalness of a decision. Another way to determine whether a specific behavior or situation has an ethical component is to ask other individuals in the business how they feel about it and whether they view it as ethically challenging. Trade associations and business self-regulatory groups such as the Better Business Bureau often provide direction for companies in defining ethical issues. Finally, it is important to determine whether the organization has adopted specific policies on the activity. An activity approved of by most members of an organization, if it is also customary in the industry, is probably ethical. An issue, activity, or situation that can withstand open discussion between many stakeholders, both inside and outside the organization, probably does not pose ethical problems.

> ***"Over time, problems can become ethical issues as a result of changing societal values."***

However, over time, problems can become ethical issues as a result of changing societal values. For instance, for decades Kraft Foods Inc. has been a staple in almost every home in the United States, with products such as Kraft Macaroni and Cheese, Chips Ahoy! cookies, Lunchables, Kool-Aid, Fruity Pebbles, and Oreos. Nothing was said about such foods until 2004. However, a problem was perceived first by parents, then schools, and then politicians who became aware that the United States has the most obese people in the world, with approximately 40 percent of the population overweight.

The fact is that since 1980 the rate of obesity in children (ages 6 to 11) has more than doubled, and it has tripled in adolescents. Children who are 10 years of age weigh 10 pounds more than they did in the 1960s. As a result, Congress has proposed legislation relative to obesity and concerning the advertising of unhealthy food products to children. Kraft realized that it now has an ethical situation regarding the advertising of such items as hotdogs, cookies, and cereals with high sugar levels. Some consumer groups might now perceive Kraft's $90 million annual advertising budget, which was primarily directed at children, as unethical. Because ignoring the situation could be potentially disastrous, Kraft instead devised a compromise: It would stop advertising some of its products to children under 12 years of age and instead market healthier foods. As a result of government recommendations, Kraft executives have continually revised their advertising guidelines regarding children and the advertisement of products containing large amounts of sugar, fat, and calories, knowing that their decisions would probably negatively affect their bottom line.[78]

Once stakeholders trigger ethical issue awareness and individuals openly discuss it and ask for guidance and the opinions of others, one enters the ethical decision making process, which we examine in Chapter 5.

SUMMARY

Stakeholders' concerns largely determine whether business actions and decisions are perceived as ethical or unethical. When government, communities, and society become involved, what was merely an ethical issue can quickly become a legal one. Shareholders can unwittingly complicate the issue of conducting business ethically by demanding that managers make decisions to boost short-term earnings to maintain or boost the value of their shares of stock.

A first step toward understanding business ethics is to develop ethical issue awareness; that is, to learn to identify which stakeholder issues contain an ethical component. Characteristics of the job, the corporate or local culture, or the organization of the society in which one does business can all create ethical issues. Recognizing an ethical issue is essential to understanding business ethics and therefore to creating an effective ethics and compliance program that will seek to minimize unethical behavior. In order to do this, people must understand the universal moral constants of honesty, fairness, and integrity, which are accepted by businesspeople everywhere. Without embracing these concepts, running a business becomes very difficult. To be honest is to tell the truth to the best of your ability without hiding anything. Confucius defined several levels of honesty: *Li*, which relates to the superficial desires of a person; *Yi*, which relates to doing business based on reciprocity; and *Ren*, which is based on empathy and understanding others. Confucianism advocates treating inferiors as you would want superiors to treat you, an idea that is later reflected in Kant's Golden Rule. Virtues such as a family's honor and a person's reputation for honesty are of paramount importance.

Fairness is the quality of being just, equitable, and impartial, and it overlaps terms such as *justice, equity, equality*, and *morality*. The three fundamental elements that motivate people to be fair are equality, reciprocity, and optimization. Equality relates to how wealth is distributed between employees, within a company or a country or globally; reciprocity relates to the return of small favors that are approximately equal in value; and integrity relates to a person's character and is made up of two basic parts: a formal relation that one has to oneself and a person's set of terminal, or enduring, values from which he or she does not deviate.

An ethical issue is a problem, situation, or opportunity that requires an individual, group, or organization to choose among several actions that must be evaluated as right or wrong, ethical or unethical, but an ethical dilemma has no right or ethical choice.

Bribery is the practice of offering something (usually money) in order to gain an illicit advantage. A conflict of interest is when an individual must choose whether to advance his or her own interests, those of the organization, or those of some other group. Corporate intelligence is the collection and analysis of information on markets, technologies, customers, and competitors, as well as on socioeconomic and external political trends. There are three intelligence models: passive, tactical, and top-management. The tools of corporate intelligence are many. One tool is hacking, which has three categories: system, remote, and physical; another is social engineering in which someone is tricked into revealing valuable corporate information; other techniques include dumpster diving, whacking, and phone eavesdropping.

Another ethical/legal issue is discrimination, which is illegal in the United States when it occurs on the basis of race, color, religion, sex, marital status, sexual orientation, public-assistance status, disability, age, national origin, or veteran status. Additionally, discrimination on the basis of political opinions or affiliation with a union is defined as harassment. Sexual harassment is a form of sex discrimination. To help build workforces that reflect their customer base, many companies have initiated affirmative action programs. Environmental issues such as air, water, and waste are becoming an ethical concern within business. In general, fraud is any purposeful communication that deceives, manipulates, or conceals facts in order to create a false impression. There are several types of fraud: accounting, marketing, and consumer.

An insider is any officer, director, or owner of 10 percent or more of a class of a company's securities. There are two types of insider trading: legal and illegal. Intellectual property rights involve the legal protection of intellectual properties such as music, books, and movies. Consumer advocates continue to warn consumers about new threats to their privacy.

IMPORTANT TERMS FOR REVIEW

honesty
fairness
equality
reciprocity
optimization
integrity
ethical issue
ethical dilemma
abusive or intimidating behavior
lying
conflict of interest
bribery
active bribery
passive bribery
facilitation payment
corporate intelligence
hacking
system hacking
remote hacking
physical hacking
social engineering
shoulder surfing
password guessing
dumpster diving
whacking
phone eavesdropping
discrimination
Equal Employment Opportunity Commission
Age Discrimination in Employment Act
affirmative action program
sexual harassment
hostile work environment
dual relationship
unethical dual relationship
environmental issue
Kyoto Protocol
water pollution
green energy
fraud
accounting fraud
marketing fraud
puffery
implied falsity
literally false
labeling issue
slamming
consumer fraud
insider trading
intellectual property rights
privacy issue

RESOLVING ETHICAL BUSINESS CHALLENGES*

Joseph Freberg had been with Alcon for 18 months. He had begun his career right out of college with a firm in the Southeast called Cala Industrial, which specialized in air compressors. Because of his work with Cala, he had been lured away to Alcon, in Omaha, as a sales manager. Joseph's first six months had been hard. Working with older salespeople, trying to get a handle on his people's sales territories and settling into the corporate culture of a new firm took 16-hour days, six days a week. During those six months, he also bought a house, and his fiancé, Ellen, furnished it, deciding almost everything from the color of the rugs to the style of the curtains.

Ellen had taken a brokerage job with Trout Brothers and seemed to be working even more hours than Joseph. But the long days were paying off. Ellen was now starting to handle some large accounts and was being noticed by the "right" crowd in the wealthier Omaha areas.

Costs for the new home had exceeded their anticipated spending limit, and the plans for their wedding seemed to be getting larger and larger. In addition, Ellen was commuting from her apartment to the new home and then to her job, and the commute killed her car. As a result, she decided to lease something that exuded success.

"Ellen, don't you think a Mercedes is a little out of our range? What are the payments?" inquired Joseph.

"Don't worry, darling. When my clients see me in this—as well as when we start entertaining at the new house once we're married—the payments on the car will seem small compared with the money I'll be making," Ellen mused as she ran her fingers through Joseph's hair and gave him a peck on the cheek.

By the time of their wedding and honeymoon, Joseph and Ellen's bank statement looked like a bullfighter's cape—red. "Don't worry, Joseph, everything will turn out okay. You've got a good job. I've got a good job. We're young and have drive. Things will straighten out after a while," said Ellen as she eyed a Rolex in a store window.

After the wedding, things did settle down—to a hectic pace, given their two careers and their two sets of parents 1,000 miles away in either direction. Joseph had realized that Alcon was a paternal type of organization, with good benefits and tremendous growth potential. He had identified whom to be friends with and whom to stay away from in the company. His salespeople seemed to tolerate him, sometimes calling him "Little Joe" or "Joey" because of his age, and his salespeople were producing—slowly climbing up the sales ladder to the number-one spot in the company.

While doing some regular checkup work on sales personnel, Joseph found out that Carl had been giving kickbacks to some of his buyers. Carl's sales volume accounted for a substantial amount of the company's existing clientele sales, and he had been a trainer for the company for several years. Carl also happened to be the vice president's son-in-law. Joseph started to check on the other reps more closely and discovered that, although Carl seemed to be the biggest offender, 3 of his 10 people were doing the same thing. The next day, Joseph looked up Alcon's policy handbook and found this statement: "Our company stands for doing the right thing at all times and giving our customers the best product for the best prices." There was no specific mention of kickbacks, but everyone knew that kickbacks ultimately reduce fair competition, which eventually leads to reduced quality and increased prices for customers.

By talking to a few of the old-timers at Alcon, Joseph learned that there had been sporadic enforcement of the "no kickback" policy. It seemed that when times were good it became unacceptable and when times were bad it slipped into the acceptable range. And then there was his boss, Kathryn, the vice president. Joseph knew that Kathryn had a tendency to shoot the bearer of bad news. He remembered a story that he had heard about a sales manager coming in to see Kathryn to explain an error in a bid that one of his salespeople had made. Kathryn called in the entire sales staff and fired the salesperson on the spot. Then, smiling, she told the sales manager: "This was your second mistake, so I hope that you can get a good recommendation from personnel. You have two weeks to find employment elsewhere." From then on, the office staff had a nickname for Kathryn—Jaws.

Trying to solve the problem that he was facing, Joseph broached the subject of kickbacks at his monthly meeting with Carl. Carl responded, "You've been in this business long enough to know that this happens all the time. I see nothing wrong with this practice if it increases sales. Besides, I take the money out of my commission. You know that right now I'm trying to pay off some big medical bills. I've also gotten tacit clearance from above, but I wouldn't mention that if I were you." Joseph knew that the chain-of-command structure in the company made it very dangerous to go directly to a vice president with this type of information.

As Joseph was pondering whether to do nothing, bring the matter into the open and state that it was wrong and that such practices were against policy, or talk to Kathryn about the situation, his cell phone rang. It was Ellen. "Honey, guess what just happened. Kathryn, your boss, has decided to use me as her new broker. Isn't that fantastic!"

What should Joseph do?

QUESTIONS • EXERCISES

1. What are Joseph's ethical problems?
2. Assume that you are Joseph and discuss your options.
3. What other information do you feel you need before making your decision?
4. Discuss in which business areas the ethical problems lie.

*This case is strictly hypothetical; any resemblance to real persons, companies, or situations is coincidental.

CHECK YOUR EQ

Check your EQ, or Ethics Quotient, by completing the following. Assess your performance to evaluate your overall understanding of the chapter material.

1. Business can be considered a game people play like basketball or boxing. **Yes** **No**
2. Key ethical issues in an organization relate to fraud, discrimination, honesty and fairness, conflicts of interest, and technology. **Yes** **No**
3. Only 10 percent of employees observe abusive behavior in the workplace. **Yes** **No**
4. Fraud occurs when a false impression exists, which conceals facts. **Yes** **No**
5. Putting one's own interests ahead of the organization is the most commonly observed type of misconduct. **Yes** **No**

ANSWERS **1. No.** People are not economically self-sufficient and cannot withdraw from the game of business. **2. Yes.** See pages 62–83 regarding these key ethical issues and their implications for the organization. **3. No.** According to Table 3-1, 21 percent of employees observe abusive behavior in the workplace. **4. No.** Fraud must be purposeful, rather than accidental, and exists when deception and manipulation of facts are concealed to create a false impression that causes harm. **5. Yes.** The most observed form of misconduct in Table 3-1 is putting one's own interests ahead of the company.

aroma and generates intense thirst. Casual users claim that khat lifts spirits, sharpens thinking, and, when its effects wear off, generates mild lapses into depression similar to those observed among cocaine users. The body appears to have a physical intolerance to khat due in part to limitations in how much can be ingested by chewing. As a result, reports suggest that there are no physical symptoms accompanying withdrawal. Advocates of khat use claim that it eases symptoms of diabetes, asthma, and disorders of the stomach and the intestinal tract. Opponents claim that khat damages health, suppresses appetite, and prevents sleep. In the United States, khat has been classified as a schedule IV substance by the Drug Enforcement Agency (DEA): freshly picked khat leaves (that is, within 48 hours of harvest) are classified as a schedule I narcotic, the most restrictive category used by the DEA.

After doing his research, Myron delivered his report to David and said, "I really think that, given the right marketing to some of the big pharmaceutical companies, we should have two huge revenue makers."

"That's great, Myron, but the pharmaceutical market is only secondary to our primary market—the two billion consumers to whom we can introduce these products."

"What do you mean, David?" Myron asked.

"I mean these products are grown legally around the world, and the countries that we are targeting have no restrictions on these substances," David explained. "Why not tailor the delivery of the product by country? For example, we find out which flavors people want the betel nut in, in North and South America or the Middle East. The packaging will have to change by country as well as branding. Pricing strategies will need to be developed relative to our branding decisions, and of course quantity usages will have to be calculated. For example, single, multiple, and super value sizes need to be explored. The same can be done for khat. Because of your research and your business background, I'm putting you on the marketing team for both. Of course, this means that you're going to have to be promoted and at least for a while live in Hong Kong. I know Quan will be excited. In fact, I told her the news this morning that she would be working on the same project in Hong Kong. Producto International tries to be sensitive to the dual-career family problems that can occur. Plus you'll be closer to relatives. I told Quan that with living allowances and all of the other things that go with international placement, you two should almost triple your salaries! You don't have to thank me, Myron. You've worked hard on these projects, and now you deserve to have some of the benefits."

Myron went back to his office to think about his and Quan's future. He had heard of another employee who had rejected a similar offer, and that person's career had languished at PI. Eventually, that individual left the industry, never to be heard from again.

QUESTIONS • EXERCISES

1. Identify the social responsibility issues in this scenario.
2. Discuss the advantages and disadvantages of each decision that Myron could make.
3. Discuss the issue of marketing products that are legal but have addictive properties associated with them.

*This case is strictly hypothetical; any resemblance to real persons, companies, or situations is coincidental.

To understand the institutionalization of business ethics it is important to understand the voluntary and legally mandated dimensions of organizational practices. In addition, there are core practices sometimes called best practices that most responsible firms—trying to achieve acceptable conduct—embrace and implement. The effective organizational practice of business ethics requires all three dimensions (legal, voluntary, and core practices) to be integrated into an ethics and compliance program. This creates an ethical culture that can effectively manage the risks of misconduct. Institutionalization relates to legal and societal forces that provide both rewards and punishment to organizations based on the stakeholder evaluations of specific conduct. Institutionalization in business ethics relates to established laws, customs, and expected organizational programs that are considered normative in establishing reputation. This means that deviations from expected conduct often are considered ethical issues and therefore concern stakeholders. Institutions provide requirements, structure, and societal expectations to reward and sanction ethical decision making.

In this chapter, we examine the boundaries of ethical conduct and focus on the voluntary, core practices, and mandated requirements for legal compliance—three important areas in developing an ethical culture. In particular, we concentrate on compliance in specific areas related to competition, consumers, safety, and the environment. We also consider the requirements of the Sarbanes–Oxley legislation and its implementation by the Securities and Exchange Commission (SEC) and how its implementation has affected companies. This chapter gives an overview of legislative and administrative actions taken to help the public maintain confidence in the financial system. We also provide an overview of the Federal Sentencing Guidelines for Organizations (FSGO) and give recommendations and incentives for developing an ethical corporate culture. The FSGO, the Sarbanes–Oxley Act, industry trade associations, and societal expectations support core practices. Finally, we examine philanthropic contributions and how strategic philanthropy can be an important core competency to manage stakeholder relationships.

MANAGING ETHICAL RISK THROUGH MANDATED AND VOLUNTARY PROGRAMS

Table 4–1 provides an overview of the three dimensions of institutionalization. **Voluntary practices** include the beliefs, values, and voluntary contractual obligations of a business. All businesses engage in some level of commitment to voluntary activities to benefit both internal and external stakeholders. Google, Inc. works hard to give its employees a positive work environment through its benefits package. In addition to being a famously great place to work, Google offices offer such health and wellness-boosting amenities as swimming pools, gyms, volleyball courts, ping-pong tables and dance classes, the company even allows employees to bring their dogs to work.[1] Most firms engage in **philanthropy**—giving back to communities and causes.

Core practices are documented best practices, often encouraged by legal and regulatory forces as well as industry trade associations. The **Better Business Bureau** is a leading self-regulatory body that provides directions for managing customer disputes and reviews advertising cases. These practices are appropriate and common practices that help ensure compliance with legal requirements and societal expectations. Although these practices are not enforced, there are consequences for not engaging in these practices when there is misconduct. For example, the Federal Sentencing Guidelines for Organizations (FSGO) suggest that the governing authority (board of directors) be

TABLE 4–1 Voluntary Boundary, Core Practices, and Mandated Boundaries of Ethical Decisions

Voluntary boundary	A management-initiated boundary of conduct (beliefs, values, voluntary policies, and voluntary contractual obligations)
Core practice	A highly appropriate and common practice that helps ensure compliance with legal requirements, industry self-regulation, and societal expectations
Mandated boundary	An externally imposed boundary of conduct (laws, rules, regulations, and other requirements)

Source: Adapted from the "Open Compliance Ethics Group (OCEG) Foundation Guidelines," v1.0, Steering Committee Update, December 2005, Phoenix, AZ.

responsible for and assess an organization's ethical and compliance activities. There is no required reporting of investigations by government regulatory bodies, but there are incentives to the firm that effectively implement this recommendation. If misconduct occurs, there may be opportunities to avoid serious punishment. On the other hand, if there has been no effort by the board to oversee ethics and compliance, this could increase and compound the level of punishment. In this way, the government in institutionalizing core practices provides organizations the opportunity to take their own approach and only takes action if there are violations. **Mandated boundaries** are the externally imposed boundaries of conduct, such as laws, rules, regulations, and other requirements. Antitrust and consumer protection laws create boundaries that must be respected by companies.

There is a need to maintain an ethical culture, and to manage stakeholder expectations for appropriate conduct in an organization. This is achieved through corporate governance compliance, risk management, and voluntary activities. The development of these drivers of an ethical culture has been institutionally supported by government initiatives and the demands of stakeholders. The compliance element represents areas that must conform to existing legal and regulatory requirements. Established laws and regulatory decisions leave limited flexibility to organizations in adhering to these standards. Corporate governance (as discussed in Chapter 2) is structured by a governing authority providing oversight as well as checks and balances to make sure that the organization meets its goals and objectives for ethical performance. Risk management analyzes the probability or chance that misconduct could occur based on the nature of the business and the exposure to risky events. Voluntary activities often represent the values and responsibilities that firms accept in contributing to stakeholder needs and expectations.

Figure 4–1 depicts the key elements of an organizational culture. The elements include values, norms, artifacts, and behavior. An ethical culture creates an environment in which to structure behavior that is then evaluated by stakeholders. Values are broad and are viewed as long-term enduring beliefs about issues such as integrity, trust, openness, diversity, and individual respect and responsibility. Norms dictate and clarify desirable behaviors through principles, rules, policies, and procedures. For example, norms could provide guiding principles for antibribery issues, sustainability, and conflicts of interest. Artifacts are visible, tangible external symbols of values and norms. Websites, codes of ethics, rituals, language, and physical settings are artifacts. These three elements have different impacts on behaviors. For example, norms prescribe specific behaviors in certain situations. Organizational decisions on such issues as governance, core practices, and legal compliance help shape the ethical culture.

FIGURE 4–1 Elements of an Ethical Culture

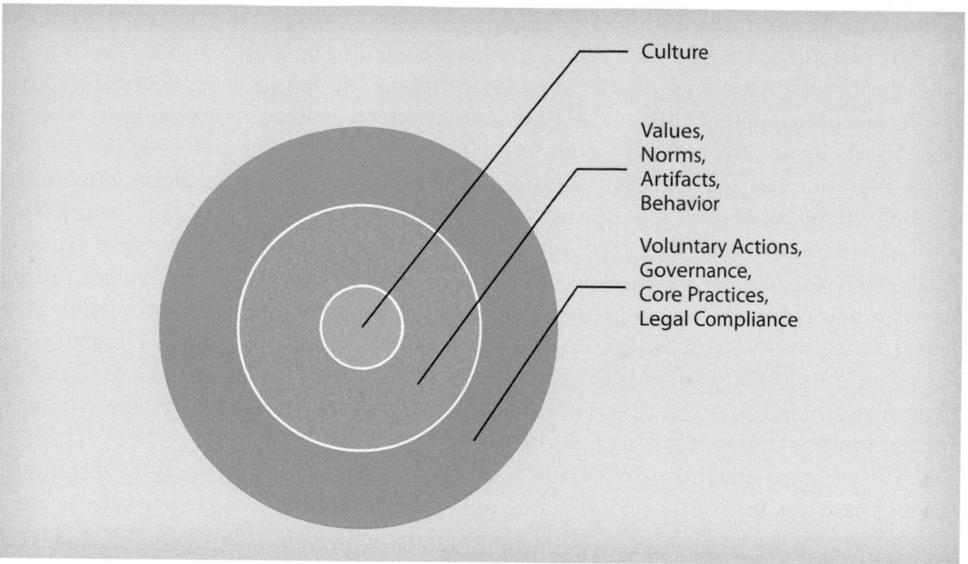

MANDATED REQUIREMENTS FOR LEGAL COMPLIANCE

Laws and regulations are established by governments to set minimum standards for responsible behavior—society's codification of what is right and wrong. Laws regulating business conduct are passed because certain stakeholders believe that business cannot be trusted to do what is right in certain areas, such as consumer safety and environmental protection. Because public policy is dynamic and often changes in response to business abuses and consumer demands for safety and equality, many laws have been passed to resolve specific problems and issues. But the opinions of society, as expressed in legislation, can change over time, and different courts or state legislatures may take diverging views. For example, the thrust of most business legislation can be summed up as follows: Any practice is permitted that does not substantially lessen or reduce competition or harm consumers or society. Courts differ, however, in their interpretations of what constitutes a "substantial" reduction of competition. Laws can help businesspeople determine what society believes at a certain time, but what is legally wrong today may be perceived as acceptable tomorrow, and vice versa. After generations of fame for its top-secret bank accounts, Swiss banks have been forced to disclose information about some of their clients. The rules are changing, however, and countries like Switzerland, Liechtenstein, and Luxembourg now must share information on potential tax dodgers with government agencies like the Internal Revenue Service. One bank alone, UBS, may harbor the secret bank accounts of 52,000 American tax dodgers.[2] However, personal views on legal and illegal activity in this area vary tremendously and explain why accounting firms struggle to advise.[3] Instructions to employees to "just obey the law" are meaningless without effective training and experience in dealing with specific legal risk areas.

Laws are categorized as either civil or criminal. **Civil law** defines the rights and duties of individuals and organizations (including businesses). **Criminal law** not only prohibits specific actions—such as fraud, theft, or securities trading violations—but also imposes fines or imprisonment as punishment for breaking the law. The primary difference between criminal and civil law is that the state or nation enforces criminal laws, whereas individuals (generally, in court) enforce civil laws. Criminal and civil laws are derived from four sources: the U.S. Constitution (constitutional law), precedents established by judges (common law), federal and state laws or statutes (statutory law), and federal and state administrative agencies (administrative law). Federal administrative agencies established by Congress control and influence business by enforcing laws and regulations to encourage competition and to protect consumers, workers, and the environment. State laws and regulatory agencies also exist to achieve these objectives. Amid the fallout from the subprime mortgage and Wall Street financial sector crises, the Securities and Exchange Commission CEO, Mary Schapiro, moved quickly to try to fill in regulatory gaps to prevent further financial crises and bank failures.[4]

The primary method of resolving conflicts and serious business ethics disputes is through lawsuits in which one individual or organization uses civil laws to take another individual or organization to court. To avoid lawsuits and to maintain the standards necessary to reduce risk and create an ethical culture, it is necessary to have both legal and organizational standards enforced. When violations of organizational standards occur, the National Business Ethics Survey (NBES) notes that many employees do not feel that their company has a strong ethics program. In fact, Figure 4–2 demonstrates that only 25 percent of companies in the United States have a well-implemented ethics program. A full 30 percent of companies do not have any ethics program at all to speak of, a serious

FIGURE 4–2 Only One in Four Companies Has a Well-Implemented Ethics Program

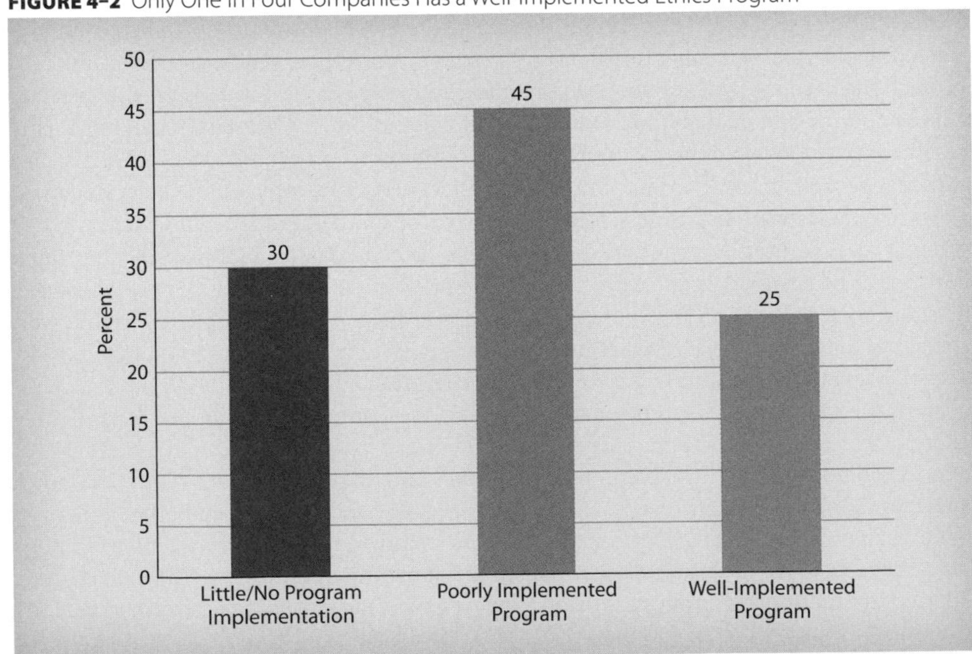

Source: 2007 National Business Ethics Survery, p. 20.

problem in this age of misconduct and ethical violations. It is important for a company to have a functioning program in place long before an ethical disaster strikes.

The role of laws is not so much to distinguish what is ethical or unethical as to determine the appropriateness of specific activities or situations. In other words, laws establish the basic ground rules for responsible business activities. Most of the laws and regulations that govern business activities fall into one of five groups: (1) regulation of competition, (2) protection of consumers, (3) promotion of equity and safety, (4) protection of the natural environment, and (5) incentives to encourage organizational compliance programs to deter misconduct, which we examine later.

Laws Regulating Competition

The issues surrounding the impact of competition on business's social responsibility arise from the rivalry among businesses for customers and profits. When businesses compete unfairly, legal and social responsibility issues can result. Intense competition sometimes makes managers feel that their company's very survival is threatened. In these situations, managers may begin to see unacceptable alternatives as acceptable, and they may begin engaging in questionable practices to ensure the survival of their organizations. Both Intel and Microsoft have been hit with fines amounting to billions of dollars for alleged antitrust activity in Europe, where the companies have been accused of engaging in behavior that prevents smaller companies from competing. The European Union is famous for being tough on companies suspected of antitrust cases, although being aware of antitrust laws is important for all large corporations around the world.

Size frequently gives some companies an advantage over others. For example, large firms can often generate economies of scale (for example, by forcing their suppliers to lower their prices) that allow them to put smaller firms out of business. Consequently, small companies and even whole communities may resist the efforts of firms like Wal-Mart, Home Depot, and Best Buy to open stores in their vicinity. These firms' sheer size enables them to operate at such low costs that small, local firms often cannot compete. Some companies' competitive strategies may focus on weakening or destroying a competitor, which can harm competition and ultimately reduce consumer choice. When the Chinese government mandated that all computers must be equipped with web-filtering software, lawyers and academics promptly challenged the law. They claimed that the software could be used to filter other content as well, such as political content the government deems unfavorable. They also worried that the measure was anticompetitive because it would favor two companies selected by the government in a nontransparent way to produce the software.[5] Other examples of anticompetitive strategies include sustained price cuts, discriminatory pricing, and price wars. The primary objective of U.S. antitrust laws is to distinguish competitive strategies that enhance consumer welfare from those that reduce it. The difficulty of this task lies in determining whether the intent of a company's pricing policy is to weaken or even destroy a competitor.[6] President Obama has promised to be tough on antitrust violations, and followed through by reversing a Bush-era policy that made it more difficult for the government to pursue antitrust violations. The Bush administration brought an historically low number of antitrust cases to trial.[7] President Obama plans to follow Europe's model for antitrust cases, which marks a return to a historic norm after eight years of Bush's noninterventionism.[8] Intense competition may also lead companies to resort to corporate espionage. Corporate espionage is the act of illegally taking information from a corporation through computer hacking, theft, intimidation, sorting through trash, and through impersonation of organizational members. Estimates show corporate espionage may cost companies nearly $50 billion annually. Unauthorized information collected includes patents in development, intellectual property, pricing strategies, customer information, unique manufacturing and technological operations, as well as marketing plans, research and development, and future plans for market and customer expansion.[9] Determining an accurate amount for losses is difficult because most companies do not report such losses for fear that the publicity will harm their stock price or encourage further break-ins. Espionage may be carried out by outsiders or by employees—executives, programmers, network or computer auditors, engineers, or janitors who have legitimate reasons to access facilities, data, computers or networks. They may use a variety of techniques for obtaining valuable information such as dumpster diving, whacking, and hacking as discussed in Chapter 3.

Laws have been passed to prevent the establishment of monopolies, inequitable pricing practices, and other practices that reduce or restrict competition among businesses. These laws are sometimes called **procompetitive legislation** because they were enacted to encourage competition and prevent activities that restrain trade (Table 4–2). The Sherman Antitrust Act of 1890, for example, prohibits organizations from holding monopolies in their industry, and the Robinson–Patman Act of 1936 bans price discrimination between retailers and wholesalers.

In law, however, there are always exceptions. Under the McCarran–Ferguson Act of 1944, for example, Congress exempted the insurance industry from the Sherman Antitrust Act and other antitrust laws. Insurance companies were allowed to join together and set insurance premiums at specific industry-wide levels. However, this legal "permission" could still be viewed as irresponsible and unethical if it neutralizes competition and if prices no longer reflect the true costs of insurance protection. This illustrates the point that what is legal is not always considered ethical by some interest groups. Even Major League Baseball has an antitrust exemption dating back to 1922. MLB is the only major sport that has such a sweeping antitrust exemption, although the major effect it has on the game these days is that sports teams cannot relocate without MLB's permission.[10]

Laws Protecting Consumers

Laws that protect consumers require businesses to provide accurate information about products and services and to follow safety standards (Table 4–3). The first **consumer protection law** was passed in 1906, partly in response to a novel by Upton Sinclair. *The Jungle* describes, among other things, the atrocities and unsanitary conditions of the meatpacking industry in turn-of-the-century Chicago. The outraged public response to this book and other exposés of the industry resulted in the passage of the Pure Food and Drug Act. Likewise, Ralph Nader had a tremendous impact on consumer protection laws with his book *Unsafe at Any Speed.* His critique and attack of General Motors' Corvair had far-reaching effects on autos and other consumer products. Other consumer protection laws emerged from similar processes.

Large groups of people with specific vulnerabilities have been granted special levels of legal protection relative to the general population. For example, the legal status of children and the elderly, defined according to age-related criteria, has received greater attention. American society has responded to research and documentation showing that young consumers and senior citizens encounter difficulties in the acquisition, consumption, and disposition of products. Special legal protection provided to vulnerable consumers is considered to be in the public interest.[11] For example, the Children's Online

TABLE 4–2 Laws Regulating Competition

Sherman Antitrust Act, 1890	Prohibits monopolies.
Clayton Act, 1914	Prohibits price discrimination, exclusive dealing, and other efforts to restrict competition.
Federal Trade Commission Act, 1914	Created the Federal Trade Commission (FTC) to help enforce antitrust laws.
Robinson–Patman Act, 1936	Bans price discrimination between retailers and wholesalers.
Wheeler–Lea Act, 1938	Prohibits unfair and deceptive acts regardless of whether competition is injured.
McCarran–Ferguson Act, 1944	Exempts the insurance industry from antitrust laws.
Lanham Act, 1946	Protects and regulates brand names, brand marks, trade names, and trademarks.
Celler–Kefauver Act, 1950	Prohibits one corporation from controlling another where the effect is to lessen competition.
Consumer Goods Pricing Act, 1975	Prohibits price maintenance agreements among manufacturers and resellers in interstate commerce.
FTC Improvement Act, 1975	Gives the FTC more power to prohibit unfair industry practices.
Antitrust Improvements Act, 1976	Strengthens earlier antitrust laws—Justice Department has more investigative authority.
Trademark Counterfeiting Act, 1980	Provides penalties for individuals dealing in counterfeit goods.
Trademark Law Revision Act, 1988	Amends the Lanham Act to allow brands not yet introduced to be protected through patent and trademark registration.
Federal Trademark Dilution Act, 1995	Gives trademark owners the right to protect trademarks and requires them to relinquish those that match or parallel existing trademarks.
Digital Millennium Copyright Act, 1998	Refines copyright laws to protect digital versions of copyrighted materials, including music and movies.

Privacy Protection Act (COPPA) requires commercial Internet sites to carry privacy policy statements, obtain parental consent before soliciting information from children under the age of 13, and provide an opportunity to remove any information provided by children using such sites. Critics of COPPA argue that children age 13 and older should not be treated as adults on the Web. In a study of children ages 10 to 17, nearly half indicated that they would give their name, address, and other demographic information in exchange for a gift worth $100 or more. Internet safety among children is another major topic of concern. Research has shown that filtering and age verification are not effective in making the Internet safer—businesses, regulators, and parents are all trying to find answers in how to protect children from dangers ranging from online predators to pornography.[12]

TABLE 4–3 Laws Protecting Consumers

Pure Food and Drug Act, 1906	Prohibits adulteration and mislabeling of foods and drugs sold in interstate commerce.
Federal Hazardous Substances Labeling Act, 1960	Controls the labeling of hazardous substances for household use.
Truth in Lending Act, 1968	Requires full disclosure of credit terms to purchasers.
Consumer Product Safety Act, 1972	Created the Consumer Product Safety Commission to establish safety standards and regulations for consumer products.
Fair Credit Billing Act, 1974	Requires accurate, up-to-date consumer credit records.
Energy Policy and Conservation Act, 1975	Requires auto dealers to have "gas mileage guides" in their showrooms.
Consumer Goods Pricing Act, 1975	Prohibits price maintenance agreements.
Consumer Leasing Act, 1976	Requires accurate disclosure of leasing terms to consumers.
Fair Debt Collection Practices Act, 1978	Defines permissible debt collection practices.
Toy Safety Act, 1984	Gives the government the power to recall dangerous toys quickly.
Nutritional Labeling and Education Act, 1990	Prohibits exaggerated health claims and requires all processed foods to have labels showing nutritional information.
Telephone Consumer Protection Act, 1991	Establishes procedures for avoiding unwanted telephone solicitations.
Children's Online Privacy Protection Act, 1998	Requires the FTC to formulate rules for collecting online information from children under age 13.
Do Not Call Implementation Act, 2003	Directs the FCC and the FTC to coordinate so that their rules are consistent regarding telemarketing call practices including the Do Not Call Registry and other lists, as well as call abandonment.

Seniors are another highly vulnerable demographic. New laws have taken aim at financial scams on seniors, such as free lunch seminars. The state of Arkansas has taken the forefront on this issue, conducting police sweeps of suspected scams, increasing fines, and amending laws to imposed increased penalties for those who prey on the elderly. Older people are the most vulnerable group when it comes to financial scams, as they rely on their savings for retirement security.[13]

The role of the FTC's Bureau of Consumer Protection is to protect consumers against unfair, deceptive, or fraudulent practices. The bureau, which enforces a variety of consumer protection laws, is divided into five divisions. The Division of Enforcement monitors compliance with and investigates violations of laws, including unfulfilled holiday delivery promises by online shopping sites, employment opportunities fraud, scholarship scams, misleading advertising for health care products, high-tech and telemarketing fraud, data security, and financial practices.

TABLE 4–4 Laws Promoting Equity and Safety

Law	Description
Equal Pay Act of 1963	Prohibits discrimination in pay on the basis of sex.
Equal Pay Act of 1963 (amended)	Prohibits sex-based discrimination in the rate of pay to men and women working in the same or similar jobs.
Title VII of the Civil Rights Act of 1964 (amended in 1972)	Prohibits discrimination in employment on the basis of race, color, sex, religion, or national origin.
Age Discrimination in Employment Act, 1967	Prohibits discrimination in employment against persons between the ages of 40 and 70.
Occupational Safety and Health Act, 1970	Designed to ensure healthful and safe working conditions for all employees.
Title IX of Education Amendments of 1972	Prohibits discrimination based on sex in education programs or activities that receive federal financial assistance.
Vocational Rehabilitation Act, 1973	Prohibits discrimination in employment because of physical or mental handicaps.
Vietnam Era Veterans Readjustment Act, 1974	Prohibits discrimination against disabled veterans and Vietnam War veterans.
Pension Reform Act, 1974	Designed to prevent abuses in employee retirement, profit-sharing, thrift, and savings plans.
Equal Credit Opportunity Act, 1974	Prohibits discrimination in credit on the basis of sex or marital status.
Age Discrimination Act, 1975	Prohibits discrimination on age in federally assisted programs.
Pregnancy Discrimination Act, 1978	Prohibits discrimination on the basis of pregnancy, childbirth, or related medical conditions.
Immigration Reform and Control Act, 1986	Prohibits employers from knowingly hiring a person who is an unauthorized alien.
Americans with Disabilities Act, 1990	Prohibits discrimination against people with disabilities and requires that they be given the same opportunities as people without disabilities.
Civil Rights Act of 1991	Provides monetary damages in cases of intentional employment discrimination.

Laws Promoting Equity and Safety

Laws promoting equity in the workplace were passed during the 1960s and 1970s to protect the rights of minorities, women, older persons, and persons with disabilities; other legislation has sought to protect the safety of all workers (Table 4–4). Of these laws, probably the most important to business is Title VII of the Civil Rights Act, originally passed in 1964 and amended several times since. Title VII specifically prohibits discrimination in employment on the basis of race, sex, religion, color, or national origin. The Civil Rights Act also created the Equal Employment Opportunity Commission (EEOC) to help enforce the provisions of Title VII. Among other things, the EEOC helps businesses design affirmative action programs. These programs aim to increase job opportunities for women and minorities by analyzing the present pool of employees, identifying areas where women and minorities are underrepresented, and establishing specific hiring and promotion goals, along with target dates for meeting those goals.

Other legislation addresses more specific employment practices. The Equal Pay Act of 1963 mandates that women and men who do equal work must receive equal pay. Wage differences are allowed only if they can be attributed to seniority, performance, or qualifications. The Americans with Disabilities Act of 1990 prohibits discrimination against people with disabilities. Despite these laws, inequities in the workplace still exist. According to the U.S. Women's Bureau and National Committee on Pay Equity, women earn 77.8 percent of what men earn.[14] The disparity in wages is even higher for African American, Hispanic, and older women.

Congress has also passed laws that seek to improve safety in the workplace. By far the most significant of these is the Occupational Safety and Health Act of 1970, which mandates that employers provide safe and healthy working conditions for all workers. The **Occupational Safety and Health Administration** (OSHA), which enforces the act, makes regular surprise inspections to ensure that businesses maintain safe working environments.

Even with the passage and enforcement of safety laws, many employees still work in unhealthy or dangerous environments. Safety experts suspect that companies underreport industrial accidents to avoid state and federal inspection and regulation. The current emphasis on increased productivity has been cited as the main reason for the growing number of such accidents. Competitive pressures are also believed to lie behind the increases in manufacturing injuries. Greater turnover in organizations due to downsizing means that employees may have more responsibilities and less experience in their current positions, thus increasing the potential for accidents. The airline industry has become a prime example of tough economic times resulting in overworked, under-trained employees. Many pilots receive low compensation, poor health benefits, and are forced to work long hours—all factors that may have played a part in a tragic crash in Buffalo, New York, in February 2009 that killed all 49 people on board and one person on the ground. Even esteemed Captain Sully Sullenberger, who safely landed a plane on the Hudson River in January 2009 after colliding with some geese, confessed that his pay had been cut 40 percent. Because the industry cannot pay for the best and the brightest, such important factors as experience and skill are less important when hiring new pilots.[15]

Laws Protecting the Environment

Environmental protection laws have been enacted largely in response to concerns over business's impact on the environment, which began to emerge in the 1960s. **Sustainability** has become a buzzword in recent years, yet many people may not even think about what it means. According to the UN's World Commission on the Environment and Development, sustainable means "meeting the present needs without compromising future generations to meet their own needs."[16] The environment and sustainability are more important topics than ever. Thirty-five percent of people say that they are more interested in environmental issues and expect companies to be more environmentally responsible than they used to be.[17] Consumer interest in sustainability is so great that many firms have even made being green a competitive issue. For example, General Electric and Siemens, two large technology companies, are fighting via their advertisements and reports for title of greenest company. GE has an Ecomagination report that allows consumers to see all the green measures it has taken. Siemens, on the other hand, claims that it has a much larger environmental report yet has been annoyed by the lack of attention it has received for its actions.[18]

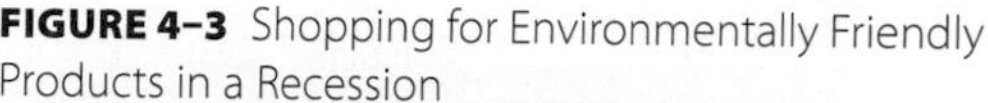

FIGURE 4–3 Shopping for Environmentally Friendly Products in a Recession

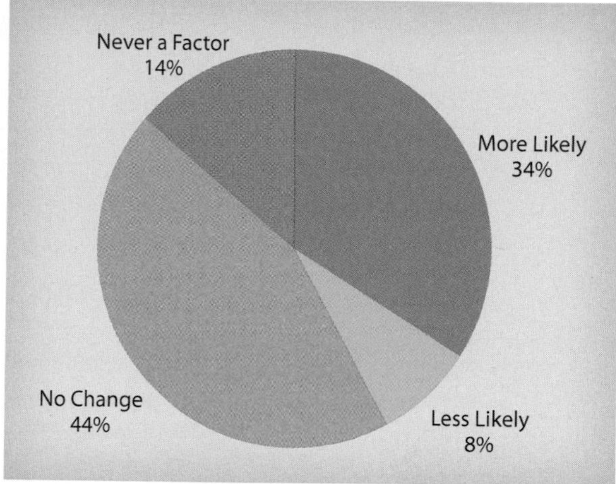

Source: 2009 Cone Consumer Environmental Survey of 1,087 adults, January 29–30.

Many people have questioned the cost-benefit analyses often used in making business decisions. Such analyses try to take into account all factors in a situation, represent them with dollar figures, calculate the costs and benefits of the proposed action, and determine whether an action's benefits outweigh its costs. The problem, however, is that it is difficult to arrive at an accurate monetary valuation of environmental damage or physical pain and injury. In addition, people outside the business world often perceive such analyses as inhumane. Figure 4–3 indicates that most consumers view environmental responsibility to be important, even during a recession. In addition, 70 percent of Americans now say that they pay attention to companies' stances toward the environment, even if they cannot afford to buy their products or services.[19]

The **Environmental Protection Agency** (EPA) was created in 1970 to coordinate environmental agencies involved in enforcing the nation's environmental laws. The major area of environmental concern relates to air, water, and land pollution. Large corporations are being encouraged to establish pollution-control mechanisms and other policies favorable to the environment. Otherwise, these companies could deplete resources and damage the health and welfare of society by focusing only on their own economic interests. For example, 3M voluntarily stopped making Scotchguard, a successful product for 40 years with $300 million in sales, after tests showed that it did not decompose in the environment.[20]

Increases in toxic waste in the air and water, as well as noise pollution, have prompted the passage of a number of laws (Table 4–5). Many environmental protection laws have resulted in the elimination or modification of goods and services. For instance, leaded gasoline was phased out during the 1990s by the EPA because catalytic converters, which reduce pollution caused by automobile emissions and are required by law on most vehicles, do not work properly with leaded gasoline. Increased Corporate Average Fuel Economy (or CAFE) standards are forcing companies to figure out ways for their cars to get better gas mileage. For many carmakers, a major part of this strategy involves increased production and sales of hybrid vehicles, as well as improving electric car and hydrogen fuel-cell technology.

The harmful effects of toxic waste on water life and on leisure industries such as resorts and fishing have raised concerns about proper disposal of these wastes. Few disposal sites meet EPA standards, so businesses must decide what to do with their waste until disposal sites become available. Some firms have solved this problem by illegal or unethical measures: dumping toxic wastes along highways, improperly burying drums containing toxic chemicals, and discarding hazardous waste at sea. For example, a five-year investigation found that ships owned by Royal Caribbean Cruises Ltd. used "secret bypass pipes" to dump waste oil and hazardous materials overboard, often at night. Justice Department officials accused the company of dumping to save the expense of properly disposing of waste at the same time that the cruise line was promoting itself as environmentally

TABLE 4–5 Laws Protecting the Environment

Law	Description
Clean Air Act, 1970	Established air-quality standards; requires approved state plans for implementation of the standards.
National Environmental Policy Act, 1970	Established broad policy goals for all federal agencies; created the Council on Environmental Quality as a monitoring agency.
Coastal Zone Management Act, 1972	Provides financial resources to the states to protect coastal zones from overpopulation.
Federal Water Pollution Control Act, 1972	Designed to prevent, reduce, or eliminate water pollution.
Noise Pollution Control Act, 1972	Designed to control the noise emission of certain manufactured items.
Federal Insecticide, Fungicide and Rodenticide Act, 1972	Provides federal control of pesticide distribution, sale, and use.
Endangered Species Act, 1973	Provides a program for the conservation of threatened and endangered plants and animals and the habitats in which they are found
Safe Drinking Water Act, 1974	Established to protect the quality of drinking water in the United States; focused on all waters actually or potentially designed for drinking use, whether from aboveground or underground sources; established safe standards of purity and required all owners or operators of public water systems to comply with primary (health-related) standards.
Toxic Substances Control Act, 1976	Requires testing and restricts use of certain chemical substances, to protect human health and the environment.
Resource Conservation and Recovery Act, 1976	Gives the EPA authority to control hazardous waste from the "cradle to grave"; includes the generation, transportation, treatment, storage, and disposal of hazardous waste, as well as a framework for the management of nonhazardous waste.
Comprehensive Environmental Response, Compensation, and Liability Act, 1980	Created a tax on chemical and petroleum industries and provides broad federal authority to respond directly to releases or threatened releases of hazardous substances that may endanger public health or the environment.
Emergency Planning and Community Right-to-Know Act, 1986	The national legislation on community safety, designed to help local communities protect public health, safety, and the environment from chemical hazards.
Oil Pollution Act, 1990	Streamlined and strengthened the EPA's ability to prevent and respond to catastrophic oil spills; a trust fund financed by a tax on oil is available to clean up spills when the responsible party is incapable or unwilling to do so.
Pollution Prevention Act, 1990	Focuses industry, government, and public attention on reducing the amount of pollution through cost-effective changes in production, operation, and raw materials use.
Food Quality Protection Act, 1996	Amended the Federal Insecticide, Fungicide and Rodenticide Act and the Federal Food Drug and Cosmetic Act; the requirements included a new safety standard—reasonable certainty of no harm—that must be applied to all pesticides used on foods.

FIGURE 4–4 Growth in Recycling Cell Phones (in millions)

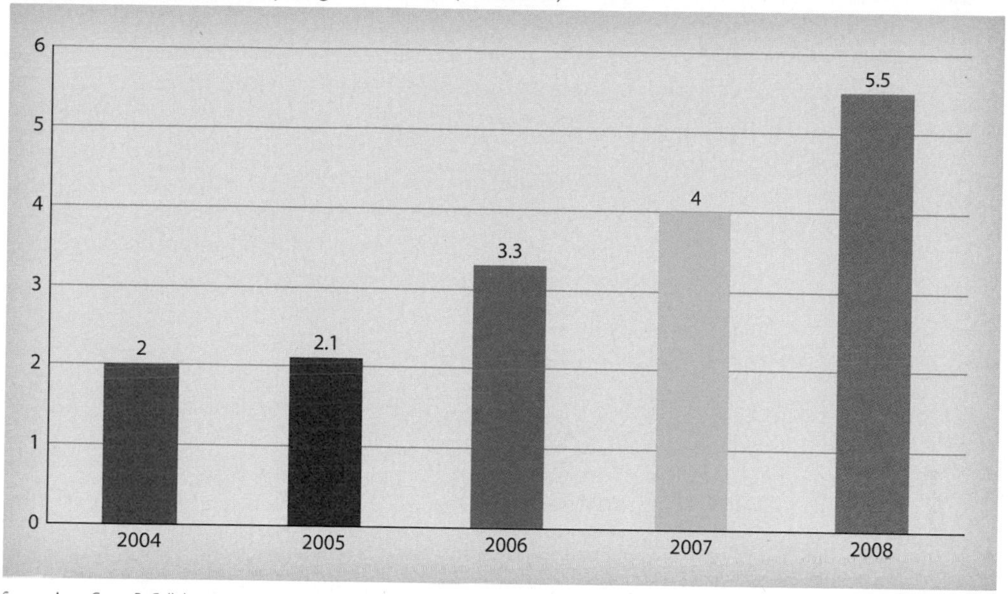

Source: Anne Carey, ReCellular.com

friendly. The company ultimately pleaded guilty to 21 felony counts, paid $27 million in fines, spent as much as $90,000 per vessel to install new oily water-treatment systems and placed an environmental officer on board each vessel.[21] Congress regularly evaluates legislation to increase the penalties for disposing of toxic wastes in this way. Disposal issues remain controversial because, although everyone acknowledges that the wastes must go somewhere, no community wants them dumped in its own backyard.

One solid-waste problem is the result of rapid innovations in computer hardware, which render machines obsolete after just 18 months. Today, hundreds of millions of computers have reached obsolescence, and tens of millions of these are expected to end up in landfills. Cell phones are another problem, with billions destined for landfills. Computers and cell phones both contain such toxic substances as lead, mercury, and polyvinyl chloride, which can leach into the soil and contaminate groundwater when disposed of improperly. While electronics recycling is not widespread, it has become increasingly available, as Figure 4–4 shows. Websites like electronicsrecycling.org help consumers find locations to recycle their phones and computers. The Environmental Protection Agency hosts its own electronics recycling program, which collects around 67 million pounds of electronics a year. Stores like Staples and Best Buy offer limited recycling programs, and companies like Dell and Samsung are all seeking to extend the availability of recycling for their products.[22]

GATEKEEPERS AND STAKEHOLDERS

Trust is the glue that holds businesses and their stakeholders together. Trust creates confidence and helps to forge relationships of reliance between businesses and stakeholders. Trust also allows businesses to depend upon one another as they make transactions or exchange value. Ethics helps create the foundational trust between two parties in a transaction. There are many people who must trust and be trusted to make business work properly. Sometimes these parties are referred to as *gatekeepers*. Gatekeepers not only include accountants, who are essential to certifying the accuracy of financial information, but also lawyers, financial rating agencies, and even financial reporting services. All of these groups are critical in providing information that allows stakeholders to gain an understanding of the financial position of an organization. Most of these gatekeepers operate with professional codes of ethics and face legal consequences, or even disbarment, if they fail to operate within agreed-upon principles of conduct. Therefore, there is a strong need for gatekeepers to retain ethical standards and independence using standard methods and procedures that can be audited by other gatekeepers, the regulatory system, and investors.

Accountants

Accountants measure and disclose financial information, with an assurance of accuracy, to the public. Managers, investors, tax authorities, and other stakeholders who make resource allocation decisions are all groups who use the information provided by accountants. Accountants assume certain basic principles about their clients. One assumption is that the corporation is an entity that is separate and distinct from its owners, and that it will continue to operate as such in the future. Another assumption is that a stable monetary system (such as the dollar) is in place and that all necessary information concerning the business is available and presented in an understandable manner. Accountants have their own set of rules, one of which is that, if there is a choice between equally acceptable accounting methods, they should use the one that is least likely to overstate or misdirect. During the 2008–2009 financial meltdown, many people lost trust in accountants and auditors because a few made unscrupulous decisions.

> *“Gatekeepers such as lawyers, financial rating agencies, and even financial reporting services must have high ethical standards.”*

Some accountants have not been adhering to their responsibilities to stakeholders. For example, Arthur Andersen was once a standard bearer for integrity. But at Andersen, growth became the priority, and its emphasis on recruiting and retaining big clients came at the expense of quality and independent audits. The company linked its consulting business in a joint cooperative relationship with its audit arm, which compromised its auditors' independence, a quality crucial to the execution of a credible audit. The firm's focus on growth generated a fundamental change in its corporate culture, one in which obtaining high-profit consulting business was regarded as more important than providing objective auditing services. This situation presents a conflict of interest, and posed a problem when partners had to decide how to treat questionable accounting practices discovered at some of Andersen's largest clients. Ultimately, Arthur Andersen was dissolved because of its ties to the Enron scandal. Gatekeepers such as lawyers, financial rating agencies, and even financial reporting services must have high ethical standards. These groups must be trusted by all stakeholders, and most operate with professional codes of ethics.

Risk Assessment

Another critical gatekeeper group in the financial meltdown was risk assessors of financial products. The top three companies in the world that independently assess financial risks are Standard & Poor's, Moody's, and Fitch. They assess risk and express it through letters ranging from "AAA," which is the highest grade, to "C," which is junk. Different rating services use the same letter grades, but use various combinations of upper- and lowercase letters to differentiate themselves.

As early as 2003, financial analysts and the three global rating firms suspected that there were some major problems with the way their models were assessing risk. In 2005, Standard & Poor's realized that its algorithm for estimating the risks associated with debt packages was flawed. As a result, it asked for comments on improving its equations. In 2006–2007 many governmental regulators and others started to realize what the rating agencies had known for years: Their ratings were not very accurate. One report stated that the high ratings given to debt were based on inadequate historical data and companies were ratings shopping between companies so as to obtain the best rating possible. It was found that investment banks were among some of the worst offenders, paying for ratings and therefore causing conflicts of interest. The amount of revenue these three companies annually receive is approximately $5 billion.

Further investigations uncovered many disturbing problems. First, Moody's, S&P's, and Fitch had all violated a code of conduct that required analysts to consider only credit factors, not "'the potential impact on Moody's, or an issuer, an investor or other market participant."' Also, these companies had become overwhelmed by an increase in the volume and sophistication of the securities they were asked to review. Finally, analysts, faced with less time to perform the due diligence expected of them, began to cut corners.

SEC Chairman Mary Schapiro believes that the SEC must take more drastic measures to implement oversight for credit-rating firms—a group that was largely blamed for not catching risky activity in the financial sector sooner. Part of the problem, as Schapiro sees it, is that credit rating firms are paid by the securities that they rank. This creates a conflict of interest problem, and can affect the reliability of the ratings.[23] No organization is exempt from criticism over how transparent it is. While large financial firms have received most of the fury over risk taking and executive pay, even nonprofits are now being scrutinized more carefully.[24]

THE SARBANES–OXLEY ACT

In 2002, largely in response to widespread corporate accounting scandals, Congress passed the Sarbanes–Oxley Act to establish a system of federal oversight of corporate accounting practices. In addition to making fraudulent financial reporting a criminal offense and strengthening penalties for corporate fraud, the law requires corporations to establish codes of ethics for financial reporting and to develop greater transparency in financial reporting to investors and other stakeholders.

Supported by both Republicans and Democrats, the Sarbanes–Oxley Act was enacted to restore stakeholder confidence after accounting fraud at Enron, WorldCom, and hundreds of other companies resulted in investors and employees losing much of their savings. During the resulting investigations, the public learned that hundreds of corporations had not reported their financial results accurately. Many stakeholders came to believe that accounting firms, lawyers, top executives, and boards of directors had developed a culture of deception to ensure investor approval and gain competitive advantage. Many boards failed to provide appropriate oversight of the decisions of their companies' top officers. At Adelphia Communications, for example, the Rigas family amassed $3.1 billion in off-balance-sheet loans backed by the company. Dennis Kozlowski, CEO of Tyco, was accused of improperly using corporate funds for personal use as well as fraudulent accounting practices.[25] At Kmart, CEO Charles Conaway allegedly hired unqualified executives and consultants for excessive fees. Kmart's board also approved $24 million in loans to various executives, just a month before the retailer filed for Chapter 11 bankruptcy protection. Conaway and the other executives have since left the company or were fired. Loans of this type are now illegal under the Sarbanes–Oxley Act.[26]

As a result of public outrage over the accounting scandals, the Sarbanes–Oxley Act garnered nearly unanimous support not only in Congress but also by government regulatory agencies, the president, and the general public. When President George W. Bush signed the Sarbanes–Oxley Act into law, he emphasized the need for new standards of ethical behavior in business, particularly among the top managers and boards of directors responsible for overseeing business decisions and activities.

At the heart of the Sarbanes–Oxley Act is the **Public Company Accounting Oversight Board,** which monitors accounting firms that audit public corporations and establishes standards and rules for auditors in accounting firms. The law gave the board investigatory and disciplinary power over auditors and securities analysts who issue reports about corporate performance and health. The law attempts to eliminate conflicts of interest by prohibiting accounting firms from providing both auditing and consulting services to the same client companies without special permission from the client firm's audit committee; it also places limits on the length of time lead auditors can serve a particular client.Table 4–6 summarizes the significant provisions of the law.

TABLE 4–6 Major Provisions of the Sarbanes–Oxley Act

1.	Requires the establishment of a Public Company Accounting Oversight Board in charge of regulations administered by the SEC.
2.	Requires CEOs and CFOs to certify that their companies' financial statements are true and without misleading statements.
3.	Requires that corporate board of directors' audit committees consist of independent members who have no material interests in the company.
4.	Prohibits corporations from making or offering loans to officers and board members.
5.	Requires codes of ethics for senior financial officers; code must be registered with the SEC.
6.	Prohibits accounting firms from providing both auditing and consulting services to the same client without the approval of the client firm's audit committee.
7.	Requires company attorneys to report wrongdoing to top managers and, if necessary, to the board of directors; if managers and directors fail to respond to reports of wrongdoing, the attorney should stop representing the company.
8.	Mandates "whistle-blower protection" for persons who disclose wrongdoing to authorities.
9.	Requires financial securities analysts to certify that their recommendations are based on objective reports.
10.	Requires mutual fund managers to disclose how they vote shareholder proxies, giving investors information about how their shares influence decisions.
11.	Establishes a ten-year penalty for mail/wire fraud.
12.	Prohibits the two senior auditors from working on a corporation's account for more than five years; other auditors are prohibited from working on an account for more than seven years. In other words, accounting firms must rotate individual auditors from one account to another from time to time.

TABLE 4–7 Benefits of the Sarbanes–Oxley Act

1.	Greater accountability of top managers and boards of directors to employees, investors, communities, and society
2.	Renewed investor confidence
3.	Clear explanations by CEOs as to why their compensation package is in the best interest of the company; the loss of some traditional senior-management perks such as company loans; greater disclosures by executives about their own stock trades
4.	Greater protection of employee retirement plans
5.	Improved information from stock analysts and rating agencies
6.	Greater penalties for and accountability of senior managers, auditors, and board members

The Sarbanes–Oxley Act requires corporations to take greater responsibility for their decisions and to provide leadership based on ethical principles. For instance, the law requires top managers to certify that their firms' financial reports are complete and accurate, making CEOs and CFOs personally accountable for the credibility and accuracy of their companies' financial statements. Similar provisions are required of corporate boards of directors, especially audit committees, and senior financial officers are now subject to a code of ethics that addresses their specific areas of risk. Additionally, the law modifies the attorney–client relationship to require lawyers to report wrongdoing to top managers and/or the board of directors. It also provides protection for "whistle-blowing" employees who might report illegal activity to authorities. These provisions provide internal controls to make managers aware of and responsible for legal and ethical problems. Table 4–7 summarizes the benefits of the legislation.

On the other hand, the Sarbanes–Oxley Act has raised a number of concerns. The complex law may impose burdensome requirements on executives; the rules and regulations already run to thousands of pages. Some people also believe that the law will not be sufficient to stop those executives who want to lie, steal, manipulate, or deceive. They believe that a deep commitment to managerial integrity, rather than additional rules and regulations, are the key to solving the current crisis in business.[27] Additionally, the new act has caused many firms to restate their financial reports to avoid penalties. Big public companies spent thousands of hours and an average of $4.4 million each annually to make sure that someone was looking over the shoulder of key accounting personnel at every step of every business process, according to Financial Executives International. Section 404 is a core provision of the 2002 corporate reform law. The number of companies that disclosed serious chinks in their internal accounting controls jumped to more than 586 in 2005 compared to 313 in 2004.[28]

Public Company Accounting Oversight Board

The Sarbanes–Oxley Act establishes an oversight board to oversee the audit of public companies in order to protect the interests of investors and further the public interest in the preparation of informative, accurate, and independent audit reports for companies. Their duties include (1) registration of public accounting firms; (2) establishment of auditing, quality control, ethics, independence, and other standards relating to preparation of audit reports; (3) inspection of accounting firms; (4) investigations, disciplinary proceedings, and imposition of sanctions; and (5) enforcement of compliance with accounting rules of the board, professional standards, and securities laws relating to the preparation and issuance of audit reports and obligations and liabilities of accountants.

The board reports to the SEC on an annual basis that includes any new established rules and any final disciplinary rulings. The board works with designated professional groups of accountants and other standard-setting advisory groups in establishing auditing, quality control, ethics, and independence rules.

Auditor and Analyst Independence

The Sarbanes–Oxley Act also seeks to eliminate conflicts of interest among auditors, security analysts, brokers, and dealers and the public companies they serve in order to ensure enhanced financial disclosures of public companies' true condition. To accomplish auditor independence, Section 201 of the act no longer allows registered public accounting firms to provide both non-audit and audit services to a public company. National securities exchanges and registered securities associations have already adopted similar conflict-of-interest rules for security analysts, brokers, and dealers, who recommend equities in research reports. The face of Wall Street is experiencing major changes. In early 2003, 10 of the nation's largest securities firms agreed to pay a record \$1.4 billion to settle government charges involving abuse of investors during the stock market bubble of the late 1990s. Wall Street firms routinely issued overly optimistic stock research to investors in order to gain favor with corporate clients and win their lucrative investment-banking business.

Enhanced Financial Disclosures

With independence, the Sarbanes–Oxley Act is better able to ensure compliance with the enhanced financial disclosures of public companies' true condition. For example, registered public accounting firms are now required to identify all material correcting adjustments to reflect accurate financial statements. Also, all material off-balance-sheet transactions and other relationships with unconsolidated entities that affect current or future financial conditions of a public company must be disclosed in each annual and quarterly financial report. In addition, public companies must also report "on a rapid and current basis" material changes in the financial condition or operations.

Whistle-Blower Protection

Employees of public companies and accounting firms, in general, are also accountable to report unethical behavior. The Sarbanes–Oxley Act intends to motivate employees through whistle-blower protection that would prohibit the employer from taking certain actions against employees who lawfully disclose private employer information to, among others, parties in a judicial proceeding involving a fraud claim. Whistle-blowers are also granted a remedy of special damages and attorneys' fees. Two years after the act, the SEC received approximately 40,000 whistle-blowing reports per month, compared with 6,400 per month in 2001.[29] With only 11,000 publicly-traded companies in the United States, it seems that even though 75 percent of the whistle-blowing reports have no validity, there are still more whistle-blowing reports every month than the number of companies listed.[30]

Also, any act of retaliation that harms informants, including interference with the lawful employment or livelihood of any person, for providing to a law enforcement officer any truthful information relating to the commission or possible commission of any federal offense, will be fined and/or imprisoned for 10 years.

Corporate and Criminal Fraud Accountability

Title VIII of the Sarbanes–Oxley Act, Corporate and Criminal Fraud Accountability, makes the knowing destruction or creation of documents to "impede, obstruct or influence" any existing or contemplated federal investigation a felony. The White-Collar Crime Penalty Enhancements Act of 2002 increased the maximum penalty for mail and wire fraud from 5 to 10 years in prison. It also makes record tampering or otherwise impeding an official a crime. If necessary, the SEC could freeze extraordinary payments to directors, officers, partners, controlling persons, and agents of employees. The U.S. Sentencing Commission reviews sentencing guidelines for securities and accounting fraud.

The act may not prevent future Enron-type businesses from occurring. However, the act's uniqueness from past legislation is its perspective to mandate accountability from the many players in the "game of business," creating more explicit rules in playing fair. The act creates a foundation to strongly discourage wrongdoing and sets ethical standards of what's expected of American business.

> ***The national cost of compliance of the Sarbanes–Oxley Act is estimated at $1 million per $1.7 billion in revenues.***

Cost of Compliance

The national cost of compliance of the Sarbanes–Oxley Act is estimated at $1 million per $1.7 billion in revenues.[31] These costs come from internal costs, external costs, and auditor fees. In a survey by Financial Executives International, nearly all the respondents (94 percent) said that the costs of compliance exceeded the benefits.[32] This act has increased external auditing costs for mid- to large-size companies between 52 and 81 percent. The section that has caused the most cost for companies has been compliance with Section 404. Section 404 has three central issues: It requires that (1) management create reliable internal financial controls, (2) that management attest to the reliability of those controls and the accuracy of financial statements that result from those controls, and (3) that an independent auditor further attests to the statements made by management. Section 404 requires companies to document both the results of financial transactions and the processes they have used to generate them. A company may have thousands of processes that may work, but they have never been written down. Writing down the processes is time consuming and costly.[33] Also, because the cost of compliance is so high for many small companies, some publicly-traded companies are even considering delisting themselves from the U.S. Stock Exchange. Companies based outside the United States have also been weighing the costs of compliance versus the savings of deregistration. Sweden-based Electrolux was among the first to delist from NASDAQ after the Sarbanes–Oxley Act was passed. Many new non-U.S. companies may be avoiding the U.S. market altogether. New listings with the SEC from companies outside the United States have dropped to almost zero since the act passed in 2002.[34] After years of complaints from firms, in spring 2009 the Supreme Court agreed to hear arguments over the constitutionality of

Sarbanes–Oxley, which has gained new critics as it failed to detect wrongdoing that led to the subprime mortgage crisis and the meltdown on Wall Street in 2008–2009.[35]

However, there are some cases where companies are benefiting from the act's implementation. Apart from the obvious increase in books and materials to help people comply with the act, there is also a growing business for people teaching and implementing ethics programs and hotlines for organizations. Companies such as Global Compliance and EthicsPoint have grown rapidly as companies seek to learn ethics, and a vast new industry of consultants and suppliers has emerged.[36] Other benefits and savings have come in the form of increased efficiency as companies such as Pitney Bowes Inc. find that they can meld various units such as combining four accounts receivable offices into one, saving more than $500,000 a year. At Genentech Inc., simply having detailed reports on financial controls sped up installation, by several months, of a new computer system that consolidates financial data, which meant that it was running months ahead of schedule. The new system allows managers to analyze data from customers rather than just collecting it. Cisco spent $50 million and 240,000 hours on its first-year audit of internal controls. The mind-numbing effort revealed opportunities to streamline steps for ordering products and services, making it easier for customers to do business with Cisco. It forced them to make sure that sales and support were integrated when a customer called, resulting in one-stop shopping for its customers. Other companies have been able to streamline steps for ordering products and services, making it easier for customers to do business with them.[37]

LAWS THAT ENCOURAGE ETHICAL CONDUCT

Violations of the law usually begin when businesspeople stretch the limits of ethical standards, as defined by company or industry codes of conduct, and then choose to engage in schemes that knowingly or unwittingly violate the law. In recent years, new laws and regulations have been passed to discourage such decisions—and to foster programs designed to improve business ethics and social responsibility (Table 4–8). The most important of these are the Federal Sentencing Guidelines for Organizations (FSGO) and the Sarbanes–Oxley Act. One of the goals of both acts is to require employees to

TABLE 4–8 Institutionalization of Ethics through the U.S. Sentencing Guidelines for Organizations

1991	*Law:* U.S. Sentencing Guidelines for Organizations created for federal prosecutions of organizations. These guidelines provide for just punishment, adequate deterrence, and incentives for organizations to prevent, detect, and report misconduct. Organizations need to have an effective ethics and compliance program to receive incentives in the case of misconduct.
2004	*Amendments:* The definition of an effective ethics program now includes the development of an ethical organizational culture. Executives and board members must assume the responsibility of identifying areas of risk, provide ethics training, create reporting mechanisms, and designate an individual to oversee ethics programs.
2007–2008	*Additional definition of a compliance and ethics program:* Firms should focus on due diligence to detect and prevent misconduct and to promote an organizational culture that encourages ethical conduct. More details are provided encouraging the assessment of risk and appropriate steps to design, implement, and modify ethics programs and training to include all employees, top management, and the board or governing authority. These modifications continue to reinforce the importance of an ethical culture in preventing misconduct.

FIGURE 4–5 Percentage of Employees Who Still DO NOT Report Observed Misconduct

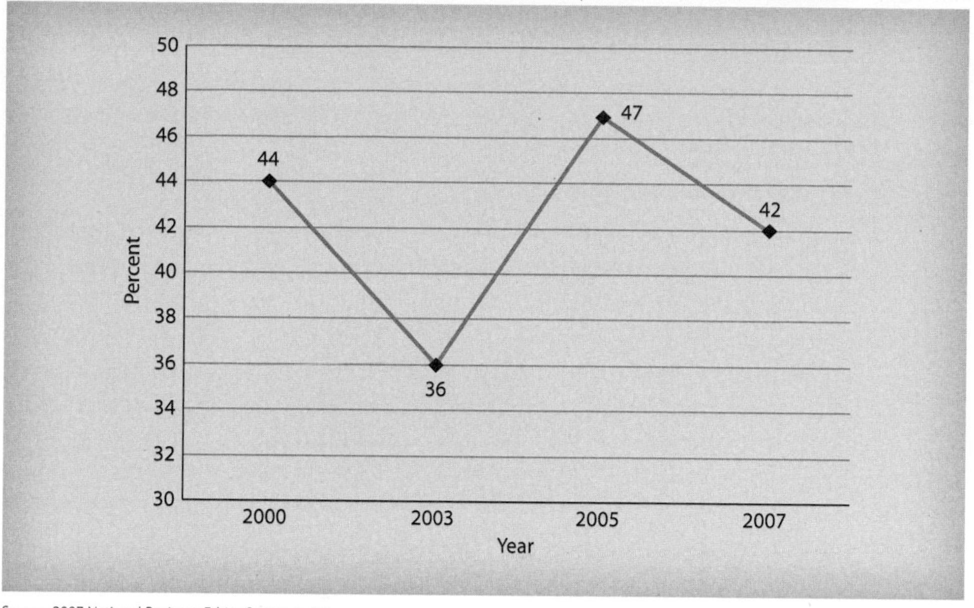

Source: 2007 National Business Ethics Survey, p. 17.

report observed misconduct. The development of reporting systems has advanced with most companies having some method for employees to report observed misconduct. While reported misconduct is up, a sizable percentage of employees still do not report misconduct, as Figure 4–5 shows.

FEDERAL SENTENCING GUIDELINES FOR ORGANIZATIONS

As mentioned in Chapter 1, Congress passed the FSGO in 1991 to create an incentive for organizations to develop and implement programs designed to foster ethical and legal compliance. These guidelines, which were developed by the U.S. Sentencing Commission, apply to all felonies and class A misdemeanors committed by employees in association with their work. As an incentive, organizations that have demonstrated due diligence in developing effective compliance programs that discourage unethical and illegal conduct may be subject to reduced organizational penalties if an employee commits a crime.[38] Overall, the government philosophy is that legal violations can be prevented through organizational values and a commitment to ethical conduct.

The commission delineated seven steps that companies must implement to demonstrate due diligence:

1. A firm must develop and disseminate a code of conduct that communicates required standards and identifies key risk areas for the organization.

2. High-ranking personnel in the organization who are known to abide by the legal and ethical standards of the industry (such as an ethics officer, vice president of human resources, general counsel, and so forth) must have oversight over the program.
3. No one with a known propensity to engage in misconduct should be put in a position of authority.
4. A communications system for disseminating standards and procedures (ethics training) must also be put into place.
5. Organizational communications should include a way for employees to report misconduct without fearing retaliation, such as an anonymous toll-free hotline or an ombudsman. Monitoring and auditing systems designed to detect misconduct are also required.
6. If misconduct is detected, then the firm must take appropriate and fair disciplinary action. Individuals both directly and indirectly responsible for the offense should be disciplined. In addition, the sanctions should be appropriate for the offense.
7. After misconduct has been discovered, the organization must take steps to prevent similar offenses in the future. This usually involves making modifications to the ethical compliance program, additional employee training, and issuing communications about specific types of conduct.

The government expects these seven steps for compliance programs to undergo continuous improvement and refinement.[39]

These steps are based on the commission's determination to emphasize compliance programs and to provide guidance for both organizations and courts regarding program effectiveness. Organizations have flexibility about the type of program they develop; the seven steps are not a checklist requiring that legal procedures be followed to gain certification of an effective program. Organizations implement the guidelines through effective core practices that are appropriate for their firms. The program must be capable of reducing the opportunity that employees have to engage in misconduct.

A 2004 amendment to the FSGO requires that a business's governing authority be well informed about its ethics program with respect to content, implementation, and effectiveness. This places the responsibility squarely on the shoulders of the firm's leadership, usually the board of directors. The board must ensure that there is a high-ranking manager accountable for the day-to-day operational oversight of the ethics program. The board must provide for adequate authority, resources, and access to the board or an appropriate subcommittee of the board. The board must ensure that there are confidential mechanisms available so that the organization's employees and agents may report or seek guidance about potential or actual misconduct without fear of retaliation. Finally, the board is required to oversee the discovery of risks and to design, implement, and modify approaches to deal with those risks. Figure 4–6 provides an overview from NBES about how prepared employees are to respond to various ethical and legal risks. Over three-quarters of employees who encounter risk feel adequately prepared to respond. If board members do not understand the nature, purpose, and methods available to implement an ethics program, the firm is at risk of inadequate oversight in the event of ethical misconduct that escalates into a scandal.[40]

A 2005 Supreme Court decision held that the sentences for violations of law were not mandatory but should serve only as recommendations for judges to use in their decisions. Some legal and business experts believe that this decision might weaken

FIGURE 4–6 Employees' Preparation to Respond to Risk

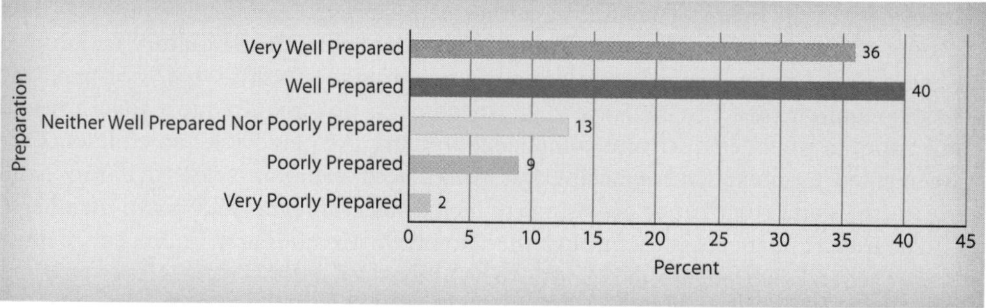

Source: National Business Ethics Survey, *How Employees View Ethics in Their Organizations 1994-2205* (Washington D.C.: Ethics Resource Center, 2005): 39.

the implementation of the FSGO, but most sentences have remained in the same range as before the Supreme Court decision. The guidelines remain an important consideration in developing an effective ethics and compliance program. An Open Compliance Group Benchmarking survey provided some insights into effective core practices, as illustrated in Table 4-9.

TABLE 4–9 Key Findings from the Open Compliance Ethics Group Benchmarking Survey

Crisis Can Help the Cause	Companies that have experienced reputation damage in the past see themselves as much further along in terms of program maturity and in relation to their peers—both today and in the future.
Pay Now or Pay Later	Companies that have experienced reputation damage invest *three* times more than their nondamaged peers in specific compliance and ethics processes.
Preference for Proactive and Values-Based Programs	Compliance and ethics programs are becoming more proactive and values based, allowing companies to prevent ethical and compliance violations before they become a crisis.
Proactive Skills Training May Need More Emphasis	To reach the objective of more proactive programs, companies must provide training to the people who are accountable for the compliance and ethics program—training that focuses on more proactive disciplines.
Set/Align Objectives for More Benefit	Companies that set explicit objectives for their compliance and ethics programs rate the benefits of their programs more highly and ascribe them more than companies that do not set explicit objectives.
Integrate/Cooperate for More Benefit	Additional benefits and performance can be realized when an organization integrates the compliance and ethics program with other aspects of the enterprise and when the program has a good working relationship with other business functions/processes.
Experience	Of the companies in this study, 54 percent have implemented a compliance and ethics program relatively recently (within the last five years). *Zero* companies in this study with a program in place for 10 years or more experienced highly visible reputation damage in the last five years, a testament to the important impact these programs can have over time.

Source: Open Compliance Ethics Group 2005 Benchmarking Study Key Findings, http://www.oceg.org/view/Benchmarking2005 (accessed June 12, 2009). Reprinted with permission.

The 2007–2008 amendments to the FSGO extend the ethics training of individuals to members of the board or governing authority, high-level personnel, employees, and the organizations' agents. This applies not only oversight but mandatory training to all levels of the organization. Merely distributing a code of ethics does not meet the training requirements. The 2007 and 2008 amendments now require most governmental contractors to provide ethics and compliance training. As new FSGO amendments are implemented, more explicit responsibility is being placed on organizations to improve and expand ethics and compliance provisions to include all employees and board members.

The Department of Justice, through the Thompson Memo (Larry Thompson, deputy attorney general, 2003 memo to U.S. Attorneys), advanced general principles to consider in cases involving corporate wrongdoing. This memo makes it clear that ethics and compliance programs are important to detect the types of misconduct most likely to occur in a particular corporation's line of business. Without an effective ethics and compliance program to detect ethical and legal lapses, the firm should not be treated leniently. Also, the prosecutor generally has wide latitude in determining when, whom, and whether to prosecute violations of federal law. U.S. Attorneys are directed that charging for even minor misconduct may be appropriate when the wrongdoing was pervasive by a large number of employees in a particular role—for example, sales staff, procurement officers—or was condoned by upper management. Without an effective program to identify an isolated rogue employee involved in misconduct, serious consequences can be associated with regulatory issues, enforcement, and sentencing.[41] Therefore, there is general agreement both from laws and administrative policy that an effective ethics and compliance program is necessary to prevent conduct and reduce the legal consequences.

HIGHLY APPROPRIATE CORE PRACTICES

The FSGO and the Sarbanes–Oxley Act provide incentives for developing core practices that help ensure ethical and legal compliance. Core practices move the emphasis from a focus on individuals' moral capability to developing structurally sound organization core practices and developing structural integrity for both financial performance and nonfinancial performance. Although the Sarbanes–Oxley Act provides standards for financial performance, most ethical issues relate to nonfinancial issues such as marketing, human resource management, and customer relationships. Abusive behavior, lying, and conflict of interest are still the top three ethical issues.

The Integrity Institute has developed an integrated model to standardize the measurement of nonfinancial performance. Methodologies have been developed to assess communications, compensation, social responsibility, corporate culture, leadership, risk, and stakeholder perceptions, as well as more subjective aspects of earnings, corporate governance, technology, and other important nonfinancial areas. The model exists to establish a standard that can predict sustainability and success of an organization. The Integrity Institute uses the measurement to an established standard as the basis of certification of integrity.[42]

The majority of executives and board members want to measure nonfinancial performance, but no standards currently exist. The Open Compliance Ethics Group (oceg.org) has developed benchmarking studies available to organizations to conduct self-assessments to develop ethics program elements. Developing organizational systems and processes is a requirement of the regulatory environment, but organizations are given considerable freedom in developing ethics and compliance programs. Core practices do exist and can be identified in every industry. Trade associations' self-regulatory groups and research studies often provide insights about the expected best core practices. The most important is for each firm to assess its legal and ethical risk areas and then develop structures to prevent, detect, and quickly correct any misconduct.

Consider McDonald's approach to answering critics about nutritional guidance. It announced a move to provide nutritional information on its product packaging worldwide. McDonald's was the first in its industry to post nutritional information on food packaging. McDonald's has been seeking to build trust and loyalty among consumers, something that the company proclaims is highly important to it. McDonald's also introduced a "Balanced Lifestyles" initiative for kids, which involved offering healthier menu options, promoting physical activity, and providing more nutritional information to its customers about its products. In 2004 it withdrew its supersize meals after a damaging portrayal of the company in the film *Super Size Me*. The product sizes available at McDonald's are small, medium, and large, but upgrading to a bigger-portion size remains cheap.[43]

Philanthropic Contributions

Philanthropic issues are another dimension of voluntary social responsibility and relate to a business's contributions to stakeholders. Philanthropy provides four major benefits to society:

1. Philanthropy improves the quality of life and helps make communities places where people want to do business, raise families, and enjoy life. Thus, improving the quality of life in a community makes it easier to attract and retain employees and customers.
2. Philanthropy reduces government involvement by providing assistance to stakeholders.
3. Philanthropy develops employee leadership skills. Many firms, for example, use campaigns by the United Way and other community service organizations as leadership- and skill-building exercises for their employees.
4. Philanthropy helps create an ethical culture and the values that can act as a buffer to organizational misconduct.[44]

> *"Philanthropy helps create an ethical culture"*

The most common way that businesses demonstrate philanthropy is through donations to local and national charitable organizations. Consistently a large philanthropic donor, Wells Fargo & Company contributes around $100 million annually in community grants for nonprofits and schools, contributes $45 million and 100,000 volunteers to Habitat for Humanity and other housing nonprofits, purchases green energy, has a website devoted to financial education, and its employees have donated hundreds of thousands of hours to charities around the nation.[45] Indeed, many companies have become concerned about the quality of education in the United States after realizing that the current pool of prospective employees lacks many basic work skills. Recognizing that today's students are tomorrow's employees and customers, firms such as Kroger, Campbell Soup Company, Eastman Kodak, American Express, Apple Computer, Xerox, and Coca-Cola have donated money, equipment, and employee time to help improve schools in their communities and throughout the nation.

The Wal-Mart Foundation, the charitable giving branch of Wal-Mart Inc., donated $378 million in 2009 to charities and communities across the globe, making it the largest corporate cash contributor in the nation, according to the Chronicle of Philanthropy. *Forbes Magazine* recognized Wal-Mart as the most generous company in the nation overall.[46] The money supported a variety of causes such as child development, education, the environment, and disaster relief. Wal-Mart feels that it can make the greatest impact on communities by supporting issues and causes that are important to its customers and associates in their own neighborhoods. Wal-Mart relies on its own associates to know which organizations are the most important to their hometowns, and it empowers them to determine how money will be spent in their communities. Wal-Mart is particularly focused on education, workforce development, sustainability, and health and wellness. By supporting communities at the local level, it encourages customer loyalty and goodwill.[47]

Strategic Philanthropy

Tying philanthropic giving to overall strategy and objectives is also known as strategic philanthropy. **Strategic philanthropy** is the synergistic and mutually beneficial use of an organization's core competencies and resources to deal with key stakeholders so as to bring about organizational and societal benefits. For example, last year Bisto, a staple of Britain's meal tables since 1908 with its instant gravy, launched a new marketing campaign. The focus was on families trying to eat one meal together a week. Bisto called it "ahh nights" based on its longtime marketing slogan of "ahh . . . Bisto." Families eat fewer and fewer meals together; this has been identified by social policy experts as playing a key role in a wide range of social problems such as teenage drug abuse, sexual promiscuity, teenage pregnancy, crime, antisocial behavior, truancy, and poor academic performance. Bisto used the new marketing slogan to extol the virtues of eating together as a family while explicitly recognizing the challenges of doing this in the modern world. It used a website, www.aahnight.co.uk, to make it easy for families to have a meal together at least once a week. It used three steps: (1) Download a contract that families can sign and stick on the refrigerator; (2) invite family or friends by e-mail; (3) make a delicious meal with recipes provided using—you guessed it—Bisto.[48]

Home Depot directs much of the money it spends on philanthropy to affordable housing, at-risk youth, the environment, and disaster recovery. In 2008 the company supported thousands of nonprofit organizations with over $50 million in contributions. The company also posts a Social Responsibility Report on its website. Home Depot works with more than 350 affiliates of Habitat for Humanity. In March 2008, Home Depot and Habitat for Humanity announced a five-year $30 million initiative to provide funding for creating at least 5,000 energy-efficient homes. Home Depot also supports YouthBuildUSA, a nonprofit organization that provides training and skill development for young people. After the 9/11 terrorist attacks in 2001, the company set up three command centers to help coordinate relief supplies such as dust masks, gloves, batteries, and tools to victims and rescue workers. After hurricanes Katrina, Rita, and Wilma, Home Depot, the Home Depot Foundation, their suppliers, and The Home Fund contributed $9.3 million in cash and materials to support recovery. Home Depot also donated $500,000 supporting the American Red Cross tsunami relief efforts in South East Asia. More recently, Home Depot donated $300,000 to the American Red Cross for disaster relief for people who suffer from hurricanes. Separately, Home Depot's Home Fund donated $500,000 to 650 associates who had suffered through Hurricane Gustav in 2008.[49]

SUMMARY

To understand the institutionalization of business ethics, it is important to understand the voluntary and legally mandated dimensions of organizational practices. Core practices are documented best practices, often encouraged by legal and regulatory forces as well as industry trade associations. The effective organizational practice of business ethics requires all three dimensions to be integrated into an ethics and compliance program. This creates an ethical culture that can effectively manage the risks of misconduct. Institutionalization in business ethics relates to established laws, customs, and expected organizational programs that are considered normative in establishing reputation. Institutions provide requirements, structure, and societal expectations to reward and sanction ethical decision making. In this way, society is institutionalizing core practices and providing organizations the opportunity to take their own approach, only taking action if there are violations.

Laws and regulations are established by governments to set minimum standards for responsible behavior—society's codification of what is right and wrong. Civil and criminal laws regulating business conduct are passed because society—including consumers, interest groups, competitors, and legislators—believes that business must comply with society's standards. Such laws regulate competition, protect consumers, promote safety and equity in the workplace, protect the environment, and provide incentives for preventing misconduct.

In 2002, largely in response to widespread corporate accounting scandals, Congress passed the Sarbanes–Oxley Act to establish a system of federal oversight of corporate accounting practices. In addition to making fraudulent financial reporting a criminal offense and strengthening penalties for corporate fraud, the law requires corporations to establish codes of ethics for financial reporting and to develop greater transparency in financial reporting to investors and other stakeholders. The Sarbanes–Oxley Act requires corporations to take greater responsibility for their decisions and to provide leadership based on ethical principles. For instance, the law requires top managers to certify that their firms' financial reports are complete and accurate, making CEOs and CFOs personally accountable for the credibility and accuracy of their companies' financial statements. The act establishes an oversight board to oversee the audit of public companies in order to protect the interests of investors and further the public interest in the preparation of informative, accurate, and independent audit reports for companies.

Congress passed the Federal Sentencing Guidelines for Organizations (FSGO) in 1991 to create an incentive for organizations to develop and implement programs designed to foster ethical and legal compliance. These guidelines, which were developed by the U.S. Sentencing Commission, apply to all felonies and class A misdemeanors committed by employees in association with their work. As an incentive, organizations that have demonstrated due diligence in developing effective compliance programs that discourage unethical and illegal conduct may be subject to reduced organizational penalties if an employee commits a crime.[50] Overall, the government philosophy is that legal violations can be prevented through organizational values and a commitment to ethical conduct. A 2004 amendment to the FSGO requires that a business's governing authority be well-informed about its ethics program with respect to content, implementation, and effectiveness. This places the responsibility squarely on the shoulders of the firm's leadership, usually the board of directors. The board must ensure that there is a high-ranking manager accountable for the day-to-day operational oversight of the ethics program. The board must provide for adequate authority, resources, and access to the board or an appropriate subcommittee of the board. The board must ensure that there are confidential mechanisms available so that the organization's employees and agents may report or seek guidance about potential or actual misconduct without fear of retaliation.

The FSGO and the Sarbanes–Oxley Act provide incentives for developing core practices that help ensure ethical and legal compliance. Core practices move the emphasis from a focus on the individual's moral capability to developing structurally sound organization core practices and developing structural integrity for both financial performance and nonfinancial performance. The Integrity Institute has developed an integrated model to standardize the measurement of nonfinancial performance. Methodologies have been developed to assess communications, compensation, social responsibility, corporate culture, leadership, risk, and stakeholder perceptions, as well as more subjective aspects of earnings, corporate governance, technology, and other important nonfinancial areas.

Philanthropic issues touch on businesses' social responsibility insofar as businesses contribute to the local community and to society. Philanthropy provides four major benefits to society: improving the quality of life, reducing government involvement, developing staff leadership skills, and building staff morale. Companies contribute significant amounts of money to education, the arts, environmental causes, and the disadvantaged by supporting local and national charitable organizations. Strategic philanthropy involves linking core business competencies to societal and community needs.

IMPORTANT TERMS FOR REVIEW

voluntary practices

philanthropy

core practices

Better Business Bureau

mandated boundaries

civil law

criminal law

procompetitive legislation

consumer protection law

Occupational Safety and Health Administration

sustainability

Environmental Protection Agency

Public Company Accounting Oversight Board

strategic philanthropy

RESOLVING ETHICAL BUSINESS CHALLENGES*

Albert Chen was sweating profusely in his Jaguar on the expressway as he thought about his options and the fact that Christmas and the Chinese New Year were at hand. He and his wife, Mary, who were on their way to meet Albert's parents at New York's John F. Kennedy International Airport, seemed to be looking up from an abyss, with no daylight to be seen. Several visits and phone calls from various people had engulfed both him and Mary.

He had graduated with honors in finance and had married Mary in his senior year. They had both obtained prestigious brokerage jobs in the New York area, and both had been working killer hours to develop their accounts. Listening to other brokers, both had learned that there were some added expenses to their professions. For example, they were told that brokers need to "look" and "act" successful. So Albert and Mary bought the appropriate clothes and cars, joined the right clubs, and ate at the right restaurants with the right people. They also took the advice of others, which was to identify the "players" of large corporations at parties and take mental notes. "You'd be surprised at what information you hear with a little alcohol in these people," said one broker. Both started using this strategy, and five months later their clients began to see significant profits in their portfolios.

Their good luck even came from strange places. For example, Albert had an uncle whose work as a janitor gave him access to many law offices that had information on a number of companies, especially those about to file for bankruptcy. Mary and Albert were able to use information provided by this uncle to benefit their clients' portfolios. The uncle even had some of his friends use Albert. To Albert's surprise, his uncle's friends often had nest eggs in excess of $200,000. Because some of these friends were quite elderly, Albert was given permission to buy and sell nonrisky stocks at will.

Because both of them were earning good salaries, the Chens soon managed to invest in the market themselves, and their investments included stock in the company for which Mary's father worked. After eighteen months, Albert decided to jump ship and start working for Jarvis, Sunni, Lamar & Morten (JSL&M). JSL&M's reputation was that of a fast mover in the business. "We go up to the line and then measure how wide the line is so that we know how far we can go into it," was a common remark at the brokerage firm.

About six months ago, Mary's father, who was with a major health care company, commented that the management team was running the company into the ground. "If only someone could buy the company and put in a good management team," he mused. After the conversation, Mary investigated the company and discovered that the stock was grossly undervalued. She made a few phone calls and found a company that was interested in doing a hostile takeover. Mary also learned from her father that if a new management were acceptable to the union, the union would do everything in its power to oust the old management—by striking, if necessary—and welcome the new one. As things started to materialize, Mary told several of her best clients, who in turn did very well on the stock. This increased her status in the firm, which kept drawing bigger clients.

Albert soon became a player in initial public stock offerings (IPOs) of new companies. Occasionally, when Albert saw a very hot IPO, he would talk to some of his best venture-capital friends, who then bought the IPOs and gained some very good returns. This strategy helped attract some larger players in the market. By this point in his young career, Albert had made a great many friends.

One of those friends was Barry, who worked on the stock floor. As they were talking, Barry mentioned that if Albert wanted to, he, as a favor, when placing orders to buy shares, would occasionally put Albert's or Mary's trade before the client order.

The first sign of trouble came when Mary told Albert about what was happening at her office. "I'm getting e-mail from some of the brokers with off-color jokes and even some nude photos of women and men. I just don't care for it."

"So what are you doing about it?" Albert asked.

"Well, I've just started not even opening my messages if they come from these people," Mary replied.

"What about messages that request that you send them on? What do you do with those?" queried Albert.

"I just e-mail them along without looking at them," was her response.

"This isn't good, Mary. A couple of analysts were just fired for doing that at a big firm last week," said Albert.

Several weeks later the people who were sending Mary the obnoxious messages were fired. Mary was also asked to see the head of her division. When she came to his office, he said, "Please shut the door, Mary. I have some bad news. I know that you weren't involved with what was happening with the e-mail scandal; however, you did forward messages that contained such material. As a result, I have no alternative but to give you your two weeks' notice. I know this is unfair, but I have my orders. Because of this mess, the SEC wants to check all your trades for the last eight months. It seems to be a formality, but it will take time, and as you well know, the chances of going to another firm with that hanging over your head are slim. I'm sorry that it's only two months until the holidays." That night Mary fell into a depression.

To exacerbate the situation, Albert's parents were flying in from the People's Republic of China. They were not happy with Albert's marriage to a non-Chinese woman, but they had consoled themselves that Mary had a good job. They had also said that if things should go badly for them in New York, they could always come to the parents' retirement home in Taiwan. However, the idea of leaving the United States, attempting to learn Mandarin, and raising children in an unfamiliar culture did not appeal to Mary.

Albert was also having some problems. Because their income was cut in half, Albert tried to make up for the loss by trading in some high-risk markets, such as commodities and precious metals. However, many of these investments turned sour, and he found himself buying and selling more and more to pull his own portfolio, as well as those of his clients, into the black. He was getting worried because some of his uncle's friends' portfolios were losing significant value. Other matters, however, were causing him even more anxiety. The previous week Barry had called him, asking for some inside information on several companies that he was working with for an IPO. Albert knew that this could be construed as insider information and had said no.

Today, Barry called again and said, "Look, Al, I've been doing you favors for a while. I need to score big because of the holidays. You probably don't know, but what I've been doing for you could be construed as spinning, which is not looked upon favorably. I'm not asking for the IPO information—I'm demanding it. Is that clear enough for you, Al? E-mail it over by tomorrow morning." Then Barry hung up.

An hour later Albert's supervisor came in and said, "Al, I need a favor from you. I want you to buy some stock for a few friends and me. When it goes to $112, I want you to sell it. We'll pay the taxes and give you a little bonus for Christmas as well. I want you to buy tomorrow as soon as the market opens. Here are the account numbers for the transaction. I must run. See you tomorrow."

QUESTIONS • EXERCISES

1. Identify the ethical and legal issues of which Albert needs to be aware.
2. Discuss the advantages and disadvantages of each decision that Albert could make and has made.
3. Identify the pressures that have brought about these issues.

*This case is strictly hypothetical; any resemblance to real persons, companies, or situations is coincidental.

CHECK YOUR EQ

Check your EQ, or Ethics Quotient, by completing the following. Assess your performance to evaluate your overall understanding of the chapter material.

1. Voluntary practices include documented best practices **Yes No**
2. The primary method for resolving business ethics disputes is through the criminal court system. **Yes No**
3. The FSGO provides an incentive for organizations to conscientiously develop and implement ethics programs. **Yes No**
4. The Sarbanes–Oxley Act encourages CEOs and CFOs to report their financial statements accurately. **Yes No**
5. Strategic philanthropy represents a new direction in corporate giving that maximizes the benefit to societal or community needs and relates to business objectives. **Yes No**

ANSWERS **1. No.** Core practices are documented best practices. **2. No.** Lawsuits and civil litigation are the primary way in which business ethics disputes are resolved. **3. Yes.** Well-designed ethics and compliance programs can minimize legal liability when organizational misconduct is detected. **4. No.** The Sarbanes–Oxley Act *requires* CEOs and CFOs to accurately report their financial statements to a federal oversight committee; they must sign the document and are held personally liable for any inaccuracies. **5. Yes.** Strategic philanthropy helps both society and the organization.

PART 3
The Decision Making Process

CHAPTER 5

Ethical Decision Making and Ethical Leadership

CHAPTER OBJECTIVES

- To provide a comprehensive framework for ethical decision making in business
- To examine the intensity of ethical issues as an important element influencing the ethical decision making process
- To introduce individual factors that may influence ethical decision making in business
- To introduce organizational factors that may influence ethical decision making in business
- To explore the role of opportunity in ethical decision making in business
- To explain how knowledge about the ethical decision making framework can be used to improve ethical leadership
- To provide leadership styles and habits that promote an ethical culture

CHAPTER OUTLINE

AN ETHICAL DILEMMA*

Bill Church was in a bind. A recent graduate of a prestigious business school, he had taken a job in the auditing division of Greenspan & Company, a fast-growing leader in the accounting industry. Greenspan relocated Bill, his wife, and their 1-year-old daughter from the Midwest to the East Coast. On arriving, they bought their first home and a second car. Bill was told that the company had big plans for him. Thus, he did not worry about being financially overextended.

Several months into the job, Bill found that he was working late into the night to complete his auditing assignments. He realized that the company did not want its clients billed for excessive hours and that he needed to become more efficient if he wanted to move up in the company. He asked one of his friends, Ann, how she managed to be so efficient in auditing client records.

Ann quietly explained: "Bill, there are times when being efficient isn't enough. You need to do what is required to get ahead. The partners just want results—they don't care how you get them."

"I don't understand," said Bill.

"Look," Ann explained, "I had the same problem you have a few years ago, but Mr. Reed [the manager of the auditing department] explained that everyone 'eats time' so that the group shows top results and looks good. And when the group looks good, everyone in it looks good. No one cares if a little time gets lost in the shuffle."

Bill realized that "eating time" meant not reporting all the hours required to complete a project. He also remembered one of Reed's classic catch phrases, "results, results, results." He thanked Ann for her input and went back to work. Bill thought of going over Reed's head and asking for advice from the division manager, but he had met her only once and did not know anything about her.

QUESTIONS • EXERCISES

1. What should Bill do?
2. Describe the process through which Bill might attempt to resolve his dilemma.
3. Consider the impact of this company's approach on young accountants. How could working long hours be an ethical problem?

*This case is strictly hypothetical; any resemblance to real persons, companies, or situations is coincidental.

To improve ethical decision making in business, one must first understand how individuals make ethical decisions in an organizational environment. Too often it is assumed that individuals in organizations make ethical decisions in the same way that they make ethical decisions at home, in their family, or in their personal lives. Within the context of an organizational work group, however, few individuals have the freedom to decide ethical issues independent of organizational pressures.

This chapter summarizes our current knowledge of ethical decision making in business and provides insights into ethical decision making in organizations. Although it is impossible to describe exactly how any one individual or work group might make ethical decisions, we can offer generalizations about average or typical behavior patterns within organizations. These generalizations are based on many studies and at least six ethical decision models that have been widely accepted by academics and practitioners.[1] Based on these models, we present a framework for understanding ethical decision making in the context of business organizations. In addition to business, this framework integrates concepts from philosophy, psychology, sociology, and organizational behavior. This framework should be helpful in understanding organizational ethics and developing ethical programs.

A FRAMEWORK FOR ETHICAL DECISION MAKING IN BUSINESS

As Figure 5–1 shows, our model of the ethical decision making process in business includes ethical issue intensity, individual factors, and organizational factors such as corporate culture and opportunity. All of these interrelated factors influence the evaluations of and intentions behind the decisions that produce ethical or unethical behavior. This model does not describe how to make ethical decisions, but it does help one to understand the factors and processes related to ethical decision making.

FIGURE 5–1 Framework for Understanding Ethical Decision Making in Business

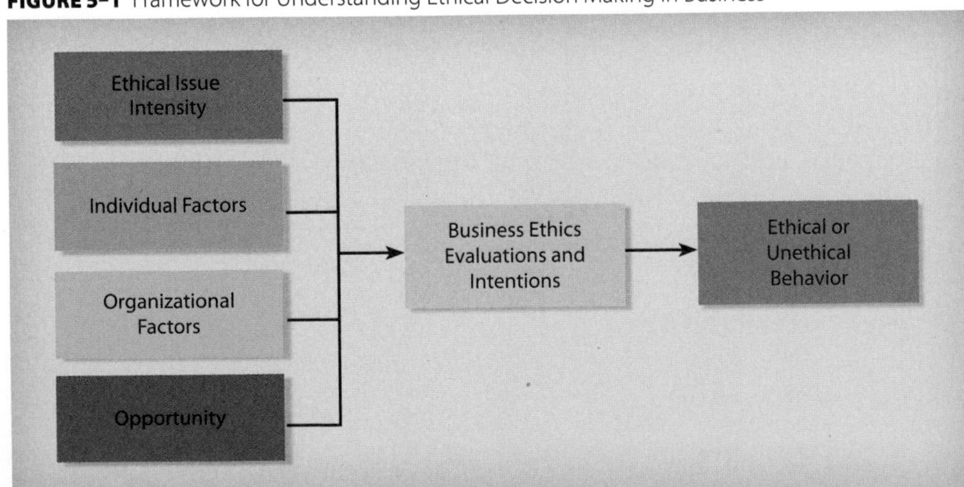

Ethical Issue Intensity

The first step in ethical decision making is to recognize that an ethical issue requires an individual or work group to choose among several actions that various stakeholders inside or outside the firm will ultimately evaluate as right or wrong. The intensity of an ethical issue relates to its perceived importance to the decision maker.[2] **Ethical issue intensity**, then, can be defined as the relevance or importance of an ethical issue in the eyes of the individual, work group, and/or organization. It is personal and temporal in character to accommodate values, beliefs, needs, perceptions, the special characteristics of the situation, and the personal pressures prevailing at a particular place and time.[3] Senior employees and those with administrative authority contribute significantly to intensity because they typically dictate an organization's stance on ethical issues. In fact, under current law, managers can be held liable for the unethical and illegal actions of subordinates. In the United States, the Federal Sentencing Guidelines for Organizations have a liability formula that judges those who are in positions of authority in regard to their action or inaction regarding the unethical and illegal activities of those around them. For example, many of the Enron employees and managers who were aware of the firm's use of off-balance-sheet partnerships—which turned out to be the major cause of the energy firm's collapse—were advised that these partnerships were legal, so they did not perceive them as an ethical issue. Although such partnerships were in fact legal at that time, the way that some Enron officials designed them and the methods they used to provide collateral (that is, Enron stock) created a scheme that brought about the collapse of the company.[4] Thus, ethical issue intensity involves individuals' cognitive state of concern about an issue, whether or not they have knowledge that an issue is unethical, which indicates their involvement in making choices.

Ethical issue intensity reflects the ethical sensitivity of the individual or work group that faces the ethical decision making process. Research suggests that individuals are subject to six "spheres of influence" when confronted with ethical choices—the workplace, family, religion, legal system, community, and profession—and that the level of importance of each of these influences will vary depending on how important the decision maker perceives the issue to be.[5] Additionally, the individual's sense of the situation's moral intensity increases the individual's perceptiveness regarding ethical problems, which in turn reduces his or her intention to act unethically.[6] **Moral intensity** relates to a person's perception of social pressure and the harm the decision will have on others.[7] All other factors in Figure 5–1, including individual factors, organizational factors, and intentions, determine why different individuals perceive ethical issues differently. Unless individuals in an organization share common concerns about ethical issues, the stage is set for ethical conflict. The perception of ethical issue intensity can be influenced by management's use of rewards and punishments, corporate policies, and corporate values to sensitize employees. In other words, managers can affect the degree to which employees perceive the importance of an ethical issue through positive and/or negative incentives.[8]

For some employees, ethical issues may not reach the critical awareness level if managers fail to identify and educate employees about specific problem areas. Subprime lenders, such as Countrywide Finance, failed to educate brokers about the damages of misrepresenting financial data to help individuals secure loans. Organizations that consist of employees with diverse values and backgrounds must train them in the way the firm wants specific ethical issues handled. Identifying the ethical issues and risks that employees might encounter is a significant step toward developing their ability to make ethical decisions. Many ethical issues are identified by industry groups or through general information available to a firm. Companies must assess areas of ethical and legal risk that are in reality ethical issues. Issues that are communicated as being high in ethical importance could trigger increases in employees' ethical issue intensity. The perceived importance of an ethical issue has been found to have a strong influence on both employees' ethical judgment and their behavioral intention. In other words, the more likely individuals are to perceive an ethical issue as important, the less likely they are to engage in questionable or unethical behavior.[9] Therefore, ethical issue intensity should be considered a key factor in the ethical decision making process.

Individual Factors

When people need to resolve ethical issues in their daily lives, they often base their decisions on their own values and principles of right or wrong. They generally learn these values and principles through the socialization process with family members, social groups, and religion and in their formal education. The actions of specific individuals in scandal-plagued companies such as AIG, Countrywide Financial, Fannie Mae, and Freddie Mac often raise questions about those individuals' personal character and integrity. They appear to operate in their own self-interest or in total disregard of the law and interests of society. Fannie Mae has become one of the high-profile figures in the 2008–2009 financial meltdown. It is a stockholder-owned corporation created to purchase and securitize mortgages, and was a key figure in the subprime mortgage debacle.[10] Many people granted mortgages by Fannie Mae were not strong candidates to receive mortgages, and their homes have since been foreclosed. Civil charges had already been filed against Fannie Mae's CEO, CFO, and the former controller, who allegedly manipulated earnings to increase their bonuses. CEO Daniel Mudd was also investigated for lying to investors about earnings. Bad decisions and managerial misconduct clearly contributed to the company's downfall.[11]

"The more likely individuals are to perceive an ethical issue as important, the less likely they are to engage in questionable or unethical behavior."

In the workplace, personal ethical issues typically involve honesty, conflicts of interest, discrimination, nepotism, and theft of organizational resources. For example, many individuals use the company computer system for several hours of work time a day for personal reasons. Most employees limit the use of their work time for personal use, and most companies probably overlook these as reasonable. Some employees, however, use times in excess of 30 minutes for personal Internet communications, which companies are likely to view as an excessive use of company time for personal reasons. The decision to use company time for personal affairs is an example of an ethical decision. It illustrates the fine line between what may be acceptable or unacceptable in a business environment. It also reflects how well an individual will assume responsibilities in the work environment. Often this decision will depend on company policy and the corporate environment.

The way the public perceives individual ethics generally varies according to the profession in question. Telemarketers, car salespersons, advertising practitioners, stockbrokers, and real estate brokers are often perceived as having the lowest ethics. Research regarding individual factors that affect ethical awareness, judgment, intent, and behavior include gender, education, work experience, nationality, age, and locus of control.

Extensive research has been done regarding the link between **gender** and ethical decision making. The research shows that in many aspects there are no differences between men and women, but when differences are found, women are generally more ethical than men.[12] By "more ethical," we mean that women seem to be more sensitive to ethical scenarios and less tolerant of unethical actions. In a study on gender and intentions for fraudulent financial reporting, females reported higher intentions to report them than male participants.[13] As more and more women work in managerial positions, these findings may become increasingly significant.

Education, the number of years spent in pursuit of academic knowledge, is also a significant factor in the ethical decision making process. The important thing to remember about education is that it does not reflect experience. Work experience is defined as the number of years within a specific job, occupation, and/or industry. Generally, the more education or work experience that one has, the better he or she is at ethical decision making. The type of education has little or no effect on ethics. For example, it doesn't matter if you are a business student or a liberal arts student—you are pretty much the same in terms of ethical decision making. Current research, however, shows that students are less ethical than businesspeople, which is likely because businesspeople have been exposed to more ethically challenging situations than students.[14]

Nationality is the legal relationship between a person and the country in which he or she is born. Within the twenty-first century, nationality is being redefined by regional economic integration such as the European Union (EU). When European students are asked their nationality, they are less likely to state where they were born than where they currently live. The same thing is happening in the United States, as someone born in Florida who lives in New York might consider him- or herself to be a New Yorker. Research about nationality and ethics appears to be significant in that it affects ethical decision making; however, the true effect is somewhat hard to interpret.[15] Because of cultural differences, it is impossible to state that ethical decision making in an organizational context will differ significantly. The reality of today is that multinational companies look for businesspeople who can make decisions regardless of nationality. Perhaps in twenty years, nationality will no longer be an issue in that the multinational's culture will replace the national status as the most significant factor in ethical decision making.

Age is another individual factor that has been researched within business ethics. Several decades ago, we believed that age was positively correlated with ethical decision making. In other words, the older you are, the more ethical you are. However, recent research suggests that there is probably a more complex relationship between ethics and age.[16] We do believe that older employees with more experience have greater knowledge to deal with complex industry-specific ethical issues.

Locus of control relates to individual differences in relation to a generalized belief about how one is affected by internal versus external events or reinforcements. In other words, the concept relates to where people view themselves in relation to power. Those who believe in **external control** (that is, externals) see themselves as going with the flow because that's all they can do. They believe that the events in their lives are due to uncontrollable forces. They consider that what they want to achieve depends on luck, chance, and powerful people in their company. In addition, they believe that the probability of being able to control their lives by their own actions and efforts is low. Conversely, those who believe in **internal control** (that is, internals) believe that they control the events in their lives by their own effort and skill, viewing themselves as masters of their destinies and trusting in their capacity to influence their environment.

Current research suggests that we still can't be sure how significant locus of control is in terms of ethical decision making. One study that found a relationship between locus of control and ethical decision making concluded that internals were positively related whereas externals were negative.[17] In other words, those who believe that their fate is in the hands of others were more ethical than those who believed that they formed their own destiny.

Organizational Factors

Although people can and do make individual ethical choices in business situations, no one operates in a vacuum. Indeed, research has established that in the workplace the organization's values often have greater influence on decisions than a person's own values.[18] Ethical choices in business are most often made jointly, in work groups and committees, or in conversations and discussions with coworkers. Employees approach ethical issues on the basis of what they have learned not only from their own backgrounds but also from others in the organization. The outcome of this learning process depends on the strength of each person's personal values, the opportunities he or she has to behave unethically, and the exposure he or she has to others who behave ethically or unethically. Although people outside the organization, such as family members and friends, also influence decision makers, an organization's culture and structure operate through the relationships of its members to influence their ethical decisions.

A **corporate culture** can be defined as a set of values, norms, and artifacts, including ways of solving problems that members (employees) of an organization share. As time passes, stakeholders come to view the company or organization as a living organism, with a mind and will of its own. The Walt Disney Company, for example, requires all new employees to take a course in the traditions and history of Disneyland and Walt Disney, including the ethical dimensions of the company. The corporate culture at American Express Company stresses that employees help customers out of difficult situations whenever possible. This attitude is reinforced through numerous company legends of employees who have gone above and beyond the call of duty to help customers. This strong tradition of customer loyalty thus might encourage an American Express employee to take unorthodox steps to help a customer who encounters a problem while traveling overseas. Employees learn that they can take some risks in helping customers. Such strong traditions and values have become a driving force in many companies, including McDonald's, IBM, Procter & Gamble, Southwest Airlines, and Hershey Foods.

> *"The more ethical employees perceive an organization's culture to be, the less likely they are to make unethical decisions."*

An important component of corporate, or organizational, culture is the company's ethical culture. Whereas corporate culture involves values and norms that prescribe a wide range of behavior for organizational members, the **ethical culture** reflects whether the firm also has an ethical conscience. Ethical culture is a function of many factors, including corporate policies on ethics, top management's leadership on ethical issues, the influence of coworkers, and the opportunity for unethical behavior. Within the organization as a whole, subclimates can develop within individual departments or work groups, but they are influenced by the strength of the firm's overall ethical culture, as well as the function of the department and the stakeholders it serves.[19]

The more ethical employees perceive an organization's culture to be, the less likely they are to make unethical decisions. Corporate culture and ethical culture are closely associated with the idea that significant others within the organization help determine ethical decisions within that organization. Research also indicates that the ethical values embodied in an organization's culture are positively related to employees' commitment to the firm and their sense that they fit into the company. These findings suggest that companies should develop and promote ethical values to enhance employees' experiences in the workplace.[20]

Those who have influence in a work group, including peers, managers, coworkers, and subordinates, are referred to as **significant others**. They help workers on a daily basis with unfamiliar tasks and provide advice and information in both formal and informal ways.

Coworkers, for instance, can offer help in the comments they make in discussions over lunch or when the boss is away. Likewise, a manager may provide directives about certain types of activities that employees perform on the job. Indeed, an employee's supervisor can play a central role in helping employees develop and fit in socially in the workplace.[21] Numerous studies conducted over the years confirm that significant others within an organization may have more impact on a worker's decisions on a daily basis than any other factor.[22]

Obedience to authority is another aspect of the influence that significant others can exercise. Obedience to authority helps to explain why many employees resolve business ethics issues by simply following the directives of a superior. In organizations that emphasize respect for superiors, for example, employees may feel that they are expected to carry out orders by a supervisor even if those orders are contrary to the employees' sense of right and wrong. Later, if the employee's decision is judged to have been wrong, he or she is likely to say, "I was only carrying out orders" or "My boss told me to do it this way." In addition, the type of industry and the size of the organization have also been researched and found to be relevant factors; the bigger the company, the more potential for unethical activities.[23]

Opportunity

Opportunity describes the conditions in an organization that limit or permit ethical or unethical behavior. Opportunity results from conditions that either provide rewards, whether internal or external, or fail to erect barriers against unethical behavior. Examples of internal rewards include feelings of goodness and personal worth generated by performing altruistic acts. External rewards refer to what an individual expects to receive from others in the social environment. Rewards are external to the individual to the degree that they bring social approval, status, and esteem.

An example of a condition that fails to erect barriers against unethical behavior is a company policy that does not punish employees who accept large gifts from clients. The absence of punishment essentially provides an opportunity for unethical behavior because it allows individuals to engage in such behavior without fear of consequences. The prospect of a reward for unethical behavior can also create an opportunity for questionable decisions. For example, a salesperson who is given public recognition and a large bonus for making a valuable sale that he or she obtained through unethical tactics will probably be motivated to use such tactics in the future, even if such behavior goes against the salesperson's personal value system. If 10 percent of employees report observing others at the workplace abusing drugs or alcohol, then the opportunity to engage in these activities exists if there is a failure to report and respond to this conduct.[24]

Opportunity relates to individuals' **immediate job context**—where they work, whom they work with, and the nature of the work. The immediate job context includes the motivational "carrots and sticks" that superiors use to influence employee behavior. Pay raises, bonuses, and public recognition act as carrots, or positive reinforcements, whereas demotions, firings, reprimands, and pay penalties act as sticks, the negative reinforcements. The United States Chamber of Commerce reports that 75 percent of employees steal from their workplaces, and most do so repeatedly.[25] As Figure 5–2 shows, many employees pilfer office-supply rooms for matters unrelated to the job. It is possible that the opportunity is provided, and in some cases, there are no concerns if employees take pens, Post-its, envelopes, notepads, and paper. Respondents to the survey by Vault.com indicated that 25 percent felt that no one cared if they took office supplies, 34 percent said that they never

FIGURE 5–2 Items that Employees Pilfer in the Workplace

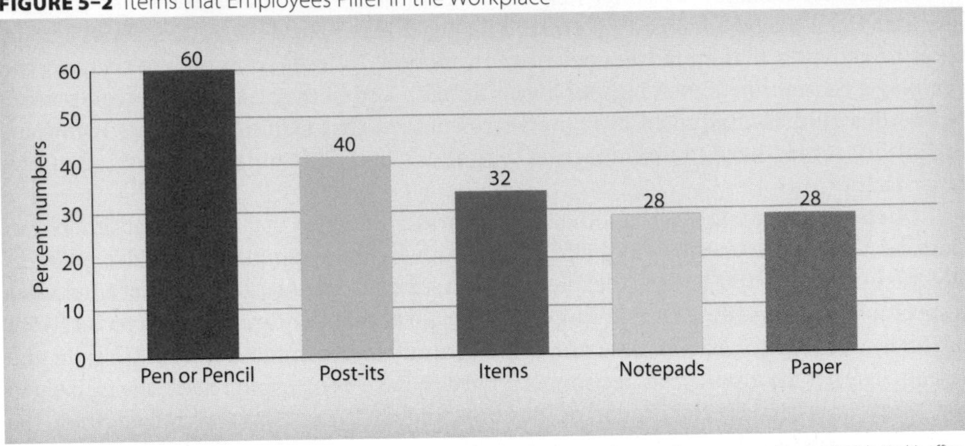

Source: "Top Items Employees Pilfer," the most popular items employees take from office-supply rooms for matters unrelated to the job. Vault's office survey of 1,152 respondents. In Snapshots, *USA Today*, March 29, 2006, B1.

got caught, and 1 percent said that they were caught and got in trouble. If there is no policy against this practice, one concern is that employees will not learn where to draw the line and will get into the habit of taking even more expensive items for personal use.

The opportunity that employees have for unethical behavior in an organization can be eliminated through formal codes, policies, and rules that are adequately enforced by management. For example, financial companies—such as banks, savings and loan associations, and securities companies—have developed elaborate sets of rules and procedures to avoid the opportunity for individual employees to manipulate or take advantage of their trusted position. In banks, one such rule requires most employees to take a vacation and stay out of the bank a certain number of days every year so that they cannot be physically present to cover up embezzlement or other diversion of funds. This rule prevents the opportunity for inappropriate conduct. Even after audits by prestigious accounting firm PricewaterhouseCoopers, the founder and chairman of one of India's largest technology companies, Satyam Computer Services Ltd., admitted he invented financial results, including a fictitious cash balance of more than $1 billion. He was able to overstate profits and understate liabilities. This was allowed to happen, even though Satyam had independent directors, including a Harvard business school professor, on its board. The question is: How did the CEO manage to blatantly manipulate financial information without anyone catching on? There had to be loopholes in the oversight of the company's accounting, audits, and corporate governance that allowed this fraud. In addition, government regulation of financial reporting allowed the opportunity for misconduct. To avoid situations like this in the future, there must be checks and balances that create transparency.[26]

Opportunity also comes from knowledge. Major misconduct observed among employees in the workplace include lying to employees, customers, vendors, or the public or withholding needed information from them.[27] A person who has an information base, expertise, or information about the competition has the opportunity to exploit this knowledge. An individual can be a source of information because he or she is familiar with the organization. Individuals who have been employed by one organization for many years become "gatekeepers" of its culture and often have the opportunity to make decisions related to unwritten traditions and rules. They help socialize newer employees to abide by the rules and norms of the company's internal and external ways of doing business, as well as understanding when the opportunity exists to cross the line. They may function as mentors or supervise managers in training. Like drill sergeants in the army, these trainers mold the new recruits into what the company wants. This can contribute to either ethical or unethical conduct.

The opportunity for unethical behavior cannot be eliminated without aggressive enforcement of codes and rules. A national jewelry store–chain president explained to us how he dealt with a jewelry buyer in one of his stores who had taken a bribe from a supplier. There was an explicit company policy against taking incentive payments in order to deal with a specific supplier. When the president of the firm learned that one of his buyers had taken a bribe, he immediately traveled to that buyer's office and terminated his employment. He then traveled to the supplier (manufacturer) selling jewelry to his stores and terminated his relationship with the firm. The message was clear: Taking a bribe is unacceptable for the store's buyers, and salespeople from supplying companies could cost their firm significant sales by offering bribes. This type of policy enforcement illustrates how the opportunity to commit unethical acts can be eliminated.

Business Ethics Evaluations and Intentions

Ethical dilemmas involve problem-solving situations in which decision rules are often vague or in conflict. The results of an ethical decision are often uncertain; no one can always tell us whether we have made the right decision. There are no magic formulas, nor is there computer software that ethical dilemmas can be plugged into for a solution. Even if they mean well, most businesspeople will make ethical mistakes. Thus, there is no substitute for critical thinking and the ability to take responsibility for our own decisions.

An individual's intentions and the final decision regarding what action he or she will take are the last steps in the ethical decision making process. When the individual's intentions and behavior are inconsistent with his or her ethical judgment, the person may feel guilty. For example, when an advertising account executive is asked by her client to create an advertisement that she perceives as misleading, she has two alternatives: to comply or to refuse. If she refuses, she stands to lose business from that client and possibly her job. Other factors—such as pressure from the client, the need to keep her job to pay her debts and living expenses, and the possibility of a raise if she develops the advertisement successfully—may influence her resolution of this ethical dilemma. Because of these other factors, she may decide to act unethically and develop the advertisement even though she believes it to be inaccurate. Because her actions are inconsistent with her ethical judgment, she will probably feel guilty about her decision.

Guilt or uneasiness is the first sign that an unethical decision has occurred. The next step is changing one's behavior to reduce such feelings. This change can reflect a person's values shifting to fit the decision or the person changing his or her decision type the next time a similar situation occurs. Finally, one can eliminate some of the situational factors by quitting. For those who begin the value shift, the following are the usual justifications that will reduce and finally eliminate guilt:

1. I need the paycheck and can't afford to quit right now.
2. Those around me are doing it so why shouldn't I? They believe it's okay.
3. If I don't do this, I might not be able to get a good reference from my boss or company when I leave.

4. This is not such a big deal, given the potential benefits.
5. Business is business with a different set of rules.
6. If not me, someone else would do it and get rewarded.

The road to success depends on how the businessperson defines *success*. The success concept drives intentions and behavior in business either implicitly or explicitly. Money, security, family, power, wealth, and personal or group gratification are all types of success measures that people use. The list described is not comprehensive, and in the next chapter, you will understand more about how success can be defined. Another concept that affects behavior is the probability of rewards and punishments. That too will be explained further in Chapter 6.

USING THE ETHICAL DECISION MAKING FRAMEWORK TO IMPROVE ETHICAL DECISIONS

The ethical decision making framework presented in this chapter cannot tell you if a business decision is ethical or unethical. It bears repeating that it is impossible to tell you what is right or wrong; instead, we are attempting to prepare you to make informed ethical decisions. Although this chapter does not moralize by telling you what to do in a specific situation, it does provide an overview of typical decision making processes and factors that influence ethical decisions. The framework is not a guide for how to make decisions but is intended to provide you with insights and knowledge about typical ethical decision making processes in business organizations.

Because it is impossible to agree on normative judgments about what is ethical, business ethics scholars developing descriptive models have instead focused on regularities in decision making and the various phenomena that interact in a dynamic environment to produce predictable behavioral patterns. Furthermore, it is unlikely that an organization's ethical problems will be solved strictly by having a thorough knowledge about how ethical decisions are made. By its very nature, business ethics involves value judgments and collective agreement about acceptable patterns of behavior.

We propose that gaining an understanding of typical ethical decision making in business organizations will reveal several ways that such decision making could be improved. With more knowledge about how the decision process works, you will be better prepared to analyze critical ethical dilemmas and to provide ethical leadership regardless of your role in the organization. One important conclusion that should be taken from our framework is that ethical decision making within an organization does not rely strictly on the personal values and morals of individuals. Knowledge of moral philosophies or principles must be balanced with business knowledge and understanding of the complexities of the dilemma requiring a decision. For example, a manager who embraces honesty, fairness, and equity has to understand the diverse risks associated with a complex financial instrument such as options or derivatives. Business competence must exist, along with personal accountability, in ethical decisions. Organizations take on a culture of their own, with managers and coworkers exerting a significant influence on ethical decisions.

THE ROLE OF LEADERSHIP IN A CORPORATE CULTURE

Top managers provide a blueprint for what a firm's corporate culture should be.[28] If these leaders fail to express desired behaviors and goals, a corporate culture will evolve on its own but will still reflect the values and norms of the company. **Leadership,** the ability or authority to guide and direct others toward achievement of a goal, has a significant impact on ethical decision making because leaders have the power to motivate others and enforce the organization's norms and policies as well as their own viewpoints. Leaders are key to influencing an organization's corporate culture and ethical posture. However, one poll found that less than half (47 percent) of employees in large (2,500 employees or more) organizations think that the senior leadership in their firm is highly ethical.[29]

Although we often think of CEOs and other top managers as the most important leaders in an organization, the corporate governance reforms discussed in Chapter 4 make it clear that a firm's board of directors is also an important leadership component. Indeed, directors have a legal obligation to manage companies "for the best interests of the corporation." To determine what is in the best interest of the firm, directors can consider the effects that a decision may have on not only shareholders and employees but also other important stakeholders.[30] Therefore, when we discuss leadership, we include the corporate directors as well as top executives.

In the long run, if stakeholders are not reasonably satisfied with a company's leader, he or she will not retain a leadership position. A leader must have not only his or her followers' respect but also provide a standard of ethical conduct to them. Former chairman of Korean electronics giant Samsung Group, Lee Kun-hee, resigned in disgraced after 20 years on the Samsung board after being accused of evading $128 million in taxes. His son and heir to the company, Lee Jae-yong, also resigned from the board. This was only the final in a long string of corruption charges against Lee. He was also convicted of bribery 10 years ago. Since his resignation, the company has sought to improve its image.[31] Table 5–1 summarizes the steps executives should take to demonstrate that they understand the importance of ethics in doing business.

TABLE 5–1 The Managerial Role in Developing Ethics Program Leadership

1. Organizational commitment from board of directors and top management
2. Organizational resources for ethics initiatives
3. Determine ethical risks and develop contingency plans
4. Develop an effective ethics program to address risks and maintain compliance with ethical standards
5. Provide oversight for implementation and audits of ethical programs
6. Communicate with stakeholders to establish shared commitment and values for ethical conduct.

LEADERSHIP STYLES INFLUENCE ETHICAL DECISIONS

Leadership styles influence many aspects of organizational behavior, including employees' acceptance of and adherence to organizational norms and values. Styles that focus on building strong organizational values among employees contribute to shared standards of conduct. They also influence the organization's transmittal and monitoring of values, norms, and codes of ethics.[32] In short, the leadership style of an organization influences how its employees act. For example, the management philosophy of Mike Armstrong, former CEO of AT&T, is characterized by the observations of its lab's chief, David Nagel: "Most bosses hate conflict. Mike is delighted when he sees us getting at each other." Armstrong has been characterized as scary, demanding, a taskmaster, and a maniac—in an affectionate way. The fast-paced, intensely competitive telecommunications industry requires a "nontraditional" leadership style to achieve success.[33] Studying a firm's leadership styles and attitudes can also help pinpoint where future ethical issues may arise. Even for actions that may be against the law, employees often look to their organizational leaders to determine how to resolve the issue.

> ***"The ethical leadership concept is not only for CEOs, boards of directors, and managers but can also be fellow employees."***

Although we often think of CEOs and other top managers as the most important leaders in an organization, a firm's board of directors is also a required leadership and an oversight component. The ethical leadership concept is not only for CEOs, boards of directors, and managers but can also be fellow employees. Ethical leadership by the CEO requires an understanding of the firm's vision and values, as well as the challenges of responsibility and the risk in achieving organizational objectives. Lapses in ethical leadership can occur even in people who possess strong ethical character, especially if they view the organization's ethical culture as being outside the realm of decision making that exists in the home, family, and community. This phenomenon has been observed in countless cases of so-called good community citizens engaging in unethical business activities. For example, Robin Szeliga, former CFO of Qwest, who pleaded guilty for insider trading, was an excellent community leader, even serving on a college of business advisory board.

Ethical leaders need both knowledge and experience to make decisions. Strong ethical leaders must have the right kind of moral integrity. Such integrity must be transparent or, in other words, do in private as if it were always public. This type of integrity relates to values and is discussed in later chapters. They must be proactive and ready to leave the organization if its corporate governance system makes it impossible to make the right choice. Such right choices are complex by definition. The ethical leader must choose a balance of all involved today as well as in the future. Such a person must be concerned with shareholders as well as the lowest-paid employee. Experience shows that no leader can always be right or judged ethical by stakeholders in every case. The acknowledgment of this may be perceived as a weakness, but in reality it supports integrity and increases the debate exchange of views on ethics and openness.

Six leadership styles that are based on emotional intelligence—the ability to manage ourselves and our relationships effectively—have been identified by Daniel Goleman.[34]

1. The coercive leader demands instantaneous obedience and focuses on achievement, initiative, and self-control. Although this style can be very effective during times of

crisis or during a turnaround, it otherwise creates a negative climate for organizational performance.

2. The authoritative leader—considered to be one of the most effective styles—inspires employees to follow a vision, facilitates change, and creates a strongly positive performance climate.

3. The affiliative leader values people, their emotions, and their needs and relies on friendship and trust to promote flexibility, innovation, and risk taking.

4. The democratic leader relies on participation and teamwork to reach collaborative decisions. This style focuses on communication and creates a positive climate for achieving results.

5. The pacesetting leader can create a negative climate because of the high standards that he or she sets. This style works best for attaining quick results from highly motivated individuals who value achievement and take the initiative.

6. The coaching leader builds a positive climate by developing skills to foster long-term success, delegating responsibility, and skillfully issuing challenging assignments.

The most successful leaders do not rely on one style but alter their techniques based on the characteristics of the situation. Different styles can be effective in developing an ethical culture depending on the leader's assessment of risks and desire to achieve a positive climate for organizational performance.

Another way to consider leadership styles is to classify them as transactional or transformational. **Transactional leaders** attempt to create employee satisfaction through negotiating, or "bartering," for desired behaviors or levels of performance. **Transformational leaders** strive to raise employees' level of commitment and to foster trust and motivation.[35] Both transformational and transactional leaders can positively influence the corporate culture.

Transformational leaders communicate a sense of mission, stimulate new ways of thinking, and enhance as well as generate new learning experiences. They consider employee needs and aspirations in conjunction with organizational needs. They also build commitment and respect for values that provide agreement on how to deal with ethical issues.

Thus, transformational leaders strive to promote activities and behavior through a shared vision and common learning experience. As a result, they have a stronger influence on coworker support for ethical decisions and building an ethical culture than do transactional leaders. Transformational ethical leadership is best suited for organizations that have higher levels of ethical commitment among employees and strong stakeholder support for an ethical culture. A number of industry trade associations—including the American Institute of Certified Public Accountants, Defense Industry Initiative on Business Ethics and Conduct, Ethics and Compliance Officer Association, and Mortgage Bankers Association of America—are helping companies provide transformational leadership.[36]

In contrast, transactional leaders focus on ensuring that required conduct and procedures are implemented. Their negotiations to achieve desired outcomes result in a dynamic relationship with subordinates in which reactions, conflict, and crisis influence the relationship more than ethical concerns. Transactional leaders produce employees who achieve a negotiated level of performance, including compliance with ethical and legal standards. As long as employees and leaders both find this exchange mutually rewarding, the relationship is likely to be successful. However, transactional leadership is best suited for rapidly changing situations, including those that require responses to ethical problems or issues. When Eric Pillmore took over as senior vice president of corporate governance at Tyco, after a major scandal involving CEO Dennis Kozlowski, the company needed transitional leadership. To turn the company around, many ethics and corporate governance decisions needed to be made quickly. The company also needed cross-functional leadership, improved accountability, and empowered leaders in order to improve corporate culture. Pillmore helped install a new ethics program that changed leadership policies and allowed him direct communications with the board in order to help implement the leadership transition.[37]

HABITS OF STRONG ETHICAL LEADERS

Archie Carroll, a University of Georgia business professor, crafted "7 Habits of Highly Moral Leaders" based on the idea of Stephen Covey's *The 7 Habits of Highly Effective People.*[38] We have adapted Carroll's "7 Habits of Highly Moral Leaders"[39] to create our own "Seven Habits of Strong Ethical Leaders" (Table 5–2). In particular, we believe that ethical leadership is based on holistic thinking that embraces the complex and challenging issues that companies face on a daily basis. Ethical leaders need both knowledge and experience to make the right decision. Strong ethical leaders have both the courage and the most complete information to make decisions that will be the best in the long run. Strong ethical leaders must stick to their principles and, if necessary, be ready to leave the organization if its corporate governance system is so flawed that it is impossible to make the right choice.

Many corporate founders—such as Sam Walton, Bill Gates, Milton Hershey, Michael Dell, and Steve Jobs, as well as Ben Cohen and Jerry Greenfield—left their ethical stamp on their companies. Their conduct set the tone, making them role models for desired conduct in the early growth of their respective corporations. In the case of Milton Hershey, his legacy endures, and Hershey Foods continues to be a role model for ethical corporate culture. In the case of Sam Walton, Wal-Mart embarked on a course of rapid growth after his death and became involved in numerous conflicts with various stakeholder groups, especially employees, regulators, competitors, and communities. Despite the ethical foundation left by Sam Walton, Wal-Mart, as well as most large corporations, deals with hundreds of reported ethical lapses every month.[40]

TABLE 5–2 Seven Habits of Strong Ethical Leaders

1. Ethical leaders have strong personal character.
2. Ethical leaders have a passion to do right.
3. Ethical leaders are proactive.
4. Ethical leaders consider stakeholders' interests.
5. Ethical leaders are role models for the organization's values.
6. Ethical leaders are transparent and actively involved in organizational decision making.
7. Ethical leaders are competent managers who take a holistic view of the firm's ethical culture.

Ethical Leaders Have Strong Personal Character

There is general agreement that ethical leadership is highly unlikely without a strong personal character. The question is how to teach or develop a moral person in a corporate environment. Thomas I. White, a leading authority on character development, believes the focus should be on "ethical reasoning" rather than on being a "moral person." According to White, the ability to resolve the complex ethical dilemmas encountered in a corporate culture requires intellectual skills.[41] For example, when Lawrence S. Benjamin took over as president of U.S. Food Service after a major ethical disaster, he initiated an ethics and compliance program to promote transparency and to teach employees how to make difficult ethical choices. A fundamental problem in traditional character development is that specific values and virtues are used to teach a belief or philosophy. This approach may be inappropriate for a business environment where cultural diversity and privacy must be respected. On the other hand, teaching individuals who want to do the right thing regarding corporate values and ethical codes, and equipping them with the intellectual skills to address the complexities of ethical issues, is the correct approach.

Ethical Leaders Have a Passion to Do Right

The passion to do right is "the glue that holds ethical concepts together." Some leaders develop this trait early in life, whereas others develop it over time through experience, reason, or spiritual growth. They often cite familiar arguments for doing right—to keep society from disintegrating, to alleviate human suffering, to advance human prosperity, to resolve conflicts of interest fairly and logically, to praise the good and punish the guilty, or just because something "is the right thing to do."[42] Having a passion to do right indicates a personal characteristic of not only recognizing the importance of ethical behavior but also the willingness to face challenges and make tough choices. Courageous leadership requires making and defending the right decision. Consider the crisis faced by Harry Kraemer, the CEO of Baxter International, after 53 dialysis patients died during treatment. "We have this situation. The financial people will assess the potential financial impact. The legal people will do the same. But at the end of the day, if we think it's a problem that a Baxter product was involved in the deaths of 53 people, then those other issues become pretty easy. If we don't do the right thing, then we won't be around to address those other issues."[43]

Ethical Leaders Are Proactive

Ethical leaders do not hang around waiting for ethical problems to arise. They anticipate, plan, and act proactively to avoid potential ethical crises.[44] One way to be proactive is to take a leadership role in developing effective programs that provide employees with guidance and support for making more ethical choices even in the face of considerable pressure to do otherwise. Ethical leaders who are proactive understand social needs and apply or even develop "the best practices" of ethical leadership that exist in their industry. One of *Fortune* magazine's Best Companies to Work For in 2009, office furniture maker Herman Miller is also known for its highly ethical culture. *Fortune* also has ranked it the Most Admired Company in its industry for the past 20 years. Its strong ethical culture has placed Herman Miller at the top of the Human Rights Campaign's Corporate Equality Index for years. Additionally, the company ranks as one of the safest, coolest, and most ethical companies in its industry.[45] Strong leadership is key in maintaining such impressive credentials over the long term.

Ethical Leaders Consider Stakeholders' Interests

Ethical leaders consider the interests of and implications for all stakeholders, not just those that have an economic impact on the firm. This requires acknowledging and monitoring the concerns of all legitimate stakeholders, actively communicating and cooperating with them, employing processes that are respectful of them, recognizing interdependencies among them, avoiding activities that would harm their human rights, and recognizing the potential conflicts between leaders' "own role as corporate stakeholders and their legal and moral responsibilities for the interests of other stakeholders."[46]

Ethical leaders have the responsibility to balance stakeholder interests to ensure that the organization maximizes its role as a responsible corporate citizen. In addition to being one of the world's most admired companies, according to *Fortune* magazine, Xerox has taken significant strides toward reducing its environmental impact, increasing social responsibility, and improving diversity. Xerox is the largest document management and technology company in the world with sales of over $17.6 billion annually, and as such a large company it produces a lot of waste every day. Xerox is aware of its carbon footprint and has produced such innovations as erasable paper to be used in testing machines so that the company does not throw away so much paper each day. The company also aims to be carbon neutral and tries to source its paper from sustainable sources.[47] The company also recently celebrated some significant diversity milestones. In 2009 Ursula Burns became the first African American female to be the CEO of a major American company, and Xerox was the first major company in history to have a female-to-female CEO sucession.[48] The company also extends its commitment to diversity to suppliers as well, because its own research has found that minority and women-owned businesses often have higher standards.[49]

Ethical Leaders Are Role Models for the Organization's Values

If leaders do not actively serve as role models for the organization's core values, then those values become nothing more than lip service. According to behavioral scientist Brent Smith, as role models, leaders are the primary influence on individual ethical behavior. Leaders whose decisions and actions are contrary to the firm's values send a signal that the firm's values are trivial or irrelevant.[50] Firms such as Countrywide Financial articulated core values that were only used as window dressing. On the other hand, when leaders model the firm's core values at every turn, the results can be powerful.

Consider Whole Foods, the world's largest organic and natural grocer. Ever since its conception in Austin, Texas, in 1980, Whole Foods has demonstrated a commitment to social responsibility and strong core values. (See Table 5–3) In addition to providing consumers with fresh, healthy foods, Whole Foods cares for its employees by creating a transparent and friendly work environment. The company encourages a sense of teamwork through imposing a salary cap for top executives. The company also works to support growers and the environment through sourcing from sustainable growers and such efforts as recycling and reducing energy whenever possible. Whole Foods donates a minimum of 5 percent of profits to local communities in which it operates. Especially in a time of repeated food contamination scares, many people are drawn to grocers like Whole Foods because of its high quality standards, educational initiatives, and close relationships with many of its suppliers.[51]

TABLE 5–3 Whole Food's Core Values

• Selling the highest quality natural and organic products
• Satisfying and delighting our customers
• Supporting team member happiness and excellence
• Creating wealth through profits and growth
• Caring about our communities and our environment
• Creating ongoing win-win partnerships with our suppliers
• Promoting the health of our stakeholders through healthy eating education.

Source: "Our Core Values," Whole Foods Markets, www.wholefoodsmarket.com/company/corevalues.php (accessed June 5, 2009).

Ethical Leaders Are Transparent and Actively Involved in Organizational Decision Making

Being transparent fosters openness, freedom to express ideas, and the ability to question conduct, and it encourages stakeholders to learn about and comment on what a firm is doing. Transparent leaders will not be effective unless they are personally involved in the key decisions that have ethical ramifications. Transformational leaders are collaborative, which opens the door for transparency through interpersonal exchange. Earlier we said that transformational leaders instill commitment and respect for values that provide guidance on how to deal with ethical issues. Herb Baum, former CEO of the Dial Corporation, says, "In today's business environment, if you're a leader—or want to be—and you aren't contributing to a values-based business culture that encourages your entire organization to operate with integrity, your company is as vulnerable as a baby chick in a pit of rattlesnakes." Baum's three remarkably simple principles of transparency are (1) tell the whole truth, (2) build a values-based culture, and (3) hire "people people."[52]

Ethical Leaders Are Competent Managers Who Take a Holistic View of the Firm's Ethical Culture

Ethical leaders can see a holistic view of their organization and therefore view ethics as a strategic component of decision making, much like marketing, information systems, production, and so on. Although his company is called Waste Management, CEO David P. Steiner is as committed to renewable energy as just about anyone working for a multibillion dollar business. Steiner was selected as one of the 100 Most Influential People in Business Ethics by the Ethisphere Institute in 2007, and his company, Waste Management, was chosen as one of the World's Most Ethical Companies in 2008.[53] Steiner likes to point out that Waste Management produces more renewable energy than the entire U.S. solar industry. In fact, nearly half of the company's revenues come from "green" services.[54] Steiner's personal commitment to social responsibility and sustainability has dramatically changed a company that was previously known primarily as a garbage collection service.

The challenge of being an effective leader is illustrated in Table 5–4. Most senior executives believe that it is much more challenging to be a leader in today's business environment compared to five years ago. Leadership continues to be one of the most important drivers of ethical conduct in organizations.

TABLE 5–4 Leadership Is More Challenging in Today's Business Environment

Do you think it is more or less challenging to be a company leader in today's business environment compared with five years ago?	
More challenging	89%
No change	9%
Less challenging	1%
Don't know	1%

Source: Robert Half Management Resources poll of 150 senior executives at companies with revenue of $1 billion to $40 billion. In *USA Today*, March 6, 2006, B1.

SUMMARY

The key components of the ethical decision making framework include ethical issue intensity, individual factors, organizational factors, and opportunity. These factors are interrelated and influence business ethics evaluations and intentions, which result in ethical or unethical behavior.

The first step in ethical decision making is to recognize that an ethical issue requires that an individual or work group choose among several actions that will ultimately be evaluated as ethical or unethical by various stakeholders. Ethical issue intensity is the perceived relevance or importance of an ethical issue to the individual or work group. It reflects the ethical sensitivity of the individual or work group that triggers the ethical decision process. Other factors in our ethical decision making framework influence this sensitivity, thus determining why different individuals often perceive ethical issues differently.

Individual factors such as gender, education, nationality, age, and locus of control can affect the ethical decision making process, with some factors being more important than others. Organizational factors such as an organization's values often have greater influence on an individual's decisions than that person's own values. In addition, decisions in business are most often made jointly, in work groups and committees, or in conversations and discussions with coworkers. Corporate cultures and structures operate through the individual relationships of the organization's members to influence those members' ethical decisions. A corporate culture can be defined as a set of values, beliefs, goals, norms, and ways of solving problems that members (employees) of an organization share. Corporate culture involves norms that prescribe a wide range of behavior for the organization's members. The ethical culture of an organization indicates whether it has an ethical conscience. Significant others—including peers, managers, coworkers, and subordinates—who influence the work group have more daily impact on an employee's decisions than any other factor in the decision making framework. Obedience to authority may explain why many business ethics issues are resolved simply by following the directives of a superior.

Ethical opportunity results from conditions that either provide rewards, whether internal or external, or limit barriers to ethical or unethical behavior. Included in opportunity is a person's immediate job context, which includes the motivational techniques superiors use to influence employee behavior. The opportunity employees have for unethical behavior in an organization can be eliminated through formal codes, policies, and rules that are adequately enforced by management.

The ethical decision making framework is not a guide for making decisions. It is intended to provide insights and knowledge about typical ethical decision making processes in business organizations. Ethical decision making within organizations does not rely strictly on the personal values and morals of employees. Organizations have a culture of their own, which when combined with corporate governance mechanisms may significantly influence business ethics.

Leadership styles and habits promote an organizational ethical climate. Leadership styles include coercive, authoritative, affiliative, democratic, and coaching elements. Transactional leaders negotiate or barter with employees. Transformational leaders strive for a shared vision and common learning experience. Strong ethical leaders have a strong personal character, have a passion to do the right thing, are proactive, focus on stakeholders' interests, are role models for the organization's values, make transparent decisions, and take a holistic view of the firm's ethical culture.

IMPORTANT TERMS FOR REVIEW

ethical issue intensity
moral intensity
gender
education
nationality
locus of control
external control
internal control
corporate culture
ethical culture
significant other
obedience to authority
opportunity
immediate job context
leadership
transactional leader
transformational leader

RESOLVING ETHICAL BUSINESS CHALLENGES*

Peter had been a human resource (HR) manager for 18 years and vice president for 2 more years for Zyedego Corporation, a small company in New Orleans. In the last decade, there have been many changes to what potential/actual employees can be asked and what constitutes fair and equitable treatment. Frankly, the situation Peter was in was partly his own fault.

The first issue began with Hurricane Katrina. In its wake, Zyedego employees had been working around the clock to get the company up and running again. The company had been calling all employees (if they could locate them) to get them to return to work. Gwyn, one of Peter's HR managers, was planning on rehiring Dana Gonzales but found out that Dana was pregnant. Because of the "rough" condition of the workplace, Gwyn was concerned for Dana's safety. Gwyn felt that if Dana were rehired, employees' hourly wages should be decreased by 25 percent because the company had experienced setbacks during the hurricane and had to work with a reduced budget. In addition, Gwyn had some concerns over Dana's citizenship because her passport appeared to be questionable. The flooding destroyed the original documents, and although Gwyn requested new documents, Dana had been slow in providing them. Gwyn had asked some difficult questions, and Dana stated that if not rehired she would go to a competitor and expected the company to pay severance of two weeks' wages for the time she was out of work during the hurricane. Another issue is the hiring of truck drivers. Zyedego hires many truck drivers and routinely requests driving records as part of the preemployment process. Several of the potential new hires have past DWI records. All have stated that they would never do it again, have maintained a clean record for at least five years, and understand the consequences of another infraction. Gwyn has hired some drivers with infractions to secure the necessary number of drivers needed for the company. However, Gwyn has some concerns over whether she is exposing the company to unnecessary risk because of the increased potential for accidents or repeat DWI violation. From Peter, Gwyn needs guidance related to continuing these hiring practices.

However, Zyedego has even deeper problems, which is what concerns Peter. The problem really started when Peter was still an HR manager, and involves one "family." Guy Martin started working for Zyedego 20 years ago. He was married with two children, and had a mortgage. A little over a year ago, Guy separated from his wife, and they divorced only to remarry six months later. When Guy was hired, Peter had made sure that Guy's son, who has asthma, would be covered by health insurance. Peter also helped out the family several times when money was tight and provided Guy with overtime work. But tragedy struck the Martins when Guy was killed in the hurricane. Police and rescue workers hunted for his body, but it was never found. Because Martha, Guy's wife, was a stay-at-home mother, their only income had been from Zyedego. The company's death benefits provide only 50 percent of the deceased's pension for a surviving spouse. Also, because the body had not been found, there was the legal question of death. Usually, it takes seven years before one can claim any type of insurance or death-benefit payments, as well as medical insurance, for the family. Even with Social Security benefits, Martha would probably lose the house and could be forced to seek employment.

Zyedego had sustained substantial losses since the hurricane. Insurance companies were extremely slow concerning payments to all the small businesses, arguing about wind versus water damage. Impeding the process of obtaining benefits was the lack of many documents destroyed in the storm.

The storm really began for Peter late last week when he met with the insurance company about medical reimbursements, death benefits, and the pension plans. Darrell Lambert was the chief adjuster for Zyedego's insurance and pension provider.

"Here's another case that we will not cover," said Darrell as he flipped the file to Peter. "We can't help the Martins for a variety of reasons. There is no body, which means no payment until after a judge declares him legally dead. That will take at least a year. While that is being settled, Mrs. Martin and her family will not be eligible for medical coverage unless Zyedego is going to pay their amount. Finally, and I know this may sound heartless, but Mrs. Martin will only get a maximum of half of Mr. Martin's pension."

"But he was killed on the job!" exclaimed Peter.

"Did you require him to work that day? Did he punch in or out? Is there any record that he was called in from Zyedego to help? The answer is no to all of the above. He helped because he felt obligated to Zyedego. But I am not Zyedego, and I do not have any obligation to the Martins," Darrell said with a smile.

"Peter," exclaimed Darrell, "I know that Zyedego is under intense financial pressure, but we are too. You have approximately 100 families that we will have to pay something to. You and I can spend the next 12 months going over every case, bit-by-bit, item-by-item, but if that's what you want, Zyedego will go into bankruptcy. We don't want that to happen. But we also are not going to pay for everything that you claim you are due. Our lawyers will stall the system until you go broke, and your 100 families will get nothing. Well, maybe something in five to seven years. What I am proposing is a way for you to stay in business and for my company to reduce its financial payouts. Remember, we have hundreds of small businesses like you to deal with."

Darrell then calmly said, "My proposal is that you look over these files and reduce your total reimbursements to us by 40 percent. To help you out, I'll start with this case [Martin's]. You decide whether we pay out 40 percent or nothing. Tomorrow at 9:00 A.M., I want you to have 25 cases, including this one, pared down by 40 percent. If not, well, I'm sure my superiors have informed your superiors about this arrangement by now. You should be getting a call within the hour. So, I'll see you here at 9:00," and Darrell walked out the door.

Several hours later, Peter received a phone call from upper management about the deal he was to implement to save the company.

QUESTIONS • EXERCISES

1. What are the legal and ethical risks associated with the decision about hiring truck drivers at Zyedego?
2. What should Peter recommend to Gwyn about Dana's case?
3. Do you think Peter is too emotionally attached to the Martin case to make an objective decision?

*This case is strictly hypothetical; any resemblance to real persons, companies, or situations is coincidental.

CHECK YOUR EQ

Check your EQ, or Ethics Quotient, by completing the following. Assess your performance to evaluate your overall understanding of the chapter material.

1.	The first step in ethical decision making is to understand the individual factors that influence the process.	**Yes**	**No**
2.	Opportunity describes the conditions within an organization that limit or permit ethical or unethical behavior.	**Yes**	**No**
3.	Transactional leaders negotiate compliance and ethics.	**Yes**	**No**
4.	The most significant influence on ethical behavior in an organization is the opportunity to engage in (un)ethical behavior.	**Yes**	**No**
5.	Obedience to authority relates to the influence of corporate culture.	**Yes**	**No**

Answers **1. No.** The first step is to become more aware that an ethical issue exists and to consider its relevance to the individual or work group. **2. Yes.** Opportunity results from conditions that provide rewards or fail to erect barriers against unethical behavior. **3. Yes.** Transactional leaders barter or negotiate with employees. **4. No.** Significant others have more impact on ethical decisions within an organization. **5. No.** Obedience to authority relates to the influence of significant others and supervisors.

CHAPTER 6

Individual Factors: Moral Philosophies and Values

CHAPTER OBJECTIVES

- To understand how moral philosophies and values influence individual and group ethical decision making in business
- To compare and contrast the teleological, deontological, virtue, and justice perspectives of moral philosophy
- To discuss the impact of philosophies on business ethics
- To recognize the stages of cognitive moral development and its shortcomings
- To introduce white-collar crime as it relates to moral philosophies, values, and corporate culture

CHAPTER OUTLINE

AN ETHICAL DILEMMA*

One of the problems that Lael Matthews has had to deal with in trying to climb the corporate ladder is the "glass ceiling" faced by minorities and women. In her current position, she must decide which of three managers to promote, a decision that, as her superior has informed her, could have serious repercussions for her future. The following people are the candidates.

Liz is a 34-year-old African American, divorced with one child, who graduated in the lower half of her college class at Northwest State. She has been with the company for four years and in the industry for eight years, with mediocre performance ratings but a high energy level. She has had some difficulties in managing her staff. In addition, her child has had various medical problems, so higher pay would be helpful. If promoted, Liz would be the first African American female manager at this level. Although Lael has known Liz only a short time, they seem to have hit it off; in fact, Lael once babysat Liz's daughter, Janeen, in an emergency. The downside to promoting Liz, though, might be a perception that Lael is playing favorites.

Roy is a 57-year-old Caucasian, married with three children, who graduated from a private university in the top half of his class. Roy has been with the company for 20 years and in the industry for 30, and he has always been a steady performer, with mostly average ratings. The reason why Roy has been passed over before was his refusal to relocate, but that is no longer a problem. Roy's energy level is average to low; however, he has produced many of the company's top sales performers in the past. This promotion would be his last before retirement, and many in the company feel that he has earned it. In fact, one senior manager stopped Lael in the hall and said, "You know, Lael, Roy has been with us for a long time. He has done many good things for the company, sacrificing not only himself but also his family. I really hope that you can see your way to promoting him. It would be a favor to me that I wouldn't forget."

Quang Yeh, a single, 27-year-old Asian American, graduated from State University in the top 3 percent of her class and has been with the company for three years. She is known for putting in 60-hour weeks and for her meticulous management style, which has generated some criticism from her sales staff. The last area that she managed showed record increases, despite the loss of some older accounts that for some reason did not like dealing with Quang.

Moreover, Quang sued her previous employer for discrimination and won. A comment that Lael heard from that company was that Quang was intense and that nothing would stop her from reaching her goals. As Lael was going over some of her notes, another upper-management individual came to her office and said, "You know, Lael, Quang is engaged to my son. I've looked over her personnel files, and she looks very good. She looks like a rising star, which would indicate that she should be promoted as quickly as possible. I realize that you're not in my division, but the way people get transferred, you never know. I would really like to see Quang get this promotion."

As she was considering the choices, Lael's immediate supervisor came to her to talk about Liz. "You know, Lael, Liz is one of a very few people in the company who is both an African American woman and qualified for this position. I've been going over the company's hiring and promotion figures, and it would be very advantageous for me personally and for the company to promote her. I've also spoken to public relations, and they believe that this would be a tremendous boost for the company."

As Lael pondered her decision, she mentally went through each candidate's records and found that each had advantages and disadvantages. While she was considering her problem, the phone rang. It was Liz, sounding frantic. "Lael, I'm sorry to disturb you at this late hour, but I need you to come to the hospital. Janeen has been in an accident, and I don't know who to turn to." When Lael got to the hospital, she found that Janeen's injuries were fairly serious and that Liz would have to miss some work to help with the recuperation process. Lael also realized that this accident would create a financial problem for Liz, which a promotion could help solve.

The next day seemed very long and was punctuated by the announcement that Roy's son was getting married to the vice president's daughter. The wedding would be in June, and it sounded as though it would be a company affair. By 4:30 that afternoon, Lael had gone through four aspirins and two antacids. Her decision was due in two days. What should she do?

QUESTIONS • EXERCISES

1. Discuss the advantages and disadvantages of each candidate.
2. What are the ethical and legal considerations for Lael?
3. Identify the pressures that have made her promotion decision an ethical and legal issue.
4. Discuss the implications of each decision that Lael could make.

*This case is strictly hypothetical; any resemblance to real persons, companies, or situations is coincidental.

Most discussions of business ethics address the role of the individual in ethical decision making. The ethical decision making model that was described in Chapter 5 placed the individual moral perspectives as a central component in making an ethical decision. In this chapter, we provide a detailed description and analysis of how individuals' backgrounds and philosophies influence their decisions. It is important to determine when one action is right and when another is viewed as wrong, and individual moral philosophies are often used to justify decisions or explain actions. To understand how people make ethical decisions, it is useful to have a grasp of the major types of moral philosophies. In this chapter, a discussion of the stages of cognitive development as they relate to these moral philosophies and their shortcomings is addressed. Finally, we examine white-collar crime as it relates to moral philosophies and personal values.

MORAL PHILOSOPHY DEFINED

When people talk about philosophy, they usually mean the general system of values by which they live. **Moral philosophy,** on the other hand, refers in particular to the specific principles or rules that people use to decide what is right or wrong. It is important to understand the distinction between moral philosophies and business ethics. A moral philosophy is a person's principles and values that define what is moral or immoral. Moral philosophies are person-specific, whereas business ethics is based on decisions in groups or those made when carrying out tasks to meet business objectives. In the context of business, ethics refers to what the group, firm, or strategic business unit (SBU) defines as right or wrong actions pertaining to its business operations and the objective of profits, earnings per share, or some other financial measure of success as defined by the group. For example, a production manager may be guided by a general philosophy of management that emphasizes encouraging workers to know as much as possible about the product that they are manufacturing. However, the manager's moral philosophy comes into play when he must make decisions such as whether to notify employees in advance of upcoming layoffs. Although workers would prefer advance warning, giving it might adversely affect the quality and quantity of production. Such decisions require a person to evaluate the "rightness," or morality, of choices in terms of his or her own principles and values.

Moral philosophies present guidelines for "determining how conflicts in human interests are to be settled and for optimizing mutual benefit of people living together in groups," guiding businesspeople as they formulate business strategies and resolve specific ethical issues.[1] However, there is no single moral philosophy that everyone accepts. Some managers, for example, view profit as the ultimate goal of an enterprise and therefore may not be concerned about the impact of their firms' decisions on society. As we have seen, the economist Milton Friedman supports this viewpoint, contending that the market will reward or punish companies for unethical conduct without the need for government regulation.[2] The emergence of this Friedman-type capitalism as the dominant and most widely accepted economic system has created market-driven societies around the world. Over the past six decades, the United States has been waging an ideological war over capitalism; first with the Soviet Union, then with Latin America in the 1980s, and finally with China. Even China's communist government has adapted capitalism and free enterprise to help it become a leading economic power. The United States has been actively exporting the idea that the invisible hand of free market capitalism can solve the troubles of mankind and lead toward greater happiness and prosperity. Such happiness is derived from the increased availability of products and services. Marketing helps consumers to understand, compare, and obtain these products and services, thereby increasing the efficiency and effectiveness of the exchange. However, free markets may not be a panacea- For example, empirical research and a study of history show that excessive consumption can have negative effects and may be psychologically, spiritually, and physically unhealthy.[3] In other words, more is not necessarily best.

Adam Smith is considered the father of free market capitalism. He was a professor of logic and moral philosophy and wrote the seminal "The Theory of Moral Sentiments" and the book *Inquiry into the Nature and Causes of the Wealth of Nations* (1776). Smith believed that business was and should be guided by the morals of good men. But in the eighteenth century, Smith could not image the complexity of modern markets or the size of multinationals, nor could he fathom the concept that four or five companies could gain control of the vast majority of the resources of the world. His ideas did not take into account the full force of democracy, nor the immense wealth and power some firms wield within countries.

Economic systems not only allocate resources and products within a society but also affect individuals and society as a whole. Thus, the success of an economic system depends both on its philosophical framework and on the individuals within the system who maintain moral philosophies that bring people together in a cooperative, efficient, and productive marketplace. Going back to Aristotle, there is a long Western tradition of questioning whether a market economy and individual moral behavior are compatible. In reality, individuals in today's society exist within the framework of social, political, and economic institutions.

People who face ethical issues often base their decisions on their own values and principles of right or wrong, most of which are learned through the socialization process with the help of family members, social groups, religions, and formal education. Individual factors that influence decision making include personal moral philosophies. Ethical dilemmas arise in problem-solving situations in which the rules governing decision making are often vague or in conflict. In real-life situations, there is no substitute for an individual's own critical thinking and ability to accept responsibility for his or her decision.

Moral philosophies are ideal moral perspectives that provide individuals with abstract principles for guiding their social existence. For example, individuals' decisions to recycle waste or to purchase or sell recycled or recyclable products are influenced by moral philosophies and attitudes toward recycling.[4] Thus, it is often difficult to implement an individual moral philosophy within the complex environment of a business organization. On the other hand, the functioning of our economic system depends on individuals coming together and sharing philosophies that create the moral values, trust, and expectations that allow the system to work. Most employees within a business organization do not think about what particular moral philosophy they are using when they are confronted with an ethical issue. Individuals learn decision making approaches or philosophies through their cultural and social development.

Many theories associated with moral philosophies refer to a value orientation and such things as economics, idealism, and relativism. The concept of the **economic value orientation** is associated with values that can be quantified by monetary means; thus, according to this theory, if an act produces more value than its effort, then it should be accepted as ethical. **Idealism,** on the other hand, is a moral philosophy that places special value on ideas and ideals as products of the mind, in comparison with the world's view. The term refers to efforts to account for all objects in nature and experience and assign to such representations a higher order of existence. Studies have found that there is a positive correlation between idealistic thinking and ethical decision making. **Realism** is the view that an external world exists independent of our perception of it. Realists work under the assumption that humankind is not inherently benevolent and kind but instead is inherently self-centered and competitive. According to realists, each person is always ultimately guided by his or her own self-interest. Research shows a negative correlation between realistic thinking and ethical decision making. Thus, the belief that all actions are ultimately self-motivated leads to a tendency toward negative ethical decision making.

MORAL PHILOSOPHIES

There are many moral philosophies, but because a detailed study of all moral philosophies is beyond the scope of this book, we limit our discussion to those that are most applicable to the study of business ethics. Our approach focuses on the most basic concepts needed to help you understand the ethical decision making process in business. We do not prescribe the use of any particular moral philosophy, for there is no one "correct" way to resolve ethical issues in business.

To help you understand how the moral philosophies discussed in this chapter may be applied in decision making, we use a hypothetical situation as an illustration. Suppose that Sam Colt, a sales representative, is preparing a sales presentation for his firm Midwest Hardware, which manufactures nuts and bolts. Sam hopes to obtain a large sale from a construction firm that is building a bridge across the Mississippi River near St. Louis. The bolts manufactured by Midwest Hardware have a 3 percent defect rate, which, although acceptable in the industry, makes them unsuitable for use in certain types of projects, such as those that may be subject to sudden, severe stress. The new bridge will be located near the New Madrid Fault line, the source of the United States' greatest earthquake in 1811. The epicenter of that earthquake, which caused extensive damage and altered the flow of the Mississippi, is less than 200 miles from the new bridge site. Earthquake experts believe there is a 50 percent chance that an earthquake with a magnitude greater than 7 on the Richter scale will occur somewhere along the New Madrid Fault by the year 2020. Bridge construction in the area is not regulated by earthquake codes, however. If Sam wins the sale, he will earn a commission of $25,000 on top of his regular salary. But if he tells the contractor about the defect rate, Midwest may lose the sale to a competitor that markets bolts with a lower defect rate. Thus, Sam's ethical issue is whether to point out to the bridge contractor that, in the event of an earthquake, some Midwest bolts could fail, possibly resulting in the collapse of the bridge.

We will come back to this illustration as we discuss particular moral philosophies, asking how Sam Colt might use each philosophy to resolve his ethical issue. We don't judge the quality of Sam's decision, nor do we advocate any one moral philosophy; in fact, this illustration and Sam's decision rationales are necessarily simplistic as well as hypothetical. In reality, the decision maker would probably have many more factors to consider in making his or her choice and thus might reach a different decision. With that note of caution, we introduce the concept of goodness and several types of moral philosophy: teleology, deontology, the relativist perspective, virtue ethics, and justice theories (see Table 6–1).

TABLE 6–1 A Comparison of the Philosophies used in Business Decisions

Teleology	Stipulates that acts are morally right or acceptable if they produce some desired result, such as realization of self-interest or utility.
Egoism	Defines right or acceptable actions as those that maximize a particular person's self-interest as defined by the individual.
Utilitarianism	Defines right or acceptable actions as those that maximize total utility, or the greatest good for the greatest number of people.
Deontology	Focuses on the preservation of individual rights and on the intentions associated with a particular behavior rather than on its consequences.
Relativist	Evaluates ethicalness subjectively on the basis of individual and group experiences.
Virtue ethics	Assumes that what is moral in a given situation is not only what conventional morality requires but also what the mature person with a "good" moral character would deem appropriate.
Justice	Evaluates ethicalness on the basis of fairness: distributive, procedural, and interactional.

Goodness—Instrumental and Intrinsic

To appreciate moral philosophy, one must understand the differing perspectives of goodness. Are there clearly defined goods and bads and, if so, what is the relationship between the ends and the means of bringing them about? Is there some intrinsic way of determining if the ends can be identified independently as good or bad? Aristotle, for example, argued that happiness is an intrinsically good end—in other words, its goodness is natural and universal, without relativity. On the other hand, the philosopher Immanuel Kant emphasized means and motivations to argue that goodwill, seriously applied toward accomplishment, is the only thing good in itself.

Two basic concepts of goodness are monism and pluralism. **Monists** believe that only one thing is intrinsically good, and the pluralists believe that two or more things are intrinsically good. Monists are often exemplified by **hedonism**—that one's pleasure is the ultimate intrinsic good or that the moral end, or goodness, is the greatest balance of pleasure over pain. Hedonism defines right or acceptable behavior as that which maximizes personal pleasure. Moral philosophers describe those who believe that more pleasure is better as **quantitative hedonists** and those who believe that it is possible to get too much of a good thing (such as pleasure) as **qualitative hedonists**.

Pluralists, often referred to as nonhedonists, take the opposite position that no *one* thing is intrinsically good. For example, a pluralist might view other ultimate goods as beauty, aesthetic experience, knowledge, and personal affection. Plato argued that the good life is a mixture of (1) moderation and fitness, (2) proportion and beauty, (3) intelligence and wisdom, (4) sciences and arts, and (5) pure pleasures of the soul.

Although all pluralists are nonhedonists, it is important to note that all monists are not necessarily hedonists. An individual can believe in a single intrinsic good other than pleasure; Machiavelli and Nietzsche, for example, each held power to be the sole good, and Kant's belief in the single virtue of goodwill classifies him as a monistic nonhedonist.

A more modern view is expressed in the instrumentalist position. Sometimes called pragmatists, **instrumentalists** reject the idea that (1) ends can be separated from the means that produce them and (2) ends, purposes, or outcomes are intrinsically good in and of themselves. The philosopher John Dewey argued that the ends–means perspective is a relative distinction, that the difference between ends and means is no difference at all but merely a matter of the individual's perspective; thus, almost any action can be an end or a means. Dewey gives the example that people eat in order to be able to work, and they work in order to eat. From a practical standpoint, an end is only a remote means, and a means is but a series of acts viewed from an earlier stage. From this it follows that there is no such thing as a single, universal end.

So how does this discussion equate to business? Isn't business about shareholder wealth and the wealth of executives? To measure success in business is to measure monetary wealth . . . right? To answer this question, let's go back to 1923 when a meeting was held at the Edgewater Beach Hotel in Chicago. Attending this meeting were nine of the richest men in the world: (1) Charles Schwab, president of the world's largest independent steel company; (2) Samuel Insull, president of the world's largest utility company; (3) Howard Hopson, president of the world's largest gas firm; (4) Arthur Cutten, the greatest wheat speculator; (5) Richard Whitney, president of the New York Stock Exchange; (6) Albert Fall, member of the president's cabinet; (7) Leon Fraizer, president of the Bank of International Settlements; (8) Jessie Livermore, the greatest speculator in the stock market; and (9) Ivar Kreuger, head of the company with the most widely distributed securities in the world. Twenty-five years later, (1) Charles Schwab had died having lived on borrowed money for the last five years of his life, (2) Samuel Insull had died a penniless fugitive,

(3) Howard Hopson had gone insane, (4) Arthur Cutten had died bankrupt, (5) Richard Whitney had spent time in prison, (6) Albert Fall had been pardoned from prison so that he could die at home, and (7) Leon Fraizer, (8) Jessie Livermore, and (9) Ivar Kreuger had committed suicide. Measured by wealth and power, these men had achieved success, at least temporarily. So this begs the question of whether money guarantees happiness; in other words, do the ends always justify the means?

A discussion of moral value often revolves around the nature of goodness—instrumental or intrinsic. Theories of moral obligation, by contrast, change the question to "What makes a given action right or obligatory?" **Goodness theories** typically focus on the *end result* of actions and the goodness or happiness created by them, whereas **obligation theories** emphasize the *means* and *motives* by which actions are justified. These obligation theories are teleology and deontology, respectively.

Teleology

Teleology (from the Greek word for "end" or "purpose") refers to moral philosophies in which an act is considered morally right or acceptable if it produces some desired result such as pleasure, knowledge, career growth, the realization of self-interest, utility, wealth, or even fame. In other words, teleological philosophies assess the moral worth of a behavior by looking at its consequences, and thus moral philosophers today often refer to these theories as **consequentialism**. Two important teleological philosophies that often guide decision making in individual business decisions are egoism and utilitarianism.

> *"Teleological philosophies assess the moral worth of a behavior by looking at its consequences"*

Egoism defines right or acceptable behavior in terms of its consequences for the individual. Egoists believe that they should make decisions that maximize their own self-interest, which is defined differently by each individual. Depending on the egoist, self-interest may be construed as physical well-being, power, pleasure, fame, a satisfying career, a good family life, wealth, or something else. In an ethical decision making situation, an egoist will probably choose the alternative that contributes most to his or her self-interest. The egoist's creed generally can be stated as "Do the act that promotes the greatest good for oneself." Many believe that egoistic people and companies are inherently unethical, are short-term oriented, and will take advantage of any opportunity. For example, some telemarketers demonstrate this negative tendency when they prey on elderly consumers who may be vulnerable because of loneliness or fear of losing their financial independence. Thousands of senior citizens fall victim to fraudulent telemarketers every year, in many cases losing all of their savings and sometimes their homes.

However, there is also **enlightened egoism**. Enlightened egoists take a long-range perspective and allow for the well-being of others although their own self-interest remains paramount. An example of enlightened egoism is helping a turtle across a highway because, if killed, the person would feel distressed. To feel good, or eliminate the chance of a feeling of distress, the person helps the turtle to cross the road.[5] Enlightened egoists may, for example, abide by professional codes of ethics, control pollution, avoid cheating on taxes, help create jobs, and support community projects. Yet they do so not because these actions benefit others but because they help achieve some ultimate goal for the egoist, such as advancement within the firm. An enlightened egoist might call management's attention to a coworker who is making false accounting reports but only to safeguard the company's reputation and thus the egoist's own job security. In addition, some enlightened egoists may become whistle-blowers and report misconduct to a government regulatory agency to keep their job and receive a reward for exposing misconduct. When businesses donate money, resources, or time to specific causes and institutions, their motives may not be purely altruistic either. For example, International Business Machines (IBM) has a policy of donating or reducing the cost of computers to educational institutions. In exchange, the company receives tax breaks for donations of equipment, which reduces the cost of its philanthropy. In addition, IBM hopes to build future sales by placing its products on campuses. When students enter the workforce, they may request the IBM products with which they have become familiar. Although the company's actions benefit society in general, in the long run they also benefit IBM.

Let's return to the hypothetical case of Sam Colt, who must decide whether to warn the bridge contractor that 3 percent of Midwest Hardware's bolts are likely to be defective. If he is an egoist, he will probably choose the alternative that maximizes his own self-interest. If he defines self-interest in terms of personal wealth, his personal moral philosophy may lead him to value a $25,000 commission more than a chance to reduce the risk of a bridge collapse. As a result, an egoist might well resolve this ethical dilemma by keeping quiet about the bolts' defect rate, hoping to win the sale and the $25,000 commission, rationalizing that there is a slim chance of an earthquake, that bolts would not be a factor in a major earthquake, and that, even if they were, no one would be able to prove that defective bolts caused the bridge to collapse.

"The utilitarian seeks the greatest good for the greatest number of people."

Like egoism, **utilitarianism** is concerned with consequences, but the utilitarian seeks the greatest good for the greatest number of people. Utilitarians believe that they should make decisions that result in the greatest total *utility,* that achieve the greatest benefit for all those affected by a decision. An argument for utilitarianism may be President Obama's 2009 economic stimulus package. Its costs to the American taxpayer may have been weighted against the greater costs of allowing the market to fall into a depression without government intervention.

Utilitarian decision making relies on a systematic comparison of the costs and benefits to all affected parties. Using such a cost–benefit analysis, a utilitarian decision maker calculates the utility of the consequences of all possible alternatives and then selects the one that results in the greatest benefit. For example, the U.S. Supreme Court has ruled that supervisors are responsible for the sexual misconduct of employees, even if the employers knew nothing about the behavior, establishing a strict standard for harassment on the job. One of the justices indicated in the ruling that the employer's burden to prevent harassment is "one of the costs of doing business."[6] Apparently, the Court has decided that the greatest utility to society will result from forcing businesses to prevent harassment.

In evaluating an action's consequences, some utilitarians consider the effects on animals as well as on human beings. This perspective is especially significant in the controversy surrounding the use of animals for research purposes by cosmetics and pharmaceutical companies. Animal rights groups have protested that such testing is unethical because it harms and even kills the animals, depriving them of their rights. Researchers for pharmaceutical and cosmetics manufacturers, however, defend animal testing on utilitarian grounds. The consequences of the research (such as new or improved drugs to treat disease, or safer cosmetics) create more benefit for society, they argue, than would be achieved by halting the research and preserving the animals' rights. Nonetheless, many cosmetics firms have responded to the controversy by agreeing to stop animal research.

Now suppose that Sam Colt, the bolt salesperson, is a utilitarian. Before making his decision, he would conduct a cost–benefit analysis to assess which alternative would create the greatest utility. On one hand, building the bridge would improve roadways and allow more people to cross the Mississippi River to reach jobs in St. Louis. The project would create hundreds of jobs, enhance the local economy, and unite communities on both sides of the river. Additionally, it would increase the revenues of Midwest Hardware, allowing the firm to invest more in research to lower the defect rate of bolts it produced in the future. On the other hand, a bridge collapse could kill or injure as many as 100 people. But the bolts have only a 3 percent defect rate, there is only a 50 percent probability of an earthquake *somewhere* along the fault line, and there might be only a few cars on the bridge at the time of a disaster.

After analyzing the costs and benefits of the situation, Sam might rationalize that building the bridge with his company's bolts would create more utility (jobs, unity, economic growth, and company growth) than would result from telling the bridge contractor that the bolts might fail in an earthquake. If so, a utilitarian would probably not alert the bridge contractor to the defect rate of the bolts.

Utilitarians use various criteria to judge the morality of an action. Some utilitarian philosophers have argued that general rules should be followed to decide which action is best.[7] These **rule utilitarians** determine behavior on the basis of principles, or rules, designed to promote the greatest utility rather than on an examination of each particular situation. One such rule might be "Bribery is wrong." If people felt free to offer bribes whenever they might be useful, the world would become chaotic; therefore, a rule prohibiting bribery would increase utility. A rule utilitarian would not bribe an official, even to preserve workers' jobs, but would adhere strictly to the rule. Rule utilitarians do not automatically accept conventional moral rules, however; thus, if they determined that an alternative rule would promote greater utility, they would advocate changing it.

Other utilitarian philosophers have argued that the rightness of each individual action must be evaluated to determine whether it produces the greatest utility for the greatest number of people.[8] These **act utilitarians** examine a specific action itself, rather than the general rules governing it, to assess whether it will result in the greatest utility. Rules such as "Bribery is wrong" serve only as general guidelines for act utilitarians. They would likely agree that bribery is generally wrong, not because there is anything inherently wrong with bribery, but because the total amount of utility decreases when one person's interests are placed ahead of those of society.[9] In a particular case, however, an act utilitarian might argue that bribery is acceptable.

For example, a sales manager might believe that his or her firm will not win a construction contract unless a local government official gets a bribe; moreover, if the firm does not obtain the contract, it will have to lay off 100 workers. The manager might therefore argue that bribery is justified because saving 100 jobs creates more utility than obeying a law. Another example may be found in the actions of farmers in China who use toxic melamine to increase milk quality. Melamine's chemical properties boost the apparent presence of protein in food. Manufacturers of melamine, an industrial chemical used in plastics, say they had noticed a rising demand for their factories' scrap. Actual protein powders are also prohibited from being added to raw milk. They are made from ground animal parts, soy, and other sources. China's biggest local seller of liquid milk, Nestlé SA, said it was aware that Chinese farmers and traders added unauthorized substances to raw milk, but that it didn't know melamine was among them. Among other common milk additives: a viscous yellow liquid containing fat and a combination of preservatives and antibiotics, known as "fresh-keeping liquid" is "very common" and hard to detect. It can be argued that everyone within the milk supply chain saw their actions as helping more people financially rather than harm them from the unknown dangers of the additives.[10]

Deontology

Deontology (from the Greek word for "ethics") refers to moral philosophies that focus on the rights of individuals and on the intentions associated with a particular behavior rather than on its consequences. Fundamental to deontological theory is the idea that equal respect must be given to all persons. Unlike utilitarians, deontologists argue that there are some things that we should *not* do, even to maximize utility. For example, deontologists would consider it wrong to kill an innocent person or commit a serious injustice against a person, no matter how much greater social utility might result from doing so, because such an action would infringe on that person's rights as an individual. The utilitarian, however, might consider as acceptable an action that resulted in a person's death if that action created some greater benefit. Deontological philosophies regard certain behaviors as inherently right, and the determination of this rightness focuses on the individual actor, not society. Thus, these perspectives are sometimes referred to as **nonconsequentialism** an ethics based on *respect for persons.*

Contemporary deontology has been greatly influenced by the German philosopher Immanuel Kant, who developed the so-called categorical imperative: "Act as if the maxim of thy action were to become by thy will a universal law of nature."[11] Simply put, if you feel comfortable allowing everyone in the world to see you commit an act and if your rationale for acting in a particular manner is suitable to become a universal principle guiding behavior, then committing that act is ethical. For example, if a person borrows money, promising to return it but with no intention of keeping that promise, he or she cannot "universalize" that act. If everyone were to borrow money without the intention of returning it, no one would take such promises seriously, and all lending would cease.[12] Therefore, the rationale for the action would not be a suitable universal principle, and the act could not be considered ethical.

> *"Teleological philosophies consider the ends associated with an action whereas deontological philosophies consider the means."*

The term *nature* is crucial for deontologists. In general, deontologists regard the nature of moral principles as permanent and stable, and they believe that compliance with these principles defines ethicalness. Deontologists believe that individuals have certain absolute rights:

- Freedom of conscience
- Freedom of consent
- Freedom of privacy
- Freedom of speech
- Due process[13]

To decide whether a behavior is ethical, deontologists look for conformity to moral principles. For example, if a manufacturing worker becomes ill or dies as a result of conditions in the workplace, a deontologist might argue that the company must modify its production processes to correct the condition, no matter what the cost—even if it means bankrupting the company and thus causing all workers to lose their jobs. In contrast, a utilitarian would analyze all the costs and benefits of modifying production processes and make a decision on that basis. This example is greatly oversimplified, of course, but it helps clarify the difference between teleology and deontology. In short, teleological philosophies consider the *ends* associated with an action whereas deontological philosophies consider the *means.*

Returning again to our bolt salesperson, let's consider a deontological Sam Colt. He would probably feel obliged to tell the bridge contractor about the defect rate because of the potential loss of life that might result from an earthquake-caused bridge collapse. Even though constructing the bridge would benefit residents and earn Sam a substantial commission, the failure of the bolts during an earthquake would infringe on the rights of any person crossing the bridge at the time of the collapse. Thus, the deontological Sam would likely inform the bridge contractor of the defect rate and point out the earthquake risk, even though, by doing so, he would probably lose the sale.

As with utilitarians, deontologists may be divided into those who focus on moral rules and those who focus on the nature of the acts themselves. **Rule deontologists** believe that conformity to general moral principles determines ethicalness. Deontological philosophies use reason and logic to formulate rules for behavior. Examples include Kant's categorical imperative and the Golden Rule of the Judeo-Christian tradition: Do unto others as you would have them do unto you. Such rules, or principles, guiding ethical behavior override the imperatives that emerge from a specific context. One could argue that Jeffery Wigand—who exposed the underside of the tobacco industry when he blew the whistle on his employer, Brown & Williamson Tobacco—was such a rule deontologist. Although it cost him both financially and socially, Wigand testified to Congress about the realities of marketing cigarettes and their effects on society.[14]

Rule deontology is determined by the relationship between the basic rights of the individual and a set of rules governing conduct. For example, a video store owner accused of distributing obscene materials could argue from a rule deontological perspective that the basic right to freedom of speech overrides the other indecency or pornography aspects of his business. Indeed, the free-speech argument has held up in many courts. Kant and rule deontologists would support a process of discovery to identify the moral issues relevant to a firm's mission and objectives. Then, they would follow a process of justifying that mission or those objectives based on rules.[15] An example of rule deontology is Kellogg's president, David Mackay. After hearing about possible salmonella contamination in peanut butter, he encouraged supermarkets not to sell Kellogg's products using peanut butter until the source of the contamination was discovered and peanut butter was deemed safe again.

Act deontologists, in contrast, hold that actions are the proper basis on which to judge morality or ethicalness. Act deontology requires that a person use equity, fairness, and impartiality when making and enforcing decisions.[16] For act deontologists, as for act utilitarians, rules serve only as guidelines, with past experiences weighing more heavily than rules upon the decision making process. In effect, act deontologists suggest that people simply *know* that certain acts are right or wrong, regardless of the consequences or any appeal to deontological rules. In addition, act deontologists regard the particular act or moment in time as taking precedence over any rule. For example, many people view data collection by Internet sites as a violation of personal privacy in itself. Regardless of any website's stated rules or policies, many Internet users want to be left alone unless they provide permission to be tracked while online.[17] A high school teacher at Hoover High in Alabama purportedly lost her job because she refused to change a football player's grade. It would have been much easier for her to do as others had done, yet the philosophy she used was within the act deontologist's range.[18] Current research suggests that rule and act deontological principles play a larger role in a person's decision than teleological philosophies.[19]

As we have seen, ethical issues can be evaluated from many different perspectives. Each type of philosophy discussed here would have a distinct basis for deciding whether a particular action is right or wrong. Adherents of different personal moral philosophies may disagree in their evaluations of a given action, yet all are behaving ethically *according to their own standards.* All would agree that there is no one "right" way to make ethical decisions and no best moral philosophy except their own. The relativist perspective may be helpful in understanding how people make such decisions in practice.

Relativist Perspective

From the **relativist perspective**, definitions of ethical behavior are derived subjectively from the experiences of individuals and groups. Relativists use themselves or the people around them as their basis for defining ethical standards, and the various forms of relativism include descriptive, metaethical, or normative.[20] **Descriptive relativism** relates to observing cultures. We may observe that different cultures exhibit different norms, customs, and values and, in so doing, arrive at a factual description of a culture. These observations say nothing about the higher questions of ethical justification, however. At this point metaethical relativism comes into play.

Metaethical relativists understand that people naturally see situations from their own perspectives and argue that, as a result, there is no objective way of resolving ethical disputes between value systems and individuals. Simply put, one culture's moral philosophy cannot logically be preferred to another because there exists no meaningful basis for comparison. Because ethical rules are relative to a specific culture, the values and behaviors of people in one culture need not influence the behaviors of people in another culture.[21] At the individual level of reasoning, we have **normative relativism**. Normative relativists assume that one person's opinion is as good as another's.[22]

> *"Normative relativists assume that one person's opinion is as good as another's."*

Basic relativism acknowledges that we live in a society in which people have many different views and bases from which to justify decisions as right or wrong. The relativist looks to the interacting groups and tries to determine probable solutions based on group consensus. When formulating business strategies and plans, for example, a relativist would try to anticipate the conflicts that might arise between the different philosophies held by members of the organization, its suppliers, its customers, and the community at large.

The relativist observes the actions of members of an involved group and attempts to determine that group's consensus on a given behavior. A positive consensus, for example, would signify that the group considers the action to be right or ethical. However, such judgments may not remain valid forever. As circumstances evolve or the makeup of the group changes, a formerly accepted behavior may come to be viewed as wrong or unethical, or vice versa. Within the accounting profession, for example, it was traditionally considered unethical to advertise. However, advertising has been gaining acceptance among accountants. This shift in ethical views may have come about as a result of the steady increase in the number of accountants, which has led to greater competition. Moreover, the federal government investigated the restrictions that accounting groups placed on their members and concluded that they inhibited free competition. Consequently, an informal consensus has emerged in the accounting industry that advertising is now acceptable. A problem with relativism is that it places too much emphasis on peoples' differences while ignoring their basic similarities. Similarities within different people and cultures—such as beliefs against incest, murder, and theft or promoting reciprocity and respect for the elderly—are hard to argue away and hard to explain from the relativist perspective.

In the case of the Midwest Hardware salesperson, if he were a relativist, he would attempt to determine the group consensus before deciding whether to tell his prospective customer about the bolts' defect rate. The relativist Sam Colt would look at both his own company's policy and at the general industry practice. He might also informally survey his colleagues and superiors as well as consulting industry trade journals and codes of ethics. Such investigations would help him determine the group consensus, which should reflect a variety of moral philosophies. If he learns that general company policy, as well as industry practice, is to discuss defect rates with those customers for whom faulty bolts may cause serious problems, he may infer that there is a consensus on the matter. As a relativist, he would probably then inform the bridge contractor that some of the bolts may fail, perhaps leading to a bridge collapse in the event of an earthquake. Conversely, if he determines that the normal practice in his company and the industry is to not inform customers about defect rates, he would probably not raise the subject with the bridge contractor.

Empirical research into the general concept of relativism suggests that it is negatively related to a person's ethical sensitivity to issues. Thus, if someone scores high on relativism, he or she will probably be less likely to detect or be sensitive to issues that are defined by others as having an ethical component.[23]

Virtue Ethics

A moral virtue represents an acquired disposition that is valued as a part of an individual's character. As an individual develops socially, he or she may become disposed to behave in the same way (in terms of reasons, feelings, and desires) as what he or she considers to be moral.[24] A person who has the character trait of honesty will be disposed to tell the truth because it is considered to be right and comfortable. This individual will always try to tell the truth because of its importance in human communication. A virtue is considered praiseworthy because it is an achievement that an individual develops through practice and commitment.[25]

This philosophy is called **virtue ethics**, and it posits that what is moral in a given situation is not only what conventional morality or moral rules (current societal definitions) require but also what the mature person with a "good" moral character would deem appropriate.

Proponents of virtue ethics frequently discuss lists of basic goods and virtues, which are generally presented as positive and useful mental habits or cultivated character traits. Aristotle named, among others, standards of loyalty, courage, wit, community, and judgment as the "excellences" that society requires. While listing the important virtues is a popular theoretical task, the philosopher Dewey cautions that virtues should not be looked at separately. The pluralism of virtues gives the businessperson a positive character and constitutes the very best idea of integrity of character. The virtue ethics approach to business can be summarized as follows:

1. Individual virtue and integrity count, but good corporate ethics programs encourage individual virtue and integrity.
2. By the employee's role in the community (organization), these virtues associated with appropriate conduct form a good person.
3. The ultimate purpose is to serve society's demands and the public good and to be rewarded in one's career.
4. The well-being of the community goes together with individual excellence because of the social consciousness and public spirit of every individual.[26]

The difference between deontology, teleology, and virtue ethics is that the first two are applied *deductively* to problems whereas virtue ethics is applied *inductively*. Virtue ethics assumes that what current societal moral rules require may indeed be the moral minimum for the beginning of virtue. The viability of our political, social, and economic systems depends on the presence of certain virtues among the citizenry that are vital for the proper functioning of a market economy.[27]

Indeed, virtue theory could be thought of as a dynamic theory of how to conduct business activities. The virtue ethicist believes that to have a successful market economy, society must be capable of carving out sanctuaries such as family, school, church, and community, where virtues can be nurtured. These virtues, including truth, trust, tolerance, and restraint, can play a role in the functioning of an individualistic, contractual economy and create obligations that make social cooperation possible. The operation of a market economy based on virtues provides a traditional existence where individuals in the economic system have powerful inducements to conform to prevailing standards of behavior. Some philosophers think that virtues may be weakened by the operation of the market, but virtue ethicists believe that institutions and society must maintain a balance and constantly add to their stock of virtues.[28] Some of the virtues that could drive a market economy are listed in Table 6–2; the list, although not comprehensive, provides examples of the types of virtues that support the business environment.

TABLE 6–2 Virtues That Support Business Transactions

Trust: The predisposition to place confidence in the behavior of others while taking the risk that the expected behavior will not be performed	Trust eliminates the need for and associated cost of monitoring compliance with agreements, contracts, and reciprocal agreements. There is the expectation that a promise or agreement can be relied on.
Self-control: The disposition to pass up an immediate advantage or gratification. It indicates the ability to avoid exploiting a known opportunity for self-interest	The trade-off is between short-term self-interest and long-term benefits.
Empathy: The ability to share the feelings or emotions of others	Empathy promotes civility because success in the market depends on the courteous treatment of people who have the option of going to competitors. The ability to anticipate needs and satisfy customers and employees contributes to a firm's economic success.
Fairness: The disposition to deal equitably with the perceived injustices of others	Fairness often relates to doing the right thing with respect to small matters in order to cultivate a long-term business relationship.
Truthfulness: The disposition to provide the facts or correct information as known to the individual	Telling the truth involves avoiding deception and contributes to trust in business relationships.
Learning: The disposition to constantly acquire knowledge internal and external to the firm, whether of an industry, culture, or other societies	Learning involves gaining knowledge to make better, more informed decisions.
Gratitude: A sign of maturity that is the beginning of civility and decency	Gratitude is the recognition that people do not succeed alone.
Civility: The disposition or essence of courtesy, politeness, respect, and consideration for others	Civility relates to the process of doing business in a culturally correct way, thus decreasing communication errors and increasing trust.
Moral leadership: Strength of character, peace of mind, heart, and happiness in life	Moral leadership is a trait of those leaders who follow a consistent pattern of behavior based on virtues

Source: Adapted from Ian Maitland, "Virtuous Markets: The Market as School of the Virtues," *Business Ethics Quarterly* (January 1997): 97; and Gordon B. Hinckley, *Standing for Something: 10 Neglected Virtues That Will Heal Our Hearts and Homes* (New York: Three Rivers Press, 2001).

The elements of virtue that are important to business transactions have been defined as trust, self-control, empathy, fairness, and truthfulness. Attributes in contrast to virtue would include lying, cheating, fraud, and corruption. In their broadest sense, these concepts appear to be accepted within all cultures. The problem of virtue ethics comes in its implementation within and between cultures, as those who practice virtue ethics go beyond social norms. For example, if a company tacitly approves of corruption, the employee who adheres to the virtues of trust and truthfulness would consider it wrong to sell unneeded repair parts despite the organization's approval of such acts. Some employees might view this truthful employee as highly ethical but, in order to rationalize their own behavior, judge his or her ethics as going beyond what is required by their job or society. They might argue that virtue is an unattainable goal and thus one should not be obliged to live up to its standards. However, to those who espouse virtue ethics, this relativistic argument is meaningless because they believe in the universal reality of the elements of virtue.

If our salesperson Sam Colt were a virtue ethicist, he would consider the elements of virtue and then tell the prospective customer about the defect rate and about his concerns regarding the building of the bridge. He would not resort to puffery to explain the product or its risks and, indeed, might suggest alternative products or companies that would lower the probability of the bridge collapsing.

Justice

Justice as it is applied in business ethics involves evaluations of fairness or the disposition to deal with perceived injustices of others. Justice is fair treatment and due reward in accordance with ethical or legal standards. In business, this means that the decision rules used by an individual to determine the justice of a situation could be based on the perceived rights of individuals and on the intentions of the people involved in a given business interaction. For that reason, justice is more likely to be based on deontological moral philosophies than on teleological or utilitarian philosophies. In other words, justice deals more with the issue of what individuals feel they are due based on their rights and performance in the workplace. For example, the U.S. Equal Employment Opportunity Commission exists to help employees who suspect they have been unjustly discriminated against in the workplace.

Three types of justice provide a framework for evaluating the fairness of different situations (see Table 6–3). **Distributive justice** is based on the evaluation of the outcomes or results of the business relationship. If some employees feel that they are paid less than their coworkers for the same work, then they have concerns about distributive justice. Distributive justice is difficult to develop when one member of the business exchange intends to take advantage of the relationship. A boss who forces his employees to do more work so that he can take more time off would be seen as unjust because he is taking advantage of his position to redistribute the workers under him. Situations such as this cause an imbalance in distributive justice.

Procedural justice is based on the processes and activities that produce the outcome or results. Evaluations of performance that are not consistently developed and applied can lead to problems with procedural justice. For instance, employees' concerns about inequitable compensation would relate to their perception that the processes of fairness or justice in their company were inconsistent. A climate that emphasizes procedural justice is expected to positively influence employees' attitudes and behaviors toward work-group cohesion. The visibility of supervisors and the work group's perceptions of its own cohesiveness

TABLE 6–3 Types of Justice

Justice Type	Evaluations of Fairness
Distributive justice: Based on the evaluation of outcomes or results of the business relationship	Benefits derived Equity in rewards
Procedural justice: Based on the processes and activities that produce the outcome or results	Decision making process Level of access, openness, and participation
Interactional justice: Based on an evaluation of the communication process used in the business relationship	Accuracy of information Truthfulness, respect, and courtesy in the process

are products of a climate of procedural justice.[29] When there is strong employee support for decisions, decision makers, organizations, and outcomes, procedural justice is less important to the individual. In contrast, when employees' support for decisions, decision makers, organizations, or outcomes is not very strong, then procedural justice becomes more important.[30] For example, Wainwright Bank and Trust Corporation in Boston has made a commitment to promoting justice to all stakeholders by providing a "sense of inclusion and diversity that extends from the boardroom to the mail room."[31] The bank, in other words, uses methods of procedural justice to establish positive stakeholder relationships by promoting understanding and inclusion in the decision making process.

Interactional justice is based on evaluating the communication processes used in the business relationship. Because interactional justice is linked to fairness in communication, it often involves the individual's relationship with the business organization through the accuracy of the information the organization provides. Employees can also be guilty in interactional justice disputes. For example, many employees admit that they stay home when they are not really sick if they feel they can get away with it. Such workplace absenteeism costs businesses millions of dollars each year. Being untruthful about the reasons for missing work is an example of an interactional justice issue.

All three types of justice—distributive, procedural, and interactional—could be used to evaluate a single business situation and the fairness of the organization involved. In the example of Sam Colt, Sam's decision to implement a justice perspective would be identical to using a deontological moral philosophy. That is, he would feel obligated to tell all affected parties about the bolt defect rate and the possible consequences of it. In general, justice evaluations result in restitution seeking, relationship building, and evaluations of fairness in business relationships.

APPLYING MORAL PHILOSOPHY TO ETHICAL DECISION MAKING

Strong evidence shows that individuals use different moral philosophies depending on whether they are making a personal decision outside the work environment or making a work-related decision on the job.[32] Two possible reasons may explain this. First, in the business arena, some goals and pressures for success differ from the goals and pressures in a person's life outside of work. As a result, an employee might view a specific action as "good" in the business sector but "unacceptable" in the nonwork environment. It is often suggested that business managers are morally different from other people. In a way, this is correct in that business has one variable that is absent from other situations: the profit motive. The weights on the various factors that make up a person's moral philosophy are shifted in a business (profit) situation. The statement "it's not personal, it's just business" demonstrates the conflict businesspeople can have when their personal values do not align with utilitarian or profit-oriented decisions. The reality is that if firms do not make a profit, they will fail. This should not be construed to be a justification for seeking excessive profits or executive pay, issues which are now being questioned by stakeholders. The second reason people change moral philosophies could be the corporate culture where they work. When a child enters school, for example, he or she learns certain rules such as raising your hand to speak or asking permission to use the restroom. So it is with a new employee. Rules, personalities, and historical precedence exert pressure on the employee to conform to the new firm's culture. As this occurs, the individual's moral philosophy may change to be compatible with the work environment. The employee may alter some or all of the values within his or her moral philosophy as he or she shifts into the firm's different moral philosophy. Many people are acquainted with someone who is known for their goodness at home or in their communities who makes unethical decisions in the workplace. Even Bernard Madoff, the perpetrator of the largest Ponzi scheme in history, had a reputation as an upstanding citizen before his fraud was uncovered.

Obviously, the concept of a moral philosophy is inexact. For that reason, moral philosophies must be assessed on a continuum rather than as static entities. Simply put, when examining moral philosophies, we must remember that each philosophy states an ideal perspective and that most individuals seem to shift to other moral philosophies in their individual interpretation of and experiencing of ethical dilemmas. In other words, implementing moral philosophies from an individual perspective is not an exact science. It requires individuals to apply their own accepted value systems to real-world situations. Individuals make judgments about what they believe to be right or wrong, but in their business lives they make decisions that may be based not only on perceived right or wrong but also on producing the greatest benefits with the least harm. Such decisions should respect fundamental moral rights as well as perspectives on fairness, justice, and the common good, but these issues become complicated in the real world.

The virtue approach to business ethics, as discussed earlier, assumes that there are certain ideals and values that everyone should strive for in order to achieve the maximum welfare and happiness of society.[33] Aspects of these ideals and values are expressed through individuals' specific moral philosophies. Every day in the workplace, employees must decide what is right or wrong and act accordingly. At the same time, as a member of a larger organization, an employee cannot simply enforce his or her own personal perspective, especially if he or she adheres narrowly to a single moral philosophy. Because individuals cannot control most of the decisions in their work environment, though they are always responsible for their own actions, they rarely have the power (especially in entry-level and middle-management positions) to impose their own personal moral perspective on others. In fact, the idea that a new employee has the freedom to make independent decisions on a variety of job responsibilities is not realistic.

Sometimes a company makes decisions that could be questionable according to individual customers' values and moral philosophies. For example, a brewery or a distributor of sexually explicit movies could be considered unethical to some stakeholders based on a personal perspective. A company's core values will determine how decisions that bring moral philosophies into conflict are made. Most businesses have developed a mission statement, a corporate culture, and a set of core values that express how they want to relate to their stakeholders, including customers, employees, the legal system, and society. It is usually impossible to please all stakeholders.

Problems arise when employees encounter ethical situations that they cannot resolve. Sometimes gaining a better understanding of the basic premise of their decision rationale can help them choose the "right" solution. For instance, to decide whether they should offer bribes to customers to secure a large contract, salespeople need to understand their own personal moral philosophies as well as their firm's core values. If complying with company policy or legal requirements is an important motivation to the individual, he or she is less likely to offer a bribe. On the other hand, if the salesperson's ultimate goal is a "successful" career and if offering a bribe seems likely to result in a promotion, then bribery might not be inconsistent with that person's moral philosophy of acceptable business behavior. Even though bribery is illegal under U.S. law, the employee may rationalize that bribery is necessary "because everyone else does it."

COGNITIVE MORAL DEVELOPMENT

> *"Problems arise when employees encounter ethical situations that they cannot resolve."*

Many people believe that individuals advance through stages of moral development as their knowledge and socialization continue over time. In this section, we examine a model that describes this cognitive moral development process—that is, the stages through which people may progress in their development of moral thought. Many models, developed to explain, predict, and control individuals' ethical behavior within business organizations, have proposed that cognitive moral processing is an element in ethical decision making. Cognitive moral processing is based on a body of literature in psychology that focuses on studying children and their cognitive development.[34] Psychologist Lawrence Kohlberg adapted Piaget's theory and developed the six-stage model of cognitive development, which, although not specifically designed for business contexts, provides an interesting perspective on the question of moral philosophy in business. According to **Kohlberg's model of cognitive moral development**, people make different decisions in similar ethical situations because they are in different stages of six cognitive moral development stages:

1. *The stage of punishment and obedience.* An individual in Kohlberg's first stage defines *right* as literal obedience to rules and authority. A person in this stage will respond to rules and labels of "good" and "bad" in terms of the physical power of those who determine such rules. Right and wrong are not associated with any higher order or philosophy but rather with a person who has power. Stage 1 is usually associated with small children, but signs of stage 1 development are also evident in adult behavior. For example, some companies forbid their buyers to accept gifts from salespeople. A buyer in stage 1 might justify a refusal to accept gifts from salespeople by referring to the company's rule that defines accepting gifts as an unethical practice, or the buyer may accept the gift if he or she believes that there is no chance of being caught and punished.
2. *The stage of individual instrumental purpose and exchange.* An individual in stage 2 defines *right* as that which serves his or her own needs. In this stage, the individual no longer makes moral decisions solely on the basis of specific rules or authority figures; he or she now evaluates behavior on the basis of its fairness to him or her. For example, a sales representative in stage 2 doing business for the first time in a foreign country

may be expected by custom to give customers "gifts." Although gift giving may be against company policy in the United States, the salesperson may decide that certain company rules designed for operating in the United States do not apply overseas. In the culture of some foreign countries, gifts may be considered part of a person's pay. So, in this instance, not giving a gift might put the salesperson at a disadvantage. Some refer to stage 2 as the stage of reciprocity because, from a practical standpoint, ethical decisions are based on an agreement that "you scratch my back and I'll scratch yours" instead of on principles of loyalty, gratitude, or justice.

3. *The stage of mutual interpersonal expectations, relationships, and conformity.* An individual in stage 3 emphasizes others rather than him or herself. Although ethical motivation is still derived from obedience to rules, the individual considers the well-being of others. A production manager in this stage might obey upper management's order to speed up an assembly line if he or she believed that this would generate more profit for the company and thus save employee jobs. This manager not only considers his or her own well-being in deciding to follow the order but also tries to put him or herself in upper management's and fellow employees' shoes. Thus, stage 3 differs from stage 2 in that fairness to others is one of the individual's ethical motives.
4. *The stage of social system and conscience maintenance.* An individual in stage 4 determines what is right by considering his or her duty to society, not just to other specific people. Duty, respect for authority, and maintaining the social order become the focal points. For example, some managers consider it a duty to society to protect privacy and therefore refrain from monitoring employee conversations.
5. *The stage of prior rights, social contract, or utility.* In stage 5, an individual is concerned with upholding the basic rights, values, and legal contracts of society. Individuals in this stage feel a sense of obligation or commitment, a "social contract," to other groups and recognize that in some cases legal and moral points of view may conflict. To reduce such conflict, stage 5 individuals base their decisions on a rational calculation of overall utilities. The president of a firm may decide to establish an ethics program because it will provide a buffer against legal problems and the firm will be perceived as a responsible contributor to society.
6. *The stage of universal ethical principles.* A person in this stage believes that right is determined by universal ethical principles that everyone should follow. Stage 6 individuals believe that there are inalienable rights, which are universal in nature and consequence. These rights, laws, or social agreements are valid, not because of a particular society's laws or customs, but because they rest on the premise of universality. Justice and equality are examples of principles that are deemed universal in nature. A person in this stage may be more concerned with social ethical issues and thus not rely on the business organization for ethical direction. For example, a businessperson at this stage might argue for discontinuing a product that has caused death and injury because the inalienable right to life makes killing wrong, regardless of the reason. Therefore, company profits would not be a justification for the continued sale of the product.[35]

Kohlberg's six stages can be reduced to three different levels of ethical concern. At the first level, a person is concerned with his or her own immediate interests and with external rewards and punishments. At the second level, an individual equates *right* with conformity to the expectations of good behavior of the larger society or some significant reference group. Finally, at the third, or "principled," level, an individual sees beyond the norms, laws, and authority of groups or individuals. Employees at this level make ethical decisions regardless of negative external pressures. However, research has shown that most workers' abilities to identify and resolve moral dilemmas do not reside at this third level and that their motives are often a mixture of selflessness, self-interest, and selfishness.

Kohlberg suggests that people continue to change their decision making priorities after their formative years, and as a result of time, education, and experience, they may change their values and ethical behavior. In the context of business, an individual's moral development can be influenced by corporate culture, especially ethics training. Ethics training and education have been shown to improve managers' cognitive development scores.[36] Because of corporate reform, most employees in *Fortune* 1000 companies today receive some type of ethics training. Training is also a requirement of the Federal Sentencing Guidelines for Organizations.

Some feel that experience in resolving moral conflicts accelerates an individual's progress in moral development. A manager who relies on a specific set of values or rules may eventually come across a situation in which the rules do not apply. For example, suppose Sarah is a manager whose policy is to fire any employee whose productivity declines for four consecutive months. Sarah has an employee, George, whose productivity has suffered because of depression, but George's coworkers tell Sarah that George will recover and soon be a top performer again. Because of the circumstances and the perceived value of the employee, Sarah may bend the rule and keep George. Managers in the highest stages of the moral development process seem to be more democratic than autocratic, more likely to consider the ethical views of the other people involved in an ethical decision making situation.

Once thought to be critical, the theory of cognitive moral development and the empirical research for the last 10 years has been mixed, suggesting both a positive and negative relationship between it and ethical decision making. The consensus appears to be that cognitive moral development is difficult at best to measure and connect with ethical decision making.[37]

WHITE-COLLAR CRIME

The terms *crime* and *criminal* normally conjure up thoughts of rape, arson, armed robbery, or murder. The news constantly reports on the damages that occur as a result of these types of crimes. But, although the devastation caused by these "crimes of the street" is more appealing to the evening news, it is no less destructive than the crimes perpetrated every year by seemingly nonviolent white-collar criminals. Referred to as **white-collar crimes** (WCCs), these "crimes of the suite" do more damage in monetary and emotional loss in one year than the crimes of the street over several years combined.[38]

WCC creates victims by establishing trust and respectability. WCCs are often considered to be different than crimes of the street. It is interesting to note in Figure 6–1 that deceptive pricing, unnecessary repairs, and credit card fraud are the three victim categories that were found in the national public household survey of consumers reporting over their lifetime. The victims of WCC are often trusting consumers who believe that businesses are legitimate. Unfortunately, senior citizens and other disadvantaged consumers fall prey to WCC perpetrators. Online white-collar crime is a growing problem around the world. Online WCC surged 33 percent during the most recent recession, accounting for

FIGURE 6–1 Top Internet Fraud Complaints

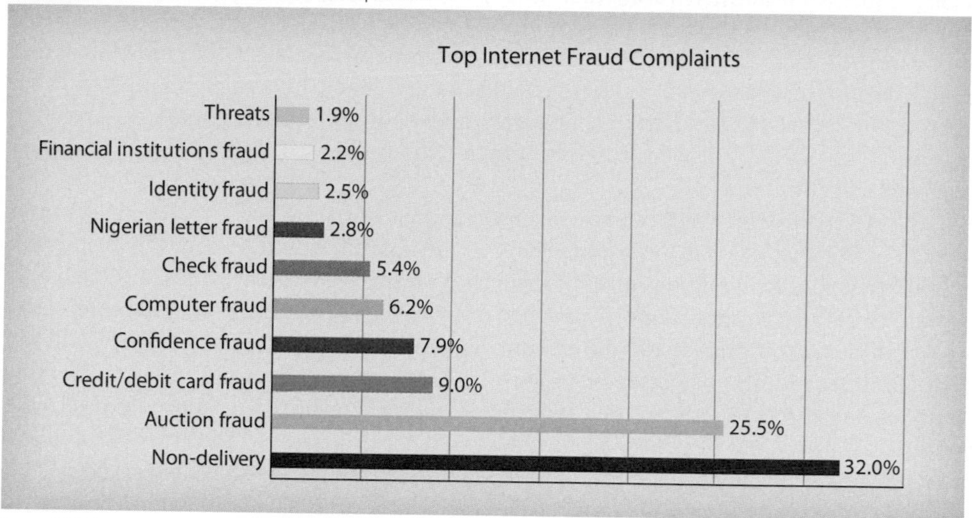

Source: "2008 Internet Crime Report," Bureau of Justice, http://www.ic3.gov/media/annualreport/2008_ic3report.pdf (accessed August 18, 2009).

nearly $265 billion in losses to U.S. households.[39] As a response to the surge in white-collar crimes, the Unites States government has stepped up its efforts to combat it, with the number of cases being investigated more than tripling since 2005. The government is concerned about the destabilizing effect that WCC has on U.S. households and the economy in general.[40]

At first glance, the job of deciding what constitutes a white-collar crime seems fairly simple. According to the glossary of legal terms for the Office of Justice Programs at the U.S. Department of Justice, a WCC is a "non-violent criminal act involving deceit, concealment, subterfuge and other fraudulent activity." The corporate executive who manipulates the stock market, the tax cheat, or the doctor who sets up an operation to swindle Medicaid are all fairly obvious candidates. However, WCC is not always so easy to define. Because government, Congress, and the American people want to better understand WCC, a number of subcategories have been created. Although the government official who accepts an illegal payment may have been wearing a white collar, he probably will be prosecuted under another title: official corruption. And while the corporate executive who orders his workers to dump illegal toxic waste materials in a nearby river also may be wearing a white collar, he probably will be classified as a violator of environmental regulations.

From various proposed definitions of WCC, the following appears to be inclusive of the main criminology literature yet parsimonious and exacting enough to be understood:

> *An individual or group committing an illegal act in relation to his/her employment, who is highly educated (college), in a position of power, trust, respectability and responsibility, within a profit/nonprofit business or government organization and who abuses the trust and authority normally associated with the position for personal and/or organizational gains.*

As one can see in Figure 6–1, many white-collar crimes are now being perpetrated via the Internet. A few of the most common white-collar offenses include antitrust violations, computer and Internet fraud, credit card fraud, bankruptcy fraud, health care fraud, tax evasion, violating environmental laws, insider trading, bribery, kickbacks, money laundering, and trade secret theft. According to the FBI, white-collar crime costs the United States an estimated $300 billion annually. The government can charge both individuals and corporations for WCC offenses. The penalties include fines, home detention, paying for the cost of prosecution, forfeitures, and even prison time. However, sanctions are often reduced if the defendant takes responsibility for the crime and assists the authorities in their investigation.

White-collar crime has become a virtual epidemic in the financial world. For example, Federal regulators charged Texas financier R. Allen Stanford and three of his firms with a fraud that centered on high-interest certificates of deposit. The Securities and Exchange Commission alleged that Stanford arranged a fraudulent investment scheme centered on an $8 billion CD program that promised unrealistically high interest rates. The SEC alleged that Stanford and his businesses lied about the security of the deposits and that Stanford was running a second scheme tied to sales of mutual funds, which allegedly used fake historical data to lure investors. The mutual fund scheme grew from under $10 million in 2004 to over $1 billion when it was discovered. According to the SEC, the fraud helped generate $25 million in revenue from fees for Stanford Group in 2007 and 2008.[41] Another example of someone committing WCC is former Illinois Governor Rod Blagojevich, who was arrested for allegedly trying to sell former Senator Obama's vacant Senate seat. He was also found guilty of taking campaign contributions to exchange for official actions.[42] He faces a maximum of 140 years in prison.

The presence of technology also seems to be giving a whole new generation of criminals the opportunity to score big. WCCs that previously originated at the top of organizations are now able to be committed at lower levels. Because of these advanced technology systems and corporate culture's increased reliance on them, anyone with the ability to hack into a system now can access the highly sensitive information necessary to commit WCC.

A classic example of WCC is the fraud perpetrated by Bernard Madoff, which was discovered in December 2008. Madoff's scam was based upon a Ponzi scheme, in which the operating principle is that you must constantly attract new investors to pay off old investors the "gains" they were promised. Most Ponzi schemes self-destruct fairly quickly as the ability to keep attracting new investors dwindles.

However, Madoff kept his scheme going for many years. The business that started with a small circle of friends and relatives was built on the promise of modest and steady returns in spite of market swings. With Madoff's social and business connections, and remarkably steady returns of 10 percent to 12 percent, investors were willing to spend billions of dollars. Part of the appeal was the aura that this investment opportunity was highly exclusive, although it later came out that thousands had given their money to Madoff.

When investors questioned Madoff about their investments, he refused to provide them online access to their accounts. Nonetheless, Madoff's well-dressed, multilingual sales representatives continued to convince European buyers to invest.

Many people indicate that one red flag would have been the fact that Madoff would have overtaken the market had he traded the options in the volumes necessary to meet his financial goals. Madoff ultimately admitted to running a 4,800-client Ponzi scheme for more than a decade. While investors thought they had nearly $65 billion invested with Madoff, his financial advisement firm never had anywhere near that much money. Incredibly, he had not invested a single penny. Instead, Madoff deposited the money in a bank account, which he then used to pay investors when they asked for their money back.

The only way he sustained the operation for as long as he did was through attracting new clients. Madoff will spend the rest of his life in prison for his crime.[43]

The focus of criminology is often the behavior of the individual and discovery of the reasons why people commit such crimes. Advocates of the organizational deviance perspective argue that a corporation is a living, breathing organism that can collectively become deviant; that companies have a life of their own, separate and distinct from biological persons; that the ultimate "actors" in an organization are individuals; and that the corporate culture of the company transcends the individuals who occupy these positions. With time, patterns of activities become institutionalized within the organization that live on after those who established them have left the firm. Table 6–4 lists some of the top justifications given by perpetrators of white collar crimes.

Another common cause of WCC is peer influence, the result of an individual's circle of acquaintances within an organization, with their accompanying views and behaviors. Employees, at least in part, self-select the people with whom they associate within an organization. For companies with a high number of ethical employees, there is a higher probability that a fence sitter (the 40 percent of businesspeople who could be persuaded to be ethical or unethical) will go along with their coworkers.

Finally, there is an argument to be made that some businesspeople may have personalities that are inherently criminal.[44] Personality tests have been used to predict behavior in individuals working within an organization, but such tests presuppose that values and philosophies are constant; thus, they seem to be ineffective as an approach to understanding the subtleties of white-collar criminals.[45] We also know that businesspeople and companies must make a profit on revenue to exist, slanting their orientation toward teleology and making them increasingly likely to commit white-collar crimes. The answer to the increase in WCC is not easy to pinpoint because many variables cause good people to make bad decisions. Many people disagree that the government is devoting enough resources to combat WCC. The current focus of the Federal Sentencing Guidelines for Organizations is that all organizations should develop effective ethics and compliance programs to prevent WCC.

TABLE 6–4 Common Justifications for White Collar Crime

1.	Denial of responsibility (Everyone can, with varying degrees of plausibility, point the finger at someone else.)
2.	Denial of injury (White-collar criminals often never meet or interact with those who are harmed by their actions.)
3.	Denial of the victim (The offender is playing tit-for-tat, and claims to be responding to a prior offense inflicted by the supposed victim.)
4.	Condemnation of the condemners (Executives dispute the legitimacy of the laws under which they are charged, or impugn the motives of the prosecutors who enforce them.)
5.	Appeal to a higher authority ("I did it for my family" remains a popular excuse.)
6.	Everyone else is doing it (Because of the highly competitive marketplace, certain pressures exist to perform that may drive people to break the law.)
7.	Entitlement (Criminals simply deny the authority of the laws they have broken.)

Source: Adapted from Daniel J. Curran and Claire M. Renzetti, *Theories of Crime* (Needham Heights, MA: Allyn & Bacon, 1994).

THE ROLE OF INDIVIDUAL FACTORS IN BUSINESS ETHICS

Of course, not everyone agrees on what the role of traditional moral philosophies in ethical decision making in an organization is. Some types such as Machiavellianism, which comes from the writing of Machiavelli, an Italian political theorist, have been found to influence ethical decisions. *The Prince* (a letter that Machiavelli wrote from exile to an Italian prince) argues against the relevance of morality in political affairs and holds that craft and deceit are justified in pursuing and maintaining political power. Machiavelli is famous for the idea that, for a leader, it is better to be feared than to be loved. This type of thinking abounds within *The Prince* because Machiavelli basically presents a guidebook for obtaining and maintaining power without the need for morality. Most business managers do not embrace this extreme philosophy, and most managers cannot communicate the exact moral philosophy that they use to make ethical decisions.

> *"Although a personal moral compass is important, it is not sufficient to prevent ethical misconduct in an organizational context."*

According to ethics consultant David Gebler, "Most unethical behavior is not done for personal gain, it's done to meet performance goals."[46] Unfortunately, many people believe that individual moral philosophies are the main driver of ethical behavior in business. This belief can be a stumbling block in assessing ethical risk and preventing misconduct in an organizational context. The moral values learned within the family and through religion and education are key factors that influence decision making, but as indicated in the models in Chapter 5, it is only one factor. The fact that many companies and business schools focus on personal character or moral development in their training programs as the main consideration reinforces the idea that employees can control the work environment. Although a personal moral compass is important, it is not sufficient to prevent ethical misconduct in an organizational context. The rewards for meeting performance goals and the corporate culture, especially for coworkers and managers, have been found to be the most important drivers of ethical decision making.[47]

Strong abilities in ethical reasoning will probably lead to more ethical business decisions in the future than trying to provide detached character education for each employee.[48] Equipping employees with intellectual skills that will allow them to understand and resolve complex ethical dilemmas that they encounter in complex corporate cultures will help them make the right decisions. This approach will hopefully keep them from being carried along by peer pressure and lulled by unethical managers to engage in misconduct.[49] The West Point model for character development focuses on the fact that competence and character must be developed simultaneously. This model assumes that ethical reasoning has to be approached in the context of a specific profession. The military has been effective in teaching skills and developing principles and values that can be used in most situations that a soldier will encounter. In a similar manner, accountants, managers, or marketers need to develop ethical reasoning in the context of their jobs.

SUMMARY

Moral philosophy refers to the set of principles, or rules, that people use to decide what is right or wrong. These principles, rules, or philosophies present guidelines for resolving conflicts and for optimizing the mutual benefit of people living in groups. Businesspeople are somewhat guided by moral philosophies as they formulate business strategies and resolve specific ethical issues.

Teleological, or consequentialist, philosophies stipulate that acts are morally right or acceptable if they produce some desired result, such as realization of self-interest or utility. Egoism defines right or acceptable behavior in terms of the consequences for the individual. In an ethical decision making situation, the egoist will choose the alternative that contributes most to his or her own self-interest. Egoism further can be classified into hedonism and enlightened egoism. Utilitarianism is concerned with maximizing total utility, or providing the greatest benefit for the greatest number of people. In making ethical decisions, utilitarians often conduct a cost–benefit analysis, which considers the costs and benefits to all affected parties. Rule utilitarians determine behavior on the basis of rules designed to promote the greatest utility rather than by examining particular situations. Act utilitarians examine the action itself, rather than the rules governing the action, to determine whether it will result in the greatest utility.

Deontological, or nonconsequentialist, philosophies focus on the rights of individuals and on the intentions behind an individual's particular behavior rather than on its consequences. In general, deontologists regard the nature of moral principles as permanent and stable, and they believe that compliance with these principles defines ethicalness. Deontologists believe that individuals have certain absolute rights that must be respected. Rule deontologists believe that conformity to general moral principles determines ethicalness. Act deontologists hold that actions are the proper basis on which to judge morality or ethicalness and that rules serve only as guidelines.

According to the relativist perspective, definitions of ethical behavior are derived subjectively from the experiences of individuals and groups. The relativist observes behavior within a relevant group and attempts to determine what consensus group members have reached on the issue in question.

Virtue ethics posits that what is moral in a given situation is not only what is required by conventional morality or current social definitions, however justified, but also what a person with a "good" moral character would deem appropriate. Those who profess virtue ethics do not believe that the end justifies the means in any situation.

Ideas of justice as applied in business relate to evaluations of fairness. Justice relates to the fair treatment and due reward in accordance with ethical or legal standards. Distributive justice is based on the evaluation of the outcome or results of a business relationship. Procedural justice is based on the processes and activities that produce the outcomes or results. Interactional justice is based on an evaluation of the communication process in business.

The concept of a moral philosophy is not exact; moral philosophies can only be assessed on a continuum. Individuals use different moral philosophies depending on whether they are making a personal or a workplace decision.

According to Kohlberg's model of cognitive moral development, individuals make different decisions in similar ethical situations because they are in different stages of moral development. In Kohlberg's model, people progress through six stages of moral development: (1) punishment and obedience; (2) individual instrumental purpose and exchange; (3) mutual interpersonal expectations, relationships, and conformity; (4) social system and conscience maintenance; (5) prior rights, social contract, or utility; and (6) universal ethical principles. Kohlberg's six stages can be further reduced to three levels of ethical concern: immediate self-interest, social expectations, and general ethical principles. Cognitive moral development may not explain as much as was once believed.

White-collar crime can be defined as an individual who is educated and in a position of power, trust, respectability, and responsibility committing an illegal act in relation to his or her employment, and who abuses the trust and authority normally associated with the position for personal and/or organizational gains. Some reasons why white-collar crime is not being heavily researched are that it doesn't come to mind when people think of crime, the offender (or organization) is in a position of trust and respectability, criminology or criminal justice systems look at white-collar crime differently, and many researchers have not moved past the definitional issues. The increase in technology use seems to be increasing the opportunity to commit white-collar crime with less risk.

Individual factors such as religion, moral intensity, and a person's professional affiliations can affect a person's values and decision making process. Other factors such as ethical awareness, biases, conflict, personality type, and intelligence have been studied, but no definitive conclusions can be made at this time about their relationship to ethical behavior. One thing we do know is that moral philosophies, values, and business are more complex than merely giving people honesty tests or value profiles that are not business oriented. Paper-and-pencil techniques do not yield accurate profiles for companies.

IMPORTANT TERMS FOR REVIEW

moral philosophy
economic value orientation
idealism
realism
monist
hedonism
quantitative hedonist
qualitative hedonist
pluralist
instrumentalist
goodness theory
obligation theory
teleology
consequentialism
egoism
enlightened egoism
utilitarianism
rule utilitarian
act utilitarian
deontology
nonconsequentialist
rule deontologist
act deontologist
relativist perspective
descriptive relativism
metaethical relativist
normative relativism
virtue ethics
justice
distributive justice
procedural justice
interactional justice
Kohlberg's model of cognitive moral development
white-collar crime

RESOLVING ETHICAL BUSINESS CHALLENGES*

Twenty-eight-year-old Elaine Hunt, who is married and has one child, has been with United Banc Corporation (UBC) for several years. During that time, she has seen the company grow from a relatively small-size to a medium-size business with domestic and international customers. Elaine's husband, Dennis, has been involved in the import–export business.

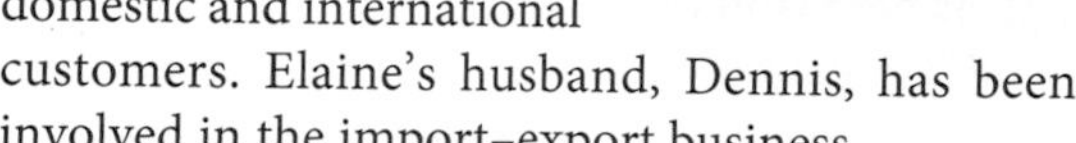

The situation that precipitated their current problem began six months ago. Elaine had just been promoted to senior financial manager, which put her in charge of 10 branch-office loan managers, each of whom had five loan officers who reported to him or her. For the most part, the branch loan officers would go through the numbers of their loan people, as well as sign off on loans under $250,000. However, recently this limit had been increased to $500,000. For loans over this amount and up to $40 million, Elaine had to sign off. For larger loans, a vice president would have to be involved.

Recently, Graphco Inc. requested a $10 million loan, which Elaine had been hesitant to approve. Graphco was a subsidiary of a tobacco firm embroiled in litigation concerning the promotion of its products to children. When reviewing the numbers, Elaine could not find any glaring problems, yet she had decided against the loan even when Graphco had offered to pay an additional interest point. Some at UBC applauded her moral stance while others did not, arguing that it was not a good financial business decision. The next prospective loan was for a Canadian company that was exporting cigars from Cuba. Elaine cited the U.S. policy against Cuba as the reason for not approving that loan. "The Helms-Burton Amendment gives us clear guidance as to what we shouldn't be doing with Cuba," she said to others in the company, even though the loan was to a Canadian firm. The third loan application she was unwilling to approve had come from Electrode International, which sought $50 million. The numbers had been marginal, but the sticking point for Elaine was Electrode's unusually high profits during the last two years. During dinner with Dennis, she had learned about a meeting in Zurich during which Electrode and others had allegedly fixed the prices on their products. Because only a handful of companies manufactured these particular products, the price increases were very successful. When Elaine suggested denying the loan on the basis of this information, she was overruled. At the same time, a company in Brazil was asking for an agricultural loan to harvest parts of the rain forest. The Brazilian company was willing to pay almost 2 points over the going rate for a $40 million loan. Because of her stand on environmental issues, Elaine rejected this application as well. The company obtained the loan from one of UBC's competitors.

Recently, Elaine's husband's decision making had fallen short of his superior's expectations. First, there was the problem of an American firm wanting to export nicotine and caffeine patches to Southeast Asia. With new research showing both these drugs to be more problematic than previously thought, the manufacturing firm had decided to attempt a rapid-penetration marketing strategy—that is, to price the products very low or at cost in order to gain market share and then over time slightly increase the margin. With 2 billion potential customers, a one-cent markup could result in millions of dollars in profits. Dennis had rejected the deal, and the firm had gone to another company. One person in Dennis's division had said, "Do you realize that you had the perfect product—one that was low cost and both physically and psychologically addictive? You could have serviced that one account for years and would have had enough for early retirement. Are you nuts for turning it down?!"

Soon afterward, an area financial bank manager wanted Elaine to sign off on a revolving loan for ABCO. ABCO's debt/equity ratio had increased significantly and did not conform to company regulations. However, Elaine was the one who had written the standards for UBC. Some in the company felt that Elaine was not quite up with the times. For example, several very good bank staff members had left in the past year because they found her regulations too provincial for the emerging global marketplace. As Elaine reviewed ABCO's credit report, she found many danger signals; however, the loan was relatively large, $30 million, and the company had been in a credit sales slump. As she questioned ABCO, Elaine learned that the loan was to develop a new business venture within the People's Republic of China, which rumor had it was also working with the Democratic People's Republic of Korea. The biotech venture was for fetal tissue research and harvesting. Recently, attention had focused on the economic benefits of such tissue in helping a host of ailments. Anticipated global market sales for such products were being estimated at $10 billion for the next decade. ABCO was also willing to go almost 2 points above the standard interest equation for such a revolving loan. Elaine realized that if she signed off on this sale, it would signal an end to her standards. However, if she did not and ABCO went to another company for the loan and paid off the debt, she would have made a gross error, and everyone in the company would know it.

As Elaine was wrestling with this problem, Dennis's commissions began to slip, putting a crimp in their cash-flow projections. If things did not turn around quickly for him, they would lose their new home, fall behind in other payments, and reduce the number of educational options for their child. Elaine had also had a frank discussion with senior management about her loan standards as well as her stand on tobacco, which had lost UBC precious income. The response was, "Elaine, we applaud your moral outrage about such products, but your morals are negatively impacting the bottom line. We can't have that all the time."

QUESTIONS • EXERCISES

1. Discuss the advantages and disadvantages of each decision that Elaine has made.
2. What are the ethical and legal considerations facing Elaine, Dennis, and UBC?
3. Discuss the moral philosophies that may be relevant to this situation.
4. Discuss the implications of each decision that Elaine could make.

*This case is strictly hypothetical; any resemblance to real persons, companies, or situations is coincidental.

CHECK YOUR EQ

Check your EQ, or Ethics Quotient, by completing the following. Assess your performance to evaluate your overall understanding of the chapter material.

1. Teleology defines right or acceptable behavior in terms of consequences for the individual. **Yes No**
2. A relativist looks at an ethical situation and considers the individuals and groups involved. **Yes No**
3. A utilitarian is most concerned with the bottom-line benefits. **Yes No**
4. Act deontology requires that a person use equity, fairness, and impartiality in making decisions and evaluating actions. **Yes No**
5. Virtues that support business transactions include trust, fairness, truthfulness, competitiveness, and focus. **Yes No**

ANSWERS **1. No.** That's egoism. **2. Yes.** Relativists look at themselves and those around them to determine ethical standards. **3. Yes.** Utilitarians look for the greatest good for the greatest number of people and use a cost–benefit approach. **4. Yes.** The rules serve only as guidelines, and past experience weighs more heavily than the rules. **5. No.** The characteristics include trust, self-control, empathy, fairness, and truthfulness—not competitiveness and focus.

CHAPTER 7

Organizational Factors: The Role of Ethical Culture and Relationships

CHAPTER OBJECTIVES

- To understand the concept of corporate culture
- To examine the influence of corporate culture on business ethics
- To determine how leadership, power, and motivation relate to ethical decision making in organizations
- To assess organizational structure and its relationship to business ethics
- To explore how the work group influences ethical decisions
- To discuss the relationship between individual and group ethical decision making

CHAPTER OUTLINE

Defining Corporate Culture

The Role of Corporate Culture in Ethical Decision Making

Ethical Frameworks and Evaluations of Corporate Culture

Ethics as a Component of Corporate Culture

Compliance versus Value-based Ethical Cultures

Differential Association

Whistle-Blowing

Leaders Influence Corporate Culture

Reward Power

Coercive Power

Legitimate Power

Expert Power

Referent Power

Motivating Ethical Behavior

Organizational Structure and Business Ethics

Group Dimensions of Corporate Structure and Culture

Types of Groups

Group Norms

Variation in Employee Conduct

Can People Control Their Own Actions Within a Corporate Culture?

AN ETHICAL DILEMMA*

Dawn Prarie had been with PCA Health Care Hospitals for three years and had been promoted to marketing director in the Miami area. She had a staff of 10 and a fairly healthy budget. Dawn's job was to attract more patients into the HMO while helping keep costs down. At a meeting with Dawn, Nancy Belle, the vice president, had explained the ramifications of the Balanced Budget Act and how it was affecting all HMOs. "Being here in Miami does not help our division," she told Dawn. "Because of this Balanced Budget Act, we have been losing money on many of our elderly patients. For example, we used to receive $600 or more a month, per patient, from Medicare, but now our minimum reimbursement is just $367 a month! I need solutions, and that's where you come in. By the end of the month, I want a list of things that will help us show a profit. Anything less than a positive balance sheet will be unacceptable."

It was obvious that Nancy was serious about cutting costs and increasing revenues within the elderly market. That's why Dawn had been promoted to marketing director. The first thing Dawn did after the meeting with Nancy was to fire four key people. She then gave their duties to six who were at lower salaries and put the hospital staff on notice that changes would be occurring at the hospital over the next several months. In about three weeks, Dawn presented Nancy with an extensive list of ideas. It included these suggestions:

1. Trimming some prescription drug benefits
2. Reducing redundant tests for terminal patients
3. Hiring physician assistants to see patients but billing patients at the physician rate
4. Allowing physicians to buy shares in PCA, thus providing an incentive for bringing in more patients
5. Sterilizing and reusing cardiac catheters
6. Instituting a one-vendor policy on hospital products to gain quantity discounts
7. Prescreening "insurance" patients for probability of payment

Dawn's assistants felt that some of the hospital staff could be more aggressive in the marketing area. They urged using more promotional materials, offering incentives for physicians who suggested PCA or required their patients to be hospitalized, and prescreening potential clients into categories. "You see," said Ron, one of Dawn's staff, "we feel that there are four types of elderly patients. There are the healthy elderly, whose life expectancies are 10 or more years. There are the fragile elderly, with life expectancies of two to seven years. Then there are the demented and dying elderly, who usually have one to three years. Finally, we have the high-cost or uninsured elderly. Patients who are designated healthy would get the most care, including mammograms, prostate-cancer screening, and cholesterol checks. Patients in the other categories would get less."

As she implemented some of the recommendations on Dawn's list, Nancy also launched an aggressive plan to destabilize the nurses' union. As a result, many nurses began a work slowdown and were filing internal petitions to upper management. Headquarters told Nancy to give the nurses and other hospital staff as much overtime as they wanted but not to hire anyone new. One floor manager suggested splitting up the staff into work teams, with built-in incentives for those who worked smarter and/or faster. Nancy approved the plan, and in three months productivity jumped 50 percent, with many of the hospital workers making more money. The downside for Nancy was an increase in worker-related accidents.

When Dawn toured the hospital around this time, she found that some of the most productive workers were using substandard procedures and poorly made products. One nurse said, "Yes, the surgical gloves are somewhat of a problem, but we were told that the quality met the minimum requirements and so we have to use them." Dawn brought this to Nancy's attention, whereupon Nancy drafted the following memo:

> **Attention Hospital Staff**
> It has come to management's attention that minor injuries to staff and patients are on the rise. Please review the Occupational Safety and Health Administration guidelines, as well as the standard procedures handbook, to make sure you are in compliance. I also want to thank all those teams that have been keeping costs down. We have finally gone into the plus side as far as profitability. Hang on and we'll be able to stabilize the hospital to make it a better place to care for patients and to work.

At Nancy's latest meeting with Dawn, she told Dawn, "We've decided on your staff's segmentation strategy for the elderly market. We want you to develop a questionnaire to prescreen incoming HMO patients, as well as existing clients, into one of the four categories so that we can tag their charts and alert the HMO physicians to the new protocols. Also, because the recommendations that we've put into practice have worked so well, we've decided to use the rest of your suggestions. The implementation phase will start next month. I want you, Dawn, to be the lead person in developing a long-term strategy to break the unions in the hospital. Do whatever it takes. We just need to do more with less. I'm firm on this—so you're either on board or you're not. Which is it going to be?"

QUESTIONS • EXERCISES

1. Discuss PCA Health Care Hospitals' corporate culture and its ethical implications.
2. What factors are affecting Dawn's options?
3. Discuss the issue of for-profit versus nonprofit health-care facilities.
4. If you were Dawn, what information would you like to have to make your decisions?

*This case is strictly hypothetical; any resemblance to real persons, companies, or situations is coincidental.

Organizations are much more than structures in which we work. Although they are not alive, we attribute human characteristics to them. When times are good, we say the company is "well"; when times are not so good, we may try to "save" the company. Understandably, people have feelings toward the place that provides them with income and benefits, challenge, satisfaction, self-esteem, and often lifelong friendships. In fact, excluding the time spent sleeping, we spend almost 50 percent of our lives in this second home with our second "family." It is important, then, to examine how the culture and structure of these organizations influence the ethical decisions made within them.

In the ethical decision making framework described in Chapter 5, we introduced the concept that organizational factors and interpersonal relationships influence the ethical decision making process. In this chapter, we take a closer look at corporate culture and the way a company's values and traditions can affect employees' ethical behavior. We also discuss the role of leadership in influencing ethical behavior within the organization. Next we describe two organizational structures and examine how they may influence ethical decisions. We discuss new organizational structures that have been created to address the global or corporate responsibility to employees and other stakeholders. Then we consider the impact of groups within organizations. Finally, we examine the implications of organizational relationships for ethical decisions.

DEFINING CORPORATE CULTURE

Culture is a common word that people generally use in relation to genealogy, country of origin, language and the way people speak, what they eat, and their customs. Many define culture as nationality or citizenship. Values, norms, artifacts, and rituals all play a role in culture. Chapter 5 defined the term corporate culture as a set of values, norms, and artifacts including ways of solving problems that members (employees) of an organization share.

Corporate culture is also viewed as "the shared beliefs top managers in a company have about how they should manage themselves and other employees, and how they should conduct their business(es)."[1] Mutual of Omaha defines corporate culture as the "personality of the organization, the shared beliefs that determine how its people behave and solve business problems."[2] Its executives believe that its corporate culture provides the foundation for the company's work and objectives, and the company has adopted a set of core values called "Values for Success." The company believes that these values form the foundation for a corporate culture that will help the organization realize its vision and achieve its goals. Corporate culture includes values, norms, and artifacts and is exhibited through the behavioral patterns, concepts, documents such as codes of ethics, and rituals that take place in the organization.[3].It gives the members of the organization meaning as well as the internal rules of behavior.[4]

Southwest Airlines has a very strong and friendly, fun-loving organizational culture that dates all the way back to the days of its key founder Herb Kelleher. Stories are legendary of Kelleher appearing in a dress and feather boa and joining baggage handlers on Southwest flights. He ran an awards ceremony for employees that many felt rivaled the Academy Awards. His employees were treated like family. Today, Southwest continues that legacy and culture. Over 1,300 Southwest employees are married couples. This family-friendly environment also relates to parents and their children working for the airline. In one case, 15 members of the same Chicago family work for the airline. Pilots willingly and enthusiastically support the "Adopt a Pilot" program whereby students in classrooms around the country adopt a Southwest pilot for a four-week educational and mentoring program, attending classes, e-mailing, and sending postcards from a variety of destinations. Southwest's culture has caused it to rank among the best companies to work for and allows it to attract some of the best talent in the industry.[5] When these values, beliefs, customs, rules, and ceremonies are accepted, shared, and circulated throughout the organization, they represent its culture. All organizations, not just corporations, have some sort of culture, and thus we use the terms *organizational culture* and *corporate culture* interchangeably.

A company's history and unwritten rules are a part of its culture. Thus, for many years, IBM salespeople adhered to a series of unwritten standards for dealing with clients. The history or stories passed down from generation to generation within an organization are like the traditions that are propagated within society. Henry Ford, the founder of Ford Motor Company, left a legacy that emphasized the importance of the individual employee and the natural environment. Just as Henry Ford pioneered the then-unheard-of high wage of $5 a day in the early years of the twentieth century, current chairman William Clay Ford, Jr., continues to affirm that employees represent the only sustainable advantage of a company.[6] William Ford has maintained his grandfather's legacy by taking a leadership role in improving vehicle fuel efficiency while reducing emissions. Ford faces many financial challenges, especially with the financial meltdown. Although it is not one of the companies receiving government financial support during the economic crisis, Ford offered some of its debtholders less than the debt was originally worth (less than one-third) to eliminate over $10 billion in financial obligations.[7]

> *"A company's history and unwritten rules are a part of its culture."*

Leaders are responsible for the actions of subordinates and corporations should have good corporate cultures. For this reason, the definition and measurement of culture is very important. For example, it is defined in the Sarbanes–Oxley Act, which was enacted after the Enron, Tyco International, Adelphia, Peregrine Systems, and WorldCom scandals. This was codified within the **Sarbanes–Oxley 404** compliance section. This section includes management's assessment of its controls, management's assertion whether these controls are effective, and an audit of these internal controls by the external auditor in conjunction with the audit of the financial statements. Section 404 forces firms into a set of values that must make up a portion of the company's culture. The evaluation of corporate culture is meant to provide insight into the character of an organization, its ethics, and level of openness.

Compliance with Sarbanes–Oxley 404 requires cultural change, not merely accounting changes. The intent is to expose mismanagement, fraud, theft, abuse, and to sustain a corporate culture that does not allow these conditions and actions to exist. Many consulting companies have filled the need of companies wanting to comply, but have not understood what culture is. Instead, they have sought to provide direction and criteria for improving an organization's ability to manage risk, not ethicalness. In many firms what is meant by a good corporate culture is measured in the following ways:

- Management and the board demonstrate their commitment to strong controls through their communications and actions.
- Every employee is encouraged and required to have hands-on involvement in the internal control system.
- Every employee is encouraged and empowered to report policy exceptions.
- Employees are expected to be in the communication loop through resolutions and corrective actions.

- Employees have the ability to report policy exceptions anonymously to any member of the organization, including the CEO, other members of management, and the board of directors.[8]

The problem with these measures of culture is that they merely measure risk, not ethics. As a result, many assume that the four aforementioned items define culture and what a good culture should be. The problem still remains of defining corporate culture and what should be measured.

In the past 50 years, scholars have developed at least 164 distinct definitions of culture. More recent reviews indicate that the number of definitions has only been increasing.[9] While these definitions of culture vary greatly, there are three common elements: (1) "culture is shared among individuals belonging to a group or society;" (2) "culture is formed over a relatively long period of time;" and (3) "culture is relatively stable."[10]

Different models of culture, and consequently different instruments for measuring it, focus on various levels (national, organizational, individual) and aspects (values, practices, observable artifacts and rituals, underlying implicit assumptions). Geert Hofstede, an important researcher of IBM's corporate culture, described it as an onion with many layers, representing different levels within the corporation.[11]

Because many researchers and experts have defined culture so many different ways, "cultural values" and "culture" are often used interchangeably, especially in the fields of management and psychology. Nevertheless, there is no single opinion as to what values and attitudes constitute culture. Despite the overlap in dimensions from different models of culture, there are differences in what is emphasized in different fields of research. Since no one has established conclusively what factors or components should represent corporate culture, we cannot infer intent or readily define what constitutes an ethical or unethical firm.

Many in business define ethics as what society states as good or bad and develop measures that manage the risk of illegal behavior. We definitely know that culture has a significant effect on the ethical decision making process of those in business, regardless of the firm's makeup. We want you to understand that managing risk is not the same as understanding what makes up a firm's culture. Ethical audits, ethical compliance, and risk culture surveys may be good tools, but they are not valid in helping to define culture or to explain an ethical/unethical organization.

THE ROLE OF CORPORATE CULTURE IN ETHICAL DECISION MAKING

The role of corporate culture has been associated with success and failure. Some cultures are so strong that to outsiders they come to represent the character of the entire organization. For example, Levi Strauss, Ben & Jerry's Homemade (the ice cream company), and Hershey Foods are widely perceived as casual organizations with strong ethical cultures, whereas Lockheed Martin, Procter & Gamble, and Texas Instruments are perceived as more formal, ethical ones. The culture of an organization may be explicitly articulated or left unspoken.

Explicit statements of values, beliefs, and customs usually come from upper management. Memos, written codes of conduct, handbooks, manuals, forms, and ceremonies are all formal expressions of an organization's culture. Many of these statements can be found on company websites, like that for Wells Fargo (Table 7–1).

TABLE 7–1 Wells Fargo's Values

We want all team members to know our values so well that if we threw out all the policy manuals, we would still make decisions based on our understanding of our culture. These are our values:
Ethics
• Maintain the highest standards with customers, team members, stockholders and our communities.
• Value and reward open, honest, two-way communication.
• Be accountable for, and proud of, your conduct and your decisions.
• Only make promises you intend to keep—do what you say you'll do.
• If things change, let people know.
• Avoid any actual or perceived conflict of interest.
• Comply with the letter and the spirit of the law.

Source: "What Are Our Values?," Wells Fargo, https://www.wellsfargo.com/invest_relations/vision_values/11 (accessed May 29, 2009).

Corporate culture is often expressed informally—for example, through comments, both direct and indirect, that communicate the wishes of management. In some companies, shared values are expressed through informal dress codes, working late, and participating in extracurricular activities. Corporate culture can even be expressed through gestures, looks, labels, promotions, programs, and legends (or the lack of these). Phil Knight, Nike co-founder and sports icon, has created a strong and appealing organizational culture. Knight has been known to seek out new employees on their first few days on the job to "borrow $20.00 for lunch." The unsuspecting new employees are astounded that Knight spoke to them. Knight used that tactic as a subtle way to let new employees know that they were on the radar. Interestingly, Knight has never paid back any of the employees. This ritual contributed to building trust, commitment, and differentiates Nike's organizational culture from that of its competitors.

The "tone at the top" is often cited as a determining factor in creating a high-integrity organization. Employees were asked, in a KPMG Forensic Integrity Survey (Figure 7–1), whether their CEO and other senior executives exhibited characteristics attributable to personal integrity and ethical leadership. Nearly two-thirds of employees believed that their leaders served as positive role models for their organizations. However, roughly half suggested a lack of confidence (based on "unsure" and "disagree" responses) that their CEOs knew about behaviors further down in the organization. Nearly half suggested a lack of confidence that their leaders would be approachable if employees had ethics concerns, and 70 percent agreed that their CEOs would respond appropriately to matters brought to their attention. Overall, nearly two-thirds of employees agreed their leaders set the right tone at the top, leaving one-third unsure or in disagreement.

Ethical Frameworks and Evaluations of Corporate Culture

Corporate culture has been conceptualized in many ways. Authors N. K. Sethia and Mary Ann Von Glinow have proposed two basic dimensions to describe an organization's culture: (1) concern for people—the organization's efforts to care for its employees' well-being; and (2) concern for performance—the organization's efforts to focus on output

FIGURE 7–1 Perceived Tone and Culture, Tone at the Top, and Perceptions of the CEO and Other Senior Executives

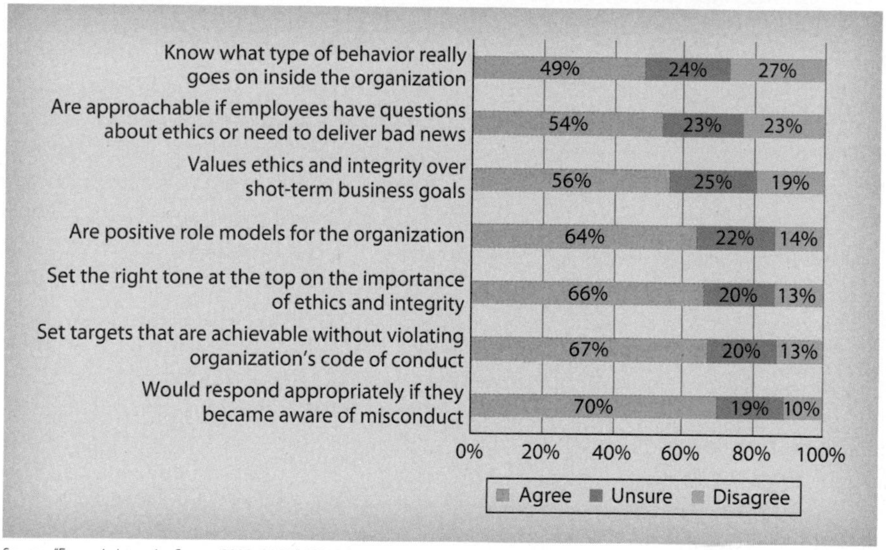

Know what type of behavior really goes on inside the organization
49%
24%
27%
Are approachable if employees have questions about ethics or need to deliver bad news
54%
23%
23%
Values ethics and integrity over shot-term business goals
56%
25%
19%
Are positive role models for the organization
64%
22%
14%
Set the right tone at the top on the importance of ethics and integrity
66%
20%
13%
Set targets that are achievable without violating organization's code of conduct
67%
20%
13%
Would respond appropriately if they became aware of misconduct
70%
19%
10%
0%
20%
40%
60%
80%
100%
Agree
Unsure
Disagree

Source: "Forensic Integrity Survey 2008–2009," KPMG, http://www.kpmg.com/SiteCollectionDocuments/Integrity-Survey-2008-2009.pdf (accessed August 19, 2009).

and employee productivity. A two-by-two matrix represents the four general types of organizational cultures (Figure 7–2).[12]

As Figure 7–2 shows, the four organizational cultures can be classified as apathetic, caring, exacting, and integrative. The **apathetic culture** shows minimal concern for either people or performance. In this culture, individuals focus on their own self-interests. Apathetic tendencies can occur in almost any organization. Steel companies and airlines were among the first to freeze employee pensions to keep their businesses operating. Sweeping changes in corporate America are impacting employee compensation and retirement plans. Simple gestures of appreciation, such as anniversary watches, rings, dinners, or birthday cards for family members, are being dropped. Many companies view

FIGURE 7–2 A Framework of Organizational Culture Typologies

High
Caring
Integrative
Concern for People
Low
Apathetic
Exacting
Low
High
Concern for Performance

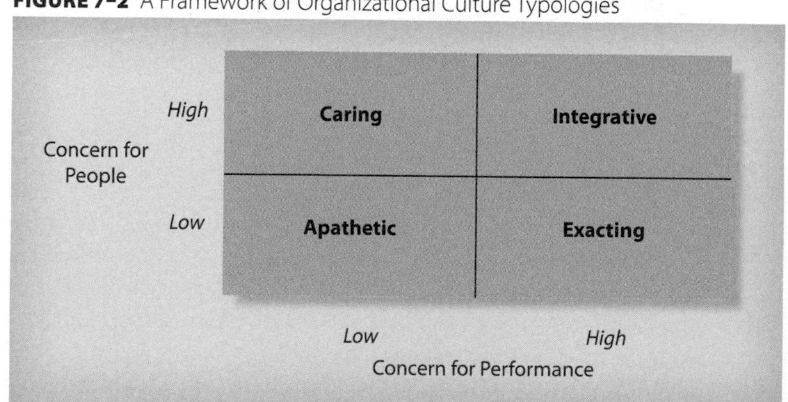

Source: From *Gaining Control of the Corporate Culture*, by N. K. Sethia and M. A. Von Glinow, 1985, Jossey-Bass, Inc. Reprinted with permission of John Wiley & Sons, Inc.

long-serving employees as dead wood and do not take into account past performance. This attitude demonstrates the companies' apathetic culture.

The **caring culture** exhibits high concern for people but minimal concern for performance issues. From an ethical standpoint, the caring culture seems very appealing. However, it is difficult to find nationally recognizable companies that maintain little or no concern for performance. In contrast, the **exacting culture** shows little concern for people but a high concern for performance; it focuses on the interests of the organization. United Parcel Service (UPS) has always been very exacting. With over 1.8 million customers shipping to 6.1 million consignees in over 200 countries, UPS knows just how many employees it needs to move its 15.5 million pieces per day worldwide.[13] To combat the uncaring, unsympathetic attitude of many of its managers, UPS developed a community service program for its employees. Global Volunteer Week gives UPS employees around the world the opportunity to help paint schools, renovate shelters, and assist with many other needed projects within their communities. An early innovator, UPS tested ways to use alternate fuels in the 1930s. Now the company operates the largest private alternative fleet in the transportation industry with over 1,600 compressed natural gas, liquefied natural gas, hybrid electric, electric, and propane powered vehicles. The goal of UPS is to dramatically reduce emissions and improve fuel efficiency.[14]

The **integrative culture** combines high concern for people and for performance. An organization becomes integrative when superiors recognize that employees are more than interchangeable parts—that employees have an ineffable quality that helps the firm meet its performance criteria. Many companies, such as the Boston Consulting Group, have such a culture. The Boston Consulting Group rated first place among *Fortune*'s "Best Companies to Work For" among the smaller organizations. The company values its employees and creates significant mentorship opportunities and extensive training that allow employees to develop rapidly. In addition, the company provides high pay and a progressive benefits package (including three months of paid maternity leave, plus a 15 percent bonus on pay to a retirement plan). The Boston Consulting Group is a financially successful global consulting firm with a strong reputation that specializes in business strategy.[15] Companies can classify their corporate culture and identify its specific values, norms, beliefs, and customs by conducting a cultural audit. A **cultural audit** is an assessment of the organization's values. It is usually conducted by outside consultants but may be performed internally as well. Table 7–2 illustrates some of the issues that an ethics audit of a corporate culture should address. The table identifies components of an organizational ethical culture, with the percentage of those employees who strongly agreed or agreed that the specific action was being displayed in their organizations. These issues can help identify a corporate culture that creates ethical conflict.

Ethics as a Component of Corporate Culture

As indicated in the framework presented in Chapter 5, ethical culture, the ethical component of corporate culture, is a significant factor in ethical decision making. If a firm's culture encourages or rewards unethical behavior, its employees may well act unethically. If the culture dictates hiring people who have specific, similar values and if those values are perceived as unethical by society, society will view the organization and its members as unethical. Such a pattern often occurs in certain areas of marketing. For instance, salespeople may be seen as unethical because they sometimes use aggressive selling tactics to get customers to buy things they do not need or want. If a company's primary objective is to make as much profit as possible, through whatever means, its culture may foster

TABLE 7–2 Ethics-Related Actions Among Levels of Employees

Statement Describing Ethics-Related Actions	Percentage of Employees Strongly Agreeing or Agreeing
Top management provides information	80
Top management keeps commitments	81
Top management communicates ethics	89
Top management sets a good example of ethics	87
Middle management keeps commitments	85
Middle management communicates ethics	89
Middle management sets good example of ethics	89
Supervisor sets good example of ethics	91
Supervisor keeps commitments	88
Supervisor talks about ethics	90
Supervisor supports standards	93
Coworkers consider ethics in decisions	91
Coworkers support standards	94
Coworkers set good example of ethics	92
Coworkers talk about ethics	80

Source: From ***2005 National Business Ethics Survey: How Employees Perceive Ethics at Work***, p. 20. Copyright © 2006, Ethics Resource Center (ERC). Used with permission of the ERC, 1747 Pennsylvania Ave., N.W., Suite 400, Washington, DC 2006, www.ethics.org.

behavior that conflicts with stakeholders' ethical values. For example, Boeing general counsel, Doug Bain, noted in an annual leadership meeting that Boeing operated with a culture of winning at any cost. He noted that 15 company vice presidents had been removed for a variety of ethical lapses. Boeing is under investigation by the Justice Department and could face heavy fines.[16] The interests of diverse Boeing stakeholders (shareholders, suppliers, and employees) may have been ignored in its efforts to boost profits.

On the other hand, if the organization values ethical behaviors, it will reward them. It is important to handle recognition and awards for appropriate behavior in a consistent and balanced manner. All employees should be eligible for the recognition, the behaviors or actions acknowledged should be noted, anyone performing at the threshold level should be acknowledged, and the praise or reward should be given as close to the performance as possible.[17] An organization's failure to monitor or manage its culture may foster questionable behavior. In a patent infringement case brought against Gateway in Utah, a federal judge reprimanded the company for destroying or losing evidence in "bad faith." A former IBM engineer brought the suit against Gateway, indicating that Gateway infringed upon his patents for addressing defects in floppy-disk drives. The engineer also added that Gateway lost or destroyed documents that would have helped prove his case. Attempts to cover up wrongdoing by destroying documents should not be tolerated.[18]

Management's sense of the organization's culture may be quite different from the values and ethical beliefs that are actually guiding the firm's employees. Table 7–3 provides an example of a corporate culture ethics audit. Companies interested in assessing their culture can use this tool and benchmark against previous years' results to measure for organizational improvements. Ethical issues may arise because of conflicts between the cultural values perceived by management and those actually at work in the organization. For example, managers may believe that the culture encourages respect for peers and subordinates. On the basis of the rewards or sanctions associated with various behaviors, however, the firm's employees may believe that the company encourages competition among organizational members. A competitive orientation may result in a less ethical corporate culture. On the other hand, employees appreciate working in an environment that is designed to enhance workplace experiences through goals that encompass more than just maximizing profits.[19] Thus, it is very important for top managers to determine what the organization's culture is and to monitor its values, traditions, and beliefs to ensure that they represent the desired culture. However, the rewards and punishments imposed by an organization need to be consistent with the actual corporate culture. As two business ethics experts have observed, "Employees will value and use as guidelines those activities for which they will be rewarded. When a behavior that is rewarded comes into conflict with an unstated and unmonitored ethical value, usually the rewarded behavior wins out."[20]

Compliance versus Value-based Ethical Cultures

During the latter twentieth century a distinction evolved between culture types. The traditional ethics-based culture revolved around compliance. The accounting professional model of rules created a **compliance culture** that fed into the notion of risk. Compliance-based cultures use their legal departments to determine ethics. They include the auditing department to create rules and procedures as well as monitoring the process. Codes of conduct are established, compliance is the focus, and auditors and lawyers establish the framework so as to attempt to match what different laws want. The compliance approach's main problem is in the measurement of its purpose. Instead of revolving around ethics it revolves around risk management. A traditional ethical compliance culture usually has an audit and financial focus; a transaction-based, compliance objective with policies and procedures; and multiyear audit coverage within a budgeted cost center with career auditors.[21] The compliance approach is good in the short term at presenting to management, stakeholders, and legal agencies that adherence to laws, rules, and the intent of compliance is fulfilled. A problem in the compliance approach is its lack of long-term focus on values and integrity.

Within the last 10 years there has been a shift from compliance towards a values-based approach. A **values-based ethics culture** approach to ethical corporate cultures relies upon an explicit mission statement that defines the firm as well as how customers and employees should be treated. From this, the board of directors as well as upper management adds to the general value statements by operationalizing them by strategic business unit (SBU), product, geography, or function within the firm's management structure. Certain areas may have rules that are associated with stated values such that employees understand the rationale between the two. The focus is on values, not rules that help employees to decide to "do the right thing". As stated by the 10-40-40-10 rule, 40 percent of employees want to do right but 40 percent can go either way. It is important when using a values-based approach to explain why rules exist, the penalties when violated, and ways for employees to help improve the ethics of the company. The crux of any ethical culture is top-down integrity for the

TABLE 7–3 Corporate Culture Ethics Audit

Answer Yes or No to each of the following questions.*		
Yes	No	Has the founder or top management of the company left an ethical legacy to the organization?
Yes	No	Does the company have methods for detecting ethical concerns within the organization and outside it?
Yes	No	Is there a shared value system and understanding of what constitutes appropriate behavior within the organization?
Yes	No	Are stories and myths embedded in daily conversations about appropriate ethical conduct when confronting ethical situations?
Yes	No	Are codes of ethics or ethical policies communicated to employees?
Yes	No	Are there ethical rules or procedures in training manuals or other company publications?
Yes	No	Are there penalties that are publicly discussed for ethical transgressions?
Yes	No	Are there rewards for good ethical decisions even if they don't always result in a profit?
Yes	No	Does the company recognize the importance of creating a culture that is concerned about people and their self-development as members of the business?
Yes	No	Does the company have a value system of fair play and honesty toward customers?
Yes	No	Do employees treat each other with respect, honesty, and fairness?
Yes	No	Do employees spend their time working in a cohesive way on what is valued by the organization?
Yes	No	Are there ethically based beliefs and values about how to succeed in the company?
Yes	No	Are there heroes or stars in the organization who communicate a common understanding about what positive ethical values are important?
Yes	No	Are there day-to-day rituals or behavior patterns that create direction and prevent confusion or mixed signals on ethics matters?
Yes	No	Is the firm more focused on the long run than on the short run?
Yes	No	Are employees satisfied or happy, and is employee turnover low?
Yes	No	Do the dress, speech, and physical work setting prevent an environment of fragmentation or inconsistency about what is right?
Yes	No	Are emotional outbursts about role conflict and ambiguity rare?
Yes	No	Has discrimination and/or sexual harassment been eliminated?
Yes	No	Is there an absence of open hostility and severe conflict?
Yes	No	Do people act on the job in a way that is consistent with what they say is ethical?
Yes	No	Is the firm more externally focused on customers, the environment, and the welfare of society than on its own profits?
Yes	No	Is there open communication between superiors and subordinates on ethical dilemmas?
Yes	No	Have employees ever received advice on how to improve ethical behavior or been disciplined for committing unethical acts?

*Add the number of Yes answers. The greater the number of Yes answers, the less ethical conflict is likely in your organization.

values, procedures, and rules. Without it a firm's reputation, its ethics within and outside its industry, and the perception of government officials will increase the likelihood that legal fees will increase, stakeholders will be disaffected, and legal agencies will start investigating.

S.C. Johnson represents a values-based culture involving five generations of Johnson family members. The company maintains a strong commitment to consumers, the general public, neighbors and host countries, world communities, and employees. It has been recognized as one of the best places to work and exemplify excellence, diversity, and work–life balance. S.C. Johnson offers flexible work schedules; "no meeting day Fridays," so that employees can catch up on work on Fridays and go into the weekend more relaxed; extended leave for maternity, paternity, and adoption; paid sabbaticals to improve employee performance; on-premise child care services; telecommuting; on-site banking; laundry pick up/drop off; support to take care of services such as oil changes; and a 146-acre park for employees offering an indoor recreation center, aquatic complex, softball fields, tennis courts, driving range, and miniature golf course.[22]

Differential Association

Differential association refers to the idea that people learn ethical or unethical behavior while interacting with others who are part of their role-sets or belong to other intimate personal groups.[23] The learning process is more likely to result in unethical behavior if the individual associates primarily with persons who behave unethically. Associating with others who are unethical, combined with the opportunity to act unethically, is a major influence on ethical decision making, as described in the decision making framework in Chapter 5.[24]

> *"Superiors have a strong influence on the ethics of their subordinates."*

Consider two cashiers working different shifts at the same supermarket. Kevin, who works in the evenings, has seen his cashier friends take money from the bag containing the soft-drink machine change, which is collected every afternoon but not counted until closing time. Although Kevin personally believes that stealing is wrong, he has often heard his friends rationalize that the company owes them free beverages while they work. During his break one evening, Kevin discovers that he has no money to buy a soda. Because he has seen his friends take money from the bag and has heard them justify the practice, Kevin does not feel guilty about taking four quarters. However, Sally, who works the day shift, has never seen her friends take money from the bag. When she discovers that she does not have enough money to purchase a beverage for her break, it does not occur to her to take money from the change bag. Instead, she borrows from a friend. Although both Sally and Kevin view stealing as wrong, Kevin has associated with others who say the practice is justified. When the opportunity arose, Kevin used his friends' rationalization to justify his theft.

A variety of studies have supported the notion that such differential association influences ethical decision making. In particular, superiors have a strong influence on the ethics of their subordinates. Consider the actions of Mark Hernandez, who worked at NASA's Michoud Assembly Facility applying insulating foam to the space shuttles' external fuel tanks. Within a few weeks on the job, coworkers taught him to repair scratches in the insulation without reporting the repairs. Supervisors encouraged the workers not to fill out the required paperwork on the repairs so that they could meet the space shuttle program's tight production schedules. After the shuttle *Columbia* broke up on reentry, killing all seven astronauts on board, investigators focused on whether a piece of foam falling off a fuel tank during liftoff may have irreparably damaged the shuttle. The final determination of the cause of the disaster may require years of investigation.[25]

Several research studies have found that employees, especially young managers, tend to go along with their superiors' moral judgments to demonstrate loyalty. In one study, an experiment was conducted to determine how a hypothetical board of directors would respond to the marketing of one of the company's most profitable drugs, which resulted in 14 to 22 unnecessary deaths a year. When the imaginary board of directors learned that a competitor's drug was coming into the market with no side effects, more than 80 percent supported continuing to market the drug and taking legal and political action to prevent a ban. When asked their personal view on this situation, 97 percent believed that continuing to market the drug was irresponsible.[26] We have made it clear that *how* people typically make ethical decisions is not necessarily the way they *should* make ethical decisions. But we believe that you will be able to improve your own ethical decision making once you understand the potential influence of your interaction with others in your intimate work groups.

Whistle-Blowing

Interpersonal conflict ensues when employees think they know the right course of action in a situation, yet their work group or company promotes or requires a different, unethical decision. In such cases, employees may choose to follow their own values and refuse to participate in the unethical or illegal conduct. If they conclude that they cannot discuss what they are doing or what should be done with their coworkers or immediate supervisors, these employees may go outside the organization to publicize and correct the unethical situation.

Whistle-blowing means exposing an employer's wrongdoing to outsiders (external to the company) such as the media or government regulatory agencies. The term *whistle blowing* is also used for internal reporting of misconduct to management, especially through anonymous reporting mechanisms, often called hotlines. Whistle-blower laws have provisions against retaliation and are enforced by a number of government agencies. For example, under the Sarbanes–Oxley Act, the U.S. Department of Labor (DOL) directly protects whistle-blowers from retaliation, reporting violations of the laws, and refusing to engage in any action made unlawful. The Corporate and Criminal Fraud Accountability (CCFA) Act protects employees of publicly-traded firms from retaliation for reporting violations of any rule or regulation of the Securities and Exchange Commission, or any provision of federal law relating to fraud against shareholders. The CCFA Act makes it a federal crime for a company to retaliate. It also requires attorneys to become internal whistle-blowers as well.

The Sarbanes–Oxley Act and the Federal Sentencing Guidelines for Organizations (FSGO) has institutionalized internal whistle-blowing to encourage discovery of internal misconduct. For example, billionaire R. Allen Stanford's worst enemies may be former employees, turned whistle-blowers, who once worked for his $50 billion Stanford Financial Group. One lawsuit alleges that an employee hired to edit the firm's corporate magazine objected to and raised concerns about firm practices that he believed violated federal and state laws. He was later fired. Others who filed industry arbitration claims alleged they were forced out of the fast-growing firm after questioning the ability of Stanford International Bank to justify high CD rates. In the Stanford case, whistle-blowers have provided pivotal evidence documenting corporate malfeasance at a number of companies.[27] Historically, the fortunes of external whistle-blowers have not been as positive; most were labeled traitors, and many lost their jobs. Even Sherron Watkins was a potential candidate for firing as the Enron investigation unfolded with law firms assessing the implications of terminating her in light of her ethical and legal concerns about Enron.[28]

TABLE 7–4 Questions to Ask Before Engaging in External Whistle-Blowing

1.	**Have I exhausted internal anonymous reporting opportunities within the organization?**
2.	**Have I examined company policies and codes that outline acceptable behavior and violations of standards?**
3.	**Is this a personal issue that should be resolved through other means?**
4.	**Can I manage the stress that may evolve from exposing potential wrongdoing in the organization?**
5.	**Can I deal with the consequences of resolving an ethical or legal conflict within the organization?**

A study of 300 whistle-blowers by researchers at the University of Pennsylvania found that 69 percent lost their jobs or were forced to retire after exposing their companies' misdeeds.[29] For example, the whistle-blower who exposed Wal-Mart chairman Thomas Coughlin of defrauding the company was terminated about a week after Coughlin resigned. Jared Bowen, a former vice president for Wal-Mart Stores, Inc., claims that he was terminated for his exposure of Coughlin, in violation of a provision of the Sarbanes–Oxley Act protecting whistle-blowers.[30] If an employee provides information to the government about the company's wrongdoing, under the Federal False Claims Act, the whistle-blower is known as a ***qui tam relator***. Upon investigation by the U.S. Department of Justice, the whistle-blower can receive between 15 and 25 percent of the recovered funds, depending upon how instrumental his or her claims were in holding the firm accountable for its wrongdoing.[31] Although most whistle-blowers do not receive positive recognition for pointing out corporate misconduct, some have turned to the courts and obtained substantial settlements. Table 7–4 provides a checklist of questions an employee should ask before blowing the whistle externally. Figure 7–3 shows that nearly one in four employees experience retaliation after reporting misconduct. Nearly half of all employees who report misconduct received positive feedback for having done so.

If whistle-blowers present an accurate picture of organizational misconduct, they should not fear for their jobs. Indeed, the Sarbanes–Oxley Act makes it illegal to "discharge, demote, suspend, threaten, harass, or in any manner discriminate against" a whistle-blower and sets penalties of up to 10 years in jail for executives who retaliate against whistle-blowers. The law also requires publicly traded companies to implement an anonymous reporting mechanism that allows employees to question actions that they believe may indicate fraud or other misconduct.[32] Additionally, the FSGO provides rewards for companies that systematically detect and address unethical or illegal activities. More recently, within the federal stimulus proposal, new whistle-blower protection was supported for state and local government employees and contractors, subcontractors, and grantees. The new law provides specific protections including the right to seek investigation and review by federal Inspectors General for "adverse actions" such as termination or demotions.[33]

Some U.S. companies are setting up computer systems that encourage internal whistle-blowing. With over 5,500 employees, Marvin Windows (one of the world's largest custom manufacturers of wood windows and doors) is concerned about employees feeling comfortable reporting violations of safety conditions, bad management, fraud, or theft. The system is anonymous and allows for reporting in native-country languages. This system is used to alert management to potential problems in the organization and facilitate an investigation.[34]

FIGURE 7–3 Outcomes for Internal Whistle-Blowers Reporting Misconduct

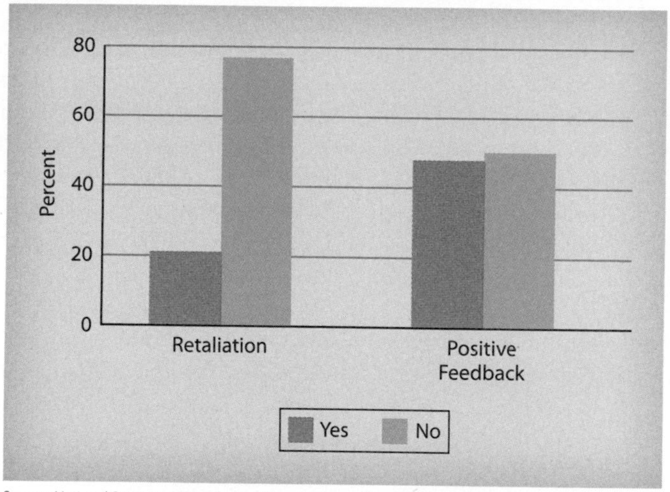

Source: National Business Ethics Survey, *How Employees View Ethics in Their Organizations 1994–2005* (Washington, DC: Ethics Resource Center, 2005), 32.

Even before the passage of the Sarbanes–Oxley Act, an increasing number of companies were setting up anonymous reporting services, normally toll-free numbers, through which employees can report suspected violations or seek input on how to proceed when encountering ambiguous situations. These internal reporting services are perceived to be most effective when they are managed by an outside organization that specializes in maintaining ethics hotlines.

Figure 7–4 indicates the reasons why employees do not report misconduct in the organization. The extent to which employees feel there will be no corrective action or there will be retaliation are leading factors influencing their decisions not to report observed misconduct.

FIGURE 7–4 Reasons why Employees do not Report Observed Misconduct

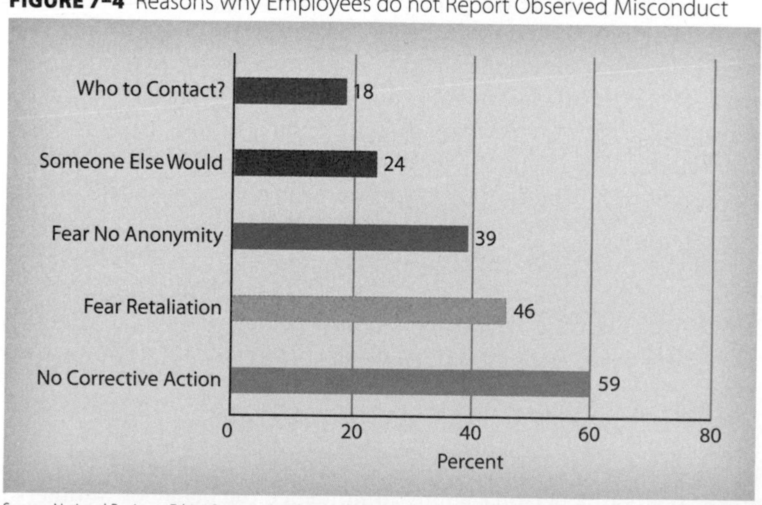

Source: National Business Ethics Survey, *How Employees View Ethics in Their Organizations 1994–2005* (Washington, DC: Ethics Resource Center, 2005), 29.

LEADERS INFLUENCE CORPORATE CULTURE

Organizational leaders can shape and influence corporate culture for the good and bad. A fundamental question about leaders is the distinction between good and ethical. A good leader is one that does well for the stakeholders of the corporation. Good leaders are effective at getting followers to their common goals or objectives in the most effective and efficient way. The stakeholders who have the most influence on the leader and his or her objectives determine the "good." In this context, Bernie Madoff could be considered a "good leader" in that he made investors happy by reporting stable and steady returns when others were not. Ken Lay and Jeffery Skilling were good in that they transformed Enron from a small oil and gas pipeline firm into one of the largest entities in its industry. They were inspirational, imaginative, creative, and they motivated their personnel to achieve. But all three were not good in the long term as it relates to ethics. Ethical leaders lead by example. They have integrity. Integrity gives way to respect. David Neeleman, founder and CEO of JetBlue Airlines, put it this way: "People do a better job if they respect the leader of the company".[35] Consistency counts as a leader. Many believe that being ethical means not being competitive. The following successful business leaders show examples to the contrary:

> *"Ethical leaders lead by example."*

- Dave Checketts, former CEO of Madison Square Garden Corporation: "Whether it is television, sports, or business, it's always about winning. I have always run very, very deep that way. When it comes to being competitive, I'm off the map, way over the top."
- David Neeleman, founder and CEO of JetBlue: "Down deep in my gut I hate it when someone else does something better than me."
- Kevin Rollins, CEO of Dell: "I hate to lose! I don't want to hurt people to win. But I want to win"

The use of power and influence shapes corporate culture. *Power* refers to the influence that leaders and managers have over the behavior and decisions of subordinates. An individual has power over others when his or her presence causes them to behave differently. Exerting power is one way to influence the ethical decision making framework described in Chapter 5 (especially significant others and opportunity).

The status and power of leaders is directly related to the amount of pressure that they can exert on employees to conform to their expectations. A superior in an authority position can put strong pressure on employees to comply, even when their personal ethical values conflict with the superior's wishes. For example, a manager might say to a subordinate, "I want the confidential data about our competitor's sales on my desk by Monday morning, and I don't care how you get it." A subordinate who values his or her job or who does not realize the ethical questions involved may feel pressure to do something unethical to obtain the data.

There are five power bases from which one person may influence another: (1) reward power, (2) coercive power, (3) legitimate power, (4) expert power, and (5) referent power.[36] These five bases of power can be used to motivate individuals either ethically or unethically.

Reward Power

Reward power refers to a person's ability to influence the behavior of others by offering them something desirable. Typical rewards might be money, status, or promotion.

Consider, for example, a retail salesperson who has two watches (a Timex and a Movado) for sale. Let's assume that the Movado is of higher quality than the Timex but is priced about the same. In the absence of any form of reward power, the salesperson would logically attempt to sell the Movado watch. However, if Timex gave him an extra 10 percent commission, he would probably focus his efforts on selling the Timex. This "carrot dangling" and incentives have been shown to be very effective in getting people to change their behavior in the long run. In the short run, however, it is not as effective as coercive power.

Coercive Power

Coercive power is essentially the opposite of reward power. Instead of rewarding a person for doing something, coercive power penalizes actions or behavior. As an example, suppose a valuable client asks an industrial salesperson for a bribe and insinuates that he will take his business elsewhere if his demands are not met. Although the salesperson believes bribery is unethical, her boss has told her that she must keep the client happy or lose her chance at promotion. The boss is imposing a negative sanction if certain actions are not performed. Many companies have used a system whereby they systematically fire the lowest performing employees in their organization on an annual basis. GE's Jack Welch is perhaps the most known for supporting a "vitality curve" that annually terminated the lowest 10 percent of employees. Enron called it "rank and yank" and annually fired the lowest 20 percent. Motorola, Dow Chemical, and Microsoft have used similar systems for firing employees.[37] Coercive power relies on fear to change behavior. For this reason, it has been found to be more effective in changing behavior in the short run than in the long run. Coercion is often employed in situations where there is an extreme imbalance in power. However, people who are continually subjected to coercion may seek a counterbalance by aligning themselves with other, more powerful persons or by simply leaving the organization. In firms that use coercive power, relationships usually break down in the long run. Power is an ethical issue not only for individuals but also for work groups that establish policy for large corporations.

Legitimate Power

Legitimate power stems from the belief that a certain person has the right to exert influence and that certain others have an obligation to accept it. The titles and positions of authority that organizations bestow on individuals appeal to this traditional view of power. Many people readily acquiesce to those who wield legitimate power, sometimes committing acts that are contrary to their beliefs and values. Betty Vinson, an accountant at WorldCom, objected to her supervisor's requests to produce improper accounting entries in an effort to conceal WorldCom's deteriorating financial condition. She finally gave in to their requests, being told this was the only way to save the company. She and other WorldCom accountants eventually pled guilty to conspiracy and fraud charges. She was sentenced to five months in prison and five months of house arrest.[38]

Such staunch loyalty to authority figures can also be seen in corporations that have strong charismatic leaders and centralized structures. In business, if a superior tells an employee to increase sales "no matter what it takes" and that employee has a strong affiliation to legitimate power, the employee may try anything to fulfill that order.

Expert Power

Expert power is derived from a person's knowledge (or the perception that the person possesses knowledge). Expert power usually stems from a superior's credibility with subordinates. Credibility, and thus expert power, is positively related to the number of years that a person has worked in a firm or industry, the person's education, or the honors that he or she has received for performance. Others who perceive a person to be an expert on a specific topic can also confer expert power on him or her. A relatively low-level secretary may have expert power because he or she knows specific details about how the business operates and can even make suggestions on how to inflate revenue through expense reimbursements.

Expert power may cause ethical problems when it is used to manipulate others or to gain an unfair advantage. Physicians, lawyers, or consultants can take unfair advantage of unknowing clients, for example. Accounting firms may gain extra income by ignoring concerns about the accuracy of financial data that they are provided in an audit.

Referent Power

Referent power may exist when one person perceives that his or her goals or objectives are similar to another's. The second person may attempt to influence the first to take actions that will lead both to achieve their objectives. Because they share the same objective, the person influenced by the other will perceive the other's use of referent power as beneficial. For this power relationship to be effective, however, some sort of empathy must exist between the individuals. Identification with others helps boost the decision maker's confidence when making a decision, thus increasing his or her referent power.

"*People typically use several power bases to effect change in others.*"

Consider the following situation: Lisa Jones, a manager in the accounting department of a manufacturing firm, has asked Michael Wong, a salesperson, to speed up the delivery of sales contracts, which usually take about one month to process after a deal is reached. Michael protests that he is not to blame for the slow process. Rather than threaten to slow delivery of Michael's commission checks (coercive power), Lisa makes use of referent power. She invites Michael to lunch, and they discuss some of their work concerns, including the problem of slow-moving documentation. They agree that if document processing cannot be speeded up, both will be hurt. Lisa then suggests that Michael start faxing contracts instead of mailing them. He agrees to give it a try, and within several weeks the contracts are moving faster. Lisa's job is made easier, and Michael gets his commission checks a little sooner.

The five bases of power are not mutually exclusive. People typically use several power bases to effect change in others. Although power in itself is neither ethical nor unethical, its use can raise ethical issues. Sometimes a leader uses power to manipulate a situation or a person's values in a way that creates a conflict with the person's value structure. For example, a manager who forces an employee to choose between staying home with his sick child and keeping his job is using coercive power, which creates a direct conflict with the employee's values. The trappings of power can become all-encompassing for some. In business, titles and salary signify power. But power and wealth often breed arrogance and are easily abused.

In a McKinsey survey, power and leadership used to support environmental, social, and governance programs was found to create shareholder value. The Vitamin Cottage, a regional health-oriented grocery store, banned all traditional shopping bags starting on Earth Day 2009. Customers have to bring their own reusable bags or take their grocery items out in recycled boxes. The grocery stores targeting the health conscious (Whole

Foods, Sunflower Market, Vitamin Cottage, etc.) have taken a leadership position in supporting minimizing their negative impact upon the environment.[39]

MOTIVATING ETHICAL BEHAVIOR

A leader's ability to motivate subordinates plays a key role in maintaining an ethical organization. **Motivation** is a force within the individual that focuses his or her behavior toward achieving a goal. **Job performance** is considered to be a function of ability and motivation, thus Job performance = ability × motivation, meaning that employees can be motivated, but resources and know-how are also needed to get the job done. To create motivation, an organization offers incentives to encourage employees to work toward organizational objectives. Understanding motivation is important to the effective management of people, and it also helps explain their ethical behavior. For example, a person who aspires to higher positions in an organization may sabotage a coworker's project so as to make that person look bad. This unethical behavior is directly related to the first employee's ambition (motivation) to rise in the organization. Employees want to feel they are a good fit with their organization, have a clear understanding of job expectations, be supported in their role, and be valued and inspired to perform well. Towers-Perrin-ISR conducted a study that showed that there was a 52 percent gap in performance in operating income between companies with highly engaged and motivated employees versus those with low engagement.[40]

As businesspeople move into middle management and beyond, higher-order needs (social, esteem, and recognition) tend to become more important than lower-order needs (salary, safety, and job security). Research has shown that an individual's career stage, age, organization size, and geographic location affect the relative priority that he or she gives to satisfying respect, self-esteem, and basic physiological needs.

From an ethics perspective, needs or goals may change as a person progresses through the ranks of the company. This shift may cause or help solve problems depending on that person's current ethical status relative to the company or society. For example, junior executives might inflate purchase or sales orders, overbill time worked on projects, or accept cash gratuities if they are worried about providing for their families' basic physical necessities. As they continue up the ladder and are able to fulfill these needs, such concerns may become less important. Consequently, these managers may go back to obeying company policy or culture and be more concerned with internal recognition and achievement than their families' physical needs.

An individual's hierarchy of needs may influence his or her motivation and ethical behavior. After basic needs such as food, working conditions (existence needs), and survival are satisfied, relatedness needs and growth needs become important. **Relatedness needs** are satisfied by social and interpersonal relationships, and **growth needs** are satisfied by creative or productive activities.[41] Consider what happens when a new employee, Jill Taylor, joins a company. At first Jill is concerned about working conditions, pay, and security (existence needs). After some time on the job, she feels she has satisfied these needs and begins to focus on developing good interpersonal relations with coworkers. When these relatedness needs have been satisfied, Jill wants to advance to a more challenging job. However, she learns that a higher-level job would require her to travel a lot. She greatly values her family life and feels that travel and nights away from home would not be good for her. She decides, therefore, not to work toward a promotion (resulting in a "need frustration"). Instead, she decides to focus on furthering good interpersonal relations with her coworkers. This is termed *frustration-regression* because, to reduce her anxiety, Jill is now focusing on an area (interpersonal relations) not related to her main problem: the need for a more challenging job. In this example, Jill's need for promotion has been modified by her values. To feel productive, she attempts to fill her needs by going back to an earlier stage in her hierarchy of needs. Whatever her present job is, Jill would continue to emphasize high performance in it. But this regression creates frustration that may lead Jill to seek other employment.

Examining the role that motivation plays in ethics offers a way to relate business ethics to the broader social context in which workers live and the deeper moral assumptions on which society depends. Workers are individuals and they will be motivated by a variety of personal interests. Although we keep emphasizing that managers are positioned to exert pressure and force individuals' compliance on ethically related issues, we also acknowledge that an individual's personal ethics and needs will significantly affect his or her ethical decisions.

ORGANIZATIONAL STRUCTURE AND BUSINESS ETHICS

An organization's structure is important to the study of business ethics because the various roles and job descriptions that comprise that structure may create opportunities for unethical behavior. The structure of organizations can be described in many ways. For simplicity's sake, we discuss two broad categories of organizational structures—centralized and decentralized. Note that these are not mutually exclusive structures; in the real world, organizational structures exist on a continuum. Table 7–5 compares some strengths and weaknesses of centralized and decentralized structures.

In a **centralized organization**, decision making authority is concentrated in the hands of top-level managers, and little authority is delegated to lower levels. Responsibility, both internal and external, rests with top-level managers. This structure is especially suited for organizations that make high-risk decisions and whose lower-level managers are not highly skilled in decision making. It is also suitable for organizations in which production processes are routine and efficiency is of primary importance. These organizations are usually extremely bureaucratic, and the division of labor is typically very well defined. Each worker knows his or her job and what is specifically expected, and each has a clear understanding of how to carry out assigned tasks. Centralized organizations stress formal rules, policies, and procedures, backed up with elaborate control systems. Their codes of ethics may specify the techniques to be used for decision making. General Motors, the Internal Revenue Service, and the U.S. Army are examples of centralized organizations.

Because of their top-down approach and the distance between employee and decision maker, centralized organizational structures can lead to unethical acts. If the centralized organization is very bureaucratic, some employees may behave according to "the letter of the law" rather than the spirit. For example, a centralized organization can have a policy about bribes that does not include wording about donating to a client's favorite charity before or after a sale. Such donations or gifts can, in some cases, be construed as a tacit bribe because the employee buyer could be swayed by the donation, or gift, to act in a less than favorable way or not to act in the best interests of his or her firm.

TABLE 7–5 Structural Comparison of Organizational Types

	Emphasis	
Characteristic	**Centralized**	**Decentralized**
Hierarchy of authority	Centralized	Decentralized
Flexibility	Low	High
Adaptability	Low	High
Problem recognition	Low	High
Implementation	High	Low
Dealing with changes	Poor environmental complexity	Good
Rules and procedures	Many and formal	Few and informal
Division of labor	Clear-cut	Ambiguous
Span of control	Many employees	Few employees
Use of managerial techniques	Extensive	Minimal
Coordination and control	Formal and impersonal	Informal and personal

Other ethical concerns may arise in centralized structures because they typically have very little upward communication. Top-level managers may not be aware of problems and unethical activity. Some companies' use of sweatshop labor may be one manifestation of this lack of upward communication. Sweatshops produce products such as garments by employing laborers, sometimes forced immigrant labor, who often work 12- to 16-hour shifts for little or no pay. The United Nations says that forced labor costs $21 billion a year in the form of children enslaved in sweatshops, migrant laborers working on farms and building homes, and illegal immigrants subservient to their smugglers. Asia is home to nearly three-quarters of all forced workers in the world. Industries that benefit the most from the cheap labor include electronics, automobiles, textiles, construction, fishing, and agriculture.[42] Another ethical issue that may arise in centralized organizations is blame shifting, or scapegoating. People may try to transfer blame for their actions to others who are not responsible. The specialization and significant division of labor in centralized organizations can also create ethical problems. Employees may not understand how their actions can affect the overall organization because they work on one piece of a much larger puzzle. This lack of connectedness can lead employees to engage in unethical behavior because they fail to understand the overall ramifications of their behavior.

In a **decentralized organization**, decision making authority is delegated as far down the chain of command as possible. Such organizations have relatively few formal rules, and coordination and control are usually informal and personal. They focus instead on increasing the flow of information. As a result, one of the main strengths of decentralized organizations is their adaptability and early recognition of external change. With greater flexibility, managers can react quickly to changes in their ethical environment. A parallel weakness of decentralized organizations is the difficulty that they have in responding

TABLE 7–6 Examples of Centralized and Decentralized Corporate Cultures

Company	Organizational Culture	Characterized by
Nike	Decentralized	Creativity, freedom, informality
Southwest Airlines	Decentralized	Fun, teamwork orientation, loyalty
General Motors	Centralized	Unions, adherence to task assignments, structured
Microsoft	Decentralized	Creative, investigative, fast paced
Procter & Gamble	Centralized	Experienced, dependable, a rich history and tradition of products, powerful

quickly to changes in policy and procedures established by top management. In addition, independent profit centers within a decentralized organization may deviate from organizational objectives. Other decentralized firms may look no further than the local community for their ethical standards. For example, if a firm that produces toxic wastes leaves decisions on disposal to lower-level operating units, the managers of those units may feel that they have solved their waste-disposal problem as long as they find a way to dump wastes outside their immediate community. Table 7–6 gives examples of centralized versus decentralized organizations and describes their corporate culture.

Due to the strict formalization and implementation of ethics policies and procedures in centralized organizations, they tend to be more ethical in their practices than decentralized organizations. Centralized organizations may also exert more influence on their employees because they have a central core of policies and codes of ethical conduct. Decentralized organizations give employees extensive decision making autonomy because management empowers the employees. However, it is also true that decentralized organizations may be able to avoid ethical dilemmas by tailoring their decisions to the specific situations, laws, and values of a particular community. If widely shared values are in place in decentralized organizations, there may be no need for excessive compliance programs. However, different units in the company may evolve diverse value systems and approaches to ethical decision making. For example, a high-tech defense firm like Lockheed Martin, which employs more than 200,000 people, might have to cope with many different decisions on the same ethical issue if it did not have a centralized ethics program. Boeing has become more centralized since the entrance of CEO W. James McNerney, Jr., and exit of previous CEO Harry Stonecipher, who carried on a relationship with a female vice president of the company, resulting in his exit. Boeing had gone through several years of ethics and legal difficulties, including the jailing of the former CFO for illegal job negotiations with Pentagon officials, indictment of a manager for stealing 25,000 pages of proprietary documents, abuse of attorney–client privilege to cover up internal studies showing pay inequities, and other scandals.[43]

Unethical behavior is possible in either centralized or decentralized structures when specific corporate cultures permit or encourage workers to deviate from accepted standards or ignore corporate legal and ethical responsibilities. Centralized firms may have a more difficult time uprooting unethical activity than decentralized organizations. The latter may have a more fluid history in which changes affect only a small portion of the company. Often, when a centralized firm uncovers unethical activity and it appears to be pervasive, the leadership is removed so that the old unethical culture can be uprooted and replaced with a more ethical one. For example, Mitsubishi Motors suggested significant management changes after it was discovered that a cover-up of auto defects had been going on for more than two decades.

Some centralized organizations are seeking to restructure to become more decentralized, flexible, and adaptive to the needs of employees and customers. In other cases, entire industries are being impacted by a trend of decentralization. For example, many software companies, such as Citrix Systems, can cut their employee costs by decentralizing and operating development centers in Florida, Washington, and California.[44] Decentralized decisions about ethics and social responsibility allow regional or local operators to set policy and establish conduct requirements.

GROUP DIMENSIONS OF CORPORATE STRUCTURE AND CULTURE

When discussing corporate culture, we tend to focus on the organization as a whole. But corporate values, beliefs, patterns, and rules are often expressed through smaller groups within the organization. Moreover, individual groups within organizations often adopt their own rules and values.

Types of Groups

Two main categories of groups affect ethical behavior in business. A **formal group** is defined as an assembly of individuals that has an organized structure accepted explicitly by the group. An **informal group** is defined as two or more individuals with a common interest but without an explicit organizational structure.

Formal Groups. Formal groups can be divided into committees and work groups and teams.

Committees A *committee* is a formal group of individuals assigned to a specific task. Often a single manager could not complete the task, or management may believe that a committee can better represent different constituencies and improve the coordination and implementation of decisions. Committees may meet regularly to review performance, develop plans, or make decisions. Most formal committees in organizations operate on an ongoing basis, but their membership may change over time. A committee is an excellent example of a situation in which coworkers and significant others within the organization can influence ethical decisions. Committee decisions are to some extent legitimized because of agreement or majority rule. In this respect, minority views on issues such as ethics can be pushed aside through the majority's authority. Committees bring diverse personal moral values into the ethical decision making process, which may expand the number of alternatives considered.

The main disadvantage of committees is that they typically take longer to reach a decision than an individual would. Committee decisions are also generally more conservative than those made by individuals and may be based on unnecessary compromise rather than on identifying the best alternative. Also inherent in the committee structure is a lack of individual responsibility. Because of the diverse composition of the group, members may not be committed or willing to assume responsibility for the group decision. Groupthink may emerge and the majority can explain ethical considerations away.

Although many organizations have financial, diversity, personnel, or social responsibility committees, only a very few organizations have committees that are devoted exclusively to ethics. An ethics committee might raise ethical concerns, resolve ethical dilemmas in the organization, and create or update the company's code of ethics. Motorola, for example, maintains a Business Ethics Compliance Committee, which interprets, classifies, communicates, and enforces the company's code and ethics initiatives. An ethics committee can gather information on functional areas of the business and examine manufacturing practices, personnel policies, dealings with suppliers, financial reporting, and sales techniques to find out whether the company's practices are ethical. Though much of a corporation's culture operates informally, an ethics committee would be a highly formalized approach for dealing with ethical issues.

Ethics committees can be misused if they are established for the purpose of legitimizing management's ethical standards on some issue. For example, ethics committees may be quickly assembled for political purposes—that is, to make a symbolic decision on some event that has occurred within the company. If the CEO or manager in charge selects committee members who will produce a predetermined outcome, the ethics committee may not help the organization resolve its ethical issues in the long run. For example, organizations have been known to quickly assemble an ethics committee to fire someone for a minor infraction because they wanted him or her out of the organization and needed an excuse for termination.

Ethics committee members may also fail to understand their role or function. If they attempt to apply their own personal ethics to complex business issues, resolving ethical issues may be difficult. Because most people's personal ethical perspectives differ, the committee may experience conflict. Even if the committee members reach a consensus, they may enforce their personal beliefs rather than the organization's standards on certain ethical issues.

Ethics committees should be organized around professional, business-related issues that occur internally. In general, the ethics committee should formulate policy, develop ethical standards, and then assess the organization's compliance with these requirements. Ethics committees should be aware of their industries' codes of ethics, community standards, and the organizational culture in which they work. Although ethics committees do not always succeed, they can provide one of the best organizational approaches to resolving internal ethical issues fairly. Texas Instruments (TI) has operated with high integrity and well-designed ethics programs and initiatives. Overseeing the corporate governance area, TI has three committees: audit and ethics, compensation, and governance and stockholder relations.[45]

Work Groups and Teams *Work groups* are used to subdivide duties within specific functional areas of a company. For example, on an automotive assembly line, one work group might install the seats and interior design elements of the vehicle while another group installs all the dashboard instruments. This enables production supervisors to specialize in a specific area and provide expert advice to work groups.

Whereas work groups operate within a single functional area, *teams* bring together the functional expertise of employees from several different areas of the organization—for example, finance, marketing, and production—on a single project, such as developing a new product. Many manufacturing firms, including General Motors, Westinghouse, and Procter & Gamble, are using the team concept to improve participative management. Ethical conflicts may arise because team members come from different functional areas. Each member of the team has a particular role to play and has probably had limited interaction with other members of the team. Members may have encountered different ethical issues in their own functional areas and may therefore bring different viewpoints when the team faces an ethical issue. For example, a production quality-control employee might believe that side-impact air bags should be standard equipment on all automobiles for safety reasons. A marketing member of the team may reply that the cost of adding the air bags would force the company to raise prices beyond the reach of some consumers. The production employee might then argue that it is unethical for an automobile maker to fail to include a safety feature that could save hundreds of lives. Such conflicts often occur when members of different organizational groups must interact. However, airing viewpoints representative of all the functional areas helps provide more options from which to choose.

Work groups and teams provide the organizational structure for group decision making. One of the reasons why individuals cannot implement their personal ethical beliefs in organizations is that work groups collectively reach so many decisions. However, those who have legitimate power are in a position to influence ethics-related activities. The work group and team often sanction certain activities as ethical or define others as unethical.

Informal Groups. In addition to the groups that businesses formally organize and recognize—such as committees, work groups, and teams—most organizations have a number of informal groups. These groups are usually composed of individuals, often from the same department, who have similar interests and band together for companionship or for purposes that may or may not be relevant to the goals of the organization. For example, four or five people who have similar tastes in outdoor activities and music may discuss their interests while working, and they may meet outside work for dinner, concerts, sports events, or other activities. Other informal groups may evolve to form a union, improve working conditions or benefits, get a manager fired, or protest work practices that they view as unfair. Informal groups may generate disagreement and conflict, or they may enhance morale and job satisfaction.

"Informal groups help develop informal channels of communication,"

Informal groups help develop informal channels of communication, sometimes called the "grapevine," which are important in every organization. Informal communication flows up, down, diagonally, and horizontally, not necessarily following the communication lines on a company's organization chart. Information passed along the grapevine may relate to the job, the organization, or an ethical issue; or it may simply be gossip and rumors. The grapevine can act as an early warning system for employees. If employees learn informally that their company may be sold or that a particular action will be condemned as unethical by top management or the community, they have time to think about what they will do. Because gossip is not uncommon in an organization, the information passed along the grapevine is not always accurate. Managers who understand how the grapevine works can use it to reinforce acceptable values and beliefs.

The grapevine is also an important source of information for individuals to assess ethical behavior within their organization. One way an employee can determine acceptable behavior is to ask friends and peers in informal groups about the consequences of certain actions such as lying to a customer about a product-safety issue. The corporate culture may provide employees with a general understanding of the patterns and rules that govern behavior, but informal groups make this culture come alive and provide direction for employees' daily choices. For example, if a new employee learns anecdotally through the grapevine that the organization does not punish ethical violations, he or she may seize the next opportunity for unethical behavior if it accomplishes the organization's objectives. There is a general tendency to discipline top sales performers more leniently than poor sales performers for engaging in identical forms of unethical selling behavior. A superior sales record appears to induce more lenient forms of discipline, despite organizational policies that state otherwise.[46] In this case, the grapevine has clearly communicated that the organization rewards those who break the ethical rules to achieve desirable objectives.

Group Norms

Group norms are standards of behavior that groups expect of their members. Just as corporate culture establishes behavior guidelines for an organization's members, group norms help define acceptable and unacceptable behavior within a group. In particular, group norms define the limit allowed on deviations from group expectations.

Most work organizations, for example, develop norms that govern groups' rates of production and communication with management as well as provide a general understanding of behavior considered right or wrong, ethical or unethical, within the group. For example, other group members may punish an employee who reports to a supervisor that a coworker has covered up a serious production error for this breach of confidence. Other members of the group may glare at the informant, who has violated a group norm, and refuse to talk to or sit by him or her.

Norms have the power to enforce a strong degree of conformity among group members. At the same time, norms define the different roles for various positions within the organization. Thus, a low-ranking member of a group may be expected to carry out an unpleasant task such as accepting responsibility for someone else's ethical mistake. Abusive behavior toward new or lower-ranking employees could be a norm in an informal group.

Sometimes group norms conflict with the values and rules prescribed by the organization's culture. For example, the organization may have policies about the personal use of computers during work hours and may use rewards and punishments to encourage this culture. In a particular informal group, however, norms may encourage using computers for personal use during work hours and avoiding management's attention. Issues of equity may arise in this situation if other groups believe they are unfairly forced to follow policies that are not enforced. These other employees may complain to management or to the offending group. If they believe management is not taking corrective action, they, too, may use computers for personal use, thus hurting the whole organization's productivity. For this reason, management must carefully monitor not only the corporate culture but also the norms of all the various groups within the organization. Sanctions may be necessary to bring in line a group whose norms deviate sharply from the overall culture.

VARIATION IN EMPLOYEE CONDUCT

Although the corporation is required to take responsibility for conducting its business ethically, a substantial amount of research indicates that significant differences exist in the values and philosophies that influence how the individuals that comprise corporations make ethical decisions.[47] In other words, because people are culturally diverse and have

TABLE 7–7 Variation in Employee Conduct*

10%	40%	40%	10%
Follow their own values and beliefs; believe that their values are superior to those of others in the company.	**Always try to follow company policies.**	**Go along with the work group.**	**Take advantage of situations if the penalty is less than the benefit and the risk of being caught is low.**

*These percentages are based on a number of studies in the popular press and data gathered by the authors. These percentages are not exact and represent a general typology that may vary by organization.

Source: From John Fraedrich and O.C. Ferrell, "Cognitive Consistency of Marketing Managers in Ethical Situations," *Journal of the Academy of Marketing Science* 20 (Summer 1992): 243–252. Copyright © 1992 by Sage Publications, Inc. Reprinted by permission of Sage Publications, Inc.

different values, they interpret situations differently and will vary in the ethical decisions they make on the same ethical issue.

Table 7–7 shows that approximately 10 percent of employees take advantage of situations to further their own personal interests. These individuals are more likely to manipulate, cheat, or be self-serving when the benefits gained from doing so are greater than the penalties for the misconduct. Such employees may choose to take office supplies from work for personal use if the only penalty they may suffer if caught is having to pay for the supplies. The lower the risk of being caught, the higher is the likelihood that the 10 percent most likely to take advantage will be involved in unethical activities.

Another 40 percent of workers go along with the work group on most matters. These employees are most concerned about the social implications of their actions and want to fit into the organization. Although they have their own personal opinions, they are easily influenced by what people around them are doing. These individuals may know that using office supplies for personal use is improper, yet they view it as acceptable because their coworkers do so. These employees rationalize their action by saying that the use of office supplies is one of the benefits of working at their particular business and it must be acceptable because the company does not enforce a policy precluding the behavior. Coupled with this philosophy is the belief that no one will get into trouble for doing what everybody else is doing, for there is safety in numbers.

About 40 percent of a company's employees, as shown in Table 7–7, always try to follow company policies and rules. These workers not only have a strong grasp of their corporate culture's definition of acceptable behavior, but also attempt to comply with codes of ethics, ethics training, and other communications about appropriate conduct. If the company has a policy prohibiting taking office supplies from work, these employees probably would observe it. However, they likely would not speak out about the 40 percent who choose to go along with the work group, for these employees prefer to focus on their jobs and steer clear of any organizational misconduct. If the company fails to communicate standards of appropriate behavior, members of this group will devise their own.

The final 10 percent of employees try to maintain formal ethical standards that focus on rights, duties, and rules. They embrace values that assert certain inalienable rights and actions, which they perceive to be always ethically correct. In general, members of this group believe that their values are right and superior to the values of others in the company, or even to the company's value system, when an ethical conflict arises. These individuals have a tendency to report the misconduct of others or to speak out when they view activities within the company as unethical. Consequently, members of this group would probably report colleagues who take office supplies.

The significance of this variation in the way individuals behave ethically is simply this: Employees use different approaches when making ethical decisions. Because of the probability that a large percentage of any work group will either take advantage of a situation or at least go along with the work group, it is vital that companies provide communication and control mechanisms to maintain an ethical culture. Companies that fail to monitor activities and enforce ethics policies provide a low-risk environment for those employees who are inclined to take advantage of situations to accomplish their personal, and sometimes unethical, objectives.

Good business practice and concern for the law requires organizations to recognize this variation in employees' desire to be ethical. The percentages cited in Table 7–7 are only estimates, and the actual percentages of each type of employee may vary widely across organizations based on individuals and corporate culture. The specific percentages are less important than the fact that our research has identified these variations as existing within most organizations. Organizations should focus particular attention on managers who oversee the day-to-day operations of employees within the company. They should also provide training and communication to ensure that the business operates ethically, that it does not become the victim of fraud or theft, and that employees, customers, and other stakeholders are not abused through the misconduct of people who have a pattern of unethical behavior.

As we have seen throughout this book, many examples can be cited of employees and managers who have no concern for ethical conduct but are nonetheless hired and placed in positions of trust. Some corporations continue to support executives who ignore environmental concerns, poor working conditions, or defective products, or who engage in accounting fraud. Executives who can get results, regardless of the consequences, are often admired and lauded, especially in the business press. When their unethical or even illegal actions become public knowledge, however, they risk more than the loss of their positions. Table 7–8 summarizes the penalties that corporate executives have experienced over the past several years.

CAN PEOPLE CONTROL THEIR OWN ACTIONS WITHIN A CORPORATE CULTURE?

Many people find it hard to believe that an organization's culture can exert so strong an influence on individuals' behavior within the organization. In our society, we want to believe that individuals control their own destiny. A popular way of viewing business ethics is therefore to see it as a reflection of the alternative moral philosophies that individuals use to resolve their personal moral dilemmas. As this chapter has shown, however, ethical decisions within organizations are often made by committees and formal and informal groups, not by individuals. Decisions related to financial reporting, advertising, product design, sales practices, and pollution-control issues are often beyond the influence of individuals alone. In addition, these decisions are frequently based on business rather than personal goals.

Most new employees in highly bureaucratic organizations have almost no input into the basic operating rules and procedures for getting things done. Along with learning sales tactics and accounting procedures, employees may be taught to ignore a design flaw in a product that could be dangerous to users. Although many personal ethics issues

TABLE 7–8 Penalties for Convictions of Organizational Wrongdoing

Executive/Company	Trial Outcome
Franklin Brown, former general counsel, Rite Aid	Convicted and sentenced to 10 years in prison.
Bernard Ebbers, former chairman and CEO, WorldCom	Convicted and sentenced to 25 years to life in prison.
Dennis Kozlowski, former CEO, Tyco	Mistrial in first trial; in second, convicted and sentenced to 8 1/3 to 25 years in prison.
Jeffery Skilling, former president of Enron	Convicted of multiple felony charges and currently serving a 24-year, 4-month prison sentence.
Joseph P. Nacchio, former CEO of Qwest Communications International	Convicted of insider trading, $19 million fine, forfeit of $52 million, and 6 years in prison.
Xujia Wang, vice president of finance, Morgan Stanley Company	Convicted of securities fraud and conspiracy to commit securities fraud, 18 months in prison and $611,248 fine.
Attorney Raymond Joseph Costanzo, Jr.	Provided false qualifying information and falsified down payments, 3 years, 5 months in prison to be followed by 4 years of supervised release and ordered to pay $7,843,184 in restitution.
Gandhi Ben Morka, real estate appraiser	Convicted of mortgage fraud, 60 months in prison, and ordered to pay more than $2.3 million in restitution.

Source: From *Wall Street Journal Online*, "White-Collar Defendants: Take the Stand, or Not?," April 2, 2006; FBI Report, http://www.fbi.gov/publications/financial/fcs_report2007/financial_crime_2007.htm (accessed August 19, 2009).

may seem straightforward and easy to resolve, individuals entering business will usually need several years of experience within a specific industry to understand how to resolve ethical close calls. For example, what constitutes misleading advertising? When Corvette introduced the new C-6 design, it wanted to reach a younger demographic. The company hired Madonna's husband, Guy Ritchie, and used the Rolling Stones singing "Jumpin' Jack Flash" to create a memorable TV commercial showing a young boy fantasizing about being able to drive the Corvette. General Motors received complaints from parents and organizations indicating that it was inappropriate for GM to show a clearly underage driver, driving recklessly, even if it was a fantasy. GM responded quickly by withdrawing the commercial from the airwaves. How could this problem have been prevented? Perhaps GM should have screened the ads to a variety of audiences, not just the target audience for the vehicle. The only thing that is certain is that one person's opinion or maybe even a work group's opinion is insufficient in dealing with complex decisions.

It is not our purpose to suggest that you ought to go along with management or the group on business ethics issues. Honesty and open discussion of ethical issues are important to successful ethical decision making. We believe that most companies and businesspeople try to make ethical decisions. However, because there is so much difference between individuals, ethical conflict is inevitable. If you manage and supervise others, it will be necessary to maintain ethical policies for your organization and report misconduct that occurs. This means that ethics is not just a personal matter.

Regardless of how a person or organization views the acceptability of a particular activity, if society judges it to be wrong or unethical, then this larger view directly affects the organization's ability to achieve its goals. Not all activities deemed unethical by society are illegal. But if public opinion decries or consumers protest against a particular activity, the result may be legislation that restricts or bans a specific business practice. For instance, concern about teen smoking prompted the government to regulate the placement of cigarette advertising and curb the use of characters and approaches designed to appeal to children. Public concern and outrage at the growth in cigarette smoking among minors spurred much of this intervention. Besieged by mounting negative opinion, numerous class action lawsuits, and a landmark settlement with 46 states, Philip Morris USA, producer of the world's best-selling cigarette, was forced to modify its marketing strategies, in particular to avoid marketing its products to minors. The company launched the Youth Tobacco Prevention Program in 1998, which uses the Internet, TV commercials, school publications, and print ads to encourage teenagers not to smoke. Philip Morris has spent hundreds of millions of dollars on youth smoking-prevention advertising, providing grants to youth development organizations, producing tools and resources to help parents talk to their children about the hazards of smoking, and supporting youth access prevention initiatives to help keep cigarettes out of children's hands.[48] While there is some debate over how effective these methods have been, the rate of underage smoking has declined dramatically since the 1990s.[49] If a person believes that his or her personal ethics severely conflict with the ethics of the work group and of superiors in an organization, that individual's only alternative may be to leave the organization. In the highly competitive employment market of the twenty-first century, quitting a job because of an ethical conflict requires courage and, possibly, the ability to survive without a job. Obviously, there are no easy answers for resolving ethical conflicts between the organization and the individual. Our goal is not to tell you what you should do. But we do believe that the more you know about how ethical decision making occurs within organizations, the more opportunity you will have to influence decisions positively and resolve ethical conflict more effectively.

SUMMARY

Corporate culture refers to the set of values, beliefs, goals, norms, and ways of solving problems that the members (employees) of an organization share. These shared values may be formally expressed or unspoken. Corporate cultures can be classified in several ways, and a cultural audit can be conducted to identify an organization's culture. If an organization's culture rewards unethical behavior, people within the company are more likely to act unethically. A company's failure to monitor or manage its culture may foster questionable behavior.

Leadership—the ability or authority to guide others toward achieving goals—has a significant impact on the ethical decision making process because leaders have the power to motivate others and enforce both the organization's rules and policies and their own viewpoints. A leader must not only gain the respect of his or her followers but also provide a standard of ethical conduct. Leaders exert power to influence the behaviors and decisions of subordinates. There are five power bases from which a leader may influence ethical behavior: reward power, coercive power, legitimate power, expert power, and referent power. Leaders also attempt to motivate subordinates; motivation is an internal force that focuses an individual's behavior toward achieving a goal. It can be created by the incentives that an organization offers employees.

The structure of an organization may create opportunities to engage in unethical behavior. In a centralized organization, decision making authority is concentrated in the hands of top managers, and little authority is delegated to lower levels. In a decentralized organization, decision making authority is delegated as far down the chain of command as possible. Centralized organizations tend to be more ethical than decentralized ones because they enforce more rigid controls such as codes of ethics and corporate policies on ethical practices. However, unethical conduct can occur in both types of structures.

In addition to the values and customs that represent the culture of an organization, individual groups within the organization often adopt their own rules and values and even create subcultures. The main types of groups are formal groups—which include committees, work groups, and teams—and informal groups. Informal groups often feed an informal channel of communication called the "grapevine." Group norms are standards of behavior that groups expect of their members. They help define acceptable and unacceptable behavior within a group and especially define the limits on deviating from group expectations. Sometimes group norms conflict with the values and rules prescribed by the organization's culture.

Sometimes an employee's own personal ethical standards conflict with what is expected of him or her as a member of an organization and its corporate culture. This is especially true given that an organization's ethical decisions are often resolved by committees, formal groups, and informal groups rather than by individuals. When such ethical conflict is severe, the individual may have to decide whether to leave the organization.

IMPORTANT TERMS FOR REVIEW

Sarbanes-Oxley 404
apathetic culture
caring culture
exacting culture
integrative culture
cultural audit
compliance culture
values-based ethics culture
differential association
whistle-blowing
qui tam relator
reward power
coercive power
legitimate power
expert power
referent power
motivation
job performance
relatedness needs
growth needs
centralized organization
decentralized organization
formal group
informal group
group norm

RESOLVING ETHICAL BUSINESS CHALLENGES*

As Gerard sat down in his expensive new chair, he was worried. What had he gotten himself into? How could things have gone so wrong so fast? It was as if he'd been walking and some truck had blindsided him. Gerard had been with Trawlers Accounting, a medium-size firm, for several years. His wife, Vicky, had a job in the pharmaceutical industry, and their first child was due any day now. The doctor had told her that she would need to stop work early because hers was a high-risk pregnancy. So three months before her due date, she asked and received a four-month leave of absence. This was great, but the leave was without pay. Luckily, Gerard had received a promotion and now headed a department.

Some interesting activities were going on in the accounting industry. For example, Gerard's superior had decided that all CPAs would take exams to become registered investment advisers. The rationale for such a new development was simple. The firm could use its relationships with clients to increase investment revenues. Because of the long-term nature of these relationships with many firms and individuals as well as the implicit sense of honesty that CPAs must bring to their jobs, clients understood that a violation of so high a trust was unlikely—or so Gerard's boss argued. Many of the people in Gerard's department didn't like this new policy; however, some who had passed the exams increased their pay by 15 percent. During lunch, one of Gerard's financial friends engaged him heatedly.

"What you're doing, Gerard, is called unfair competition," the friend accused him. "For example, your CPAs have exclusive access to confidential client taxpayer information, which could give you insight into people's financial needs. Besides, you could easily direct clients to mutual funds that you already own in order to keep your own personal investments afloat. Also, if your people start chasing commissions and fees on mutual funds that go bad, your credibility will become suspect, and you won't be trusted. Plus, your people will now have to keep abreast of financial, tax, and accounting changes."

When Gerard got to his office, he found that some of his people had been recommending a group of mutual funds that Trawlers had been auditing. Then someone from another of his company's accounting clients, CENA Mutual Funds, telephoned.

"What's the idea of having your people suggest PPI Mutual Funds when they are in direct competition with us?" the caller yelled. "We pay you a lot, Gerard, to do our accounting procedures, and that's how you reward us? I want to know by the end of the day if you are going to continue to push our competitor's product. I don't have to tell you that this will directly affect your department and you. Also, things like this get around the business circles, if you know what I mean."

With these words, the caller hung up on Gerard.

QUESTIONS • EXERCISES

1. Identify any ethical and legal issues of which Gerard needs to be aware.
2. Discuss the advantages and disadvantages of each decision Gerard has made and could make.
3. Discuss the issue of accounting firms going into the financial services market.
4. Discuss the type of groups that are influencing Gerard.

*This case is strictly hypothetical; any resemblance to real persons, companies, or situations is coincidental.

CHECK YOUR EQ

Check your EQ, or Ethics Quotient, by completing the following. Assess your performance to evaluate your overall understanding of the chapter material.

1. Decentralized organizations tend to put the blame for unethical behavior on lower-level personnel. **Yes No**
2. Decentralized organizations give employees extensive decision making autonomy. **Yes No**
3. Corporate culture provides rules for behaving within the organization. **Yes No**
4. An integrative culture shows high concern for performance and little concern for people. **Yes No**
5. Coercive power works in the same manner as reward power. **Yes No**

ANSWERS **1. No.** This is more likely to occur in centralized organizations. **2. Yes.** This is known as empowerment. **3. Yes.** Values, beliefs, customs, and ceremonies represent what is acceptable and unacceptable in the organization. **4. No.** This describes an exacting culture. An integrative culture combines high concern for people and production. **5. No.** Coercive power is the opposite of reward power. One offers rewards and the other punishment to encourage appropriate behavior.

PART 4
Implementing Business Ethics in a Global Economy

CHAPTER 8

Developing an Effective Ethics Program

CHAPTER OBJECTIVES

- To understand the responsibility of the corporation to be a moral agent
- To understand why businesses need to develop ethics programs
- To list the minimum requirements for an ethics program
- To describe the role of codes of ethics in identifying key risk areas for the organization
- To identify the keys to successful ethics training, including program types and goals
- To examine the ways that ethical standards are monitored, audited, and enforced and to understand the need for continuous improvement

CHAPTER OUTLINE

The Responsibility of the Corporation as a Moral Agent

The Need for Organizational Ethics Programs

An Effective Ethics Program

An Ethics Program Can Help Avoid Legal Problems

Values versus Compliance Programs

Codes of Conduct

Ethics Officers

Ethics Training and Communication

Systems to Monitor and Enforce Ethical Standards

Continuous Improvement of the Ethics Program

Common Mistakes in Designing and Implementing an Ethics Program

AN ETHICAL DILEMMA*

Victoria was starting to wonder about the implications of her actions as well as her company's strategy. She had begun working for Koke International (KI) after graduating from Pacific West University with degrees in both finance and marketing. KI was the leader in franchised home repair outlets in the United States. In 25 years, KI had grown from several stores in the Pacific Northwest to 250 over much of the United States and Canada. Koke International came to dominate the markets that it entered by undercutting local competitors on price and quality. The lower prices were easy to charge because KI received large quantity discounts from its vendors. The franchise concept also helped create another barrier to entry for KI's competitors. By expanding rapidly, KI was able to spread the costs of marketing to many more stores, giving it still another differential advantage. This active nourishment of its brand image coupled with some technological advances such as just-in-time inventory, electronic scanners, and electronic market niching had sent KI's stock soaring. As a result, it had a 50 percent share of the market. Koke International had done such an excellent job of positioning itself in its field that articles in major business newspapers were calling it "the Microsoft of home improvements." The view was that "KI is going to continue to be a very profitable endeavor, with less expected direct competition in a slow-growth, high-margin market for the future."

Wendy, Victoria's boss, had brought her in on KI's next potential conquest: the New England states of Maine, Vermont, New Hampshire, Connecticut, and Massachusetts.

"This is the last big potential market," Wendy said at a planning session with her senior staff. "I want you to realize that when we launch into these states we're going to have to be ruthless. I'd like your suggestions as to how we're going to eliminate the competition."

One person spoke up: "We first need to recognize that there are only five major players (multiple-store chains), with Home Designs being the largest."

"The top corporate people want us to attack Maine, New Hampshire, and Vermont first and then make a secondary attack on the other two states," interjected Victoria.

"Our buildings are four months from completion," Wendy pointed out, "and the media blitz is due to start one month prior to the 20-store grand opening. With that much exposed capital from our franchises, we need to make sure everything goes well. Vicky, have you completed your price analysis of all of the surrounding home repair stores?"

"Yes, and you're not going to like the news," Victoria replied. "Many of the stores are going to be extremely competitive relative to our normal pricing. In a few cases, they seem to have an edge."

Wendy turned to Ed. "Ed, how much cash flow/reserves have you been able to calculate from the five players?"

"Well, Wendy, it looks like if we slash our prices for about six months to a year, we could drive all but Home Designs into near bankruptcy, providing that our promotional campaign doesn't have a misstep."

"What about personnel, Frank?" Wendy cut in. "Have you done the usual research to see about hiring away the five players' key personnel?"

"Yes, but many won't go unless they get a 50 percent raise, which is way out of line with our other stores."

At this point, Wendy slammed her fist on the table and shouted, "I'm tired of hearing negative reports! It's our job to drive out the competition, so I want solutions!"

There was a long silence in the room. Wendy was noted for her quick temper and her quick firings when things didn't go as planned. She had been the first woman to make it this high in the company, and it wasn't the result of being overly pleasant.

"So this is what we're going to do," Wendy said softly. "Frank, you're going to hire those key people at a 50 percent increase. You're going to keep the unions away from the rest of the people. In 18 months, when these overpriced employees have trained the others, we'll find some way of getting rid of them. Ed, you're going to lean on the players' bankers. See if we do business with them as well. See what other information you can squeeze out of them. Victoria, since you're the newest, I'm putting you in charge of breaking the pricing problem. I want you to come up with a unique pricing strategy for each of the 20 stores that will consistently undercut the competition for the next 18 months, even if we have to lose money on everything in the stores! The franchisees will go with this once we explain the payout."

One of the newer staff members asked, "If we're successful, doesn't that make us a monopoly in the area? Don't we have to worry about antitrust issues?"

Wendy raised her eyebrow a little and said, "We don't mention the word *monopoly* around here as if it were wrong. It took the Feds decades to break up AT&T. Microsoft was next on their list, and now it's MasterCard. We're in retail. No one has ever had problems with the Feds in this industry. By the time they deal with what we're doing, we will all be retired."

QUESTIONS • EXERCISES

1. Identify the issues of which Victoria needs to be aware.
2. Discuss the implications of each decision that Wendy made.
3. Discuss the issue of monopolies and whether they are right or wrong.

*This case is strictly hypothetical; any resemblance to real persons, companies, or situations is coincidental.

Programs that are designed to foster ethical decision making in business are controversial today because much unethical and illegal business conduct has continued to occur, even in organizations that have adopted such programs. Enron, for example, had a code of ethics and was a member of the Better Business Bureau, yet the company was ruined by unethical activities and corporate scandal. Many business leaders believe that ethics initiatives should arise naturally from a company's corporate culture and that hiring good employees will limit unethical conduct. Moreover, many business executives and board members often do not understand how organizational ethics can be systematically implemented. We believe, however, that a customized ethics and compliance program will help many businesses provide guidance so that employees from diverse backgrounds will understand what behaviors are acceptable (or unacceptable) within the organization. In business, many ethical issues are complex and require that organizations reach a consensus on appropriate action. Top executives and boards of directors must provide the leadership and a system to resolve these issues.

Business ethics programs have the potential to help top managers establish an ethical culture and eliminate the opportunity for unethical conduct. This chapter therefore provides a framework for developing an ethics program that is consistent with research, best practices, and the decision making process described in Chapter 5, as well as the Federal Sentencing Guidelines for Organizations (FSGO) and the Sarbanes–Oxley Act in Chapter 4. These legislative reforms require both executives and boards of directors to assume responsibility and ensure that ethical standards are properly implemented on a daily basis.

In this chapter, we first provide an assessment of the corporation as an entity in society, and then we give an overview of why businesses need to develop an organizational ethics program. Next, we consider the factors that must be part of such a program: a code of conduct, an ethics officer and the appropriate delegation of authority, an effective ethics-training program, a system for monitoring and supporting ethical compliance, and continual efforts to improve the ethics program. Finally, we consider common mistakes made in designing and implementing ethics programs.

THE RESPONSIBILITY OF THE CORPORATION AS A MORAL AGENT

Increasingly, corporations are viewed not merely as profit-making entities but also as moral agents that are accountable for their conduct to their employees, investors, suppliers, and customers. Companies are more than the sum of their parts or participants. Because corporations are chartered as citizens of a state and/or nation, they generally have the same rights and responsibilities as individuals. Through legislation and court precedents, society holds companies accountable for the conduct of their employees as well as for their decisions and the consequences of those decisions. Publicity in the news media about specific issues such as employee benefits, executive compensation, defective products, competitive practices, and financial reporting contribute to a firm's reputation as a moral agent.

Viewed as moral agents, companies are required to obey the laws and regulations that define acceptable business conduct. However, it is important to acknowledge that they are not human beings who can think through moral issues. Because companies are not human, laws and regulations are necessary to provide formal structural restraints and guidance on ethical issues. Although individuals may attempt to abide by their own values and moral philosophy, as employees they are supposed to act in the company's best interests. Thus, the individual as a moral agent has a moral obligation beyond that of the corporation because it is the individual, not the company, who can think responsibly through complex ethical issues.[1] Figure 8–1 illustrates the basic causes of individual misconduct, the key reason why individuals engage in misconduct to do "whatever it takes to meet business targets."

FIGURE 8–1 Root Causes of Misconduct

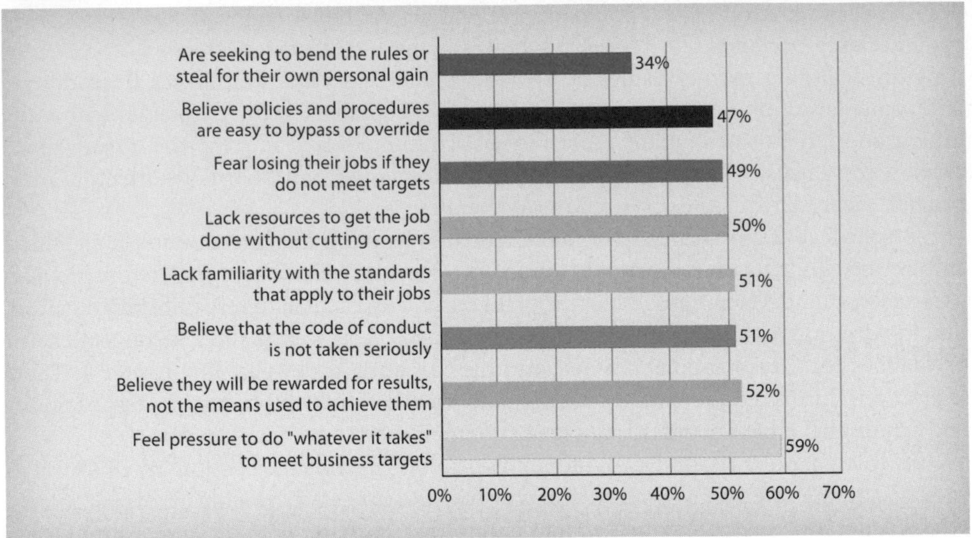

Source: KPMG Forensic Integrity Survey: 2008–2009, http://www.kpmg.com/SiteCollectionDocuments/Integrity-Survey-2008-2009.pdf, p. 6 (accessed August 20, 2009).

Though obviously not a person, a corporation can be considered a societal moral agent that is created to perform specific functions in society and is therefore responsible to society for its actions. Because corporations have the characteristics of agents, responsibility for ethical behavior is assigned to them as legal entities as well as to individuals or work groups they employ. As Figure 8–1 indicates, a corporate culture without values and appropriate communication about ethics can facilitate individual misconduct. As such, companies may be punished for wrongdoing and rewarded for good business ethics. The FSGO holds corporations responsible for conduct they engage in as an entity. Some corporate outcomes cannot be tied to one individual or even a group, and misconduct can be the result of a collective pattern of decisions supported by a corporate culture. Therefore, corporations can be held accountable, fined, and even receive the death penalty when they are operating in a manner inconsistent with major legal requirements. Some organizations receive such large fines and negative publicity that they have to go out of business because there is no way to survive under these pressures. On the other hand, companies that have been selected as top corporate citizens, including Bristol-Myers Squibb, General Mills, IBM, Merck, and HP, receive awards and recognition for being responsible moral agents in society.[2] One major misunderstanding in studying business ethics is to assume that a coherent ethical corporate culture will evolve through individual and interpersonal relationships. Because ethics is often viewed as an individual matter, many reason that the best way to develop an ethical corporate culture is to provide character education to employees or to hire individuals with good character and sensitize them to ethical issues. This assumes that ethical conduct will develop through company-wide agreement and consensus. Although these assumptions are laudable and have some truth, the companies that are responsible for most of the economic activity in the world employ thousands of culturally diverse individuals who will never reach agreement on all ethical issues. Many ethical business issues are complex close calls, and the only way to ensure consistent decisions that represent the interests of all stakeholders is to require ethical policies. This chapter provides support for the belief that implementing a centralized corporate ethics program can provide a cohesive, internally consistent set of statements and policies representing the corporation as a moral agent.

THE NEED FOR ORGANIZATIONAL ETHICS PROGRAMS

To understand why companies need to develop ethics programs, judge whether each of the following actions is unethical or illegal:

1. You want to skip work to go to a baseball game, but you need a doctor's excuse, so you make up some symptoms so that your insurance company pays for the doctor's visit. (unethical, illegal)
2. While having a latte at Starbucks, you run into an acquaintance who works as a salesperson at a competing firm. You wind up chatting about future product prices. When you get back to your office, you tell your supervisor what you heard. (unethical, illegal)
3. You are fired from your company, but before leaving to take a position with another company, you take a confidential list of client names and telephone numbers that you compiled for your former employer. (unethical, illegal)
4. You receive a loan from your parents to make the down payment on your first home, but when describing the source of the down payment on the mortgage application, you characterize it as a gift. (unethical, illegal)
5. Your manager asks you to book some sales revenue from the next quarter into this quarter's sales report to help reach target sales figures. You agree to do so. (unethical, illegal)

You probably labeled one or more of these five scenarios as unethical rather than illegal. The reality is that all of them are illegal. You may have chosen incorrectly because it is nearly impossible to know every detail of the highly complex laws relevant to these situations. Consider that there are 10,000 laws and regulations associated with the processing and selling of a single hamburger. Unless you are a lawyer who specializes in a particular area, it is difficult to know every law associated with your job. However, you can become more sensitized to what might be unethical or, in this case, illegal. One reason why ethics programs are required in one form or another is to help sensitize employees to the potential legal and ethical issues within their work environments.

As we have mentioned throughout this book, recent ethics scandals in U.S. business have destroyed trust in top management and significantly lowered the public's trust of business. Table 8–1 shows the Caux Round Table's Seven Point Plan to Restore Trust in Business. Pepsi CEO Indra Nooyi believes that all businesses are challenged to help restore consumer confidence and trust. She stated that rebuilding trust will require "all companies to think again about what they do to build trust, and to think again about how they make, give, and add value. And most of all, it will require all companies to ensure that they embrace not just the commercial idea of value, but the ethical ideal of values too."[3] Understanding the factors that influence the ethical decision making process, as discussed in Chapter 5, can help companies encourage ethical behavior and discourage undesirable

TABLE 8–1 The Caux Round Table's Seven Point Reform Plan to Restore Trust in Business and in the Global Financial System

1. Require board directors to consider interests beyond shareholders, which may affect the company's success by codifying the principle of "enlightened shareholder value" in company law.
2. Require minimum standards of corporate governance knowledge and expertise for corporate board directors.
3. Require corporate boards to have a dedicated board committee responsible for risk oversight across the full spectrum of risks—financial, governance, social, environmental.
4. Regulate executive remuneration structures to ensure that they are consistent with prudent risk management, align with long-term wealth creation, and do not reward poor performers.
5. Implement stronger and globally coordinated financial and banking regulatory reforms to prevent systematic risk build-up or market manipulation.
6. Regulate all financial markets instruments and investment activities that materially impact on financial system stability.
7. Reform and adequately resource the International Monetary Fund and other multilateral institutions to ensure they are effective forces for economic and social justice globally.

Source: "Seven Point Reform Plan to Restore Trust in Business and in the Global Financial System," March 31, 2009, http://www.cauxroundtable.org/newsmaster.cfm?&menuid=99&action=view&retrieveid=11 (accessed June 8, 2009).

conduct. Fostering ethical decision making within an organization requires terminating unethical persons and improving the firm's ethical standards. Consider the "bad apple–bad barrel" analogy. Some people are simply "bad apples" who will always do things in their own self-interest regardless of their organization's goals or accepted standards of conduct. Eliminating such bad apples through screening techniques and enforcement of the firm's ethical standards can help improve the firm's overall behavior.[4] For example, Countrywide Financial CEO Angelo Mozilo created a corporate culture focused on low documentation and subprime mortgages. Until its demise, Mozilo made positive statements about the company, although he had sold $474 million of his company's stock prior to its sale to Bank of America. Additionally, "liar loans," where borrowers' financial information is altered, were widespread in the company, putting the focus on the rewards of commissions for making loans with little concern for stakeholders.[5]

Organizations also can become "bad barrels," not because the individuals within them are bad, but because the pressures to succeed create opportunities that reward unethical decisions. In the case of such bad barrels, the firms must redesign their image and culture to conform to industry and social standards of acceptable behavior.[6] Most companies attempt to improve ethical decision making by establishing and implementing a strategic approach to improving their organization's ethics. Companies as diverse as Texas Instruments, Starbucks, Ford Motor Company, and Johnson & Johnson have adopted a strategic approach to organizational ethics and also continuously monitor their programs and make improvements when problems occur.

To promote legal and ethical conduct, an organization should develop an organizational ethics program by establishing, communicating, and monitoring the ethical values and legal requirements that characterize its history, culture, industry, and operating environment.

Without such programs, uniform standards, and policies of conduct, it is difficult for employees to determine what behaviors are acceptable within a company. As discussed in Chapters 6 and 7, in the absence of such programs and standards, employees generally will make decisions based on their observations of how their coworkers and superiors behave. A strong ethics program includes a written code of conduct, an ethics officer to oversee the program, careful delegation of authority; formal ethics training; and rigorous auditing, monitoring, enforcement, and revision of program standards. Without a strong program, problems likely will occur. Such is the case in Latin America where a survey by a Latin American business magazine found that Argentine businesses have the greatest number of ethical problems. In Latin America, there is no method, rule, or corporate internal policy that controls in absolute terms what business managers plan, execute, or do, and only 26 percent of all executives follow the values of the founder or owner of the business in which they are employed.[7]

Although there are no universal standards that can be applied to organizational ethics programs, most companies develop codes, values, or policies to provide guidance on business conduct. However, it would be naïve to think that simply having a code of ethics will solve all the ethical dilemmas that a company might face.[8] Indeed, most of the companies that have experienced ethical and legal difficulties in recent years have had formal ethics codes and programs. The problem is that top managers have not integrated these codes, values, and standards into their firms' corporate culture where they can provide effective guidance for daily decision making. Merrill Lynch CEO John Thain spent over 1.2 million in decorating his Manhattan offices at a time when the company was facing record losses. In addition, Thain worked to provide large bonuses to company employees before the Bank of America acquisition. Thain resigned from Merrill Lynch shortly after the Bank of America acquisition. Thain's actions were in contrast to companies like Citigroup, which began system-wide cutbacks in the face of declining income by eliminating BlackBerrys and color copies.[9]

If a company's leadership fails to provide the vision and support needed for ethical conduct, then an ethics program will not be effective. Ethics is not something to be delegated to lower-level employees while top managers break the rules.

To satisfy the public's escalating demands for ethical decision making, companies need to develop plans and structures for addressing ethical considerations. Some directions for improving ethics have been mandated through regulations, but companies must be willing to have in place a system for implementing values and ethics that exceeds the minimum requirements.

AN EFFECTIVE ETHICS PROGRAM

Throughout this book, we have emphasized that ethical issues are at the forefront of organizational concerns as managers and employees face increasingly complex decisions. These decisions are often made in a group environment composed of different value systems, competitive pressures, and political concerns that contribute to the opportunity for misconduct. Almost half of the employees in the KPMG Forensic Ethics Survey stated that they had observed misconduct that could cause "a significant loss of public trust if discovered." The number soared to 60 percent in the banking and finance industry.[10] When opportunity to engage in unethical conduct abounds, companies are vulnerable to both ethical problems and legal violations if their employees do not know how to make the right decisions.

A company must have an effective ethics program to ensure that all employees understand its values and comply with the policies and codes of conduct that create its ethical culture. Because we come from diverse business, educational, and family backgrounds, it cannot be assumed that we know how to behave appropriately when we enter a new organization or job. Pharmaceutical company Merck requires all employees to be responsible for supporting its Code of Business Conduct, which is available in 27 languages. All employees receive ethics delivery through classroom training to help employees understand how to resolve ethical dilemmas in the workplace, as well as online training to raise awareness of ethical issues and assist in maintaining an ethical organizational culture.[11] According to a study by the Open Compliance Ethics Group (OCEG), among companies with an ethics program in place for 10 years or more, none have experienced "reputation damage" in the last 5 years—"a testament to the important impact these programs can have over time." Companies that have experienced reputation damage in the past are much further along compared to their peers in establishing ethics and compliance programs.[12]

An Ethics Program Can Help Avoid Legal Problems

As mentioned in Chapter 7, some corporate cultures provide opportunities for or reward unethical conduct because their management lacks concern or the company has failed to comply with the minimum requirements of the FSGO (Table 8–2). In such cases, the company may face penalties and the loss of public confidence if one of its employees breaks the law. The guidelines encourage companies to assess their key risk areas and to customize a compliance program that will address these risks and satisfy key effectiveness criteria. The guidelines also hold companies responsible for the misconduct of their employees. The KPMG Forensic Integrity Survey found that around half of those surveyed felt that their company would not discipline workers guilty of an ethical infraction, and 59 percent said that they felt pressure to do "whatever it takes" to meet business goals.[13]

At the heart of the FSGO is a "carrot-and-stick" philosophy. Companies that act to prevent misconduct by establishing and enforcing ethical and legal compliance programs

TABLE 8–2 Minimum Requirements for Ethics and Compliance Programs

1. Standards and procedures, such as codes of ethics, that are reasonably capable of detecting and preventing misconduct
2. High-level personnel who are responsible for an ethics and compliance program
3. No substantial discretionary authority given to individuals with a propensity for misconduct
4. Standards and procedures communicated effectively via ethics-training programs
5. Establishment of systems to monitor, audit, and report misconduct
6. Consistent enforcement of standards, codes, and punishment
7. Continuous improvement of the ethics and compliance program

Source: Adapted from U.S. Sentencing Commission, *Federal Sentencing Guidelines Manual*, effective November 1, 2004 (St. Paul: West, 2008).

TABLE 8-3 Mean and Median Fines Imposed on Sentenced Organizations in Three Offense Categories

	Cases with Fine Imposed							
	Cases with Fine Imposed (2003)				Cases with Fine Imposed (2007)			
Offense	Total Number of Cases (including those with no fine)	Number of Cases with Fine Imposed	Mean Fine ($)	Median Fine ($)	Total Number of Cases (including those with no Fine)	Number of Cases with Fine Imposed	Mean Fine ($)	Median Fine ($)
Antitrust	12	7	58,944	30,000	15	11	115,691	50,000
Fraud	7,035	674	707,470	33,816	7,726	1,047	1,621,654	45,177
Environmental/ wildlife	140	62	19,234	2,500	192	133	14,364	5,000

Source: 2003 Annual Report, Table 15, U.S. Sentencing Commission, http://www.ussc.gov/ANNRPT/2003/SBTOC03.htm (accessed August 20, 2009); 2007 Annual Report, Table 15, U.S. Sentencing Commission, www.ussc.gov/ANNRPT/2007/Table15.pdf (accessed August 20, 2009).

may receive a "carrot" and avoid penalties should a violation occur. The ultimate "stick" is the possibility of being fined or put on probation if convicted of a crime. Organizational probation involves using consultants on-site to observe and monitor a company's legal compliance efforts as well as to report the company's progress toward avoiding misconduct to the U.S. Sentencing Commission. Table 8–3 shows the fines that have been imposed on sentenced organizations for leading offenses, including antitrust violations and fraud. The table compares two years of data; as can be seen from the table, cases of fraud, antitrust, and environmental wildlife offenses have all increased.

The FSGO also requires federal judges to increase fines for organizations that continually tolerate misconduct and to reduce or eliminate fines for firms with extensive compliance programs that are making due diligence attempts to abide by legal and ethical standards. Until the guidelines were formulated, courts were inconsistent in holding corporations responsible for employee misconduct. There was no incentive to build effective programs to encourage employees to make ethical and legal decisions. Now companies earn credit for creating ethics programs that meet a rigorous standard. The effectiveness of a program is determined by its design and implementation: It must deal effectively with the risk associated with a particular business and has to become part of the corporate culture.

An ethics program can help a firm avoid civil liability, but the company still bears the burden of proving that it has an effective program. A program developed in the absence of misconduct will be much more effective than one imposed as a reaction to scandal or prosecution. A legal test of a company's ethics program is possible when an individual employee is charged with misconduct. The court system or the U.S. Sentencing Commission evaluates the organization's responsibility for the individual's behavior during the process of an investigation. If the courts find that the company contributed to the misconduct or failed to show due diligence in preventing misconduct, then the firm may be convicted and sentenced.

The Sarbanes–Oxley Act of 2002, as discussed in Chapter 3, established new requirements for corporate governance to prevent fraudulent behavior in business. The heart of this act is an accounting oversight board that establishes financial reporting requirements including instituting a code of conduct for senior financial officers. This legislation covers many issues related to corporate governance, including the role of board members relative to the oversight of ethics programs. It also requires public corporations to file their code of ethics with the accounting oversight board or explain why they do not have a code of ethics.

Values versus Compliance Programs

No matter what their goals, ethics programs are developed as organizational control systems, the aim of which is to create predictability in employee behavior. Two types of control systems can be created. A **compliance orientation** creates order by requiring that employees identify with and commit to specific required conduct. It uses legal terms, statutes, and contracts that teach employees the rules and penalties for noncompliance. The other type of system is a **values orientation**, which strives to develop shared values. Although penalties are attached, the focus is more on an abstract core of ideals such as accountability and commitment.

Research into compliance- and values-based approaches reveals that both types of programs can interact or work toward the same end but that a values orientation influences employees and creates ethical reasoning among employees. Values-based programs increase employees' awareness of ethics at work, their integrity, their willingness to deliver bad news to supervisors, and the perception that better decisions are made. Compliance-based programs are linked to employees' awareness of ethical issues at work, to their perception that decision making is better because of the program, and to their explicit knowledge of rules and expectations that makes decision making easier. In the final analysis, both orientations can be used to help employees and managers; however, it appears that a values-based program may be better for companies in the long run.

CODES OF CONDUCT

Most companies begin the process of establishing organizational ethics programs by developing **codes of conduct**, which are formal statements that describe what an organization expects of its employees. Such statements may take three different forms: a code of ethics, a code of conduct, and a statement of values. A **code of ethics** is the most comprehensive and consists of general statements, sometimes altruistic or inspirational, that serve as principles and the basis for rules of conduct. A code of ethics generally specifies methods for reporting violations, disciplinary action for violations, and a structure of due process. A code of conduct is a written document that may contain some inspirational statements but usually specifies acceptable or unacceptable types of behavior. A code of conduct is more akin to a regulatory set of rules and, as such, tends to elicit less debate about specific actions. Some of the key reasons that codes of ethics fail are that (1) the code is not promoted and employees do not read; (2) the code is not easily accessible; (3) the code is written too legalistically and therefore is not understandable by average employees; (4) the code is written too vaguely, providing no accurate direction; and (5) top management never refers to the code in body or spirit.[14]

The final type of ethical statement is a **statement of values**, which serves the general public and also addresses distinct groups such as stakeholders. Values statements are conceived by management and are fully developed with input from all stakeholders. Despite the distinction made in this book between a code of ethics

FIGURE 8-2 Percentage of Employees Who Identify Comprehensive Ethics and Compliance Programs in Their Own Companies

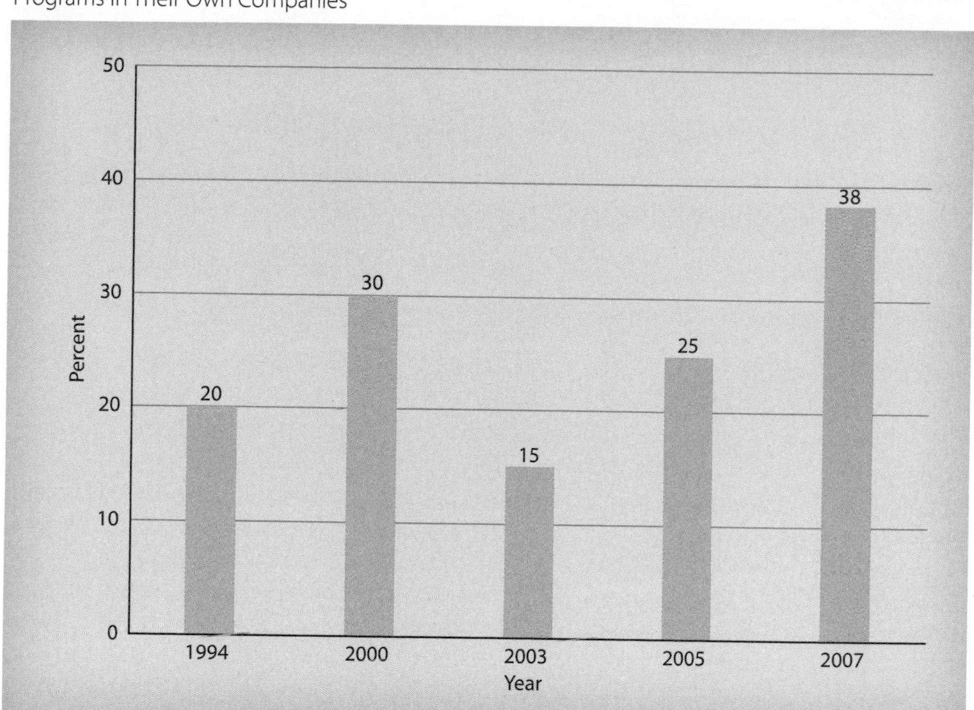

Source: National Business Ethics Survey, How Employees View Ethics in their Organizations, (Washington DC: Ethics Resource Center, 2007), 18.

and a values statement, it is important to recognize that these terms are often used interchangeably. Figure 8–2 indicates that most employees do not feel their company's code of conduct is comprehensive. While 38 percent appears low, this represents a 13 percent improvement over 2005. Because of legal regulations, 55 percent of publicly-held organizations have comprehensive codes, as opposed to a mere 27 percent in privately-held organizations.[15]

Regardless of the degree of comprehensiveness, a code of ethics should reflect upper managers' desire for compliance with the values, rules, and policies that support an ethical culture. The development of a code of ethics should involve the president, board of directors, and chief executive officers who will be implementing the code. Legal staff should also be called on to ensure that the code has correctly assessed key areas of risk and that it provides buffers for potential legal problems. A code of ethics that does not address specific high-risk activities within the scope of daily operations is inadequate for maintaining standards that can prevent misconduct. Table 8–4 shows factors to consider when developing and implementing a code of ethics.

These codes may address a variety of situations, from internal operations to sales presentations and financial disclosure practices. Research has found that corporate codes of ethics often contain about six core values or principles in addition to more detailed descriptions and examples of appropriate conduct.[16] The six values that have been suggested as being desirable for codes of ethics include (1) trustworthiness, (2) respect, (3) responsibility, (4) fairness, (5) caring, and (6) citizenship.[17] These values will not be

TABLE 8–4 Developing and Implementing a Code of Ethics

1. Consider areas of risk and state the values as well as conduct necessary to comply with laws and regulations. Values are an important buffer in preventing serious misconduct.
2. Identify values that specifically address current ethical issues.
3. Consider values that link the organization to a stakeholder orientation. Attempt to find overlaps in organizational and stakeholder values.
4. Make the code understandable by providing examples that reflect values.
5. Communicate the code frequently and in language that employees can understand.
6. Revise the code every year with input from organizational members and stakeholders.

effective without distribution, training, and the support of top management in making these values a part of the corporate culture. Employees need specific examples of how these values can be implemented. Table 8–5 lists the top 10 corporate codes of ethics, according to *Ethisphere Magazine*.

Codes of conduct will not resolve every ethical issue encountered in daily operations, but they help employees and managers deal with ethical dilemmas by prescribing or limiting specific activities. Many companies have a code of ethics, but it is not communicated effectively. A code that is placed on a website or in a training manual is useless if it is not reinforced every day. By communicating to employees both what is expected of them and what punishments they face if they violate the rules, codes of conduct curtail opportunities for unethical behavior and thereby improve ethical decision making. For example, the American Society for Civil Engineers Code of Ethics specifies that engineers must act with zero tolerance toward bribery, fraud, and corruption in all engineering and construction projects in which they are engaged.[18] Codes of conduct do not have to be so

TABLE 8–5 Top 10 Codes of Ethics

1. Verizon Wireless
2. Granite Construction Company
3. BP PLC
4. Datapath Inc.
5. Sprint Nextel
6. Accenture
7. Pepsico
8. Cardinal Health Inc.
9. Rockwell Collins
10. Fluor Corporation

Source: "Ten Best Codes of Ethics and Business Conduct," *Ethisphere*, http://ethisphere.com/10-best-codes-of-ethics-and-business-conduct-government-contractors/ (accessed June 8, 2009).

detailed that they take into account every situation, but they should provide guidelines and principles that are capable of helping employees achieve organizational ethical objectives and addressing risks in an accepted way.

In the United States, Texas Instruments has gained recognition as having one of the nation's leading ethics programs. The company has won numerous ethics awards as well as being listed on the *Fortune* list of America's most admired companies, where it ranked number one in the semiconductor industry for three years. It was also on the *Business Ethics* "100 Best Corporate Citizens" list in the last four years. Texas Instruments is extremely focused on ethics and social responsibility, it ensures that its employees are educated in ethics, and it does this through its "Code of Ethics" booklet and the ethics quick test that is an integral part of everything that Texas Instruments does. It is not only large companies that need to develop an ethics and compliance program; small companies need to and are doing it too.

ETHICS OFFICERS

Organizational ethics programs also must have oversight by high-ranking persons known to respect legal and ethical standards. These individuals—often referred to as **ethics officers**—are responsible for managing their organizations' ethics and legal compliance programs. They are usually responsible for (1) assessing the needs and risks that an organization- wide ethics program must address, (2) developing and distributing a code of conduct or ethics, (3) conducting training programs for employees, (4) establishing and maintaining a confidential service to answer employees' questions about ethical issues, (5) making sure that the company is in compliance with government regulation, (6) monitoring and auditing ethical conduct, (7) taking action on possible violations of the company's code, and (8) reviewing and updating the code. Ethics officers are also responsible for knowing thousands of pages of relevant regulations as well as communicating and reinforcing values that build an ethical corporate culture. The Ethics Resource Center reports that having a comprehensive ethics program in place, one that includes an ethics officer, helps companies reduce incidences of misconduct by as much as 75 percent. However, only 9 percent of corporations included in the survey have an ethics program deemed comprehensive by the ERC.[19] Corporate wrongdoings and scandal-grabbing headlines have a profound negative impact on public trust. To ensure compliance with state and federal regulations, many corporations are now appointing chief compliance officers and ethics and business conduct professionals to develop and oversee corporate compliance programs.[20]

The Ethics and Compliance Officer Association (ECOA) has over 1,350 members who are frontline managers of ethics programs in over 30 industries and 600 organizations.[21] Ethics officers often move into their position from other jobs in their company rather than having formal ethics training. Ethics and compliance officers have backgrounds in law, finance, and human resource management. Sarbanes- Oxley has increased the responsibility that ethics officers and boards of directors have for oversight of financial reporting. Ethics officers' positions are still relatively new and somewhat ill-defined. Although tough economic times call all expenditures into question, economic uncertainty brings about the greatest need for the investment and formalization of the ethics and compliance roles within the organization. Times of economic distress tend to generate significant organizational and individual wrongdoing.[22] Although recommended as best practice, it is not common for ethics officers to report directly to the board of directors. Ethics officers often report directly to the chief executive officer and may have some access to the board. In a survey of chief financial officers, more than 30 percent indicated their operations had been impacted or disrupted by unexpected circumstances in the past year. Oversight, monitoring, and review of operating procedures and outcomes by the ethics and compliance function can prevent such surprises.[23]

ETHICS TRAINING AND COMMUNICATION

A major step in developing an effective ethics program is implementing a training program and communication system to educate employees about the firm's ethical standards. The National Business Ethics Survey looked at 18 dimensions of ethical culture and formal programs and found that companies with strong ethical cultures and formal ethics programs are 36 percentage points less likely to observe misconduct than employees in organizations with weak cultures and ethics programs.[24] A significant number of employees report that they frequently find such training useful. Training can educate employees about the firm's policies and expectations, relevant laws and regulations, and general social standards. Training programs can make employees aware of available resources, support systems, and designated personnel who can assist them with ethical and legal advice. They can also empower employees to ask tough questions and make ethical decisions. Many companies are now incorporating ethics training into their employee and management development training efforts. KPMG strives to operate a model ethics and compliance program. KPMG focuses on the "tone at the top," ethical leadership from top managers, as well as the "tone at the middle," recognizing the importance of the influence and leadership of mid-level managers. KPMG strives to integrate ethics training throughout many "touch points," including orientation, company-wide meetings, technical training, employee letter, publications, as well as its website. KPMG also finds the best of these opportunities to address ethics training is through technical training, which covers 20–100 hours each year and allows ethical issues to be presented in the context of daily decision making.[25]

> *"The existence and enforcement of company rules and procedures limit unethical practices in the organization."*

As we emphasized in Chapters 5 and 7, ethical decision making is influenced by corporate culture, by coworkers and supervisors, and by the opportunities available to engage in unethical behavior. Ethics training can affect all three types of influence. Full awareness of the philosophy of management, rules, and procedures can strengthen both the corporate culture and the ethical stance of peers and supervisors. Such awareness, too, arms employees against opportunities for unethical behavior and lessens the likelihood of misconduct. Thus, the existence and enforcement of company rules and procedures limit unethical practices in the organization. If adequately and thoughtfully designed, ethics training can make employees aware of ethical issues and increase the importance of ethics training to employees and increase employees' confidence that they can make the correct decision when faced with an ethical dilemma.[26] If ethics training is to be effective, it must start with a foundation, a code of ethics, a procedure for airing ethical concerns, line and staff involvements, and executive priorities on ethics that are communicated to employees. Managers from every department must be involved in the development of an ethics-training program. Training and communication initiatives should reflect the unique characteristics of an organization: its size, culture, values, management style, and employee base. It is important for the ethics program to differentiate between personal and organizational ethics. Discussions in ethics-training programs sometimes break down into personal opinions about what should or should not be done in particular situations. To be successful, business ethics programs should educate employees about formal ethical frameworks and models for analyzing business ethics issues. Then employees can base ethical decisions on their knowledge of choices rather than on emotions.

Some of the goals of an ethics-training program might be to improve employees' understanding of ethical issues and their ability to identify them, to inform employees of related procedures and rules, and to identify the contact person who could help employees resolve ethical problems. Texas Instruments operates a comprehensive ethics office that supports ethical conduct in the organization. The office is responsible for assisting in aligning business policies and practices with ethical principles, clearly communicating ethical expectations, and promoting multiple channels for feedback on concerns and resolution of ethical issues. The office is responsible for the following publications: The TI Procurement Policy; Expense Reporting; Acceptance of Gifts, Travel, and Entertainment; Use of TI Employees and Assets to Perform Personal Work; Conflicts of Interest; and Ethical Inquiries and Issues.[27]

A key part of managing an effective and efficient ethics and compliance program is understanding techniques that deliver employee understanding of the culture, policies, and procedures for dealing with ethical issues. Many feel that "hands on" experience where employees are forced to face actual or hypothetical ethical dilemmas train them as to how an organization would like for them to deal with such potential problems. Lockheed Martin, for example, developed a training game called "Gray Matters" that includes dilemmas that can be resolved in teams. Each team member can offer his or her perspective, thereby helping other team members understand the ramifications of a decision for coworkers and the organization.

A relatively new training device is behavioral simulation, which gives participants a short, hypothetical ethical issue situation to review. Each participant is assigned a role within a hypothetical organization and is provided with varying levels of information about the scenario. Participants then must interact to develop recommended courses of action representing short-term, mid-term, and long-term considerations. Such simulations recreate the complexities of organizational relationships as well as the realities of having to address difficult situations with incomplete information. They help participants gain awareness of the ethical, legal, and social dimensions of business decision making; develop analytical skills for resolving ethical issues; and gain exposure to the complexity of ethical decision making in organizations. Research indicates that "the simulation not only instructs on the importance of ethics but on the processes for managing ethical concerns and conflict."[28]

Top executives must communicate with managers at the operations level (in production, sales, and finance, for instance) and enforce overall ethical standards within the organization. Table 8–6 lists the goals for successful ethics training. Making employees aware of the key risk areas for their occupation or profession is a key challenge in any ethics training. In addition, employees need to know who to contact for guidance when they encounter "gray areas" where the organization's rules, policies, and training do not provide adequate direction.

Although training and communication should reinforce values and provide employees with opportunities to learn about rules, they represent just one part of an effective ethics program. Moreover, ethics training will be ineffective if conducted solely because it is required or because it is something that competing firms are doing. The majority of ethics officers surveyed by the Conference Board said that even ethics training could not have

TABLE 8–6 Key Goals of Successful Ethics-Training Programs

1. Identify key risk areas that employees will face.
2. Provide experience in dealing with hypothetical or disguised ethical issues within the industry through mini-cases, online challenges, CD-ROMs, or other experiential learning opportunities.
3. Let your employees know that wrongdoing will never be supported in the organization and that employee evaluations will take their conduct in this area into consideration.
4. Let employees know that they are individually accountable for their behavior.
5. Align employee conduct with organizational reputation and branding.
6. Provide ongoing examples through communication with employees of how employees are handling ethical issues appropriately.
7. Allow a mechanism for employees to voice their concerns that is anonymous, but allows for the provision of feedback to key questions (24 hour hotlines)
8. Provide a hierarchy of leadership for employees to contact when they are faced with an ethical dilemma that they do not know how to resolve.

prevented the high-profile collapses such as Enron or AIG, which were due to accounting improprieties.[29] For example, Enron had an ethics program in place. However, executives knew they had the support of Arthur Andersen, the firm's auditing and accounting consulting partner, as well as that of law firms, investment analysts, and in some cases, government regulators. Enron's top managers therefore probably believed that their efforts to hide debt in off-balance-sheet partnerships would not be exposed.

In the Conference Board survey, 56 percent of ethics officers responded that they do not survey their employees to assess the effectiveness of their ethics programs, and 54 percent do not have ethics measurements as part of their performance appraisal systems.[30] Both of these activities could help determine the effectiveness of a firm's ethics training. If ethical performance is not a part of regular performance appraisals, this sends the message that ethics is not an important component of decision making. For ethics training to make a difference, employees must understand why it is conducted, how it fits into the organization, and what their own role in implementing it is.

SYSTEMS TO MONITOR AND ENFORCE ETHICAL STANDARDS

An effective ethics program employs a variety of resources to monitor ethical conduct and measure the program's effectiveness. Observing employees, internal audits, surveys, reporting systems, and investigations can assess compliance with the company's ethical code and standards. An external audit and review of company activities may sometimes be helpful in developing benchmarks of compliance. (We examine the process of ethical auditing in Chapter 9.)

To determine whether a person is performing his or her job adequately and ethically, observers might focus on how the employee handles an ethically charged situation. For example, many businesses employ role-playing exercises in training salespeople and managers. Ethical issues can be introduced into the discussion, and the results can be videotaped so that both participants and their superiors can evaluate the outcome of the ethics dilemma.

Questionnaires can serve as benchmarks in an ongoing assessment of ethical performance by surveying employees' ethical perceptions of their company, their superiors, their coworkers, and themselves, as well as gaining their ratings of ethical or unethical practices within the firm and industry. Then, if unethical conduct appears to be increasing, management will have a better understanding of what types of unethical practices may be occurring and why. A change in the company's ethics training may then be necessary.

The existence of an internal system by which employees can report misconduct is especially useful for monitoring and evaluating ethical performance. Many companies set up ethics assistance lines, also known as "hotlines," to provide support and give employees the opportunity to ask questions or report concerns. The most effective ethics hotlines operate on an anonymous basis and are supported 24 hours a day, 365 days a year. Approximately 50 percent of hotline calls occur at night or on the weekends. Many times troubling ethical issues can cause you to lose sleep or ponder conduct during free time.[31] Although there is always some concern that employees may misreport a situation or abuse a hotline to retaliate against a coworker, hotlines have become widespread, and employees do use them. An easy-to-use hotline or help desk can serve as a safety net that increases the chance of detecting and responding to unethical conduct in a timely manner. Hotlines serve as a central contact point where critical comments, dilemmas, and advice can be assigned to the person most appropriate for handling a specific case.[32] Figure 8–3 provides an overview of changes in employee propensity to report misconduct. Employees prefer to deal with ethical issues through their supervisor or manager or try to resolve the matter directly before using an anonymous reporting system such as a hotline.

Companies are increasingly using firms that provide professional case-management services and software. Software is becoming popular because it provides reports of employee concerns, complaints, or observations of misconduct, which can then be tracked and managed.

FIGURE 8-3 Percentage of Employees Nationally Who Report Misconduct between 2000 and 2005 in the propensity of employees to report misconduct

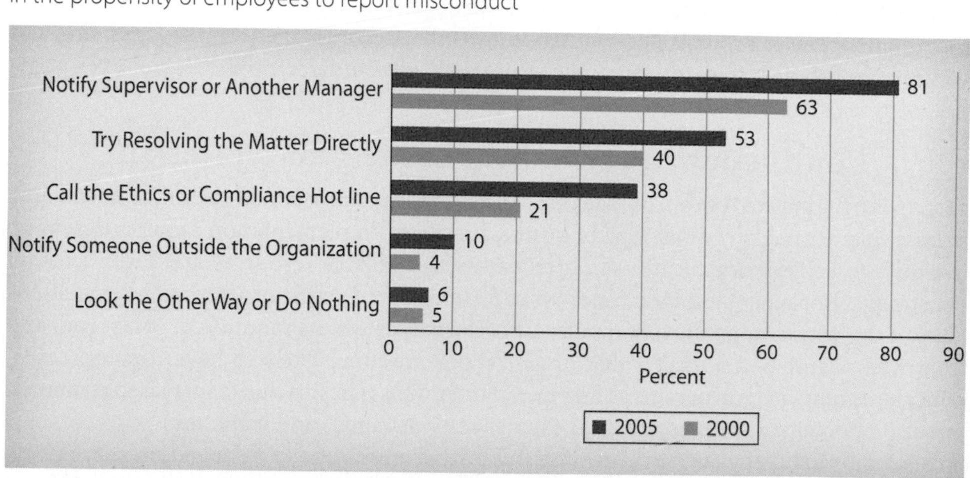

Source: "KPMG Forensic Integrity Survey 2005–2006," http://www.kpmginsiders.com/display_analysis.asp?cs_id=148597 (accessed March 9, 2006).

It then allows the company to track investigations, analysis, resolutions, and documentation of misconduct reports. This helps prevent lawsuits, and the shared management and prevention can help a company analyze and learn about ethical lapses. However, it is important for companies to choose the right software for their company. They need to assess their current position and determine what they need going forward. Although only 10 to 15 percent of companies currently use some type of compliance management tool, many companies are moving toward the automated process that technology and software provide.

If a company is not making progress toward creating and maintaining an ethical culture, it needs to determine why and take corrective action, either by enforcing current standards more strictly or by setting higher standards. Corrective action may involve rewarding employees who comply with company policies and standards and punishing those who do not. When employees abide by organizational standards, their efforts should be acknowledged through public recognition, bonuses, raises, or some other means. On the other hand, when employees violate organizational standards, they must be reprimanded, transferred, docked, suspended, or even fired. If the firm fails to take corrective action against unethical or illegal behavior, the inappropriate behavior is likely to continue. In the Ethics Resource Center Survey, 54 percent of employees who observe misconduct but do not report it choose inaction because they are skeptical that their report will make a difference.[33] Additionally, 36 percent of non-reporters fear retaliation.

Consistent enforcement and necessary disciplinary action are essential to a functional ethics or compliance program. The ethics officer is usually responsible for implementing all disciplinary actions for violations of the firm's ethical standards. Many companies are including ethical compliance in employee performance appraisals. During performance appraisals, employees may be asked to sign an acknowledgment that they have read the company's current ethics guidelines. The company must also promptly investigate any known or suspected misconduct. The appropriate company official, usually the ethics officer, needs to make a recommendation to senior management on how to deal with a particular ethical infraction. In some cases, a company may be required to report substantiated misconduct to a designated government or regulatory agency so as to receive credit. Under the FSGO, such credit for having an effective compliance program can reduce fines.[34]

Efforts to deter unethical behavior are important for companies' long-term relationships with their employees, customers, and community. If the code of ethics is aggressively enforced and becomes part of the corporate culture, it can effectively improve ethical behavior within the organization. If a code is not properly enforced, it becomes mere window dressing and will accomplish little toward improving ethical behavior and decisions.

Continuous Improvement of the Ethics Program

Improving the system that encourages employees to make more ethical decisions differs little from implementing any other type of business strategy. Implementation requires designing activities to achieve organizational objectives using available resources and given existing constraints. Implementation translates a plan for action into operational terms and establishes a means by which an organization's ethical performance will be monitored, controlled, and improved. Figure 8–4 indicates that organizations are more likely to have comprehensive ethics and compliance programs as they grow larger. This is in part due to increased resources, but also undoubtedly to increased stakeholder responsibilities and liabilities.

A firm's ability to plan and implement ethical business standards depends in part on how it structures resources and activities to achieve its ethical objectives. People's attitudes and

FIGURE 8-4 Percentage of Employees Recognizing Own Companies as Having Comprehensive Ethics Programs Increases with Company Size

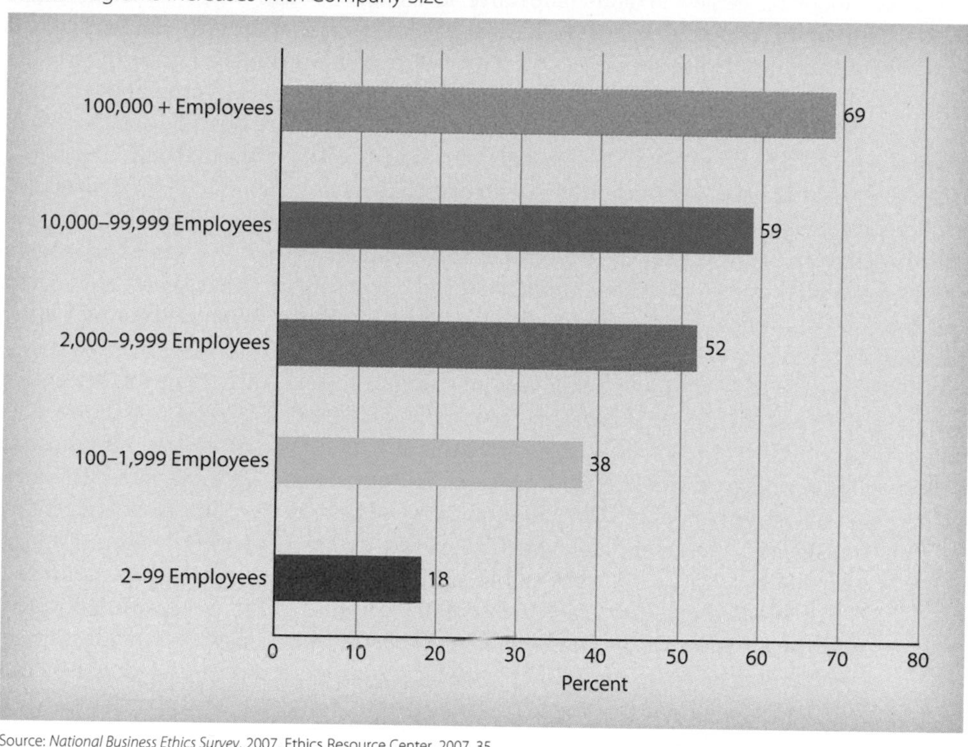

Source: *National Business Ethics Survey*, 2007, Ethics Resource Center, 2007, 35.

behavior must be guided by a shared commitment to the business rather than mere obedience to traditional managerial authority. Encouraging diversity of perspectives, disagreement, and the empowerment of people helps align the company's leadership with its employees.

If a company determines that its ethical performance has been less than satisfactory, executives may want to change how certain kinds of decisions are made. For example, a decentralized organization may need to centralize key decisions, at least for a time, so that upper managers can ensure that the decisions are ethical. Centralization may reduce the opportunities that lower-level managers and employees have to make unethical decisions. Executives can then focus on initiatives for improving the corporate culture and infuse more ethical values throughout the firm by rewarding positive behavior and sanctioning negative behavior. In other companies, decentralizing important decisions may be a better way to attack ethical problems so that lower-level managers, familiar with the forces of the local business environment and local culture and values, can make more decisions. Whether the ethics function is centralized or decentralized, the key need is to delegate authority in such a way that the organization can achieve ethical performance.

Common Mistakes in Designing and Implementing an Ethics Program

Many business leaders recognize that they need to have an ethics program, but few take the time to answer fundamental questions about the goals of such programs. As mentioned previously, some of the most common program objectives are to deter and detect unethical behavior as well as violations of the law; to gain competitive advantages through improved relationships with customers, suppliers, and employees; and, especially for multinational corporations, to link employees through a unifying and shared corporate culture. Failure to understand and appreciate these goals is the first mistake that many firms make when designing ethics programs.

A second mistake is not setting realistic and measurable program objectives. Once a consensus on objectives is reached, companies should solicit input through interviews, focus groups, and survey instruments. Finding out what employees might do in a particular situation can help companies better understand how to correct unethical or illegal behavior either reactively or proactively. Research suggests that employees and senior managers often know that they are doing something unethical but rationalize their behavior as being "for the good of the company." As a result, ethics program objectives should contain some elements that are measurable.[35]

The third mistake is senior management's failure to take ownership of the ethics program. Maintaining an ethical culture may be impossible if CEOs do not support an ethical culture. In recent years, many firms, particularly in the telecommunications industry, have falsified revenue reports by recording sales that never took place, shipping products before customers agreed to delivery, or recording all revenue from long-term contracts up front instead of over the life of the contracts in order to keep earnings high and boost their stock prices. In a number of cases, top executives encouraged such fraud because they held stock options or other bonus packages tied to the company's performance. Thus, reporting higher revenues ensured that they earned larger payoffs. Of the most highly visible accounting fraud cases brought by the SEC, more than half involved falsifying revenue records. For example, the SEC, along with the Department of Justice and a congressional committee, investigated whether Qwest improperly recorded revenues from the sale of fiber-optic capacity as immediate gains even though most of the deals involved long-term leases.[36] If top managers behave unethically, creating and enforcing an ethical culture will be difficult, if not impossible.

"If top managers behave unethically, creating and enforcing an ethical culture will be difficult, if not impossible."

The fourth mistake is developing program materials that do not address the needs of the average employee. Many compliance programs are designed by lawyers to ensure that the company is legally protected. These programs usually yield complex "legalese" that few within the organization can understand. To avoid this problem, ethics programs—including codes of conduct and training materials—should include feedback from employees from across the firm, not just the legal department. Including a question-and-answer section in the program, referencing additional resources for guidance on key ethical issues, and using checklists, illustrations, and even cartoons can help make program materials more user-friendly.

The fifth common mistake made in implementing ethics programs is transferring an "American" program to a firm's international operations. In multinational firms, executives should involve overseas personnel as early as possible in the process in order to help foster an understanding of the company's values and to minimize potential from misconduct stemming from misunderstandings. This can be done by developing an inventory of common global management practices and processes and examining the corporation's standards of conduct in this international context.

A final common mistake is designing an ethics program that is little more than a series of lectures. In such cases, participants typically recall less than 15 percent the day after the lecture. A more practical solution is to allow employees to practice the skills they learn through case studies or small-group exercises.

A firm cannot succeed solely by taking a legalistic approach to ethics and compliance with sentencing guidelines. Top managers must seek to develop high ethical standards that serve as a barrier to illegal conduct. Although an ethics program should help reduce the possibility of penalties and negative public reaction to misconduct, a company must want to be a good corporate citizen and recognize the importance of ethics to success in business.

SUMMARY

Ethics programs help sensitize employees to potential legal and ethical issues within their work environments. To promote ethical and legal conduct, organizations should develop ethics programs by establishing, communicating, and monitoring ethical values and legal requirements that characterize the firms' history, culture, industry, and operating environment. Without such programs and such uniform standards and policies of conduct, it is difficult for employees to determine what behaviors a company deems acceptable.

A company must have an effective ethics program to ensure that employees understand its values and comply with its policies and codes of conduct. An ethics program should help reduce the possibility of legally enforced penalties and negative public reaction to misconduct. The main objective of the Federal Sentencing Guidelines for Organizations is to encourage companies to assess risk and then self-monitor and aggressively work to deter unethical acts and punish unethical employees. Ethics programs are developed as organizational control systems to create predictability in employee behavior. These control systems may have a compliance orientation—which uses legal terms, statutes, and contracts that teach employees the rules and the penalties for noncompliance—or a values orientation—which consists of developing shared values.

Most companies begin the process of establishing organizational ethics programs by developing codes of conduct, which are formal statements that describe what an organization expects of its employees. Variations of codes of conduct include the code of ethics and the statement of values. A code of ethics must be developed as part of senior management's desire to ensure that the company complies with values, rules, and policies that support an ethical culture. Without uniform policies and standards, employees will have difficulty determining what is acceptable behavior in the company.

Having a high-level manager or committee who is responsible for an ethical compliance program can significantly enhance its administration and oversight. Such ethics officers are usually responsible for assessing the needs of and risks to be addressed in an organization-wide ethics program, developing and distributing a code of conduct or ethics, conducting training programs for employees, establishing and maintaining a confidential service to answer questions about ethical issues, making sure the company is complying with government regulation, monitoring and auditing ethical conduct, taking action on possible violations of the company's code, and reviewing and updating the code.

Successful ethics training is important in helping employees identify ethical issues and in providing them with the means to address and resolve such issues. Training can educate employees about the firm's policies and expectations, available resources, support systems, and designated ethics personnel, as well as about relevant laws and regulations and general social standards. Top executives must communicate with managers at the operations level and enforce overall ethical standards within the organization.

An effective ethics program employs a variety of resources to monitor ethical conduct and measure the program's effectiveness. Compliance with the company's ethical code and standards can be assessed through observing employees, performing internal audits and surveys, instituting reporting systems, and conducting investigations, as well as by external audits and review, as needed. Corrective action involves rewarding employees who comply with company policies and standards and punishing those who do not. Consistent enforcement and disciplinary action are necessary for a functioning ethical compliance program.

Ethical compliance can be ensured by designing activities that achieve organizational objectives, using available resources and given existing constraints. A firm's ability to plan and implement ethics business standards depends in part on its ability to structure resources and activities to achieve its ethics and objectives effectively and efficiently.

In implementing ethics and compliance programs, many firms make some common mistakes including failing to answer fundamental questions about the goals of such programs, not setting realistic and measurable program objectives, failing to have its senior management take ownership of the ethics program, developing program materials that do not address the needs of the average employee, transferring an "American" program to a firm's international operations, and designing an ethics program that is little more than a series of lectures. Although an ethics program should help reduce the possibility of penalties and negative public reaction to misconduct, a company must want to be a good corporate citizen and recognize the importance of ethics to successful business activities.

IMPORTANT TERMS FOR REVIEW

compliance orientation

values orientation

code of conduct

code of ethics

statement of values

ethics officers

RESOLVING ETHICAL BUSINESS CHALLENGES*

Jim, now in his fourth year with Cinco Corporation, was made a plant manager three months ago after completing the company's management-training program. Cinco owns pulp-processing plants that produce various grades of paper from fast-growing, genetically altered trees. Jim's plant, the smallest and oldest of Cinco's, is located in upstate New York, near a small town. It employs between 100 and 175 workers, mostly from the nearby town. In fact, the plant boasts about employees whose fathers and grandfathers have also worked there. Every year Cinco holds a Fourth of July picnic for the entire town.

Cinco's policy is to give each manager a free hand in dealing with employees, the community, and the plant itself. Its main measure of performance is the bottom line, and the employees are keenly aware of this fact.

Like all pulp-processing plants, Cinco is located near a river. Because of the plant's age, much of its equipment is outdated. Consequently, it takes more time and money to produce paper at Jim's plant than at Cinco's newer plants. Cinco has a long-standing policy of breaking in new managers at this plant to see if they can manage a work force and a mill efficiently and effectively. The tradition is that a manager who does well with the upstate New York plant will be transferred to a larger, more modern one. As a result, the plant's workers have had to deal with many managers and have become hardened and insensitive to change. In addition, most of the workers are older and more experienced than their managers, including Jim.

In his brief tenure as plant manager, Jim learned much from his workers about the business. Jim's secretary, Ramona, made sure that reports were prepared correctly, that bills were paid, and that Jim learned how to perform his tasks. Ramona has been with the plant for so long that she has become a permanent fixture. Jim's three foremen are all in their late 40s and keep things running smoothly. Jim's wife, Elaine, is having a difficult time adjusting to upstate New York. Speaking with other managers' wives, she learned that the "prison sentence," as she called it, typically lasted no longer than two years. She had a large calendar in the kitchen and crossed off each day they were there.

One morning as Jim came into the office, Ramona didn't seem her usual stoic self.

"What's up?" Jim asked her.

"You need to call the EPA," she replied. "It's not really important. Ralph Hoad said he wanted you to call him."

When Jim made the call, Ralph told him the mill's waste disposal into the river exceeded Environmental Protection Agency (EPA) guidelines, and he would stop by next week to discuss the situation. Jim hung up the phone and asked Ramona for the water sample results for the last six months from upstream, from downstream, and at the plant. After inspecting the data and comparing them with EPA standards, he found no violations of any kind. He then ordered more tests to verify the original data. The next day Jim compared the previous day's tests with the last six months' worth of data and still found no significant differences and no EPA violations. As he continued to look at the data, however, something stood out on the printouts that he hadn't noticed before. All the tests had been done on the first or second shifts. Jim called the foremen of the two shifts to his office and asked if they knew what was going on. Both men were extremely evasive in their answers and referred him to the third-shift foreman. When Jim phoned him, he, too, was evasive and said not to worry—that Ralph would explain it to him.

That night Jim decided to make a spot inspection of the mill and test the wastewater. When he arrived at the river, he knew by the smell that something was very wrong. Jim immediately went back to the mill and demanded to know what was happening. Chuck, the third-shift foreman, took Jim down to the lowest level of the plant. In one of the many rooms stood four large storage tanks. Chuck explained to Jim that when the pressure gauge reached a certain level, a third-shift worker opened the valve and allowed the waste to mix with everything else.

"You see," Chuck told Jim, "the mill was never modernized to meet EPA standards, so we have to divert the bad waste here; twice a week it goes into the river."

"Who knows about this?" asked Jim.

"Everyone who needs to," answered Chuck.

When Jim got home, he told Elaine about the situation. Elaine's reaction was, "Does this mean we're stuck here? Because if we are, I don't know what I'll do!" Jim knew that all the managers before him must have had the same problem. He also knew that there would be no budget for installing EPA-approved equipment for at least another two years. The next morning Jim checked the EPA reports and was puzzled to find that the mill had always been in compliance. There should have been warning notices and fines affixed, but he found nothing.

That afternoon Ralph Hoad stopped by. Ralph talked about the weather, hunting, fishing, and then he said, "Jim, I realize you're new. I apologize for not coming sooner, but I saw no reason to because your predecessor had taken care of me until this month."

"What do you mean?" Jim asked.

"Ramona will fill you in. There's nothing to worry about. I know no one in town wants to see the mill close down, and I don't want it to either. There are lots of memories in this old place. I'll stop by to see you in another couple of months." With that, Ralph left.

Jim asked Ramona about what Ralph had said. She showed him a miscellaneous expense of $100 a month in the ledgers. "We do this every month," she told him.

"How long has this been going on?" asked Jim.

"Since the new EPA rules," Ramona replied. She went on to clarify Jim's alternatives. Either he could continue paying Ralph, which didn't amount to much, or he could refuse to, which would mean paying EPA fines and a potential shutdown of the plant. As Ramona put it, "Headquarters only cares about the bottom line. Now, unless you want to live here the rest of your life, the first alternative is the best for your career. The last manager who bucked the system lost his job. The rule in this industry is that if you can't manage Cinco's upstate New York plant, you can't manage. That's the way it is."

QUESTIONS • EXERCISES

1. Identify the ethical and legal issues of which Jim needs to be aware.
2. Discuss the advantages and disadvantages of each decision that Jim could make.
3. Identify the pressures that have brought about the ethical and legal issues.
4. What is Jim's power structure and leadership position at the plant?

*This case is strictly hypothetical; any resemblance to real persons, companies, or situations is coincidental.

CHECK YOUR EQ

Check your EQ, or Ethics Quotient, by completing the following. Assess your performance to evaluate your overall understanding of the chapter material.

1. A compliance program should be deemed effective if it addresses the seven minimum requirements for ethical compliance programs. **Yes No**
2. The accountability and responsibility for appropriate business conduct rests with top management. **Yes No**
3. Ethical compliance can be measured by observing employees as well as through investigating and reporting mechanisms. **Yes No**
4. The key goal of ethics training is to help employees identify ethical issues. **Yes No**
5. An ethical compliance audit is designed to determine the effectiveness of ethics initiatives. **Yes No**

ANSWERS **1. No.** An effective compliance program has the seven elements of a compliance program in place and goes beyond those minimum requirements to determine what will work in a particular organization. **2. Yes.** Executives in the organization determine the culture and initiatives that support ethical behavior. **3. Yes.** Sometimes external monitoring is necessary, but internal monitoring and evaluation are the norm. **4. No.** It is much more than that—it involves not only recognition but also an understanding of the values, culture, and rules in the organization as well as the impact of ethical decisions on the company. **5. Yes.** It helps in establishing the code and in making program improvements.

CHAPTER 9

Implementing and Auditing Ethics Programs

CHAPTER OBJECTIVES

- To define ethics auditing
- To identify the benefits and limitations of ethics auditing
- To examine the challenges of measuring nonfinancial performance
- To explore the stages of the ethics-auditing process
- To understand the strategic role that the ethics audit can play

CHAPTER OUTLINE

AN ETHICAL DILEMMA*

Chantal has been with Butterfly Industries for 13 years. She started out as an assistant buyer and was later promoted to buyer. She threw herself into her work, and within a few years she had moved into the corporate offices.

During Chantal's tenure, Butterfly Industries grew from fewer than 500 employees to more than 35,000. The company expanded all over the world and opened offices on every continent; it had nearly exclusive arrangements with suppliers from six different countries. Such rapid growth eroded the freedoms of a small firm in which one could do anything one wanted. So many employees—with different cultures, languages, time zones, and varied clients—from so many countries, each with its own political realities, made corporate life much more complicated.

To Chantal, it seemed that the firm had grown at a whirlwind pace, and sometimes she thought that whirlwind had become an ugly black cloud. She had heard, for example, that some of Butterfly's suppliers in Puerto Rico mistreated their workers. In other foreign locations, Butterfly's products were bringing changes to the environment, as well as to local culture and gender roles. Because these workers tended to be women, children were being left to fend for themselves. In some Latin American countries, husbands were angry because their wives earned more than they did. And then there were the rumors that retailers in some countries were selling Butterfly products without adequate service or, worse, diluting the products and selling them as "full strength."

After Butterfly went public, Chantal's sense of a foreboding whirlwind grew darker as headquarters' employees scrambled to satisfy shareholders' demands for specific information about products, projected earnings, employee benefit policies, and equal employment opportunity records. Chantal was also troubled that so many of the corporate people were men; only she and one other woman were directly involved in the inner workings of the increasingly complex firm.

Six months ago, Chantal began hearing that some plant employees were suffering pay cuts while others weren't. In some cases, employees who had been working for Butterfly for 15 years had been cut to 36-hour workweeks, losing their full-time benefits. She began to notice political alliances being erected between marketing, finance, manufacturing, and corporate headquarters. Because each plant operated as an independent profit-making entity, each was guarded in its communication with other plants, knowing that if it could increase its profits it could also increase overall pay.

Chantal was not the only one to recognize that Butterfly needed guidance in a variety of areas, but no one had stepped forward. Then a month ago, Butterfly's president, Jermaine, asked Chantal to lunch. This was not unusual, but the conversation soon took a significant twist that Chantal was unprepared for.

"Chantal, you've been with the company for 13 years now, right?" asked Jermaine.

"Yes, that's right," Chantal answered.

"You know as well as anyone that I haven't kept pace with the growth," Jermaine continued with a mixture of sadness and determination. "When I founded this company, I could tell a few staffers to check out an idea, and several weeks later we'd talk about whether it would work. There was a time when I knew every employee, and even their families, but not anymore. Chantal, I think Butterfly has outgrown my style of management. What this company needs is a comprehensive set of rules and guidelines for every part of the company. I need to delegate more. That's why I wanted to talk to you."

Chantal, noticing her mouth was open, closed it and asked, "Jermaine, what are you saying to me?"

"Chantal, I've always been impressed with your work ethic and your sense of values. You know this company and its culture so well. I know you've heard some of the same rumors, so we both know that all is not well at Butterfly. What I'd like is for you to become the head of Butterfly's new ethics committee. Of course, you know that we don't have an ethics committee, so that's where you come in."

"Me!?" Chantal asked with surprise.

"Yes, you. If you're willing, I want you to create this entity and run it so that we all can be proud of Butterfly again. So that people inside and outside the company know that we stand for what is right. You will be promoted to vice president, your salary will be doubled, and you can select your own team. Chantal, this is your chance to really make a huge difference. What's your answer?" asked Jermaine.

Chantal hesitated for a moment and then said, "Yes."

"Great! I knew I could count on you. The first thing I need is a proposed outline of the responsibilities of the new ethics committee, enforcement procedures—the works—and I want it in two weeks along with a list of people for the committee."

That night, Chantal began to plan.

QUESTIONS • EXERCISES

1. Prioritize the issues that Butterfly needs to address. How can an ethics program address these issues?
2. Develop an outline of who should be on the new ethics committee and describe what the committee's first steps should be toward implementing an effective ethics program.
3. Should the new ethics committee commission an ethics audit? If yes, when should this audit be conducted? If no, why not?

*This case is strictly hypothetical; any resemblance to real persons, companies, or situations is coincidental.

In Chapter 8, we introduced the idea of ethics programs as a way for organizations to improve ethical decision making and conduct in business. To properly implement these programs and ensure their effectiveness, companies need to measure their impact. Increasingly, companies are applying the principles of auditing to ascertain whether their ethics codes, policies, and corporate values are having a positive impact on the firm's ethical conduct. These audits can help companies identify risks, noncompliance with laws and company policies, and areas that need improvement. An audit should provide a systematic and objective survey of the firm's ethical culture and values.

In this chapter, we examine the concept of an ethics audit as a way to implement an effective ethics program. We begin by defining the term *ethics audit* and exploring its relationship to a social audit. Next, we examine the benefits and limitations of this implementation tool, especially with regard to avoiding a management crisis. The challenges of measuring nonfinancial ethical performance are examined and evolving standards are reviewed from AA1000, the Integrity Institute, and the Open Compliance Ethics Group. We then detail our framework for the steps of an ethics audit, including securing the commitment of directors and top managers; establishing a committee to oversee the audit; defining the scope of the audit process; reviewing the firm's mission, values, goals, and policies and defining ethical priorities; collecting and analyzing relevant information; verifying the results; and reporting them. Finally, we consider the strategic importance of ethics auditing.

THE ETHICS AUDIT

An **ethics audit** is a systematic evaluation of an organization's ethics program and performance to determine whether it is effective. A major component of the ethics program described in Chapter 8, the ethics audit includes "regular, complete, and documented measurements of compliance with the company's published policies and procedures."[1] As such, the audit provides an opportunity to measure conformity to the firm's desired ethical standards. An audit can even be a precursor to setting up an ethics program in that it identifies the firm's current ethical standards and policies and risk areas so that an ethics program can effectively address problem areas. Although few companies have so far conducted ethics audits, recent legislation will encourage greater ethics auditing as companies attempt to demonstrate to various stakeholders that they are abiding by the law and have established programs to improve ethical decision making.

The concept of ethics auditing emerged from the movement to audit and report on companies' broader social responsibility initiatives, particularly with regard to the natural environment. An increasing number of companies are auditing their social responsibility programs and reporting the results so as to document their efforts to be more responsible to various interested stakeholder groups. A **social audit** is the process of assessing and reporting a business's performance in fulfilling the economic, legal, ethical, and philanthropic responsibilities expected of it by its stakeholders.[2] Social reports often discuss issues related to a firm's performance in the four dimensions of social responsibility as well as to specific social responsibility and ethical issues such as staff issues, community economic development, volunteerism, and environmental impact.[3] In contrast, ethics audits focus on more narrow issues related to assessing and reporting on a firm's performance in terms of ethical and legal conduct. However, an ethics audit can be a component of a social audit, and, indeed, many companies include ethical issues in their social audits. British Petroleum, for example, includes ethical performance in its Sustainability Report.[4]

Regardless of the breadth of the audit, ethics auditing is a tool that companies can employ to identify and measure their ethical commitment to stakeholders. Employees, customers, investors, suppliers, community members, activists, the media, and regulators are increasingly demanding that companies be ethical and accountable for their conduct. In response, businesses are working to incorporate accountability into their actions, from long-term planning, everyday decision making, and rethinking processes for corporate governance and financial reporting to hiring, retaining, and promoting employees and building relationships with customers. The ethics audit provides an objective method for demonstrating a company's commitment to improving strategic planning, including its compliance with legal and ethical standards and social responsibility. The auditing process is important to business because it can improve a firm's performance and effectiveness, increase its attractiveness to investors, improve its relationships with stakeholders, identify potential risks, and decrease the risk of misconduct and adverse publicity that could harm its reputation.[5]

Ethics auditing is similar to financial auditing in that it employs similar procedures and processes to create a system of integrity that includes objective reporting. Like an accounting audit, someone with expertise from outside the organization may conduct an ethics audit. Although the standards used in financial auditing can be adapted to provide an objective foundation for ethics reporting, there are significant differences between the two audit types. Whereas financial auditing focuses on all systems related to money flow and on financial assessments of value for tax purposes and managerial accountability, ethics auditing deals with the internal and broad external impact of the organization's ethical performance. Another significant difference is that ethics auditing is not usually associated with regulatory requirements, whereas financial audits are required of public companies that issue securities. Because ethics and social audits are voluntary, there are fewer standards that a company can apply with regard to reporting frequency, disclosure requirements, and remedial actions that it should take in response to results. This may change as more companies build ethics programs in the current environment—where regulatory agencies support giving boards of directors oversight of corporate ethics. For boards to track the effectiveness of ethics programs, audits will be required. In addition, nonfinancial auditing standards are developing with data available for benchmarking and comparing a firm's nonfinancial ethical performance.

BENEFITS OF ETHICS AUDITING

There are many reasons why companies choose to understand, report on, and improve their ethical conduct. Recent accounting scandals and legal and ethical transgressions have encouraged companies to better account for their actions in a wide range of areas, including corporate governance, ethics programs, customer relationships, employee relations, environmental policies, and community involvement. Cadence Design Systems, an electronics design company, restated its earnings in 2008, admitting that it had noted $24 million in revenue too early. A shareholder-filed lawsuit against the company alleges that Cadence inflated the stock price, violated federal securities laws, and took advantage of shareholders by causing the 25 percent stock price decline.[6]

At one extreme, a company may want to achieve the most ethical performance possible, whereas another firm may use an ethics audit merely to project a good image to hide its corrupt culture. Other firms may want to comply with the Federal Sentencing Guidelines for Organizations (FSGO) requirements that the board of directors oversee the discovery of ethical risk, design and implement an ethics program, and evaluate performance. Versus compliance with the law, some companies see the auditing process as tied to continuous improvement that is closely related to improved financial performance. The range of reasons for supporting the FSGO is complex and diverse. For example, it is common for firms to conduct audits of business practices with legal ramifications such as employee safety, environmental impact, and financial reporting. Although these practices are important to a firm's ethics and social responsibility, they are also legally required and thus constitute the minimum level of commitment. However, because stakeholders are demanding increased transparency and taking a more active role through external organizations that represent their interests, government regulators are calling on companies to improve their ethical conduct and make more decisions based on principles rather than laws alone. The assessment of the ethical culture of an organization is necessary to improve ethical performance and to document in legal proceedings that a firm has an effective ethics program.

The auditing process can highlight trends, improve organizational learning, and facilitate communication and working relationships.[7] As such, auditing provides benefits for both organizations and their stakeholders. Auditing can help companies assess the effectiveness of their programs and policies, which often improves their operating efficiencies and reduces costs. Information from audits and reports can also help identify priorities among various activities so that the company can ensure that it is achieving the greatest possible impact with available resources.[8] The process of ethics auditing can also help an organization identify potential risks and liabilities and improve its compliance with the law. Furthermore, the audit report may help document the firm's compliance with legal requirements as well as demonstrate its progress in areas where it previously failed to comply, such as by describing the systems it is implementing to reduce the likelihood of a recurrence of misconduct.[9]

For organizations, one of the greatest benefits of the auditing process is improved relationships with stakeholders who desire greater transparency. Many stakeholders have become wary of corporate public relations campaigns. Verbal assurances by corporate management are no longer sufficient to gain the trust of stakeholders. An ethics audit could have saved Enron if it identified and questioned millions of dollars in debt in off-balance-sheet partnerships. When companies and their employees, suppliers, and investors trust each other, the costs of monitoring and managing these relationships are lower. Companies experience less conflict with these stakeholders, which results in a heightened capacity for innovation and relationship building.

As a result, shareholders and investors have welcomed the increased disclosure that comes with corporate accountability. Figure 9–1 illustrates issues that are expected to have the most impact on shareholder value over the next five years. These issues can be considered major risk areas for ethics initiatives. Therefore, they represent subject matter areas that could be important in an ethics audit. A growing number of investors are considering nonfinancial measures—such as the existence of ethics programs, legal compliance, board diversity and independence, and other corporate governance issues such as CEO compensation—when they analyze the quality of current and potential investments. Research suggests that investors may be willing to pay higher prices for the stock of companies that they deem to be accountable.[10] *Fortune's* "World's Most Admired Companies" include Apple, Berkshire Hathaway, Toyota Motors, Google, Johnson & Johnson, Procter & Gamble, FedEx, Southwest Airlines, General Electric, and Microsoft, who have generally avoided major ethical disasters.[11] However, some companies have experienced legal issues or had their ethics questioned. Former Wal-Mart CEO Lee Scott was recognized for his leadership in the business ethics area by investing heavily in renewable energy and environmental causes. Under his leadership, Wal-Mart began to use wind power to supply up to 15 percent of its energy needs in 360 Texas stores. The company has strived to learn from past mistakes, settling over 60 wage and hour abuse

FIGURE 9–1 Top Issues Over the Next Five Years

Rank	Likely to Impact Shareholder Value	Likely to Gain Public Attention
1	Environmental issues, climate change	Environmental issues, climate change
2	Political influence/ involvement of companies	Privacy and data security
3	Privacy and data security (tied for 3rd)	Demand for safer products (tied for 3rd)
4	Healthcare/benefits for workers (tied for 3rd)	Healthcare/benefits for workers (tied for 3rd)
5	Job losses from offshoring (tied for 5th)	Job losses from offshoring
6	Pension and retirement benefits (tied for 5th)	Affordable products for poor consumers
7	Demand for safer products	Demand for ethically produced
8	Demand for investment in developing countries	Pension and retirement benefits
9	Affordable products for poor consumers	High executive pay/compensation
10	High executive pay/compensation	Political influence/ involvement of companies

Adapted from "From Risk to Opportunity—How Global Executives View Sociopolitical Issues: McKinsey Global Survey Results," *McKinsey Quarterly*, October 2008, http://www.mckinseyquarterly.com/Strategy/Strategic_Thinking/ McKinsey_Global_Survey_Results_From_risk_to_opportunity_How_global_executives_view_sociopolitical_issues_2235 (accessed January 15, 2009).

lawsuits. Wal-Mart consistently ranks near the top of *Fortune's* Most Admired Companies in spite of past ethical and legal concerns.[12] Regular audits permit shareholders and investors to judge whether a firm is achieving the goals that it has established and whether it abides by the values that it has specified as important. Moreover, it permits stakeholders to influence the organization's behavior.[13] Increasingly, a broad range of stakeholder groups are seeking specific, often quantifiable, information from companies. These stakeholders expect companies to take a deeper look at the nature of their operations and to publicly disclose both their progress and problems in addressing these issues. Some investors are using their rights as stockholders to encourage companies to modify their plans and policies to address specific ethical issues. On a broader scale, the Obama administration sought to impose limits on executive compensation of those firms seeking government financial support.[14]

Ethical Crisis Management and Recovery

A significant benefit of ethics auditing is that it may help prevent crises resulting from ethical or legal misconduct, crises that can potentially be more devastating than traditional natural disasters or technological disruptions. Just as companies develop *crisis management* plans to respond to and recover from natural disasters, they should also prepare for ethical disasters, which can result not only in substantial legal and financial costs but also disrupt routine operations, paralyze employees, reduce productivity, destroy organizational reputation, and erode stakeholder confidence. Ethical and legal crises have resulted in the demise or acquisition of a number of well-known companies, including Lehman Brothers, Wachovia, Merrill Lynch, and Washington Mutual. Many other companies—HealthSouth, Firestone, Waste Management, Rite Aid, U.S. Foodservice, Qwest, Kmart, Mitsubishi Motors, Xerox, Daiwa Bank of Japan, and Archer Daniels Midland, to name but a few—survived ethical and legal crises. However, they paid a high price not only financially but also in terms of compromised reputation and declining stakeholder trust. In recent years, companies have spent up to $7 million a month on outside legal counsel to defend against alleged organizational wrongdoing. One study found that publicity about unethical corporate behavior lowers stock prices for at least six months.[15]

Organizational members who engage in questionable or even illegal conduct cause ethical misconduct. These rogue employees can threaten the overall integrity of the organization. Top leaders in particular can magnify ethical misconduct to disastrous dimensions. Organizational disasters resulting from individuals' misconduct include Madoff family members at Madoff Investments, Andrew Fastow at Enron, Dennis Kozlowski at Tyco, and Bernie Ebbers at WorldCom.[16] An ethics audit can discover rogue employees who are violating the firm's ethical standards and policies or laws and regulations.

Ethical disasters follow recognizable phases of escalation, from ethical issue recognition and the decision to act unethically to the organization's discovery of and response to the act. Appropriate anticipation of and intervention during these can stave off organizational disaster. Such contingency planning assesses risks, plans for these potential occurrences, and provides ready tools for responding to ethical crises. The process of ethical disaster-recovery planning involves assessing the organization's values, developing an ethics program, performing an ethics audit, and developing contingency plans for potential ethical disasters. The ethics audit itself provides the key link to preventing ethical disasters.

The global financial crisis has impacted U.S. businesses and their ability to effectively compete. Table 9–1 shows areas where the United States has been impacted in comparison to three years earlier. Roughly 60 percent of U.S. business executives feel that the country has lost competitiveness over the past five years. Of great concern to many is the fact that 38 percent feel we are losing ground in the business ethics and corporate governance areas. The deterioration in the effectiveness of ethics and compliance programs creates

TABLE 9–1 Where the United States has Lost Its Competitive Edge
Percent of executives surveyed who feel the U. S. has lost competitiveness in the following areas:

	2006	2009
Worker health care and pension costs	65	75
Access to capital	8	73
Quality of U.S. capital markets	NA	71
Alternate energy sources	38	39
Business ethics and corporate governance	13	38
Costs to customers and end users	30	37
Government policies that are pro-business	NA	35

Source: PricewaterhouseCoopers, Measuring American Competitiveness, 2009, http://www.pwc.com/extweb/pwcpublications.nsf/docid/B3C7B78DCB0AF4E285257583005001A7 (accessed June 12, 2009).

an opportunity for companies to do a better job of assessing their risks and programs through comprehensive ethics and compliance audits. The global financial crisis has only heightened the need for organizations to implement due diligence ethics and compliance programs to restore confidence and competitiveness. The ethics audit becomes a key part of this review and management process.[17]

Challenges of Measuring Nonfinancial Performance

Although much of the regulatory focus of corporate ethics and compliance is driven by financial measures, the integrity of an organization also has to focus on nonfinancial areas of performance. The word *integrity* implies a balanced organization that not only makes ethical financial decisions but also is ethical in the more subjective aspects of its corporate culture. For example, the Sarbanes–Oxley Act has focused on questionable accounting and the metrics that destroy shareholder value. On the other hand, models have been developed—such as Six Sigma, the Balanced Scorecard, and the Triple Bottom Line—to capture structural and behavioral organizational ethical performance. *Six Sigma* is a methodology to manage process variations that cause defects, defined as unacceptable deviations from the mean or target, and to systematically work toward managing variation to eliminate those defects. The objective of Six Sigma is to deliver world-class performance, reliability, and value to the end customer. The *Balanced Scorecard* is a management system that focuses on all the elements that contribute to organizational performance and success including financial, customer, market, and internal processes. The goal is to develop a broader perspective on performance factors and a culture of learning and growth that improves all organizational communication. The *Triple Bottom Line* provides a perspective that takes into account the social, environmental, and financial impact of decisions made within the organization. When making an increased commitment to social responsibility, sustainability, or ethics, companies consider implementing Triple Bottom Line reporting to confirm that investments and initiatives are supporting organizational success and values. The purpose of a variety of measures of performance and goal achievement is to determine the quality and effectiveness of environmental, social, and ethics initiatives. Many believe that there is an inherent gain realized by companies with strong ethical cultures and environmental commitments that is paid back not only in customer commitment, but in avoiding the negative publicity and costs associated with wrongdoing.

AccountAbility is an international membership organization committed to enhancing the performance of organizations and to developing the competencies of individuals in social and ethical accountability and sustainable development. Figure 9–2 illustrates the AccountAbility AA1000 framework for ethics and social responsibility. The AA1000 process standards link the definition and embedding of an organization's values to the development of performance targets and to the assessment and communication of organizational performance. By this process, focused around the organization's engagement with stakeholders, AA1000 ties social and ethical issues into the organization's strategic management and operations. AA1000 recognizes these different traditions. It combines the terms *social* and *ethical* to refer to the systems *and* individual behavior within an organization and to the *direct* and *indirect* impact of an organization's activities on stakeholders. *Social and ethical issues* (relating to systems, behavior and impacts) are defined by an organization's values and aims through the influence of the interests and expectations of its stakeholders and by societal norms and expectations. *Assessment* is

FIGURE 9–2 AA1000 Framework for Ethics and Social Accountability

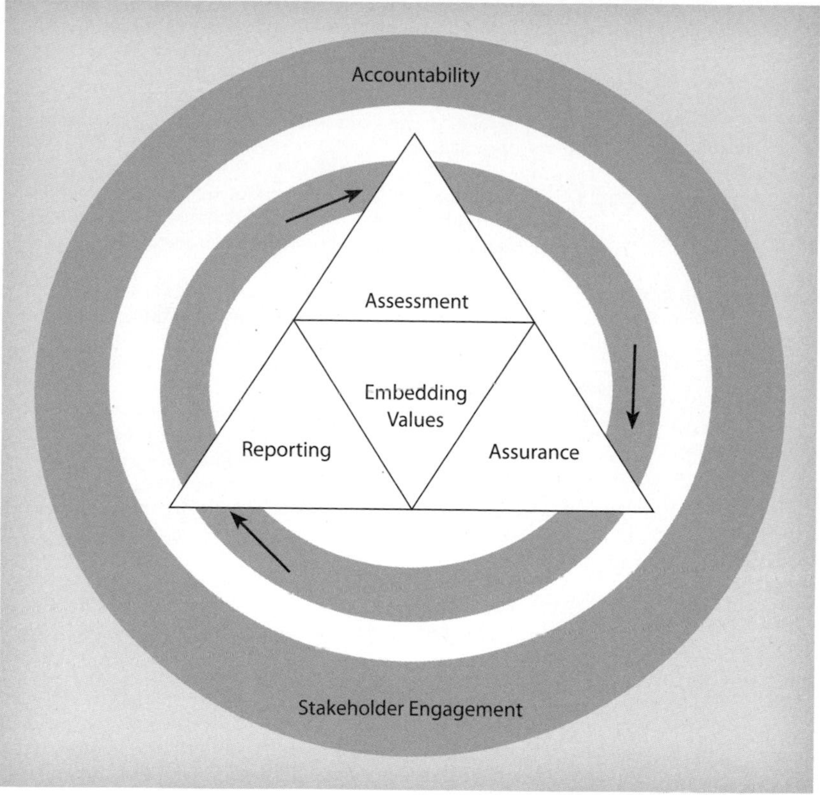

Source: Adapted from AccountAbility AA1000 Series of Standards, http://www.accountability21.net/aa1000series (accessed March 12, 2009). Reprinted with permission of The Institute of Social and Ethical Accountability.

measuring organizational responsiveness or the extent to which an organization takes action on the basis of stakeholder engagement. This is followed by *assurance,* including control mechanisms, and then reporting to document the process. *Embedding* of an organization's values to assure performance is a continuous process.

The Integrity Institute has developed 10 validated models that create a diagnostic tool to help organizations recognize the structural weaknesses early on in order to avoid or address problems appropriately rather than to respond to and recover from a crisis, which often proves too late. Rather than focusing on *single-issue* assessments, a comprehensive model provides nonfinancial information that discovers and assesses the soundness, wholeness, and incorruptibility of a corporation, making it possible to pinpoint more accurately the weaknesses that may influence the health and welfare of a company and its sustainability. By measuring these components, it is possible to assess an organization's ability to withstand market forces (for example, ethical misconduct disasters) that may influence the company and destroy shareholder value.[18]

Table 9–2 illustrates the Integrity Institute's integrated model to standardize the measure of integrity. The model integrates 10 drivers, or markers, that have the potential to weaken the overall structural soundness of the organization. These components include (1) communication, (2) compensation, (3) compliance and ethics, (4) corporate citizenship, (5) culture, (6) earnings, (7) governance, (8) leadership, (9) risk, and (10) stakeholder

TABLE 9–2 The Integrity Institute Integrated Model to Standardize the Measure of Integrity

Communication integrity	Communicated information, messages, metamessages, and processes.
Compensation integrity	Excessive compensation, tactics used to motivate employees to take certain actions that can jeopardize the integrity of an organization.
Compliance and ethical integrity	Organizations that fail to comply with minimum legal requirements on a variety of fronts are being regularly dropped from investment and insurance portfolios.
Corporate citizenship integrity (environmental and social responsibility)	Integrity of the environmental policies and social responsibility practices of an organization. It measures the structure, not the morality, of corporate citizenship and identifies pressure being placed on companies to do the right thing.
Cultural integrity	Collective consciousness and values define the culture of the organization and whether it has integrity; whether the culture is sound, whole, and incorruptible and what predictive markers exist that may weaken the organization's ability to stand strong.
Earnings integrity	The extent to which corporate earnings are managed vs. manipulated has long been of interest to analysts, regulators, researchers, and other investment professionals.
Leadership integrity	Behavioral complexity in leadership and the strategy of leadership.
Risk integrity	Risks associated with intelligence and the sharing of data and related privacy issues. Risk integrity begins and ends with information and the transfer of that information.
Stakeholders perceptions of organizational integrity	After analyzing the nine nonfinancial performance indicators outlined above, measure them against the stakeholders' perceptions.

Source: From *Managing Risks for Corporate Integrity: How to Survive An Ethical Misconduct Disaster* 1st edition by Brewer, Chandler, and Ferrell. Copyright © 2006. Reprinted with permission of South-Western, a division of Thomson Learning: www.thomsonrights.com. Fax 800 730-2215.

perceptions. While investors may already use many of these variables, the Integrity Institute Integria™ model establishes a standard that can predict the sustainability and success of the organization. This measurement to an established standard is used as a basis of certification of integrity by the Integrity Institute.

Figure 9–3 shows the Open Compliance Ethics Group framework overview. The Open Compliance Ethics Group (OCEG) (http://www.oceg.org) has worked with over 100 companies to create a universal framework for compliance and ethics management. The OCEG focuses on nonfinancial compliance and the more qualitative elements of internal controls. The OCEG framework deals with complex issues of compliance and actual solutions to address the development of organizational ethics. The OCEG framework integrates some of the best thinking in several disciplines to address compliance and ethics management. Using expertise from these disciplines, guidelines were developed. By establishing guidelines, rather than standards, OCEG provides a tool for each company to use as it sees fit, given its size, scope, structure, industry, and other factors that create individualized needs. The OCEG guidelines and benchmarking studies can be very valuable

FIGURE 9–3 The Open Compliance Ethics Group Framework Overview

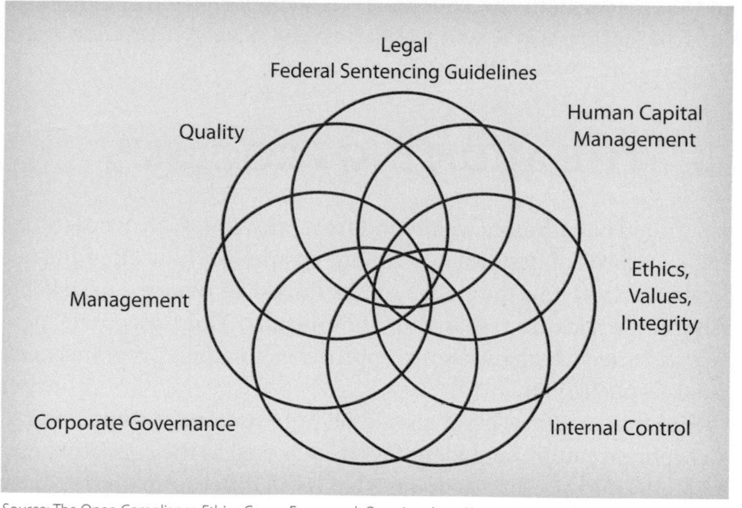

Source: The Open Compliance Ethics Group Framework Overview, http://www.oceg.org/framework.asp (accessed April 4, 2006). Reprinted with permission.

to a firm conducting an ethics audit. Most significant is the opportunity to benchmark an organization's current activities to those of other organizations.

Risks and Requirements in Ethics Auditing

Although ethics audits provide many benefits for individual companies and their stakeholders, they do have the potential to create risks. For example, a firm may uncover a serious ethical problem that it would prefer not to disclose until it can remedy the situation. It may find that one or more of its stakeholders' criticisms cannot be dismissed or easily addressed. Occasionally, the process of conducting an ethics audit may foster stakeholder dissatisfaction rather than stifle it. Moreover, the auditing process imposes burdens (especially with regard to record keeping) and costs for firms that undertake it. Auditing, although a prudent measure, provides no assurance that ethical risks and challenges can be avoided. In addition, there have been some initiatives to benchmark risk assessment and best practices, but this process is in its early stages.

Many companies that engage in suspected misconduct find that public scrutiny of their practices causes them to conduct an ethics audit to show concern and respond appropriately to weaknesses in their ethics program. Companies in the public eye because of questionable conduct or legal violations, such as Countrywide Financial, AIG, Fannie Mae, Freddie Mac, and Merrill Lynch, should conduct an ethics audit to demonstrate their visible commitment to improving decision making and business conduct.

Although ethics and social responsibility are defined and perceived differently by various stakeholders, a core of minimum standards for ethical performance is evolving. These standards represent a fundamental step toward the development of minimum ethics requirements that are specific, measurable, achievable, and meaningful to the business's impact on communities, employees, consumers, the environment, and economic systems. These standards help companies set measurable and achievable targets for improvement and form an objective foundation for reporting the firm's efforts to all direct stakeholders. There may still be disagreements on key issues and standards, but through these standards progress should be made. Both the FSGO's seven steps for effective ethical compliance, as discussed in Chapters 3 and 8, and the Sarbanes–Oxley Act provide standards that organizations can use in ethics auditing.

THE AUDITING PROCESS[19]

Many questions should be addressed when conducting an audit, such as how broad the audit should be, what standards of performance should be applied, how often the audit should be conducted, whether and how the audit's results should be reported to stakeholders, and what actions should be taken in response to audit results. Thus, corporate approaches to ethics audits are as varied as organizations' approaches to ethics programs and responses to improve social responsibility.

It is our belief that an ethics audit should be unique to each company, reflecting its size, industry, corporate culture, and identified risks as well as the regulatory environment in which it operates. Thus, an ethics audit for a bank will differ from one for an automobile manufacturer or a food processor. Each has different regulatory concerns and unique risks stemming from the nature of its business. For this reason, we have mapped out a framework (see Table 9–3) that is somewhat generic and that most companies can therefore expand on when conducting their own ethics audit. The steps in our framework can also be applied to a broader social audit that includes specific ethical issues as well as other economic, legal, and philanthropic concerns of interest to various stakeholders. As with any new initiative, companies may choose to begin their effort with a smaller, less-formal audit and then work up to a more comprehensive social audit. For example, a firm may choose to focus on primary stakeholders in its initial audit year and then expand to secondary groups in subsequent audits.

Our framework encompasses a wide range of business responsibilities and relationships. The audit entails an individualized process and outcomes for a particular firm, as it requires the careful consideration of the unique issues that face a particular organization. For example, the auditing process at Kellogg Company includes the following:

TABLE 9–3 Framework for an Ethics Audit

- **Secure commitment of top managers and board of directors.**
- **Establish a committee to oversee the ethics audit.**
- **Define the scope of the audit process, including subject matter areas important to the ethics audit.**
- **Review the organization's mission, policies, goals, and objectives and define its ethical priorities.**
- **Collect and analyze relevant information in each designated subject matter area.**
- **Have the results verified by an independent agent.**
- **Report the findings to the audit committee and, if approved, to managers and stakeholders.**

Sources: These steps are compatible with the social auditing methods prescribed by Warren Dow and Roy Crowe, *What Social Auditing Can Do for Voluntary Organizations* (Vancouver, Canada: Volunteer Vancouver, July 1999); Sandra Waddock and Neil Smith, "Corporate Responsibility Audits: Doing Well by Doing Good," *Sloan Management Review*, 41 (2000): 79.

> The Social Responsibility Committee of the Board of Directors shall identify, evaluate and monitor the social, political, environmental, occupational safety and health trends, issues, and concerns, domestic and foreign, which affect or could affect the Company's business or performance.
>
> The Committee shall make recommendations to assist in the formulation and adoption of policies, programs, and practices concerning the matters set forth above including, but not limited to, environmental protection, employee and community health and safety, ethical business conduct, consumer affairs, alcohol and drug abuse, equal opportunity matters, and government relations, and shall monitor the Company's charitable contributions.[20]

As you can see in Figure 9–4, Kellogg's takes a sweeping approach to identify risk areas and audit issues across the value chain incorporating the interests of diverse stakeholders.

Thus, although this chapter presents a structure and recommendations for both general social and ethics-specific audits, there is no generic approach that will satisfy every firm's circumstances. Nevertheless, the benefits and limitations that companies derive from auditing are relatively consistent.

Secure Commitment of Top Managers and Board of Directors

The first step in conducting any audit is securing the commitment of the firm's top management and, if it is a public corporation, its board of directors. Indeed, the push

FIGURE 9–4 Kellogg Identifies Corporate Social Responsibility, Ethics, and Governance Issues

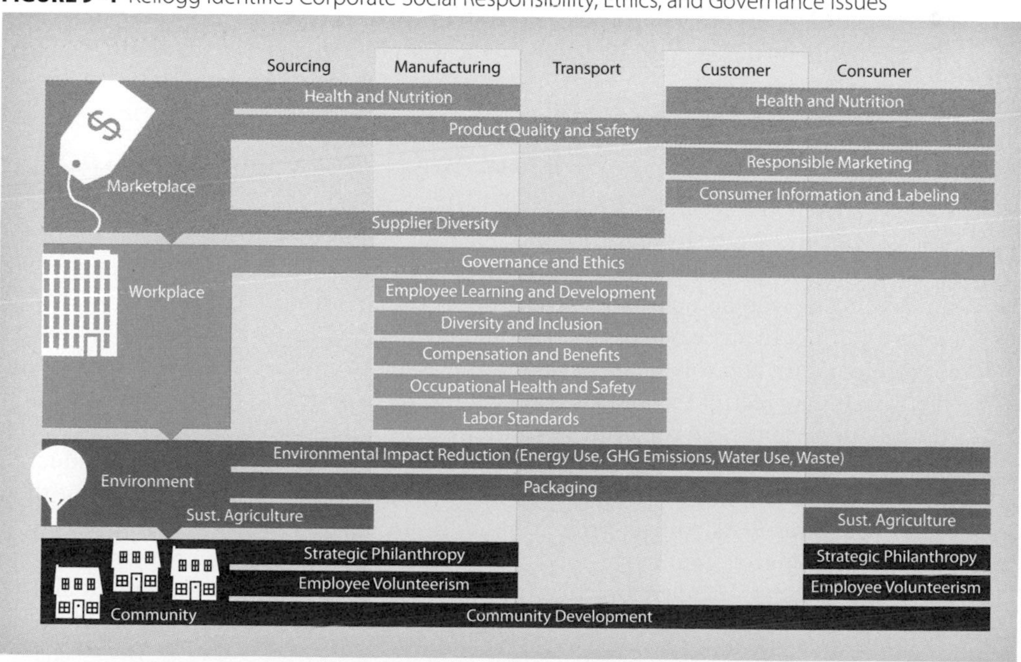

Source: Kellogg Company, "Analyzing Our Issues," http://www.kelloggcompany.com/corporateresponsibility.aspx?id=1507 (accessed June 12, 2009).

for an ethics audit may come directly from the board of directors in response to specific stakeholder concerns or in response to corporate governance reforms related to the Sarbanes–Oxley Act, which suggests that boards of directors should provide oversight for *all* auditing activities. In addition, court decisions related to the FSGO hold board members responsible for the ethical and legal compliance programs of the firms they oversee. New rules and regulations associated with the Sarbanes–Oxley Act require that boards include members who are knowledgeable and qualified to oversee accounting and other types of audits to ensure that these reports are accurate and include all material information. Although a board's financial audit committee will examine ethical standards throughout the organization as they relate to financial matters, it will also deal with the implementation of codes of ethics for top financial officers. Many of those issues relate to such corporate governance issues as compensation, stock options, and conflicts of interest. An ethics audit can demonstrate that a firm has taken steps to prevent misconduct, which can be useful in cases where civil lawsuits blame the firm and its directors for the actions of a rogue employee.

"An external auditor should not have other consulting or conflict-of-interest relationships with top managers or board members."

Pressure for an audit can also come from top managers who are looking for ways to track and improve ethical performance and perhaps give their firm an advantage over competitors that are facing questions about their ethical conduct. Additionally, under the Sarbanes–Oxley Act, CEOs and CFOs may be criminally prosecuted if they knowingly certify misleading financial statements. They may request an ethics audit as a tool to help improve their confidence in their firm's reporting processes. Some companies have established a high-level ethics office in conjunction with an ethics program, and the ethics officer may campaign for an ethics audit as a way to measure the effectiveness of the firm's ethics program. Regardless of where the impetus for an audit comes from, its success hinges on the full support of top management, particularly the CEO and the board of directors. Without this support, an ethics audit will not improve the ethics program and corporate culture.

Establish a Committee to Oversee the Ethics Audit

The next step in our framework is to establish a committee or team to oversee the audit process. Ideally, the board of directors' financial audit committee would oversee the ethics audit, but this is not the case in most companies. In most firms, managers or ethics officers, who do not always report to the board of directors, conduct social and ethics auditing. In any case, this team should include members who are knowledgeable about the nature and role of ethics audits and come from various departments within the firm. It may recruit individuals from within the firm or hire outside consultants to coordinate the audit and report the results directly to the board of directors. The Ethics Resource Center, a nonprofit organization engaged in supporting ethical conduct in the public and private sector, assists companies with assessments and audits of their ethics programs.[21] As with the financial audit, an external auditor should not have other consulting or conflict-of-interest relationships with top managers or board members. Based on the best practices of corporate governance, audits should also be monitored by an independent board of directors' committee, as recommended by the Sarbanes–Oxley Act.

Define the Scope of the Audit Process

The ethics audit committee should establish the scope of the audit and monitor its progress to ensure that it stays on track. The scope of an audit depends on the type of business, the risks faced by the firm, and the opportunities available to manage ethics. This step includes defining the key subject matter or risk areas that are important to the ethics audit (for example, environment, discrimination, product liability, employee rights, privacy, fraud, financial reporting, legal compliance) as well as the bases on which they should be assessed. Assessments can be made on the basis of direct consultation, observation, surveys, or focus groups.[22] Table 9–4 lists some sample subject matter areas and the audit items for each.

Review Organizational Mission, Values, Goals, and Policies and Define Ethical Priorities

Because ethics audits generally involve comparing an organization's ethical performance to its goals, values, and policies, the audit process should include a review of the current mission statement and strategic objectives. The company's overall mission may incorporate ethics objectives, but these may also be found in separate documents, including those that focus on social responsibility. For example, the firm's ethics statement or statement of values may offer guidance for managing transactions and human relationships that support the firm's reputation, thereby fostering confidence from the firm's external stakeholders.[23] Franklin Energy, for example, specifies five core values in managing its business which contribute to its success: ingenuity, results orientation, frugality, integrity, and environmental stewardship.[24]

This review step should examine all formal documents that make explicit commitments to ethical, legal, or social responsibility, as well as less formal documents, including marketing materials, workplace policies, and ethics policies and standards for suppliers or vendors. This review may reveal a need to create additional statements to fill the identified gaps or to create a new comprehensive mission statement or ethical policy that addresses any deficiencies.[25]

It is also important to examine all of the firm's policies and practices with respect to the specific areas covered by the audit. For example, in an audit whose scope includes discrimination issues, this review step would consider the company's goals and objectives regarding discrimination, its policies on discrimination, the means available for communicating these policies, and the effectiveness of this communication. This assessment should also look at whether and how managers are rewarded for meeting their goals and the systems that employees have available to give and receive feedback. An effective ethics audit should review all these systems and assess their strengths and weaknesses.[26] Concurrent with this step in the auditing process, the firm should define its ethical priorities. Determining these priorities is a balancing act because identifying the needs and assessing the priorities of each stakeholder can be difficult. Because there may be no legal requirements for ethical priorities, it is up to management's strategic planning processes to determine risks, appropriate standards, and communication with stakeholders required to deal with ethics issues. It is very important in this stage to articulate these priorities and values as a set of parameters or performance indicators that can be objectively and quantitatively assessed. Because the ethics audit is a structured report that offers quantitative and descriptive assessments, actions should be measurable by quantitative indicators. However, it is sometimes not possible to go beyond description.[27]

TABLE 9–4 The Ethics Audit

Organizational Issues*		
Yes	No	1. Does the company have a code of ethics that is reasonably capable of preventing misconduct?
Yes	No	2. Does the board of directors participate in the development and evaluation of the ethics program?
Yes	No	3. Is there a person with high managerial authority responsible for the ethics program?
Yes	No	4. Are there mechanisms in place to avoid delegating authority to individuals with a propensity for misconduct?
Yes	No	5. Does the organization effectively communicate standards and procedures to its employees via ethics-training programs?
Yes	No	6. Does the organization communicate its ethical standards to suppliers, customers, and significant others that have a relationship with the organization?
Yes	No	7. Do the company's manuals and written documents guiding operations contain ethics messages about appropriate behavior?
Yes	No	8. Is there formal or informal communication within the organization about procedures and activities that are considered acceptable ethical behavior?
Yes	No	9. Does top management have a mechanism to detect ethical issues relating to employees, customers, the community, and society?
Yes	No	10. Is there a system for employees to report unethical behavior?
Yes	No	11. Is there consistent enforcement of standards and punishments in the organization?
Yes	No	12. Is there a committee, department, team, or group that deals with ethical issues in the organization?
Yes	No	13. Does the organization make a continuous effort to improve its ethical compliance program?
Yes	No	14. Does the firm perform an ethics audit?
Examples of Specific Issues That Could Be Monitored in an Ethics Audit†		
Yes	No	1. Are there any systems and operational procedures to safeguard individual employees' ethical behavior?
Yes	No	2. Is it necessary for employees to break the company's ethical rules in order to get the job done?
Yes	No	3. Is there an environment of deception, repression, and cover-ups concerning events that would embarrass the company?
Yes	No	4. Are there any participatory management practices that allow ethical issues to be discussed?
Yes	No	5. Are compensation systems totally dependent on performance?
Yes	No	6. Is there sexual harassment?

Yes	No	7. Is there any form of discrimination—race, sex, or age—in hiring, promotion, or compensation?
Yes	No	8. Are the only standards about environmental impact those that are legally required?
Yes	No	9. Do the firm's activities show any concern for the ethical value systems of the community?
Yes	No	10. Are there deceptive and misleading messages in promotion?
Yes	No	11. Are products described in misleading or negative ways or without communicating their limitations to customers?
Yes	No	12. Are the documents and copyrighted materials of other companies used in unauthorized ways?
Yes	No	13. Are expense accounts inflated?
Yes	No	14. Are customers overcharged?
Yes	No	15. Is there unauthorized copying of computer software?

*A high number of yes answers indicates that ethical control mechanisms and procedures are in place within the organization.
†The number of yes answers indicates the number of possible ethical issues to address.

At some point, the firm must demonstrate action-oriented responsiveness to those ethics issues it has given top priority. For example, National Grid, formerly Niagara Mohawk Power Company has a long history of working to minimize damage to the environment. The firm adopted the international standard for environmental management systems, ISO 14001. The guidelines specified by ISO 14001 require external auditing by a certified auditor.[28]

Collect and Analyze Relevant Information

The next step in the ethical audit framework is to identify the tools or methods for measuring the firm's progress in improving employees' ethical decisions and conduct. In this step, the firm should collect relevant information for each designated subject matter area. To understand employee issues, for example, the auditing committee will work with the firm's human resources department to gather employee survey information and other statistics and feedback. A thorough ethics audit will review all relevant reports, including external documents sent to government agencies and others. The information collected in this measurement step will help determine baseline levels of compliance as well as the internal and external expectations of the company. This step will also identify where the company has, or has not, met its commitments, including those dictated by its mission statement and other policy documents. The documents reviewed in this process will vary from company to company, depending on the firm's size, the nature of its business, and the scope of the audit process.[29] At Green Mountain Coffee, the audit committee of the board of directors is responsible for providing oversight of reporting procedures and audits. Green Mountain's code of ethics provided in Table 9–5 provides a framework for the principles that are the backbone of the ethics audit.[30]

TABLE 9–5 Green Mountain Coffee's Code of Ethics

• **Respect individual rights and the property of others**
• **Maintain accurate records and report any unethical behavior**
• **Comply with all laws, rules, and regulatory requirements**
• **Avoid conflicts of interest and refrain from any appearance of impropriety**
• **Be responsible stewards in the use, protection, and management of GMCR's assets and resources**
• **Be aware of anti-trust laws and their implications and uphold fair competitive practices**
• **Share our story while following the Media Relations guidelines that promote consistent communications**
• **Act with integrity while still maintaining the confidentiality of GMCR information**
• **Support GMCR's Purpose, Principles, Policies and Procedures and encourage our business partners to do the same.**

Source: Adapted from GMC's Code of Ethics, http://www.greenmountaincoffee.com/ContentPage.aspx?Name=CodeOfEthics (accessed June 17, 2009).

Some techniques for collecting evidence might involve examining both internal and external documents, observing the data-collection process (such as by consulting with stakeholders), and confirming information in the organization's accounting records. Auditors may also employ ratio analysis of relevant indicators to identify any inconsistencies or unexpected patterns. The importance of objective measurement is the key consideration of the ethics auditor.[31]

Figure 9–5 indicates the communication channels that employees feel comfortable using in providing feedback during data collection. Employees were asked to whom they would "feel comfortable" reporting misconduct if they suspected or became aware of it. Supervisors and local managers received the most favorable response, suggesting the need for organizations to ensure that frontline managers are equipped to respond appropriately to allegations. It is worth noting that those functions that are primarily charged with taking action in response to alleged misconduct (legal, internal audit, and board or audit committee functions) were cited among the less likely channels that employees would feel comfortable using to report allegations.

Because integrating stakeholder feedback in the ethics audit process is so crucial, these stakeholders must first be defined and then interviewed during the data-collection stage. For most companies, stakeholders include employees, customers, investors, suppliers, community groups, regulators, nongovernment organizations, and the media. Both social and ethics audits typically interview and conduct focus groups with these stakeholders to gain an understanding of how they perceive the company. For example, the Chris Hani Baragwanath Hospital (CHBH) in Johannesburg, South Africa, conducted an ethics audit that included focus groups with the hospital's management, doctors, nurses, related health professionals, support staff, and patients. Using the trends uncovered in these focus groups, CHBH then developed a questionnaire for an ethics survey, which it administered to a larger group of individual stakeholders.[32] The more stakeholders that auditors include in this measurement stage, the more time and resources the audit will consume. However, a larger sample of stakeholders may yield a more useful variety of opinions about the

FIGURE 9–5 Employee-Preferred Channels for Reporting Misconduct

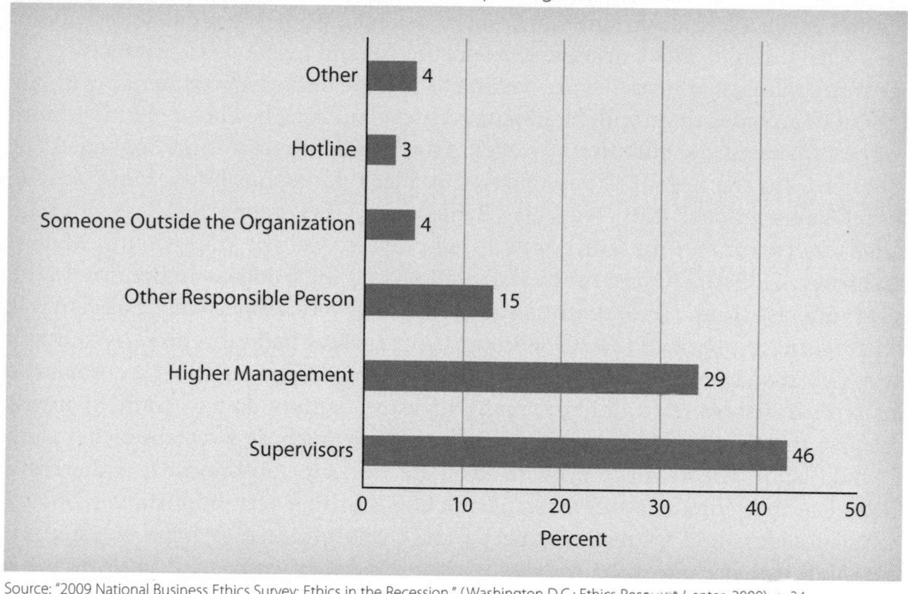

Source: "2009 National Business Ethics Survey: Ethics in the Recession," (Washington D.C.: Ethics Resource Center, 2009): p. 34.

company. In multinational corporations, a decision must also be made regarding whether to include in the audit only the main office or headquarters region or all facilities around the globe.[33]

Because employees carry out a business's operations, including its ethics initiatives, understanding employee issues is vital to a successful audit. Useful indicators for assessing employee issues include staff turnover and employee satisfaction. High turnover rates could indicate poor working conditions, an unethical culture, inadequate compensation, or general employee dissatisfaction. Companies can analyze these factors to determine key areas for improvement.[34] Questionnaires that survey employees' ethical perception of their company, their superiors, coworkers, and themselves, as well as ratings of ethical or unethical practices within the firm and industry, can serve as benchmarks in an ongoing assessment of ethical performance. Then, if unethical behavior is perceived to increase, management will better understand what types of unethical practices may be occurring and why. For example, the CHBH ethics survey asked employees about many issues including corporate culture and values, their physical workplace, human resources issues, misconduct, standards of patient care, and problems and sources of stress.[35] Most organizations recognize that employees will behave in ways that lead to recognition and rewards and avoid behavior that results in punishment. Thus, companies can design and implement human resources policies and procedures for recruiting, hiring, promoting, compensating, and rewarding employees that encourage ethical behavior.[36]

Customers are another primary stakeholder group because their patronage and loyalty determines the company's financial success. Providing meaningful feedback is critical to creating and maintaining customer satisfaction. Through surveys and customer-initiated communication systems such as response cards, online social networks, email, and toll-free telephone systems, an organization can monitor and respond to customer issues and its perceived social performance. Procter & Gamble uses online social networking sites such as MySpace and Facebook to determine which social issues consumers are passionate about, as well as to gain insights into consumers' product needs and reactions to products.

A growing number of investors are seeking to include in their investment portfolios the stocks of companies that conduct ethics and social audits. They are becoming more aware of the financial benefits that can stem from socially responsible management systems—as well as the negative consequences of a lack of responsibility. For example, President Obama praised City National Bancshares CEO Leonard Abess after he distributed his entire $60 million bonus to employees, On the other hand, Martin Sullivan, former CEO of AIG, approved $165 million and $121 million in bonuses to the Financial Products Group and executives and other employees, respectively. Sullivan was ousted before the company took $200 billion in government bailout money, which was funded by U.S. taxpayers.[37] Thus, even the hint of wrongdoing can affect a company's relations with investors. Additionally, many investors simply do not want to invest in companies that engage in certain business practices, such as sweatshops or using child labor, which fail to provide adequate working conditions. It is therefore critical that companies understand the issues of this very important group of stakeholders and what they expect from corporations they have invested in, both financially and socially.

> *Even the hint of wrongdoing can affect a company's relations with investors.*

Organizations can obtain feedback from stakeholders through standardized surveys, interviews, and focus groups. Companies can also encourage stakeholder exchanges by inviting specific groups together for discussions. Such meetings also may include an office or facility tour or a field trip by company representatives to sites in the community. Regardless of how companies collect information about stakeholders' views, the primary objective is to generate a variety of opinions about how the company is perceived and whether it is fulfilling stakeholders' expectations.[38]

Once these data have been collected, the firm should compare its internal perceptions to those discovered during the stakeholder assessment stage and summarize these findings. During this phase, the audit committee should draw some conclusions about the information it obtained in the previous stages. These conclusions may involve descriptive assessments of the findings, such as the costs and benefits of the company's ethics program, the strengths and weaknesses of the firm's policies and practices, feedback from stakeholders, and issues that should be addressed in future audits. In some cases, it may be appropriate to weigh the findings against standards identified earlier, both quantitatively and qualitatively.[39]

Data analysis should also include an examination of how other organizations in the industry are performing in the designated subject matter areas. For example, the audit committee can investigate the successes of some other benchmark firm that is considered the best in a particular area and compare the auditing company's performance to it. Some common examples of the benchmark information available from most corporate ethics audits are employee or customer satisfaction, how community groups perceive the company, and the impact of the company's philanthropy. For example, the Ethics and Compliance Officer Association (ECOA) conducts research on legal and ethical issues in the workplace. These studies allow ECOA members to compare their responses to the aggregate results obtained through the study.[40] Such comparisons can help the audit committee identify best practices for a particular industry or establish a baseline for minimum requirements for ethics. It is important to note that a wide variety of standards are emerging that apply to ethics accountability. The aim of these standards is to create a tool for benchmarking and a framework for businesses to follow.

Verify the Results

The next step is to have an independent party—such as a social/ethics audit consultant, a financial accounting firm that offers social auditing services (for example, KPMG), or a nonprofit special interest group with auditing experience (for example, the New Economics Foundation)—verify the results of the data analysis. Business for Social Responsibility, a nonprofit organization supporting social responsibility initiatives and reporting, has defined *verification* as an independent assessment of the quality, accuracy, and completeness of a company's social report. Independent verification offers a measure of assurance that the company has reported its ethical performance fairly and honestly, as well as an assessment of the company's social and environmental reporting systems.[41] As such, verification by an independent party gives stakeholders confidence in a company's ethics or social audit and lends the audit report credibility and objectivity.[42] British Petroleum, for example, had its "Environmental and Social Report," which includes ethical performance issues, verified by the accounting firm Ernst & Young.[43] However, a survey conducted by one of the Big Four accounting firms found that only a few social reports contained any form of external verification. This lack of third-party assurance may have contributed to the criticism that social and ethics auditing and reporting has more to do with public relations than genuine change. However, the number of outside verified reports is increasing.[44]

Although the independent validation of ethics audits is not required, an increasing number of companies are choosing to do so, much as they have their financial reports certified by a reputable auditing firm. Many public policy experts believe that an independent, objective audit can be provided only if the auditor has played no role in the reporting process—in other words, consulting and auditing should be distinctly separate roles. The Sarbanes–Oxley Act essentially legalized this belief.

The process of verifying the results of an audit should involve standard procedures that control the reliability and validity of the information. As with a financial audit, auditors can apply substantive tests to detect material misstatements in the audit data and analysis. The tests commonly used in financial audits—confirmation, observation, tracing, vouching, analytical procedures, inquiry, and recomputing—can be used in ethics and social audits as well. For example, positive confirmations can be requested from the participants of a stakeholder focus group to affirm that the reported results are consistent with what the focus group believes it found. Likewise, an ethics auditor can actually observe a company's procedures for handling ethical disputes to verify statements made in the report. And, just as a financial auditor traces from the supporting documents to the financial statements to test their completeness, an ethics auditor or verifier may examine employee complaints about an ethics issue to attest whether the reporting of such complaints was complete. An auditor can also employ analytical procedures by examining plausible relationships such as the prior year's employee turnover ratio or the related ratio commonly reported within the industry. With the reporting firm's permission, an auditor can contact the company's legal counsel to inquire about pending litigation that may shed light on ethical and legal issues currently facing the firm.[45]

Additionally, a financial auditor may be asked to provide a letter to the company's board of directors and senior managers to highlight inconsistencies in the reporting process. The auditor may request that management reply to particular points in the letter to indicate the actions it intends to take to address problems or weaknesses. The financial auditor is required to report to the board of directors' financial audit committee (or equivalent) any significant adjustments or difficulties encountered during the audit and any disagreements with management. Therefore, ethics auditors should be required to report to the company's board of directors' audit committee the same issues that a financial auditor would report.[46] Green Mountain Coffee uses this method.

Report the Findings

The final step in our framework is issuing the ethics audit report. This involves reporting the audit findings through a formal report to the relevant internal parties—namely, the board of directors and top executives—and, if approved, to external stakeholders. Although some companies prefer not to release the results of their auditing efforts to the public, more companies are choosing to make their reports available to a broad group of stakeholders. Some companies, including UK-based The Co-operative Bank and newspaper *The Guardian*, integrate the results of the social audit with their annual report of financial documents and other important information. Many other companies, including Johnson & Johnson, Shell, and Green Mountain Coffee, also make their audit reports available on their corporate websites.[47]

Based on the guidelines established by the Global Reporting Initiative and Accountability, the report should spell out the purpose and scope of the audit, the methods used in the audit process (evidence gathering and evaluation), the role of the (preferably independent) auditor, any auditing guidelines followed by the auditor, and any reporting guidelines followed by the company.[48] The ethics audit of Johannesburg's Chris Hani Baragwanath Hospital follows these guidelines.[49] The report is more meaningful if it is integrated with other organizational information available, such as financial reports, employee surveys, regulatory filings, and customer feedback. The use of information such as the OCEG Benchmarking Study, discussed earlier in the chapter, evaluates key elements of corporate and ethics programs that could help assess best practices across industry.[50]

As mentioned earlier, ethics audits may resemble financial audits, but they take quite different forms. In a financial audit, the Statement of Auditing Standards dictates literally every word found in a financial audit report in terms of content and placement. Based on the auditor's findings, the report issued can take one of the following four forms, among other variations. An *unqualified opinion* states that the financial statements are fairly stated, and a *qualified opinion* asserts that although the auditor believes the financial statements are fairly stated an unqualified opinion is not possible because of limitations placed on the auditor or minor issues involving disclosure or accounting principles. An *adverse opinion* states that the financial statements are not fairly stated, and, finally, a *disclaimer of opinion* qualifies that the auditor didn't have full access to records or discovered a conflict of interest. The technical difference between these various opinions has enormous consequences to the company.

THE STRATEGIC IMPORTANCE OF ETHICS AUDITING

Although the concept of auditing implies an official examination of ethical performance, many organizations audit their performance informally. Any attempt to verify outcomes and to compare them with standards can be considered an auditing activity. Many smaller firms probably would not use the word *audit*, but they do perform auditing activities.

Organizations such as the Better Business Bureau (BBB) provide awards and assessment tools to help any organization evaluate their ethical performance. Companies with fewer resources may wish to use the judging criteria from the BBB's Torch Award Criteria for Ethical Companies (Table 9–6) as benchmarks for their informal self-audits. Past winners of this award include large companies such as American Honda Motor Company, Target Corporation, and Freescale Semiconductor, Inc. The award criteria even provide a category for companies with less than 10 employees.

The ethics audit, like the financial audit, should be conducted regularly rather than in response to problems involving or questions about a firm's priorities and conduct. In other words, the ethics audit is not a control process to be used during a crisis although it can pinpoint potential problem areas and generate solutions in a crisis situation. As mentioned earlier, an audit may be comprehensive and encompass all the ethics and social responsibility areas of a business, or it can be specific and focus on one or two areas. One specialized audit could be an environmental impact audit in which specific environmental issues, such as proper waste disposal, are analyzed. According to the KPMG International Survey of Corporate Responsibility Reporting, 80 percent of the 2,200 companies in 22 countries surveyed include CSR in their reporting, up from 50 percent in 2005.[51] Examples of other specialized audits include diversity, employee benefits, and conflicts of interest. Ethics audits can present several problems. They can be expensive and time consuming, and selecting the auditors may be difficult if objective, qualified personnel are not available. Employees sometimes fear comprehensive evaluations, especially by outsiders, and in such cases, ethics audits can be extremely disruptive.

Despite these problems, however, auditing ethical performance can generate many benefits, as we have seen throughout this chapter. The ethics audit provides an assessment of a company's overall ethical performance as compared to its core values, ethics policy, internal operating practices, management systems, and, most important, key stakeholders' expectations.[52] As such, ethics and social audit reports are a useful management tool for helping companies identify and define their impact and facilitate important improvements.[53] This assessment can be used to reallocate resources and activities as well as focus on new

TABLE 9–6 Better Business Bureau's Torch Award Criteria for Ethical Companies

A business should demonstrate its superior commitment to exceptional standards that benefit its customers, employees, suppliers, shareholders, and surrounding communities. The business must provide supporting documentation in four areas for consideration in the Marketplace Excellence category. While examples from all four areas must be provided, the bullet points below are only suggestions and not all bullet points are required to be addressed in order for a business to compete in this category.
Management Practices
• Pertinent sections from an employee handbook, business manual, or training program (formal or informal) showing how the business's commitment to exceptional standards are communicated to and implemented by employees
• A vision, mission, or core values statement describing the business's commitment to exceptional standards that benefit its customers, employees, suppliers, shareholders, and surrounding communities
• Formal training and/or procedures used to address concerns an employee may have in dealing with ethical issues

(continued)

TABLE 9–6 Better Business Bureau's Torch Award Criteria for Ethical Companies *(continued)*

- Management practices and policies that foster positive employee relations
- Employee benefits and/or workplace practices contributing to the quality of family life
- Actions taken to assess and mitigate risks, and prevent workplace injury
- Examples of sound environmental practices
- Examples of operational practices focused on security and privacy issues—on and offline
- Illustrations of your business's commitment to standards that build trust in the marketplace (i.e., customer service program, employee relation policy or practice, vendor/supplier relationship, etc.)

Customer/Vendor/Supplier/Shareholder Relations

- Examples of the business's vision, mission, and/or core values statement in action—describing how the business's beliefs have been leveraged for the benefit of consumers, employees, suppliers, shareholders, and surrounding communities
- Business policies and practices that demonstrate accountability and responsibility to communities, investors, and other stakeholder audiences
- Corporate governance practices address accountability and responsibility to shareholders
- Complimentary feedback from customers, vendors, suppliers, and /or community leaders
- Actions taken by the business demonstrating service "beyond the call of duty"
- Brief case study examples of circumstances in which the business made tough decisions that had negative short-term consequences, but created long-term value and benefits
- Examples of, and results produced by, pro bono work
- Examples of the business working closely within the community and making a positive social impact—and any recognition for charitable and/or community service projects.

Marketing/Advertising/Communications/Sales Practices

- Descriptions of methods the business uses to ensure all sales, promotional materials, and advertisements are truthful and accurate
- Sales training policies and/or codes of ethics used by sales personnel that ensure all transactions are made in a transparent, honest manner
- Crisis communications efforts and associated marketing actions that educated audiences, prevented negative outcomes, and restored trust and confidence in the business, its products, and services
- Examples of internal communications practices benefiting employees and contributing to overall business effectiveness and efficiency

Reputation Within Industry and Community

- Media coverage reflecting the business's industry and community reputation as a trustworthy business
- Awards, recognition, and/or complimentary letters from within the business's industry, trade group, or community

Source: Adapted from "International Torch Award Judging Criteria," Better Business Bureau, http://www.bbb.org/international-torch-awards/critera.html (accessed June 18, 2009).

opportunities. The audit process can also help companies fulfill their mission statements in ways that boost profits and reduce risks.[54] More specifically, a company may seek continual improvement in its employment practices, customer and community relations, and the ethical soundness of its general business practices.[55] Thus, the audit can pinpoint areas where improving operating practices can improve both bottom-line profits and stakeholder relationships.[56]

Most managers view profitability and ethics and social responsibility as a trade-off. This "either/or" mindset prevents them from taking a more proactive "both/and" approach.[57] However, the auditing process can demonstrate the positive impact of ethical conduct and social responsibility initiatives on the firm's bottom line, convincing managers—and other primary stakeholders—of the value of adopting more ethical and socially responsible business practices.[58]

SUMMARY

An ethics audit is a systematic evaluation of an organization's ethics program and/or performance to determine its effectiveness. Such audits provide an opportunity to measure conformity to the firm's desired ethical standards. The concept of ethics auditing has emerged from the movement toward auditing and reporting on companies' broader social responsibility initiatives. Social auditing is the process of assessing and reporting a business's performance in fulfilling the economic, legal, ethical, and philanthropic social responsibilities expected of it by its stakeholders. An ethics audit may be conducted as a component of a social audit. Auditing is a tool that companies can employ to identify and measure their ethical commitment to stakeholders and to demonstrate their commitment to improving strategic planning, including their compliance with legal, ethical, and social responsibility standards.

The auditing process can highlight trends, improve organizational learning, and facilitate communication and working relationships. It can help companies assess the effectiveness of programs and policies, identify potential risks and liabilities, improve compliance with the law, and demonstrate progress in areas of previous noncompliance. One of the greatest benefits for businesses is improved relationships with stakeholders. A significant benefit of ethics auditing is that it may help prevent the public relations crises associated with ethical or legal misconduct. Although ethics audits provide many benefits for companies and their stakeholders, they do have the potential to create risks. In particular, the process of auditing cannot guarantee that the firm will not face challenges. Additionally, there are few common standards for judging disclosure and effectiveness or for making comparisons.

An ethics audit should be unique to each company based on its size, industry, corporate culture, identified risks, and the regulatory environment in which it operates. The chapter offered a framework for conducting an ethics audit that can also be used for a broader social audit.

The first step in conducting an audit is securing the commitment of the firm's top management and/or its board of directors. The push for an ethics audit may come directly from the board of directors in response to specific stakeholder concerns or corporate governance reforms or from top managers looking for ways to track and improve ethical performance. The audit's success hinges on the full support of top management.

The second step is establishing a committee or team to oversee the audit process. Ideally, the board of directors' financial audit committee would oversee the ethics audit, but in most firms, managers or ethics officers conduct auditing. This committee will recruit an individual from within the firm or hire an outside consultant to coordinate the audit and report the results.

The third step is establishing the scope of the audit, which depends on the type of business, the risks faced by the firm, and available opportunities to manage ethics. This step includes defining the key subject matter or risk areas that are important to the ethics audit.

The fourth step should include a review of the firm's mission, values, goals, and policies. This step should include an examination of both formal documents that make explicit commitments with regard to ethical, legal, or social responsibility and less formal documents including marketing materials, workplace policies, and ethics policies and standards for suppliers or vendors. During this step, the firm should define its ethical priorities and articulate them as a set of parameters or performance indicators that can be objectively and quantitatively assessed.

The fifth step is identifying the tools or methods that can be employed to measure the firm's progress and then collecting and analyzing the relevant information. Some evidence-collection techniques might involve examining both internal and external documents, observing the data-collection process (such as stakeholder consultation), and confirming the information in the organization's accounting records. During this step, a company's stakeholders need to be defined and interviewed to understand how they perceive the company. This can be accomplished through standardized surveys, interviews, and focus groups. Once these data have been collected, they should be analyzed and summarized. Analysis should include an examination of how other organizations in the industry are performing in the designated subject matter areas.

The sixth step is having an independent party—such as a social/ethics audit consultant, a financial accounting firm that offers social auditing services, or a nonprofit special interest group with auditing experience—verify the results of the data analysis. Verification is an independent assessment of the quality, accuracy, and completeness of a company's audit process. Such verification gives stakeholders confidence in a company's ethics audit and lends the audit report credibility and objectivity. The process of verifying the results of an audit should employ standard procedures that control the reliability and validity of the information.

The final step in the audit process is reporting the audit findings to the board of directors and top executives and, if approved, to external stakeholders. The report should spell out the purpose and scope of the audit, the methods used in the audit process (evidence gathering and evaluation), the role of the (preferably independent) auditor, any auditing guidelines followed by the auditor, and any reporting guidelines followed by the company.

Although the concept of auditing implies an official examination of ethical performance, many organizations audit informally. The ethics audit should be conducted regularly. Although social auditing may present problems, it can generate many benefits. Through the auditing process, a firm can demonstrate the positive impact of ethical conduct and social responsibility initiatives on its bottom line, which may convince stakeholders of the value of adopting more ethical and socially responsible business practices.

IMPORTANT TERMS FOR REVIEW

ethics audit **social audit**

RESOLVING ETHICAL BUSINESS CHALLENGES*

As Jerry looked around at the other members of the board, he wondered if it was too late to resign. How could he have been stupid enough to be dragged into this ethics audit quagmire? It had started innocently enough. With the passing of the Sarbanes–Oxley Act, everyone was aware of the consequences of accounting problems and their potential negative impact on a company, its board members, and its employees. So when Jerry's friend John, the president of Soumey Corporation, had asked him to be on the company's board of directors, Jerry had checked out the company. It wasn't that he didn't trust John; he just felt that he should never take unnecessary chances. But when Jerry's investigation of Soumey uncovered nothing unusual, he accepted the board position.

Soumey's board of directors included John Jacobs, Soumey's president; Alan Kerns, a retired Soumey executive; Alice Finkelstein, a retired executive from a similar company; Latisha Timme, a consultant within the industry; and Jerry. With Jerry on board, one of the board's first tasks was to conduct an ethics audit. The directors decided to contract the task to Teico, Inron, and Wurrel (TIW), an accounting firm highly recommended by Latisha. A few months later, TIW filed its final report of the audit with the board. The report indicated that, with a few exceptions, Soumey was doing a good job of monitoring ethical issues. Among the recommendations that the report offered were that the company should appoint a person with high managerial authority to be responsible for its ethical compliance program, that it establish a confidential hotline for employees who had ethical or legal concerns, and that it create an ethics committee to address ethical issues in the organization.

At the next board meeting, John suggested that Alan be the ethics compliance officer because he lived close to the main offices and had time to do it. Alan quickly agreed, provided there was substantial remuneration for his time, which John affirmed. Jerry asked a few questions such as whether Alan had sufficient managerial authority.

Alice responded, "Jerry, this industry is rather small with only a few large players, Soumey being one of them. Trust me when I say that Alan, as a retired president of the company, will definitely have the respect of the employees."

Jerry had no more questions, and Alan became Soumey's new compliance officer. The confidential hotline was quickly installed, and announcements about its existence were widely distributed around the various offices and plant buildings to ensure it reached all of the firm's several thousand employees. The board also discussed TIW's final suggestion for an ethics committee, and all but Jerry agreed that the board could handle that task as well.

Jerry pointed out, "I don't think this is wise, John. This is a conflict of interest for you, isn't it?"

After a moment of hesitation, John replied, "You're right, Jerry, it is a conflict of interest that I be on the ethics committee." After another bit of silence, John suggested, "Wouldn't you agree that

I should not be on the committee, Alan, Alice, and Latisha?" They all discussed the matter and agreed that Jerry's suggestion made perfect sense.

Time passed and the board held its quarterly meetings. Nothing unusual was brought up, just the same old issues that any publicly held company must deal with relative to shareholders, lawyers, regulators, and the public. Alan had suggested that the ethics compliance committee meet twice a year so that he could fill everyone in on what was happening. At these meetings, Alan would usually report the number of calls to the hotline, the status of complaints, and whether there were any serious allegations such as sexual harassment or any reported forms of race, sex, or age discrimination in hiring personnel.

After two years of quarterly board meetings and semiannual ethics meetings, Jerry suggested to Alan that they conduct another ethics audit.

"Why would we want to do that, Jerry? Things are going smoothly with the approach we're taking. Why have another outside audit? Do you think that we're doing a bad job?"

Jerry hedged, "I'm not saying that, Alan. What I'm saying is that we may need to have an outside audit just to make sure everything looks good to the public. Why don't we discuss this with Latisha and Alice this week?"

Alan agreed but when the ethics committee met that week it was obvious to Jerry that Alan had spoken to Alice and Latisha about his and Alan's meeting. He wasn't surprised when the committee decided another audit would diminish the confidence in Alan's performance as ethics compliance officer. Several weeks later, John sent all the board members a letter announcing an increase in their pay as board directors as well as doubling their pay as ethics committee members. The letter stated, "Soumey Corporation has decided that your service to the company has been exemplary both as board members and as an ethics committee."

In Jerry's third year on the board of directors, he was finally able to attend Soumey's annual company picnic with his wife and children. They arrived late after all of the introductions, and everyone was already in the buffet line. As a result, no one really knew who he was. The kids were having fun, and Jerry and his wife, Rosa, were too. However, after a while Jerry began to overhear some interesting comments. In one conversation, a production worker spoke about a toxic spill that had occurred because of the lack of safeguards. He told his companion, "Yeah, I know it was pretty messy, but only a few of my crew were hurt."

His friend asked, "Did they or you report it to management?"

He exclaimed, "Are you kidding? My guys don't want to lose their bonuses. Remember what happened to Bob's crew when the same thing happened and some of his guys complained. They had them filling out paperwork for a whole day, and the next week they were assigned a project with no incentives. They lost 40 percent of what they had been making with all the overtime and performance-based stuff. The guys and I agreed not to report it for those reasons."

Jerry couldn't help interrupting, "So why didn't the company fix the problem after it happened the first time?"

One of the men asked, "Are you new here?"

"Yeah, been here only a few weeks," Jerry lied.

The production worker answered, "You want to boost your pay, right? So you cut a few corners to get by."

Later that evening after Jerry and his family returned home, Rosa told him about a conversation she had overheard. "These women were talking about how unfair it is that most of the incentive-based pay seems to go to men with families. One woman said that she heard of a man over 55 who should have gotten a promotion but who was turned down because his supervisor was told not to give it to him. Rumor was that this guy had bucked the last president of Soumey, and this was his payback. Jerry, you should have heard what they say about Alan, that he's like Santa Claus and the Grinch. You never see him, and if you do, it's not a pleasant experience. One woman told me that when she was working for him, he used to be a little too friendly. She said that's why no one really uses the ethics hotline for certain issues: They know that the fox is guarding the hen house."

A little later, one of Jerry's sons bounced into the room and asked him a question about the picnic. "Dad, how come all the Spanish workers are on the night shift? It really makes it hard for a couple of my friends to get their parents to drop them off for soccer."

The picnic had opened Jerry's eyes about an uglier side of Soumey. At the next board meeting, he indirectly addressed some of the problems he had noticed. But John responded, "We're going into a recession, and we have to cut a few corners to keep our dividends up to the market's expectations. Latisha has been watching and consulting me on the best way to keep ahead of the pack on this."

Latisha and Alice both commented, "Thank goodness we have a large Spanish workforce to offset some price increases. They're hard workers and don't complain."

"You're absolutely right," said Alan. "We don't have the EPA, OSHA, or other agencies on our backs because these people know how to work and keep quiet. If some federal agencies do start to poke around, I have some contingency plans to prevent any type of ethical disaster."

That evening Jerry and Rosa were talking about the situation. He told Rosa, "I think Soumey has some potentially ethical issues that need to be addressed, but what can I do?"

"Well," sighed Rosa, "We've lived in this town for a long time. We know the families that are on the board. They're good people. However, there's one thing you didn't hear at that picnic because of your lack of Spanish. I've told you that it's important to learn it, even if it's just for my family. A few of the people I overheard were talking about how the hotline isn't really anonymous. That's just not right, Jerry. You need to do something even if it does mean losing the extra income." Rosa's points struck a nerve because Jerry knew they were a little overextended financially.

"I'll see what I can do," he told her.

Still, she warned him, "That's good, honey, but remember I don't want you to make too many waves. We still have to live here, and you know we can't swing a dead cat and not hit one of the people at Soumey."

QUESTIONS • EXERCISES

1. What areas of its ethics audit should Soumey change?
2. Does Jerry have a legal duty to report any of the items that he has heard to an outside authority?
3. Discuss the makeup of Soumey's board of directors. Is it ethical?
4. Is Jerry liable for the problems associated with Soumey over the last three years? Explain why or why not.

*This case is strictly hypothetical; any resemblance to real persons, companies, or situations is coincidental.

CHECK YOUR EQ

Check your EQ, or Ethics Quotient, by completing the following. Assess your performance to evaluate your overall understanding of the chapter material.

1. The ethics audit is required by the Sarbanes–Oxley Act of 2002. Yes No
2. In public corporations, the ethics audit should be reported to the board of directors. Yes No
3. The ethics audit helps identify risks and rogue employees. Yes No
4. The scope of the ethics audit depends on the type of risks and the opportunities to manage them. Yes No
5. Smaller companies can skip the step of verifying the results of the ethics audit. Yes No

ANSWERS **1. No.** Financial audits are required, and these may address some ethical issues. **2. Yes.** This is consistent with good corporate governance but not required. **3. Yes.** This is the main benefit of an ethics audit. **4. Yes.** The scope determines the risks unique to the organization. **5. No.** Verification is necessary to maintain integrity and accuracy.

Sid was barely surviving. Then one of his contacts in the government repaid a favor by recommending several stocks to buy and sell. The information paid off, and Sid gained some breathing room from Ron. Around the same time, some of Sid's Japanese clients lost a considerable amount of money in the U.S. markets and wanted a "discount"—the term used for the practice in some large Japanese brokerage houses of informally paying off part of their best clients' losses. When Glenna was still in Tokyo, she had dipped into the company's assets several times to fund such discounts. Because everything required Ron's approval, Sid and his colleagues believed that this practice would not be tolerated. However, late one afternoon Sid and a few others provided the proper forms, and Ron signed them without realizing what he had done.

Several months passed and the three survivors had resorted to lowering their expenses by using their own funds. This in turn led to Sid churning some of his accounts; that is, he bought and sold stocks for the express purpose of increasing his own revenues. Churning was tolerated in Japan, along with other practices that would be deemed questionable in the United States. Ron was oblivious to what Sid was doing because his focus was on reducing expenses. In the previous month, a group of important D&R clients had thrown a party for a few of their favorite brokers at one of their local haunts. After the customary toasts and small talk, it was suggested to Sid that a Japanese cartel might be interested in D&R. Sid was cautious and nothing else was mentioned. Several weeks later at another party, Sid and the two remaining D&R people were told that a takeover was imminent. But to make the takeover painless, the cartel needed certain sensitive information. Sid's reward for providing it would be a high position in the new, reorganized company and a "wink/nod" agreement that he could go anywhere in the world for his next assignment.

That week Ron announced that headquarters was pleased with the productivity of the Tokyo group. "It's only a matter of time before I get transferred, and I want out of Tokyo," he told them. The office knew that if Ron were successful, his next position would be that of vice president. He also informed the group that corporate representatives would be coming to Tokyo the following week.

"It seems that they've heard rumors of a possible hostile takeover attempt on D&R from someone in Japan, and they want us to check it out," Ron said, adding with a tight smile. "There will be some changes next week."

Sid suspected that this meant there would be even fewer people working even harder. It might also mean, however, that someone knew that Sid and the two representatives had been talking to the wrong people. Or maybe one of the three had sold out the other two. If Sid was to gather the information sought by the cartel, he would have to act quickly.

QUESTIONS • EXERCISES

1. What are the ethical issues here?
2. What moral philosophies were Sid, Glenna, and Ron using?
3. What are some control options that D&R could have introduced to create a more ethical culture?
4. Discuss the advantages and disadvantages of each decision that Sid could make.
5. Identify the pressures that have caused the ethical issues to develop.
6. Discuss Sid's power structure and leadership position at D&R and what it might be at the new D&R.

*This case is strictly hypothetical; any resemblance to real persons, companies, or situations is coincidental.

Advances in communication, technology, and transportation have minimized the world's borders, creating a new global economy as more and more countries industrialize and compete internationally. These transactions across national boundaries define **global business,** a practice that brings together people from countries that have different cultures, values, laws, and ethical standards. Thus, the international businessperson must not only understand the values, culture, and ethical standards of his or her own country, but must also be sensitive to those of other countries. In addition, although about 90 percent of American companies have a written code of ethics, surveys indicate that ethical codes are found less frequently outside the United States. For example, only 51 percent of German firms, 41 percent of British firms, and 30 percent of French firms surveyed had ethics codes in place.[1] The emphases of codes of ethics are also shifting within various cultures. For example, ethical codes are increasingly concerned with conduct against the firm rather than with conduct on behalf of the firm. Also becoming increasingly important are environmental affairs, a legal or values approach to ethics codes, and enforcement/compliance procedures.

In this chapter, we explore the ethical complexities and challenges facing businesses that operate internationally. As you read this chapter you will see some of the same ethical issues that were discussed in Chapter 3, but this chapter goes a step further. We try to help you understand how global business ethics can have more complexity than business in just one country. The global business complexity, if not understood, can destroy the trust needed to do business. Simple transactions with one well-understood culture or country can become disastrous in the global arena. Our goal in this chapter is to help you avoid, or at least become aware of, the many ethical quagmires that lurk in this domain. To help you become more ethically sensitive to this reality we start at the basics by explaining the global debate concerning capitalism, economics, and business ethics. A discussion of common values and goals and their relationship to business practices follows; as well as a general framework for developing global ethical frameworks. Also, we help you understand that there are global entities that do not necessarily conform to your country's view of the world or the way to do business. In this chapter we explain the current and future ethical problems facing global businesses and examine multinational corporations and the ethical problems they face. From these topics we discuss the International Monetary Fund, and the World Trade Organization. As stated in earlier chapters, we do not attempt to offer absolute answers to the ethical issues. Our goal is to help you understand how international business activities can create ethical conflict and to help you improve your ethical decision making ability.

CAPITALISM, ECONOMICS, AND BUSINESS ETHICS

At the close of the first decade of the 21st century, the world economy found itself mired in a quagmire of red ink. Over a six-month period the largest banks and brokerage houses around the globe became victims of what many called an "unforeseeable" set of events. Regardless of whether the financial meltdown could have been accurately predicted, governments, analysts, executives, and stakeholders have been left to sort through the mess.

A major part of the problem was an excessive focus on rewards and the bottom line that pervaded the global financial industry. The global financial market is a highly interconnected system that can exhibit too little transparency in decision making, lack of accountability, and unreliable accounting methods. This system combined with rampant leveraging and the widespread use of complex financial computer models that many experts did not even fully understand resulted in a global financial meltdown.

It did not take much to bring the entire system to its knees. Many who should have known were ignorant because of risk compartmentalization. **Risk compartmentalization** occurs when various profit centers within corporations become unaware of the overall consequences of their actions on the firm as a whole. As a result, no one person, company, or agency should be blamed in that problems were systemic. Prior to the financial meltdown, most companies tried to remain in compliance with legal systems, while many simultaneously looked for legal loopholes and unregulated means of maximizing profits and financial rewards. Many companies tried to do what was ethical; however, because of the complex nature of the global economy, many did not see the disaster coming because everyone was too focused on their own bottom line.

The meltdown caused many to question the stability of governmental institutions as well as the responsibility of those who manage the money of individuals, corporations, and countries. Some countries, such as Iceland, Zimbabwe, Hungary, Ukraine, and Serbia, even declared a form of bankruptcy.[2] Lack of trust, honesty, and fairness caused major investors to question the competence of regulatory institutions, which in turn caused instability and mistrust in the entire financial system. As a result, many questioned the foundations of capitalism and the policies needed to make it function. Today some of the fundamental concepts and assumptions of capitalism are being discussed and even revised. Because you will enter this new reality, we briefly explain the global economic debate.

We cannot give a full review of economics' wide range of axioms, theories, and models; however, to understand capitalism, you must understand three forms of economics as well as socialism. The main forms of capitalism and socialism are derived from the works of Adam Smith, John Maynard Keynes, and Milton Friedman.

Adam Smith was a Professor of Logic and Moral Philosophy during the late eighteenth century and he published critical economic ideas in *The Theory of Moral Sentiments* and the *Inquiry into the Nature and Causes of the Wealth of Nations*, which are still considered important today. Smith observed the supply and demand, contractual efficiency, and division of labor of various companies within England. Smith's writings formed the basis of modern economics. Smith's idea of **laissez-faire,** or the invisible hand, is critical to capitalism in that it assumes the market, through its own inherent mechanisms, will keep commerce in equilibrium.

The second form of capitalism gained support at the beginning of the Great Depression. During the 1930s **John Maynard Keynes** argued that the state could stimulate economic growth and improve stability in the private sector—through, for example, controlling interest rates, taxation and public projects.[3] Keynes argued that government policies could be used to increase aggregate demand, thus increasing economic activity and reducing unemployment and deflation. He argued that the solution to depression was to stimulate the economy through some combination of a reduction in interest rates or government investment in infrastructure. President Franklin D. Roosevelt employed Keynesian economic theories during his tenure as president when he was seeking to pull the United States out of the Great Depression.

The third and most recent form of capitalism was developed by **Milton Friedman,** and represented a swing to the right on the political spectrum. Friedman had lived through the Great Depression but rejected the Keynesian conclusion that the market sometimes needs some intervention in order to function most efficiently. Friedman instead believed in deregulation because he thought that the system could reach equilibrium without government intervention.[4] Friedman's ideas were the guiding principles for government policy making in the United States, and increasingly throughout the world, starting in the second half of the twentieth century.

Both Keynes and Friedman agreed that "(1) People have rational preferences among outcomes that can be identified and associated with a value; (2) Individuals maximize utility and firms maximize profits; (3) People act independently on the basis of full and relevant information." Today these assumptions are being questioned.[5]

Socialism refers to economic theories advocating the creation of a society in which wealth and power are shared and distributed evenly based on the amount of work expended in production. Modern socialism originated in the late nineteenth century and was a working-class political movement that criticized the effects of industrialization and private ownership. Karl Marx was one of socialism's most famous and strongest advocates. Marxism was Marx's own interpretation of socialism that was then transformed into communism in countries such as the U.S.S.R. and Cuba. History has shown that communism, strictly interpreted, causes economies to fail. In the 1940s **social democracy** formed as an offshoot of socialism, which allows for private ownership of property and also features a large government equipped to offer such services as education and health care to its citizens. Social democracies take on such problems as disease, ignorance, squalor, and idleness and advocates governmental intervention. Scandinavian countries like Sweden and Finland are examples of social democracies.

Past economists could not have imagined the multinational corporation, or that the world's energy resources would ever be concentrated under the control of a handful of corporations. Our world has grown increasingly bimodal in wealth distribution. **Bimodal wealth distribution** occurs when the middle class shrinks, resulting in highly concentrated wealth amongst the rich and large numbers of poor people with very few resources. This is not a desirable scenario and can result in instability. Economists of the early twentieth century and before could not have imagined the size and power of today's multinational corporations. Companies can pit one government against another for strategic advantages. One can see the same strategy by country group in trade blocs such as NAFTA (North American Free Trade Agreement), EU (European Union), and ASEAN (Association of Southeast Nations). These trade blocs give economic leverage to country groups and use the same economic principles as multinationals. To understand the future global perspective we next discuss the difference between rational and behavioral economics.

Rational economics is based upon the assumption that people are predictable and will maximize the utility of their choices relative to their needs and wants. For example, if you are hungry and have $10 to spend, rational economics suggests you spend the money on food that satisfies your hunger needs and wants (it tastes good). Time, effort, convenience, tastes, and preferences are part of the equation so that one can predict what a person will buy with his or her $10. But people are not always rational. For example, no one wants to go to jail. Even those who have stolen millions admit that the reward was probably not worth the punishment. In one case, Michael Fisher, owner of Fisher Sand & Gravel in North Dakota, paid for personal expenses such as construction and furnishing his house from company accounts. He also used company funds to pay for improvements to another business he owned, Tiger Discount gas station. Mr. Fisher did not report these payments to the IRS and pled guilty to one count of conspiracy to defraud and four counts of filing false individual and federal tax returns. His punishment was five years in prison and a $250,000 fine for each count.[6]

The second assumption is that people act independently on the basis of full and relevant information. In Mr. Fisher's case, we can assume that he did not have full or relevant information concerning his actions. If he did, then we must assume he felt his actions were worth a potential 45 years in jail and $2.25 million in fines.

Behavioral economics assumes that humans may not act rationally because of genetics, learned behavior, and heuristics, or rules of thumb. In addition, behavioral economics states that the way something is presented to a consumer can affect choice. This is called a **framing effect.** Figure 10–1 depicts where countries may be in the economic philosophy process and helps to understand where they may want to go. For example, China, Sweden, and the Soviet Union are in the lower left quadrant representing socialism as a society with behavioral economics as the vehicle towards happiness. As we mentioned, each of these country's definition of happiness is derived from social democratic goals. They are behavioral, in that they believe very little in laissez-faire. The dates on these points are important because they show that countries can change their position over time. In the upper right quadrant, Figure 10-1 shows countries and how their economics and tools have defined happiness and government's role. Finally, in the upper left quadrant is the United States and Sweden, representing Sweden's shift to capitalism and more laissez-faire economics and the United State's shift to a less laissez-faire economy.

The conflict between capitalism and socialism in the United States is due, in part, to the cold war. Many in the United States perceive socialism as Marxism; it is not. Outside the United States, most see socialism as group oriented as it relates to social problems. Socialism argues for the good of the community with government

FIGURE 10–1 The Economic Capitalism Country Differential

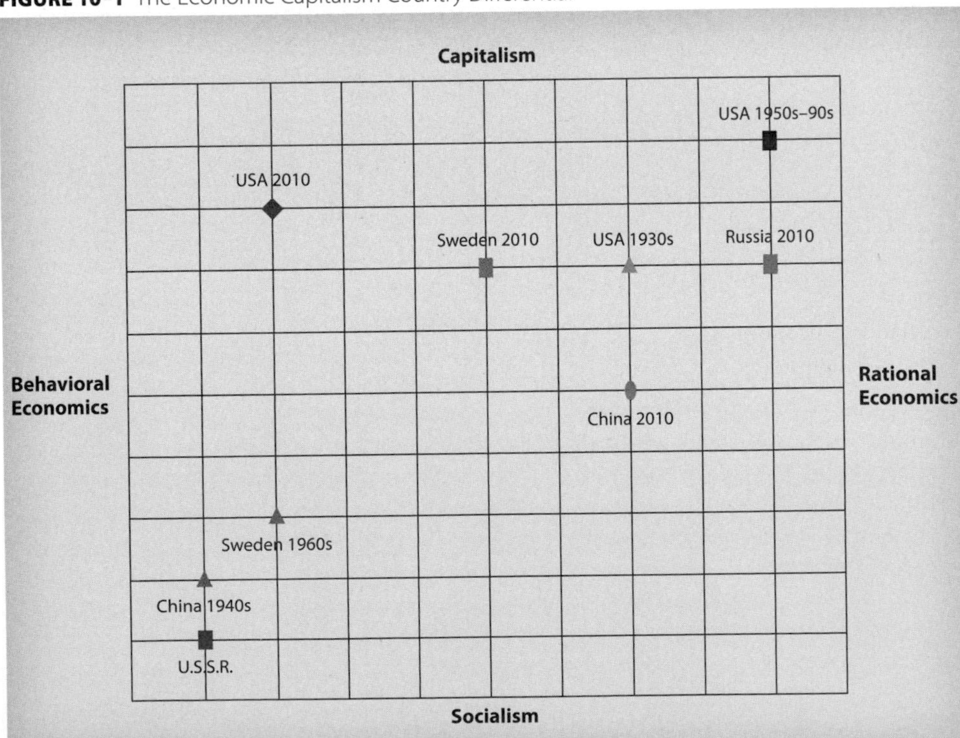

helping the people through the economy. The U.S. form of capitalism is grounded in individualism where government is perceived not so much as a help but as a hindrance to happiness.

Today, capitalism is one of the United States' many exports. While the United States practices one kind of capitalism, there are many forms with no one single best type. The success of the U.S. model of capitalism during the 1990s and 2000s led many businesses and countries to uphold it at the premier capitalistic model. However, the 2008–2009 recession and the collapse of some of the world's largest financial firms has dampened global enthusiasm for the U.S. model. It is likely that in the future more attention will be paid to other forms of capitalism.[7]

Sweden was one of the poorest countries in Western Europe in the 1880s. During the 1890s it became more worker friendly. From 1918–1970 Sweden's standard of living rose faster than most countries.[8] After 1970, it changed some of its worker policies to become more corporate-friendly and has continued to have one of the highest standards of living in the world. For some countries, behavioral capitalism can increase living standards faster than rational capitalism.

India and China have introduced the free market into their systems, although their models are very different. China has a very large communist government that blurs the lines between organizations, businesses, and government because organizations must comply with government mandates. India, on the other hand, is democratic and has a lively civil society that is often empowered to stand up against the government and against capitalism. These two countries represent around one-third of the world's population and are considered rising powers—yet their forms of capitalism are radically dissimilar. China's government involvement in business, combined with the rapid growth of its economy, may cause us to question the notion that large governments stand in the way of business success—in fact, in China government often seems to be the premier entrepreneur.[9]

Is capitalism of minimal government interaction and the free flow of goods and services across national boundaries best? Or should governments be more protectionist in order to give local businesses the upper hand? Corporations can create competitive barriers via government legislation or by collusion to form oligopolies for managed competition. Certain forms of capitalism argue that the corporation should pay shareholders as much as possible and other stakeholders are of secondary importance. Stakeholders' concerns may appear on the income statement as an expense.

There is a general consensus amongst experts, academics, and businesspeople that corporations that operate with social responsibility in mind must take into account the norms and mores of the societies in which they operate. Corporations may take varying views of CSR.[10] A broad view would include thinking about the consequences of their actions on a broad selection of stakeholders and using the corporation as a tool for public policy; while a very narrow view would involve only looking at the number of jobs created, for example. These are some of the ethical questions that business and governments need to address. There is no agreement that one form of free market system is more ethical or better than others. Ethical business systems are not restricted to capitalist models either; socialist countries also develop ethical businesses. The countries, institutions, social systems, technology, and other cultural factors can have a major effect on organizational ethics. To better understand global ethics, we start at the elemental level of values that yield business goals and that are judged to be legal or not by countries, and ethical or unethical by industries and firms.

COMMON VALUES, GOALS, AND BUSINESS PRACTICES

The term *common values* refers to two distinct concepts. The first is **global common values** that are shared across most cultures. Most laws are directly or indirectly the result of values derived from the major religions of Hinduism, Buddhism, Confucianism, Judaism, Islam, and Christianity. It is beyond our scope to explain all religious forms; however, there appears to be a consensus on the following desirable and undesirable global common values.[11]

> Desirable Global Common Values: Integrity, family and community unity, equality, honesty, fidelity, sharing, and unselfishness.
>
> Undesirable Global Common Values: Ignorance, pride and egoism, selfish desires, lust, greed, adultery, theft, deceit, lying, murder, hypocrisy, slander, and addiction.

The second type of common value is **country cultural values** that are specific to groups, sects, regions, or countries that express actions, behavior, and intent. **Culture** consists of everything in our surroundings that is made by people—both tangible items and intangible things including values, norms and artifacts. Language, law, politics, technology, education, social organizations, general values, and ethical standards are all included within this definition. Each nation contains unique cultures and, consequently, distinctive beliefs about what business activities are acceptable or unethical. Subcultures can also be found within many nations, ethnic groups, and religious groups. Thus, when transacting international business, individuals encounter values, beliefs, and ideas that may diverge from their own because of cultural differences. When someone from another culture mentions words such as integrity or democracy, most listeners feel reassured because these are familiar concepts. However, these concepts mean different things to different people depending on the perspective of his or her culture. To further complicate this discussion, you must keep in mind that organizational culture is different from national culture. Often organizational cultures, based on values, norms and artifacts, are derived from and influenced by national cultures.

Consider, for example, that honesty is valued in both Japan and the United States. Honesty begets trust. In Japan's banking industry, businesspeople demonstrated trust by hiring retired Japanese bureaucrats to become auditors, directors, executives, and presidents—a practice known as **amakudari**, or "descent from heaven." Because the men in charge of oversight were trusted, bankers felt nothing bad or unethical could happen. Later, the relationship between regulated and regulator became fuzzy and conflicts of interest started to arise. To help clarify this problem, in the United States businesspeople may trust former superiors, but they also believe there should be a separation between those who regulate and those who are regulated.

From global to cultural values come business ethics. Table 10–1 lists six documents that mirror global and cultural values such as truthfulness, integrity, fairness, and equality. When applied, global businesses have a clearer understanding of desirable and undesirable behaviors that yield ethical codes. From a country-corporate level, the Caux Round Table in Switzerland created an international ethics code (http://www.cauxroundtable.org). In addition, 50 of the world's largest corporations have signed the UN Global Compact, the purpose of which is to support free-trade unions, abolish child labor, and protect the

TABLE 10–1 Global Management Ethics

1993 Parliament of the World's Religions, The Declaration of a Global Ethic	State of California Handbook on Moral and Civic Education	Michael Josephson, Character Counts, Ethics: Easier Said Than Done
Nonviolence (love)	Morality	Trustworthiness
Respect for life	Truth	Honesty
Commitment	Justice	Integrity
Solidarity	Patriotism	Promise keeping
Truthfulness	Self-esteem	Loyalty
Tolerance	Integrity	Respect for others
Equal rights	Empathy	Responsibility
Sexual morality	Exemplary conduct	Fairness
	Reliability	Caring
	Respect for family, property, law	Citizenship
William J. Bennett, *The Book of Virtues*	**Thomas Donaldson,** *Fundamental International Rights*	**Rushworth W. Kidder,** *Shared Values for a Troubled World*
Self-discipline	Physical movement	Love
Compassion	Property, ownership	Truthfulness
Responsibility	No torture	Fairness
Friendship	Fair trial	Freedom
Work	Nondiscrimination	Unity
Courage	Physical security	Tolerance
Perseverance	Speech and association	Responsibility
Honesty	Minimal education	Respect for life
	Loyalty	Political participation
	Faith	Subsistence

Source: Andrew Sikula, "Global Management Ethics," in *Applied Management Ethics* (1996), 127. Used by permission of the author, Andrew Sikula.

natural environment. Signatory companies are required to post an annual update on their progress in these areas and are expected to cooperate with UN agencies on social projects in the developing countries in which they operate. The International Organization for Standardization (ISO) has begun the process of developing an international standard on social responsibility.[12] From this level, global companies have established global business codes of ethics. Another set of global principles were developed by Revered Leon Sullivan as a way to rise above the discrimination and struggles in post-apartheid South Africa. Revered Sullivan worked with the UN Secretary General to revise the principles to meet global needs, and since 1999 both large and small companies have agreed to abide by the Global Sullivan Principles (Table 10–2) that encourage social responsibility around the world.

The Association to Advance Collegiate Schools of Business, or AACSB, an international organization that represents over 1,100 business schools, has taken these common values and developed six principles for responsible business education. These principles are encapsulated under the title "Principles for Responsible Management Education."

TABLE 10–2 The Global Sullivan Principles

As a company which endorses the Global Sullivan Principles we will respect the law, and as a responsible member of society we will apply these Principles with integrity consistent with the legitimate role of business. We will develop and implement company policies, procedures, training and internal reporting structures to ensure commitment to these principles throughout our organization. We believe the application of these Principles will achieve greater tolerance and better understanding among peoples, and advance the culture of peace.
Accordingly, we will:
• Express our support for universal human rights and, particularly, those of our employees, the communities within which we operate, and parties with whom we do business.
• Promote equal opportunity for our employees at all levels of the company with respect to issues such as color, race, gender, age, ethnicity or religious beliefs, and operate without unacceptable worker treatment such as the exploitation of children, physical punishment, female abuse, involuntary servitude, or other forms of abuse.
• Respect our employees' voluntary freedom of association.
• Compensate our employees to enable them to meet at least their basic needs and provide the opportunity to improve their skill and capability in order to raise their social and economic opportunities.
• Provide a safe and healthy workplace; protect human health and the environment; and promote sustainable development.
• Promote fair competition including respect for intellectual and other property rights, and not offer, pay or accept bribes.
• Work with government and communities in which we do business to improve the quality of life in those communities—their educational, cultural, economic and social well-being—and seek to provide training and opportunities for workers from disadvantaged backgrounds.
• Promote the application of these principles by those with whom we do business.
We will be transparent in our implementation of these principles and provide information which demonstrates publicly our commitment to them.

Source: Reprinted from *Ethikos: Examining Ethical and Compliance Issues in Business*, The Sullivan Foundation, http://www.thesullivanfoundation.org/gsp/principles/gsp/default.asp (accessed June 2, 2009).

The first principle calls for developing students to be future generators of sustainable value for business and society and work toward a sustainable global economy. Other principles include incorporating global social responsibility into curricula, creating educational materials that cultivate responsible leaders, and interacting with corporate managers to learn about the problems facing them and to develop approaches for addressing these issues. These six principles heavily relate to the concept of sustainable development. Also, AACSB is helping to facilitate and support dialogue and debate among educators, business, government, consumers, media, civil society organizations, and other interested groups and stakeholders on critical issues related to global social responsibility and sustainability. Such cooperation is demonstrated by AACSB's involvement with the United Nations Global Compact, which is a policy initiative that aims to align corporate goals with universally accepted principles of human rights, labor, and the environment.[13]

If such business codes exist, then why do businesspeople have trouble understanding what is ethical or unethical? The answer about these variations between values and business practices is derived from organizational goals and culture. In an attempt to maximize profit, an organization may adopt values that do not take into account long-term relationships with stakeholders. Honesty, charity, virtue, and beneficence may be universally desirable values, but the profit motive in business can result in an organizational culture that misinterprets these values.

GLOBAL BUSINESS PRACTICES

When businesspeople travel, they sometimes perceive that other business cultures have different modes of operation. The perception exists that American companies are different from those in other countries, and some people perceive U.S. companies as being superior to their foreign counterparts. This implied perspective of ethical superiority—"us" versus "them"—is also common in other countries. Table 10–3 indicates the countries that businesspeople, risk analysts, and the general public perceived as the most and least corrupt. In business, the idea that "we" differ from "them" is called the **self-reference criterion** (SRC).

The SRC is the unconscious reference to one's own cultural values, experiences, and knowledge. When confronted with a situation, we react on the basis of knowledge we

TABLE 10–3 Perceptions of Countries as Least/Most Corrupt

Least Corrupt Country	Most Corrupt Country
1. Denmark	1. Somalia
1. New Zealand	2. Myanmar
1. Sweden	2. Iraq
4. Singapore	4. Haiti
5. Finland	5. Afghanistan
5. Switzerland	6. Sudan
7. Iceland	6. Guinea
7. Netherlands	6. Chad
9. Australia	9. Equatorial Guinea
9. Canada	9. Congo, Democratic Republic
11. Luxembourg	11. Zimbabwe
12. Austria	11. Uzbekistan
12. Hong Kong	11. Turkmenistan
14. Germany	11. Kyrgyzstan
14. Norway	11. Cambodia

Source: Transparency International Corruptions Index, 2008, http://www.transparency.org/policy_research/surveys_indices/cpi/2008 (accessed June 22, 2009).

Note: The U.S. ranks as the 18th least corrupt country.

have accumulated over a lifetime, which is usually grounded in our culture of origin. Our reactions are based on meanings, values, and symbols that relate to our culture but may not have the same relevance to people of other cultures.

In the United States, for example, **dumping**—the practice of charging high prices for products in domestic markets while selling the same products in foreign markets at low prices, often below cost—is viewed as anticompetitive. The United States has a number of antidumping laws. The U.S. Congress passed the Byrd amendment, which allows U.S. Customs to distribute money generated from foreign companies accused of dumping products to U.S. firms harmed by the dumping. However, the World Trade Organization (WTO) ruled that this distribution of funds to U.S. firms violates its international trade rules and regulations. The WTO recommended that the United States repeal the Byrd amendment, but the United States officially rejected this recommendation. Although the United States is a member of the WTO, in this case, it rejected its rules.[14] The WTO ruled that the amendment was inconsistent with the U.S. WTO obligations, and it authorized eight WTO members to retaliate against the United States.[15]

One of the critical ethical business issues linked to cultural differences is the question of whose values and ethical standards take precedence during international negotiations and business transactions. When conducting business outside their home country, should businesspeople impose their own values, ethical standards, and laws on members of other cultures? Or should they adapt to the values, ethical standards, and laws of the country in which they are doing business? As with many ethical issues, there are no easy answers to these questions.

When in Rome, do as the Romans do or *you must adapt to the cultural practices of the country in which you are operating* are rationalizations businesspeople sometimes offer for straying from their own ethical values when doing business abroad. By defending the payment of bribes or "greasing the wheels of business" and other questionable practices in this fashion, they are resorting to **cultural relativism,** the concept that morality varies from one culture to another and that business practices are therefore differentially defined as right or wrong by particular cultures. The U.S. Justice Department has stepped up its crackdown on corporate bribes, something that is tolerated to varying degrees in different cultures. The Foreign Corrupt Practices Act, a law that was passed in the aftermath of Watergate but which was largely ignored until the Obama administration took office, prohibits U.S. companies from paying or offering to pay bribes to foreign officials or employees of state-owned companies to gain business. The law can be interpreted broadly enough to include gifts. As a result, hundreds of companies have undergone government investigations into whether or not they have engaged in bribery.[16]

Although companies in the United States installed whistle-blower hotlines to meet Securities and Exchange (SEC) requirements under the Sarbanes–Oxley Act, rulings in France and Germany challenged the legality of such hotlines.[17] French authorities assert that the hotlines violate French privacy law because accusations can be anonymous, thus creating concern that persons named by a whistle-blower do not have a chance to prove their innocence. Across Europe there are concerns about personal data and data protection. Xerox has an ethics help line in every country in which it operates, including Germany and France. The difference is that it is a *help* line, not a hotline, where people can ask general questions about policies. Xerox has had its code of conduct approved in every country where it applies.[18]

Other aspects of ethics compliance have been challenged. A German labor court ruled that parts of Wal-Mart Stores Inc.'s ethics code, including a ban on relationships between

TABLE 10–4 Writing an Effective Global Code of Conduct

1. *Form an international advisory group.* The group needs to provide content expertise and become local "champions" for the code. It should be a functionally diverse group that is geographically representative of the target markets as well as the company and management structure.
2. *Set clear objectives for the code.* It is important to establish some clear and realistic objectives for the document. Some of the most common objectives for codes of conduct are compliance, corporate social responsibility, suppliers, and partners or a values-based code. Companies need to make sure that they can follow through with enforcing a code once it is in place. If this does not occur, employees may become very cynical.
3. *Draft content.* This stage includes determining the issues, developing standards, and reviewing the preliminary draft of the code. There are four key components that should be included in each major standard: provide a rationale to explain the need for the standard, provide a clear definition of the issue, provide clear guidance (through examples, questions and answers, and the like), and discuss additional resources for information.
4. *Have knowledge about graphic design.* Cultural sensitivity plays a key role in graphic design and is required especially for the following areas: (1) the use of color—companies should be aware that color can have different meanings in different cultures; (2) use of symbols—the document should not rely on country-specific symbols such as the dollar symbol to represent currency; (3) use of photos—it is important to ensure that the photos represent the international character of the company and not one or two particular geographies.
5. *Hold focus groups and finalize content.* It is best to conduct focus groups in the native language and if possible with a translated code of conduct. Companies can use internal personnel or external personnel to conduct the focus group, but when using internal personnel, it is important to avoid using a member of management, which could stifle discussion and dissent.
6. *Translate the code.* It is important that companies understand when to translate the code and how to select translators. When there are fewer than 25 employees, it is best to provide a translation, but it is not necessary to reprint the code with graphics or in color. With more than 100 employees, it is important to invest in translation and color reprinting of the code.

Source: From Lori Tansey Martens, "Writing an Effective Code of Conduct," *International Business Ethics Review*, Vol. 8, No. 1, Spring/Summer 2005, pp. 1, 9–14. Reprinted with permission.

employees, violate German law. The same court also ruled against a proposed hotline for employees to report on colleagues' violations of the code of conduct. Labor representatives from the 91 German Wal-Mart stores sued the retail giant over the code after it was introduced without their prior approval. Under German law, employee–management councils must sign off on a wide range of workplace conditions.[19]

Writing a code of conduct for a global workforce can be challenging. Table 10–4 provides a general framework for writing an effective global code of conduct. Individuals may adjust to the ethics of a particular foreign culture or use their own culture as a defense against something unethical as perceived in the foreign country. The disadvantage is that they may be in conflict with their own individual moral standards and perhaps with their own culture's values and legal system. Figure 10–2 is a two-by-two matrix showing the global potential for unethical and illegal decisions.

Rapid growth and poverty reduction in China, India, and other countries has been a positive aspect of globalization. But globalization has also generated significant international opposition over concerns that it has increased inequality and environmental

FIGURE 10–2 Matrix for Global Relativists When Making Cross-Cultural Ethics Decisions

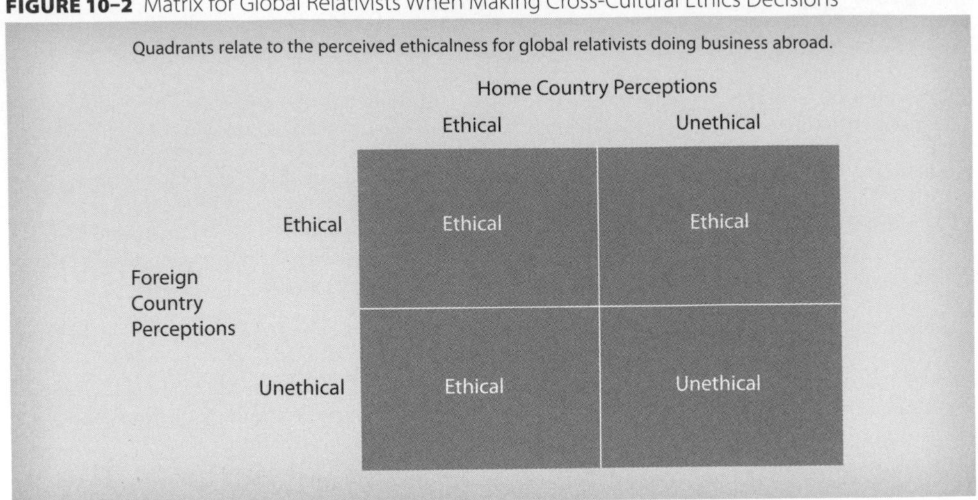

degradation. No company, country, or culture is immune to ethics issues. Some are obvious while others are not. The following list of topics is not inclusive, rather it includes items perceived to become illegal in the future. The first, in no special order is consumerism.

Consumerism

Consumerism is the belief that consumers, rather than the interests of producers, should dictate the economic structure of a society. It refers to the theory that an increasing consumption of goods is economically desirable and equates personal happiness with the purchase and consumption of material possessions. Consumption in the past 50 years has placed significant strains on the environment. Some argue that human factors such as the increase in fossil fuel emissions from industrialization and rising meat and dairy consumption in the United States, China, and India has caused global warming. Many countries argue that consumer choices are moral choices, and that choosing a high rate of consumption will affect vulnerable groups like the poor, and that the world will be increasingly less habitable if people refuse to change their behavior.[20]

As nations increase their wealth, consumers increase their quality of living with luxury items and technological innovations that improve the comfort, convenience, and efficiency of their lives. Such consumption beyond basic needs is not necessarily a bad thing in and of itself; however, as more people engage in this type of behavior waste and pollution increase. Some important issues must be addressed in relation to consumerism. For example:

- What are the impacts of production on the environment, society, and individuals?
- What are the impacts of certain forms of consumption on the environment, society, and individuals?
- Who influences consumption and how and why they are produced?
- What are truly necessities and what are luxuries?

- How much of what we consume is influenced by corporations versus our needs?
- What is the impact on poorer nations of the consumption patterns of wealthier nations?

The last question has many ethical ramifications, especially because many developing countries hold the debt of the United States and Europe. For example, China holds over $1 trillion of U.S. debt.[21]

China's rise to dominance in manufacturing and world trade has resulted in its outpacing the United States as a consumer. It now leads the United States in consumption of basic goods such as grain, meat, coal, and steel. China has also surpassed the United States in greenhouse gas emissions. Some fear that China's newfound consumerism will push up global prices for goods, as well as speed up global warming, even as other more developed nations take measures to stop it. While Chinese consumption patterns are currently more in line with those in Europe, the ideology of development through mass consumption is comparable to the United States.[22] For example, Hummer, formerly owned by GM, manufactures vehicles based on the U.S. Army's Humvee. Because of the perceived demand for Hummers in China, an obscure Chinese machinery maker, Sichuan Tengzhong Heavy Industrial Machinery Co., purchased the Hummer Vehicle Unit. The Hummer epitomizes the U.S. gas-guzzler and in China has become a status symbol for wealthy Chinese. Hummer owner Liu Haiyun of Shanghai explains, ""Nowadays, from the point of view of doing business, it's all about image. Buying Hummer proves your power. It shows your value.[23]

But the Hummer concept runs contrary to the Chinese government's policy of increased efficiency and ecologically friendly cars. The new generation of "Chuppies"—Chinese yuppies—is riding a wave of unprecedented commercialism. It is estimated that there are over 200 million Chuppies in China.[24] Technologically savvy, they are the first generation to use credit cards and do not save like their parents did. China historically has one of the world's highest savings rates, but Chuppies are changing that. Marketers estimate that China's youth will become the most powerful consumer force in the world within the next 20 years.

Consumption patterns are being created by business in China that will cause large resource requirements. For example, there are 640 million cell phone users in China, and, on average, they replace their phones every three to six months. Consumers in China can choose from nearly 1,000 different models, compared with fewer than 100 in the United States.[25]

India, with its 1.1 billion people, is following China and the western consumerism path as well. Half of India's 1.1 billion people are under the age of 25. An estimated 2.1 million people graduate from college each year: 200,000 as engineers and 40,000 in management.[26] The country's economy has been growing at an average of 8 percent a year. India has the world's fastest-growing information technology market, creating skilled, high-wage jobs for software engineers, business process experts, and call center workers. India has joined the rush for greater consumerism as well. In fact, the country is well-situated to weather global recessions because much of the country's demand for goods is domestic. With over 1 billion people, India has the second largest domestic market for goods in the world. The country is also well-poised for future growth with a young, dynamic, and highly educated workforce.[27]

The ethics of these consumerism issues for business are many. These large emerging economies are the profit-making centers of the future. Most in business understand that it is in the best interest of the firm that consumer needs and desires are never completely or permanently fulfilled, so the consumer can repeat the consumption process and purchase more products. For example, **made-to-break,** or planned obsolescence, products are better for business, in that they keep consumers returning to buy more. It is also profitable to make products part of a continuously changing fashion market. By doing this, items that are still in good condition and can last for many years are deemed in need of constant replacement, in order to keep in sync with current fashion trends. In this way, steady profits are assured. The top 20 percent of consumers in the highest income countries account for 86 percent of global consumption expenditures. The poorest 20 percent account for 1.3 percent of consumption expenditures. The richest fifth consume 45 percent of all meat and fish, 58 percent of total energy, have 74 percent of all telephone lines, consume 84 percent of all paper, and own 87 percent of the world's vehicles.[28]

An ethical question that is being asked by more people and countries is: Does consumerism lead to happiness? Consumer detractors are gaining ground globally and the United States is their example of global non-sustainable consumption. They cite that while the United States comprises 4.6 percent of the world's population, they consume 33 percent of the world's resources. The world's poorest 2.3 billion people only consume 3 percent of the world's resources. The average American generates twice as much waste per person per year than the average European.[29]

The consumption statistics point to a very different lifestyle for the future and global business will drive it. The moral conflict between countries, especially the United States and the developing world, will increase with corresponding ethical challenges for business. The future may be one of cross-class, country violence with business responding, or it may be a lifestyle that global business creates and markets to avoid civil and global war. It will be up to you and others to decide.

Human Rights

Human rights have been codified into a United Nations document and are defined as an inherent dignity with equal and inalienable rights as the foundation of freedom, justice, and peace in the world. Human rights is not a new concept. It was established decades ago, but few companies took it into consideration until recently. Today, businesses are paying attention to the following points: Table 10–5 provides three articles from the UN Human Rights Declaration.

The three human rights articles mentioned appear to be benign but, as explained earlier, their business implementation can have serious ethical ramifications. For example Article 18 concerns freedom of religion; from a western perspective this

TABLE 10–5 Selected Articles from the UN Human Rights Declaration

Article 18. Freedom of religion . . . either alone or in community . . . in public or private . . .
Article 23. The right to work . . . to just and favorable conditions of work and to protection against unemployment . . . equal pay for equal work . . . ensuring for himself and his family an existence worthy of human dignity . . . right to form and to join trade unions . . .
Article 25. Right to a standard of living adequate for the health and well-being . . . Motherhood and childhood are entitled to special care and assistance.

Source: United Nations Human Rights Declaration, http://www.un.org/en/rights/ (accessed June 22, 2009).

appears to be straightforward. However, how should firms respond to employees from countries where it is acceptable to have multiple wives—should they all be granted health insurance? The right to freedom of religion, women's rights, and health care, as well as other legal questions become more complex. For example, Ford Motor Company started the Ford Interfaith Network, an organization for employees from eight major religions, including Hinduism and Buddhism. The organization has designated areas in Ford workplaces where Muslims, for example, can perform ablution, a ritual cleansing, before praying.[30] But if you are in Saudi Arabia, such an interfaith group does not exist. The Saudi government prohibits the public practice of non-Muslim religions. In general, they recognize the right of non-Muslims to worship in private; however, this right is not extended to the public domain. Within Saudi Arabia freedom of religion is not legally defined.

Article 23 appears benign to firms as well. Few would argue against the right to work and equal pay. Upon closer inspection it also mentions the right to join trade unions. Within the European Union trade unions are accepted, but in many other countries, such as Burma, Burundi, China, Cuba, Iran, South Korea, Tunisia, Turkey, and Zimbabwe, trade unionists risk imprisonment.[31] European companies having employees in these countries will face many ethically charged decisions. Trade unions are an ethically charged issue in the United States as well. For example, McDonald's and Wal-Mart discourage attempts to unionize in the United States, but they acquiesced to China's suggestion of unions. Both companies have unions in all of their Chinese facilities, yet outside China both are fighting to block unions in their home country.[32]

Article 25 mentions a standard of living and special rights to pregnancy. To help understand how firms can become entangled in implementing such concepts, take, for example, the U.S. Supreme Court ruling that maternity leave cannot count towards pensions.[33] In the United States employees are allowed to take unpaid maternity leave with the guarantee their jobs will not be affected. Some countries have been arguing for allowing men to take off the same amount of leave (either paid or unpaid) as women. This debate would never happen in Sweden because parents get a total of 480 days that can be split between parents at 100 percent pay.[34]

Another global human rights issue is privacy. The Internet has allowed data to be moved around the globe at an unprecedented rate with few safety measures. Different countries have different privacy laws causing business ethical and legal challenges. For example, in Europe personal information cannot be collected without permission. If collected, the person has the right to review the data and correct inaccuracies. Companies that process data must register their activities with the government. Employers cannot read workers' private email or share personal information without the individual's permission. Such restrictions are not codified in laws in the United States.

In China, privacy has become an international issue. For example, the Chinese government mandated that any Microsoft computer imported into China must include Green Dam Software, which was designed to filter out sexually explicit images and words. Zhang Chenming of Jinhui Computer System Engineering, one of the creators of the software, said the purpose of Green Wall is to help enforce China's "Great Firewall," which is controlled by China's security ministry and military.[35] China is attempting to limit its people's access to information via the Internet. Some companies doing business in China risk government backlash if they attempt to uphold their home country's protections freedoms of speech.

Health Care

Another human right is health care. Globally, one billion people lack access to health care systems and approximately 11 million children under the age of 5 die from malnutrition and mostly preventable diseases each year.[36] However, global concern about the priorities of pharmaceutical companies, which are supposed to provide life-saving drugs to those who need them, is on the rise. The first concern is their profits. Opponents suggest that the quest for ever-greater profits have led pharmaceuticals to emphasis research for drugs aimed at markets that can afford things such as cures for baldness or impotence, rather than focusing on widespread deadly diseases like malaria, HIV, and AIDs. Activists have been more successful than ever in demonstrating and alleging that pharmaceutical companies are unethical and globally immoral. For example, a documentary released by True Vision, an international documentary film company, features a child in Honduras who ultimately dies from the ravages of AIDs.[37] Pfizer produces one of the drugs that he needs, but it costs $29 per tablet. The family only earns $19 a week. The generic version of the drug is available for 30 cents in neighboring Guatemala, but the drug maker has no license to produce or sell in Honduras. The implication is that Pfizer controls international licensing rights so as to maximize its profits, with little concern for the people who need the medications. The Internet has helped to inform consumers and expose these kinds of inequalities and injustices. In order to survive in the long term, businesses must learn to deal with the ethics of this new reality.

> *"Rising health care costs continue to pose a critical challenge, particularly in the United States."*

A related issue affecting both poor and wealthy countries is health care affordability. Rising health care costs continue to pose a critical challenge, particularly in the United States. Health care in the United States costs people approximately $2 trillion a year, and 45 million people are currently uninsured.[38] Employees, businesses, states, and the federal government cannot meet the expanding costs of public programs like Medicaid and Medicare and many people are clamoring for an overhaul to the system. The United States spends more than twice as much per person for health care as other industrialized countries, and has fallen to last place among those countries in preventing deaths through effective medical care.[39]

The fundamental issue driving some businesses into ethical and legal trouble around the world is whether health care is a right or privilege. For example, many people in the United States see health care as a privilege, not a right, thus it is the responsibility of individuals to provide for themselves. Other countries such as Germany disagree. German employees have been guaranteed access to high-quality comprehensive health care since 1883.[40] Many countries believe that health care is important because it increases productivity and that government ought to provide it. As health care costs continue to increase, the burden either falls on companies, employees, or both. The global ethics of health care has been going forward with U.S. firms becoming less competitive because of these costs. Another global issue businesses must adjust to is labor; specifically employees.

Labor

Today, more people live and work in a country other than their homeland. In the European Union, for example, workers can carry benefits across countries within the EU without any reductions or changes. Multinationals are training more people in the way they do business than at any other time. Many businesspeople are asking the question, am I a multinational employee first and then a citizen of a country, or am I a citizen first and an employee second? Later in the chapter we bring up the same question but with more complexity. Because businesses must make a profit there are increasing occasions where nationality no longer is a deciding factor. In business, we are becoming global citizens. As a result, firms need to understand that certain employee issues, once country specific, have become global. For example, the debate over gender pay inequality has spread around the globe. As China industrializes, blue-collar gender pay differences are becoming an issue most striking among blue-collar workers.[41]

Multinationals with high-level international employees have a unique set of ethical issues that will need to be addressed. For example, corporations will have to deal with stricter executive compensation regulations, temporary defined benefit plans or funding relief, and subsidized health coverage for laid-off workers.[42] Since the financial meltdown, workers in countries around the globe, especially in places without strong employee protections, are asking why they are getting fired as a result of the poor decisions of their superiors. Furthermore, many workers have begun to question why so may high-level executives get paid so much when their real incomes have stayed the same or even fallen. The executive pay issue began with the U.S. government. When companies agreed to take bailout money a plan was developed that restricts "golden parachutes" for dismissed executives and requires the disclosure of policies on so-called luxury spending (e.g., holiday parties, corporate jets, and office renovations). "This is America," President Obama declared. "We don't disparage wealth. We don't begrudge anybody for achieving success. And we believe success should be rewarded. But what gets people upset—and rightfully so—are executives being rewarded for failure, especially when those rewards are subsidized by U.S. taxpayers."[43]

Some companies have begun to heed the call to reduce compensation. GM directors reduced their $200,000 annual retainer by half.[44] Ford directors gave up the $40,000 cash portion of their annual retainers, as well as payments for committee chairmen.[45] Internationally, China's government said executives of its state-owned banks and insurers are paid too much and ordered them to cut their salaries to promote income fairness. Chinese executive pay is modest by Western standards but many times that of ordinary workers. For example, the chairman and chief executive of China's biggest insurer, China Life Insurance Co., was paid 1.7 million yuan ($248,000) last year. That was a reduction from Yang Chao's 2 million yuan the year before in salary and bonuses. China's second-largest insurer, Ping An Insurance Co. of China Ltd., suffered a major loss because of the global crisis. Ping An's chairman, Ma Mingzhe, announced he would give up his yearly salary because of the loss.[46] Another pay issue is associated with standard of living.

Although most in the west believe this to be a non-issue, forced labor is a very large problem in other parts of the world. Corporations that perceive this as not relevant to them will find themselves in many ethical and legal problems. The International Labor Organization (ILO) estimates 12.3 million men, women, and children worldwide are currently enslaved.[47] Oftentimes workers are lured into traps that promise work abroad. Countries such as the Philippines, Indonesia, Bangladesh, and Sri Lanka are the leading suppliers of forced labor going to wealthier Asian and Middle Eastern countries. Once there, it becomes nearly impossible for people to leave either because of economic or legal issues. Combine this fact with the global manufacturing chain and problems can easily occur. For example, Gap Inc. came under fire when it was discovered that children as young as 10 were producing children's goods for the chain in India. Gap took responsibility and said a manufacturer used an unauthorized subcontractor. Gap quickly made sure that all garments made were never sold.[48]

SUSTAINABLE DEVELOPMENT

Another concept related to the ethical issues discussed in Chapter 3 is sustainable development. **Sustainable development** is a systematic approach to achieving human development in such a way that the earth's resources are preserved for future generations. It is an approach that acknowledges that the earth's resources are finite and that human consumption is occurring at a rate beyond Earth's capacity to support it over the long term. The concept of sustainability is based on the notion that human health is dependent on the healthy functioning of the earth's ecosystems. Notions of sustainability call for sharply reduced waste and consumption in the world's wealthiest nations because the earth's systems will become overwhelmed if more people continue to match consumption rates of wealthier nations. Sustainable development requires alterations in the lifestyle of the wealthy to live within what is called the carrying capacity of the environment. In other words, if population continues to grow, governments or the markets must discover ways to do more with less and to do it more efficiently for everyone to obtain their fair share of resources. Many fear that the failure to achieve global sustainable development will result in dire consequences such as increased conflicts, starvation, and lowered standards of living. As discussed in prior chapters, businesses want to reduce transactional risk and get products to the right place, at the right time, in the right amounts, to the right people, at the right prices. It is therefore in businesses' long-term interests to work toward becoming more sustainable.

The sustainable development concept gained a high level of international recognition through The Millennium Ecosystem Assessment (MA) initiated by the United Nations' Secretary-General Kofi Annan. Table 10–6 illustrates some of the questions asked by the report.

Some global businesses have taken the report and initiative very seriously as a tool that lays the blueprint for what countries and governments will be stressing in the next 50 years. It helps to tell business which industries will become more or less desirable, as well as what will be the most important ethical and legal issues in coming years. For example, one item mentioned in the report was deforestation. If a firm produces or

TABLE 10–6 The Millennium Ecosystem Assessment

1.	What are the current condition and trends of ecosystems, ecosystem services, and human well-being?
2.	What are plausible future changes in ecosystems and their ecosystem services and the consequent changes in human well-being?
3.	What can be done to enhance well-being and conserve ecosystems?
4.	What are the strengths and weaknesses of response options that can be considered to realize or avoid specific futures?
5.	What are the key uncertainties that hinder effective decision making concerning ecosystems?

Source: Overview of the Millennium Ecosystem, Assessment, http://www.maweb.org/en/About.aspx # 1(accessed June 9, 2009).

depends on paper products, serious ethical and legal issues lie ahead. Some companies are therefore working to create standards now that anticipate future problems. For example, Stora Enso, the world's largest paper company, is addressing such issues as its carbon footprint, developing sustainable suppliers, and recovering and recycling the more than 579 square miles of corrugated packing material it produces annually. Even though the company has an independent sustainability auditor, Csrnetwork, giving an assessment of their Sustainability Performance Reports, it has remaining ethical issues to address. For example, the company was accused of not helping in Brazil's land reform policies. Brazil's Landless Worker's Movement (MST) and Via Campesina, another rural workers' group, together with the Friends of the Earth in Finland, began a letter campaign against Stora Enso's operations to draw attention to allegations that it was interfering with land reform resolutions by purchasing private land. The MST and other groups felt that Stora Enso was taking land that rightfully belonged to Brazilian landless workers. Stora Enso asserted that it never purchased any land that was set aside for land reform or redistribution. Although not settled in the way these groups wanted, Stora Enso made the ethical issue transparent to stakeholders; something that is rare for corporations.[49] Other companies are also heeding the call to be better for the environment. For example, after tests showed that Scotchguard does not decompose, therefore representing an environmental contaminant, 3M announced a voluntary end to production of the popular product, which had generated $300 million in sales.

INTERNATIONAL MONETARY FUND (IMF)

The **International Monetary Fund** (IMF) originated from the Bretton Woods agreement of July 1944, where a group of international leaders decided that the primary responsibility for the regulation of monetary relationships among national economies should rest in an extra-national body, the IMF. Member states provide resources to fund the IMF through a system of quotas that are proportional to the size of their respective economies. Member states also receive IMF voting power relative to these quota contributions. Under this rule the United States has just under one-fifth of the votes.

In the 1980s the IMF became the key institution in the management of the Less Developed Country (LDC) debt crisis, which plunged most of Latin America into a decade of economic decline. IMF policy has been sharply criticized, although its often-painful structural adjustment policies in weaker economies have worked. Countries using the IMF have frequently faced numerous periods of crisis and adjustment. The strings attached to the loans often force sharp budget cuts or interest-rate increases. An ethical issue surrounding the IMF is the argument that global liberalization has created more inequality and poverty in the countries seeking its help. Some contend that corporations offload their foreign debt, via IMF bailouts.

"Today, our tools are limited," said Treasury Secretary Paulson in a recent speech. Policy makers could ultimately find themselves in a situation similar to one they faced a decade ago when a global financial crisis was sweeping from country to country.[50] The IMF, pushed by the U.S. Treasury, mounted multibillion-dollar bailouts of Thailand, Indonesia, and Korea. It is now urging a new system of government oversight of big hedge funds, private-equity firms, and other financial firms whose failures pose major risk to the global economy. The IMF is suggesting governments adopt a "binding code of conduct across nations" to coordinate how and when they would intercede in troubled firms, and how to share losses from major financial institutions that operate across borders. The IMF has also proposed limiting the number of newly regulated firms to the biggest ones posing systemic risk. "We need to regulate systemic risk better, but at the same time avoid a rush to regulation," said Jaime Caruana, the IMF's top banking official.[51] The IMF has become the international coordinator of regulatory policy for the world.

Other countries are challenging assumed practices created in large part by the United States. One such practice that will be ethically challenging for some is the argument that the world needs to reduce its dominance of a few individual currencies, such as the dollar, euro, and yen, in international trade and finance. Most nations concentrate their assets in those reserve currencies, which exaggerates the size of flows and makes financial systems overall more volatile. By moving to a currency that belongs to no individual nation it would be easier for all nations to manage their economies better. It could also be the basis for a more equitable way of financing the IMF. In the future the IMF could dictate monetary terms for countries in a capricious way. However, many would argue that far less has been achieved in the receiving nations than was expected, but they would disagree as to why that was the case. Some argue that too much of the money has been spent on projects that have proven to be of little real benefit. Also, whether development assistance is given to a particular country is often determined by political or military considerations than by social or humanitarian ones. Finally, and all too often, government officials in recipient countries, their family members, and their close associates have illegally enriched themselves at the expense of those who were supposed to have benefited.

WORLD TRADE ORGANIZATION (WTO)

The **World Trade Organization** (WTO) was established in 1995 at the Uruguay round of negotiations of the General Agreement on Tariffs and Trade (GATT). Today, the WTO has 133 member nations and an additional 33 nations that have applied for membership and hold observer status. On behalf of its membership, the WTO administers its own trade agreements, facilitates future trade negotiations, settles trade disputes, and monitors the trade policies of member nations. The WTO addresses economic and social issues involving agriculture, textiles and clothing, banking, telecommunications, government purchases, industrial standards, food sanitation regulations, services, and intellectual property. It also provides legally binding ground rules for international commerce and trade policy. The organization attempts to reduce barriers to trade between and within nations and settle trade disputes.

Although its goals are certainly lofty, the WTO has been criticized by a number of groups, especially environmental organizations. For example, after the U.S. Marine Mammal Act placed an embargo on tuna caught using methods that can also kill dolphins, Mexico denounced the act and sued the United States. In its Tuna–Dolphin Ruling, the WTO declared the U.S. law illegal under GATT rules, forcing the United States to rescind the law. A similar set of circumstances resulted in the WTO's Shrimp–Turtle Ruling. After the U.S. Environmental Protection Act required that all shrimp fishers use nets with turtle-excluder devices to protect endangered sea turtles, several Asian nations that refused to use the nets were excluded from selling shrimp in the United States. They filed suit, arguing that the United States cannot use import bans to influence fishing practices outside its own borders. The WTO agreed, and the United States eliminated this portion of the law.[52] Rulings such as these have led environmental organizations to question the effectiveness of the WTO.

The WTO has not been able to manage the decreased global commitment to free trade. "There have been increases in tariffs, new nontariff measures and more resort to trade defense measures such as antidumping actions," says its director, Pascal Lamy.[53] During the past year there have been European import tariffs on Asian plastic bags to a ban on Chinese toys in India. South Korea raised import tariffs on oil; Mexico raised tariffs on 89 U.S. goods; Ukraine added an extra 13 percent tariff on all imports; the United States raised duties on imports of Chinese steel pipes; and Argentina mandated a special license for toy imports. The WTO says shoes, cars, and steel are among the goods most vulnerable to protectionism. Argentina, Brazil, Canada, Russia, Ecuador, and Ukraine raised import duties on shoes, mostly from China and Vietnam.[54] During global downturns more countries tend to restrict trading. As usual firms will find ways around such tariffs. For example, if a company wants instant free trade access to both the EU and the USA, manufacture in Israel. If you have a low-tech product and want free trade access to the EU, make it in Senegal, since they have a free trade agreement with France. The list of bypasses around tariffs is long and grows as NAFTA and the EU expand.

THE MULTINATIONAL CORPORATION (MNC)

Multinational corporations (MNCs), as discussed earlier in the chapter as well throughout this book, are public companies that operate on a global scale without significant ties to any one nation or region. MNCs represent the highest level of international business commitment and are characterized by a global strategy of focusing on opportunities throughout the world. Examples of U.S.-based multinational corporations include Nike, Monsanto, and Cisco Systems. Some of these firms have grown so large that they generate higher revenues than the gross domestic product (GDP)—the sum of all the goods and services produced in a country during one year—of some of the countries in which they do business, as shown in Table 10–7.

TABLE 10–7 World's Largest Countries and Corporations Based on Gross Domestic Products and Revenues

Country	GDP (millions $ U.S.)	Company	Revenues (millions $ U.S.)
1. The United States	14,264,600	1. Wal-Mart Stores	378,799
2. Japan	4,923,761	2. Exxon Mobil	372,824
3. China	4,401,614	3. Royal Dutch Shell	355,782
4. Germany	3,667,513	4. BP	291,438
5. France	2,865,737	5. Toyota Motor	230,201
26. Taiwan	392,552	6. Chevron	210,783
27. Greece	357,549	7. ING Group	201,516
28. Iran	344,820	8. Total	187,280
29. Denmark	342,925	9. General Motors	182,347
30. Argentina	326,474	10. ConocoPhillips	178,558

Source: Adapted from "2008 IMF Country Rankings by GDP," Global Fortune 500, 2008, http://money.cnn.com/magazines/fortune/global500/2008/full_list/ (accessed June 22, 2009); CIA World Factbook, https://www.cia.gov/library/publications/the-world-factbook/ (accessed September 4, 2009).

Based on revenues versus GDP, Wal-Mart Stores, Inc. is roughly the same size as the 26th largest country economy in the world, Taiwan, and Wal-Mart and Exxon Mobil are both larger than the economy of Greece. Because of their size and financial power, MNCs have been the subject of much ethical criticism, and their impact on the countries in which they do business has been hotly debated. Both American and European labor unions argue that it is unfair for MNCs to transfer jobs overseas, where wage rates are lower. Other critics have charged that multinationals use labor-saving devices that increase unemployment in the countries where they manufacture. MNCs have also been accused of increasing the gap between rich and poor nations and of misusing and misallocating scarce resources. Their size and financial clout enable MNCs to control money supplies, employment, and even the economic well-being of less-developed countries. In some instances, MNCs have controlled entire cultures and countries. For example, a Los Angeles judge ruled that Unocal may be liable for the conduct of the government of Myanmar (formerly known as Burma) because documents presented in court contended that forced labor was commonly used in Myanmar to build Unocal projects and that workers' refusal to work resulted in their imprisonment and/or execution at the hands of the Myanmar army. Unocal's financial size and determination to complete certain projects at any cost compelled the Myanmar government to sanction the use of forced labor.[55] Years later, Unocal announced that it had reached a final settlement with the parties regarding several lawsuits related to the company's investment through subsidiaries in the Yadana natural gas pipeline project. The court documents have been sealed.

> *"In some instances, MNCs have controlled entire cultures and countries."*

Critics believe that the size and power of MNCs create ethical issues involving the exploitation of both natural and human resources. One question is whether MNCs should be able to pay a low price for the right to remove minerals, timber, oil, and other natural resources and then sell products made from those resources for a much higher price. In many instances, only a small fraction of the ultimate sale price of such resources comes back to benefit the country of origin. This complaint led many oil-producing countries to form the Organization of Petroleum Exporting Countries (OPEC) in the 1960s to gain control over the revenues from oil produced in those lands.

Critics also accuse MNCs of exploiting the labor markets of host countries. As conveyed in prior paragraphs, MNCs have been accused of paying inadequate wages. Sometimes MNCs pay higher wages than local employers can afford to match; then local businesses complain that the most productive and skilled workers go to work for multinationals. Measures have been taken to curtail such practices. For example, many MNCs are trying to help organize labor unions and establish minimum-wage laws. In addition, host governments have levied import taxes that increase the price that MNCs charge for their products and reduce their profits. Import taxes are meant to favor local industry as sources of supply for an MNC manufacturing in the host country. If such a tax raises the MNC's costs, it might lead the MNC to charge higher prices or accept lower profits, but such effects are not the fundamental goal of the law. Host governments have also imposed export taxes on MNCs to force them to share more of their profits.

The activities of MNCs may also raise issues of unfair competition. Because of their diversified nature, MNCs can borrow money from local capital resources in much higher volume than smaller local firms. MNCs have also been accused of failing to carry an appropriate share of the cost of social development. They frequently apply advanced, high-productivity technologies that local companies cannot afford or cannot implement because they lack qualified workers. The MNCs thus become more productive and can afford to pay higher wages to workers. Because of their technology, however, they require fewer employees than the local firms would hire to produce the same product. And, given their economies of scale, MNCs can also negotiate lower tax rates. By manipulating transfer payments among their affiliates, they may pay little tax anywhere. All these special advantages explain why some claim that MNCs compete unfairly. For example, many heavy-equipment companies in the United States try to sell construction equipment to foreign companies that build major roads, dams, and utility complexes. They argue that this equipment will make it possible to complete these projects sooner, thus benefiting the country. Some less-developed countries counter that such equipment purchases actually remove hard currency from their economies and increase unemployment. Certain nations, such as India, therefore believe that it is better in the long run to hire laborers to do construction work than to buy a piece of heavy equipment. The country keeps its hard currency in its economy and creates new jobs, which increases the quality of life more than does having a project completed sooner.

Although it is unethical or illegal conduct by MNCs that grabs world headlines, some MNCs also strive to be good global citizens with strong ethical values. Texas Instruments (TI), for example, has adopted a three-level global approach to ethical integrity that asks (1) Are we complying with all legal requirements on a local level? (2) Are there business practices or requirements at the local level which impact how we interact with co-workers in other parts of the world? and (3) Do some of our practices need to be adapted based on the local laws and customers of a specific locale? (4) On what basis do we define our universal standards that apply to TI employees everywhere? Texas Instruments generally follows conservative rules regarding the giving and receiving of gifts. However, what may be considered an excessive gift in the United States may be viewed differently according to the local customs of other parts of the world. Texas Instruments used to define gift limits in terms of U.S. dollars, but now it just specifies that gift-giving should not be used in a way that exerts undue pressure to win business or implies a quid pro quo.[56]

Many companies, including Coca-Cola, DuPont, Hewlett-Packard, Levi Strauss & Co., Texaco, and Wal-Mart, endorse following responsible business practices abroad. These companies support a globally based resource system called **Business for Social Responsibility** (BSR). BSR tracks emerging issues and trends, provides information on corporate leadership and best practices, conducts educational workshops and training, and assists organizations in developing practical business ethics tools. It addresses such issues as community investment, corporate social responsibility, the environment, governance, and accountability. BSR has also established formal partnerships with other organizations that focus on corporate responsibility in Brazil, Israel, the United Kingdom, Chile, and Panama.[57]

Although MNCs are not inherently unethical, their size and power often seem threatening to people and businesses in less-developed countries. The ethical problems that MNCs face arise from the opposing viewpoints inherent in multicultural situations. Differences in cultural perspectives may be as important as differences in economic interests. Because of their size and power, MNCs must therefore take extra care to make ethical decisions that not only achieve their own objectives but also benefit the countries where they manufacture or market their products. Even the most respected MNCs sometimes find themselves in ethical conflict and face liability as a result.

The American model of the MNC, exported throughout the world by the United States, is fading as developing countries such as China, India, Brazil, and South Korea form

MNCs as alliances, joint ventures, and wholly-owned subsidiaries.[58] The turn away from the American model does not mean less concern for ethics and social responsibility. As corporations expand internationally, ethics and social responsibility are important firm-specific capabilities that can be a resource and lend a company an advantage for future growth and profits. The development of trust and corporate citizenship is a necessary capability like technology or marketing. A number of Chinese businesses, for example, have learned that long-term success cannot be achieved by selling products that are unsafe or of inferior quality. Ethical and responsible business conduct is a requirement for long-term success in global business.

SUMMARY

In this chapter we have tried to sensitize you to why some basic assumptions are being questioned. The spark that ignited the questioning was the global financial meltdown. The world is a highly interconnected system, but with little transparency in decision making, lack of accountability, and unreliable accounting methods it became flammable. The set of assumptions used were rational economics. Starting with Adam Smith, then to Keynes, and then Friedman economics assumed (1) People have rational preferences among outcomes that can be identified and associated with a value; (2) Individuals maximize utility and firms maximize profits; (3) People act independently on the basis of full and relevant information. Capitalism bases its models on these assumptions. Then behavioral economics argued humans may not act rational because of genetics, learned behavior, and heuristics or rules of thumb. In addition, behavioral economics states that the way something is presented to a consumer can also affect choice.

A basic question in business ethics is whether there is a set of common values. We explained that there are. The first is global common values that are found within the major world religions; the second is country common values that are specific to groups, sects, regions, or countries that express actions, behavior, and intent. In general integrity, family and community unity, equality, honesty, fidelity, sharing, and unselfishness are globally shared. Some operationalize these in business to be honesty, charity, virtue, and beneficence. Although universally desirable qualities, in business they can raise ethical issues in that they may not maximize profits.

We explained some of the major global ethical issues such as consumerism, human rights, health care, labor, and sustainable development. Consumerism is the belief that consumers should dictate the economic structure of a society, rather than the interests of producers. It refers to the theory that an increasing consumption of goods is economically desirable and equates personal happiness with the purchase and consumption of material possessions. The United Nations has codified human rights as an inherent dignity with equal and inalienable rights as the foundation of freedom, justice, and peace in the world. Global businesses may think the articles in this code are easily understood, but as explained they can become very problematic in their business implantation. Health care and labor were explained globally to help understand that when different cultures and laws interact, business practices and their assumptions can cause unethical and illegal consequences.

Sustainable development's argument is that human consumption is occurring at a rate beyond Earth's capacity to support it. These systems would be overwhelmed if all of the Earth's inhabitants were to match the consumption patterns of wealthier nations. Sustainable development requires alterations in the lifestyle of the wealthy to live within the carrying capacity of the environment. The premise is based on population growth and equal wealth distribution.

Global entities, such as the World Trade Organization, are in the process of redefining themselves in relation to the new global environment. Ethics in the twenty-first century has taken on a new importance and is seen as critical to the economic sustainability of corporations and countries. Business reality in the twenty-first century is filled with international organizations that have more impact than before. Our interconnectedness via business demands transparency both from governments and multinationals. As has been discussed in this chapter, multinationals can and will fill leadership vacuums within governments. The new reality for both is that ethics is real and both entities will face global scrutiny from the global consumer and citizen. It is up to you to determine our economic future.

Multinationals (MNCs) represent the highest level of international business commitment and are characterized by a global strategy of focusing on opportunities throughout the world. Multinational corporations operate on a global scale without significant ties to any one nation or region. Because of their size and financial power, MNCs can have a serious impact on the countries where they do business, which may create ethical issues.

IMPORTANT TERMS FOR REVIEW

global business
risk compartmentalization
Adam Smith
laissez-faire
John Maynard Keynes
Milton Friedman
socialism
social democracy
bimodal wealth distribution
rational economics
behavioral economics
framing effect
global common values
country cultural values
culture
amakudari
self-reference criterion
dumping
cultural relativism
consumerism
made-to-break
human rights
sustainable development
International Monetary Fund
World Trade Organization
multinational corporation
Business for Social Responsibility

RESOLVING ETHICAL BUSINESS CHALLENGES*

George Wilson, the operations manager of the CornCo plant in Phoenix, Arizona, has a dilemma. He is in charge of buying corn and producing chips marketed by CornCo in the United States and elsewhere. Several months ago, George's supervisor, CornCo's vice president Jake Lamont, called to tell him that corn futures were on the rise, which would ultimately increase the overall costs of production. In addition, a new company called Abco Snack Foods had begun marketing corn chips at competitive prices in CornCo's market area. Abco had already shown signs of eroding CornCo's market share. Jake was concerned that George's production costs would not be competitive with

Abco's—hence, profitability would decline. Jake had already asked George to find ways to cut costs. If he couldn't, Jake said, then layoffs would begin.

George scoured the Midwest looking for cheap corn and finally found some. But when the railcars started coming in, one of the company's testers reported the presence of aflatoxin—a naturally occurring carcinogen that induces liver cancer in lab animals. Once corn has been ground into corn meal, however, the aflatoxin is virtually impossible to detect. George knew that by blending the contaminated corn with uncontaminated corn he could reduce the aflatoxin concentrations in the final product, which, he had heard, other managers sometimes did. According to U.S. law, corn contaminated with aflatoxin cannot be used for edible products sold in the United States, and fines are to be imposed for such use. So far, no one has been convicted. No law, however, prohibits shipping the contaminated corn to other countries.

George knows that, because of his competitors' prices, if he doesn't sell the contaminated corn his production costs will be too high. When he spoke to Jake, Jake's response was, "So how much of the corn coming in is contaminated?"

"It's about 10 percent," replied George. "They probably knew that the corn was contaminated. That's why we're getting such good deals on it."

Jake thought for a moment and said, "George, call the suspected grain elevators, complain to them, and demand a 50 percent discount. If they agree, buy all they have."

"But if we do, the blends will just increase in contamination!" said George.

"That's OK. When the blends start getting high, we'll stop shipping into the U.S. market and go foreign," Jake told him. "Remember, there are no fines for contaminated corn in Mexico."

George learned that one other person, Lee Garcia, an operations manager for the breakfast cereals division, had sold the contaminated corn once.

"Yeah, so what about it? I've got a family to support and house payments. For me there was no alternative. I had to do it or face getting laid off," Lee said.

As George thought about the problem, word spread about his alternatives. The following notes appeared in the plant suggestion box:

Use the corn or we all get laid off!

Process it and ship it off to Mexico!

It's just wrong to use this corn!

When George balked at Jake's proposed solution, Jake said, "George, I understand your situation. I was there once—just like you. But you've got to look at the bigger picture. Hundreds of workers would be out of a job. Sure, the FDA [Food and Drug Administration] says that aflatoxin is bad, but we're talking rats eating their weight in this stuff. What if it does get detected—so what? The company gets a fine, the FDA tester gets reprimanded for screwing up, and it's back to business as usual."

"Is that all that will happen?" asked George.

"Of course, don't worry," replied Jake.

But George's signature, not Jake's, was on the receipts for the contaminated railcars. "So if I do this, at what aflatoxin percentage do I stop, and will you sign off on this?" asked George.

"Look," said Jake, "that's up to you. Remember that the more corn chips that are produced for the U.S. market, the more profit the company gets and the higher your bonus. As for me signing off on this, I'm shocked that you would even suggest something like that. George, you're the operations manager. You're the one who's responsible for what happens at the plant. It just isn't done that way at CornCo. But whatever you do, you had better do it in the next several hours because, as I see it, the contaminated corn has to be blended with something, and the longer you wait, the higher the percentages will get."

QUESTIONS • EXERCISES

1. Discuss the corporate ethical issue of providing questionable products to other markets.
2. Discuss the suggestions submitted in the suggestion box in light of the decision that George must make. Should the suggestions have an influence?
3. Identify the pressures that have caused the ethical and legal issues in this scenario to arise.

*This case is strictly hypothetical; any resemblance to real persons, companies, or situations is coincidental.

CHECK YOUR EQ

Check your EQ, or Ethics Quotient, by completing the following. Assess your performance to evaluate your overall understanding of the chapter material.

1. Most countries have a strong orientation toward ethical compliance or laws. **Yes No**
2. The self-reference criterion is an unconscious reference to one's own cultural values, experience, and knowledge. **Yes No**
3. One of the critical ethical business issues linked to cultural differences is the question of whose values and ethical standards take precedence during international negotiations and business transactions. **Yes No**
4. Multinational corporations have identifiable home countries but operate globally. **Yes No**
5. Certain facilitating payments are acceptable under the Foreign Corrupt Practices Act. **Yes No**

ANSWERS **1. No.** That's an ethnocentric perspective; in other countries laws may be viewed more situationally. **2. Yes.** We react based on what we have experienced over our lifetimes. **3. Yes.** Ethical standards and values differ from culture to culture, and this can be a critical point in effective business negotiations. Some people believe in cultural relativism, which means that the standards of the host country hold sway. However, many MNCs are legally bound to adhere to the standards of the host country. **4. No.** Multinational corporations have no significant ties to any nation or region. **5. Yes.** A violation of the FCPA occurs when the payments are excessive or are used to persuade the recipients to perform other than normal duties.

PART 5

Daryl Benson

CASES

CASE 1

Monsanto Attempts to Balance Stakeholder Interests

Daryl Benson

Think Monsanto, and you probably do not think about small farms. Rather, the phrase *genetically modified* likely comes to mind. The Monsanto Company is the world's largest seed company, with sales of over $8.6 billion. It specializes in biotechnology, or the genetic manipulation of organisms. Monsanto scientists have spent the last few decades modifying crops, often by inserting new genes or adapting existing genes within plant seeds, to better meet certain aims such as higher yield or insect resistance. Monsanto produces plants that can survive weeks of drought, ward off weeds, and kill invasive insects. Monsanto's genetically modified (GM) seeds have increased the quantity and availability of crops, helping farmers worldwide increase food production and revenues.

Today, 90 percent of the world's GM seeds are sold by Monsanto or by companies that use Monsanto genes. Monsanto also holds 70–100 percent market share on certain crops. Yet Monsanto has met with its share of criticism from sources as diverse as governments, farmers, activists, and advocacy groups. Monsanto supporters say it is creating solutions to world hunger by generating higher crop yields and hardier plants. Critics accuse the multinational giant of trying to take over the world's food supply, and destroying biodiversity. Since biotechnology is relatively new, they also express concerns about the possibility of negative health and environmental effects from biotech food. However, such criticisms have not deterred Monsanto from becoming one of the world's most successful companies.

The following analysis first looks at the history of Monsanto as it progressed from a chemical company to an organization focused on biotechnology, and then examines Monsanto's current focus on developing genetically modified seeds, including stakeholder concerns regarding the safety and environmental effects of these seeds. The controversy surrounding the drug Posilac is also examined. Next, some ethical concerns, including organizational misconduct and patent issues, are discussed. The analysis also looks at

Jennifer Sawayda, under the direction of O.C. Ferrell and Jennifer Jackson, prepared this case for classroom discussion, rather than to illustrate either effective or ineffective handling of an administrative, ethical, or legal decision by management. All sources used for this case were obtained through publicly available material.

some of Monsanto's corporate responsibility initiatives. It concludes by examining the challenges and opportunities Monsanto may face in the future.

HISTORY: FROM CHEMICALS TO FOOD

The original Monsanto was very different from the current company. It was started by John F. Queeny in 1901 in St. Louis and was named after his wife, Olga Monsanto Queeny. The company started making artificial food additives. Its first product was the artificial sweetener saccharine, which it sold to Coca-Cola. Monsanto followed by selling Coca-Cola caffeine extract and vanillin, an artificial vanilla flavoring. At the start of WWI, company leaders realized the growth opportunities in the industrial chemicals industry and renamed the company The Monsanto Chemical Company. The company began specializing in plastics, its own agricultural chemicals, and synthetic rubbers.

Due to its expanding product lines, Monsanto was renamed again the Monsanto Company in 1964. By this time, Monsanto was producing such diverse products as petroleum, fibers, and packaging. A couple years later, Monsanto created its first Roundup herbicide, a successful product that would propel the company even more into the public's consciousness.

However, during the 1970s, Monsanto hit a major legal snare. The company had produced a chemical known as Agent Orange that was used during the Vietnam War to quickly deforest the thick Vietnamese jungles. Agent Orange contained dioxin, a chemical that caused a legal nightmare for Monsanto. Dioxin was found to be extremely carcinogenic, and in 1979, a lawsuit was filed against Monsanto on behalf of hundreds of veterans who claimed they were harmed by the chemical. Monsanto and several other manufacturers agreed to settle for $180 million. The repercussions of dioxin would continue to plague the company for decades.

In 1981, Monsanto leaders determined that biotechnology would be the company's new strategic focus. The quest for biotechnology was on, and in 1994 Monsanto introduced the first biotechnology product to win regulatory approval. Soon the company was selling soybean, cotton, and canola seeds that were engineered to be tolerant to Monsanto's Roundup Ready herbicide. Many other herbicides killed the good plants as well as the bad ones. Roundup Ready seeds allowed farmers to use the herbicide to eliminate weeds while sparing the crop.

In 1997, Monsanto spun off its chemical business as Solutia, and in 2000 the company entered into a merger and changed its name to the Pharmacia Corporation. Two years later, a new Monsanto, focused entirely on agriculture, broke off from Pharmacia, and the companies became two separate legal entities. The company before 2000 is often referred to as "old Monsanto," while today's company is known as "new Monsanto."

The emergence of new Monsanto was tainted by some disturbing news about the company's conduct. It was revealed that Monsanto had been covering up decades of environmental pollution. For nearly forty years, the Monsanto Company had released toxic waste into a creek in an Alabama town called Anniston. It had also disposed of polychlorinated biphenyls (PCBs), a highly toxic chemical, in open-pit landfills in the area. The results were catastrophic. Fish from the creek were deformed, and the population had elevated PCB levels that astounded environmental health experts. A paper trail showed that Monsanto leaders had known about the pollution since the 1960s, but had not stopped production. Once the cover-up was discovered, thousands of plaintiffs from the city filed a lawsuit against the company. In 2003, Monsanto and Solutia agreed to pay a settlement of $700 million to more than 20,000 Anniston residents. However, no amount of money will give people back their health or the health of their environment.

When current CEO Hugh Grant took over in 2003, scandals and stakeholder uncertainty over Monsanto's GM products had tarnished the company's reputation. The price of Monsanto's stock had fallen by almost 50 percent, down to $8 a share. The company had lost $1.7 billion the previous year. Grant knew the company was fragile; yet through a strategic focus on GM foods, the company has recovered and is now prospering.

In spite of their controversial nature, GM foods have become popular both in developed and developing countries. Monsanto became so successful with its GM seeds that it acquired Seminis, Inc., a leader in the fruit and vegetable seed industry. The acquisition transformed Monsanto into a global leader in the seed industry. Today, Monsanto employs nearly 20,000 people in 160 countries. It has been recognized as the top employer in Argentina, Mexico, India, and, for eight times in a row, Brazil.

THE SEEDS OF CHANGE: MONSANTO'S EMPHASIS ON BIOTECHNOLOGY

> *"Approximately 282 million acres worldwide are now devoted to biotech crops."*

While the original Monsanto made a name for itself through the manufacturing of chemicals, new Monsanto took quite a different turn. It switched its emphasis from chemicals to food. Today's Monsanto owes its $8.6 billion in sales to biotechnology, specifically to its sales of genetically modified (GM) plant seeds. These seeds have revolutionized the agriculture industry.

Throughout history, weeds, insects, and drought have been the bane of the farmer's existence. In the past century, herbicides and pesticides were invented to ward off pests. Yet applying these chemicals to an entire crop was both costly and time-consuming. Then Monsanto scientists, through their work in biotechnology, were able to implant seeds with genes that make the plants themselves kill bugs. They also created seeds containing the herbicide Roundup Ready, an herbicide that kills weeds but spares the crops.

The broad introduction of these GM seeds in the 1990s unleashed a stream of criticism. Monsanto was nicknamed "Mutanto," and GM produce was called "Frankenfood." Critics believed that influencing the gene pools of plants we eat could result in negative health consequences, a fear that remains to this day. Others worried about the health effects on beneficial insects and plants. Could pollinating GM plants have an effect on nearby insects and non-GM plants? CEO Hugh Grant decided to curtail the tide of criticism by focusing biotechnology on products that would not be directly placed on the dinner plate, but instead on seeds that produce goods like animal feed and corn syrup. In this way, Grant was able to reduce some of the opposition. Today, the company invests largely in four crops: corn, cotton, soybeans, and canola.

Thus far, the dire predictions of critics have not occurred. Monsanto owes approximately 60 percent of its revenue to its work in GM seeds, and today, more than half of U.S. crops, including most soybeans and 70 percent of corn, are genetically modified. Approximately 282 million acres worldwide are now devoted to biotech crops, and the fastest growth is in developing countries. However, critics are wary that long-term effects still might be discovered.

Farmers who purchase GM seeds can now grow more crops on less land and with less left to chance. GM crops have saved farmers billions by preventing loss and increasing crop yields. For example, in 1970 the average corn harvest yielded approximately 70 bushels an acre. With the introduction of biotech crops, the average corn harvest has increased to roughly 150 bushels an acre. Monsanto predicts even higher yields in the future, possibly up to 300 bushels an acre by 2030. "As agricultural productivity increases, farmers are able to produce more food, feed, fuel, and fiber on the same amount of land, helping to ensure that agriculture can meet humanity's needs in the future," said Monsanto CEO Hugh Grant concerning Monsanto technology.

As a result of higher yields, the revenues of farmers in developing countries have increased dramatically. According to company statistics, the cotton yield of Indian farmers rose by 50 percent, doubling their income in one year. Additionally, the company claims that its insect-protected corn has raised the income level in the Philippines to above poverty level. Critics argue that these numbers are inflated; they say the cost of GM seeds is dramatically higher than that of traditional seeds, and therefore they actually reduce farmers' take-home profits.

Monsanto's GM seeds have not been accepted everywhere. Attempts to introduce them into Europe have been met with extreme consumer backlash. Consumers have gone so far as to destroy fields of GM crops and arrange sit-ins. Greenpeace has fought Monsanto for years, especially in the company's efforts to promote GM crops in developing countries. This animosity toward Monsanto's products is generated by two main concerns: worries about the safety of GM food, and concerns about the environmental effects.

Concerns About the Safety of GM Food

Of great concern for many stakeholders are the moral and safety implications of GM food. Many skeptics see biotech crops as unnatural, with the Monsanto scientist essentially "playing God" by controlling what goes into the seed. Also, because GM crops are relatively new, critics maintain that the health implications of biotech food may not be known for years to come.

They also contend that effective standards have not been created to determine the safety of biotech crops. Some geneticists believe the splicing of these genes into seeds could create small changes that might negatively impact the health of humans and animals that eat them. Also, even though the FDA has declared biotech crops safe, critics say they have not been around long enough to gauge their long-term effects.

One major health concern is the allergenicity of GM products. Critics fear that a lack of appropriate regulation could allow allergens to creep into the products. Another concern is toxicity, particularly considering that many Monsanto seeds are equipped with a gene to allow them to produce their own Roundup Ready herbicide. Could ingesting this herbicide, even in small amounts, cause detrimental effects on consumers? Some stakeholders say yes, and point to statistics on glyphosate, Roundup's chief ingredient, for support. According to an ecology center fact sheet, glyphosate exposure is the third most commonly reported illness among California agriculture workers, and glyphosate residues can last for a year. Yet the EPA lists glyphosate as having a low skin and oral toxicity, and a study from the New York Medical College states that Roundup does not create a health risk for humans.

Despite consumer concerns, the FDA has proclaimed that GM food is safe to consume. As a result, it also has determined that Americans do not need to know when they are consuming GM products. Thus, this information is not placed on labels in the United

States, although other countries, most notably Great Britain and the European Union, do require GM food products to state this fact in their labeling.

Bovine Growth Hormone Concerns. Monsanto has also come under scrutiny for its synthetic hormone Posilac, the brand name of a Monsanto drug that contains recombinant bovine growth hormone (rBST). This hormone is a supplement to the naturally occurring hormone BST in cows. Posilac causes cows to produce more milk, a boon to dairy farmers but a cause of concern to many stakeholders who fear that Posilac may cause health problems in cows and in the humans who drink their milk. After numerous tests, the FDA has found that milk from Posilac-treated cows is no different in terms of safety than milk from rBST-free cows. Yet these assurances have done little to alleviate stakeholder fears, especially since some studies maintain that rBST increases health problems in cows.

Public outcry from concerned consumers has become so loud that many grocery stores and restaurants have stopped purchasing rBST-treated milk. Starbucks, Kroger, Ben & Jerry's, and even Wal-Mart have responded to consumer demand by only using or selling rBST-free milk, which has put a damper on Monsanto's Posilac profits.

In the past few years, certain groups, including Monsanto, have fought back against the popularity of rBST-free milk. They maintain that consumers are being misled by implications that rBST-free milk is safer than rBST-treated milk. The grassroots organization AFACT, short for American Farmers for the Advancement and Conservation of Technology, has pressured the government to pass laws forbidding the use of labels that state that milk is free of rBST. Their efforts have been met with some support from legislators. In 2006, Pennsylvania senator and agriculture secretary Dennis Wolff tried to ban milk that was labeled as rBST-free, but stakeholder outrage prevented the law from being enforced. Instead, tighter restrictions on labels have been initiated. All rBST-free milk must now contain the following FDA claim: "No significant difference has been shown between milk derived from rBST-treated and non-rBST-treated cows."

Although Monsanto denies influencing AFACT in any way, many have accused the company of secretly governing the organization. Lori Hoag, spokeswoman for the dairy unit of Monsanto, admitted that the company did provide funds to AFACT, but says that the company has nothing to do with the governing decisions AFACT makes. In fact, on its website, Monsanto stresses that it has no problem with milk labels listed as rBST-free as long as the label contains the claim of the FDA. However, critics are still accusing Monsanto of being behind AFACT in what they say is an attempt to curtail the unpopularity of Posilac.

Concerns About Environmental Effects of Monsanto Products

Studies have supported the premise that Roundup herbicide, which is used in conjunction with the hearty GMO seeds called Roundup Ready, can be harmful to birds, insects, and particularly amphibians. Such studies have revealed that small concentrations of Roundup may be deadly to tadpoles, which is a major concern, as frog and toad species are rapidly disappearing around the globe. A test using Roundup, performed by University of Pittsburgh assistant professor of biological sciences Rick Relyea and his doctoral students, killed 71 percent of tadpoles in outdoor tanks at one-third the maximum concentrations found in nature. Relyea also maintains that soil does not lessen the herbicide's negative effects. Roundup was never approved for water use; however, Relyea and others fear that water runoff may carry Roundup into water sources.

Another concern with GM seeds in general is the threat of environmental contamination. Bumblebees, insects, and wind can carry a crop's seeds to other areas, sometimes to fields containing non-GM crops. These seeds and pollens might then mix in with the farmer's crops. In the past, organic farmers have complained that genetically modified seeds from nearby farms have "contaminated" their crops. This environmental contamination could pose a serious threat. Some scientists fear that GM seeds that are spread to native plants may cause those plants to adopt the GM trait, thus creating new genetic variations of those plants that could negatively influence (through genetic advantages) the surrounding ecosystem. Andrew Kimbrell, director of the Centre for Technology Assessment in Washington, predicts that "biological pollution will be the environmental nightmare of the twenty-first century."

Monsanto has not been silent on these issues and has acted to address some of these concerns. The company maintains that the environmental impact of everything it creates has been studied by the EPA and approved. Monsanto officials claim that glyphosate in Roundup Ready does not usually end up in ground water, and cites a study which revealed that less than 1 percent of glyphosate contaminates ground water through runoff. The company also claims that when it does contaminate ground water, it is soluble and will not have much effect on aquatic species. This conflicts with Relyea's study, leaving stakeholders unsure about what to believe.

> ***Some scientists fear that GM seeds that are spread to native plants may cause those plants to adopt the GM trait***

Crop Resistance to Pesticides and Herbicides. Another environmental problem that has emerged is the possibility of weed and insect resistance to the herbicides and pesticides on Monsanto crops. Critics fear that continual use of the chemicals could result in "super weeds" and "super bugs," much like overuse of antibiotics in humans has resulted in drug-resistant bacteria. The company's Roundup Ready line, in particular, has come under attack. Monsanto points out, and rightly so, that Roundup herbicide has been used for thirty years, largely without resistance issues. However, GMO plants labeled Roundup Ready are genetically engineered to withstand large doses of the herbicide Roundup. As Roundup is being used more frequently and exclusively because of the Roundup Ready plants' tolerance, even weeds have started developing a resistance to this popular herbicide. As early as 2003, significant numbers of Roundup resistant weeds had been found in the United States and Australia.

To combat "super bugs," the government requires farmers using Monsanto's GMO products to create "refuges," in which they plant 20 percent of their fields with a non-genetically modified crop. The theory is that this allows nonresistant bugs to mate with those that are resistant, preventing a new race of super bugs. To prevent resistance to the Roundup herbicide, farmers are supposed to vary herbicide use and practice crop rotations. However, since Roundup is so easy to use, particularly in conjunction with Roundup Ready seeds, many farmers do not take the time to institute these preventative measures. When they do rotate their crops, some will rotate one Roundup Ready crop with another type of Roundup Ready crop, which does little to solve the problem. This is of particular concern in Latin America, Africa, and Asia where farmers may not be as informed of the risks of herbicide and pesticide overuse.

Monsanto has taken action to deter weed herbicide resistance. In 2009, the company agreed to offer rebates, up to $12/acre, to farmers in thirteen states who use combinations of herbicides on their crops. Monsanto is offering rebates on six of the products, only one of which is a Monsanto product. The company is taking a proactive stance to show that it cares about preventing resistance; however, this does little to stem what might become a global problem.

DEALING WITH ORGANIZATIONAL ETHICAL ISSUES

In addition to concerns over the safety of GM seeds and environmental issues, Monsanto has had to deal with concerns about organizational conduct. Organizations face significant risks from strategies and also from employees striving for high performance standards. Such pressure sometimes encourages employees to engage in illegal or unethical conduct. All firms have these concerns, and in the case of Monsanto, bribes and patents have resulted in legal, ethical, and reputational consequences.

Bribery Issues

Bribery presents a dilemma to multinational corporations because different countries have different perspectives on it. While it is illegal in the United States, other countries allow it. Monsanto faced such a problem with Indonesia, and its actions resulted in the company being fined a large sum.

In 2002, a senior manager at Monsanto instructed an Indonesian consulting firm to pay a bribe of $50,000 to a high-level official in the country's environment ministry. The bribe apparently was for the company to disguise an invoice, which showed that Monsanto was facing opposition from farmers and activists in regard to the introduction of GM cotton in Indonesia.

It was later revealed that such bribery was not an isolated event; the company had paid off many officials between 1997 and 2002. Monsanto first became aware of the problem after discovering some irregularities at their Indonesian subsidiary in 2001. As a result, the company launched an internal investigation and reported the bribery to the U.S. Department of Justice and the Securities and Exchange Commission (SEC).

Monsanto accepted full responsibility for its employees' behavior and agreed to pay $1 million to the Department of Justice and $500,000 to the SEC. It also agreed to three years of close monitoring of its activities by American authorities. The incident showed that although Monsanto has not been immune to scandals, it has been willing to work with authorities to correct them.

Patent Issues

Like most businesses, Monsanto wants to patent its products. A problem arises, however, when it comes to patenting seeds. As bioengineered creations of the Monsanto Company,

Monsanto's seeds are protected under patent law. Under the terms of the patent, farmers using Monsanto seeds are not allowed to harvest seeds from the plants for use in upcoming seasons. Instead, they must purchase new Monsanto seeds each season. By issuing new seeds each year, Monsanto ensures it will secure a profit as well as maintain control over its property.

Unfortunately, this is a new concept for most farmers. Throughout agricultural history, farmers have collected and saved seeds from previous harvests to plant the following year's crops. Critics argue that requiring farmers to suddenly purchase new seeds year after year puts an undue financial burden on them and allows Monsanto too much power. However, the law protects Monsanto's right to have exclusive control over its creations, and farmers must abide by these laws. When they are found guilty of using Monsanto seeds from previous seasons, either deliberately or out of ignorance, they are often fined.

Since it is fairly easy for farmers to violate the patent, Monsanto has found it necessary to employ investigators from law firms to investigate suspected violations. The resulting investigations are a source of contention between Monsanto and accused farmers. According to Monsanto, investigators approach the farmers suspected of patent infringement and ask them some questions. The investigators must practice transparency with the farmers and tell them why they are there and who they represent. If after the initial interview is completed, suspicions still exist, the investigators may pull the farmer's records (after assuring the farmer they will do so in a respectful manner). Sometimes they bring in a sampling team, with the farmer's permission, to test the farmer's fields. If found guilty, the farmer often has to pay Monsanto. According to Monsanto, in the past ten years, it has only filed suit against farmers 120 times, and only eight of these suits have proceeded to trial. Each time the ruling was in Monsanto's favor.

> ***Farmers using Monsanto seeds are not allowed to harvest seeds from the plants for use in upcoming seasons.***

Some farmers, on the other hand, tell a different story about Monsanto and its seed investigators, calling the investigators the "seed police" and even referring to them with such harsh words as "Gestapo" or "mafia." One controversial suit was a case involving storeowner Gary Rinehart from Missouri. As Rinehart relates it, a Monsanto seed investigator entered his store and accused him of saving seeds from previous seasons. The investigator then threatened him with a suit if he did not settle. The company filed suit but eventually found it had the wrong man. Monsanto dropped the suit against him but never apologized. Rinehart also claims the investigators were inspecting other farmers in the area. Other complaints against investigators include similar acts of intimidation, with some farmers even going so far as to accuse investigators of following them and secretly videotaping them.

Such accusations are disturbing, but Monsanto has countered them with its own stories. It claims that Rinehart refused to cooperate and became irate, finally throwing the investigators out of his store. Monsanto filed suit, but eventually found that it was Rinehart's nephew who was transporting the saved seed. The company dropped the suit against Rinehart, and the nephew eventually agreed to settle. According to their website, the nephew still has not paid the settlement.

In order to prevent so many instances of patent infringement, some have suggested that Monsanto make use of GURT, or gene use restriction technology. This technology would let Monsanto create "sterile" seeds. Dubbed by stakeholders as "Terminator seeds," these seeds have several risks and have spurred much controversy among the public, including a concern that these sterile seeds might somehow get transported to other plants, which could create sterile plants that would reduce genetic diversity. In 1999, Monsanto pledged not to commercialize sterile seed technology in food crops. The company has promised that it will only do so in the future after consulting with experts, stakeholders, and relevant NGOs.

CORPORATE RESPONSIBILITY AT MONSANTO

It is a common expectation today for multinational companies to take actions to advance the interests and well-being of the people in the countries in which they do business. Monsanto is no exception. The company has given millions of dollars in programs to help improve the communities in developing countries. In fact, *Corporate Responsibility Magazine* ranked Monsanto number 20 on its 100 Best Corporate Citizens list of 2009, a jump from number 88 the previous year.

In addition, as an agricultural company, Monsanto must address the grim reality facing the world in the future: The world's population is increasing at a fast rate, and the amount of available land and water for agriculture is decreasing. Some experts believe that our planet will have to produce more food in the next 50 years to feed the world's population than it has grown in the past 10,000 years, requiring us to double our food output. As a multinational corporation dedicated to agriculture, Monsanto is expected to address these problems. In fiscal year 2008, the company expended $980 million for researching new farmer tools. The company has also developed a three-tiered commitment policy: (1) produce more yield in crops, (2) conserve more resources, and (3) improve the lives of farmers. The company hopes to achieve these goals by taking some initiatives in sustainable agriculture.

Sustainable Agriculture

> *Agriculture intersects the toughest challenges we all face on the planet. Together, we must meet the needs for increased food, fiber and energy while protecting the environment. In short, the world needs to produce more and conserve smarter.*

This quote by Monsanto CEO Hugh Grant demonstrates the challenges agriculture is facing today, along with Monsanto's goals to meet these challenges head-on. For instance, Monsanto is quick to point out that its biotech products added more than 100 million tons to worldwide agriculture production between 1996 and 2006, which they estimate has increased farmer's incomes by $33.8 billion. Monsanto has also created partnerships between nonprofit organizations across the world to enrich the lives of farmers in developing countries. Two regions on which Monsanto is focusing are India and Africa.

The need for better agriculture is apparent in India, where the population is estimated to hit 1.3 billion by 2017. Biotech crops have helped to improve the size of yields in India, allowing some biotech farmers to increase their yields by 50 percent. Monsanto estimates that cotton farmers in India using biotech crops earn approximately $176 more in revenues per acre than their non-biotech contemporaries. In February 2009, Monsanto announced that it would launch Project SHARE, a sustainable yield initiative done in conjunction with the nonprofit Indian Society of Agribusiness, to try and improve the lives of 10,000 cotton farmers in 1,100 villages.

In Africa, Monsanto has helped many farmers prosper and thrive through difficult periods. For example, in 2007 the government of Malawi provided farmers with vouchers worth about $3 each, which farmers could exchange for Monsanto seeds. Some of the farmers using these seeds saw their crop yields increase from a few bags to hundreds. Monsanto has also provided help to Project Malawi, a program to improve food security and health care to thousands of Malawians. Monsanto has provided the program with hybrid maize seed and has sent experts from the company to provide training for farmers in how to use the seed. Additionally, the large seed company has agreed to donate 240 tons of hybrid corn seed through 2010 to villages in Malawi, Tanzania, and Kenya. The goal of Monsanto is to improve farmers' lives in a way that will help them become self-sufficient.

Not all view Monsanto's presence in Africa as an outreach in corporate responsibility. Some see it as another way for Monsanto to improve the bottom line. Critics see the company as trying to take control of African agriculture and destroy African agricultural practices that have lasted for thousands of years. Yet, despite this criticism, there is no denying that Monsanto has positively affected African farmers' lives, along with increasing the company's profits for its shareholders. As CEO Hugh Grant writes, "This initiative isn't simply altruistic; we see it as a unique business proposition that rewards farmers and shareowners."

Charitable Giving

In 1964, the Monsanto Company established the Monsanto Fund. Much of the Monsanto Fund's contributions fund the company's projects in Africa. In 2006, the Fund awarded a $15 million gift to the Donald Danforth Plant Science Center, which will help to support crop research in Africa. Other projects of the Fund include the "Healthy Children, Healthy Future" program, which seeks to reduce diseases in Brazilian children through education on good health and basic hygiene, and the funding of the Monsanto Insectarium at the St. Louis Zoo.

The Monsanto Company also supports youth programs. In the first decade of the twenty-first century, the company donated nearly $1.5 million in scholarships to students who want to pursue agriculture-related degrees. The company also supports Future Farmers of America, the 4-H program, and the program Farm Safety 4 Just Kids, a program which helps teach rural children about safety while working on farms.

THE FUTURE OF MONSANTO

Monsanto faces some challenges that it needs to address, including lingering concerns over the safety and the environmental impact of its products. The company needs to enforce its code of ethics effectively to avoid organizational misconduct (like bribery) in the future. Monsanto also may be facing increased competition from other companies. The seed company Pioneer Hi-Bred International Inc. is using pricing strategies and seed sampling to attract price-conscious customers. Additionally, lower grain prices may convince farmers to switch from Monsanto to less expensive brands.

Yet, despite the onslaught of criticism from Monsanto detractors and the challenge of increased competition from other companies, Monsanto has numerous opportunities to thrive in the future. The company is currently working on new innovations that could increase its competitive edge as well as provide enormous benefits to farmers worldwide.

In 2009, the company announced that it had finished regulatory submissions for the planet's first biotech drought-tolerant corn. This corn could be a major boon to farmers in areas where drought is prevalent. Monsanto is also working with the African Agriculture Technology Foundation to bring drought-resistant technology to Africa (without having them pay royalties).

Although Monsanto has made ethical errors in the past, it is trying to portray itself as a socially responsible company dedicated to improving agriculture. As noted, the company still has some problems. The predictions from Monsanto critics about biotech food have not yet come true, but that has not totally eradicated the fears of stakeholders. With the increasing popularity of organic food and staunch criticism from opponents, Monsanto will need to continue working with stakeholders to promote its technological innovations and to eliminate fears concerning its industry.

QUESTIONS

1. Does Monsanto maintain an ethical culture that can effectively respond to various stakeholders?
2. Compare the benefits of growing GMO seeds for crops with the potential negative consequences of using them.
3. How should Monsanto manage the potential harm to plant and animal life from using products such as Roundup?

SOURCES

"Agriculture Scholarships," Monsanto, http://www.monsanto.com/responsibility/youth/scholarship.asp (accessed April 1, 2009); "Backgrounder: Glyphosate and Environmental Fate Studies," Monsanto, 2005, http://www.monsanto.com/monsanto/content/products/productivity/roundup/gly_efate_bkg.pdf (accessed April 1, 2009); Barlett, Donald L., and James B. Steele, "Monsanto's Harvest of Fear," May 5, 2008, Vanity Fair, http://www.vanityfair.com/politics/features/2008/05/monsanto200805 (accessed August 25, 2009); "Biotech Cotton Improving Lives of Farmers, Villages in India." Monsanto, http://www.monsanto.com/responsibility/sustainable-ag/biotech_cotton_india.asp (accessed March 31, 2009); "Corporate Profile," Monsanto, http://www.monsanto.com/investors/corporate_profile.asp (accessed March 15, 2009); Environmental Protection Agency, "R.E.D. Facts," September 1993, http://www.epa.gov/oppsrrd1/REDs/factsheets/0178fact.pdf (accessed April 1, 2009); Etter, Lauren, and Rebecca Townsend, "Monsanto's Profits Shoot Higher," January 8, 2009; Etter, Lauren, and Rebecca Townsend, "Monsanto: Winning the Ground War," *BusinessWeek*, pp. 35–41; "Even Small Doses of Popular Weed Killer Fatal to Frogs, Scientist Finds," *ScienceDaily*, August 5, 2005, http://www.sciencedaily.com/releases/2005/08/050804053212.htm (accessed March 24, 2009); "Farm Safety 4 Just Kids," Monsanto, http://www.monsanto.com/responsibility/youth/fs4jk.asp (accessed April 1, 2009); "Follow-Up to Monsanto Lawsuits," Monsanto, http://www.monsanto.com/monsanto_today/for_the_record/monsanto_farmer_lawsuits_followup.asp (accessed March 30, 2009); Gibson, Ellen, "Monsanto," *BusinessWeek*, December 22, 2008, p. 51; "GMOs Under a Microscope," Science & Technology in Congress, October 1999, http://www.aaas.org/spp/cstc/pne/pubs/stc/bulletin/articles/10-99/GMOs.htm (accessed March 25, 2009); "Great Place to Work," Monsanto, http://www.monsanto.com/careers/culture/great_place.asp (accessed April 2009); "Growing Hope in Africa," Monsanto, http://www.monsanto.com/responsibility/our_pledge/stronger_society/growing_self_sufficiency.asp (accessed March 31, 2009); Grunwald, Michael, "Monsanto Hid Decades of Pollution," *Washington Post,* January 1, 2002, p. A1; "Healthy Children, Healthy Future Project—Brazil," Monsanto Fund, http://www.monsantofund.org/asp/pop_ups/BRAZIL_HealthyChildren_Project.asp (accessed April 1, 2009); "Is Monsanto Going to Develop or Sell 'Terminator' Seeds?," Monsanto, http://www.monsanto.com/monsanto_today/for_the_record/monsanto_terminator_seeds.asp (accessed March 28, 2009); Martin, Andrew, "Fighting on a Battlefield the Size of a Milk Label," *New York Times,* March 9, 2008, http://www.nytimes.com/2008/03/09/business/09feed.html?ex=1362805200&en=56197f6ee92b4643&ei=5124&partner=permalink&exprod=permalink (accessed March 2, 1999); "Milk Labeling—Is Monsanto Opposed to Truth in Labeling?," Monsanto, http://www.monsanto.com/monsanto_today/for_the_record/rbst_milk_labeling.asp (accessed March 2, 2009); "Monsanto & NGO ISAP Launch Project Share—Sustainable Yield Initiative to Improve Farmer Lives," Monsanto, http://monsanto.mediaroom.com/index.php?s=43&item=693 (accessed March 31, 2009); "Monsanto Company—Company Profile, Information, Business Description, History, Background Information on Monsanto Company," http://www.referenceforbusiness.com/history2/92/Monsanto-Company.html (accessed March 20, 2009); "Monsanto Completes Regulatory Submissions in U.S. and Canada for World's First Biotech Drought-Tolerant Corn Product," Monsanto, March 9, 2009, http://monsanto.mediaroom.com/index.php?s=43&item=695 (accessed April 1, 2009); "Monsanto Expanding Residual Herbicide Rebates," *Delta Farm Press,* January 12, 2009, http://deltafarmpress.com/cotton/herbicide-rebates-0112/ (accessed March 2, 2009); "Monsanto Fined $1.5M for Bribery," *BBC News,* January 7, 2005, http://news.bbc.co.uk/2/hi/business/4153635.stm (accessed March 15, 2009); "Monsanto Fund," Monsanto Fund, http://www.monsantofund.org/asp/About_the_Fund/Main_Menu.asp (accessed April 1, 2009); "Monsanto Mania: The Seed of Profits," *iStockAnalyst,* http://www.istockanalyst.com/article/viewarticle.aspx?articleid=1235584&zoneid=Home (accessed April 12, 2009); Oxborrow, Claire, Becky Price, and Peter Riley, "Breaking Free," *Ecologist* 38, no. 9 (November 2008): 35–36; "Phinizy Swamp Nature Park," Monsanto Fund, http://www.monsantofund.org/asp/Priorities/pop_ups/science.asp (accessed April 1, 2009); Pollack, Andrew, "So What's the Problem with Roundup?" Ecology Center, January 14, 2003, http://www.ecologycenter.org/factsheets/roundup.html (accessed March 25, 2009); Pollan, Michael, "Playing God in the Garden," *New York Times Magazine,* October 25, 1998, http://www.michaelpollan.com/article.php?id=73; "Produce More," Monsanto, http://www.monsanto.com/responsibility/sustainable-ag/produce_more.asp (accessed April 1, 2009); "Report on Animal Welfare Aspects of the Use of Bovine Sematotrophin," Report of the Scientific Committee on Animal Health and Animal Welfare, March 10, 1999, http://ec.europa.eu/food/fs/sc/scah/out21_en.pdf (accessed August 25, 2009); "Seed Police?," Monsanto, http://www.monsanto.com/seedpatentprotection/monsanto_seed_police.asp (accessed March 30, 2009); "$700 Million Settlement in Alabama PCB Lawsuit," *New York Times,* August 21, 2001, http://www.nytimes.com/2003/08/21/business/700-million-settlement-in-alabama-pcb-lawsuit.html (accessed March 15, 2009); Weintraub, Arlene, "The Outcry over 'Terminator' Genes in Food," *BusinessWeek,* July 14, 2003, http://www.businessweek.com/magazine/content/03_28/b3841091.htm (accessed March 25, 2009); "Widely Used Crop Herbicide Is Losing Weed Resistance," *New York Times,* January 14, 2003, http://www.nytimes.com/2003/01/14/business/widely-used-crop-herbicide-is-losing-weed-resistance.html (accessed August 25, 2009); Williams, G. M., R. Kroes, and I. C. Monro, "Safety Evaluation and Risk Assessment of the Herbicide Roundup and Its Active Ingredient, Glyphosate, for Humans," NCBI, April 2000, http://www.ncbi.nlm.nih.gov/pubmed/10854122 (accessed April 1, 2009).

CASE 2

Wal-Mart: The Future Is Sustainability

Daryl Benson

Wal-Mart Stores, Inc., is an icon of American business. From small-town business to multinational, from hugely controversial to a leader in renewable energy, Wal-Mart has long been a lightning rod for news and criticism. With 2008 sales of over $405.6 billion and more than two million employees worldwide, the world's largest public corporation must carefully manage many different stakeholder relationships. It is a challenge that has sparked significant debate.

Although Wal-Mart reportedly can save the average family $3,200 annually, the company has historically received plenty of criticism regarding its treatment of employees, suppliers, and economic impacts on communities. Feminists, activists, and labor union leaders have all voiced their beliefs that Wal-Mart has engaged in misconduct in order to provide low prices. However, Wal-Mart has been turning over a new leaf. New emphases on diversity, charitable giving, and sustainability have contributed to Wal-Mart's revitalized image.

The story of Wal-Mart and its low prices includes both positive and negative impacts on society. Positively, Wal-Mart reportedly saves consumers over $287 billion annually, equating to about $950 per person. On the flip side, research shows that communities can be negatively impacted by Wal-Mart's arrival in their areas.

This analysis attempts to show both sides of the controversy. It begins by briefly examining the growth of Wal-Mart, and then discusses Wal-Mart's various relationships with its stakeholders, including competitors, suppliers, and employees. Some of the ethical issues concerning these stakeholders include accusations of discrimination, illegal immigration issues, and leadership misconduct as demonstrated by Wal-Mart former vice chair Thomas Coughlin. Yet, in an effort to show Wal-Mart's attempts to position itself as a socially responsible company, this case also examines Wal-Mart's sustainability plans,

This case was prepared by O.C. Ferrell, with the editorial assistance of Jennifer Jackson and Jennifer Sawayda. Melanie Drever, Lisa Heldt, Tabitha Payton, and Rob Boostrom made significant contributions to previous editions of this case, which was prepared for classroom discussion, rather than to illustrate either effective or ineffective handling of an administrative, ethical, or legal decision by management. All sources used for this case were obtained through publicly available material and the Wal-Mart website.

its ethical initiatives, and former CEO Lee Scott's impressive leadership qualities. The analysis concludes by highlighting Wal-Mart's strategy during the most recent recession and recovery.

HISTORY: THE GROWTH OF WAL-MART

The story of Wal-Mart began in 1962, when founder Sam Walton opened the first Wal-Mart Discount Store in Rogers, Arkansas. Although it had a slow start due to lack of funds, Wal-Mart grew at an accelerated rate during the next forty years. The company grew from a small chain to more than 7,000 facilities in thirteen countries. In 2008 Wal-Mart opened its 3,000th international store. Only Exxon Mobil had more revenue than Wal-Mart did in 2008. The company now serves more than 176 million customers per year.

Much of the success that Wal-Mart has experienced can be attributed to its founder. A shrewd businessman, Walton believed in customer satisfaction and hard work. He convinced many of his associates to abide by the "ten-foot rule," where employees pledged that whenever they got within ten feet of a customer, they would look the customer in the eye, greet him or her, and ask if he or she needed help with anything. Walton's famous mantra, known as the "sundown rule," was: "Why put off until tomorrow what you can do today?" Due to this staunch work ethic and dedication to customer care, Wal-Mart claimed early on that a formal ethics program was unnecessary because the company had Mr. Sam's ethics to follow.

In 2002 Wal-Mart officially became the largest grocery chain, topping the Fortune 500 (a position it held seven times between 2002 and 2009). The company also has become known for its efforts toward sustainability growth. Former Wal-Mart CEO Lee Scott was even ranked seventh in the Ethisphere list of 100 top contributors to business ethics, based on his support of sustainability. Additionally, *Fortune* named Wal-Mart the "most admired company in America" in 2003 and 2004. Although it has slipped since then, it remained high on the list in 2009, when it was ranked eleventh most admired.

EFFECTS ON COMPETITOR STAKEHOLDERS

Possibly the greatest complaint against Wal-Mart is that it puts other companies out of business. With its low prices, Wal-Mart makes it harder for local stores to compete. Wal-Mart is often accused of being responsible for the downward pressure on wages and benefits in towns in which the company is located. Some businesses have tried to file lawsuits against Wal-Mart with mixed success, claiming that the company uses predatory pricing to put competing stores out of business. Wal-Mart counters by defending its pricing, asserting that its purpose is to provide quality, low-cost products to the average consumer. Yet, although Wal-Mart has saved consumers millions of dollars and is a popular shopping spot for many, there is no denying that many competing stores go out of business once Wal-Mart comes to town.

In order to compete against the retail giant, other stores must reduce wages. Studies have shown that overall payroll wages, including Wal-Mart wages, are reduced by 5 percent after Wal-Mart enters a new market. As a result, some activist groups and citizens have refused to allow Wal-Mart to take up residence in their towns.

RELATIONSHIPS WITH SUPPLIER STAKEHOLDERS

Wal-Mart focuses on keeping costs low to achieve its "everyday low prices" (EDLPs) by streamlining its company. Well-known for operational excellence in its ability to handle, move, and track merchandise, Wal-Mart expects its suppliers to continually improve their systems as well. Wal-Mart often works closely with suppliers to cut prices in order to save the consumer money. For instance, Wal-Mart typically works with suppliers to reduce costs of packaging and shipping, which lessens costs for consumers. In 2006, Wal-Mart launched a plan to reduce packaging by 5 percent, an initiative reflecting Wal-Mart's desire to improve sustainability.

In 2008, Wal-Mart introduced its "Global Responsible Sourcing Initiative," which contains the following policies and requirements that will be included in new supplier agreements:

"Many companies depend on Wal-Mart for the bulk of their business."

- "Manufacturers' facilities must certify compliance with laws and regulations where they operate as well as rigorous social and environmental standards, set by government agencies, beginning with suppliers in China in January 2009 and for all other Wal-Mart suppliers in 2011."
- "By 2012, suppliers must work with Wal-Mart to make a 20 percent improvement in the energy efficiency inside the top 200 factories in China that Wal-Mart directly sources from."
- "Suppliers must create a plan to eliminate, by 2012, defective merchandise reaching the Wal-Mart supply chain."
- "And by 2012, all suppliers Wal-Mart buys from must source 95 percent of their production from factories that receive the highest ratings on environmental and social practices."

If achieved, these goals will increase the sustainability of Wal-Mart suppliers significantly.

Some critics, however, believe that pressures to achieve these standards will shift more of a cost burden onto suppliers. Since Wal-Mart is specifically targeting its largest supplier network in China, many believe these lofty goals will be hard to implement in the allotted time period and will be hard to enforce and track due to the intricate maze of suppliers in China and other countries. When suppliers do not meet its demands, Wal-Mart ceases to carry the supplier's product or, often, will find another supplier for the product at the desired price.

Wal-Mart's power centers around its size and the volume of products needed. Many companies depend on Wal-Mart for the bulk of their business. Examples are Clorox, which does 23 percent of its business with Wal-Mart, Revlon (22 percent), and Kellogg's (12 percent). This type of relationship allows Wal-Mart to influence terms with its vendors. Indeed, there are benefits to suppliers; as they become more efficient and streamlined for Wal-Mart, they help their other customers as well. Numerous companies believe that supplying Wal-Mart has been the best thing for their businesses. However, many have found the amount of power that Wal-Mart wields to be disconcerting.

The constant drive by Wal-Mart for lower prices can have a negative effect on suppliers. Many have been forced to move production from the United States to less expensive locations in Asia. Wal-Mart imports around $20 billion in products from China and encourages its suppliers to move production there in order to lower costs. China's annual exports amount to $583 billion, and Wal-Mart ranks as China's eighth-largest trading partner. Companies such as Master Lock, Fruit of the Loom, and Levi's, as well as many other Wal-Mart suppliers, have moved production overseas at the expense of U.S. jobs.

This was not founder Sam Walton's original intention. In the 1980s, after learning that his stores were putting other American companies out of business, founder Sam Walton started his "Buy American" campaign in which much of Wal-Mart's merchandise would come from American stores. However, the quest to maintain low prices has pushed many Wal-Mart suppliers overseas, and some experts now estimate that as much as 80 percent of Wal-Mart's global suppliers are stationed in China.

ETHICAL ISSUES INVOLVING EMPLOYEE STAKEHOLDERS

Employee Benefits

Much of the Wal-Mart controversy over the years has focused on the way the company treats its employees, or "associates" as Wal-Mart refers to them. Although Wal-Mart is the largest retail employer in the world, it also has been highly criticized for its low wages and benefits. Wal-Mart has been accused of failing to provide health insurance to more than 60 percent of its employees. Many part-timers are not eligible, although efforts have been made to increase the coverage of part-time workers. In a Wal-Mart memo sent to the board of directors by Susan Chambers, Wal-Mart's executive vice-president for benefits, Chambers encouraged the hiring of more part-time workers while also encouraging the hiring of "healthier, more productive employees." After this bad publicity, Wal-Mart's stock decreased 27 percent between 2000 and 2005.

Because of the deluge of bad press, Wal-Mart has taken action to improve relations with its employee stakeholders. In 2006, Wal-Mart raised pay tied to performance in about one-third of its stores. The company also improved its health benefits package for 2008 by offering lower deductibles and implementing a generic prescription plan estimated to save employees $25 million. A Wal-Mart spokesperson claims that more than 90 percent of employees are currently insured and that the company is taking steps to increase that number.

Wal-Mart's Stance on Unions

Some critics believe that workers' benefits could be improved if workers could become unionized. However, unions have been discouraged since Wal-Mart's foundation. Sam Walton believed that unions were a divisive force and might render the company uncompetitive. Wal-Mart maintains that it is not against unions in general, but that it sees no need for unions to come between workers and managers. The company says that it supports an "open-door policy" in which associates can bring problems to managers without having to resort to third parties. Wal-Mart associates have voted against unions in the past.

Although the company officially states that it is not opposed to unions, Wal-Mart often seems to fight against them. Critics claim that when the word *union* surfaces at a Wal-Mart location, the top dogs in Bentonville are called in to instantly thwart union movement. In 2000, seven of ten Wal-Mart butchers in Jacksonville, Texas, voted to join the United Food Workers Union. Wal-Mart responded by announcing it would only sell precut meat in its Supercenters, getting rid of its meat-cutting department. Although Wal-Mart offers justifiable claims for actions such as this, many see the company as aggressively working to prevent unionization in its stores.

However, Wal-Mart's stance against unions has not always held up in foreign countries. In China, Wal-Mart faced a similar decision regarding unions. To grow in China, it appeared necessary to accept a union. Poor working conditions and low wages were generating social unrest and the government was attempting to craft a new set of labor laws giving employees greater protection and giving the All-China Federation of Trade Unions (ACFTU) more power. In 2004, the Chinese Labor Federation pushed Wal-Mart to allow the formation of unions. As a result, Wal-Mart technically allowed this, but critics claim that Wal-Mart made it increasingly difficult for the workers to form new unions. In 2006, employees announced the first formation of a Wal-Mart union, and within a week, four more branches had announced their formations of unions. Wal-Mart initially reacted to these announcements by stating it would not renew the contracts of unionized workers. However, the pressure mounted, and later that year Wal-Mart signed a memorandum with the ACFTU allowing unions in stores. Chinese Wal-Marts are now some of the few worldwide Wal-Marts that have unionized workers.

“*Wal-Mart's stance against unions has not always held up in foreign countries.*”

Workplace Conditions and Discrimination

Despite accusations of low employee benefits and a strong stance against unions, Wal-Mart remains the largest nongovernment employer in the United States, Mexico, and Canada. It provides jobs to millions of people and has been a mainstay of *Fortune*'s "Most Admired Companies" list since the start of the twenty-first century. However, in December 2005, Wal-Mart was ordered to pay $172 million to more than 100,000 California employees in a class-action lawsuit claiming that Wal-Mart routinely denied meal breaks. The California employees also alleged that they were denied rest breaks and that Wal-Mart managers deliberately altered time cards to prevent overtime. Similar accusations began to pop up in other states as well. Wal-Mart denied the allegations and filed an appeal in 2007. In 2008, Wal-Mart agreed to pay up to $640 million to settle sixty-three such lawsuits.

Wal-Mart also has received accusations of discrimination from its female employees. Although women account for more than two-thirds of all Wal-Mart employees, they make up less than 10 percent of store management. Wal-Mart insists it trains and promotes women fairly, but in 2001 an internal study showed that the company paid female store managers less than males in the same positions. In 2004, a federal judge in San Francisco granted class-action status to a sex-discrimination lawsuit against Wal-Mart involving 1.6 million current and former female Wal-Mart employees. The plaintiffs claimed that Wal-Mart discriminated against them in regard to promotions, pay, training, and job assignments. Wal-Mart argued against the class-action suit, claiming that promotions were made on an individual basis by each store. So far, the company has not been able to appeal the case.

Yet, interestingly enough, Wal-Mart also has received recognition for its good treatment of female workers. Between 2007 and 2009, the National Association for Female

Executives recognized the company three years in a row as a "Top Company for Executive Women." It makes one wonder if Wal-Mart truly is trying to turn over a new leaf in how it treats its female employees.

Illegal Immigrants

In October 2003, a series of raids by U.S. Immigration and Customs Enforcement officials revealed that 250 illegal immigrants were working on cleaning crews at 61 Wal-Mart stores in 21 states. Several Wal-Mart contractors had hired the undocumented workers from Mexico, Eastern Europe, and other countries. In March 2005, this investigation ended in a landmark $11 million civil settlement. According to a *Wall Street Journal* article, three top Wal-Mart executives knew the company's cleaning contractors used illegal immigrants yet did nothing to stop the practice. The immigrants worked as many as seven days a week for less than minimum wage.

Wal-Mart answered these charges with an unusual response. It admitted that it knew about the illegal immigrants because it had been cooperating with the federal government for three years prior to the raids. Wal-Mart officials also remarked that the reason why they did not end ties with the contractors was because the federal government asked them not to do so. Additionally, Wal-Mart pointed to a prior lawsuit against Wal-Mart by the Immigration and Naturalization Service (INS) because the company required immigrants to show more verification than required by law. "Accordingly, our company was very hesitant to ask for more assurances about the status of our contractors' employees," stated Wal-Mart spokeswoman Mona Williams.

Sweatshop Workers

Wal-Mart has taken measures to show that it is against sweatshop labor. In 2003, it hired an anti-sweatshop expert to expand its global inspection program. The following year, Wal-Mart teamed up with the nonprofit Business for Social Responsibility to reinforce its global monitoring programs.

However, in December 2007, Wal-Mart fell prey to criticism after Senator Byron Dorgan accused the company of selling Christmas decorations made in Chinese sweatshops. The information came from a National Labor Committee study indicating that workers as young as 12 were working 15-hour days for as little as 26 cents an hour. In response, Wal-Mart stated that it was investigating the allegations and emphasized its code against such practices.

ETHICAL LEADERSHIP ISSUES

Aside from Sam Walton, many other distinguished people have been associated with Wal-Mart. One of them is Hillary Clinton, who served on Wal-Mart's board six years before her husband took the presidency. Another is former board vice chair Thomas Coughlin, although Coughlin achieved his fame for the corporate scandal he caused.

In March 2005, Coughlin was forced to resign from the board of directors for stealing as much as $500,000 from Wal-Mart in the form of bogus expenses, reimbursements, and the unauthorized use of gift cards. Coughlin, a protégé and hunting buddy of Sam Walton, was a legend at Wal-Mart. He often spent time on the road with Sam Walton expanding SAM's CLUB locations. At one time he was the second highest-ranking Wal-Mart executive and was a candidate for CEO.

In January 2006, Coughlin agreed to plead guilty to federal wire-fraud and tax-evasion charges. Although he took home millions of dollars in compensation, Coughlin secretly had been using Wal-Mart funds to pay for a range of his personal expenses, including hunting vacations, a $2,590 dog enclosure at his home, and a pair of handmade alligator boots. Coughlin's deceit was discovered when he asked a subordinate to approve $2,000 in expense payments without receipts.

Wal-Mart rescinded Coughlin's retirement agreement worth more than $10 million; and for his crimes, he was sentenced to 27 months of home confinement, $440,000 in fines, and 1,500 hours of community service. Wal-Mart spokesperson Mona Williams said the experience was "embarrassing and painful. Someone we expected to operate with the highest integrity let us down in a very public way." The case created concerns about leadership, corporate governance, and the ethical culture of Wal-Mart.

PROBLEMS WITH ENVIRONMENTAL STAKEHOLDERS

> *"The greatest environmental concern associated with Wal-Mart has been urban sprawl."*

Like many large corporations, Wal-Mart has been targeted as a violator of safe environmental practices. The Environmental Protection Agency (EPA) has cited Wal-Mart for violating storm water regulations and air quality restrictions. In 2005, Wal-Mart received a grand jury subpoena from the U.S. Attorney's Office in Los Angeles, California, seeking documents and information relating to the company's receipt, transportation, handling, identification, recycling, treatment, storage, and disposal of certain merchandise constituting hazardous material or hazardous waste.

However, probably the greatest environmental concern associated with Wal-Mart has been urban sprawl. The construction of a Wal-Mart can stress a city's infrastructure of roads, parking, and traffic flow. There have been concerns about the number of acres of city green space devoured by Wal-Mart construction (Wal-Mart Supercenters occupy about twenty to thirty acres of land). Another issue is the number of abandoned stores (between 350 and 400 annually), deserted when the company outgrows locations. Currently, over 26 million square feet of empty Wal-Mart space exists—enough to fill 534 football fields. Allegedly, Wal-Mart goes out of its way to prevent other retail companies from buying its abandoned stores, contributing to the empty spaces.

Sustainability 360

Wal-Mart has attempted to address its environmental stakeholders by becoming a "greener" company. Some of the company goals include the following:

- Reducing greenhouse gases at existing store, club, and distribution center bases around the world by 20 percent by 2012
- Designing new prototypes to be 25 to 30 percent more efficient by the end of 2009
- Developing and implementing innovative energy-efficient technology into existing and new stores

- Reducing the amount of packaging in the supply chain by 5 percent by 2013 (which the company has promoted through annual packaging expos)

Currently Wal-Mart is working on four main green areas: waste improvement and recycling, natural resources, energy, and social/community impact. Wal-Mart's long-term goals are to be supplied 100 percent by renewable energy, create zero waste, and carry products that sustain the environment and its resources.

Sustainability Leadership

Wal-Mart has already taken strides to obtain its sustainability objectives. It has opened two environmentally friendly stores in McKinney, Texas, and Aurora, Colorado—locations chosen for their different weather and climate considerations. The stores get electricity from solar panels and wind turbines. The company hopes these experiments will provide examples of the ways building owners, scientists, engineers, architects, contractors, and landscape designers can work together to create stores designed to save energy, conserve natural resources, and reduce pollution. According to Wal-Mart vice president Kim Saylors-Laster, this is one step in Wal-Mart's plan of being supplied by 100 percent renewable energy. Wal-Mart intends to take information gained at these stores and apply it to new stores.

To reduce energy consumption, Wal-Mart facilities are conserving energy in two major ways. First, most new stores include a "daylighting" feature enabling stores to dim or turn off lights as daylight increases and enters through skylights, thereby reducing the demand for electricity during peak hours. Second, Wal-Mart manages energy consumption by centrally controlling the heating and cooling of U.S. Wal-Mart stores.

Wal-Mart is also attempting to reduce fossil fuel use and to sell more "green" products. Throughout 2009 Wal-Mart tested new technologies, including two types of hybrid trucks and two alternatively fueled heavy-duty trucks, in order to achieve its goals of creating a more environmentally friendly trucking fleet. Wal-Mart is proud to point out that between 2005 and 2008 the company increased its fleet efficiency by 25 percent through its use of new technologies, routes, and loading procedures. Wal-Mart's new goal is to double its fleet efficiency by 2015.

Additionally, Wal-Mart has announced a goal to reduce phosphates, a water pollutant that encourages the growth of oxygen-depleting algae and can kill fish and other wildlife, in laundry and dish detergents by 70 percent by 2011. The company hopes to use its worldwide influence to make a global difference in sustainability initiatives. "Our reach around the world puts us in a unique position to drive sustainable change across national boundaries and into the global supply chain," said Craig Herkert, Wal-Mart President and CEO of the Americas.

Wal-Mart is also trying to get its associates personally involved with sustainability. Approximately 500,000 Wal-Mart associates throughout the United States have participated in the Personal Sustainability Project (PSP), a voluntary program encouraged by former CEO Lee Scott. Associates at Wal-Mart stores would select sustainability goals and make commitments to monitor their progress for several weeks. The PSP counts successes, such as recycling over 3 million pounds of plastic, and encouraging people to winterize their homes and switch to low-energy fluorescent light bulbs, but also includes health goals. Healthier employees are better for the environment, for the health-care system, and for the business. Participants have lost a collective 184,000 pounds and 20,000 have quit smoking. The PSP has also been launched in Brazil, Canada, and Japan.

To measure how its eco-friendly products are faring with consumers, Wal-Mart launched the Wal-Mart Sustainability Live Better Index in 2007. This index allows Wal-Mart to track, on a state-by-state basis, consumers' demand for low-cost products, health and welfare products, and green products. In the sustainability category, consumers can track adoption rates at Wal-Mart in the following categories: compact florescent light bulbs, organic milk, extended-life paper products, organic baby food, organic cleaning products, and organic coffee. Wal-Mart believes that consumers can "make a conscious decision to purchase them for their environmentally friendly and cost-saving benefits versus conventional versions." So far results have been good, with a 66 percent increase in average adoption rates.

Even during the 2008–2009 economic recession, Wal-Mart tried to portray itself as a firm that cares about green initiatives. It continued to partner with other large companies to promote green jobs. In 2009, Wal-Mart announced its intention to contribute $5.7 million in grants to the U.S. Conference of Mayors and Veterans Green Jobs to support the creation of green jobs in the United States. Wal-Mart expects the money to be used to train the workforce in the growing sector of the green industry. The company believes it is making a profitable investment, as 10 percent of job growth in the United States is expected to be in the "green-collar" sector by 2032. With this investment, Wal-Mart hopes to encourage mayors to promote jobs in their cities' green industries and provide veterans with training in green skills. It is clear that Wal-Mart is trying to improve its relationship with environmental activists and stakeholders.

Savings: Is Going Green Cost-Effective?

Wal-Mart's green initiatives have secured it the goodwill of many environmentally conscious consumers, but does going green save the company costs in other ways? So far Wal-Mart's initiatives have racked up the following savings:

- $25 million/year in savings from auxiliary power systems on trucks to run the air conditioning when trucks are stopped. The store further plans to double the fuel efficiency of its new heavy-duty trucks by 2015.
- $7 million/year in savings from replacing all incandescent bulbs in store display ceiling fans with compact fluorescent bulbs.

WHAT IS WAL-MART DOING TO IMPROVE ETHICS AND SOCIAL RESPONSIBILITY?

Although it has received much criticism in the past years, Wal-Mart has been working to improve its ethical reputation along with its reputation for sustainability and corporate governance. In 2004, Wal-Mart formed the Global Ethics Office and released a revised Global Statement of Ethics. The intent of the Global Ethics Office is to spread an ethical corporate culture among its global stakeholders. The Global Ethics Office provides guidance on ethical decision making based on the Global Statement of Ethics and an ethics helpline. The helpline is an anonymous and confidential way for associates to contact the company regarding ethical issues. Additionally, Wal-Mart has an Ethical Standards Team that consists of 200 associates. The intent of the team is to monitor the compliance of supplier factories with the company's "Standards for Suppliers" and local laws.

In 2005, Wal-Mart introduced a full-page newspaper ad that promoted the company's concern with ethics and its stakeholders. Its newspaper ad was a direct letter from Wal-Mart CEO Lee Scott. The ad stated that it was time for the public to read the "unfiltered truth" about Wal-Mart and time for it to stand up on behalf of a workforce that included 1.2 million Americans. Scott called for Congress to increase the minimum wage and noted that Wal-Mart had increased spending on employee health insurance.

Wal-Mart also has contributed significantly to disaster management projects. The company donated millions to relief efforts for Hurricane Katrina, $300,000 to support flood relief efforts in Southern Brazil, and $3 million for earthquake relief in China. Wal-Mart attempts to help its associates who are caught in disasters, allocating $2 million in grants for associates whose homes have been damaged and creating a toll-free number for associates who need help.

Despite its efforts, Wal-Mart's reputation was significantly tarnished again with the Coughlin scandal. It was therefore eager to reestablish its credibility with stakeholders. It found its solution in the person of Lee Scott, CEO of Wal-Mart from January 2002 to January 2009. Lee Scott was recognized as a leader in investing in clean energy. Due to him, many California facilities are now powered by solar energy, and the energy needs of 15 percent of Texas stores can now be met with wind power. Scott's leadership had such a positive effect on the company that he was given one of the top spots in the 100 Most Influential People in Business Ethics in 2008. Wal-Mart has taken great strides to portray itself as an ethically responsible business with good leadership.

> *"Wal-Mart claims a commitment to improving the standard of living for customers worldwide"*

The company's reputation for low prices helped Wal-Mart to remain a healthy business even during the 2008–2009 recession. Wal-Mart claims a commitment to improving the standard of living for customers worldwide, and has backed that claim with large charitable donations, amounting to $423 million globally in fiscal year 2009. Its key retailing strategy is offering a broad assortment of merchandise and services at everyday low prices (EDLP) while fostering a culture claiming to reward and embrace mutual respect, integrity, and diversity. Wal-Mart has always targeted lower-income customers, a strategy that paid dividends during the 2008–2009 recession. While many companies struggled to re-brand themselves as affordable, Wal-Mart had an early advantage. Wal-Mart is known for excellent market orientation—focusing on consumers, defeating competitors, and increasing shareholder value.

WAL-MART'S RESPONSE TO THE FINANCIAL CRISIS

Interestingly enough, the financial meltdown of 2008–2009 may have enhanced Wal-Mart's reputation. Unlike many stores, Wal-Mart's sales increased by 2 percent in 2008 as shoppers sought good deals. An influx of new shoppers forced Wal-Mart to create better crowd-control measures in its New York stores after an employee was trampled to death and others were injured on Black Friday 2008 by a mob of shoppers. Although refusing to admit any wrongdoing in the incident, Wal-Mart agreed to have its crowd-control measures approved by safety consultants (in addition to providing $400,000 to victims of the incident). Wal-Mart is also donating $1.5 million to a Nassau County social service program.

In addition to creating better safety measures, Wal-Mart has launched new initiatives targeting families facing financial dilemmas. For example, the company formed the Wal-Mart MoneyCard, a reloadable Visa debit card to help lower-income consumers who do not use traditional checking accounts. Because of the economic crisis, Wal-Mart has decreased the fees for this card; consumers can now purchase it for $3, rather than the $9 it cost originally. The card has no overdraft fees, and the fees for maintenance and reloading are low. With this move, Wal-Mart hopes to save consumers $500 million in money service fees each year.

The Wal-Mart Foundation has partnered with United Way and One Economy Corporation to provide free filing and tax services for low-income consumers. The Wal-Mart Foundation is donating a $3.6 million grant to this endeavor in an attempt to demonstrate social responsibility while increasing the popularity of its stores.

THE FUTURE OF WAL-MART

Wal-Mart can be viewed through two very different lenses. Some think that the company represents all that is wrong with America, and others love it. In response to criticism and in an attempt to initiate goodwill with consumers, the company has continued to improve stakeholder relationships and made efforts to exhibit itself as an ethically responsible company. Although it has faced controversy regarding competition, suppliers, employees, and workplace discrimination, it has increasingly demonstrated concern for its stakeholders.

Wal-Mart's endeavors that have sparked consumer attention deal with sustainability initiatives and social responsibility. Its goals to decrease its waste and carbon emissions extend to all facets of its operations, including suppliers. Though some consider these objectives to be unrealistic, the effort demonstrates Wal-Mart's desire (whether through genuine concern for the environment or for its own bottom-line profits) to become a more sustainable company.

Similarly, Wal-Mart's creation of an ethics and compliance program shows it has come a long way since its beginning when formal ethics programs were deemed unnecessary. Likewise, its initiatives to help families during the recession helped to reinforce its image as a caring company. Both critics and supporters of Wal-Mart alike are waiting to see whether Wal-Mart's efforts will position the company as a large retail company dedicated to social responsibility.

QUESTIONS

1. Do you think Wal-Mart is doing enough to become more sustainable?
2. What are the problems that Wal-Mart has faced, and what has the company done to address them?
3. Why has Wal-Mart tended to improve performance when other retail outlets have been suffering financially?

SOURCES

Associated Press, "Ex-Wal-Mart Vice Chairman Pleads Guilty in Fraud Case," *Wall Street Journal,* January 31, 2006, www.online.wsj.com. Bandler, James, "Former No. 2 at Wal-Mart Set to Plead Guilty," *Wall Street Journal,* January 7, 2006, p. A1; Bandler, James, and Ann Zimmerman, "A Wal-Mart Legend's Trail of Deceit," *Wall Street Journal,* April 8, 2005, p. A10; Barbaro, Michael, "Image Effort by Wal-Mart Takes a Turn," *New York Times,* May 12, 2006, pp. C1, C4; Barbaro, Michael, "Return to Low-Price Basics Pays Off Well for Wal-Mart," Wal-MartStores.com, January 12, 2009, http://www6.lexisnexis.com/publisher/EndUser?Action=UserDisplayFullDocument&orgId=2708&topicId=100019774&docId=l:728129992 (accessed February 20, 2009); "Buy Blue: Wal-Mart," http://www.buyblue.org/node/2137/view/summary (accessed January 10, 2006); Chan, Anita, "Made in China: Wal-Mart Unions," *Yale Global Online,* October 12, 2006, http://yaleglobal.yale.edu/display.article?id=8283 (accessed February 21, 2009); Coleman-Lochner, Lauren, "Independent Look at Wal-Mart Shows Both Good and Bad. With Savings and Jobs Come Falling Wages and Rising Medicaid Costs," *San Antonio Express-News,* November 5, 2005, p. 4D; Connolly, Ceci, "At Wal-Mart, a Health-Care Turnaround," *Washington Post,* February 13, 2009, http://www.washingtonpost.com/wp-dyn/content/article/2009/02/12/AR2009021204096_pf.html (accessed February 21, 2009); "Ethical Sourcing," Wal-Mart, http://walmartstores.com/Sustainability/7785.aspx (accessed May 12, 2009); Etter, Lauren, "Gauging the Wal-Mart Effect," *Wall Street Journal,* December 3–4, 2005, p. A9; "Event Highlights the Wal-Mart Health Care Crisis: New Study Declares Wal-Mart in Critical Condition," November 16, 2005, http://Wal-Martwatch.com (accessed January 18, 2006); Fishman, Charles, "The Wal-Mart You Don't Know; Why Low Prices Have a High Cost," *Fast Company,* December 2003, pp. 68–80; Fong, Mei, and Ann Zimmerman, "China's Union Push Leaves Wal-Mart with Hard Choice," *Wall Street Journal,* May 13–14, 2006, pp. A1, A6; "Global Ethics Office," Wal-Mart, https://www.walmartethics.com/ (accessed December 13, 2008); "Global Insight Releases New Study on the Impact of Wal-Mart on the U.S. Economy," http://www.globalinsight.com/MultiClientStudy/MultiClientStudyDetail2438.htm (accessed January 23, 2005); Gold, Russell, and Ann Zimmerman, "Papers Suggest Wal-Mart Knew of Illegal Workers," *Wall Street Journal,* November 5, 2005, p. A3; Grant, Lorrie, "Wal-Mart Faces a New Class Action," *USA Today,* September 14, 2005, p. 63; Heldt, Lisa, and Tabitha Peyton, "Wal-Mart's Green Marketing Strategy," April 27, 2009; "Is Wal-Mart Really a 'Green' Company?" Wal-Mart Watch, http://walmartwatch.com/img/blog/environmental_fact_sheet.pdf (accessed December 13, 2008); "Judah Schiller on Sustainability: Make It Personal," Sustainable Brands 09, http://www.sustainablelifemedia.com/people/innovators/strategy/judah_schiller_on_sustainability_make_it_personal (accessed February 23, 2009); Kabel, Marcus, "Wal-Mart at War: Retailer Faces Bruised Image, Makes Fixes," *Marketing News,* January 15, 2006, p. 25; "Live Better Index," Wal-Mart, Inc., http://www.livebetterindex.com/ (accessed August 27, 2009); McGinn, Daniel, "Wal-Mart Hits the Wall," *Newsweek,* November 14, 2005, pp. 44–46; Morrison, Kimberly, "Coughlin's Sentence Will Stand: U.S. Attorney Will Not Appeal," March 28, 2008, http://www.nwaonline.net/articles/2008/03/29/news/032908wzcouglinappeal.txt (accessed February 21, 2009); "Most Admired Companies," *Fortune,* http://money.cnn.com/magazines/fortune/mostadmired/2009/snapshots/2255.html (accessed August 27, 2009); Much, Marilyn, "Wal-Mart Holds Up in Sharp Recession, Beating EPS Views; Rare Winner: Shares Up 4%; Middle Class Now Willing to Shop at Discount King for Low Prices on Basics," Wal-MartStores.com, http://www6.lexisnexis.com/publisher/EndUser?Action=UserDisplayFullDocument&orgId=2708&topicId=100019774&docId=l:928281151 (accessed February 20, 2009); Norman, Al, "The Case Against Wal-Mart," Raphel Marketing, 2004; Olsson, Karen, "Up Against Wal-Mart," www.MotherJones.com, March/April 2003, http://www.motherjones.com/news/feature/2003/03/ma_276_01.html (accessed January 10, 2006); "100 Most Influential People in Business Ethics 2008," *Ethisphere,* December 31, 2009, http://ethisphere.com/100-most-influential-people-in-business-ethics-2008/#6 (accessed February 20, 2009); "Personal Sustainability Project Fact-Sheet," Wal-Mart, Inc., http://walmartstores.com/FactsNews/FactSheets/#Sustainability (accessed August 27, 2009); PR Newswire, "Wal-Mart Foundation Donates $5.7 Million to Support the Creation of Green Jobs in U.S.," CNBC, http://www.cnbc.com/id/28993728/site/14081545 (accessed February 20, 2009); Quinn, Steve, "Wal-Mart Green with Energy," *Fort Collins Coloradoan,* July 24, 2005, pp. E1–E2; Sebok, Anthony J., "Wal-Mart Wants to Declassify Lawsuit," CNN.com, August 11, 2004, http://www.cnn.com/2004/LAW/08/11/sebok.walmart.suit/index.html (accessed December 13, 2008); Shine, Tom, and Z. Byron Wolf, "Report Cites Holiday Abuse in Chinese Factory," ABC News, December 12, 2007, http://abcnews.go.com/Business/HolidayTheme/story?id=3989096&page=1 (accessed December 13, 2008); "Sustainability Progress to Date 2007–2008," Wal-Mart, http://walmartfacts.com/reports/2006/sustainability/associatesPersonal.html (accessed February 23, 2009); "Top Companies: The 2009 List," National Association for Female Executives, http://www.nafe.com/web?service=vpage/3847 (accessed August 27, 2009); "2009 Fortune 500," *Fortune,* http://money.cnn.com/magazines/fortune/fortune500/2009/snapshots/2255.html (accessed August 27, 2009); Wailgum, Thomas, "Wal-Mart's Green Strategy: Supply Chain Makeover Targets Chinese Manufacturers," *CIO,* http://www.cio.com/article/456625/Wal_Mart_s_Green_Strategy_Supply_Chain_Makeover_Targets_Chinese_Manufacturers?page=1 (accessed May 13, 2009); "Wal-Mart Americas Aim to Reduce Detergent Phosphates 70%," Wal-MartStore.com, January 26, 2009, http://walmartstores.com/FactsNews/NewsRoom/8938.aspx (accessed February 20, 2009); "Wal-Mart Annual Report 2008," Wall-MartStores.com, http://walmartstores.com/sites/AnnualReport/2008/, (accessed February 21, 2009); "Wal-Mart Concedes China Can Make Unions," *China Daily,* November 23, 2004, http://www.chinadaily.com.cn/english/doc/2004-11/23/content_394129.htm (accessed February 21, 2009); "Wal-Mart Foundation Teams Up with United Way and One Economy to Provide Free Tax Preparation and Filing Services," Wal-MartStores.com, February 10, 2009, http://walmartstores.com/FactsNews/NewsRoom/8962.aspx (accessed February 20, 2009); "Wal-Mart Steps Up Efforts to Help Americans Manage Their Finances with $3 Rollback Price on Key Money Service," Wal-MartStores.com, February 8, 2009, http://walmartstores.com/FactsNews/NewsRoom/8982.aspx (accessed February 20, 2009); "Wal-Mart Stores, Inc.," United States Security and Exchange Commission, January 31, 2008, http://msnmoney.brand.edgar-online.com/EFX_dll/EDGARpro.dll?FetchFilingHTML1?ID=5835838&SessionID=5RgcWZDBP11rCl9 (accessed February 21, 2009); "Wal-Mart Stores, Inc. Recognized as Top Company for Executive Women by the National Association for Female Executives," Wal-Mart, April 3, 2007, http://walmartstores.com/FactsNews/NewsRoom/6374.aspx (accessed May 12, 2009); "Wal-Mart Tests New Hybrid Trucks, Alternative Fuels," Wal-MartStores.com, http://walmartstores.com/FactsNews/NewsRoom/8949.aspx (accessed February 20, 2009); "Wal-Mart Will Pay $640M to Settle Wage Lawsuits," *Newser,* December 23, 2008, http://www.newser.com/story/46142/wal-mart-will-pay-640m-to-settle-wage-lawsuits.html?utm_source=ssp&utm_medium=cpc&utm_campaign=story (accessed May 12, 2009); Zimmerman, Anne, "Federal Officials Asked to Probe Wal-Mart Firing," Wake-Up Wal-Mart, April 28, 2005, http://www.wakeupwalmart.com/news/20050428-wsj.html (accessed February 21, 2009); Zimmerman, Anne, "Labor Pains: After Huge Raid on Illegals, Wal-Mart Fires Back at U.S.," *Wall Street Journal*, December 19, 2003, p. A1.

CASE 3

The American Red Cross

Daryl Benson

The American Red Cross (ARC) is an independent organization, supported by public financial donations and volunteerism. Its mission is to "provide relief to victims of disasters and help people prevent, prepare for and respond to emergencies." The ARC responds to more than 70,000 disasters annually. However, the ways in which it handled 9/11 in 2001 and Hurricane Katrina in 2005 were widely criticized as being inadequate and poorly managed. The ARC has had to address allegations of fraud, bribery, and even theft on the part of volunteers and employees working for the organization. The ARC also has faced a number of internal challenges due to high turnover, as well as charges of overcompensation and possible corruption among its board of directors and upper management.

A BRIEF HISTORY

Clara Barton initially founded the ARC in 1881. She was inspired by the work of the International Red Cross while on a trip to Europe during the Franco-Prussian War of 1870–1871. Barton brought the model back to the United States, and subsequently led the organization through its first domestic and international relief missions, including assisting the U.S. military during the Spanish-American War in 1898. The ARC is one of a handful of organizations chartered by the U.S. government, receiving its first federal charter in 1900.

As a member of the International Federation of Red Cross and Red Crescent Societies, the ARC joins more than 175 other national societies in bringing aid to victims of disasters throughout the world. The ARC follows the seven fundamental bylaws to which all Red Cross societies must conform: humanity, impartiality, neutrality, independence, voluntary service, unity, and universality.

This case was prepared by Michelle Watkins and John-Paul Schilling under the direction of O.C. Ferrell and the development of Jennifer Jackson. This case was prepared for classroom discussion, rather than to illustrate either effective or ineffective handling of an administrative, ethical, or legal decision by management. All sources used for this case were obtained through publicly available material.

ORGANIZATIONAL STRUCTURE

Today the American Red Cross consists of roughly half a million volunteers and 35,000 employees. For many years the ARC has had a fifty-member, all-volunteer board of governors. The president of the United States is the honorary chair of the Red Cross and appoints eight governors, including the chair of the board. The chair nominates and the board elects the president of the ARC, who is responsible for carrying into effect the policies and programs of the board. This arrangement is undergoing changes that will be discussed later in the case.

The ARC is made up of more than 700 local chapters across the country. These chapters receive funding from the national Red Cross. Directors of local chapters are authorized to run day-to-day operations. Representatives of the local chapters nominate members of the local boards of governors. In recent history, members of the local boards of directors have clashed with top national management.

ORGANIZATIONAL AND LEADERSHIP UPHEAVAL

Trouble at the Top: Executive Turnover

> *"The constant change in leadership is debilitating and does nothing to address the real problem."*

The first decade of the twenty-first century saw a high rate of turnover in the boardroom at the Red Cross. Since Elizabeth Dole's resignation as chair in 1999, the ARC has had seven different permanent or acting heads. President Bernadine Healy (1999–2001) was forced to resign following mismanagement of the response to the September 11 attacks. Similarly, president and chief executive officer Marsha J. Evans (2002–2005) was ousted after the ARC's botched handling of Hurricane Katrina, though the official reason for her departure was communication problems with the board. Mark W. Everson was president and CEO for the brief period between May 29 and November 27, 2007. He was forced to resign after an inappropriate sexual relationship with a subordinate came to light.

This frequent executive turnover has significantly weakened the organization's ability to carry out its federal mandate. Some blame the oversized board of directors. "The board seems to think it is a hiring and firing agency, and does not see its role as building a strong Red Cross," said Paul C. Light, a professor of public service at New York University. "The constant change in leadership is debilitating and does nothing to address the real problem, which is years and years of underinvestment in telecommunications, technology and other infrastructure to help the organization with its mission." In the cases of both Healy and Everson, the board spent a considerable amount of time and money conducting a search for the "right person," nearly two years and eighteen months, respectively.

The agency's reputation has been further tarnished by the ARC's history of awarding large severance packages for ousted executives, no matter how short the term served. Bernadine Healy received $1.9 million in salary and severance pay upon her departure in late 2001. Marsha Evans received a total of $780,000 in 2005; this comprised eighteen months' severance pay and a $36,495 unpaid bonus. Speaking of the damage to the organization, Diana Aviv, president and chief executive of the Independent Sector, a nonprofit trade association, said, "The tragedy of this is that the American Red Cross is probably the best-known nonprofit organization in this country. When the stories about it are more about governance and management and less about how it saves lives, it's sad and not just for the Red Cross."

Leadership troubles have extended into the local chapters as well, indicating systemic problems. In a story on the ARC, CBS News cited a laundry list of misconduct: "the fundraiser in Louisiana caught padding her own bank account with donations; the manager in Pennsylvania who embezzled to support her crack cocaine habit; and the executive in Maryland who forged signatures on purchase orders meant for disaster victims." One of the biggest charity frauds in history occurred at the ARC's Hudson County chapter in New Jersey. Chief executive Joseph Lecowitch and bookkeeper Catalina Escoto stole well over $1 million in Red Cross funds, squandering it on gambling and gifts to themselves. Escoto also gave herself at least $75,000 in bonuses. Even after Congress mandated changes meant to do away with such problems, in 2007 an executive in Orange County pleaded guilty to federal charges that she embezzled at least $110,000 of the organization's money.

The systemic problems at the American Red Cross have continued, with the nonprofit running about a $200 million deficit and eliminating 1,000 jobs in 2008 alone. Management turmoil and a slow economy combined to dampen fundraising, and the new CEO, Gail McGovern, split the organization's number-two executive position into three separate president-level positions. McGovern filled two of these positions with former AT&T executives with whom she had worked. The ARC was forced to ask for a $150 million appropriation, along with funding to help victims of wildfires, tornados, and floods.

Organizational Changes at the Top

In 2006 Congress took action to try to improve the ARC's effectiveness and efficiency after the scandals of September 11, Hurricane Katrina, and the myriad problems at local chapters when Senator Charles E. Grassley filed legislation to overhaul the organization. Grassley's legislation also forced the organization to become more transparent. In 2006 the ARC disclosed thousands of pages of documents that had not previously been available to the public. This marked the first time in almost sixty years that Congress had moved to amend the organization's charter. The legislation sought to assuage the difficulties in the board by cutting its numbers by more than half, to twenty members by the year 2012. It also restructured the role of the president of the United States in making board appointments. In the past, the president appointed the chair and eight board members, typically cabinet secretaries who rarely attended meetings. Under the legislation, the board nominates a chair for approval and appointment by the president. All other presidential appointments to the board were abolished. An independent ombudsman position was created to take charge of annually reporting to Congress as well as assisting whistle-blowers should agency misconduct be reported.

The American Red Cross Code of Business Ethics and Conduct was updated in January 2007. All employees and volunteers are required to read and sign the two-page document. The ARC offers a twenty-four-hour, confidential, anonymous hotline, the "Concern Connection Line," that provides American Red Cross staff, volunteers, and members of the public a way to report concerns or ask questions regarding potentially illegal, unsafe, or unethical conduct. The ARC also published an eight-page "Ethics

Rules and Policies," which outlines how business funds, property, and time may be allocated, as well as addressing conflicts of interest, recordkeeping, and addressing media inquiries. By far the longest section of this document is the page addressing writings by employees and volunteers about September 11, 2001, which details a policy for "creating, marketing and selling books and other literary works relating to the events of September 11, 2001."

The word *ethics* does not appear a single time in the main promotional document the ARC provides to governmental agencies. *Compliance* appears only in reference to the ARC's requirements related to the collection of blood donations. No mention is made of employee or volunteer ethics training in any official ARC documents available at its website, making it clear that this is not a high priority for the organization.

In light of the scandals that have plagued the ARC, stakeholders must be assured repeatedly of the genuine efforts the organization is making to institutionalize ethical best practices. It may be the ARC believes that because its mission is to respond to and assist people in need, organizational ethics will automatically occur. Perhaps the assumption is that all employees will be ethical without direction or training.

SEPTEMBER 11, 2001

Slow Response

After the September 11 attacks on New York City's World Trade Center, the ARC was widely criticized for its response. The criticisms began the very day of the incident, as the Pentagon called the office of Red Cross President Bernadine Healy at noon to ask, "Where the hell are you guys? Where is the Red Cross?" The Virginia-based command center known as the Disaster Operations Center (DOC) had, for more than a day afterward, failed to activate the specialized teams normally sent out after a plane crash or similar disaster. The trouble did not stop there. In the days and weeks following the attacks, the ARC was continually criticized for its management of the financial donations from thousands of Americans.

Monetary Donation Mismanagement

After September 11, monetary donations poured in at an unprecedented rate. Healy set up a separate fund, the "Liberty Fund," for donations earmarked for victims. By the end of October, the fund had received $543 million in pledges. It had, however, distributed less than one third of those funds to 9/11 relief efforts. The ARC announced that more than half would be spent to increase the organization's ability to prepare for and respond to future catastrophes instead.

Angry outcries prompted a U.S. congressional hearing in November 2001. Healy attempted to defend the use of the money, saying it was clear to donors that not all gifts would go directly to immediate relief efforts. To this Representative Billy Tauzin replied, "It was specially funded for this event, for September 11, and we're also being told parenthetically, 'by the way, we're going to give two thirds of it away to other important Red Cross needs.'" The ethical issue of asking for funds for 9/11 relief efforts, and then appropriating those funds for other purposes, created an explosive debate. At the time of the hearing, Healy had already been forced to resign as ARC president. The ARC subsequently announced that all Liberty Funds monies would go to September 11 victims and their families.

HURRICANE KATRINA

ARC and FEMA Miscommunication

During August and September of 2005, the American Red Cross responded to the disastrous effects of Hurricanes Katrina and Rita, the largest national emergencies in the history of the organization. Katrina hit New Orleans on August 23 as a category 3 storm, making it the sixth strongest hurricane ever recorded in the Atlantic. It was also the costliest hurricane in history. Hurricane Rita hit the coast of Louisiana and Texas only a month later and was an even larger category 3 storm. The ARC raised more than $2 billion in private donations to fund massive relief efforts for both these disasters.

Yet again, following this outpouring of charitable giving, the American public was left largely unsatisfied by the inadequate and untimely relief efforts depicted in the media. These subpar emergency responses were the outcome of a host of fraudulent, questionable, and inefficient decisions made by the ARC, as well as its federal, state, and local disaster relief counterparts. As a result of these faulty responses, and at the request of various congressional committees, the Government Accountability Office (GAO) wrote a report detailing the inadequacies of the ARC and the Federal Emergency Management Agency (FEMA).

The GAO found that the National Response Plan written by the Department of Homeland Security (DHS) in December 2004 was not properly followed and that coordination between the ARC and FEMA was not satisfactory. The DHS plan depicted the ARC as the primary agency responsible for coordinating federal mass care assistance in support of state and local governments and other voluntary organizations in charge of meeting needs such as shelter, food, and emergency first aid. During their disaster relief efforts, FEMA and ARC officials disagreed about their roles and responsibilities and failed to communicate appropriate points of contact for each agency. Additionally, ARC staff was criticized for rotating support positions every two to three weeks. This made it difficult for ARC staff to maintain working relationships with counterparts or to gain expertise in their job functions. Lastly, FEMA failed to implement a comprehensive system to track requests for assistance received from the ARC. One of the ARC's main objectives is properly categorizing and responding to requests for specific goods or necessary services by state and local governments as well as other voluntary organizations.

“*FEMA failed to implement a comprehensive system to track requests for assistance received from the ARC.*”

Mismanagement of Funds and Volunteers

Along with the failures in communication between FEMA and the ARC, there have been numerous accusations about the improper management of donated funds and of volunteers following Hurricanes Katrina and Rita. A *New York Times* article summarizes these actions as follows: “The accusations include the improper diversion of relief supplies, failure to follow Red Cross procedures in tracking and distributing supplies, and use of felons as volunteers in the disaster area in violation of Red Cross rules.”

Numerous Katrina volunteers reported the disappearance of rented cars, electricity generators, and even some 3,000 air mattresses. During the relief efforts, the ARC had more than 235,000 volunteers working in the hurricane disaster areas, more than five times the previous peak of 40,000 volunteers for other relief efforts. It was reported that several of these volunteers had arrest warrants or other felony charges in their backgrounds. The ARC has a screening process that normally would detect potential volunteers with criminal backgrounds, but during Katrina, the organization was so overwhelmed with people seeking to volunteer that it dropped its usual standards.

Other volunteers complained of unauthorized possession and use of Red Cross computer equipment by staff and volunteers. This equipment was equipped with software to add donated money to debit cards for immediate use by hurricane victims and could easily be misused by unscrupulous volunteers. Other incidents included an ARC call center employee writing money orders in the names of various relief victims and fraudulently cashing them herself.

The ARC launched an investigation into claims that, as an organization, it had virtually no cost controls, little oversight of inventory, and no mechanism for basic background checks on volunteers that were given substantial responsibilities. These examples of mismanagement of charitable funds and volunteers pose questions regarding the ARC's ability to prevent fraud and protect resources amid the chaos of major national disasters.

Encouragement of Corporate Partnerships

"As a nonprofit organization, the ARC should always take steps to ensure impartiality."

Another story that emerged from relief efforts for Hurricane Katrina victims regards the ARC's acceptance and choice of corporate partnerships. During the national emergency situation, many corporations were eager to help. Corporate donations not only help victims, but they also cast companies in a good light as the companies demonstrate their compassion and concern for stakeholders. As a nonprofit organization, and the lead agency in charge of various aspects of the disaster relief, the ARC had a duty to scrutinize the corporate donations. Examples of corporate partnerships during the Katrina disaster relief efforts included Coca-Cola donating water, Anheuser Busch canning and delivering water in Anheuser Busch cans, Master Card and J.P. Morgan issuing ATM cards with access to ARC-donated funds for relief victims, and the Southwest Drycleaners Association (SDA) donations of funds that were intended to help the SDA portray themselves as a compassionate and community-involved industry.

In a national emergency, these corporate partnerships help to provide access to resources that otherwise may not be available. The ARC deserves praise for incorporating the generosity of private corporations effectively into its overall disaster relief strategy. However, it should be noted that in the future a more active approach to monitoring private firms' donations would benefit the transparency and overall goals of keeping the ARC apolitical and independent from large businesses. The danger of large corporate donations is that they could make the ARC appear to be in collusion with or biased toward certain corporations. As a nonprofit organization, the ARC should always take steps to ensure impartiality. A greater level of transparency would allow the ARC to assure regular citizens that their charitable donations will not be affected or misused, regardless of corporate involvement. The ARC must be especially careful with whom it is willing to partner during times of national disaster so as not to appear to be using a disaster as a means to promote corporate products.

An article published in the *Harvard Business Review* states that entities such as the ARC would benefit from greater cooperation and partnerships with private businesses. "It's a good thing when companies pitch in after natural or other calamities. It would be a far better thing if they partnered with aid agencies to make plans before disaster struck." As an example, the authors use the agreement for a partnership between Abbott Laboratories and the ARC to supply blood-screening equipment to prove their point that preplanned private partnerships with aid agencies could expedite relief efforts to disaster victims. Through this agreement, Abbott Laboratories will donate a variety of pharmaceutical products ranging from antibiotics to baby food.

Donation Acceptance and Insufficient Capacity

The last point worth mentioning in this analysis of the ARC's donation management involves the organization's capacity to electronically accept donations. The ARC's website has become the main source for receiving individual charitable donations. After September 11, 2001, the organization had to expand its Web-based infrastructure to accommodate additional web traffic. After the tsunami in Southeast Asia, the ARC found itself once again overwhelmed with Internet traffic to donate money. Internet technology staff was forced to offload some of the expansion capabilities work to contractors in the technology processing industry.

The magnitude of donations for Hurricane Katrina victims was unprecedented in the ARC's history. Internet donors immediately overwhelmed the ARC website's capacity. More than fifty Internet technology staff members worked around-the-clock to expand capacity sixfold. The ARC once again outsourced some of the workload to Akamai Technologies, Inc.

There is a lesson to be learned from these continued action-and-reaction scenarios regarding online donation acceptance capacity. The lesson is that the ARC would benefit greatly from a plan outlining how to deal with the next crisis of insufficient capacity. Dave Clark, the chief technology officer at the ARC, believes that it would be a good idea to install a collaboration system. This would consist of a plan to effectively partner with various Internet technology firms to alleviate long-term problems regarding online capacity needs, as well as to deter the ARC from dealing with each disaster on a case-by-case basis, thus better serving the increasingly large online donor community.

MARKETING CHALLENGES AT THE RED CROSS

After much bad press, the ARC faces many challenges in marketing itself as a prominent, ethical, and transparent nonprofit organization. The ARC must effectively reduce perceived risk associated with giving to it, and must carefully choose partnerships with private corporations that will continue to encourage blood donations. The organization also must overcome any frivolous lawsuits that might damage its reputation. Lastly, the ARC must focus on marketing the positive impacts the organization has on society, including the vital role it plays in disaster relief. These marketing efforts will ideally translate into increased positive exposure and enhanced support for the organization.

Perceived Risks of Charitable Giving

Unfortunately for the ARC, many donors have been irritated by the numerous reports of fraudulent use of donations. Donors now associate a degree of uncertainty with giving to the ARC, as they question whether the funds will be used properly. The ARC has increased competition for funding as well. The number of nonprofit organizations searching for donor funds has increased dramatically in the past twenty years. In 1987 there were 422,000 nonprofit organizations in the United States; by 2005 the number had nearly doubled to 800,000. This growth obviously increases competition for charitable donations, especially in tough economic times. In order to maintain a strong donor base and continue to increase the monetary amount of donations, the ARC must increase transparency to assure donors that their money is being used responsibly.

Partnerships and the Red Cross Symbol

In 2004 the ARC joined in a unique marketing partnership with the independent film studio Lionsgate to co-market the release of a horror film entitled *Saw IV* while promoting blood collection services. The *Saw* "Give Till It Hurts" blood drive was a key element of the marketing campaign for the fourth installment of the most successful horror franchise of all time. Due in large part to promotions like the *Saw* blood drive in 2004, filmgoers' blood donations increased from 4,200 pints to 41,000 pints by 2007. In 2008, the *Saw* franchise again held a nationwide blood drive to draw attention to the release of *Saw V*. Marketing efforts such as these benefit both the film producers and the ARC by adding to the ARC's main goal of increasing blood supplies while also promoting the film. Many marketers believe that this sort of age-specific marketing strategy, accompanied by word-of-mouth advertising, is the best way to reach a new pool of potential volunteers.

"ARC must increase transparency to assure donors that their money is being used responsibly."

Lastly, the ARC benefits from brand recognition in the form of its internationally recognized Red Cross symbol, although this symbol also has generated controversy in the form of a lawsuit filed by Johnson & Johnson Company regarding licensing the Red Cross icon for use on commercial products. In 1887, Johnson & Johnson began using a red cross symbol on its surgical packages and registered the trademark for commercial use with the U.S. Patent Office in 1906. The ARC, on the other hand, cites its federal charter from the year 1900 as the adoption date for its emblem, and further points out that the image was developed in Switzerland in 1863 by the International Committee of the Red Cross, where the group decided that "volunteer nurses braving battlefields shall wear in all countries, as a uniform distinctive sign, a white armlet with a red cross."

In total, the ARC has sold first aid kits, preparedness kits, and related products that have generated over $2 million in revenue. Johnson & Johnson believed that the ARC was benefiting from consumers confusing the ARC packages for those of Johnson & Johnson, which has very similar packaging. The lawsuit was resolved in 2008, with both parties dismissing their suits and countersuits.

Focusing on Positive International Effects

From a marketing perspective, the greatest strength the ARC possesses is its ability to focus on the positive doings of its sister international organizations. The International Federation of Red Cross and Red Crescent Societies (IFRC) wrote a report discussing discrimination against women, the elderly, and the disabled in disasters. The IFRC concluded in this report that these situations, as well as sexual violence, can be prevented with an improvement in disaster-preparedness programs. This conclusion states that with stronger support by charitable organizations, such harsh discriminations can be reduced or eliminated in the future.

Even in incidents where the International Committee of the Red Cross (ICRC) is forced to evacuate a country, such as the case of Myanmar in 2006, the ARC has gained publicity from write-ups on the international association. An article in *The Economist,* for example, summarized Myanmar's decision regarding removal of the ICRC: "Last year the organization paid individual visits to more than 3,000 prisoners in 55 places. It has also been providing aid—foods, medicines, help with sanitation, and so on—to villages on the border." The article went on to state that "the ICRC announced that the ruling junta last month ordered it to close its five field offices in the country." Thus, even in negative circumstances, the positive coverage on the ICRC has benefitted the overall marketability of the ARC.

ETHICAL RISKS AND CHALLENGES

The American Red Cross faces many ethical risks and challenges. Some are common challenges for any organization of its size, such as executive compensation, preventing and handling employee misconduct, and considering all stakeholders in its operating model. Other risks are unique to the Red Cross, such as transparent and accurate representation of the organization's need for, and use of, monetary donations, volunteer time, and blood donations. Also, the ARC has the ethical challenges of maintaining effective and efficient operations to respond to disasters and transparently reporting the organization's accomplishments, failures, and opportunities for improvement in disaster response activities.

The executive turnover experienced by the ARC has brought to light the compensation awarded top executives. Bernadine Healy was given $1.9 million in salary and severance pay when she left in 2001. Marsha Evans was given $780,000 when she left in 2005. Much time and money was also spent in the search for and training of these top executives.

Employee misconduct also has been an issue, from the discrimination in disbursing relief after disasters to employee embezzlement. Such misconduct has occurred from New Orleans to Maryland and New Jersey, indicating a systemic problem. Addressing stakeholder needs, particularly those of the ARC's thousands of donors, is an ongoing challenge. Donors have a multitude of choices among nonprofits to support with their money and their time. They need open, honest, and transparent communication about how their resources are allocated and why such decisions are made. Issues like misrepresenting the use of the "Liberty Fund" collected after September 11 must be prevented if the ARC wishes to continue to be relevant.

The ARC must also address the specific ethical risks with its disaster response duties. Clear and efficient communications with federal and local government agencies is a challenge, as shown by the breakdown of communications in the aftermath of Hurricane Katrina. The ARC must develop strategic plans to better accomplish disaster response goals. These plans must include how to respond to organizational missteps and failures. Transparent, honest reporting of the ARC's goals, accomplishments, opportunities for improvement, and mistakes would go a long way to restoring the country's trust in the organization.

CONCLUSION

In short, the American Red Cross has a stakeholder obligation to fulfill its charter's expectations and deliver these promises effectively and efficiently. Charitable donations fund the nonprofit's operations and volunteers comprise 95 percent of its workers. The ARC staff and volunteers need to be well managed by capable directors and executives within ARC. Improvements to the ARC as an organization must begin with executive leadership and flow downward to every level of the group. Congressional oversight and interaction with federal, state, and local organizations must continue to be reviewed and modified to suit current needs.

Disaster relief cooperation in the form of partnering with private corporations to provide efficient and effective responses to victims of disasters should be continued. Joint marketing practices between the ARC and private businesses should also continue, as long unethical interactions or associations do not compromise the mission of the ARC. Close monitoring must be carried out by the many stakeholders of the ARC, including donors, staff, volunteers, and society in general.

QUESTIONS

1. Explain the possible problems in the ethical culture of the Red Cross that created the issues discussed in this case.
2. Name some of the problems the ARC has encountered with handling donation money.
3. What are some of the reasons for the ARC's ethical dilemmas, and how can the organization guarantee that these problems will not recur in the future?
4. What effect does organizational structure and compensation have on ethical behavior among chief executives at ARC?

SOURCES

"About Us," ARC, http://www.redcross.org/aboutus (accessed November 27, 2008); American Red Cross, "Ethics Rules and Policies," http://www.redcross.org/www-files/Documents/Governance/file_cont5874_lango_2226.pdf, pp. 7–8; Archibold, Randal C., "California: Ex-Executive at Red Cross Pleads Guilty," *New York Times,* May 26, 2007, http://www.nytimes.com/2007/05/26/us/26brfs-EXEXECUTIVEA_BRF.html?_r=1 (accessed December 22, 2008); Attkisson, Sharyl, "Disaster Strikes in Red Cross Backyard," CBS Evening News, July 29, 2002, http://www.cbsnews.com/stories/2002/07/29/eveningnews/main516700.shtml (accessed April 21, 2008); "The Battle Stations of the Cross," *Modern Healthcare* (August 20, 2007): 36; Breitkopf, David, "Stored-Value Cards for Katrina Victims," *American Banker* 170, no. 173 (2005): 20; "Caveat, Donor," *Searcher* 15, no. 2 (2007): 14; "Discrimination in Disasters," *Time,* December 31, 2007, p. 31; "Red Cross Does Not Mark the Spot," *The Economist* (December 2, 2006): 47; Dreazen, Yochi, "More Katrina Woes: Incidents of Fraud at Red Cross Centers," *Wall Street Journal,* October 14, 2005, p. B1; Hackl, Franz, and Gerald Josef Pruckner, "Demand and Supply of Emergency Help: An Economic Analysis of Red Cross Services," *Health Policy* 77, no. 3 (2006): 338; "Johnson & Johnson and American

Red Cross Announce Resolution to Lawsuit," *Fox Business Online,* June 17, 2008, http://www.foxbusiness.com/story/markets/industries/health-care/johnson--johnson-american-red-cross-announce-resolution-lawsuit (accessed December 22, 2008); Mullman, Jeremy, "Shoe on the Other Foot for Marin Institute," *Advertising Age* 77, no. 20 (2006): 8; Nobel, Carmen, "Donations Test Red Cross Staff," *Eweek* 22, no. 37 (2005): 23; "Overview of Red Cross Services," American Red Cross, 2008, http://www.redcross.org/portal/site/en/menuitem.86f46a12f382290517a8f210b80f78a0/?vgnextoid=1aa644e75215b110VgnVCM10000089f0870aRCRD&vgnextfmt=default, p. 3; "Red Crossing the Line," *Brandweek* (September 3, 2007, p. 38); Salmon, Jacqueline L., "Red Cross Gave Ousted Executive $780,000 Deal," *Washington Post,* March 4, 2006, p. A9; Sontag, Deborah, "What Brought Bernadine Healy Down?," *New York Times,* December 21, 2001, http://query.nytimes.com/gst/fullpage.html?res=9C02EEDC173EF930A15751C1A9679C8B63 (accessed December 22, 2008); Spector, Mike, "Red Cross CEO Shuffles Executive Ranks," *Wall Street Journal,* September 23, 2008, http://online.wsj.com/article/SB122220688507068655.html (accessed October 21, 2008); Strom, Stephanie, "Bill Would Restructure Red Cross," *New York Times,* December 5, 2006, http://www.nytimes.com/2006/12/05/washington/05cross.html (accessed April 17, 2008); Strom, Stephanie, "Firing Stirs New Debate Over Red Cross," *New York Times,* November 29, 2007, http://www.nytimes.com/2007/11/29/us/29cross.html?ref=us (accessed April 14, 2008); Strom, Stephanie, "President of Red Cross Resigns; Board Woes, Not Katrina, Cited," *New York Times,* December 14, 2005, http://www.nytimes.com/2005/12/14/politics/14redcross.html (accessed December 22, 2008); Strom, Stephanie, "Red Cross Sifting Internal Charges Over Katrina Aid," *New York Times,* March 24, 2006, p. A2; Suarez, Ray, "Red Cross Woes," The NewsHour with Jim Lehrer, December 19, 2001; Thomas, Anisya, and Lynn Fritz, "Disaster Relief, Inc.," *Harvard Business Review* 84, no. 11 (2006): 121; U.S. Government Accountability Office, "Coordination Between FEMA and the Red Cross Should Be Improved for the 2006 Hurricane Season," Report to Congressional Committees: Hurricanes Katrina and Rita, June 2006, p. 2.

CASE 4

Countrywide Financial: The Subprime Meltdown

Daryl Benson

Not too long ago, Countrywide Financial seemed to have everything going for it. Co-founded in part by Angelo Mozilo in 1969, it had become the largest provider of home loans in the United States within a few decades. By the early 2000s, one in six U.S. loans originated with Countrywide. In 1993, loan transactions reached the $1 trillion mark. Additionally, it was the number-one provider of home loans to minorities in the United States and had lowered the barriers of home ownership for lower-income individuals. Countrywide also offered loan closing, capital market, insurance, and banking services to its clients. In the 1970s, Countrywide had diversified into the securities market as well.

In 1992, Countrywide created a program called "House America" that enabled more consumers to qualify for home loans, as well as to make smaller down payments. In 2003, the company proposed the "We House America" program with a goal to provide $1 trillion in home loans to low-income and minority borrowers by 2010.

At the time, Countrywide's reputation in the industry was stellar. *Fortune* magazine called it the "23,000% stock" because between 1982 and 2003, Countrywide delivered investors a 23,000 percent return, exceeding the returns of Washington Mutual, Wal-Mart, and Warren Buffett's Berkshire Hathaway. In 1999, the company serviced $216.5 billion in loans. By 2000 the continued increase in revenues was attributed, in part, to home equity and subprime loans. The annual report for that year states: "Fiscal 2000 shows a higher margin for home equity and sub-prime loans (which, due in part to their higher cost structure charge a higher price per dollar loaned)."

Subprime loans were a key factor to Countrywide's immense success and rapid growth. However, the company's reliance on what was originally intended to aid low-income individuals also ended up contributing to its downfall.

This case was prepared by John Fraedrich, O.C. Ferrell, and Jennifer Jackson, with the editorial assistance of Jennifer Sawayda. This case was prepared for classroom discussion, rather than to illustrate either effective or ineffective handling of an administrative, ethical, or legal decision by management. All sources used for this case were obtained through publicly available material.

UNDERSTANDING SUBPRIME LOANS

To understand Countrywide's failure, one must first understand the concept of subprime lending. Simply put, subprime lending means lending to borrowers, generally people who would not qualify for traditional loans, at a rate higher than the prime rate (market rate), although how far above depends on factors like credit score, down payment, debt-to-income ratio, and payment delinquencies. Subprime lending is risky because clients are less likely to be able to pay back their loans.

Although subprime loans can be made for a variety of purposes, mortgages have gained the most news coverage. Subprime mortgages fall into three categories. First is the interest-only mortgage, through which borrowers pay only the loan's interest for a set period of time. The second type allows borrowers to pay monthly, but this often means that borrowers opt to pay an amount smaller than that needed to reduce the amount owed on the loan. Third, borrowers can find themselves with mortgages featuring a fixed interest rate for a period, converting to variable rates after a while.

Typically, subprime loans are offered to high-risk clients who do not qualify for conventional loans. The average borrower has a credit score of below 620 and is generally in the low-income bracket. However, a 2007 *Wall Street Journal* study revealed that from 2004 to 2006, the rate of middle- and upper-income subprime loan borrowers rose dramatically. During the early to mid 2000s, when real estate prices were booming and confidence levels were high, even clients who could have qualified for regular loans chose to take out subprime loans to finance their real estate speculations. As real estate prices peaked, more well-to-do investors turned to subprime mortgages to finance their expensive homes.

Although they have caused an immense amount of damage in the financial sector, in relation to the loan market as a whole, subprime loans comprise a relatively small part. In 2008, more than 6 million U.S. homeowners had subprime loans with a combined value of over $600 billion. In comparison, all other U.S. loans amounted to over $10 trillion. Although these loans make up only a small chunk of the overall loan market, many consider subprime loans to be a key contributor to the 2008 financial crisis.

One of the tools of the subprime loan is the adjustable rate mortgage (ARM) that allows borrowers to pay low introductory payments for three to five years, which would then be adjusted annually as the prime interest rate increases or decreases. Another type of ARM involves paying interest for a set number of years with balloon payments, meaning that people would make interest payments only for the life of the loan, and then would be expected to pay the entire principal at once upon maturity of the loan. These tools worked as long as the housing market remained on an upward trajectory, but when housing prices fell or interest rates increased, people discovered that they were unable to pay.

Many financial experts contributed to the problem by telling clients that in the future they would certainly have more income because of the increases in their property's value. They assured home buyers that even if their monthly payments increased, they would be able to afford them because the value of their homes would have increased so much. Even consumers with good credit looking to refinance were attracted to the attractive interest rates of these mortgages without fully recognizing the possible consequences.

THE SUBPRIME CRISIS

When first popularized, the financial tool of subprime loans was praised for lowering barriers to home ownership. The U.S. Department of Housing and Urban Development stated that the subprime loan was helping many minorities afford homes, and was therefore a good tool.

Although subprime lending became a major news topic only in the early part of the twenty-first century, the subprime concept began in the 1970s in Orange County, California. At this time, rural farmland was being converted into suburbs, and subprime loans were a way for people to buy homes even if their credit was poor. The typical subprime recipient would not have met normal lending standards. At that time, the subprime loans made sense as a means to fuel southern California's growth. Homes were appreciating rapidly, so if a family decided to buy a house and live there for three to five years, they could reasonably expect that home to sell for over 50 percent more than what they had paid. In addition, Congress passed the Equal Credit Opportunity Act in 1974 to help ensure that all consumers had an equal chance to receive a loan. Potential homeowners, in theory, would no longer be rejected based on sex, race, national origin, or any other factor considered discriminatory.

Contractors also wanted a part of the action. They began to build houses and "flip" them. Flipping is when the contractor builds homes without buyers on credit, and then takes the sale of the homes to the lending institution as collateral to obtain more credit to build more homes. Speculators also flipped existing homes by buying them on credit with no intention of keeping them, waiting until the value had increased, and selling them at a profit.

Industries that supplied homebuilders were profiting as well, and costs of materials increased with the high demand. Realtors were motivated to push sales through because of commissions they could earn (on average 6 percent of the sales price). Commissions were a significant part of many mortgage officers' compensation. Even real estate appraisers began to inflate the value of homes to ensure loans would go through. This was to become one of the chief accusations against Countrywide during the financial crisis.

But then something happened that no one had considered. The U.S. economy began to slow. People started working more and earning less money. Jobs started moving abroad, health insurance became more expensive, gas prices increased, and the baby boomers began to sell their homes to fund their retirement. In spite of this, builders kept on building, and the financial industry continued to lend to increasingly risky buyers. Homeowners found that they had less and less disposable income to make housing payments.

The result was a surplus of housing in which homeowners could no longer afford their homes. Banks began to foreclose on houses when the homeowners could not pay. As the demand for housing decreased, banks lost significant amounts of money. Many other industries, like the automobile industry and insurance companies, were also negatively affected as struggling citizens tried to cope with the economic downturn. With plummeting stock prices, the United States began experiencing a financial crisis that had a rippling effect across the world. Economist Alan Greenspan said the crisis could be "the most wrenching since the end of the Second World War."

Late 2007 marked the tipping-point for the burgeoning mortgage crisis. Foreclosure rates skyrocketed, and borrowers and investors began to feel the full ramifications of taking the subprime risk. Mortgage defaults played a part in triggering a string of serious bank and financial institution failures as well. Investors began to abandon their mortgage-backed securities, causing huge institutions such as Morgan Stanley, Merrill Lynch, and Citigroup to lose large sums of money. Morgan Stanley, for example, lost over $265 billion internationally. Bear Stearns required government intervention to stay afloat. Analysts have attributed the banks' failings to poor intra-bank communication and a lack of effective risk management.

Although the chief financial officer (CFO) is supposed to be in charge of risk management, it appears that many institutions viewed the role as merely advisory. It was highly risky for these firms to downplay the importance of the CFO. Not only did many of these banks fail at risk management, but they also were in violation of the Sarbanes-Oxley Act—which requires that a company verify its ability to internally control its financial reporting. A CFO not directly in charge of a company's finances is signing off on something that he or she actually knows little about. The extent of the 2008–2009 financial crisis has made it clear to many that a massive overhaul of the financial industry's regulatory system is needed.

COUNTRYWIDE'S INVOLVEMENT IN THE SUBPRIME CRISIS

During the early 2000s, Countrywide reaped the benefits of subprime loans. In 2001, mortgages contributed to 28 percent of Countrywide's earnings, with subprime loans up to $280 million (the year before, subprime loans represented $86.9 million). In 2002, Countrywide's loan portfolio to minorities and low- to moderate-income borrower tracts had dramatically and rapidly increased. Countrywide had also increased its commissioned sales force by nearly 60 percent, to 3,484 salespeople in 2003, with the goal of increasing overall market share.

"By 2008, the company had accrued over $8 billion in subprime loans with a 7 percent delinquency rate."

Some critics have argued that salespeople were given incentives to undertake riskier transactions in order to continue to grow the company at a rapid rate. One allegation against Countrywide is that, in order to increase its profit, it would even offer subprime loans to people who qualified for regular loans. Leading the day-to-day operations of the Consumer Markets Division was David Sambol, who would later be implicated in the scandal.

After years of fast growth and upbeat projections, Countrywide's 2007 annual report had a somber tone. The financial crisis had begun and the company was feeling its negative effects. A significant amount of the report focused on the details of accounting for its mortgage portfolio and default rates. In one year, Countrywide depreciated over $20 billion and absorbed over $1 billion in losses. By 2008, the company had accrued over $8 billion in subprime loans with a 7 percent delinquency rate. The industry average was 4.67 percent delinquency. That year foreclosures doubled, and the firm laid off 10 to 20 percent of its employees, or 10,000 to 20,000 people.

The company attempted to ease loan terms on more than 81,000 homeowners with a program called the Countrywide Comprehensive Home Preservation Program. The program allowed consumers to refinance or modify loans with an adjustable rate mortgage for a lower interest rate or switch to a fixed-rate mortgage. The president and chief operating officer, David Sambol, stated, "Countrywide believes that none of our subprime borrowers that have demonstrated the ability to make payments should lose their home to foreclosure solely as a result of a rate [increase]. This is yet another step in our continuing effort to identify and improve existing programs that assist our customers."

Countrywide also created special divisions to help borrowers, and actively informed its customers about their options. The company offered phone counseling teams, personalized resource mailings, and counselors within communities who could meet face-to-face. Countrywide appeared to be genuine in its attempts to help homeowners, but it was too little too late. By then questions and accusations had begun to develop against company leaders.

In 2008, Alphonso Jackson, Secretary of Housing and Urban Development (HUD), reported that more than 500,000 Countrywide consumers were in danger of facing foreclosure. The blame for this was focused primarily on subprime lending and adjustable rate mortgages. Countrywide Financial countered that there were other reasons for delinquencies and foreclosures. It maintained the main causes of delinquencies and foreclosures were unrelated to the company's investment decisions—issues like medical problems, divorce, and unemployment—not adjustable rate mortgages. It further claimed that less than 1 percent of its consumers had defaulted on account of adjustable rate mortgages. Still, consumers began to question whether Countrywide's risky lending played a role in the larger financial crisis.

ISSUES RELATED TO THE BANK OF AMERICA ACQUISITION

In 2008, Bank of America, one of the United States' top financial institutions with $683 billion in assets, offered to buy Countrywide Financial for $4 billion. The price tag was a substantial discount on what the company was actually worth. Bank of America paid approximately $8/share while shares were valued at $20/share earlier in the year. Kenneth D. Lewis, chair, president, and CEO of Bank of America, said at the time, "We are aware of the issues within the housing and mortgage industries. The transaction reflects those challenges. Mortgages will continue to be an important relationship product, and we now will have an opportunity to better serve our customers and to enhance future profitability."

At the time, Bank of America held $1.5 trillion in assets, which better equipped them to deal with the crisis. "Their balance sheet can take a shock much better than Countrywide," said CreditSights senior analyst David Hendler. "When you take the shocks at Countrywide, they have a big, busting consequence that's negative." Bart Narter, senior analyst at Celent, a Boston-based financial research and consulting firm, said, "There's still plenty of risk involved. He's brave to do it. But I think that it's very likely down the road to be profitable, maybe not immediately, but long-term."

However, there may have been other reasons why Countrywide allowed Bank of America to acquire it. It may be that Countrywide thought Bank of America was better able to handle the ethical investigations concerning Countrywide taken on by the government. Among other issues, Countrywide was coming under increased scrutiny for giving out so-called *liar loans*. Liar loans are mortgages that require no proof of the borrower's income or assets. These loans allowed consumers to purchase homes while having few or no assets. With the additional burden of the financial crisis, many homeowners with liar loans could not pay their mortgages, nor were they able to refinance their homes because housing prices plummeted. Some were forced into foreclosure, generating substantial losses for mortgage companies and the economy. One economic website estimated that the true cost of liar loans totaled over $100 billion in losses.

Countrywide Financial was one of the top providers of liar loans. These loans allowed the industry to profit, at least for a little while, because people with liar loans were riskier clients, and therefore had to pay higher fees and interest rates to the mortgage company. Many accuse Countrywide of negligence, of giving out highly risky loans to people who could not afford them for the sake of quick profits. Others accuse the company of even more unethical dealings. Some homeowners who are now struggling under liar loans are accusing Countrywide of *predatory lending*, saying the company misled them.

Although some homeowners may have been truly misled into liar loans, an estimated 90 percent of liar loan applicants knowingly overstated their income, with three out of five overstating it by at least 50 percent. This rampant dishonesty, critics charge, could not have occurred without the mortgage company's awareness. It has sparked new investigations into whether Countrywide *aided* borrowers in falsifying information. Hence, some attest that Countrywide's buyout by Bank of America may have been more than just an economic choice. Instead, it could have been a way to prepare for the onslaught of criticism that would arise against Countrywide.

In March 2008, Bank of America decided to retain David Sambol, Executive Managing Director of Business Segment Operations at Countrywide, as well as to pay him a hefty compensation package. Sambol received a bachelor's degree in Business Administration and Accounting from California State University, Northridge, in 1982. Prior to joining Countrywide in 1985, Sambol served as a certified public accountant with the accounting firm of Ernst & Whinney. After getting hired at Countrywide, his unit led all revenue-generating functions of the company. He was instrumental in Countrywide's mortgage division expanding to become the most comprehensive in the industry.

> ***Countrywide Financial was one of the top providers of liar loans.***

In March 2008, Bank of America agreed to set up a $20 million retention account for Sambol, payable in equal installments on the first and second anniversaries of the merger, plus $8 million in restricted stock. Sambol's retention package also included the use of a company car or car allowance, country club dues, and financial consulting services through the end of 2009. He was also to continue to have access to a company airplane for business and personal travel.

Much of the public was outraged that Sambol would receive such high compensation after taking part in Countrywide's questionable business dealings. The outcry over Countrywide Financial and other companies that had participated in the subprime mortgage market was so great that the U.S. Congress held a series of hearings to investigate dealings in the subprime market. Senator Charles E. Schumer, D–NY, chair of Congress' Joint Economic Committee, asked Bank of America to reconsider the decision to put Sambol in charge of home lending. "There seem to be two economic realities operating in our country today," said Representative Henry A. Waxman, D–CA, the committee chair. "Most Americans live in a world where economic security is precarious and there are real economic consequences for failure. But our nation's top executives seem to live by a different set of rules. The question before the committee was: when companies fail to perform, should they still give millions of dollars to their senior executives?" After the hearings, Bank of America announced that Barbara Desoer, Bank of America's chief technology and operations officer, would replace Sambol. Sambol would continue to receive some, though not all, of his perks.

THE ROLE OF COUNTRYWIDE'S CEO ANGELO MOZILO

Angelo Mozilo is being investigated by the SEC for potential fraud, although Mozilo maintains his innocence. Particularly, the SEC is concerned about the sale of company stock options that netted Mozilo over $400 million between 2002 and 2008. Mozilo has always maintained his innocence. In a 2007 *Business Week* interview, Mozilo was asked about allegations that he profited over $100 million on stock sales in the previous year. Mozilo asserted, "I have not sold any stock, to my recollection, in 10 years. Everything I've sold was options. The selling is because [when the options] expire, I no longer have the benefit of what I have built and what this team has built for the last 40 years. Up until this debacle, I created $25 billion in value for shareholders. There have been very few—only about 11 stocks—that have performed better over the last 25 years than Countrywide. I could have sold all of those shares at 40 bucks a share and didn't because I want to be aligned with the shareholders."

The public did not seem to believe Mozilo's defense, especially after he received a $100 million severance package when Countrywide was sold to Bank of America. In 2007–2008, Mozilo was named as a defendant in many lawsuits. The plaintiffs included:

- International Brotherhood of Electrical Workers Local 98 Pension Fund
- Norfolk County Retirement System
- Arkansas Teacher Retirement System
- Fire & Police Pension Association of Colorado
- Public Employees' Retirement System of Mississippi
- Argent Classic Convertible Arbitrage Fund
- New Jersey Carpenters' Pension Fund
- New York City Employees' Retirement System

One lawsuit alleged misconduct and disregard of fiduciary duties, including a lack of good faith and lack of oversight of Countrywide's lending practices. The lawsuit also accused Countrywide of improper financial reporting and lack of internal controls, alleging that Mozilo was paid $10 million more than was disclosed. Additionally, the company claimed that Countrywide's officers and directors unlawfully sold over $848 million of stock between 2004 and 2008 at inflated prices using insider information.

Mozilo's pay also drew heavy scrutiny from members of Congress. Federal securities regulators and congressional investigators found that easy bonus targets and other underhanded methods helped him inflate his pay. In the hearings about executive pay, Congressman Elijah E. Cummings of Maryland said, "We've got golden parachutes drifting off to the golf course and have people I see every day who are losing their homes and wondering where their kids will do their homework." He then asked Mozilo about an e-mail message he sent demanding that the taxes due on his wife's travel on the corporate jet be covered by the company. "It sounds out of whack today because it is out of whack, but in 2006 the company was going great," said Mozilo. "In today's world I would never write that memo." He also apologized for another e-mail message in which he complained about his compensation. "It was an emotional time," he said. But in the same hearings, Mozilo also reminded the audience that Countrywide's stock price had appreciated over 23,000 percent from 1982 to 2007. Shareholders did approve

Mozilo's performance-based bonuses and he exercised the options as he prepared for retirement. "In short, as our company did well, I did well," he said.

BANK OF AMERICA PLANS A RECOVERY

In July 2008, Bank of America bought Countrywide without Sambol or Mozilo. Since 2001, Bank of America has been focused on profit, not growth. However, it might be a while before Bank of America profits from the acquisition of Countrywide. According to the Securities and Exchange Commission, Bank of America has taken on $16.6 billion in Countrywide's debts. Exiting the subprime lending market is part of Bank of America's long-term plan. The company liquidated $26.3 billion of its subprime real estate portfolio in 2008–2009 and has managed its existing $9.7 billion portfolio over its remaining term.

Bank of America clearly understood that by buying Countrywide, it inherited a volatile earning stream that had become unattractive from a risk-reward standpoint. Kenneth Lewis, CEO of Bank of America said at the time, "We are committed to achieving consistent, above-average shareholder returns and these actions are aimed at achieving that mission." Bank of America plans to replace Countrywide's brand with its own.

In addition to managing Countrywide's debt, Bank of America must also handle the stream of lawsuits being filed against the company. Many of these lawsuits claim that the company duped homeowners with predatory loan practices. Countrywide has agreed to provide $8 billion in loan and foreclosure relief to more than 397,000 homeowners. It also has agreed to adjust the terms of ARMs according to borrowers' income. Bank of America's Barbara Doeser, who replaced David Sambol, said the company is committed to helping homeowners and is cutting interest rates to as low as 2.5 percent.

"Countrywide has agreed to provide $8 billion in loan and foreclosure relief to more than 397,000 homeowners."

Countrywide is facing additional investigations for other alleged cases of misconduct. In March 2008, the FBI started an investigation to find out whether Countrywide misrepresented its financial information. Additionally, the FBI is investigating Countrywide's VIP program that, according to an insider, provided special mortgage deals to certain high-up officials, known as "Friends of Angelo's." These deals included discount rates and fees not offered to ordinary Countrywide customers. Those implicated in these dealings include Democratic senators Chris Dodd and Kent Conrad, two former cabinet members, and two CEOs from Fannie Mae. These officials have denied that they knew they were getting special discounts. Prosecutors are looking into whether these discounts constituted improper gifts and whether they qualified as illegal on Countrywide's part.

Despite these proceedings, Bank of America Barbara Doeser remains optimistic about the future. Like so many others, Bank of America suffered massive losses as 2008 came to a close, with a drop in net income of 95 percent in the fourth quarter. Yet Doeser has cited some improvements. She said, "But last quarter, the first quarter that Countrywide and Bank of America operated as one company, we made 250,000 first mortgages, worth $51 billion of principal, plus $6 billion of home-equity loans." The company is predicting that home prices will stabilize by late 2009.

CONCLUSION

Countrywide was not the only cause of the financial crisis. Numerous Wall Street companies are being investigated for unethical practices related to this scandal. (This list includes the Bank of America, which has been investigated for potential breaches of fiduciary duty concerning employee retirement funds.) However, Countrywide's unethical behavior was a key contributor to the problems with the economy in 2008–2009. Many consider it to be one of the central villains in this crisis. They allege that Countrywide knowingly engaged in risky loans, offering subprime loans even to those who qualified for regular loans, in order to profit from the higher rates. In the process, it may have helped to falsify lender information, allowing those with no assets to obtain loans. The consequence was a surplus of housing, plummeting housing prices, and a slew of foreclosures, all of which placed the economy in a precarious state. The result is that the United States has lost global credibility as an economic superpower of the free world.

The Countrywide scandal has brought up other issues, including that of executive compensation. Should executives receive hefty compensation packages and severance pay when their companies flounder? Should they be called into account for not exercising due care? Many people think so, as evidenced by the enormous public outrage facing those like David Sambol and Angelo Mozilo. It is clear that Countrywide has failed the majority of its stakeholders. Ethical misconduct and high-risk business practices helped to create the disaster at Countrywide. It remains to be seen whether its acquisition by the Bank of America will be enough to salvage its reputation and to save the business that was once Countrywide Financial.

QUESTIONS

1. Are subprime loans an unethical financial instrument, or are they ethical but misused in a way that created ethical issues?
2. Discuss the ethical issues that caused the downfall of Countrywide Financial.
3. How should Bank of America deal with potential ethical and legal misconduct discovered at Countrywide?

SOURCES

"Bank of America Assumes $16.6B in Countrywide Debt," *Dayton Business Journal*, November 10, 2008, http://www.bizjournals.com/dayton/stories/2008/11/10/daily7.html (accessed November 14, 2008); Bartiromo, Maria, "Countrywide Feels the Heat," *BusinessWeek*, August 29, 2007, http://www.businessweek.com/bwdaily/dnflash/content/aug2007/db20070829_117563.htm?chan=search (accessed March 16, 2008); Caputo, Angela, "Countrywide Accord Paves Way for More Loan Remodifications," *Progress Illinois*, November 12, 2008, http://progressillinois.com/2008/11/12/loan-modification-plan; Countrywide Financial, http://about.countrywide.com (accessed September 1, 2009); "Countrywide Moves to Ease Mortgage Misery," *BusinessWeek*, October 23, 2007, www.businessweek.com/investor/content/oct2007/pi20071023_454573.htm (accessed March 16, 2008); Colvin, Geoff, "Signs of Life from the Mortgage Frontline," *Forbes*, November 13, 2008, http://money.cnn.

com/2008/11/12/magazines/fortune/colvin_desoer.fortune/?postversion=2008111311 (accessed November 14, 2008); Equal Credit Opportunity Act, Federal Trade Commission, http://www.ftc.gov/bcp/edu/pubs/consumer/credit/cre15.shtm (accessed September 1, 2009); Farzad, Roben, "In Search of a Subprime Villain," *BusinessWeek*, January 24, 2008, http://www.businessweek.com/magazine/content/08_05/b4069077193810.htm?chan=search (accessed March 16, 2008); Gimein, Mark, "Inside the Liar's Loan: How the Mortgage Industry Nurtured Deceit," *Slate*, April 24, 2008, http://www.slate.com/id/2189576/ (accessed November 14, 2008); Greenspan, Alan, "We Will Never Have a Perfect Model of Risk," *Financial Times*, March 16, 2008, http://www.ft.com/cms/s/edbdbcf6-f360-11dc-b6bc-0000779fd2ac,Authorised=false.html?_i_location=http%3A%2F%2Fwww.ft.com%2Fcms%2Fs%2F0%2Fedbdbcf6-f360-11dc-b6bc-0000779fd2ac.html%3Fnclick_check%3D1&_i_referer=http%3A%2F%2Fsearch.yahoo.com%2Fsearch%3Fp%3Dthe%2Bmost%2Bwrenching%2Bsince%2Bthe%2Bend%2Bof%2Bthe%2Bsecond%2Bworld%2Bwar%252C%2BAlan%2BGreenspan%26fr%3Dyfp-t-501%26toggle%3D1%26cop%3Dmss%26ei%3DUTF-8&nclick_check=1 (accessed November 15, 2008); Gutierrez, Carl, "Countrywide's New Bad News," *Forbes*, March 10, 2008, http://www.forbes.com/markets/2008/03/10/countrywide-fbi-mortgage-markets-equity-cx_cg_0310markets26.html (accessed September 1, 2009); "Judge Rules Mozilo and Countrywide Execs Must Face Multi-Million Dollar Federal Lawsuit," *New York Times*, May 22, 2008, http://www.nytimes.com/2008/03/07/business/07cnd-pay.html?_r=1&oref=slogin (accessed September 1, 2009); "Kansas, 11 Other States Reach Agreement with Countrywide Financial Corporation," *Kansas City Info Zine*, November 14, 2008, http://www.infozine.com/news/stories/op/storiesView/sid/31858/ (accessed September 1, 2009); "'Liar Loans' Threaten to Prolong Mortgage Mess," MSNBC, August 18, 2008, http://www.msnbc.msn.com/id/26270434/ (accessed November 14, 2008); Marco, Meg, "Subprime Meltdown: Inside the Countrywide Subprime Lending Frenzy," *The Consumerist*, August 27, 2008, http://consumerist.com/consumer/subprime-meltdown/inside-the-countrywide-subprime-lending-frenzy-293902.php (accessed November 13, 2008); Mortgage Industry Statistics, LenderRATEMATCH, freeratesearch.com/en/newsroom/mortgage_statistics/ (accessed April 1, 2008); Moyer, Liz, "A Subprime Solution," *Forbes*, December 6, 2007, http://www.forbes.com/wallstreet/2007/12/05/subprime-paulson-bush-biz-wall-cx_lm_1206subprime.html (accessed March 25, 2008); Myers, Lisa, and Amna Nawaz, "Feds Probe Countrywide's 'VIP' Program," NBC News, October 30, 2008, http://deepbackground.msnbc.msn.com/archive/2008/10/30/1613877.aspx (accessed November 14, 2008); Reckard, Scott, "Countrywide Head Ousted by Bank of America," *Los Angeles Times*, May 29, 2008, http://www2.tbo.com/content/2008/may/29/bz-countrywide-head-ousted-by-bank-of-america/?news-money (accessed June 2008); Subprime Lending, United States Department of Housing and Urban Development, http://www.hud.gov/offices/fheo/lending/subprime.cfm (accessed March 16, 2008); Wartzman, Rick, "The Countrywide Conundrum," *BusinessWeek*, November 9, 2007, http://www.businessweek.com/managing/content/nov2007/ca2007119_693870.htm?chan=search (accessed March 16, 2008).

CASE 5

Arthur Andersen: Questionable Accounting Practices

Arthur Andersen LLP was founded in Chicago in 1913 by Arthur Andersen and partner Clarence DeLany. Over a span of nearly 90 years, the Chicago accounting firm would become known as one of the "Big Five" largest accounting firms in the United States, together with Deloitte & Touche, PricewaterhouseCoopers, Ernst & Young, and KPMG. For most of those years, the firm's name was synonymous with trust, integrity, and ethics. Such values are crucial for a firm charged with independently auditing and confirming the financial statements of public corporations, whose accuracy investors depend on for investment decisions.

In its earlier days, Andersen set standards for the accounting profession and advanced new initiatives on the strength of its then undeniable integrity. One example of Andersen's leadership in the profession occurred in the late 1970s when companies began acquiring IBM's new 360-mainframe computer system, the most expensive new computer technology available at the time. Many companies had been depreciating computer hardware on the basis of an assumed 10-year useful life. Andersen, under the leadership of Leonard Spacek, determined that a more realistic life span for the computers was five years. Andersen therefore advised its accounting clients to use the shorter time period for depreciation purposes, although this resulted in higher expenses charged against income and a smaller bottom line. Public corporations that failed to adopt the more conservative measure would receive an "adverse" opinion from Andersen's auditors, something they could ill afford.

Arthur Andersen once exemplified the rock-solid character and integrity that was synonymous with the accounting profession. However, high-profile bankruptcies of clients such as Enron and WorldCom capped a string of accounting scandals that eventually cost investors nearly $300 billion and hundreds of thousands of people their jobs. As a result, the Chicago-based accounting firm closed its doors in 2002, after 90 years of business.

This case was prepared by O. C. Ferrell, with the assistance of Jennifer Jackson and Jennifer Sawayda, The University of New Mexico. Heather Stein, Colorado State University, helped to draft a previous edition of this case. This case was prepared for classroom discussion rather than to illustrate either effective or ineffective handling of an administrative, ethical, or legal decision by management. All sources used in this case were obtained through publicly available material.

THE ADVENT OF CONSULTING

Leonard Spacek joined the company in 1947 following the death of founder Arthur Andersen. He was perhaps best known for his uncompromising insistence on auditor independence, which stood in stark contrast to the philosophy of combining auditing and consulting services that many firms, including Andersen itself, later adopted. Andersen began providing consulting services to large clients such as General Electric and Schlitz Brewing in the 1950s. Over the next 30 years, Andersen's consulting business became more profitable on a per-partner basis than its core accounting and tax services businesses.

According to the American Institute of Certified Public Accountants (AICPA), the objective of an independent audit of a client's financial statements is "the expression of an opinion on the fairness with which [the financial statements] present, in all material respects, financial position, results of operations, and its cash flows in conformity with generally accepted accounting principles." The primary responsibility of an auditor is to express an opinion on a client firm's financial statements after conducting an audit to obtain reasonable assurance that the client's financial statements are free of misstatements. It is important to note that financial statements are the responsibility of a company's management and not the outside auditor.

However, at Andersen growth became the highest priority, and its emphasis on recruiting and retaining big clients might have come at the expense of quality and independent audits. The company linked its consulting business in a joint cooperative relationship with its audit arm, which compromised its auditors' independence, a quality crucial to the execution of a credible audit. The firm's focus on growth also generated a fundamental change in its corporate culture, one in which obtaining high-profit consulting business seems to have been regarded more highly than providing objective auditing services. Those individuals who could deliver the big accounts were often promoted before those people who were concerned with conducting quality audits.

Andersen's consulting business became recognized as one of the fastest-growing and most profitable consulting networks in the world. Revenues from consulting surpassed the auditing unit for the first time in 1984. Although Andersen's consulting business was growing at a rapid pace, its audit practice remained the company's bread and butter. Ten years later, Arthur Andersen merged its operational and business systems consulting units and set up a separate business consulting practice in order to offer clients a broader range of integrated services. Throughout the 1990s, Andersen reaped huge profits by selling consulting services to many clients whose financial statements it also audited. This lucrative full-service strategy would later pose an ethical conflict-of-interest dilemma for some Andersen partners, who had to decide how to treat questionable accounting practices discovered at some of Andersen's largest clients.

Thanks to the growth of Andersen's consulting services, many viewed it as a successful model that other large accounting firms should emulate. However, this same model eventually raised alarm bells at the Securities and Exchange Commission (SEC), concerned over its potential for compromising the independence of audits. In 1998, then SEC chairman Arthur Levitt publicly voiced these concerns and recommended new rules that would restrict the non-audit services that accounting firms could provide to their audit clients—a suggestion that Andersen vehemently opposed.

Nonetheless, in 1999 Andersen chose to split its accounting and consulting functions into two separate—and often competing—units. Reportedly, under this arrangement, competition between the two units for accounts tended to discourage a team spirit and instead fostered secrecy and self-interestedness. Communication suffered, hampering the firm's ability to respond quickly and effectively to crises. As revenues grew, the consulting unit demanded greater compensation and recognition. Infighting between the consulting and auditing units grew until the company was essentially split into two opposing factions.

In August 2000, following an arbitration hearing, a judge ruled that Andersen's consulting arm could effectively divorce the accounting firm and operate independently. By that time, Andersen's consulting business consisted of about 11,000 consultants and brought in global revenues of nearly $2 billion. Arthur Andersen, as a whole, employed more than 85,000 people worldwide. The new consulting company promptly changed its name to Accenture the following January. The court later ordered Arthur Andersen to change its name to Andersen Worldwide in order to better represent its new global brand of accounting services.

> *"News that Enron had overstated earnings became public, sending shock waves through the financial markets."*

Meanwhile, in January 2001, Andersen named Joseph Berardino as the new CEO of the U.S. audit practice. His first task was to navigate the smaller company through a number of lawsuits that had developed in prior years. The company paid $110 million in May 2001 to settle claims brought by Sunbeam shareholders for accounting irregularities and $100 million to settle with Waste Management shareholders over similar charges a month later. In the meantime, news that Enron had overstated earnings became public, sending shock waves through the financial markets." Over the following year, many companies, a number of them Andersen clients, were forced to restate earnings. The following sections describe a few of the cases that helped lead to Andersen's collapse.

BAPTIST FOUNDATION OF ARIZONA

In what would become the largest bankruptcy of a nonprofit charity in U.S history, the Baptist Foundation of Arizona (BFA), which Andersen served as auditor, lost $570 million of donor funds. BFA, an agency of the Arizona Southern Baptist Convention, was founded in 1948 to raise and manage endowments for church work in Arizona. It operated like a bank, paying interest on deposits that were used mostly to invest in Arizona real estate. The foundation also offered estate and financial planning services to the state's more than 400 Southern Baptist churches, and was one of the few foundations to offer investments to individuals.

BFA invested heavily in real estate, a more speculative investment strategy than other Baptist foundations in the state traditionally used. Profits from investments were supposed to be used to fund the churches' ministries and numerous charitable causes. Problems began when the real estate market in Arizona suffered a downturn, and BFA's management came under pressure to show a profit. To do so, foundation officials allegedly concealed losses from investors beginning in 1986 by selling some properties at inflated prices to entities that had borrowed money from the foundation and were unlikely to pay for the properties unless the real estate market turned around. In what court documents would later dub a Ponzi scheme, foundation officials allegedly took money from new investors to pay off existing investors in order to keep cash flowing. All the while, the foundation's top officers continued to receive six-figure salaries. With obligations to investors mounting, the scheme eventually unraveled, leading to criminal investigations and investor lawsuits against BFA and Andersen; more than half of the foundation's 133 employees were laid off.

Finally, the foundation petitioned for Chapter 11 bankruptcy protection in 1999, listing debts of about $640 million against assets of about $240 million.

The investor lawsuit against Andersen accused the auditing firm of issuing false and misleading approvals of BFA's financial statements, which allowed the foundation to perpetuate the fraud. Andersen, in a February 2000 statement, responded that it sympathized with BFA investors but stood by the accuracy of its audit opinions. The firm blamed BFA management for the collapse, arguing that it was given misleading information on which to conduct the audits. However, during nearly two years of investigation, reports surfaced that Andersen had been warned of possible fraudulent activity, and the firm eventually agreed to pay $217 million to settle the shareholder lawsuit in May 2002.

SUNBEAM

Andersen's troubles over Sunbeam Corp. began when its audits failed to address serious accounting errors that eventually led to a class-action lawsuit by Sunbeam investors and the ouster of CEO Albert Dunlap in 1998. Boca Raton–based Sunbeam is the maker of such home appliance brands as Mr. Coffee, Mixmaster, Oster, Powermate, and others. Both the lawsuit and a civil injunction filed by the SEC accused Sunbeam of inflating earnings through fraudulent accounting strategies such as "cookie jar" revenues, recording revenue on contingent sales, and accelerating sales from later periods into the present quarter. The company was also accused of using improper "bill and hold" transactions, which involves booking sales months ahead of actual shipment or billing, temporarily inflating revenue through accounts receivable, and artificially boosting quarterly net income. As a result, Sunbeam was forced to restate six quarters of financial statements. The SEC's injunction also accused Phillip Harlow, then a partner at Arthur Andersen, of authorizing clean or "unqualified" opinions on Sunbeam's 1996 and 1997 financial statements despite his awareness of many of Sunbeam's accounting and disclosure improprieties.

In August 2002, a federal judge approved a $141 million settlement in the case. In it, Andersen agreed to pay $110 million to resolve the claims without admitting fault or liability. Losses to Sunbeam shareholders amounted to about $4.4 billion, with job losses of about 1,700.

WASTE MANAGEMENT

Andersen also found itself in court over questionable accounting practices with regard to $1.4 billion of overstated earnings at Waste Management. A complaint filed by the SEC charged Waste Management with perpetrating a "massive" financial fraud over a period of more than five years. According to the complaint, the company's senior management aided and abetted others' violations of antifraud, reporting, and record keeping provisions of federal securities laws, resulting in a loss to investors of more than $6 billion. Andersen was named in the case as having assisted in the fraud by repeatedly issuing unqualified audit opinions on Waste Management's materially misleading financial statements.

According to SEC documents, Waste Management capped the amount of fees it would pay for Andersen's auditing services, but it advised Andersen that it could earn additional fees through "special work." At first, Andersen identified improper accounting practices and presented them to Waste Management officials in a report called "Proposed

Adjusting Journal Entries," which outlined entries that needed to be corrected to avoid understating Waste Management's expenses and overstating its earnings. However, Waste officials refused to make the corrections, and instead allegedly entered into a closed-door agreement with Andersen to write off the accumulated errors over a 10-year period and change its underlying accounting practices, but only in future periods. The SEC viewed this agreement as an attempt to cover up past frauds and to commit future frauds.

The result of these cases was that Andersen paid some $220 million to Waste Management shareholders and $7 million to the SEC. Four Andersen partners were sanctioned, and an injunction was obtained against the firm. Andersen, as part of its consent decree, was forced to promise not to sign off on spurious financial statements in the future or it would face disbarment from practicing before the SEC—a promise that it would later break with Enron. After the dust settled, Waste Management shareholders lost about $20.5 billion and about 11,000 employees were laid off.

ENRON

In October 2001, the Securities and Exchange Commission announced that it was launching an investigation into the accounting of Enron, one of Andersen's biggest clients. Indeed, Andersen's new CEO, Joseph Berardino, had perhaps viewed the $1 million a week in audit fees Enron paid to Andersen, along with the consulting fees it paid to Andersen's spin-off firm, Accenture, as a significant opportunity to expand revenues at Andersen. Plus, with Enron as a client, Andersen had been able to make 80 percent of the companies in the oil and gas industry its clients. However, on November 8, 2001, Enron was forced to restate five years' worth of financial statements that Andersen had signed off on, accounting for $586 million in losses. Within a month, Enron had filed for bankruptcy. The U.S. Justice Department began a criminal investigation into Andersen in January 2002, prompting both Andersen's clients and its employees to jump ship. The auditing firm eventually admitted to destroying a number of documents concerning its auditing of Enron, which led to an indictment for obstruction of justice on March 14, 2002. CEO Bernardino stepped down by the end of the month.

> *"Enron was forced to restate five years' worth of financial statements that Andersen had signed off on"*

As Andersen's obstruction-of-justice trial progressed, Nancy Temple, Andersen's Chicago-based lawyer, demanded Fifth Amendment protection and thus did not have to testify. Many others named her as the "corrupt persuader" who led others astray. She allegedly instructed David Duncan, Andersen's supervisor of the Enron account, to remove her name from memos that could have incriminated her. On June 15, 2002, the jury found Andersen guilty of obstruction of justice, the first accounting firm ever to be convicted of a felony. The company agreed to stop auditing public companies by August 31, 2002, essentially shutting down the business.

TROUBLE WITH TELECOMS

Unfortunately for Andersen, the accusations of accounting fraud did not end with Enron. News soon surfaced that WorldCom, Andersen's largest client, had improperly accounted for nearly $3.9 billion of expenses and had overstated earnings in 2001 and the first part of 2002. After WorldCom restated its earnings, its stock price plummeted, and investors launched a barrage of lawsuits that sent the telecom into bankruptcy court. WorldCom's bankruptcy filing eclipsed Enron's as the largest in U.S. history. Andersen blamed WorldCom for the scandal, insisting that the expense irregularities had not been disclosed to its auditors and that it had complied with SEC standards in its auditing of WorldCom. WorldCom, however, pointed the finger of blame not only at its former managers but also at Andersen for failing to find the accounting irregularities. The SEC filed fraud charges against WorldCom, which fired its CFO.

While the Enron and WorldCom scandals continued, more telecommunications firms, including Global Crossing and Qwest Communications, came under investigation for alleged accounting improprieties. At the heart of both cases is the issue of fake asset swaps, in which the accused telecom companies allegedly exchanged fiber-optic broadband capacity at inflated prices in order to show huge gains. An investor lawsuit was filed against Global Crossing and Andersen, alleging that Global Crossing had artificially inflated earnings and that Andersen had violated federal securities laws by issuing unqualified (positive) audit opinions on Global Crossing's financial statements, though it knew or failed to discover that they contained material misstatements. Global Crossing filed for Chapter 11 bankruptcy protection and fired Andersen as its auditor. Qwest, which avoided bankruptcy court, admitted to using improper accounting methods and was forced to restate profits for 1999, 2000, and 2001, including $950 million in relation to the swaps and up to $531 million in cash sales of optical capacity.

CORPORATE CULTURE AND ETHICAL RAMIFICATIONS

As the details of these investigations into accounting irregularities and fraud came to light, it became apparent that Andersen was more concerned about its own revenue growth than where the revenue came from or whether its independence as an auditor had been compromised. One of the reasons for this confusion in its corporate culture may have been that numerous inexperienced business consultants and untrained auditors were sent to client sites, which were largely ignorant of company policies. Another factor may have been its partners' limited involvement in the process of issuing opinions. As the company grew, the number of partners stagnated. There is also evidence that Andersen had limited oversight over its audit teams and that such visibility was impaired by a relative lack of checks and balances that could have identified when audit teams had strayed from accepted policies. Audit teams had great discretion in terms of issuing financials and restatements.

In February 2002, Andersen hired former Federal Reserve Board chairman Paul Volcker to institute reform and to help restore its reputation. Soon after Volcker came on board, however, Andersen was indicted for obstruction of justice in connection with the shredding of Enron documents. During the investigations, Andersen had been trying to negotiate merger deals for its international partnerships and salvage what was left of its U.S operations. However, amid a mass exodus of clients and partners and the resignation of Berardino, the company was forced to begin selling off various business units, and ultimately laid off more than 7,000 employees in the United States.

During this time, Alaska Air Group, an Andersen client, restated its 2001 results, which resulted in an increase in shareholder equity of $31 million. Alaska Air made the restatement on the recommendation of its new auditor, Deloitte and Touche, which had replaced Andersen in May 2002.

After Andersen was convicted of obstruction of justice, it was fined $500,000, among other penalties. Andersen agreed to cease auditing public corporations by the end of August 2002. Accenture, its spin-off consulting unit, is free and clear of all charges, although the consulting firm remains reluctant to mention its origins and association with Andersen: nowhere on Accenture's Web site is the word Andersen to be found.

In 2005, the Supreme Court threw out Arthur Andersen's obstruction of justice conviction. A federal jury found Andersen guilty of obstructing justice by "corruptly persuading" workers to shred documents related to alleged improprieties by Enron. However, the Supreme Court said the jury instructions diluted the meaning of "corruptly" to the point that it could have covered the type of innocent shredding that companies do each day. The Supreme Court did not rule on whether Andersen's shredding was wrong; rather, the case revolved entirely around the adequacy of the jury instructions at the company's trial.

While some experts believe that the Supreme Court's ruling was strictly based on technical issues rather than whether Andersen was guilty of obstruction of justice, the fact remains that Andersen may not have gone out of business if this ruling had been made available during the trial. Looking back at this event, accounting consultants and many business executives believe that the quick rush to destroy Arthur Andersen's accounting and auditing business may have had a negative effect on competition and the cost of auditing for all public corporations. On the other hand, Arthur Andersen's involvement with so many accounting fraud cases could have caused regulatory agencies to overreact. Unfortunately, the lives of many thousands of Arthur Andersen employees not involved in accounting fraud were affected by all of the events associated with this case.

IMPLICATIONS FOR REGULATION AND ACCOUNTING ETHICS

The string of accounting scandals of the early twenty-first century sent many Andersen clients into bankruptcy court and subjected even more to greater scrutiny. They also helped spur a new focus on business ethics, driven largely by public demands for greater corporate transparency and accountability. In response, Congress passed the Sarbanes-Oxley Act of 2002, which established new guidelines and direction for corporate and accounting responsibility. The act was enacted to combat securities and accounting fraud and includes, among other things, provisions for a new accounting oversight board, stiffer penalties for violators, and higher standards of corporate governance. Table 1 discusses some of the components of the act and how it could prevent these types of situations from occurring again.

For the accounting profession, Sarbanes–Oxley emphasizes auditor independence and quality, restricts accounting firms' ability to provide both audit and non-audit services for the same clients, and requires periodic reviews of audit firms. All are provisions that the Arthur Andersen of the past would likely have supported wholeheartedly. Some are concerned, however, that such sweeping legislative and regulatory reform may be occurring too quickly in response to intense public and political pressure. The worry is that these reforms may not have been given enough forethought and cost-benefit consideration for those public corporations that operate within the law, which comprise the vast majority of corporate America. The 2008–2009 financial provided evidence that Sarbanes-Oxley does not provide comprehensive protection for excessive risk taking. Firms were able to find regulatory loopholes and to mislead investors through the financial reports.

TABLE 1 Sarbanes–Oxley Act Intended to Prevent Accounting Misconduct

Sarbanes–Oxley Act	What it does	What It Could Prevent
Section 104: Inspection of Registered Public Accounting Firms	Verify that financial statements are accurate	Use of questionable/illegal accounting practices
Section 201: Services Outside the Scope of Auditors; Prohibited Activities	Restrict auditors to audit activities only	Improper relationships, reduce likelihood of compromising good audit for more revenue
Section 203: Audit Partner Rotation	Rotate partners assigned to client, so fresh eyes see work papers	"Partner in Crime" relationship
Section 204: Auditor Reports to Audit Committees	Auditors must report to committee, who work for the board, not the company	Powerlessness of auditors by giving board power to investigate and rectify
		Companies from publishing misleading statements
Section 303: Improper Influence on Conduct of Audits	Removes power from company personnel	Withholding of information from auditors by making this illegal
Section 404: Management Assessment of Internal Controls	Gives auditor a voice outside of the audit to attest to policies demonstrated by the company	Information slipping by the SEC and stakeholders by giving more visibility to the firm
Title VIII: Corporate and Criminal Fraud Accountability Act of 2002	Makes it a felony to impede federal investigation, provides whistle-blower protection	Destruction of documents, will allow investigators to review work of auditors
Section 1102: Tampering with a Record or Otherwise Impeding an Official Proceeding	Persons acting to corrupt or destroy evidence liable for extended prison term	Others from attempting to interfere in an official investigation

Source: Table adapted from Mandy Storeim, *Andersen LLP: An Assessment of the Company's Dilemmas in Corporate Crisis*, BG660 Final Project, Colorado State University, November 13, 2002.

QUESTIONS

1. Describe the legal and ethical issues surrounding Andersen's auditing of companies accused of accounting improprieties.
2. What evidence is there that Andersen's corporate culture contributed to its downfall?
3. How can the provisions of the Sarbanes–Oxley Act help minimize the likelihood of auditors failing to identify accounting irregularities?

SOURCES

"$141M Sunbeam Fraud Case Settled," Parker Waichman Alonso LLP, August 9, 2002, http://www.yourlawyer.com/articles/read/1318 (accessed September 4, 2009); ARTHUR ANDERSEN LLP v THE UNITED STATES, FindLaw, http://caselaw.lp.findlaw.com/scripts/getcase.pl?court=US&vol=000&invol=04-368, (accessed September 4, 2009); "Alaska Air Restatement Adds Shareholder Value," Seattle Times, January 11, 2003, p. C1; "Andersen's Fall from Grace," BBC News, June 17, 2002, http://news.bbc.co.uk/2/low/business/2049237.stm (accessed September 4, 2009); Byrne, John A. "Fall from Grace," Business Week, August 12, 2002, pp. 50–56; Nanette Byrnes, Mike McNamee, Diane Brady, Louis Lavelle, Christopher Palmeri, et al., "Accounting in Crisis," Business Week, January 28, 2002, pp. 44–48; Dave Carpenter, "Andersen's WorldCom Story Familiar to Enron Excuse," Houston Chronicle, June 27, 2002, http://www.chron.com/disp/story.mpl/special/andersen/1474232.html (accessed September 4, 2009); Elizabeth Douglass, "FBI, SEC Probe Global Crossing," Los Angeles Times, February 9, 2002, http://articles.latimes.com/2002/feb/09/business/fi-techbrfs9.1 (accessed September 4, 2009); "The Fall of Andersen," Chicago Tribune, September 1, 2002, http://www.chicagotribune.com/news/chi-0209010315sep01,0,538751.story (accessed September 4, 2009); Greg Farell, "A Posthumous Victory," USA Today, May 31, 2005, http://www.usatoday.com/money/industries/banking/2005-05-31-andersen-cover_x.htm (accessed September 4, 2009); Greg Farrell, "Jury Will Hear of Andersen's Past Scandals," USA Today, May 8, 2002, http://www.usatoday.com/money/energy/enron/2002-05-07-andersen-trial.htm (accessed September 4, 2009); "First Trial of Arizona Baptist Foundation Case Starts This Week," Baptist Standard, March 4, 2002, http://baptiststandard.com/2002/3_4/print/arizona.html (accessed September 4, 2009); Jonathan D. Glater, "Auditor to Pay $217 Million to Settle Suits," Yahoo News, March 2, 2002, http://www.nytimes.com/2002/03/02/business/auditor-to-pay-217-million-to-settle-suits.html (accessed September 4, 2009); "Global Crossing Announces Results for First Half of 2002," Global Crossing, http://www.globalcrossing.com/news/2002/august/Release_MOR_for_June_2002_TK_08-01-02_final.pdf (accessed September 4, 2009); Floyd Norris, "$217 Million New Settlement by Andersen in Baptist Case," The New York Times, May 7, 2002, http://www.nytimes.com/2002/05/07/business/217-million-new-settlement-by-andersen-in-baptist-case.html (accessed September 4, 2009); Bruce Nussbaum, "Can You Trust Anybody Anymore?" Business Week, January 28, 2002, pp. 31–32; Penelope Patsuris, "The Corporate Scandal Sheet," Forbes, August 26, 2002, http://www.forbes.com/2002/07/25/accountingtracker.html (accessed September 4, 2009); "Q&A: What Now for Andersen?" BBC News, June 16, 2002, http://news.bbc.co.uk/1/hi/business/2048325.stm (accessed September 4, 2009); "Qwest Admits Improper Accounts," BBC News, July 29, 2002, http://news.bbc.co.uk/2/hi/business/2158135.stm (accessed September 4, 2009); David Schepp, "Analysis: Verdict Signals Andersen's End," BBC News, June 15, 2002, http://news.bbc.co.uk/1/hi/business/2047381.stm (accessed September 4, 2009); "SEC Sues Former CEO, CFO, Other Top Officers of Sunbeam Corporation in Massive Financial Fraud," U.S. Securities and Exchange Commission, May 15, 2001, http://www.sec.gov/news/headlines/sunbeamfraud.htm (accessed September 4, 2009); "Telecoms Bosses Deny 'Fake' Swap Deals," BBC News, October 1, 2002, http://news.bbc.co.uk/2/hi/business/2290679.stm (accessed September 4, 2009); Kathy Booth Thomas, "Called to Account," Time, June 18, 2002, pp. 43–45; "WorldCom, Andersen Play Blame Game," USA Today, July 8, 2002, http://www.usatoday.com/money/telecom/2002-07-08-worldcom-hearings-ap.htm (accessed September 4, 2009); Wendy Zellner, Stephanie Forest Anderson, and Laura Cohn, "A Hero—And a Smoking-Gun Letter," Business Week, January 28, 2002, pp. 34–35.

CASE 6

Coping with Financial and Ethical Risks at American International Group (AIG)

Daryl Benson

When American International Group (AIG) collapsed in September 2008 and was subsequently saved by a government bailout, it became one of the most controversial players in the 2008–2009 financial crises. The corporate culture at AIG had been involved in a high-stakes risk-taking scheme supported by managers and employees that appeared entirely focused on short-term financial rewards. Out of a firm of 116,000 employees, one unit with around 500 employees, AIG Financial Products, was chiefly to blame. Current CEO Ed Liddy, who was summoned by former Treasury Secretary Hank Paulson, estimates that only twenty to thirty people were directly involved in bringing down the company.

The AIG Financial Products unit specialized in derivatives and other complex financial contracts that were tied to subprime mortgages or commodities. While its dealings were risky, the unit generated billions of dollars of profits for AIG. Nevertheless, during his long tenure as CEO of AIG, Maurice "Hank" Greenberg had been open about his suspicions of the AIG Financial Products unit. However, after Greenberg resigned as chief executive of AIG in 2005, the Financial Products unit became even more speculative in its activities.

Immediately before its collapse, AIG had exposure to $64 billion in potential subprime mortgage losses. The perfect storm formed with the subprime mortgage crisis and a sudden sharp downturn in the value of residential real estate in 2008. Since much of the speculation in the Financial Products unit was tied to derivatives, even small movements in the value of financial measurements could result in catastrophic losses.

In this case, we trace the history of AIG as it evolved into one of the largest and most respected insurance companies in the world, and the more recent events that led to its demise. AIG had a market value of close to $200 billion in 2007, and by 2009 this amount had fallen to a mere $3.5 billion. Only a government rescue of what has amounted to $180 billion in loans, investments, guarantees, and financial injections prevented AIG from facing total bankruptcy in late 2008.

O.C. Ferrell and John Fraedrich prepared this case with the assistance of Jennifer Jackson. This case was prepared for classroom discussion, rather than to illustrate either effective or ineffective handling of an administrative, ethical, or legal decision by management. All sources used for this case were obtained through publicly available material.

Saving AIG was not meant as a reward, however. The government rescued the company not to keep it from bankruptcy, but to prevent the bankruptcies of many other global financial institutions that depended on AIG as counterparty on collateralized debt obligations. If AIG had been allowed to fail, it is possible that the financial meltdown that occurred in 2008–2009 would have been worse.

This case first examines the events leading up to the 2008 meltdown, including the philosophy of top management and the corporate culture that set the stage for AIG's demise. Then it reviews the events that occurred in 2008, including ethical issues related to transparency and failed internal controls. Finally, the analysis looks at the role of the government and its decision to bail out AIG, taking 79.9 percent ownership in a company that grossly mishandled its responsibility to its stakeholders.

AIG'S HISTORY

The saga of American International Group (AIG) began in 1919 with the U.S.-born Cornelius Vander Starr, who founded a company in Shanghai representing American insurance companies selling fire and marine coverage in Asia. Starr's success in Shanghai quickly led to expansion across Asia, and to the United States in 1926. While AIG began as a representative of American insurance companies abroad, in the United States it provided insurance risk coverage to insurance companies as a way to disperse liabilities. Reinsurers such as AIG were created to remove some of the risk associated with large disasters. Because of AIG and others, insurance companies could grow faster than ever before.

Insurance companies are educated risk takers. When insurance companies feel they have too much risk, they go to their reinsurance companies, such as AIG, to take out insurance so that if something catastrophic happens, they can still pay their clients. AIG utilizes models to determine how much insurance it can sell to insurers and still pay out. To put it simply, AIG charges insurance companies a premium in order to allow them to spread their risk so that they can sell insurance policies and grow more rapidly.

In 1968, Maurice "Hank" Greenberg, a native New Yorker and experienced insurance executive who had been with AIG for many years, took over as CEO. AIG grew exponentially during his tenure. By the end of the 1980s, the company had become the largest underwriter of commercial and industrial coverage in the United States and the leading international insurance organization.

AIG continued to expand throughout the 1990s, led by its return to China as the first foreign insurance organization granted a license by the Chinese authorities to operate a wholly-owned insurance business in Shanghai. AIG later expanded to Guangzhou, Shenzhen, Beijing, and Vietnam. In 2001 AIG established two joint ventures in general insurance and life insurance in India with the Tata Group, the leading Indian industrial conglomerate. New AIG subsidiary companies followed the fall of the Soviet Union into Eastern Europe, with general and life insurance companies formed in Russia, Poland, Hungary, and the Czech Republic, among other emerging markets.

In 2001 AIG purchased American General Corporation, a top U.S. life insurer. This acquisition made AIG a leader in the U.S. life insurance industry and consumer lending. Today, the four principal business areas of AIG are: General Insurance, Life Insurance and Retirement Services, Financial Services, and Asset Management. For the individual consumer, business, financial professional, or insurance professional, AIG provides: Accident and Health Insurance, Auto Insurance, Life Insurance, Banking and Loans, Retirement Services, Travel Insurance, Additional Services, and Annuities. Immediately before its 2008 collapse, AIG had revenues exceeding $110 billion, with total assets of over $1 trillion, and 116,000 employees around the world.

AIG'S CULTURE

Maurice "Hank" Greenberg was the CEO of AIG for 38 years, and was therefore a key player in shaping the modern face and corporate culture of the company. Many considered Greenberg a genius in the insurance business, and arguably he was one of the most successful and influential executives in the business. But critics called him autocratic in his drive to expand the company into an international powerhouse.

> *"Greenberg was always known for utilizing his contacts and influence to help advance the company."*

During his career, Greenberg championed innovative products that insure almost any type of risk, including Internet identity theft and hijacking. At least four U.S. presidents sought Greenberg's advice on international affairs and financial markets. And Greenberg was always known for utilizing his contacts and influence to help advance the company. Over the years, Greenberg aggressively lobbied for laws and rulings favorable to AIG. He was very involved with international politics and helped the U.S. government to secure information and develop back-door channels for classified dealings. In return, AIG was given the benefit of the doubt when regulatory agencies came questioning the company's doings. When billions or trillions of dollars are involved, global corporations have powers equal to or greater than those of governments and regulatory agencies.

In spite of Greenberg's active networking, the early 2000s found AIG under investigation by the Securities and Exchange Commission for its "finite insurance" deals—contracts that covered specific amounts of losses rather than unexpected losses of indeterminate size—and what appeared to be loans (since premiums were structured to match policy payouts and eliminate risk) rather than genuine risk allocation vehicles. A federal inquiry later found information that Greenberg might have been personally involved in creating a bogus reinsurance transaction with General Re to fraudulently boost AIG's reserves. New York Attorney General Spitzer subpoenaed Greenberg, who treated the summons far more lightly than he should have. As rumors swirled, AIG's stock began to plummet, and the AIG board started to become concerned.

In 2005, Greenberg was forced out as CEO. Martin Sullivan succeeded him and held the CEO position for three years, followed by Robert Willumstad for three months. Willumstad was forced to step down in 2008 in the wake of the corporation's meltdown. The current CEO is Edward Liddy, the former CEO of The Allstate Corporation. The SEC leveled charges of fraud against Greenberg resulting from the circumstances surrounding his departure. In order to settle the charges that AIG manipulated financial statements in 2005, the company paid the SEC $1.6 billion in 2006, and Greenberg agreed to pay an additional $15 million in 2009.

WHAT HAPPENED AT AIG TO CAUSE ITS DEMISE?

AIG's troubles leading up to the 2008 bailout were, at the heart, caused by a kind of derivative called credit default swaps (CDSs). Credit default swaps are financial products that transfer the credit exposure (risk) of fixed-income products (bonds) between parties. The buyer of a credit swap receives credit protection, whereas the seller of the swap guarantees the creditworthiness of the product. By doing this, the risk of default is transferred from the holder of the fixed-income security to the seller of the swap. One single credit default swap can be valued at hundreds of millions of dollars.

> *"AIG did not have a large enough safety net to weather the subprime mortgage collapse."*

As a reinsurer, AIG used CDSs as a kind of insurance policy on complex collateralized debt obligations (CDOs). The company issued the swaps and promised to pay these institutions, AIG's counterparties, if the debt securities defaulted. However, AIG did not have a large enough safety net to weather the subprime mortgage collapse. These insurance contracts became essentially worthless because many people could not pay back their subprime mortgages and AIG did not have the creditworthiness for the big collateral call.

The government took the drastic step to bail out the company, providing the funds to purchase the CDOs that were being held by banks, hedge funds, and other financial institutions, and in the process ended up with 79.9 percent ownership of AIG. The U.S. government is now the senior partner in a special-purpose entity that will receive interest and share liability in the ownership of these tainted investment instruments. The fear behind this move was that if AIG had been allowed to go bankrupt, many banks throughout the world would have gone bankrupt as well.

Although overall AIG had a diversified insurance business, one unit, AIG Financial Products, was the source of many of the company's woes. Formed more than twenty years ago to trade over-the-counter derivatives, its creation was timed perfectly to ride the derivatives market boom. By and large, Financial Products was run like a hedge fund out of London and Wilton, Connecticut. Hedge funds are a special type of fund available to a select range of investors. They seek to utilize a wide variety of investment tools to mitigate, or *hedge,* risk—oftentimes the term refers to funds that use short selling as a means of increasing investment returns. Short selling is betting that the stock price of a company will change during a specified period of time. When the stocks move the expected direction, the investor makes money.

AIG Financial Products specialized in derivatives that generated billions of dollars in profits over the years. Derivatives are financial contracts or instruments whose value is derived from something else such as commodities (corn, wheat, soybeans, etc.), stocks, bonds, and even home mortgages. Gains or losses from derivatives come from betting correctly on the movement of these values. The unit also dealt in mortgage securities, a sector that turned rancid with the collapse of the housing bubble. Former New York Attorney General Eliot Spitzer, a champion of financial sector reform, claimed that AIG Financial Products was "the black hole of AIG."

The AIG Financial Products unit was founded in 1987 by Howard Sosin. When Sosin joined AIG he was given an unusual deal: a 20 percent stake in the unit and 20 percent of its profits. While AIG can be described as a conservative global conglomerate selling insurance policies to businesses and individuals, the Financial Products unit was staffed by quantitative specialists with doctorates in finance and math who, it seems, were very willing to take risks. This unit thought it was above the insurance operations, and its employees conducted themselves like investment bankers.

In the late 1990s under the leadership of Joseph Cassano, AIG Financial Products ramped up its business of selling credit default swaps, which were at the heart of the 2008–2009 financial meltdown. AIG Financial Products expanded into writing swaps to cover debt that was backed by mortgages. The unit sold swaps to large institutional investors. These collateralized debt obligations were backed by mortgages, and the swaps issued by AIG backed some $440 billion worth of obligations. To put this in perspective, the entire market worth of AIG was around $200 billion at the time. AIG made millions selling collateralized debt obligations (CDOs) and was able to post modest margin requirements, which is the amount the company keeps as a deposit to protect against the risk of loan defaults or nonpayments. For example, to buy stock on margin, you must have at least 50 percent of the purchase price in your account. AIG was able to make these CDO deals with a very small fraction of actual money on hand. Unfortunately, some of these CDOs were attached to home mortgages.

In spite of the risk, the company involved itself in bad mortgage lending by financial institutions that did not have sufficient capital to cover the loans, which in turn had bought this type of insurance from AIG that created an unstable financial environment. The loans and the CDOs were often sold to people who could not repay their debt. CEO Greenberg became concerned about this unit's derivative dealings and asked a group to shadow its trades. Greenberg was uncomfortable with the results and thought the unit was taking too many risks. However, Greenberg left the company in 2005 because of regulators investigating AIG over its accounting practices.

AIG sold credit protection on CDOs by simply writing pieces of paper that stated that AIG would cover the losses in case these obligations went bad. AIG agreed to either take over the obligations or cover the losses on CDOs. While AIG made billions of dollars in profits and managers received millions of dollars in compensation for selling these so-called insurance policies, it turned out to be a high-risk house of cards. The tools, CDOs and CDSs, were used recklessly and failed to assess systemic risk of counterparties not measuring their own exposures and not paying their obligations. The Financial Products unit has been under ongoing investigations around the world, including by the United Kingdom's Serious Fraud Office.

Although they have gained notoriety now, before 2008 derivatives were not widely understood by the public, mass media, regulators, and many of the executives who were providing the oversight for their use. AIG could have taken another approach by buying mortgages or CDOs and then having some other party package them into a credit default swap as insurance, but since AIG was an insurer it simply wrote policies on CDOs, thus increasing revenues with the hope that only a few would default. Of course, AIG guessed wrong and became the epicenter of a financial nightmare that has caused many bank failures and a worldwide financial depression.

AIG Lacked Transparency

There is evidence that AIG knew of potential problems in valuing derivative contracts before the 2008–2009 financial meltdown occurred. Outside auditors raised concerns about being excluded from conversations on the evaluation of derivatives. But during this time period, AIG executives Cassano and Sullivan continued to reassure investors and auditors that AIG had accurately identified all areas of exposure to the U.S. residential housing market and stated their confidence in their evaluation methods. PricewaterhouseCoopers (PwC), AIG'S auditor, had a right to know about the models and about market indicators that indicated that the value of AIG swaps should be lowered. If prosecutors find evidence that investors and PwC were misled, it could be considered a criminal fraud.

The market indicators in question came in the form of demands for collateral by AIG trading partners. At a congressional hearing, Sullivan stated that he believed the evaluations to be accurate, based on the information he possessed at the time. This situation is similar to executives at Enron who claimed that they did not know that Enron utilized derivatives and off-the-book balance sheet partnerships that caused its demise. Many Enron executives ended up being found guilty of crimes.

AIG Provided Incentives to Take Risks

"The AIG culture was focused on a reward system that placed little responsibility on executives who made very poor decisions."

What were the factors within the corporate culture of AIG that promoted speculative risk-taking? Part of the problem may have been AIG's incentives. The AIG culture was focused on a reward system that placed little responsibility on executives who made very poor decisions." Although they produced nearly $40 billion in losses in 2008, a number of managers were selected to receive large bonuses. AIG offered cash awards and other perks to thirty-eight executives and a retention program with payments from $92,500 to $4 million for employees earning salaries between $160,000 and $1 million.

After receiving more than $152 billion in federal rescue funds, AIG publicly claimed that it would eliminate some of these bonuses for senior executives while all the time planning to hand out cash awards that doubled or tripled the salaries of some. AIG asserted that these types of payments were necessary to keep top employees at AIG, even as control of the company was being handed over to the government. The ethical ramifications of the rewards doled out in the face of excessive risk-taking and possible misconduct has been highly criticized by most stakeholders.

The central reason AIG was bailed out at all was that the government was seeking to prevent the failure of some of the world's largest banks, thereby potentially causing a global financial catastrophe. AIG's actions reflect an ethical culture that neglects the most important stakeholders that support a business.

The demise of AIG's Financial Products unit, in part, resulted from excessive risk-taking by economists and financial scholars using computer models that failed to take into account real-world market risks. For example, Gary Gorton, a finance professor at the Yale School of Management, was a scholar whose work was cited in speeches by Federal Reserve Chairman Ben Bernanke. AIG paid him large consulting fees for developing computer models to gauge risk for more than $400 billion in complicated credit default swaps. Remember that a single swap can be valued at hundreds of millions of dollars. AIG relied on Gorton's models to determine which swap deals were low risk. Unfortunately, his models did not anticipate how market forces and contract terms could turn swaps into huge financial liabilities. It was not Gorton's failing, as AIG did not assign him to assess those threats, and therefore his models did not consider them. However, the failure to assess the risk of credit default swaps correctly caused the demise of AIG and pushed the federal government to rescue it and the U.S. banking system.

Like other major firms, AIG entered a very lucrative but perilous new market without truly understanding the sheer complexity of the financial products that it was selling. What the company learned too late is that computers and academic experts cannot determine all of the variables, forces, and weights that cause a high- or low-risk investment to go bad. The blame lies with business placing too much trust in models with faulty assumptions. Models cannot predict with absolute certainty what humans will do because humans are not always rational. Warren Buffett, chief executive of Berkshire Hathaway and a billionaire many times over, said, "All I can say is, beware of geeks. . .bearing formulas."

AIG ultimately owed Wall Street's biggest firms about $100 billion dollars for speculative trades turned bad; $64 billion of it was tied to losses on subprime mortgages. This debt is particularly challenging because the rescue package for AIG does not include provisions for them. Questions remain about how the insurer will cover these debts. The company allegedly placed billions of dollars at risk through speculation on the movements of various mortgage pools, and the bottom line is that there are no actual securities backing these speculative positions on which AIG is losing money. The losses stem from market wagers that were essentially bets on the performance of bundles of derivatives linked to subprime residential mortgages.

The government rescue of AIG protected many of its policyholders and counterparties from immediate losses on traditional insurance contracts, but these speculative trades by AIG were not a part of the government risk rescue. AIG's activities indicate that managers and traders were focused on financial rewards for assembling high-risk contracts and that the Financial Products division was conducting itself like a gambler in a casino that irrationally expected all bets to pay off. AIG had lost its underlying mission, the importance of strong moral principles, and good compliance programs that respect stakeholders.

The controversies regarding AIG did not end with government ownership. In fact, the problems critics identified regarding the company's culture and reckless spending were put on full display a mere two months after receiving its bailout money. Top AIG executives were spotted holding a lavish conference at a posh Point Hilton Squaw Peak Resort in Phoenix for 150 financial planners and top AIG executives. The three-day event reportedly cost over $343,000. Representatives of the corporation defend the conference, stating that most of the costs were underwritten by sponsors—however, such an episode mere weeks after receiving its government bailout did not sit well with stakeholders. Many believe that it demonstrates how little remorse AIG has for the decisions leading up to the failure, and how little has changed since the company received government money.

AIG'S CRISIS AND BAILOUT

AIG's problems came to a boil in September 2008. Due to the many issues outlined earlier, AIG's stock was downgraded by the rating companies, which caused the stock to drop, causing a run on the reinsurer's liquid assets (cash on hand) that revealed its lack of liquidity. Simply put, AIG did not have the capital to repay investors asking for their money back.

The federal government came to the rescue—as stated earlier, not out of concern for AIG, but to prevent the string of bank failures that would surely follow an AIG bankruptcy. Over the course of a month, the government doled out over $152 billion of taxpayer money, creating a line of credit for the company and buying up AIG stock.

This was a highly controversial decision, particularly since the government did not do the same thing for the other financial giant Lehman Brothers. In March 2009, the government made the controversial decision to dole out another $30 billion in capital to the failing institution. The decision was made even more contentious when it was revealed that $165 million of the bailout money went to bonuses of employees of the failed Financial Products unit.

While the government concluded that it could not get the money back, it did resolve to increase the oversight of new bailout funds. When questioned about the decision to repeatedly bail out AIG, Federal Reserve Chair Ben Bernanke told U.S. lawmakers that "AIG exploited a huge gap in the regulatory system. There was no oversight of the financial products division. This was a hedge fund, basically, that was attached to a large and stable insurance company." He stated that AIG was the single case out of the entire 2008–2009 financial crisis that made him the angriest. However, Bernanke went on to say, "We had no choice but to try to stabilize the system because of the implications that the failure would have had for the broad economic system."

Although the bailouts were massive, they did not cover all that AIG owed and the company has had to sell off numerous assets. Two-thirds of the company needed to be sold in a tough market for sellers, resulting in auctions of dozens of the company's units around the world. Many of these sales resulted in disappointing prices for AIG. For example, Munich Re, the world's biggest reinsurer, agreed to buy AIG Inc.'s Hartford unit for $742 million, about a third less than AIG paid for it eight years before. The company also has given more than 2,000 employees cash incentives to stop them from quitting, saying that the payments are necessary. "Anybody who wants to start an insurance company or beef up their position, they will come to our organization and pick people off," Edward Liddy, the current CEO, said in the interview. "If that happens, we can't maintain the businesses we want to keep and we won't be able to sell them for the kinds of values that we need."

Former CEO Greenberg maintains his innocence, and insists that the company's upper management was the root cause of the collapse after he left. "AIG had a unique culture when I was its CEO, particularly in comparison with the way many large public companies operate today," he said. "Neither I nor other members of my senior management team had employment contracts. I received no severance package in connection with my retirement, and I never sold a single share of AIG stock during the more than 35 years that I served as CEO." Greenberg continues to hold substantial stock in the company. At the end of 2008, he and his firm, Starr International, owned more than 268 million shares, or nearly 10 percent.

In a 2008 interview, Greenberg explained what he sees as the real cause of the financial collapse. He blames low interest rates and excessively easy credit for the reckless risk-taking and poor decisions made within the financial industry. He also cites excessive leveraging and mark-to-market accounting practices as contributing to the meltdown. Mark-to-market is assigning a value to a position held in a financial instrument based on the current market price for the instrument. For example, the final value of a financial contract (grain futures) that expires in nine months will not be known until it expires. If it is marked to market, for accounting purposes, it is assigned the value that it would have at the end of each day. Greenberg believes that all these factors grew out of control to the point where the entire system had nowhere to go but toward failure.

CONCLUSION

The question remains: Was a bailout really necessary? Some say yes, like Greenberg himself. "You have to have a bailout. But I would call it something else rather than a bailout. That implies the wrong thing. It is really also helping Main Street, not just Wall Street, because if the economy doesn't grow, jobs are going to be lost and we're going to go into a depression rather than a recession. The taxpayer is not going to take a hit long-term because the money involved will be repaid over a period of time."

Others are not so certain. Critics of the AIG and auto industry bailouts, for example, cite lack of accountability in how the funds are used. Many also oppose this level of government intervention in corporations because it seems to be rewarding companies that have blatantly ignored the needs and desires of their stakeholders in favor of enriching themselves in the short term. Even months after the bailout, AIG continued to lose massive amounts of money. The company managed to slow the rate of its losses to $4.35 billion in the first quarter of 2009, but the damage to the company's reputation over this matter has been massive, and some critics wonder if it will ever recover.

The company has also had a difficult time selling off its assets in order to repay its debts, as many of its potential buyers also have been working to recover from the 2008–2009 recession. Without a doubt, the failure of AIG was massive and, bailout or not, its effects have rippled across the globe.

QUESTIONS

1. Discuss the role that AIG's corporate culture played, if any, in its downfall.
2. Discuss the ethical conduct of AIG executives, and how a stronger ethics program might help the company to strengthen the ethics of its corporate culture.
3. What could AIG have done differently to prevent its failure and subsequent bailout?

SOURCES

Anderson, Jenny, "A.I.G. Profit Is Reduced by $4 Billion," *New York Times*, June 1, 2005, http://query.nytimes.com/gst/fullpage.html?res=9C01E1D81F39F932A35755C0A9639C8B63 (accessed December 10, 2008); Anderson, Jenny, "Greenberg Fires Back at Directors," *New York Times*, August 5, 2005, http://query.nytimes.com/gst/fullpage.html?res=9A02E7DE163EF936A3575BC0A9639C8B63&sec=&spon=&pagewanted=2 (accessed December 10, 2008); Behan, Beverly, "Memo to the Board of AIG," *BusinessWeek*, November 16, 2008, http://www.businessweek.com/managing/content/nov2008/ca20081118_408443.htm (accessed December 22, 2008); Browning, Lynnley, "A.I.G.'s House of Cards," *Portfolio*, September 29, 2008, http://www.portfolio.com/news-markets/top-5/2008/09/29/AIGs-Derivatives-Run-Amok? (accessed December 22, 2008); Byrnes, Nanette, "The Unraveling of AIG," *BusinessWeek*, September 16, 2008, http://www.businessweek.com/bwdaily/dnflash/content/sep2008/db20080915_552271.htm (accessed December 22, 2008); Desmond, Mauma, "AIG. CDOs. CDS. It's a Mess," *Forbes.com*, November 15, 2008, http://www.forbes.com/markets/2008/11/15/aig-credit-default-markets-equity-cx_md_1110markets24.html (accessed November 19, 2008); Drucker, Jesse, "AIG's Tax Dispute with U.S. Has Twist of Irony," *Wall Street Journal*, November 14, 2008, p. C2; Eichenwald, Kurt, and Jenny Anderson, "How a Titan of Insurance Ran Afoul of the Government," *New York Times*, April 4, 2005, http://www.nytimes.com/2005/04/04/business/04aig.html?scp=1&sq=%22how+a+titan+of+insurance%22&st=nyt (accessed January 7, 2009); "The Great Untangling," *The Economist*, November 8, 2008, pp. 85–86; Henry, David, Matthew Goldstein, and Carol Matlack, "How AIG's Credit Loophole Squeezed Europe's Banks," *BusinessWeek*, October 16, 2008, http://www.businessweek.com/magazine/content/08_43/b4105032835044.htm (accessed December 22, 2008); Kroft, Steve, "Why AIG Stumbled, and Taxpayers Now Own It" CBS News, March 17, 2009, http://www.cbsnews.com/stories/2009/05/15/60minutes/main5016760_page2.shtml (accessed March 18, 2009); Loomis, Carol J., "AIG: The Company That Came to Dinner," *Fortune*, January 19, 2009, pp. 70–78; Mollenkamp, Carrick, Serena Ng, Liam Pleven, and Randall Smith, "Behind AIG's Fall, Risk Models Failed to Pass Real-World Test," *Wall Street Journal*, November 3, 2008, pp. A1, A16; Morgenson, Gretchen, "A.I.G.: Whiter Shade of Enron," *New York Times*, April 3, 2005, http://www.nytimes.com/2005/04/03/business/yourmoney/03gret.html?_r=1&scp=1&sq=%22whiter%20shade%20of%20enron%22&st=cse (accessed January 7, 2009); Ng, Serena, Carrick Mollenkamp, and Michael Siconolfi, "AIG Faces $10 Billion in Losses on Trades," *Wall Street Journal*, December 10, 2008, pp. A1–A2; Ng, Serena, and Liam Pleven, "Revised AIG Rescue Is Bank Boon," *Wall Street Journal*, November 12, 2008, pp. C1, C5; O'Brian, Timothy L., "Guilty Plea Is Expected in A.I.G.-Related Case," *New York Times*, June 10, 2005, http://query.nytimes.com/gst/fullpage.html?res=9801E3DC1138F933A25755C0A9639C8B63&sec=&spon=&pagewanted=2 (accessed December 10, 2008); Pleven, Liam, and Amir Efrati, "Documents Show AIG Knew of Problems with Valuations," *Wall Street Journal*, October 11–12, 2008, pp. B1–B2; Rosenthal, Justine A., "Maurice Greenberg on What's Next for Wall Street," *National Interest Online*, October 2, 2008, http://www.nationalinterest.org/Article.aspx?id=19970 (accessed December 22, 2008); Scherer, Ron, "A Top Insurance Company as the New Enron? An Accounting Probe at AIG Worries Wall Street, and Involves Some of America's Richest Men," *Christian Science Monitor*, April 1, 2005, http://www.csmonitor.com/2005/0401/p03s01-usju.html (accessed January 7, 2009); Son, Hugh, "AIG Plans to Repay U.S. in 2009, Liddy Tells CNBC," *Bloomberg.com*, December 22, 2008, http://www.bloomberg.com/apps/news?pid=20601087&sid=aDXR6Ayuezx4&refer=home (accessed December 22, 2008); Son, Hugh, "AIG Says More Managers Get Retention Payouts Topping $4 Million," *Bloomberg.com*, December 9, 2008, http://www.bloomberg.com/apps/news?pid=newsarchive&sid=aKIvmgvNl6zA (accessed December 10, 2008); Sweet, Ken, "Bernanke Tells Congress He's 'Angry' About AIG," Fox Business, March 03, 2009, http://www.foxbusiness.com/story/markets/economy/bernanke-recovery-hinges-financial-turnaround/ (accessed March 5, 2009); Walsh, Mary Williams, "A.I.G. Cuts Losses Sharply to $4.35 Billion in First Quarter," *New York Times*, May 8, 2009, p. B5; Walsh, Mary Williams, "Bigger Holes to Fill," *Wall Street Journal*, November 11, 2008, pp. B1, B5; Weisman, Jonathan, Sudeep Reddy, and Liam Pleven, "Political Heat Sears AIG," *Wall Street Journal*, March 17, 2009, http://online.wsj.com/article/SB123721970101743003.html (accessed March 17, 2009).

CASE 7

Starbucks' Mission: Social Responsibility and Brand Strength

Daryl Benson

Starbucks was founded in 1971 by three partners in Seattle's renowned open-air Pike Place Market and was named after the first mate in Herman Melville's *Moby Dick*. Howard Schultz joined Starbucks in 1982 as director of retail operations and marketing. Returning from a trip to Milan, Italy, with its 1,500 coffee bars, Schultz recognized an opportunity to develop a similar retail coffee-bar culture in Seattle.

In 1985, the company tested the first downtown Seattle coffeehouse, served the first Starbucks Café Latté, and introduced its Christmas Blend. Since then, Starbucks has been expanding across the United States and around the world, now operating nearly 17,000 stores in 49 countries. Historically, Starbucks has grown at a rate of about three stores a day, although the company cut back on expansion during 2009 in response to the global economic recession. In fact, in 2009 Starbucks made the decision to close 600 underperforming stores in the United States and 61 in Australia. The company nevertheless serves 50 million customers a week and has net revenues of approximately $10.4 billion a year.

Starbucks purchases and roasts high-quality whole coffee beans and resells them, along with freshly brewed coffee, Italian-style espresso beverages, cold blended beverages, bottled water, complementary food items, coffee-related accessories and equipment, premium teas, and a line of CDs primarily through company-operated retail stores. It also sells coffee and tea products and licenses its trademark through other channels and through some of its partners. Additionally, Starbucks produces and sells bottled Frappuccino coffee drinks, Starbucks Doubleshot espresso drinks, and a line of super-premium ice creams.

Starbucks locates its walk-in stores in high-traffic, high-visibility locations. While Starbucks can be found in a few shopping malls, the company generally focuses on locations that provide convenient access for pedestrians and drivers. The stores are designed to

Ben Siltman and Melanie Drever prepared the original draft of this case under the direction of Linda Ferrell. The current edition was updated and edited by Jennifer Jackson, with the help of Jennifer Sawayda. This case is for classroom discussion, rather than to illustrate either effective or ineffective handling of an administrative, ethical, or legal decision by management. All sources used for this case were obtained through publicly available material and the Starbucks website.

provide an inviting coffee-bar environment that is an important part of the Starbucks product and experience. Because the company is flexible regarding size and format, it can locate stores in or near a variety of settings, including downtown and suburban retail centers, office buildings, and university campuses. It can also situate retail stores in select rural and off-highway locations to serve a broader array of customers outside major metropolitan markets and to further expand brand awareness. To provide a greater degree of access and convenience for non-pedestrian customers, the company has increased development of stores with drive-through lanes.

A common criticism of Starbucks has to do with the company's strategy for location and expansion. Its "clustering" strategy, placing a Starbucks literally on every corner in some cases, has forced many smaller coffee shops out of business. This strategy was so dominant for most of the 1990s and 2000s that Starbucks became the butt of jokes. Many people began to wonder whether we really need two Starbucks directly across the street from each other. The 2008–2009 recession brought a change in policy, however. Starbucks began to pull back on expansion and, as stated, closed hundreds of stores around the United States.

Although Starbucks is always developing new products, a few drinks have fallen flat. In 2006 Starbucks pulled Chantico, its "drinkable dessert," from the menu. Chantico was marketed to resemble the thick, sweet, hot chocolate drinks found in European cafés, but it was available without any variation in a 6-ounce size. The limitations proved fatal. Customers are accustomed to dictating not only the size of their drinks, but also how they want them.

Seeking to get away from the high-priced drinks and back to its essentials, Starbucks introduced the Pike Place Blend, a bold-flavored coffee that Starbucks hoped would bring the company back to its roots of distinctive, expertly blended coffee. In order to get the flavor perfect, Starbucks enlisted the input of 1,000 customers over 1,500 hours. To kick off the new choice, Starbucks held the largest nationwide coffee tasting in history. Any customer who visited a Starbucks store at noon Eastern Standard Time on April 8, 2008, received a free 8-ounce cup of Pike Place roast. To make the brew even more appealing, Starbucks joined forces with Conservation International to ensure that the beans were sustainably harvested.

One of Starbuck's endeavors to respond to the 2008–2009 global recession was to create a value meal, Starbucks style. Called Breakfast Pairings, customers can order oatmeal or coffee cake and a latte or a breakfast sandwich and a drip coffee for $3.95. The offerings have proven popular. Oatmeal has become one of the most popular food offerings at Starbucks, as people continue to focus on their health while cutting back on fancier food items.

Starbucks is also seeking to ride another recession-spawned trend. As people cut back on their expenditures, many are choosing to brew their own coffee rather than purchase more expensive coffee shop concoctions. To gain a foothold in the potentially lucrative instant coffee market, Starbucks introduced VIA instant coffee. VIA is different from competing instant coffees in that it is processed in such a way as to retain that distinctive Starbucks taste. VIA is also aiming for a more premium market, as it retails for around $1 per serving. Only time will tell if VIA can ultimately be deemed a success. However, Starbucks has already experienced some triumphs with its new product. For instance, VIA became the official brew aboard select JetBlue flights in the United Kingdom and Spain.

Starbucks executives believe that the experience customers have in their stores should be the same in any country. During the 2008–2009 recession, Starbucks refocused on the customer experience as one of the key competitive advantages of the Starbucks brand. To enhance the European coffee shop experience for which Starbucks is known, shops are replacing their old espresso machines with new high-tech ones, and some Starbucks are switching over to Clover Brand single-cup brewing machines so that each customer receives a freshly brewed cup of coffee made to his or her specifications.

Additionally, Starbucks tries to foster brand loyalty by increasing repeat business. One of the ways it has done this is through the Starbucks Card, a reloadable card that was introduced in 2001. It has exceeded $2 billion in total activations and reloads, and more than 100 million cards have been activated. The typical Starbucks customer visits Starbucks about eighteen times a month.

STARBUCKS CULTURE

In 1990, Starbucks' senior executive team created a mission statement that laid out the guiding principles behind the company. They hoped that the principles included in the mission statement would help their partners determine the appropriateness of later decisions and actions. As Starbucks CEO Orin Smith explained, "Those guidelines are part of our culture and we try to live by them every day." After drafting the mission statement, the executive team asked all Starbucks partners to review and comment on the document. Based on their feedback, the final statement put "people first and profits last." In fact, the number one guiding principle in Starbucks' mission statement was to "provide a great work environment and treat each other with respect and dignity."

Starbucks has done three things to keep the mission and guiding principles alive over the decades. First, it distributes the mission statement and comment cards for feedback during orientation to all new partners. Second, Starbucks continually relates decisions back to the guiding principle or principles that they support. And finally, the company has formed a "Mission Review" system so any partner can comment on a decision or action relative to its consistency with one of the six principles. This continual emphasis on the guiding principles and the underlying values has become the cornerstone of a very strong culture of predominately young and educated workers who are extremely proud to work for Starbucks. Their pride comes from working for a famous and successful company that tries to act in accordance with the values they share.

> ***"Starbucks continually relates decisions back to the guiding principle or principles that they support."***

Starbucks founder and chair Howard Schultz has long been a public advocate for increased awareness of ethics in business. In a 2007 speech at Notre Dame, he spoke to an audience of students about the importance of balancing "profitability and social consciousness." Schultz is a true believer that ethical companies do better in the long run, something that has been borne out by research. Schultz also spoke about how his early childhood experiences shaped the kind of businessperson he became. As a child in a housing project in Brooklyn, New York, Schultz remembers seeing his father struggle after he was injured on the job. He received no health benefits or workers' compensation from his employers. Watching his father's travails showed Schultz how important something like health care is to the health and happiness of employees. Having grown up poor, Schultz is also committed to helping to improve the lives of the poor farmers from whom Starbucks buys its beans. Schultz has always maintained that, while it can be difficult to do the right thing at all times, it is better for a company to take some short-term losses than to lose sight of its core values in the long term.

Starbucks has been ranked on *Fortune*'s "100 Best Companies to Work For" list for nearly a decade; and in 2009, the company ranked 24th. The care the company shows its employees is a large part of what sets it apart. Starbucks offers most employees a comprehensive benefits package that includes stock option grants through *Bean Stock*, as well as health, medical, dental, and vision benefits. It also embraces diversity as an essential component of doing business. The company has more than 146,000 U.S. employees and nearly 71,000 outside the United States. Of these, around 31 percent are minorities, and 67 percent are women.

> *Shared Planet has three main goals: to achieve ethical sourcing, environmental stewardship, and greater community involvement.*

Another key part of the Starbucks image involves its commitment to ethics and sustainability. To address concerns related to these issues, Starbucks launched the Shared Planet website. Shared Planet has three main goals: to achieve ethical sourcing, environmental stewardship, and greater community involvement. The website is a means of keeping customers up-to-date on initiatives within the company. It describes how well Starbucks is faring on achieving its social responsibility goals, and it even provides a means for customers to learn about things like the nutrition data of Starbucks' offerings and other concerns related to Starbucks products.

Starbucks also actively partners with nonprofits around the globe. Currently, 5 percent of total coffee purchases are Fair Trade Certified. Starbucks joined with Bono's Product RED in an effort to raise money for HIV and AIDs research. Starbucks makes $12.5 million in loans to poor farmers around the world, and plans to increase that number in the future. Conservation International joined with Starbucks in 1998 to promote sustainable agricultural practices, namely, shade-grown coffee, and to prevent deforestation in endangered regions around the globe. The results of the partnership proved to be positive for both the environment and farmers. For example, in Chiapas, Mexico, shade-grown coffee acreage (which reduces the need to cut down trees for coffee plantations) has increased well over 220 percent, while farmers receive a price premium above the market price. Since the beginning of the partnership Starbucks made loan guarantees that helped provide nearly $1 million in loans to farmers. This financial support enabled those farmers to nearly double their income.

Starbucks works with many other organizations as well, including The African Wildlife Foundation and Business for Social Responsibility. The company's efforts at transparency, the treatment of its workers, and its dozens of philanthropic commitments demonstrate how genuine Starbucks is in its mission to be an ethical and socially responsible company.

CORPORATE SOCIAL MISSION

Although Starbucks has supported responsible business practices virtually since its inception, as the company has grown so has the importance of defending its image. At the end of 1999, Starbucks created a Corporate Social Responsibility department, now known as the Global Responsibility Department. Global Responsibility releases an annual report in order to allow shareholders to keep track of its performance, which can be accessed through the Shared Planet website. Starbucks is concerned about the environment, its employees, suppliers, customers, and its communities.

Environment

In 1992, long before it became trendy to be "green," Starbucks developed an environmental mission statement to articulate more clearly the company's environmental priorities and goals. This initiative created the Environmental Starbucks Coffee Company Affairs team tasked with developing environmentally-responsible policies and minimizing the company's "footprint." Additionally, Starbucks was active in using environmental purchasing guidelines, reducing waste through recycling and energy conservation, and continually educating partners through the company's "Green Team" initiatives. Concerned stakeholders can now track the company's progress and setbacks through its Shared Planet website, which clearly outlines Starbuck's environmental goals and how the company is faring in living up to those goals.

Employees

Growing up poor with a father whose life was nearly ruined by an unsympathetic employer that did not offer health benefits, Howard Schultz has always considered the creation of a good work environment a top priority. "I watched what would happen to the plight of working class families when society and companies turned their back on the worker," Schultz said. "I wanted to build the kind of company my father never got to work for." The result is one of the best health-care programs in the coffee shop industry. All Starbucks employees who work more than twenty hours per week are entitled to receive health benefits (including health, medical, dental, and vision benefits) and to receive stock options, known as *Bean Stock*. Schultz's key to maintaining a strong business is by "creating an environment where everyone believes they're part of something larger than themselves but believes they also have a voice." Understanding how vital employees are, Shultz is the first to admit that his company centers on personal interactions. "We are not in the coffee business serving people, but in the people business serving coffee."

However, being a great employer does take its toll on the company. In 2005, Starbucks spent more on health insurance for its employees than on raw materials required to brew its coffee. The company has faced double-digit increases in insurance costs for multiple years running. Nonetheless, the Starbucks benefits package is a key reason why it has remarkably low employee turnover and high productivity.

Suppliers

Even though it is one of the largest coffee brands in the world, Starbucks maintains a good reputation for social responsibility and business ethics throughout the international community of coffee growers. It attempts to build positive relationships with small coffee suppliers, while also working with governments and nonprofits wherever it operates. Starbucks practices conservation as well as Starbucks Coffee and Farmer Equity practices (C.A.F.E.), which is a set of socially responsible coffee buying guidelines that ensure preferential buying status for participants who receive high scores in best practices. Starbucks pays coffee farmers premium prices to help them make profits and support their families.

The company is also involved in social development programs, investing in programs to build schools, health clinics, and other projects that benefit coffee-growing communities. Starbucks collaborates directly with some of its growers through the Farmer Support Center, located in Costa Rica, which provides technical support and training to ensure high-quality coffee into the future. It also is a major purchaser of Fair Trade Certified, shade-grown, and certified organic beans, which further supports environmental and economic efforts.

In 1991, Starbucks began contributing to CARE, a worldwide relief and development foundation, as a way to give back to coffee-origin countries. By 1995, Starbucks was CARE's largest corporate donor. Starbucks' donations help with projects like clean-water systems, health and sanitation training, and literacy efforts. Starbucks continues its long-term relationship with CARE, making Pike Place Blend its first CARE-certified brew.

Customers

Starbucks continually works to please customers. Strengthening its brand and customer satisfaction is more important than ever as Starbucks seeks to regroup after the 2008–2009 recession forced the company to rethink its strategy. In addition to shutting down stores, Starbucks refocused the brand by upgrading its coffee-brewing machines, introducing new food and drink items for the budget-conscious consumer, and refocusing on its core product. While Starbucks had for years been looking for ways to branch out into music, movies, and other merchandise, 2009 found Starbucks thinking small for the first time. The company started to focus more on the quality of the coffee, the atmosphere of the coffee shops, and the overall Starbucks experience, rather than on continuing its rapid expansion of stores and products.

Enhancing the customer experience in its stores also became a high priority. As a way to encourage people to relax and spend time there, Starbucks offers wireless Internet access with T1 speeds in more than 4,300 coffee houses in U.S. and European stores. Additionally, Starbucks supports discussions in their coffee houses through "The Way I See It," a collection of thoughts, opinions, and expressions provided by notable figures that appear on Starbucks cups. Starbucks focuses most of its efforts on the customer, as a way to enhance their experience and to build loyalty.

"Starbucks focuses most of its efforts on the customer"

Communities

Starbucks coffee shops have long sought to become the "instant gathering spot" wherever they locate, a "place that draws people together." To enhance the local, community-oriented feel of Starbucks shops, store managers are encouraged to donate to local causes. For example, one Seattle store donated more than $500,000 to Zion Preparatory Academy, an African American school for inner-city youth. Howard Schultz believes that literacy has the power to improve lives and to give hope to underprivileged children. Schultz even used the advance and ongoing royalties from his book, *Pour Your Heart Into It,* to create the Starbucks Foundation, which provides "opportunity grants" to nonprofit literacy groups, sponsors young writers programs, and partners with Jumpstart, an organization helping children to prepare developmentally for school.

SUCCESS AND CHALLENGES

For decades, Starbucks has been revolutionizing our leisure time. Starbucks is not only the most prominent brand of high-end coffee in the world, but it is also one of the defining brands of our time. Is there anyone in the United States, or any part of the developed world for that matter, who has not heard of Starbucks?

Psychologist Joyce Brother says that "there is a sense of security when you go there." This sense is consistent across all Starbucks stores because the experience is remarkably consistent. In most large cities, it is impossible to go more than a few blocks without seeing the familiar mermaid logo.

For nearly two decades, Starbucks achieved amazing levels of growth, creating financial success for shareholders. Starbuck's reputation is built on product quality, stakeholder concern, and a balanced approach to all of its business activities. Of course, Starbucks does receive criticism for its ability to beat the competition, putting other coffee shops out of business, and creating a uniform retail culture in many cities. Yet Starbucks excels in its relationship with its employees and is a role model for the fast-food industry in employee benefits. In addition, in an age of shifts in supply chain power, Starbucks is as concerned about its suppliers and meeting their needs as it is about any other primary stakeholder.

In spite of Starbucks' strides at sustainability and maintaining high ethical standards, being one of the best-known brands in the world and operating in forty-four countries places it at risk for criticism. In the past, Starbucks has garnered harsh criticism on issues such as fair-trade coffee, generically modified milk, Howard Shultz's alleged financial links to the Israeli government, and the accusations that the relentless growth is forcing locally run coffee shops out of business. To counter these criticisms in the early 2000s, Starbucks began offering Fair Trade certified coffee in 2002, a menu item that was quickly made permanent. However, Starbucks has been slow to increase the share of Fair Trade products it purchases. While some competitors have switched to 100 percent Fair Trade coffee, Starbucks still buys only around 5 percent Fair Trade. However, offerings like the Pike Place Roast may increase that percentage somewhat.

Yet, starting in late 2008, Starbucks' proportion of Fair Trade offerings suddenly became the least of the company's worries. A global recession caused the market to bottom out for expensive coffee drinks. The company has responded by paring down and focusing on its core product, which is coffee, along with offering the low-priced breakfast pairings, the VIA instant coffee, and more affordably priced tall coffees. In conjunction with rolling out these lower-priced options, while still attempting to hold onto its trademark high-end coffee shop feel, Starbucks has had to rethink its rapid expansion strategy. The company has slowed its global growth plans after sixteen years of expanding at a nonstop pace in order to refocus on strengthening its brand, satisfying customers, and building consumer loyalty. As stated, the new plan included closing hundreds of underperforming stores in the United States and Australia.

Starbucks, like many businesses, is focusing on its core strengths until it can be sure that the global economy is ready for it to expand again. The company is treating this slower time in its history as an opportunity to focus on such things as community involvement, outreach work, and on improving its overall image and offerings.

QUESTIONS

1. Why do you think Starbucks has been so concerned with social responsibility in its overall corporate strategy?
2. Is Starbucks unique in being able to provide a high level of benefits to its employees?
3. Do you think that Starbucks has grown rapidly because of its ethical and socially responsible activities or because it provides products and an environment that customers want?

SOURCES

"C.A.F.E. Practices (Coffee and Farmer Equity Practices)," Starbucks Coffee Company, http://www.starbucks.ca/en-ca/_Social+Responsibility/C.A.F.E.+Practices.htm (accessed May 7, 2009); "Coca-Cola May Take on Starbucks," MSNBC.com, January 30, 2006, http://www.msnbc.msn.com/id/11101825/ (accessed May 5, 2009); "Health Care Takes Its Toll on Starbucks," MSNBC.com, September 14, 2005, http://www.msnbc.msn.com/id/9344634/ (accessed May 5, 2009); Horovitz, Bruce, "Starbucks Aims Beyond Lattes to Extend Brand to Films, Music and Books," *USA Today*, May 19, 2006, pp. A1, A2; Horovitz, Bruce, "Starbucks Unveils Menu Deal to Halt Slide," *USA Today*, February 8, 2009, www.usatoday.com/money/industries/food2009-02-08-value-menu-starbucks_N.htm (accessed May 5, 2009); Horowitz, Adam, David Jacobson, Mark Lasswell, and Owen Thomas, "101 Dumbest Moments in Business," *Business 2.0*, February 1, 2006, http://money.cnn.com/magazines/business2/101dumbest/full_list/page6.html (accessed May 5, 2009); McClelland, Kate, "Starbucks Founder Speaks on Ethics," *Notre Dame Observer*, March 30, 2007, http://media.www.ndsmcobserver.com/media/storage/paper660/news/2007/03/30/News/Starbucks.Founder.Speaks.On.Ethics-2814792.shtml (accessed September 1, 2009); "100 Best Companies to Work For," *Fortune*, http://money.cnn.com/magazines/fortune/bestcompanies/2009/full_list/ (accessed April 1, 2009); "100 Best Corporate Citizens," *Business Ethics*, http://www.business-ethics.com/node/75 (accessed April 1, 2009); "The Proof Is in the Cup: Starbucks Launched Historic New Pike Place Roast™," Starbucks.com, April 7, 2008, http://news.starbucks.com/article_display.cfm?article_id=51, (accessed May 4, 2009); "In Rare Flop, Starbucks Scraps Chocolate Drink," MSNBC.com, February 10, 2006, http://www.msnbc.msn.com/id/11274445/ (accessed May 5, 2009); "Shade Grown Coffee," Eartheasy.com, http://www.eartheasy.com/eat_shadegrown_coffee.htm (accessed May 7, 2009); "Starbucks Company Fact Sheet," http://www.starbucks.com/aboutus/Company_Factsheet.pdf (accessed May 5, 2009); "Starbucks VIA Ready Brew Launches on EasyJet Airline Across Selected Routes in United Kingdom and Spain," Starbucks.com, April 21, 2009, http://news.starbucks.com/article_display.cfm?article_id=209 (accessed May 4, 2009); "2008 Annual Report," Starbucks.com, http://media.corporate-ir.net/media_files/irol/99/99518/AR2008.pdf (accessed April 1, 2009).

CASE 8

The Fraud of the Century: The Case of Bernard Madoff

Daryl Benson

The fraud perpetrated by Bernard Madoff that was discovered in December 2008 was what is known as a Ponzi scheme. A Ponzi scheme works similarly to a pyramid scheme. Madoff took money from new investors to pay earnings for existing customers, without ever actually investing the money. In order to keep making payouts to older clients, Madoff had to continually attract new investors. The Ponzi scheme was named after Charles Ponzi, who in the early twentieth century saw a way to profit from international reply coupons. International reply coupons were a guarantee of return postage in response to an international letter. Charles Ponzi determined that he could make money by swapping out these coupons for more expensive postage stamps in countries where the stamps were of higher value. Ponzi convinced investors to provide him with capital to trade coupons for higher-priced postage stamps. His promise to investors who joined in his scheme was a 50 percent profit in a few days.

Touted as a financial wizard, Ponzi lived a fairly opulent life outside of Boston. He would often bring in as much as $250,000 a day. Part of Ponzi's success came from his personal charisma and ability to con even savvy investors. People trusted Ponzi because he created an image of power, trust, and responsibility—much like Bernard Madoff did nearly a century later. The largest problem with his scheme is that it did not work, much like Madoff's did not. In order to keep giving earlier investors their promised return, he had to continually draw new people into the scheme. In July of 1920, the *Boston Post* ran an article exposing the scheme, and soon after that regulators raided his offices and charged him with mail fraud, knowing that his fabricated investment reports were mailed to his clients. Most Ponzi schemes self-destruct fairly quickly as the ability to keep attracting new investors dwindles. Bernard Madoff's case was unusual because he was able to continue his fraud for many years.

Linda Ferrell developed this case with the editorial assistance of Jennifer Jackson and Jennifer Sawayda. This case was prepared for classroom discussion, rather than to illustrate either effective or ineffective handling of an administrative, ethical, or legal decision by management. All sources used for this case were obtained through publicly available material.

BERNARD L. MADOFF INVESTMENT SECURITIES LLC: "ALL IN THE FAMILY"

Bernard Madoff was not merely a criminal. He was also a highly successful, legitimate businessperson. He started a legal, investment business in 1960 by buying and selling over-the-counter stocks that were not listed on the New York Stock Exchange (NYSE). These stocks were traded via the telephone with no automation. This meant that an in-the-know individual such as Madoff could profit from variations between different quotes. Basically, he served as a "wholesaler" between institutional investors. In the early days, working with investment firms such as A.G. Edwards, Charles Schwab, and others, Madoff made his money based on the variance between the offer price and sales price of stocks.

In the 1990s, Madoff Securities was trading up to 10 percent of the NASDAQ (National Association of Securities Dealers Automated Quotations) shares on certain days. Early success and competitive advantage came from Bernie working with his brother Peter (the first of several family members to join his firm), who after graduating from law school joined Madoff's company and developed superior technology for trading, buying, and selling at the best prices. Madoff controlled the funds in-house and made his money, in this division, from commissions on sales and profits. The profits were not based on fraud; however, there is evidence that Madoff occasionally injected funds from his illegal business into his legal one during times of low revenues.

"Madoff made every client feel like he or she was his only client."

As Madoff became more successful, he moved the company's headquarters from Wall Street to the famous "Lipstick Building" on Third Avenue built by famed architect Philip Johnson. Not unlike Enron's Ken Lay and his lobbying efforts to deregulate the energy and gas industry, Bernie also became more involved in lobbying for regulatory changes that would make it easier to trade electronically. Brother Peter took on more oversight of the firm's securities business. Bernie served as chair of the NASDAQ in 1990, 1991, and 1993. In addition, he held a seat on the government advisory board on stock market regulation, served on charitable boards, and started his own foundation, all of which added to his credibility. He developed respectability and trust as a highly knowledgeable investment specialist.

For years Madoff had been using his legitimate success and high visibility to start a second business managing money. He seemed trustworthy and promised consistent returns of 10 to 12 percent, attracting billions of dollars from hundreds of investors. Part of the appeal of investing with Bernie was the appeal of exclusivity. Madoff made every client feel like he or she was his only client. His inaccessibility and "invitation only" approach to new investors created an air of exclusivity and desire to be involved. Ruth Madoff, Bernie's wife, also worked at the firm for a time, and often functioned as a friendly face of the companies. Madoff was frequently excessively focused on work and order, while Ruth was pretty, gregarious, and smart.

Bernie's niece and Peter's daughter, Shana Madoff, was a rules and compliance officer at Madoff's legitimate firm and worked under her father, who was head of compliance in the market-making arm (not the firm's money management business). Shana, was not charged with any crimes, is married to Eric Swanson, a former Securities and Exchange Commission (SEC) compliance lawyer. Shana Madoff has a respected career and was honored by the Girl Scouts of America as a "woman of distinction."

Although also under investigation, neither of Madoff's sons, Mark and Andrew, has been charged with any wrongdoing. It was to them that Madoff confessed his crime, and they were responsible for turning in their father to the authorities. The two deny any knowledge of the fraud and did not speak to their father or mother for months after Bernie's arrest. The family emphasizes the separation of the legitimate, stock-trading business (run on the nineteenth floor) and the illegitimate, investment management business (run on the seventeenth floor) by Bernie Madoff.

In March 2009, when Bernard Madoff stated his guilt in court, he never indicated the involvement of any other company employees or family members. He stated in the allocution that "I want to emphasize today that while my investment advisory business—the vehicle of my wrongdoing—was part of Bernard L. Madoff Securities, the other businesses that my firm engaged in, proprietary trading and market making, were legitimate, profitable and successful in all respects. Those businesses were managed by my brother and two sons" (Madoff Plea Allocution, p. 2). Further investigation will determine the extent and level of external support that Madoff had in defrauding thousands. Madoff chose to hire inexperienced, sometimes uneducated individuals with no background in finance to work in his investment management business. Some speculate that he did this so as to surround himself with unknowing participants.

EXPLAINING THE GROWTH NUMBERS

Madoff staked his investment business on claims that he could consistently generate 10 to 12 percent returns for investors, no matter what the economic climate. Many of his clients were already wealthy and just looking for a stable and constant rate of return. To these people, his friends at the Palm Beach Country Club, for example, reliable constant returns managed by one of their own seemed like the perfect way to go. His stated investment strategy was to buy stocks, while also trading options on those stocks as a way to limit the potential losses. His market timing strategy was called the "split strike-conversion." With the large financial portfolio Madoff managed, many indicate at least one "red flag" would have been the fact that he would have had to make more trades than the market would physically allow just to meet his everyday financial goals. Shocking to all of his clients, Madoff confessed in his "Plea Allocution" statement that he never invested any of his client's funds. All of the money was deposited in banks, and Madoff simply moved money between Chase Manhattan Bank in New York and Madoff Securities International Ltd., a United Kingdom Corporation. During his confession, Madoff stated that his fraud began in the early 1990s.

To help continuously draw in new clients, Madoff developed relationships with intermediaries, also known as "feeders" to his investment fund. They were other investment managers who trusted Madoff to take care of their clients' money, and it does not appear that they were integrally involved in the fraud. Many of these feeders had themselves invested money with Madoff. One such middleperson, Rene-Thierry Magon de la Villehuchet, committed suicide after losing his life savings to Madoff. These feeders profited by receiving fees and ensuring that Madoff had a stream of money flowing into his operation. Robert Jaffe operated as a middleperson for Madoff starting in 1989 when he became the manager of Boston-based Cohmad Securities, a firm co-owned by Madoff to attract investors. Jaffe was the son-in-law of one of Madoff's earliest investors and was a member of the Palm Beach Country Club. Jaffe earned a small commission whenever Madoff took on an investor introduced to him by Jaffe.

FINANCIAL SUPPORT NEAR THE END AND THE ARREST

Toward the end of Madoff's fraud, he was getting desperate for funds. As the economy collapsed in late 2008, more and more clients were requesting deposits back. In order to pay them and to not be exposed, Madoff needed more cash quickly. He resorted to soliciting, and sometimes subtlety threatening, clients for more deposits—making them feel guilty for not being better clients of such a distinguished investment firm.

A week and a half before Madoff admitted to his sons that he was operating a Ponzi scheme, 95-year-old Palm Beach philanthropist and entrepreneur Carl Shapiro gave Madoff $250 million. Shapiro lost that money, as well as $100 million in additional funds that had belonged to a charitable organization. Martin Rosenman, the president of a fuel company in New York, also provided an additional $10 million in deposits. Rosenman is suing Madoff for the money. He alleges that Madoff told him that his funds would be invested in a new fund, and was even sent a nineteen-page promotional piece in advance of the investment.

Of course, even these hundreds of millions in additional deposits would not be enough to cover Madoff's losses. Possibly because he knew that the act was up, he turned himself in to his sons. Madoff was arrested on December 11, accused of operating a $65 billion Ponzi scheme. The official charge is criminal securities fraud. Madoff declared to his sons that he had roughly $200–300 million left in the business and that he wanted to provide the money to employees before turning himself over to authorities. This was news to his sons; they thought the investment arm of the business held between $8 billion and $15 billion in assets. The SEC records showed that the firm had $17 billion in assets at the beginning of 2008.

THE INVESTIGATION AND CHARGES

Investigators in this case included the SEC, FBI, federal prosecutors from the U.S. attorney's office for the Southern District of New York, and the Financial Industry Regulatory Authority. Forensic accountants will try to pull together the trail of investments and spending to determine where the money went. There is a belief that multiple offshore funds were created by Madoff to shelter assets prior to the collapse of the firm. Madoff's business was not registered with the SEC until 2006, after an SEC investigation.

Bernard Madoff has been charged with criminal securities fraud, and investigators are now evaluating documents dating back to 2000. The charges did not come as a surprise to the SEC when Madoff was finally exposed, however; beginning in 1992, federal regulators had been investigating allegations of wrongdoing by Madoff. Table 1 provides a summary of the nature of these investigations.

It is believed that much of the money invested with Madoff went either to offset losses in his legal business or to fund the Madoff family's lavish lifestyle. There is growing evidence that although family members may not have known that Bernie was running a Ponzi scheme, they thought nothing of treating his businesses like their personal piggy banks. Investigators may pursue Ruth Madoff and their two sons in order to recover some of the money owed to bilked investors.

TABLE 1 Government and Regulatory Investigations of Bernard Madoff

Year	Nature of Investigation
1992	SEC—Madoff's name came up in a Florida accounting investigation.
1999	SEC reviewed Madoff's trading practices.
2001	SEC—Harry Markopolos, securities industry executive, raised questions regarding Madoff's returns.
2004	SEC reviewed allegations of improper trading practices.
2005	SEC interviewed Madoff and family but found no improper trading activities.
2005	Industry-based regulatory group found no improper trading activities.
2005	SEC met with Harry Markopolos, who claimed Madoff was operating the world's largest Ponzi scheme.
2006	An SEC enforcement investigation found misleading behavior, and Madoff registered as an investment advisor.
2007	Financial Industry Regulatory Authority investigated Madoff, but no regulatory action was taken.

Source: Associated Press, "The Many Fruitless Probes into Bernie Madoff," APNewswire, January 5, 2009, http://news.moneycentral.msn.com/provider/providerarticle.aspx?feed=AP&date=20090105&id=9486677, accessed January 5, 2009

INVESTORS IMPACTED

The very long list of Madoff clients is a who's who of organizations, nonprofits, successful entrepreneurs and businesspeople, as well as entertainers. The Fairfield Greenwich Group, one of Madoff's largest feeder funds, had around $7.5 billion, or more than half of its assets, invested in the firm. The Noel family, owners of Fairfield Greenwich, has been so disgraced by their association with the Madoffs that their membership to the Round Hill Country Club in Greenwich, Connecticut, was revoked. Tremont Group Holdings, owned by Oppenheimer, had $3.3 billion invested. Ezra Merkin, head of a GMAC-operated hedge fund, lost $1.8 billion to Madoff.

Several victims have shared information about their history and relationship with Bernie Madoff. Richard Sonking met with Madoff in the mid 1990s after his father, who had an account with Madoff, recommended the investment firm for its steady 8–14 percent returns. Sonking pulled together the minimum $100,000 required for investment at that time, feeling confident that he was joining a highly select group of investors. Sonking continued to place money in Madoff's hands as he accumulated greater wealth. As with all of Madoff's clients, he was happy with the constant returns and with the detailed statements that were mailed to him each month. Like everyone else, he never questioned why Madoff did not make online records available, and he did not question the secrecy to which Madoff swore his investors. Upon retiring in 2005, Sonking requested quarterly distributions from his account. As with most of Madoff's loyal investors, Sonking received no warnings of fraudulent activity until he heard the news of Madoff's arrest.

Loretta Weinberg, a New Jersey state senator, was a conservative investor who embraced her late husband's philosophy that you should live on half of what you make and save the rest.

She had no investments with Madoff, but she did place money in the hands of Stanley Chais, a Los Angeles money manager who provided quarterly investment reports and a 10–14 percent annual return. It just so happened that Chais was a feeder with Madoff, funneling much of his clients' money Madoff's way. Until the Madoff scandal hit the press, Weinberg had not even heard of Madoff. As a 73-year-old state senator making $49,000/year, she is coming to terms with what it means to lose her entire $1.3 million in life savings.

> *Madoff had a tremendous reputation for secure and conservative financial management.*

Joseph Gurwin is 88 years old and lives in Palm Beach. Like many in Palm Beach, he came to know Madoff and had become his friend through the local social and philanthropic community. Madoff had a tremendous reputation for secure and conservative financial management, and it was considered a huge honor among the elites in Palm Beach to be invested with Madoff. Gurwin's foundation (The J. Gurwin Foundation, Inc.), operating with around $28 million in assets, donated $1.2 million annually to Jewish health care, services, and programs for frail, elderly, or disabled younger adults. After investing heavily with Madoff, Gurwin's charitable foundation lost all of its assets when Madoff's Ponzi scheme crashed.

Law firms in Florida are representing clients who believed they were investing with Westport National Bank (a regulated banking institution in Connecticut), and not with Madoff, but who have received a letter from Westport National indicating that the bank had a custodial agreement with Madoff giving full discretionary authority to Bernard L. Madoff Investment Securities. Madoff's sweep went far beyond his immediate circle.

RESTITUTION FOR INVESTORS

So far, close to 9,000 people have submitted claims for restitution in the Madoff case. Some are suing the SEC for not catching this fraud sooner. However, paying back all these investors will be a difficult task. Although Madoff's fraud is being billed as a $65 billion Ponzi scheme, Madoff never had anywhere near that amount of money. The figure of $65 billion is the total amount Madoff told people they had invested and earned with him. The actual amount may be well below $10 billion. Investigators have considered pursuing legal action against Madoff family members in order to pay all of these claims.

In reaction to all the ethical scandals being uncovered in the investment and finance industries, the SEC is considering a new proposal that would place investment advisors under more government scrutiny. The proposal would require that advisors like Madoff demonstrate evidence to an independent accountant that they actually have the funds they claim to have. Although Madoff was investigated by the SEC repeatedly over the years, and in spite of skeptics providing the SEC with strong evidence that Madoff was indeed running a Ponzi scheme, investigators never thought to verify whether Madoff actually had all the money he claimed to have. This proposal to increase regulatory oversight comes at a time when it has become clear how easy it is for investment professionals to misuse client funds and then send them false reports to cover up their misdeeds.

Investigators are also looking into potential misconduct on the part of some of Madoff's clients. According to investigations, Madoff feeder funds withdrew over $12 billion in 2008, with half of that money being withdrawn in the three months leading up to his arrest—a huge sum that probably led to Bernie's confession when he could no longer pull together cash to make payments. Under federal law, the trustee for the

Madoff bankruptcy suit can sue to retrieve this money in what are called "clawback" suits. The argument is that $12 billion was essentially "stolen" from other investors who actually owned the money. Hence, to protect their assets from seizure, many who received payout funds from Madoff are transferring the money to irrevocable trusts, homes, annuities, or life insurance policies.

One of these cases seeks repayment of $5.1 billion from a prominent Madoff client and Palm Beach investor named Picower. Although Picower's charitable fund was one of the highest-profile victims of the Madoff downfall, investigators suspect some foul play. Part of the concern is that as a professional investor, Picower should have known that the profits he was getting from Madoff were too high. The accusations further state that Picower was getting payments from Madoff to help perpetuate the Ponzi scheme, which means Picower would have known about the scheme all along. This is only one of what will surely amount to dozens of lawsuits related to the attempt to recover and redistribute funds from Madoff clients. Undoubtedly this web will take years to untangle as investigators seek to learn who knew about Madoff's scheme and which ones are, therefore, guilty of being complicit.

As mentioned earlier, some investors are suing the SEC for negligence in its regulatory responsibility and not being able to identify the fraud. Such attempts represent the first time investors have sought restitution from a regulatory agency. Christopher Cox, SEC chair at the start of the fraud investigation, has indicated that the SEC examiners missed "red flags" in reviewing the Madoff firm. Allegations of wrongdoing started in the early 1990s, and Madoff confirms fraud dating back to that time. Repeated investigations and examinations by the SEC showed no investment fraud. Because many SEC employees have ended up working in the investment business on Wall Street, there has been speculation that an overall lack of objectivity clouded these investigations. Some suspect incompetence on the part of the SEC as well. In the wake of the Madoff fallout, it has become clear that some SEC investigators were sufficiently knowledgeable about the kinds of complex financial instruments used on Wall Street. Thus, they should have been knowledgeable enough to be able to detect the fraud.

Perhaps the greatest restitution for some investors came as Bernard Madoff was handcuffed and taken to prison after his twelve-minute-long confession of guilt in a Lower Manhattan courthouse. Some victims asked the judge for a trial to uncover more about this extensive fraud and to determine why the government regulatory system failed so many investors. Judge Chin indicated there would be no trial since Madoff pleaded guilty and there was an ongoing investigation at hand. Madoff was sentenced to 150 years in prison.

THE FUTURE OF CHARITABLE GIVING

Due to the widespread impact of the Madoff-related losses upon charities, nonprofits, and educational institutions, donor skepticism and withdrawal are not unexpected consequences. Some of the organizations affected included the Elie Wiesel Foundation for Humanity, Yeshiva University, and Wunderkinder Foundation (Steven Spielberg's fund). This wariness comes at a time when the global recession resulted in losses of around 30 percent for many foundations' endowments. The vast majority of nonprofits indicate that the economy had a negative impact on fundraising, even before the Madoff scandal was exposed. In the future, it is certain that charities and donors alike will approach the donation process with greater care. One way to evaluate responsible charities is to develop guidelines for giving, which would include knowing what materials are readily available to potential investors/donors from the organization, who is running the fund/charity, and who is auditing the fund/charity. Another guideline is to diversify the investment portfolio, which avoids putting all investments in one basket. This is exactly what many of Madoff's victims *did not do,* choosing instead to place all their assets into Madoff's company and losing their investments in the resulting scandal.

CONCLUSION

Bernard Madoff is accused of creating a Ponzi scheme that destroyed $65 billion in investments. Many people are trying to understand how so many experienced investors, including banks, insurance companies, and nonprofit foundations, lost billions of dollars to an individual who was able to deceive them as well as regulators. Investigators are trying to determine who helped Madoff carry off what some say could have been a 30-year scheme that caused the $65 billion in losses that have affected thousands of people around the world. Accountants, auditors, and regulators are supposed to be gatekeepers that protect the public interest. Investigators believe that Madoff had a trading strategy that failed, then after a while, he made few trades for many years and his operation consisted of taking money from new clients and paying it out to existing clients, a classic Ponzi scheme.

From an ethical perspective, this would be an example of white-collar crime. White-collar criminals create victims by establishing trust and respectability. As in this case, victims of white-collar crime are trusting clients who believe there are many checks and balances to certify that an operation is legitimate. Madoff is an example of the classic white-collar criminal. He was an educated and experienced individual in a position of power, trust, respectability, and responsibility who abused his trust for personal gains. From the inception of his investment business, he knew that he was operating a Ponzi scheme and defrauding his clients. In the end, he said he "knew this day would come."

An important question is how one individual could deceive so many intelligent people and authorities that certified his operation as legitimate. Madoff's accountants, family, and other employees will have to answer to authorities about their knowledge of the operations. For example, investigators have issued a subpoena for David Friehling, a New York accountant who audited Madoff's financial statements. Although only Madoff was originally charged with misconduct and was adamant that he acted alone, other participants will undoubtedly be discovered and charged. Madoff's right-hand man, Frank DiPascali, has admitted to knowing of individuals and firms complicit in Madoff's scheme who knowingly broke the law.

White-collar crime is unique in that it is often perpetrated by a rogue individual who knowingly steals, cheats, or manipulates in order to damage others. Often, the only way to prevent white-collar crime is to have internal controls and compliance standards that detect misconduct. Perhaps the most difficult white-collar crime and fraud to expose is that perpetrated by the top executive. We count on leadership within an organization to create, manage, and motivate an ethical organizational culture with all the checks and balances in place. In the Madoff case, there was the opportunity to deceive others without effective audits, transparency, or understanding of the true nature of his operations. As a result of this case, individual investors, institutions, and hopefully regulators will exert more diligence in demanding transparency and honesty from those who manage investments.

QUESTIONS

1. What are the ethical issues involved in the Madoff case?
2. Do you believe that Bernard Madoff worked alone, or do you think he had help in creating and sustaining his Ponzi scheme? Would this represent a conflict of interest?
3. What should be done to help ensure that Ponzi schemes like this one do not happen in the future?

SOURCES

Bandler, James, and Nicholas Varchaver with Doris Burke, "How Bernie Did It," *Fortune,* May 11, 2009, pp. 50–71; Bernstein, Elizabeth, "After Madoff, Donors Grow Wary of Giving," *Wall Street Journal,* December 23, 2008, http://online.wsj.com/article/SB122999068109728409.html (accessed September 2, 2009); Bryan-Low, Cassel, "Inside a Swiss Bank, Madoff Warnings," *Wall Street Journal,* January 14, 2009, p. 1A; Catan, Thomas, Christopher Bjork, and Jose De Cordoba, "Giant Bank Probe Over Ties to Madoff," *Wall Street Journal,* January 13, 2009, http://online.wsj.com/article/SB123179728255974859.html (accessed September 2, 2009); Efrati, Amir, "Q&A on the Madoff Case," *Wall Street Journal,* March 12, 2009, http://online.wsj.com/article/SB123005811322430633.html (accessed September 2, 2009); Efrati, Amir, "Scope of Alleged Fraud Is Still Being Assessed," *Wall Street Journal,* December 18, 2008, http://online.wsj.com/article/SB122953110854314501.html (accessed September 2, 2009); Efrati, Amir, and Chad Bray, "U.S.: Madoff Had $173 Million in Checks," *Wall Street Journal,* January 9, 2009, http://online.wsj.com/article/SB123143634250464871.html (accessed September 2, 2009); Efrati, Amir, Aaron Luccchetti, and Tom Lauricella, "Probe Eyes Audit Files, Role of Aide to Madoff," *Wall Street Journal,* September 2, 2009, http://online.wsj.com/article/SB122999256957528605.html (accessed December 23, 2008); Frank, Robert, and Amir Efrati, "Madoff Tried to Stave Off Firm's Crash Before Arrest," *Wall Street Journal,* January 7, 2009, http://online.wsj.com/article/SB123129835145559987.html (accessed September 2, 2009); Frank, Robert, and Tom Lauricella, "Madoff Created Air of Mystery," *Wall Street Journal,* December 20, 2008, http://online.wsj.com/article/SB122973208705022949.html (accessed September 2, 2009); Goldfarb, Zachary, "Investment Advisors Would Face More Scrutiny Under SEC Proposal," *Washington Post,* May 15, 2009, http://www.washingtonpost.com/wp-dyn/content/article/2009/05/14/AR2009051403970.html?hpid=topnews (accessed September 2, 2009); Hays, Tom, "Trustee: Nearly 9,000 Claims in Madoff Scam," *San Francisco Chronicle,* May 14, 2009, http://www.sfgate.com/cgi-bin/article.cgi?f=/n/a/2009/05/14/financial/f090030D98.DTL&feed=rss.business (accessed September 2, 2009); Henriques, Diana B., and Zachery Kouwe, "Billions Withdrawn Before Madoff Arrest," *New York Times,* May 12, 2009, http://www.nytimes.com/2009/05/13/business/13madoff.html?_r=1&scp=1&sq=madoff%20%2412%20billion&st=cse, September 2, 2009); Kim, Jane J., "As 'Clawback' Suits Loom, Some Investors Seek Cover," *Wall Street Journal,* March 12, 2009, p. C3; Lucchetti, Aaron, "Victims Welcome Madoff Imprisonment," *Wall Street Journal,* March 13, 2009, http://online.wsj.com/article/SB123687992688609801.html (accessed September 2, 2009); "Madoff's Victims," *Wall Street Journal,* March 6, 2009, http://s.wsj.net/public/resources/documents/st_madoff_victims_20081215.html (accessed September 2, 2009); "Plea Allocution of Bernard L. Madoff," *Wall Street Journal,* March 12, 2009, http://online.wsj.com/public/resources/documents/20090315madoffall.pdf (accessed September 2, 2009); Scannell, Kara, "Investor Who Lost Money in Alleged Scheme Seeks Relief from SEC," *Wall Street Journal,* December 23, 2008, http://online.wsj.com/article/SB122999646876429063.html (accessed September 2, 2009); Shapiro, Adam, "Who Are 'The Others' Who Helped Madoff?" Fox News, August 12, 2009, http://www.foxbusiness.com/story/personal-finance/financial-planning/helped-madoff/ (accessed September 8, 2009); Stapleton, Christine, "Madoff Scandal Ripples Among Palm Beach County Foundations," *Palm Beach*

Post, February 8, 2009, http://www.palmbeachpost.com/localnews/content/local_news/epaper/2009/02/08/a1b_foundations_0209.html, (accessed September 2, 2009); Strasburg, Jenny, "Madoff 'Feeders' Under Focus," *Wall Street Journal,* December 27–28, 2008, pp. A1, A8; Strasburg, Jenny, "Mass Mutual Burned by Madoff," *Wall Street Journal,* December 22, 2008, p. C1; Trex, Ethan, "Who Was Ponzi—What the Heck Was His Scheme?" CNN.com, December 23, 2008, http://www.cnn.com/2008/LIVING/wayoflife/12/23/mf.ponzi.scheme/index.html (accessed September 2, 2009); "Victims of Scandal Reflect on Shocking Turnabout," *Wall Street Journal,* December 23, 2008, http://online.wsj.com/article/SB122972955226822819.html (accessed September 2, 2009); Williamson, Elizabeth, "Shana Madoff's Ties to Uncle Probed," *Wall Street Journal,* December 22, 2008, http://online.wsj.com/article/SB122991035662025577.html (accessed September 2, 2009).

APPENDIX Selected Group of Madoff Investor Losses

Fairfield Greenwich Advisors	An investment management firm	$7,500,000,000
Tremont Group Holdings	Asset management firm	$3,300,000,000
Banco Santander	Spanish bank	$2,870,000,000
Bank Medici	Austrian bank	$2,100,000,000
Ascot Partners	A hedge fund founded by billionaire investor, philanthropist, and GMAC chief J. Ezra Merkin	$1,800,000,000
Fortis	Dutch bank	$1,350,000,000
HSBC	British bank	$1,000,000,000
Carl Shapiro	The founder and former chair of apparel company Kay Windsor, Inc., and his wife	$500,000,000
Fairfield, Conn.	Town pension fund	$42,000,000
Jewish Community Foundation of Los Angeles	The largest manager of charitable gift assets for Los Angeles Jewish philanthropists	$18,000,000
Korea Teachers Pension	A 10 trillion won Korean pension fund	$9,100,000
Fred Wilpon	Owner of the New York Mets	N/A
Steven Spielberg	The Spielberg charity—the Wunderkinder Foundation	N/A
Chais Family Foundation	A charity that gave to Jewish causes	N/A
Allianz Global Investors	The asset management unit of German insurer Allianz SE	N/A
UBS AG	Swiss bank	N/A
Yeshiva University	A New York–based private university	$14,500,000
Elie Wiesel Foundation for Humanity	The charitable foundation of Nobel laureate Elie Wiesel	$15,200,000
Leonard Feinstein	The co-founder of retailer Bed Bath & Beyond	N/A
Sen. Frank Lautenberg	The charitable foundation of the New Jersey senator's family	N/A
Norman Braman	Former owner of the Philadelphia Eagles	N/A

Jeffrey Katzenberg	The chief executive of DreamWorks Animation SKG Inc.	N/A
Gerald Breslauer	The Hollywood financial advisor to Steven Spielberg and Jeffrey Katzenberg	N/A
Royal Dutch Shell pension fund	Global energy and petrochemical company	N/A
New York Law School	Law school in New York City	$300,000
J. Gurwin Foundation	Charity	N/A
Fire and Police Pension Association of Colorado	Pension fund	N/A
International Olympic Committee	Olympic organizer	$4,800,000
Kevin Bacon and wife Kyra Sedgwick	Hollywood actors	N/A
Eric Roth	Hollywood screenwriter	N/A
Henry Kaufman	Individual investor, former Salomon Brothers chief economist	N/A
New York University	University	$24,000,000
Burt Ross	Former mayor of a town in New Jersey	$5,000,000
Gabriel Partners	Money-management firm run by GMAC Chair Ezra Merkin	N/A
Diocese of St. Thomas	Catholic church in the U.S. Virgin Islands	$2,000,000
Members of the Hillcrest Golf Club of St. Paul, Minn., and Oak Ridge Country Club in Hopkins, Minn.	Country clubs	N/A
Bard College	University in New York	$3,000,000
Martin Rosenman	New York City–based heating oil distributor	$10,000,000

Source: WSJ reporting; Associated Press; the companies and charities, wsj.net/public/resources/documents/st_madoff_victims_20081215.html, accessed January 9, 2009.

CASE 9

NIKE: Managing Ethical Missteps—Sweatshops to Leadership in Employment Practices

Daryl Benson

Phil Knight and his University of Oregon track coach Bill Bowerman founded Blue Ribbon Sports, later renamed Nike, in 1964. The idea, born as a result of a paper written by Knight during his Stanford MBA program, was to import athletic shoes from Japan into the U.S. market otherwise dominated by German competitors Puma and Adidas. The company initially operated as a distributor for a Japanese athletic shoe company, Onitsuka Tiger, but also developed its own brand of athletic footwear to promote in the American market. The company's relationship with Onitsuka Tiger ended in 1971, and the Nike brand was created in 1972 ("Nike" after the Greek goddess of victory). The company was renamed Nike in 1978, and has grown to be the largest worldwide seller of athletic goods, with approximately 19,000 retail accounts in the United States and about 160 countries around the world.

Nike's main popularity came from celebrity athlete sponsors. As the popularity of the Nike product grew, so did its product demands and the need to produce more apparel to meet the demands of customers. In contrast to its meteoric rise in the 1980s after going public, the late 1990s began a period composed of combating allegations about labor and human rights violations in Third World countries in which manufacturing had been subcontracted. Nike's response to this issue has been considered by critics to be more of a damage-control stunt than a sincere attempt at labor reform.

This case was prepared by O.C. Ferrell and Jennifer Jackson, based on work by Lisa Kiscaden and Megan Long, the University of New Mexico. We appreciate the editorial assistance of Jennifer Sawayda on this edition of the case, and of Melanie Drever and Alexi Sherrill on the previous edition. This case was prepared for classroom discussion, rather than to illustrate either effective or ineffective handling of an administrative, ethical, or legal decision by management. All sources used for this case were obtained through publicly available material and the Nike website.

CRITICISMS OF NIKE'S MANUFACTURING PRACTICES

In order to remain competitive and keep manufacturing costs low, athletic footwear production has moved to areas of the world with low labor costs. Assembly of shoes (as well as low-cost apparel, footwear, radios, TVs, toys, sporting goods equipment, and consumer electronics) began shifting offshore in the 1960s: first to Japan, then to Korea and Taiwan, and starting in the 1980s to Southern China. By the mid 1980s, Taiwan and Korea supplied 45 percent of the world footwear exports, and the trend has continued for production to continually shift to lower-cost Asian nations.

Because of its history and experience with Japanese manufacturing and production, Nike was a pioneer in overseas manufacturing as a way to cut costs on sports gear manufacturing. When Japan became too expensive, Nike shifted its contracts to Vietnam, Indonesia, and China. Now, around 700 independent contract factories, most of which are in poor Asian nations, manufacture the majority of Nike's products. The working conditions for the workers in these factories have been a source of heated debate. Allegations of poor conditions, child labor, widespread harassment, and abuse have all been issues for the company. Because the Asian factories have further subcontracted out the work, it has become increasingly difficult for Nike to keep track of and regulate the working conditions and wages in these factories.

Sweatshop labor is not merely an issue for Nike. It permeates the public consciousness across all manufacturing. Perhaps the incident that brought sweatshop labor to the forefront of American consciousness was the Kathy Lee Gifford debacle in 1996 when the human rights group, the National Labor Committee, uncovered that Gifford's clothing line was made in Honduran sweatshops that used child labor.

Since the mid 1990s, Nike has faced a barrage of criticism from labor rights activists, the mainstream media, and others for human and labor rights violations in its factories. The accusations have included deficiencies in health and safety conditions, extremely low wages, and indiscriminate hiring and firing practices. While much of the firestorm has died down as Nike and other athletic wear manufacturers have sought to clean up their images, the media criticisms have damaged the company's reputation.

In Indonesia, where Korean suppliers owned a majority of Nike factories, reports by labor activists and other nongovernmental organizations revealed several cases of human rights abuses and labor violations. Through the use of the mass media, these conditions came to the attention of the general public, one of the prominent instances being that of Roberta Baskin's CBS report on the conditions in Nike's manufacturing facilities in Indonesia in 1993.

In 1996, *Life* magazine published an exposé article complete with photos of Pakistani children stitching soccer balls for Nike, Adidas AG, and other companies. The images of these children, working in factories instead of being in school, had a devastating impact on Nike's sales and corporate reputation. Customers who had previously held the American athletics brand in high regard began to develop a lower opinion of the company. Another well-publicized critique against Nike was Bob Herbert's op-ed article in the *New York Times* in 1996. This report led to further public interest, accompanied by protests and demonstrations all over the United States. Several demonstrations occurred at "Nike Towns," the Nike retail mega stores.

Nike also experienced problems with factory conditions in Vietnam. This was especially serious since the discovery came as a result of a report commissioned by Nike as part of an audit by Ernst and Young of one of its factories. The private report was leaked to the press, resulting in the *New York Times* running it as a front-page article. The audit reported unacceptable levels of exposure to chemicals in the factory and documented cases of resulting employee health problems, as well as other infringements of the established code of conduct.

In response to the criticisms of the 1990s, Nike had to take rapid measures not only to redeem its reputation, but also to rectify problematic policies and lack of international oversight of its operations. Nike's new priorities changed to make certain that its factories were not taking advantage of its workers as well as to ensure that each worker has a safe work environment and competitive wage.

ENVIRONMENTAL PROBLEMS RELATED TO THE TEXTILE INDUSTRY

"The demand for cheap labor in manufacturing plants can lead to the increased prevalence of child labor and abusive practices"

Because of the nature of the textile industry, Nike faces numerous challenges and potentially critical problems. Because of the processes involved in making the materials, the textile industry negatively impacts the environment wherever manufacturing is located. Problems generated by the textile industry in general, and Nike specifically, are increased water deficits; climate change; pollution of land, air, and waterways; and large fossil fuel and raw material consumption. In addition to these environmental hazards, today's electronic textile plants expend significant amounts of energy. All of these issues are exacerbated by Western cultures that have a consumption-based mentality that clothing is disposable and that one must buy each new season's "must-have" items.

In addition to environmental considerations are the physical work conditions for employees. The demand for cheap labor in manufacturing plants can lead to the increased prevalence of child labor and abusive practices, especially in developing countries such as Pakistan, Indonesia, Vietnam, and China, where workplaces are not as regulated as in the United States.

In her book, *No Logo*, published in 2002, Naomi Klein targets Nike regulation policies quite extensively, alleging that Nike abandons manufacturing sites in favor of cheaper ones as these countries work to develop better pay and employment rights. She refers back to the 1996 photo from *Life* magazine of Pakistani children as an example of the exploitation of child labor. Many critics have suggested that Nike should improve transparency measures in all of its factories, allow independent inspection to verify conditions, and make all audits public. Nike has complied to a limited extent. For example, audits of Nike generally have determined that Nike pays wages above the legal minimum. Critics are not satisfied, however, arguing that in most cases the wages still do not constitute a fair living wage.

NIKE RESPONDS TO THE CHALLENGES

Public protests against Nike have taken the forms of boycotts and picketing of Nike stores. Universities have even been known to cancel their deals with Nike to produce branded athletic goods. In 1998, Nike revenues and stock prices decreased by approximately

50 percent, leading to the laying off of 1,600 workers. Nike's first reaction to all of the bad press was to do damage control. Nike launched a large public relations campaign involving individual consumer retailers and large university contracts to combat the damaging allegations of child labor, inhospitable working conditions, and low or nonexistent wages. In an effort to directly address the concerns of student activists, Nike visited several college campuses, opening dialog with students and university administration about its manufacturing policies. Nike even invited teams of Dartmouth graduate students to tour the Indonesian and Vietnamese factories for three weeks at Nike's expense.

The company has spent considerable resources focusing on improving the labor standards in each of its factories. It must weigh the expense of labor in nations where product manufacturing is available. However, no matter where it chooses, as these factories subcontract out to the local workforce, it becomes increasingly difficult for Nike to regulate their working environment. Nike must take extra measures to ensure that the independent subcontractors used to supply the workforce in their factories do not engage in any illegal activities such as child labor, excessive work hours, hostile work environments, inappropriate payment, or other unethical actions.

Nike also has implemented a code of conduct for all of its suppliers, and has been working with the Global Alliance to help review its factories. In August 1996, Nike Corporation joined the Apparel Industry Partnership, a coalition of companies and labor and human rights groups assembled by the Clinton administration, to draft an industry-wide code of conduct.

Nike believes that sharing factory locations with independent third parties on a confidential basis enables them to monitor their supply chain properly. It states that disclosure of the factory names, plus details of audits of those factories, would be used by nongovernmental organizations (NGOs) simply to make further attacks rather than as part of a dialog to help the company to address and resolve those problems that exist. As for wage rates, Nike feels that establishing what constitutes a "fair" wage is by no means as easy as critics would have the public believe—and disparages the constant quoting of wage rates in U.S. dollar equivalents, when these are meaningless given the different costs of living in the countries concerned.

Nike has used many other tactics to repair its tarnished image. Like other athletics brands, Nike has used celebrity endorsers to support its products. Most famously, Michael Jordan was a Nike spokesperson for years, and Kobe Bryant and LeBron James have worked with Nike as well.

Since universities form a core segment of Nike's market, and repercussions were felt in this area with several canceled deals, letters detailing the acceptable conditions in the factories and stressing Nike's commitment to corporate responsibility were sent to universities around the country. Representatives from Nike also visited campuses and spoke to students, assuring them of Nike's intention toward responsible corporate citizenship. A key visit in this context was that of Mr. Knight to the campus of the University of North Carolina at Chapel Hill. Numerous press conferences were also held with college newspapers across the United States.

Nike is clearly distressed at how it has become a central focus in this controversy. The company requests that people look at Nike's competitors to see how many of them have taken the kind of measures that Nike has in the past decade.

Amid the stress of trying to control the negative impact of Nike's increasingly controversial reputation, Nike's public relations department also has faced legal repercussions for its attempts to control damaging allegations. When media criticism began to arise, Nike launched a reputation management campaign to defend its corporate reputation. Its campaign included writing op-ed pieces, letters to the university, and press releases to defend its reputation and to refute critics' claims. It also hired an independent review by Goodworks International, LLC, which subsequently determined that the claims against Nike were false.

Marc Kasky, a California activist, maintained that Nike's claims were misleading and deceptive to the public. He subsequently filed a lawsuit, claiming that Nike's actions should be classified as commercial speech that violated California's unfair competition and advertising laws. The legal controversy culminated in the California Supreme Court's decision in *Kasky v. Nike.* This case is important because the courts assumed that public relations communication may constitute "commercial speech" that can be interpreted as "false advertising," even if there was disagreement about whether Nike's specific defense-of-reputation campaign could be legitimately so designated. As commercial speech is afforded less protection under the First Amendment, Nike could thus become liable for any claims under its public relations campaign that could be construed as misleading the public. After the ruling, Nike settled the lawsuit at approximately $2 million.

NIKE'S CORPORATE SOCIAL RESPONSIBILITY

> *"Nike has increased its efforts to be more ethical in its manufacturing practice"*

Despite the challenges Nike has faced in the past few decades, the company has come far. Indeed, Nike's corporate social responsibility (CSR) practices have been evolving since 1991. At first Nike's approach to CSR could be characterized as insufficient and generally lacking in any true forms of regulation and implementation throughout its global supply chain. Manufacturers in foreign locations were simply trying to comply with the minimal contract requirements, while at times overlooking fair labor practices in order to perform as low-cost suppliers. Nike's initial response to criticism was reputation management rather than wide-scale changes in its practices. However, as more and more issues have surfaced and been brought to the attention of not only the corporation but also its consumers, Nike has increased its efforts to be more ethical in its manufacturing practices and has become somewhat of an industry leader in certain areas.

Corporate responsibility can evolve through five stages:

1. Defensive: "It's not our fault."
2. Compliance: "We'll do only what we have to."
3. Managerial: "It's the business."
4. Strategic: "It gives us a competitive edge."
5. Civil: "We need to make sure everybody does it."

Nike could be classified as having evolved from the defensive stage, through the compliance stage, to the managerial stage. The company's initial CSR report in 2001 was intended to show how Nike had handled complaints by labor rights and student groups who wanted to see better conditions at contract factories worldwide. In its second report in 2005, the company disclosed the names and locations of factories that produced its sneakers, apparel, and other products—a first for the industry and an appeal to critics. This represented a genuine effort to invite critics to review its factories. By its third CSR report, Nike officials said they were moving away from using corporate responsibility as a crisis-management tool and were instead using it as an opportunity for innovation and growth.

Nike must now grow fully into the fourth and fifth CSR stages. The company must continue to develop its corporate responsibility strategies and increase enforcement of its policies in its factories to ensure its market share dominance in the footwear industry. With its new emphasis on corporate responsibility as an innovative tool, Nike is migrating into the notion that implementing further CSR initiatives will make the company an industry leader and thus give it a competitive edge in the footwear industry.

The following sections further discuss some of Nike's CSR practices. The areas covered include environmental sustainability, Nike's code of conduct, audit tools used to evaluate Nike contractor practices, factory transparency, Nike's corporate responsibility board, and philanthropy.

Environmental Sustainability

In 1990, Nike began development of the ReUse-A-Shoe Program to help reduce the company's environmental footprint and reduce the amount of shoes that end up in landfills. The purpose of the program was to find an environmentally-friendly way to dispose of worn-out shoes. The material made from the recycled shoes was coined "Nike Grind." In 1995, Reuse-A-Shoe began collecting old shoes in Nike retail stores. In 2002, Nike expanded Reuse-A-Shoe by partnering with the National Recycling Coalition, as well as beginning plans to go international with drop-off stations in Europe and Australia. Since the program was created, more than 1.5 million pairs of used shoes are collected for recycling each year. This is in addition to thousands of tons of manufacturing scrap material that is recycled. Nike has collected more than 21 million pairs of used athletic shoes since 1995.

Code of Conduct

Initially drafted in 1991, Nike's Code of Conduct was its first step toward improving working conditions in their factories. It is the foundation of Nike's corporate ethic. The company founded its code of conduct on the belief that Nike is comprised of many different kinds of people, and in order to reach the desired level of employer responsibility, it was necessary to appreciate individual diversity and become more dedicated to offering equal opportunity for each individual.

Nike designs, manufactures, and markets products for sports and fitness consumers. The company is striving to satisfy not only what is required by law, but also the expectations of what is necessary as a leader. Nike shares this goal with its business partners and contractors and requires them to embrace the same commitment to best practices and continuous improvement in four key areas: management practices, environmental responsibility, safety in the workplace, and promoting the overall well-being of all employees. Contractors are required to recognize the dignity of each employee, and the right to a workplace free of harassment, abuse, or corporal punishment. Decisions on hiring, salary, benefits, advancement, termination, and retirement must be based solely on the employee's ability to do the job, free from discrimination based on race, creed, gender, marital or maternity status, religious or political beliefs, age, or sexual orientation.

Audit Tools

In 1998, Nike developed three main auditing tools to help provide increasing transparency and insight into the manner in which Nike contract factories are evaluated for compliance with company standards. Management Audit Verification (MAV) combines audit and verification into one tool. It helps to identify issues related to work hours, wages and benefits, freedom of association, and grievance systems, as well as to follow up on these issues and to create an action plan to correct them according to local law and Nike's Code Leadership Standards. The Safety, Health, Attitude of Management, People and Environment (SHAPE) tool is an audit tool used quarterly by contract factories to determine their compliance with Nike's Code Leadership Standards. This tool involves inspections that help to improve work conditions, for example, by reducing workers' exposure to toxic solvents and glues. The Environment, Safety and Health (ESH) audit is an in-depth audit tool used by Nike compliance teams to determine compliance with Nike's Code Leadership Standards. In addition to its own auditing tools, external organizations such as NGOs frequently audit Nike as well.

Factory Transparency

In 2000, Nike became even more proactive by becoming the first company to respond to college requests to publicly disclose the names and locations of its contracted factories that produced licensed collegiate products. A contract factory making Nike products could be producing for as many as thirty different schools. By disclosing its supply chain, Nike believes it can be more successful at monitoring and making changes once issues have been uncovered not only in its own factories but on an industry-wide basis. The company hopes that by disclosing its own supply chain, it can encourage other companies to do the same. The company also feels that transparency should work as a motivator for contract factories. Those with high compliance rankings can be confident that business will come their way.

With multiple brands, and many universities represented, contract factories must decide which company's code(s) of conduct to follow. This is not an easy task, as standards for the varying corporate codes of conduct can contradict each other. Nike has attempted to make it easier for contract factories to comply with its code of conduct by guaranteeing that its code aligns with that of the Fair Labor Association. The company hopes that eventually a standardized code of conduct followed by all companies in the industry can be implemented, creating widespread compliance and better working conditions. Even as Nike has taken dramatic steps to increase its transparency and accountability, activists have continued putting pressure on the company to improve its standards and practices.

Nike also has implemented the Balanced Scorecard for its suppliers. The Balanced Scorecard is a lettered grading system used to better assess factory compliance with the code of conduct. Rather than simply assessing financial factors, the Balanced Scorecard also measures labor, health, and environmental standards of factories. This system gives the company a reliable method for rewarding high-performance, compliant factories. The card measures cost, delivery, and quality, all of which need to be addressed equally for the work in factories to flow smoothly. The Balanced Scorecard gives factories incentives to improve working conditions, and Nike rewards those that show improvement.

Corporate Responsibility Board

In 2001, Nike developed a Corporate Responsibility (CR) Board to review policies and activities and to make recommendations to the board of directors regarding labor and environmental practices, community affairs, charitable and foundation activities, diversity and equal opportunity, and environmental and sustainability initiatives. The Board is currently composed of ten members, eight of whom are independent directors. Nike's Vice President of Corporate Responsibility reports directly to the CEO of Nike Inc., who in turn is a member of the board of directors. Nearly 120 Nike employees work on CR issues as their primary function or have CR work as a significant portion of their workload.

Thanks to the efforts of the CR board and other Nike social responsibility initiatives, the workers in factories manufacturing Nike products are now aware of their rights, such as the right to minimum wages, and other entitlements, like food at subsidized rates. The workers also have access to basic education. Nearly all of Nike's factories offer education and training programs, and the remaining factories have similar programs in the pipeline.

Philanthropy

One of Nike's newest goals to increase its CSR is by building a social network "where innovations are shared, new funds are mobilized and human and social capital is exchanged in support of a global movement based on the power of sport to unleash human potential." Nike's goal is to encourage the use of sports as a means of empowering individuals and building skills such as leadership, conflict resolution, equity, and trauma relief. Nike partners with various individuals and groups that work directly with low-income youth, minorities, young women, and youth living in conflict situations around the world. Nike is building networks that include consumer activism, strong research evidence, and advocacy to shift policies and funding.

Because sports require access to safe spaces, good coaches, safe equipment, and education, Nike is forming partnerships in the areas of sports, youth, and education. Nike's new philanthropy initiatives have resulted in $315 million in grants, product donations, and other support through 2011 to give underprivileged youth greater access to sport programs. Nike contributes an additional $100 million annually in cash and products to nonprofit partners around the world. While contributing to the global community, the company also strives to invest in its own local communities of Portland, Oregon; Memphis, Tennessee; Hilversum, Holland; Laakdal, Belgium; and other places around the world with corporate offices.

"Nike's goal is to encourage the use of sports as a means of empowering individuals and building skills"

With a continued focus on corporate responsibility, Nike hopes to build and improve its relationships with consumers, to achieve a high-quality supply chain, and to create top-quality, innovative products. Although this evolution is a rocky one filled with lessons learned along the way, the benefits are being seen for employees all around the world, and for the company itself.

NEW CHALLENGES IN THE FUTURE

In 2006, Nike veteran Mark Parker, formerly co-president, took over as CEO and director. Parker has been with Nike for nearly thirty years, has been part of most of Nike's top innovative plans, and is recognized as a product visionary. *Ethisphere* magazine praised him for his leadership under which Nike shoes have become more eco-friendly and questionable suppliers have been fired.

As a result of its positive changes, Nike appeared in *Business Ethics* magazine's "100 Best Corporate Citizens" list for 2005–2007. *Business Ethics* magazine cited its reasons for listing Nike as the strength of Nike's commitment to community and environment.

Nike was actually ranked number one in the magazine's environmental category due to its efforts to eliminate waste and toxic substances from production processes. Nike also has made *Fortune* magazine's "100 Best Companies to Work For" list, coming in at number 100 in 2006, but rising to 82nd in 2008. *Fortune*'s 2009 list of "The World's Most Admired Companies" ranked Nike as the number one most-admired apparel company, and ranked it 23 for overall most-admired. Nike also was listed as number 26 in *CRO (Corporate Responsibility Officer)* magazine's "Best Corporate Citizens" in 2009.

The news has not all been good for Nike, however. In March 2008, one of Nike's contract factories in China was found to have underage workers, unpaid wages for employees, and to have falsified documents for worker permits. In response, Nike has detailed the efforts it has made to enforce compliance with its code of conduct and with Chinese law. China is Nike's largest single-sourcing country, with some 180 manufacturers and about 210,000 employees.

Also in 2008 Nike's contract factory in Malaysia reported that workers were living in substandard housing conditions and that their passports were being withheld and wages not paid in full. The spokesperson for the factory blamed local government labor policies and lack of enforcement as the reasons these labor abuses were being committed.

The fact is that Nike's current supply chain has major flaws in both contract negotiation and supplier oversight. Even though some experts herald Nike as a leader in CSR, its use of hundreds of international contractors make detection and enforcement of abuses incredibly difficult. While Nike has come a long way since the 1990s, its ethics and compliance system still has a lot of room for improvement. For example, Nike employs only one compliance staff member for every ten factories. Nike tries to perform two inspections per year per active factory, but in reality it inspects only about 25 percent of factories per year. Nike also contracts third parties to inspect roughly 5 percent of its factories per year.

Social and environmental responsibility involves not only doing the right thing. It also can be good for a company's bottom line in a highly competitive industry. Being perceived as a company that goes farther than the minimum required on social issues can attract and retain customers. Nike's target audience has broadened from mainly male athletes to females and more fashion-oriented offerings as well. As Nike's target audience widens, being perceived as an ethical company will help attract and retain new customers.

One of Nike's innovative product approaches is the Stand-Off Distance Singlet—a tank top for long-distance runners that uses a high-tech fabric designed to keep runners cool. It is made of 75 percent recycled soda bottles and uses 43 percent less energy to produce than standard fabrics. The tank is ultrasonically welded at the seams, which eliminates sewing thread, and does not contain any artificial dyes or toxic substances. Nike plans to develop more innovative and sustainable products like the singlet in the future.

Where wages, conditions, and other worker rights such as unions are concerned, Nike continues to strive to raise the bar and improve operations. Nike has worked hard to implement new policies, ensuring that in countries where it operates, the factories are considered the fairest and safest working environments. Nike also has joined coalitions that help them achieve this goal, such as Global Alliance. The company's ultimate goal is that everybody will benefit from their association with Nike. Customers are buying into an ideal, not just the product. In addition to customers' concerns for value, many also demand to know about the labor issues surrounding the production of their purchases. Brand management, customer awareness, and loyalty are all directly linked, and therefore maintenance of the relationship among brand images, quality, and corporate ethics has to be consistent.

Nike itself admits that it has a long way to go in the area of corporate responsibility, including continuing to improve its monitoring systems. However, the company is being rewarded for its efforts toward improvement by both positive results and industry response.

QUESTIONS

1. Why did Nike fail to address corporate social responsibility earlier?
2. Evaluate Nike's response to societal and consumer concerns about its contract manufacturing.
3. What are the challenges facing Nike in the future?

SOURCES

Balfour, Frederick, "Acting Globally but Selling Locally: Chinese Athletic Wear Maker Li Ning Is Raising Its International Profile to Win Over Shoppers at Home," *BusinessWeek*, May 12, 2008, pp. 27–29; "*Business Ethics* 100 Best Corporate Citizens 2007," *Business Ethics,* http://www.business-ethics.com/node/75 (accessed September 3, 2009); Casey, Nicholas, and Raphael Pura, "Nike Addresses Abuse Complaints at Malaysia Plant," *Wall Street Journal*, August 4, 2008, http://online.wsj.com/article/SB121779204898108093.html?mod=dist_smartbrief (accessed September 3, 2009); "Citizen Nike," *Fortune,* http://money.cnn.com/2008/11/17/news/companies/levenson_nike.fortune/index.htm (accessed September 3, 2009); Collins, E. L., L. M. Zoch, and C. S. McDonald, "A Crisis in Reputation Management: The Implications of *Kasky v. Nike,*" presented at the meeting of the International Communication Association, May 27, 2004, New Orleans Sheraton, New Orleans, LA, http://www.allacademic.com/meta/p113246_index.html (accessed September 3, 2009); "Corporate Social Responsibility in Emerging Markets: The Role of Multinational Corporations," Foreign Policy Centre, http://fpc.org.uk/fsblob/919.pdf (accessed September 3, 2009); "Corporate Social Responsibility Profile—Nike," CSR Wire, http://www.csrwire.com/profile/1262.html (accessed September 3, 2009); DeTienne, Kristen B., and Lee W. Lewis, "The Pragmatic and Ethical Barriers to Corporate Social Responsibility Disclosure: The Nike Case," *Journal of Business Ethics* 60, no. 4 (2005): 359–376; Elsasser, John, "Watching Nike Sweat," *Public Relations Tactics* 6 (1998): 1–4; "FY05–06 Corporate Responsibility Report, 2005–2006," Nike, http://www.nikebiz.com/responsibility/documents/Nike_FY05_06_CR_Report_C.pdf (accessed September 8, 2009); "Innovate for a Better World," *Nike FY05–06 Corporate Responsibility Report, 2005–2006,* http://www.nikebiz.com/responsibility/documents/Nike_FY05_06_CR_Report_C.pdf (accessed September 3, 2009); Klein, Naomi, *No Logo* (New York: Riemann Verlag, 2002); Krentzman, Jackie, "The Force Behind the Nike Empire," *Stanford Magazine,* http://www.stanfordalumni.org/news/magazine/1997/janfeb/articles/knight.html (accessed September 3, 2009); "Labors' Pains," PBS, April 14, 1997, http://www.pbs.org/newshour/bb/business/jan-june97/sweatshops_4-14.html (accessed September 3, 2009); "The Long Case for Nike—'Just Do It'" Seeking Alpha, http://seekingalpha.com/article/23192-the-long-case-for-nike-just-do-it, (accessed September 3, 2009); "Mark Parker (President & CEO, Nike)," *Ethisphere,* December 11, 2008, http://ethisphere.com/mark-parker/ (accessed September 3, 2009); "Nike Answers Critics on Corporate Responsibility," B & T Marketing, http://www.bandt.com.au/news/25/0c00d225.asp (accessed September 3, 2009); "NIKE Failed on Sweatshop Reform Promises," *Albion Monitor,* http://www.albionmonitor.com/0105b/copyright/nikereport.html, (accessed September 3, 2009); "Nike-Funded Study Claims Workers at

Nike's Indonesian Factories Are Subject to Abuse and Harassment," *Ethics Newsline*, February 26, 2001, http://www.globalethics.org/newsline/2001/02/26/nike-funded-study-claims-workers-at-nikes-indonesian-factories-are-subject-to-abuse-and-harassment/ (accessed September 3, 2009); "Nike's Corporate Social Responsibility Efforts Falling Short?," The World Is Green, http://worldisgreen.com/2007/06/05/csr-and-business-startegy-with-nike/ (accessed September 3, 2009); "Nike's New CSR Report. They Just Did It—Again," Perspectives in Responsible Sourcing, http://cscc.typepad.com/responsiblesourcing/2007/06/nikes_new_csr_r.html, (accessed September 3, 2009); "Nike University: Hooked on Sweatshops," Jonathon Speaks, http://irregulartimes.com/nike.html (accessed September 3, 2009); "Nike in Vietnam: The Tae Kwang Vina Factory," World Bank, http://siteresources.worldbank.org/INTEMPOWERMENT/Resources/14826_Nike-web.pdf (accessed April 11, 2009); "100 Best Companies to Work For," CNNMoney.com, http://money.cnn.com/magazines/fortune/bestcompanies/2008/full_list/index.html (accessed September 3, 2009); "100 Best Corporate Citizens 2009," Corporate Responsibility Officer, http://www.thecro.com/files/100BestGatefold.pdf (accessed September 3, 2009); "Our Community Programs: Reuse-A-Shoe & Nike Grind," nikebiz.com, October 28, 2008, http://www.nikebiz.com/responsibility/community_programs/reuse_a_shoe.html (accessed September 3, 2009); "Shoes Sought in Recycling Project," *Wicked Local Lexington*, April 29, 2008, http://www.wickedlocal.com/lexington/news/business/x883026486 (accessed September 3, 2009); "Social Responsibility: The Nike Story," Branding Strategy, http://www.brandingstrategyinsider.com/2008/07/social-responsi.html (accessed September 3, 2009); "World's Most Admired Companies 2009: Apparel," *Fortune,* http://money.cnn.com/magazines/fortune/mostadmired/2009/industries/3.html (accessed September 3, 2009); Zwolinski, Matt, "The Promise and Perils of Globalization: The Case of Nike," in *Social Issues in America: An Encyclopedia,* ed. James Ciment (Armonk, NY: M.E. Sharpe, 2006).

CASE 10

Banking Industry Meltdown: The Ethical and Financial Risks of Derivatives

Daryl Benson

The 2008–2009 global recession was caused in part by a failure of the financial industry to take appropriate responsibility for its decision to utilize risky and complex financial instruments. Corporate cultures were built on rewards for taking risks rather than rewards for creating value for stakeholders. Unfortunately, most stakeholders, including the public, regulators, and the mass media, do not always understand the nature of the financial risks taken on by banks and other institutions to generate profits.

Problems in the subprime mortgage markets sounded the alarm in the 2008–2009 economic downturn. Very simply, the subprime market was created by making loans to people who normally would not qualify based on their credit ratings. The debt from these loans was often repackaged and sold to other financial institutions in order to take it off lenders' books and reduce their exposure. When the real estate market became overheated, many people were no longer able to make the payments on their variable rate mortgages. When consumers began to default on payments, prices in the housing market dropped and the values of credit default swaps (the repackaged mortgage debt, also known as CDSs) lost significant value. The opposite was supposed to happen. CDSs were sold as a method of insuring against loss. These derivatives, investors were told, would act as an insurance policy to reduce the risk of loss. Unfortunately, losses in the financial industry were so widespread that even the derivative contracts that had been written to cover losses from unpaid subprime mortgages could not be covered by the financial institutions that had written these derivatives contracts. The financial industry and managers at all levels had become focused on the rewards for these transactions without concerns about how their actions could potentially damage others.

In addition to providing a simplified definition of what derivatives are, this case allows for a review of questionable, often unethical or illegal, conduct associated with a number of respected banks in the 2008–2009 financial crisis. First, we review the financial terminology

This case was prepared by John Fraedrich, O.C. Ferrell, and Jennifer Jackson, with the editorial assistance of Jennifer Sawayda, for classroom discussion, rather than to illustrate either effective or ineffective handling of an administrative, ethical, or legal decision by management. All sources used for this case were obtained through publicly available material.

associated with derivatives, as they were an integral part of the downfall of these financial institutions. Derivatives were, and still are, considered a legal and ethical financial instrument when used properly, but they inherently hold a lot of potential for mishandling. When misused, they provide a ripe opportunity for misconduct. To illustrate the types of misconduct that can result, this case employs a number of examples. First, we examine Barings Bank, which ceased to exist because of a rogue trader using derivatives. Next, we look at United Bank of Switzerland (UBS) and its huge losses from bad mortgages and derivatives. Bear Stearns, an investment bank that suffered its demise through derivatives abuse, is the third example. Finally, Lehman Brothers is an investment bank that was involved with high-risk derivatives that also led to its bankruptcy. At the conclusion of this case, we examine the risk of derivatives and potential ethical risks associated with the use of these instruments in the financial industry.

DERIVATIVES DEFINED

Derivatives are financial instruments with values that change relative to underlying variables, such as assets, events, or prices. In other words, the value of derivatives is based on the change in value of something else, called the *underlying* trade or exchange.

The main types of derivatives are futures, forwards, options, and swaps. A *futures* contract is an agreement to buy or sell a set quantity of something at a set rate at a predetermined point in the future. The date on which this exchange is scheduled to take place is called the delivery, or settlement, date. Futures contracts are often associated with buyers and sellers of commodities who are concerned about supply, demand, and changes in prices. They can be traded only on exchanges. Almost any commodity, such as oil, gold, corn, or soybeans, can have a futures contract defined for a specific trade.

> *"The value of derivatives is based on different types of underlying values"*

Forwards are similar to futures, except they can be traded between two individuals. A forward contract is a commitment to trade a specified item at a specific price in the future. The forward contract takes whatever form to which the parties agree.

An *option* is a less binding form of derivative. It conveys the right, but not the obligation, to buy or sell a particular asset in the future. A *call option* gives the investor the right to buy at a set price on delivery day. A *put option* gives the investor the option to sell a good or financial instrument at a set price on the settlement date. It is a financial contract with what is called a *long position,* giving the owner the right but not the obligation to sell an amount at a preset price and maturity date.

Finally, *swaps* live up to their name. A swap can occur when two parties agree to exchange one stream of cash flows against another one. Swaps can be used to hedge risks such as changes in interest rates, or to speculate on the changing prices of commodities or currencies. Swaps can be difficult to understand, so here is an example. JP Morgan developed CDSs that bundled together as many as 300 different assets, including subprime loans. Credit default swaps were meant as a form of insurance. In other words, securities were bundled into one financial package, and companies such as JP Morgan were essentially paying insurance premiums to the investors who purchased them, who were now on the hook if payments of any of the securities included in the CDSs did not come through.

As mentioned before, the value of derivatives is based on different types of underlying values, including assets such as commodities, equities (stocks), bonds, interest rates, exchange rates, or indexes such as a stock market index, consumer price index (CPI), or even an index of weather conditions. For example, a farmer and a grain storage business enter into a futures contract to exchange cash for grain at some future point. Both parties have reduced a future risk. For the farmer it is the uncertainty of the future grain price, and for the grain storage business it is the availability of the grain at a predetermined price.

Some believe derivatives lead to market volatility because enormous amounts of money are controlled by relatively small amounts of margin or option premiums. The job of a derivatives trader is something like a bookie taking bets on how people will bet. *Arbitrage* is defined as attempting to profit by exploiting price differences of identical or similar financial instruments, on different markets, or in different forms. As a result, derivatives can suffer large losses or returns from small movements in the underlying asset's price. Investors are like gamblers in that they can bet for or against the price (going up or down) and can consequently lose or win large amounts.

BARINGS BANK

Barings Bank, which had been in operation in the United Kingdom for 233 years, ceased to exist in 1995 when a futures trader named Nick Leeson lost approximately $1.4 billion in company assets. The extinction was due, in part, to a large holding position in the Japanese futures market. Leeson, chief trader for Barings Futures in Singapore, accumulated a large number of opening positions on the Nikkei Index. He then generated losses in the first two months of 1995 when the Nikkei dropped more than 15 percent. To try and recover these losses, Leeson placed what is called a short "straddle" on the Singapore and Tokyo stock markets. He was betting that the stock market would not move significantly in the short term. This strategy is risky but can be profitable in stable markets. However, when the Kobe earthquake hit and sent the Japanese stock market plummeting, Leeson lost a lot of money. He did not, however, change his approach. In fact, Leeson tried to cover his losses through a series of other risky investments that, instead, only increased the losses. When he finally quit his job, Leeson sent a fax to his manager, stating "sincere apologies for the predicament that I have left you in." Barings was purchased by ING, a Dutch bank for £1 (approximately $1), which then sold it under the name Baring Asset Management (BAM) to MassMutual and Northern Trust in 2005.

Nick Leeson's life is a rags-to-riches tale. Son of a plasterer, he started his career in 1984 as a clerk with royal bank Coutts and later worked briefly for Morgan Stanley. He then got a position in operations at Barings, and later was transferred to Jakarta. Leeson worked in a back office solving clients' problems of wrongly denominated certificates and difficulties of delivery. Before long, Leeson was appointed manager of a new operation in the futures markets on the Singapore Monetary Exchange (SIMEX). Leeson had the authority to hire traders and staff and to sell six financial products, but his main business was doing inter-exchange arbitrage or "switching." Switching is betting on small differences between contracts by buying and selling futures simultaneously on two different stock exchanges. For example, if a contract was worth the equivalent of $3 in London and $2.75 in Singapore, Leeson would buy in Singapore and sell in London, making a 25-cent profit.

The key to Leeson's strategy in the 1980s was the knowledge that one stock market was slower in processing trades than the other. To hide any bad bets, Leeson created an error account (named 8888 for its auspiciousness in Chinese numerology) for his losses. Because no one could see the losses hidden by this account, Leeson was widely regarded as a brilliant trader. He had assured Barings that he was not trading with company money and that all the positions were perfectly hedged and virtually risk-free. Barings managers had little knowledge in trading and did not suspect Leeson of deception. Based on their trust, Barings put a billion dollars into Leeson's account and made no attempt to check his statements. All it took to bring down this house of cards was one earthquake.

When the Kobe earthquake hit in 1995, Leeson's luck finally ran out. He fled to Malaysia, Thailand, and then Germany, and was finally arrested for fraud in Frankfurt. He was extradited back to Singapore and sentenced to six-and-a-half years in Singapore's Changi prison where he was diagnosed with colon cancer and divorced by his wife. During that time, Leeson wrote *Rogue Trader: How I Brought Down Barings Bank and Shook the Financial World*, which was later made into a movie. He was released from prison in 1999. Since then he has become CEO of the Galway United Football Club. Although he has tried to atone for his actions, to many he is still considered to be the rogue trader who, through his misuse of derivatives, destroyed the United Kingdom's oldest bank.

UBS

United Bank of Switzerland (UBS) is a diversified global financial services company, headquartered in Switzerland. It is the world's largest manager of private wealth assets and the second-largest bank in Europe with overall invested assets of approximately $3.167 trillion.

In 2000, UBS acquired PaineWebber Group Inc. to become the world's largest wealth management firm for private clients. Three years later, all UBS business groups rebranded under the UBS name as the company began operating as one large firm. As a result of the rebranding, UBS took a $1 billion write-down for the loss of goodwill associated with the retirement of the PaineWebber brand. (Write-downs represent a reduction in an asset's book value.) UBS is no longer an acronym but is the company's brand name. Its logo of three keys stands for confidence, security, and discretion. UBS had offices in the world's financial centers in 50 countries, and employed approximately 82,000.

In the late 2000s, UBS came under scrutiny for questionable practices. In 2008, Internal Revenue Service investigators asked for the names of some 20,000 American clients suspected of hiding as much as $20 billion in assets to avoid at least $300 million in federal taxes on funds in offshore accounts. The issue is complicated because using offshore accounts is not illegal in the United States, but hiding income in undeclared accounts is. However, Switzerland does not consider tax evasion a crime, and using undeclared accounts is legal. In 2008, former UBS banker Bradley Birkenfeld and Liechtenstein banker Mario Staggl were indicted in Florida for helping an American property developer evade taxes by creating bogus trusts and corporations to hide the ownership and control of offshore assets. They also were accused of advising clients to destroy bank records and of helping them to file false tax returns. UBS had asked the bankers to sign papers saying that they, not the bank, would be responsible if they broke non-Swiss tax laws.

Indian authorities also are probing suspected violations of foreign exchange controls involving accounts held at UBS by two companies controlled by India's richest man. The accusations involve transactions that were allegedly arranged by unspecified parties by taking overdrafts on accounts held with UBS London.

However, tax evasion accusations are not the only problems UBS faces. Like other banks, it has suffered from the subprime crisis due to its heavy dependence on derivatives and mortgage-related securities. In fact, UBS has suffered more losses than any other lender in Europe. By the end of 2008, the bank had been forced to write-down over $46 billion in losses on bad mortgages and derivatives. The bank blamed weak risk controls and risky investment dealings for its loss.

In 2008, UBS appealed to the Swiss government, which doled out an aid package of approximately $59.2 billion to the ailing bank. In exchange, UBS agreed to forgo nearly $27.7 million in pay to the company's top three executives. From then on, the bank promised, bonuses would depend more on the bank's performance, a decision that came to the relief of those who had criticized what they saw as the bank's excessive pay for CEOs. Additionally, some CEOs who resigned promised to return some of the compensation they received. Time will tell whether these combined decisions will be able to resolve the bank's burgeoning problems.

BEAR STEARNS

Unlike many companies that existed before the Great Depression of 1929, Bear Stearns thrived through much of the twentieth century. Unfortunately, in the early twenty-first century, Bear Stearns encountered another severe economic crisis that it did not survive. JP Morgan acquired the company in March 2008 after Bear Stearns lost billions in the subprime crisis.

Bear Stearns was a global investment bank and a securities and brokerage firm. Located in New York City, it was founded as an equity trading-house in 1923 by Joseph Bear, Robert Stearns, and Harold Mayer. With an initial $500,000 in capital, the company thrived in the twenties and even in the post–stock market crash of the 1930s. In fact, the company did so well that while other banks were failing by the dozens, Bear Stearns was able to pay out bonuses. By 1933, the company employed seventy-five people and opened its first regional office in Chicago. About twenty years later, the company began operating international offices. Bear Stearns continued to grow and prosper, and in 1985 it formed a holding company known as Bear Stearns Companies, Inc. In 2002, while other firms were struggling, Bear Stearns was the only securities firm to report a first-quarter profit increase. It also began focusing more on the housing industry, which would spell out its doom a mere five years later.

In 2005, Bear Stearns was listed as *Fortune* magazine's "America's Most Admired Securities Firm" for the second time in three years. At the end of 2006, the company's total capital was $66.7 billion and its assets totaled $350.4 billion. The subprime crisis first hit Bear Stearns early in 2007. Previously, the bank had seen a fifty-two-week high of $133.20 per share. By late 2007, two Bear Stearns hedge funds had collapsed, the company's third-quarter profit had decreased by 61 percent, and it had written off $1.2 billion in mortgage securities. In 2008, the Federal Reserve attempted to bail out the company, but it could not save Bear Stearns. JP Morgan agreed to buy the company for a mere $2 per share, which was a decrease of $131 per share in about a year. After lawsuits and intense negotiations, JP Morgan raised the buying price to $10 per share.

What caused a long-standing institution like Bear Stearns to fall? Its investment in subprime loans was a significant factor, but derivatives could also be a major reason. Since its failure, information has come out that Bear Stearns widely misrepresented clients' information on loan applications in order to make them appear more desirable mortgage recipients. Once these risky subprime loans were given out, the company packaged and sold the debt as securities to other institutions. In this way, Bear Stearns managed to keep the risky subprime lending debt off its books and moved the onus to investors. Bear Stearns had derivatives amounting to $13.4 trillion at the end of 2007. These securities were backed by cash flow from the loans, but that only works when loan payments come in as they are supposed to.

Since its failure, the Bear Stearns scheme has been exposed as a risky "house of cards." Executives have been charged with misleading investors by concealing that hedge funds were failing as the mortgage market crumbled. Investors lost $1.6 billion in assets. Executives Ralph R. Cioffi and Matthew M. Tannin were arrested and face criminal charges. Yet this has done little to console investors or Bear Stearns' employees as they have watched the company's fall and acquisition by JP Morgan.

LEHMAN BROTHERS

Another firm that had been around for a long time, more than 150 years in this case, found that it could not survive the subprime mortgage crisis either. In 2008, Lehman Brothers, the fourth-largest investment bank in the United States, filed for chapter 11 bankruptcy.

Lehman Brothers was founded by Henry, Emanuel, and Mayer Lehman, German immigrants who migrated to America in the mid-nineteenth century. It opened its first store in Montgomery, Alabama, in 1850. As cotton was the cash crop of the South, the brothers often accepted payment in cotton and began acting as brokers for those who were buying and selling the crop. The brothers' business expanded quickly, and they opened an office in New York in 1858. Soon they had transformed from brokerage to merchant banking, and Lehman Brothers became a member of the New York Stock Exchange in 1887.

> *"By late 2008, the company's shares had lost 73 percent of their value"*

The company continued to thrive even through the stock market crash of 1929. It advised and financed several other businesses, including Halliburton, Digital Equipment, and Campbell Soup. The firm opened its first international office in Paris in 1960. After going public in 1994, Lehman Brothers joined the S&P 100 Index in 1998 and watched its stock rise to $100 per share by the early 2000s. In 2007, the year the subprime crisis began, Lehman Brothers was ranked as number one in the "Most Admired Firms" list by *Fortune* magazine. CEO Richard Fuld was placed on the list of the world's thirty best CEOs. For its third quarter, Lehman Brothers possessed assets worth $275 billion.

Then the subprime mortgage crisis came to a head. By late 2008, the company's shares had lost 73 percent of their value. Even as the company asked for government aid, its executives continued to pocket millions of dollars in bonuses, an action that caused public outrage. The company filed for bankruptcy that year, with $613 billion in debt. Company shares rapidly fell 90 percent to 21 cents per share. The bank received some relief after Barclay PLC agreed to purchase much of Lehman Brothers for $1.75 billion. The purchase of Lehman Brothers was welcome news for some workers, as many of them thought they were going to lose their jobs. Yet this did little to help many shareholders, who had already seen their stocks reduced to nothing. Even CEO Fuld had lost $600 million between 2007 and 2008.

What caused such a well-established company like Lehman Brothers to go belly-up? Its dependence on subprime mortgages was the central factor. Additionally, some are accusing the firm of unethical behavior in its dealings with First Alliance Mortgage, a company accused of "predatory lending." Lehman Brothers helped bundle millions of dollars in mortgages into derivatives instruments for First Alliance and helped make them seem like appealing investment vehicles for Wall Street. When the loans defaulted, these investments contributed to the massive financial crisis.

Lehman Brothers had also acquired several credit default swaps (CDSs), a type of derivative contract. The company had acquired large amounts of subprime mortgage debt and other lower-rated assets when securitizing the underlying mortgages. Even though Lehman had closed its subprime mortgage division in 2007, it maintained much of its subprime mortgage liability through 2008, resulting in large losses from the collapse of the subprime market. Creditors of Lehman Brothers, AIG among them, had taken out CDSs to hedge against the case of a Lehman bankruptcy. The estimated amount of settling these swaps stands at $100 to $400 billion.

Additionally, many major money market funds had significant exposure to Lehman Brothers. Lehman's bankruptcy caused the investors in these money market accounts to lose millions. Undoubtedly, the fall of Lehman Brothers will have severe effects on businesses across the world for a long time, a negative legacy of this once great company.

ETHICAL ISSUES WITH DERIVATIVES

Derivatives (especially swaps) expose investors to counter-party risk. For example, if a business wants a fixed-interest loan but banks only offer variable rates, the business swaps payments with another business that wants a variable rate, creating a fixed rate for the first business. However, if the second business goes bankrupt, the first business loses its fixed rate and has to pay the variable rate. If interest rates increase to the point where the first business cannot pay back the loan, it causes a chain reaction of failures.

Derivatives also can pose high amounts of risk for small or inexperienced investors. Because derivatives offer the possibility of large rewards, they are attractive to individual investors. However, the basic premise of derivatives is to transfer risk among parties based on their willingness to assume additional risk, or hedge against it. Many small investors do not comprehend this until they lose. As a result, a chain reaction leading to a domestic or global economic crisis can occur.

Warren Buffett, a well-known investor, has stated that he regards derivatives as "financial weapons of mass destruction." Derivatives have been used to leverage the debt in an economy, sometimes to a massive degree. When something unexpected happens, an economy will find it very difficult to pay its debts, thus causing a recession or even depression. Marriner S. Eccles, U.S. Federal Reserve chair from 1934 to 1948, stated that an excessively high level of debt was one of the primary causes of the Great Depression.

Some experts believe derivatives have significant benefits as well. Although it is always the case with derivatives that someone loses while someone else gains, under normal circumstances, derivatives should not adversely affect the economic system because it is not a zero-sum game—derivatives theoretically allow for absolute economic growth. In other words, while one party gains in relation to the other, both gain relative to their previous positions. Former Federal Reserve Board chair Alan Greenspan commented in 2003 that he believed that derivatives softened the impact of the economic downturn at the beginning of the twenty-first century, and UBS believed that derivatives were part of its future.

However, derivatives have a checkered history. In the 1900s, derivatives trading and bucket shops were rampant. Bucket shops are small operators in options and securities that lure clients into transactions and then flee with the money, setting up shop elsewhere. In 1922 the federal government attempted to stop this practice with the Grain Futures

Act, and in 1936 options on grain futures were temporarily banned in the United States as well as in other countries. In 1972 the Chicago Mercantile Exchange (the Merc) created the International Monetary Market, allowing trading in currency futures, representing the first futures contracts associated with nonphysical commodities. In 1975 the Merc introduced the Treasury bill futures contract that was based purely on interest rate futures. In 1977 and 1982, T–bond (Treasury) futures contracts, Eurodollar contracts, and stock index futures were created. The 1980s marked the beginning of swaps and other over-the-counter derivatives. Soon every large, and even some not-so-large, corporations were using derivatives to hedge a wide variety of investment risks. Derivatives soon became too complex for the average person to understand, and Wall Street turned to mathematicians and physicists to create models and computer programs that could analyze these exotic instruments.

In the end, the ethical issues in using derivatives hinge on the managers and traders who use these highly complex and risky financial instruments. Derivatives are used in sales transactions where there is an opportunity of great financial rewards. However, managers and traders often do not take into account the level of risk for investors or other stakeholders. If the risk associated with a derivative is not communicated to the investor, this can result in deception or even fraud. It has become apparent that the use of derivatives such as credit default swaps became so profitable that traders and managers lost sight of anything but their incentives for selling these instruments. In other words, financial institutions were selling what could be called defective products because the true risk of these financial instruments was not understood by or disclosed to the customer. In some cases, these defective products were given to traders to sell without any due diligence from the company as to the level of risk.

CONCLUSION

While derivatives, including credit default swaps, were not the only cause of the failure of the banks discussed in this case, the use of these instruments by decision makers resulted in these banks taking enormous risks. In hindsight, these actions seem to be unwise and unfair to stakeholders. An ethical issue relates to the level of transparency that exists in using complex financial instruments to create profits for customers. If purchasers do not understand the potential risks and the possibility of the loss of their money, then a chance for deception exists. In the banks examined in this case, there is no doubt that a number of key decision makers not only pushed the limits of legitimate risk-taking, but also engaged in manipulation, and in some cases fraud, to deceive stakeholders.

At this point, it is doubtful whether banks have learned enough about the 2008– 2009 financial crises to avoid future failures. Investors and shareholders need to start looking beyond short-term results and understand the value of long-term thinking. CEOs and boards of directors need to develop a transparent business model that balances risk with market opportunity. The ethical risks of lower-level managers using deception and manipulation to create profits, often through loopholes and unregulated areas of decision making, are high. Through ethical leadership and compliance programs, all these risks can be minimized.

QUESTIONS

1. What are the ethical risks associated with derivatives?
2. What is the difference between making a bad business decision associated with derivatives and engaging in unethical conduct using derivatives?
3. What kinds of investment decisions drove Barings Bank, UBS, Bear Stearns, and Lehman Brothers to financial disasters?
4. How can an ethical corporate culture with adequate internal controls, including ethics and compliance policies, prevent future disasters in financial companies?

SOURCES

Aldrick, Philip, "UBS Sub-Prime Warning Fails to Rattle Markets," *Telegraph.co.uk*, October 3, 2007, http://www.telegraph.co.uk/finance/markets/2816866/UBS-sub-prime-warning-fails-to-rattle-markets.html (accessed September 3, 2009); Bart, Katharina, "UBS Joins the 'Bonus Chop' for Executives," *Wall Street Journal*, November 17, 2008, http://online.wsj.com/article/SB122693338045733273.html (accessed September 3, 2009); Bhugaloo, Sam, "Commodities Trading: Nick Leeson, Internal Controls and the Collapse of Barings Bank," Trade Futures, Ltd., http://www.tradefutures.co.uk/Nick_Leeson_Barings_Bank.pdf (accessed September 3, 2009); Browning, Lynnley, "Federal Prosecutors Declare European Banker a Fugitive," *New York Times*, May 23, 2008, http://www.nytimes.com/2008/05/23/business/worldbusiness/23bank.html?scp=1&sq=Federal+Prosecutors+Declare+European+Banker+a+Fugitive&st=nyt (accessed September 3, 2009); Browning, Lynnley, "Wealthy Americans Under Scrutiny in UBS Case," *New York Times*, June 6, 2008, http://www.nytimes.com/2008/06/06/business/worldbusiness/06tax.html?scp=1&sq=Wealthy%20Americans%20Under%20Scrutiny%20in%20UBS%20Case&st=cse (accessed September 3, 2009); Cane, Jeffrey, "A Pilot for UBS Foundering Ship," *Conde Nast Portfolio*, February 13, 2008, http://www.portfolio.com/news-markets/top-5/2008/02/13/A-Pilot-for-UBS-Foundering-Ship (accessed September 3, 2009); Chua-Eoan, Howard, "The Top 25 Crimes of the Century: #18 The Collapse of Barings Bank, 1995," *Time*, November 18, 2007, http://www.time.com/time/2007/crimes/18.html (accessed September 3, 2009); Dealbook Blog, "Could Bear Stearns Do Better?" *New York Times*, http://www.nytimes.com/2008/03/17/business/17dealbook-could-be21779.html?_r=1 (accessed September 3, 2009); "Down the Matterhorn: UBS Falls from Grace," *The Economist*, July 12, 2007, http://www.economist.com/finance/displaystory.cfm?story_id=E1_JQRPGNT (accessed September 3, 2009); Downey, John, "BofA Asks $20M in Dispute vs. Ex-Employees," *Charlotte Business Journal*, July 22, 2002, http://www.bizjournals.com/charlotte/stories/2002/07/22/story7.html (accessed September 3, 2009); Drennan, Lynn T., "Ethics, Governance, and Risk Management: Lessons from Mirror Group Newspapers and Barings Bank," *Journal of Business Ethics* 52, no. 3 (2004): 257–266; Eisinger, Jesse, "The $58 Trillion Elephant in the Room," November 20, 2008, http://www.portfolio.com/views/columns/wall-street/2008/10/15/Credit-Derivatives-Role-in-Crash#page1 (accessed September 3, 2009); Gomstyn, Alice, "Bleeding Green: The Fall of Fuld," ABC News, October 6, 2008, http://abcnews.go.com/Business/Economy/Story?id=5951669&page=1 (accessed September 3, 2009); Gresko, Jessica, "Ex-UBS Banker Pleads Guilty in US Tax Evasion Case," *USA Today*, June 19, 2008, http://www.usatoday.com/money/economy/2008-06-19-992401281_x.htm?csp=34 (accessed September 3, 2009); Grynbaum, Michael, "Bear Stearns Profit Plunges 61% on Subprime Woes," *New York Times*, http://www.nytimes.com/2007/09/21/business/20cnd-wall.html?scp=1&sq=Bear%20Stearns%20Plunges%2061%%20on%20Subprime%20Woes&st=cse (accessed September 3, 2009); Gwynne, S. C., "Total Risk: Nick Leeson and the Fall of Barings Bank," Book Review, *Washington Monthly*, January–February

1996, http://findarticles.com/p/articles/mi_m1316/is_/ai_17761531 (accessed September 3, 2009); Kennedy, Simon, Greg Morcroft, and Robert Schroeder, "Lehman Failure, AIG Struggle Drive Financials Lower," Market Watch, September 15, 2008, http://www.marketwatch.com/news/story/lehman-falls-80-firm-readies/story.aspx?guid={8E886D48-E3C7-4CE2-95F4-7099CE1A49DB}&dist=msr_2 (accessed September 4, 2009); Koenig, David, "Case Study: Nick Leeson and Barings Bank," Ductilibility, 2008, http://www.scribd.com/doc/16606536/Case-Study-Barings-Bank-and-Nick-Leeson (accessed September 4, 2009); Landon, Thomas, Jr., "Prosecutors Build Bear Stearns Case on E-Mails," *New York Times,* June 20, 2008, http://www.nytimes.com/2008/06/20/business/20bear.html?_r=1&hp&oref=slogin (accessed September 4, 2009); Landon, Thomas, Jr., and Eric Dash, "Seeking Fast Deal, JPMorgan Quintuples Bear Stearns Bid," *New York Times,* March 25, 2008, http://www.nytimes.com/2008/03/25/business/25bear.html?scp=1&sq=Seeking+Fast+Deal%2C+JPMorgan+Quintuples+Bear+Stearns+Bid&st=nyt (accessed September 4, 2009); "Lehman's CDS Mess: Who's on the Hook?" Seeking Alpha, October 13, 2008, http://seekingalpha.com/article/99619-lehman-s-cds-mess-who-s-on-the-hook (accessed September 4, 2009); Lengle, Kim, "A Warning Sign from Lehman," CBS News, October 20, 2008, http://www.cbsnews.com/stories/2008/10/20/cbsnews_investigates/main4535072.shtml (accessed September 4, 2009); Mamudi, Sam, "Lehman Folds with Record $613 Billion Debt," Market Watch, September 15, 2008, http://www.marketwatch.com/news/story/lehman-folds-613-billion-debt/story.aspx?guid={2FE5AC05-597A-4E71-A2D5-9B9FCC290520} (accessed September 4, 2009); "Nick Leeson Blames the Banks," SOX First, April 11, 2008, http://www.soxfirst.com/50226711/nick_leeson_blames_the_banks.php (accessed September 4, 2009); Ross, Brian, "Lehman Had Long Relationship with Suspect Mortgage Brokers," ABC News, September 15, 2008, http://abcnews.go.com/Blotter/story?id=5807408&page= (accessed September 4, 2009); Smith, Randall, Diya Gullapalli, and Jeffery McCracken, "Lehman, Workers Score Reprieve," *Wall Street Journal,* September 17, 2008, http://online.wsj.com/article/SB122156586985742907.html (accessed September 4, 2009).

CASE 11

The Coca-Cola Company Struggles with Ethical Crises

Daryl Benson

As one of the most valuable brand names worldwide, Coca-Cola has generally excelled as a business over its long history. However, in recent decades the company has had difficulties meeting its financial objectives and has been associated with a number of ethical crises. As a result, some investors have lost faith in the company. For example, Warren Buffet (board member and strong supporter of and investor in Coca-Cola) resigned from the board in 2006 after years of frustration over Coca-Cola's failure to overcome its challenges.

Since the 1990s, Coca-Cola has been accused of unethical behavior in a number of areas such as product safety, anti-competitiveness, racial discrimination, channel stuffing, distributor conflicts, intimidation of union workers, pollution, and depletion of natural resources. A number of these issues have been dealt with, some via private settlements and some via court battles, while others still besmirch the Coca-Cola name. Although its handling of different ethical situations has not always been lauded, Coca-Cola generally has responded by seeking to improve its detection and compliance systems. However, it remains to be seen whether the company can permanently rise above its ethical problems, learn from its mistakes, make necessary changes, avoid further problems, and still emerge as the leader among beverage companies.

HISTORY OF THE COCA-COLA COMPANY

Founded in 1886, the Coca-Cola Company is the world's largest beverage company. In addition to Coca-Cola and Diet Coke, it also sells other profitable brands including Powerade, Minute Maid, and Dasani water. To service global demand, the company has the world's largest distribution system, which reaches customers and businesses in nearly

This case was developed under the direction of Debbie Thorne, O.C. Ferrell, and Jennifer Jackson. Kevin Sample and Rob Boostrum helped draft previous editions of this case. Thanks also to Jennifer Sawayda and Alexi Sherrill for their editorial assistance. This case was prepared for classroom discussion, rather than to illustrate either effective or ineffective handling of an administrative, ethical, or legal decision by management. All sources used for this case were obtained through publicly available material and the Coca-Cola website.

every country on the planet. Coca-Cola estimates that more than one billion servings of its products are consumed every day.

Until the mid-twentieth century, Coca-Cola focused on expanding market share within the United States. After World War II, however, the company began to recognize the opportunities in global sales. In the last part of the twentieth century, Coca-Cola extended this global push, taking advantage of international revenue opportunities and fierce soft drink competition, in an effort to dominate the global soft drink industry. By the late 1990s, Coca-Cola had gained more than 50 percent global market share in the soft drink industry, while PepsiCo, Coke's greatest rival, stood around 15 to 20 percent. Coca-Cola remains largely focused on carbonated and sugary beverages, while PepsiCo has diversified into snack foods and New Age drinks like waters, teas, and fruit juices. While Pepsi has tended to focus more on American markets, the largest portion of Coca-Cola's sales have come from outside the United States. As the late Roberto Goizueta, former CEO of Coca-Cola, once said, "Coca-Cola used to be an American company with a large international business. Now we are a large international company with a sizable American business."

> *"By the late 1990s, Coca-Cola had gained more than 50 percent global market share in the soft drink industry"*

In spite of international recognition and a strong brand, Coca-Cola has run into numerous difficulties. The company's problems began in the mid-1990s at the executive level. In 1997, Doug Ivester became CEO. Ivester, heralded for his ability to handle the financial flows and details of the soft drink giant, had been groomed for the position by former CEO Roberto Goizueta. However, Ivester's tenure as CEO did not last. He was not well equipped to handle the tough competition from Pepsi combined with the many ethical disasters Coke faced throughout the 1990s. Some people even began to doubt "Big Red's" reputation and its future prospects. For a company with a history of successful marketing and strong financial performance, Ivester's departure in 1999 represented a high-profile aberration in a relatively strong 100-year record.

In 2000, Doug Daft, the company's former president and chief operating officer (COO), replaced Ivester as CEO. Daft's tenure too was rocky, and the company continued to have problems throughout the early 2000s. For example, the company was allegedly involved in racial discrimination, misrepresentations of market tests, manipulation of earnings, and the disruption of long-term contractual arrangements with distributors.

By 2004, Neville Isdell was called out of retirement to improve Coca-Cola's reputation; however, the company continued to face ethical crises. Problems aside, Coca-Cola's overall performance seemed to improve under CEO and Chair Isdell's tenure. In 2008, Isdell relinquished the roll of CEO to then president and COO Muhtar Kent. Isdell also decided to step down as chair of the board in order to return to retirement. In 2009, under Kent's leadership, Coca-Cola, along with companies around the globe, sought to re-strategize in order to cope with the 2008–2009 global recession.

PEPSICO: SERIOUS COMPETITION TO COKE'S SUPREMACY

Historically, Coca-Cola has been a success for more than 120 years. In contrast, PepsiCo (founded at roughly the same time) did not become a serious competitor until after World War II, when it came up with the idea to sell its product in larger portions for the same price as Coke. The "cola wars" picked up more speed by the mid 1960s and have not abated since.

Today, the two American companies wage war primarily on international fronts. While the fight occasionally grows ugly, with accusations of anticompetitive behavior, generally the two companies remain civil. They may even appreciate the serious competition the other represents. Without fierce competition, neither company would be as successful.

However, PepsiCo has surged ahead of Coke. By early 2006 PepsiCo enjoyed a market value greater than Coca-Cola for the first time. Pepsi's strategy of focusing on snack foods and innovative approaches in the non-cola beverage market has helped the company gain market share and surpass Coca-Cola in overall performance. During the 2008–2009 recession, PepsiCo's diversification strategy continued to pay off. Many analysts now see greater long-term strength for PepsiCo. On the other hand, some investors fear for Coca-Cola's long-term prospects because of how much the company depends on international sales and the fluctuating values of the dollar Combined with the global recession in 2009, these are liabilities that may hurt Coca-Cola's long-term profitability. Because PepsiCo does 60 percent of its business in North America, a strong dollar does not adversely affect the company as much as it does Coca-Cola. These factors may give PepsiCo more of an upper-hand over Coca-Cola in the future.

COCA-COLA'S REPUTATION

Coca-Cola remains one of the most-recognized brand names in the world today, worth an estimated $68.73 billion in 2009. The company has always demonstrated strong market orientation, making strategic decisions and taking action to attract, satisfy, and retain customers. During World War II, for example, then company president Robert Woodruff distributed Coke around the world to sell to members of the armed services for a nickel a bottle. This strategy gave soldiers an affordable taste of home, created lifelong loyal customers, and increased global brand recognition in one of the first steps to creating a truly global brand. The presence of Coca-Cola products in almost every corner of the globe today shows how successful the company's international marketing strategy has been. Savvy marketing and a reputation for quality have always been hallmarks of Coca-Cola and have helped to make the product ubiquitous.

However, in the 1990s and 2000s, poor decisions, mismanagement, and alleged misconduct cast a shadow over the company. In 2000, Coca-Cola failed to make the top ten of *Fortune*'s annual "America's Most Admired Companies" list for the first time in ten years, although it still ranked first in the beverage industry. By 2009 Coca-Cola was in twelfth place and had fallen to third in the beverage industry. Leadership issues, disappointing economic performance, and other upheavals likely affected its standing on the *Fortune* list. In 2001, the company disappeared from the top 100 in *Business Ethics* magazine's annual list of "100 Best Corporate Citizens." For a company that had been on both lists for years, this was disappointing but not unexpected, given its several ethical crises. In 2007, Coca-Cola was still absent from the *Business Ethics* "100 Best Corporate Citizens" list, but PepsiCo was number forty-two.

CRISIS SITUATIONS

The following sections document the alleged misconduct and questionable behavior that have affected Coca-Cola stakeholders and possibly the company's financial performance. In 1996, Coca-Cola traded just below $50 a share. In the first half of 2009, it ranged from

$59 to $37, showing little growth over a dozen years and underperforming against both the S&P 500 and NASDAQ. This slow growth may be attributed to various internal problems associated with top management turnover and departure of key investors, as well as external problems that have led to a loss of reputation. The following incidents exemplify some of the key crises Coca-Cola has faced in the last several years.

Contamination Scare

Perhaps the most damaging of Coca-Cola's crises—and a situation dreaded by every company—began in June 1999 when about thirty Belgian children became ill after consuming Coke products. Although the company issued an isolated product recall, the problem escalated. The Belgian government eventually ordered the recall of all Coca-Cola products, which prompted officials in Luxembourg and the Netherlands to recall Coke products as well. Coca-Cola finally determined that the illnesses were the result of an improperly processed batch of carbon dioxide. Coca-Cola was slow to issue a response to the problem, taking several days to address the media. Initially, Coca-Cola had not wanted to overreact over what it at first judged to be a minor problem and did not immediately investigate the extent of the issue. The slow response time led to a public relations nightmare. France soon reported more than 100 people sick from bad Coke and temporarily banned all Coca-Cola products as well. Soon thereafter, a shipment of Bonaqua, a new Coca-Cola water product, arrived in Poland contaminated with mold. In each of these instances, the company's slow responses and failure to acknowledge the severity of the situation harmed its reputation and cast doubt on then CEO Ivester's ability to successfully lead.

The contamination crisis was exacerbated in December 1999 when Belgium ordered Coca-Cola to halt the "Restore" marketing campaign it had launched in order to regain consumer trust and sales in Belgium. A rival firm claimed the campaign strategy—which included free cases of the product, discounts to wholesalers and retailers, and extra promotion personnel—was unlawful. Under Belgium's strict antitrust laws, the claim was upheld; Coca-Cola abandoned the campaign to avoid further problems. This decision, following the previous crisis, further reduced Coca-Cola's market standing in Europe.

Competitive Issues

Questions concerning Coca-Cola's market dominance and government inquiries into its marketing tactics plagued the company throughout Europe. Because the European Union countries have strict antitrust laws, all firms must pay close attention to market share and position when considering joint ventures, mergers, and acquisitions. During the summer of 1999, when Coca-Cola began an aggressive expansion push in France, the French government responded by refusing Coca-Cola's bid to purchase Orangina, a French beverage company. French authorities also forced Coca-Cola to scale back its acquisition of Cadbury Schweppes, maker of Dr. Pepper.

Moreover, in late 1999 Italy successfully won a court case against Coca-Cola over anticompetitive prices, prompting the European Commission to launch a full-scale probe into the company's competitive practices. In addition, PepsiCo and Virgin Cola accused Coca-Cola of using rebates and discounts to crowd their products off the shelves. Coca-Cola's strong-arm tactics were again found to be in violation of European laws, once again demonstrating the company's lack of awareness of European culture and laws.

Despite these legal tangles, Coca-Cola products, along with many other U.S. products, dominate foreign markets worldwide. The growing omnipresence of U.S. products, especially in highly competitive markets, makes corporate reputation, both perceived and actual, essential to building relationships with business partners, government officials, and other stakeholders.

Racial Discrimination Allegations

In 1999, Coca-Cola's reputation was dealt another blow when 1,500 African American employees sued for racial discrimination. The lawsuit, which eventually grew to include 2,000 current and former employees, accused the company of discriminating in areas of pay, promotion, and performance evaluation. Plaintiffs charged that the company grouped African American workers at the bottom of the pay scale and that they earned around $26,000 a year less than Caucasian employees in comparable jobs. The suit also alleged that top management had known about companywide discrimination since 1995 but had done nothing about it. In 1992, Coca-Cola had pledged to spend $1 billion on goods and services from minority vendors, an action designed to show the public that Coca-Cola did not discriminate, but the lawsuit from its own employees painted a different picture. Although Coca-Cola strongly denied the allegations, the lawsuit provoked unrest within the company. In response, Coca-Cola created a diversity council and the company paid $193 million to settle the racial discrimination lawsuit.

> ***Coca-Cola products, along with many other U.S. products, dominate foreign markets worldwide.***

Inflated Earnings Related to Channel Stuffing

Coca-Cola was also accused of channel stuffing during the early 2000s. Channel stuffing is the practice of shipping extra, nonrequested inventory to wholesalers and retailers before the end of a quarter. A company counts the shipments as sales although the product often remains in warehouses or is later returned. Because the goods have been shipped, the company counts them as revenue at the end of the quarter. Channel stuffing creates the appearance of strong demand (or conceals declining demand), and results in inflated financial statement earnings and the subsequent misleading of investors.

In 2004, Coca-Cola was accused of sending extra concentrate to Japanese bottlers between 1997 and 1999 in an effort to inflate its profits. The company was already under investigation; in 2000, a former employee filed a lawsuit accusing the company of fraud and improper business practices. The company settled the allegations, but the Securities and Exchange Commission (SEC) did find that channel stuffing had occurred. Coca-Cola had pressured bottlers into buying additional concentrate in exchange for extended credit.

Trouble with Distributors

In early 2006, Coca-Cola once again faced problems—this time on its home front. Fifty-four of its U.S. bottlers filed lawsuits against Coke and the company's largest bottler Coca-Cola Enterprises (CCE). The suit sought to block Coke and CCE, both based in Atlanta, from expanding delivery of Powerade sports drinks directly to Wal-Mart warehouses instead of to individual stores. Bottlers alleged that the Powerade bottler contract did not permit warehouse delivery to large retailers. They claimed that Coke breached the agreement by committing to provide warehouse delivery of Powerade to Wal-Mart and by proposing to use CCE as its agent for delivery. The main problem was that Coke was attempting to step away from the century-old tradition of direct-store delivery (DSD), in which bottlers deposit drinks at individual stores, stock shelves, and build merchandising displays. Bottlers claimed that if Coke and CCE went forward, it would greatly diminish the value of their businesses.

In their defense, Coke and CCE asserted they were simply trying to accommodate a request from Wal-Mart for warehouse delivery (how PepsiCo distributes its Gatorade brand). CCE had also proposed making payments to other bottlers in return for taking over Powerade distribution in their territories. However, bottlers feared such an arrangement violated antitrust laws. An undisclosed agreement between the bottlers and Coca-Cola was reached in 2007. Reports suggest warehouse deliveries were considered acceptable in some situations, and guidelines were developed for assessing those situations.

> *When the reputation of one company suffers, all those within the supply chain suffer in some way.*

When addressing problems faced by Coca-Cola, the media tends to focus primarily on its reputation rather than on its relations with bottlers, distributors, suppliers, and other partners. Without these strategic partnerships, Coca-Cola would not be where it is today. Such partnerships involve sharing in risks and rewards. Issues such as the contamination scare and racial discrimination allegations, especially when handled poorly, can reflect on business relationships beyond the key company's business. When the reputation of one company suffers, all those within the supply chain suffer in some way. This is especially true because Coca-Cola adopted an enterprise-resource system that linked Coca-Cola's once highly secret information to a host of partners. Thus, the company's less-than-stellar handling of ethical crises may have introduced lax integrity standards to its partnerships. The interdependence between Coca-Cola and its partners requires a diplomatic and considerate view of the business and its effects on various stakeholders. Therefore, these crises harmed Coke's partner companies, their stakeholders, and eventually their bottom lines.

International Problems Related to Unions

Between 2001 and 2004, a more sinister accusation against Coke surfaced in Colombia. Since 1989 eight union Coca-Cola workers had died there, 48 were forced into hiding, and 65 had received death threats. Many believe the deaths and threats were the results of intimidation against union workers employed at the Coca-Cola bottling plant in Colombia. The union, which alleged that Coke and its local bottler were complicit in the intimidation and the deaths, is seeking reparations for the families of the slain and displaced Colombian workers. However, Coke completely denies the allegations and notes that only one of the eight workers was killed on the bottling plant premises. Also, the company maintains that the other deaths were by-products of Colombia's four-decade-long civil war. In 2007, a group of hundreds of people made up of Teamsters, environmentalists, human rights proponents, and student activists gathered in New York City to protest against Coca-Cola in regard to the problems in Colombia, among other concerns.

Issues Regarding Water Usage and Pollution

Coca-Cola has also encountered trouble at its bottling plants in India, fielding accusations of both groundwater depletion and contamination. In 2003, the Centre for Science and Environment (CSE) tested soft drinks produced in India by Coca-Cola and other companies; findings indicated extreme levels of pesticides from using contaminated groundwater. Supported in 2004 by an Indian parliamentary committee, the first set of standards for pesticides in soft drinks was developed. Although Coca-Cola denied allegations, stating that its water is filtered and its final products are tested before being released, sales dropped temporarily by 15 percent.

In the Indian city of Varanasi, Coca-Cola was also accused of contaminating the groundwater with wastewater. Officials at the company admitted that the plant did have a wastewater issue but insisted that a new pipeline had been built to eliminate the problem. However, during the early 2000s, a number of tests were conducted regarding "sludge" produced at Coca-Cola's Indian plants. These tests, conducted by the Central Pollution Control Board of India and the British Broadcasting Corporation, came up with toxic results.

The company runs bottling plants in a handful of drought-plagued areas around India, and groups of officials blame the plants for a dramatic decline in available water. In 2004, local officials closed a Coca-Cola plant in Kerala; however, the closure was overturned by Kerala's court. Although the court agreed that Coca-Cola's presence contributed to water depletion, the company was not solely to blame. Farmers and local residents, forced to vie with Coca-Cola for water, have protested Coca-Cola's presence there and throughout India.

In 2005, students at the University of Michigan asked the university to cancel its contracts with Coca-Cola based on these issues in India. In response, the university requested that the Energy and Resources Institute out of New Delhi research the issue. Findings indicated that Coca-Cola's soda did not contain higher-than-normal levels of pesticides. However, the report did indicate that the company's bottling plants were stressing water resources and suggested that the company do a better job of considering a plant's location based on resources and future impact. Protests regarding Coca-Cola's impact on India have continued in areas around the globe for years.

Coca-Cola's Impact on Health

In 2008, Coca-Cola launched a "Motherhood and Myth-Busting" campaign in Australia, attempting to convince the public that a diet including soda was healthy for children. The Australian Competition and Consumer Commission promptly took Coca-Cola to court after the Obesity Policy Coalition, the Parents' Jury, and the Australian Dental Association all filed complaints. As a result, in 2009 the company was forced to release new advertisements in a number of Australian newspapers correcting information such as the amount of caffeine found in Diet Coke. In response, Coca-Cola admits that it did not supply consumers with detailed information during its campaign. Also in 2008, the FDA declared the company had violated the Federal Food, Drug, and Cosmetic Act when naming the Coca-Cola Diet Plus beverage. Using "plus" in the name indicated an unsubstantiated nutritional claim. The next year, Coca-Cola was sued by the Center for Science in the Public Interest regarding misleading marketing that concerned the contents of its VitaminWater. Although the beverage is marketed as healthy, it contains a high quantity of sugar. However, attacks on Coca-Cola for the health impacts of its products are nothing new. The company has been under fire since the 1940s regarding its products' impacts on human health.

RECOVERY FROM ETHICAL CRISES

Arguments abound on both sides as to whether Coca-Cola has recovered from its ethical crises. The following information indicates that the company has addressed the majority of its issues; however, some believe Coca-Cola is still not doing enough.

Regarding the health scare, Belgian officials closed their investigation involving Coca-Cola and announced that no charges would be filed. A Belgian health report indicated that no toxic contamination had been found inside Coke bottles. The bottles did contain tiny traces of carbonyl sulfide, producing a rotten-egg smell, but to be toxic the amount of carbonyl sulfide would have to have been a thousand times higher. Officials also reported no structural problems within Coca-Cola's production plant and said that the company had cooperated fully throughout the investigation.

Coca-Cola has taken strides toward countering diversity protests. The racial discrimination lawsuit, along with the threat of a boycott by the National Association for the Advancement of Colored People (NAACP), led to this correction. When Coca-Cola settled the racial discrimination lawsuit, the agreement stipulated that Coke would donate $50 million to a foundation supporting programs in minority communities, hire an ombudsman reporting directly to the CEO to investigate complaints of discrimination and harassment, and set aside $36 million to form a seven-person task force with authority to oversee the company's employment practices. The task force, which includes business and civil rights experts, has unprecedented power to dictate company policy regarding hiring, compensating, and promoting women and minorities. Despite the unusual provision granting such power, then-CEO Daft defended his company's measures to increase diversity, saying, "We need to have outside people helping us. We would be foolish to cut ourselves off from the outside world." It is worth noting that, as of May 2009, the task force had not issued a report since 2006.

> ***"Coca-Cola's responsibility is to disclose honest, detailed information regarding its products"***

In response to the SEC's findings regarding channel stuffing, the company created an ethics and compliance office and is required to verify quarterly that it has not altered the terms of payment or extended special credit. Additionally, the company agreed to work to reduce the amount of concentrate held by international bottlers.

Coca-Cola has defended itself against allegations of violence in Colombia, and the Colombian court and the Colombian attorney general support the company. In 2004, the company was dismissed as a defendant in the 2001 lawsuit; the case was dismissed two years later due to insufficient evidence. An appeal has been filed. According to Coca-Cola's company website, it does everything it can to protect its employees and works to aid Colombian children and families.

Although Coca-Cola's issues in India did cause a temporary dip in sales and ongoing protests, the company insists that it has taken measures to ensure safety and quality. Coca-Cola has partnered with local governments, NGOs, schools, and communities to establish 320 rainwater-harvesting facilities. The goal is to work toward renewing and returning all groundwater. In addition, as recommended by the University of Michigan study, the company is strengthening its plant requirements and working with local communities to ensure sustainability of local water resources. The company recently launched the Coca-Cola India Foundation for Sustainable Development and Inclusive Growth. In 2008, Coca-Cola received the Golden Peacock Global Award for corporate social responsibility in water conservation, management, and community development initiatives.

Responding to health issues related to Coca-Cola's products is more complex. The company itself cannot be held responsible for how many sugary or artificially sweetened beverages the public consumes. Ultimately, Coca-Cola's responsibility is to disclose honest, detailed information regarding its products so that consumers may make educated beverage choices. Coca-Cola does make an effort to encourage consumers to exercise and embrace a healthy lifestyle through nutritional education and physical activity programs and engages in ongoing discussions with government, NGO, and public health representatives regarding obesity and health.

SOCIAL RESPONSIBILITY FOCUS

Because Coca-Cola is so globally recognized, the industry in which it operates is so pervasive, and it has a strong history of market orientation, the company has developed a number of social responsibility initiatives to further enhance its business. These initiatives are guided by the company's core beliefs in marketplace, workplace, community, and environment. As stated in its Mission, Vision & Values statements, Coca-Cola wants to "Inspire Moments of Optimism" through brands and actions as well as to create value and to make a difference in the countries in which it does business. The company seeks to provide sustainable growth by providing a great place to work, inspiring employees to use innovation to provide a portfolio of brands meeting consumer needs worldwide. At the same time, the company strives to be a responsible business. For instance, Coca-Cola has made local education and community improvement programs top priorities—some of which are implemented through various Coca-Cola foundations. For example, Coca-Cola is involved in Education On Wheels in Singapore. This program brings history to life through an interactive discovery adventure for kids, which also enhances communication skills as children discover new insights into life in Singapore.

Coca-Cola offers grants to various colleges and universities both nationally and internationally. In addition to grants, Coca-Cola provides scholarships to hundreds of colleges, including thirty tribal colleges belonging to the American Indian College Fund. Coca-Cola also has become involved with the Hispanic Scholarship Fund. Such initiatives help enhance the Coca-Cola name, and ultimately benefit shareholders. Through the Coca-Cola Scholars Foundation, 250 new Coca-Cola Scholars are named each year and brought to Atlanta for interviews. Fifty students are then designated National Scholars, receiving awards of $20,000 for college; the remaining 200 are designated Regional Scholars, receiving $4,000 awards.

Like many other companies, Coca-Cola is addressing the issues of recycling and climate change. In 2007, the company launched "Drink2Wear" clothing made from recycled plastic bottles. In 2008, the company added bags, loungewear, and hats to the recycled line. As of 2009, the company had reused more than five million PET bottles in this fashion. Also in 2007, Coca-Cola signed the UN Global Compact's "Caring for Climate: The Business Leadership Platform." In doing so, the company pledged to increase energy efficiency and reduce emissions. To this end, Coca-Cola has co-founded the Refrigerants, Naturally! Initiative—a food and beverage industry alliance aimed to address climate change through the promotion of HFC-free alternative refrigeration technologies. In 2009, the company opened the world's largest plastic bottle-to-bottle recycling plant in South Carolina. Also in 2009, Coca-Cola released the PlantBottle™. This new bottle, made from 30 percent plant-based material, is fully recyclable and reduces use of nonrenewable resources and carbon emissions. The bottles are in use in a limited capacity, and the company plans to expand.

Coca-Cola chair Neville Isdell received the 2008 Ethics Advocate Award issued by the Center for Ethics and Corporate Responsibility at Georgia State University. Isdell was chosen thanks to his efforts to promote and address corporate social responsibility and environmental sustainability while at Coca-Cola. He was also being thanked for encouraging corporate responsibility throughout the business community.

In addition, Coca-Cola recognizes its responsibilities on a global scale and takes action to uphold this responsibility. The company remains proactive on issues such as the HIV/AIDS epidemic in Africa. Coca-Cola has partnered with UNAIDS and other nongovernment organizations, putting into place important initiatives and programs to help combat the threat of HIV/AIDS. The company is also working to create new jobs throughout the developing world in an effort to help combat poverty. In 2007 Coca-Cola joined the World Wildlife Fund (WWF) and pledged to reduce the amount of water Coca-Cola uses, to improve the recycling of water at Coca-Cola plants, and to replenish natural water sources. Coca-Cola pledged $20 million dollars to the initiative; these resources will be used in part to protect seven of the world's most important freshwater river basins.

Because consumers generally respect Coca-Cola, trust its products, and have strong attachments through brand recognition and product loyalty, Coca-Cola's actions foster relationship marketing. Because of this, problems at a firm like Coca-Cola can stir the emotions of many stakeholders.

CURRENT SITUATION AT COCA-COLA

In the early part of the twenty-first century, Coca-Cola's financial performance was positive, with the company maintaining a sound balance sheet. However, earnings across the soft drink industry have been on a slow decline because of decreased consumption, increased competition, and the 2008–2009 global recession. Nevertheless, Coca-Cola is confident of its long-term viability and remains strong in the belief that the company is well positioned to succeed regardless of the economic situation.

In order to remain a successful company long into the future, Coca-Cola must resolve conflicts and lawsuits associated with ethical crises. While Coca-Cola is trying to establish its reputation based on quality products and socially responsible activities, it has failed its numerous stakeholders on a number of occasions over the years. Can Coca-Cola's strong emphasis on social responsibility, especially philanthropic and environmental concerns, help the company maintain its reputation in the face of highly public ethical conflicts and crises?

CONCLUSION

For more than a decade, Coca-Cola has been fighting for its reputation against allegations of lack of health and safety of its products, unlawful competitive practices, racial discrimination and employee intimidation, channel stuffing, unfair distributor treatment, and the pollution and pillaging of natural resources. It is difficult to decipher all available information and come to a clear conclusion. Under Nevill Isdell and Muhtar Kent's leadership, Coca-Cola has rebounded and begun to take strides toward improving its image. The company is focusing more on environmental stewardship, for example. However, the company's critics say that Coca-Cola is not doing enough—that its efforts are merely window dressing to hide its corruption. Case in point: Although the company claims to have addressed all issues in India and claims to be making an effort to aid the country's population, the Internet is rich with real-time criticism of Coca-Cola's practices in that country. People worldwide are caught up in emotional reactions—both positive and negative—to this massive corporation.

Regardless of emotion, it is clear that Coca-Cola is not a perfect company and that it has been involved in its share of ethical misconduct. Shareholder reactions have altered many times over the company's history, but the company has retained a large loyal base. The company hopes that its current leadership is strong enough to move Coca-Cola past this focus on ethics and into a profitable start to the twenty-first century. Thus, the question is whether leadership is doing what it takes to burnish Coca-Cola's image and practice what it preaches.

QUESTIONS

1. What role does corporate reputation play within organizational performance and social responsibility? Develop a list of factors or characteristics that different stakeholders may use in assessing corporate reputation. Are these factors consistent across stakeholders? Why or why not?
2. Assume you have just become CEO at Coca-Cola. Outline the strategic steps you would take to remedy the concerns emanating from the company's board of directors, consumers, employees, and business partners; governments; and the media. What elements of social responsibility would you draw from in responding to these stakeholder issues?
3. What do you think of Coca-Cola's environmental initiatives? Are they just window dressing, or does the company seem to be sincere in its efforts?

SOURCES

"America's Most Reputable Companies," *Fortune*, April 29, 2009, http://www.forbes.com/2009/04/28/america-reputable-companies-leadership-reputation_table.html (accessed September 4, 2009); Ames, Paul, "Case Closed on Coke Health Scare," Associated Press, April 22, 2000, HighBeam Research, http://www.highbeam.com/doc/1P1-26137611.html (accessed September 4, 2009); "Another Coke Plant, More Pollution Dumping," *South Asian*, June 10, 2007, http://www.thesouthasian.org/archives/2007/another_coke_plant_more_pollut.html (accessed September 4, 2009); Beucke, Dan, "Coke Promises a Probe in Colombia," *BusinessWeek*, February 6, 2006, p. 11; Brooker, Katrina, "The Pepsi Machine," *Fortune*, February 6, 2006, pp. 68–72; Burke, Kelly, "Coca-Cola Busted for Big Fat Rotten Lies," *Sydney Morning Herald*, April 2, 2009, http://www.smh.com.au/national/cocacola-busted-for-big-fat-rotten-lies-20090402-9kn6.html?page=1 (accessed September 4, 2009); Chase, Randall, "Judge Dismisses Shareholder Suit Against Coca-Cola," Associated Press via SignOnSanDiego.com, October 22, 2007, http://www.signonsandiego.com/news/business/20071022-1441-coca-cola-lawsuit.html (accessed September 8, 2009); "Coca Cola Appears to Have Settled Lawsuit over Distribution to Retail Distribution Centers," *Supply Chain Digest*, February 14, 2007, http://www.scdigest.com/assets/newsViews/07-02-14-2.cfm?cid=896&ctype=content (accessed September 4, 2009); Coca Cola Company, http://www.thecoca-colacompany.com (accessed May 16, 2009); Doyle, T. C., "Channel Stuffing Rears Its Ugly Head," *VARBusiness*, May 6, 2003, http://www.crn.com/

it-channel/18823602;jsessionid=TC1LHY0F4LAXYQSNDLPSKHSCJUNN2JVN (accessed September 4, 2009); Faier, James, "The Name Is the Game," Retail Traffic, http://retailtrafficmag.com/mag/retail_name_game/index.html (accessed September 4, 2009); Foust, Dean, and Geri Smith, "'Killer Coke' or Innocent Abroad? Controversy over Anti-Union Violence in Colombia Has Colleges Banning Coca-Cola," *BusinessWeek*, January 23, 2006, pp. 46–48; Glovin, David, and Duane D. Stanford, "PepsiCo Sues Coca-Cola over Powerade Advertisements (Update3)," Bloomberg.com, April 13, 2009, http://www.bloomberg.com/apps/news?pid=20601110&sid=aYXGQIH6Hisk (accessed September 4, 2009); "Grand Jury to Investigate Coke on Channel Stuffing Allegations," *Atlanta Business Chronicle*, May 3, 2004, atlanta.bizjournals.com/atlanta/stories/2004/05/03/daily2.html (accessed September 4, 2009); Kelly, Marjorie, "100 Best Corporate Citizens," *Business Ethics* (Spring 2007): 23–24; "Neville Isdell, Chairman of The Coca-Cola Company, to Receive Ethics Advocate Award," J. Mack Robinson College of Business, Georgia State University, http://robinson.gsu.edu/news/08/isdell.html (accessed September 4, 2009); Peer, Melinda, "In Downturn, Pepsi May Beat Coke," *Forbes*, February 19, 2009, http://www.forbes.com/2009/02/19/coca-cola-pepsico-markets-equity_dividend_outlook_49.html (accessed September 4, 2009); Simons, Craig, "Report Examines Coke Water Use in India," Cox News Service, January 15, 2008, http://www.statesman.com/business/content/shared/money/stories/2008/01/COKE_INDIA15_1STLD_COX_F4362_1.html (accessed September 4, 2009); Srivastava, Amit, "Reality Check for Coca-Cola's Public Relations," India Resource Center, April 16, 2009, http://www.indiaresource.org/campaigns/coke/2009/realitycheck.html (accessed September 4, 2009); "Teamsters Converge on Times Square to Protest Coke's Anti-Worker Tactics; Teamsters Put Coke on Notice for Possible Job Actions over Worker Abuses," *PR Wire*, April 2, 2007, http://www.prnewswire.com/cgi-bin/stories.pl?ACCT=104&STORY=/www/story/04-02-2007/0004557941&EDATE= (accessed September 4, 2009); Terhune, Chad, "Bottlers' Suit Challenges Coke Distribution Plan," *Wall Street Journal*, February 18–19, 2006, p. A5; Terhune, Chad, "A Suit by Coke Bottlers Exposes Cracks in a Century-Old System," *Wall Street Journal*, March 13, 2006, p. A1; Waldman, Amy, "India Tries to Contain Tempest over Soft Drink Safety," *New York Times*, August 23, 2003, http://query.nytimes.com/gst/fullpage.html?res=9A04E6DC1439F930A1575BC0A9659C8B63 (accessed September 4, 2009); "WWF and Coca-Cola Embark on Water Conservation Initiative," June 5, 2007, http://www.ens-newswire.com/ens/jun2007/2007-06-05-07.asp (accessed September 4, 2009).

CASE 12

Enron: Questionable Accounting Leads to Collapse

Daryl Benson

Once upon a time, there was a gleaming headquarters office tower in Houston, with a giant tilted "E" in front, slowly revolving in the Texas sun. Enron's "E" suggested to Chinese *feng shui* practitioner Meihwa Lin a model of instability, which was perhaps an omen of things to come. The Enron Corporation, which once ranked among the top *Fortune* 500 companies, collapsed in 2001 under a mountain of debt that had been concealed through a complex scheme of off-balance-sheet partnerships. Forced to declare bankruptcy, the energy firm laid off four thousand employees; thousands more lost their retirement savings, which had been invested in Enron stock. The company's shareholders lost tens of billions of dollars after the stock price plummeted. The scandal surrounding Enron's demise engendered a global loss of confidence in corporate integrity that continues to plague markets, and eventually it triggered tough new scrutiny of financial reporting practices. To understand what went wrong, we'll examine the history, culture, and major players in the Enron scandal.

ENRON'S HISTORY

The Enron Corporation was created out of the merger of two major gas pipeline companies in 1985. Through its subsidiaries and numerous affiliates, the company provided products and services related to natural gas, electricity, and communications for its wholesale and retail customers. Enron transported natural gas through pipelines to customers all over the United States. It generated, transmitted, and distributed electricity to the northwestern United States, and marketed natural gas, electricity, and

This case was developed under the direction of O.C. Ferrell with the assistance of Jennifer Jackson and Jennifer Sawayda, University of New Mexico. Neil Herndon, helped to draft the original version of this case. The author conducted personal interviews with Ken Lay in 2006. This case is for classroom discussion, rather than to illustrate either effective or ineffective handling of an administrative, ethical, or legal decision by management. All sources used for this case were obtained through publicly available material.

other commodities globally. It was also involved in the development, construction, and operation of power plants, pipelines, and other energy-related projects all over the world, including the delivery and management of energy to retail customers in both the industrial and commercial business sectors.

Throughout the 1990s, Chair Ken Lay, chief executive officer (CEO) Jeffrey Skilling, and Chief Financial Officer (CFO) Andrew Fastow transformed Enron from an old-style electricity and gas company into a $150 billion energy company and Wall Street favorite that traded power contracts in the investment markets. From 1998 to 2000 alone, Enron's revenues grew from about $31 billion to more than $100 billion, making it the seventh-largest company of the *Fortune* 500. Enron's wholesale energy income represented about 93 percent of 2000 revenues, with another 4 percent derived from natural gas and electricity. The remaining 3 percent came from broadband services and exploration. However, a bankruptcy examiner later reported that although Enron claimed a net income of $979 million in that year, it really earned just $42 million. Moreover, the examiner found that despite Enron's claim of $3 billion in cash flow in 2000, the company actually had a cash flow of negative $154 million.

ENRON'S CORPORATE CULTURE

When describing the corporate culture of Enron, people like to use the word *arrogant*, perhaps justifiably. A large banner in the lobby at corporate headquarters proclaimed Enron "The World's Leading Company," and Enron executives blithely believed that competitors had no chance against it. Jeffrey Skilling even went so far as to tell utility executives at a conference that he was going to "eat their lunch." There was an overwhelming aura of pride, carrying with it the deep-seated belief that Enron's people could handle increasing risk without danger. The culture also was about a focus on how much money could be made for executives. For example, Enron's compensation plans seemed less concerned with generating profits for shareholders than with enriching officer wealth. Enron's corporate culture reportedly encouraged flouting, possibly even breaking, the rules.

> *"Enron's corporate culture reportedly encouraged flouting, possibly even breaking, the rules."*

Skilling appears to be the executive who created a system in which Enron's employees were rated every six months, with those ranked in the bottom 20 percent forced out. This "rank and yank" system helped create a fierce environment in which employees competed against rivals not only outside the company but also at the next desk. Delivering bad news could result in the "death" of the messenger, so problems in the trading operation, for example, were covered up rather than being communicated to management.

Enron Chair Ken Lay once said that he felt that one of the great successes at Enron was the creation of a corporate culture in which people could reach their full potential. He said that he wanted it to be a highly moral and ethical culture and that he tried to ensure that people did in fact honor the values of respect, integrity, and excellence. On his desk was an Enron paperweight with the slogan "Vision and Values." Despite these intentions, however, ethical behavior was not put into practice. Instead, integrity was pushed to the side at Enron, particularly by top managers. Some employees at the company believed that nearly anything could be turned into a financial product and, with the aid of complex statistical modeling, traded for profit. Short on assets and heavily reliant on intellectual capital, Enron's corporate culture rewarded innovation and punished employees deemed weak.

ENRON'S ACCOUNTING PROBLEMS

Enron's bankruptcy in 2001 was the largest in U.S. corporate history at the time. The bankruptcy filing came after a series of revelations that the giant energy trader had been using partnerships, called *special-purpose entities (SPEs),* to conceal losses. In a meeting with Enron's lawyers in August 2001, the company's then chief financial officer Andrew Fastow stated that Enron had established the SPEs to move assets and debt off its balance sheet and to increase cash flow by showing that funds were flowing through its books when it sold assets. Although these practices produced a very favorable financial picture, outside observers believed they constitutes fraudulent financial reporting because they did not accurately represent the company's true financial condition. Most of the SPEs were entities in name only, and Enron funded them with its own stock and maintained control over them. When one of these partnerships was unable to meet its obligations, Enron covered the debt with its own stock. This arrangement worked as long as Enron's stock price was high, but when the stock price fell, cash was needed to meet the shortfall.

After Enron restated its financial statements for fiscal year 2000 and the first nine months of 2001, its cash flow from operations was changed from a positive \$127 million in 2000 to a negative \$753 million in 2001. In 2001, with its stock price falling, Enron faced a critical cash shortage. In October 2001, after it was forced to cover some large shortfalls for its partnerships, Enron's stockholder equity fell by \$1.2 billion. Already shaken by questions about lack of disclosure in Enron's financial statements and by reports that executives had profited personally from the partnership deals, investor confidence collapsed, taking Enron's stock price with it.

For a time, it appeared that Dynegy might save the day by providing \$1.5 billion in cash, secured by Enron's premier pipeline Northern Natural Gas, and then purchasing Enron for about \$10 billion. However, when Standard & Poor's downgraded Enron's debt below investment grade on November 28, 2001, some \$4 billion in off-balance-sheet debt came due, and Enron didn't have the resources to pay. Dynegy terminated the deal. On December 2, 2001, Enron filed for bankruptcy. Enron now faces 22,000 claims totaling about \$400 billion.

The Whistle-Blower

Assigned to work directly with Andrew Fastow in June 2001, Enron vice president Sherron Watkins, an eight-year Enron veteran, was given the task of finding some assets to sell off. With the high-tech bubble bursting and Enron's stock price slipping, Watkins was troubled to find unclear, off-the-books arrangements backed only by Enron's deflating stock. No one seemed to be able to explain to her what was going on. Knowing she faced difficult consequences if she confronted then CEO Jeffrey Skilling, she began looking for another job, planning to confront Skilling just as she left for a new position. Skilling, however, suddenly quit on August 14, saying he wanted to spend more time with his family. Chair Ken Lay stepped back in as CEO and began inviting employees to express their concerns and put them into a box for later collection. Watkins prepared an anonymous memo and placed it into the box. When CEO Lay held a companywide meeting shortly thereafter and did not mention her memo, however, she arranged a personal meeting with him.

On August 22, Watkins handed Lay a seven-page letter she had prepared outlining her concerns. She told him that Enron would "implode in a wave of accounting scandals" if nothing was done. Lay arranged to have Enron's law firm, Vinson & Elkins, look into the questionable deals, although Watkins advised against having a party investigate that might be compromised by its own involvement in Enron's scam. Near the end of September, Lay sold some $1.5 million of personal stock options, while telling Enron employees that the company had never been stronger. By the middle of October, Enron was reporting a third-quarter loss of $618 million and a $1.2 billion write-off tied to the partnerships about which Watkins had warned Lay.

For her trouble, Watkins had her computer hard drive confiscated and was moved from her plush executive office suite on the top floor of the Houston headquarters tower to a sparse office on a lower level. Her new metal desk was no longer filled with the high-level projects that had once taken her all over the world on Enron business. Instead, now a vice president in name only, she faced meaningless "make work" projects. In February 2002, she testified before Congress about Enron's partnerships and resigned from Enron in November of that year.

The Chief Financial Officer

Chief Financial Officer Andrew Fastow was indicted in 2002 by the U.S. Justice Department on ninety-eight federal counts for his alleged efforts to inflate Enron's profits. These charges included fraud, money laundering, conspiracy, and one count of obstruction of justice. Fastow originally faced up to 140 years in jail and millions of dollars in fines if convicted on all counts. Federal officials attempted to recover all of the money Fastow earned illegally, and seized some $37 million.

> ***"Fastow eventually pleaded guilty to two counts of conspiracy"***

Federal prosecutors argue that Enron's case is not about exotic accounting practices but fraud and theft. They contend that Fastow was the brain behind the partnerships used to conceal some $1 billion in Enron debt and that this led directly to Enron's bankruptcy. The federal complaints allege that Fastow defrauded Enron and its shareholders through the off-balance-sheet partnerships that made Enron appear to be more profitable than it actually was. They also allege that Fastow made about $30 million both by using these partnerships to get kickbacks that were disguised as gifts from family members who invested in them and by taking income himself that should have gone to other entities.

Fastow denied any wrongdoing and maintained that he was hired to arrange the off-balance-sheet financing and that Enron's board of directors, chair, and CEO directed and praised his work. He also claimed that both lawyers and accountants reviewed his work and approved what was being done and that "at no time did he do anything he believed was a crime." Jeffrey Skilling, chief operating officer (COO) from 1997 to 2000 before becoming CEO, reportedly championed Fastow's rise at Enron and supported his efforts to keep up Enron's stock prices.

Fastow eventually pleaded guilty to two counts of conspiracy, admitting to orchestrating myriad schemes to hide Enron debt and inflate profits while enriching himself with millions. He surrendered nearly $30 million in cash and property, and agreed to serve up to ten years in prison once prosecutors no longer needed his cooperation. He was a key government witness against Lay and Skilling. His wife Lea Fastow, former assistant treasurer, quit Enron in 1997 and pleaded guilty to a felony tax crime, admitting to helping hide ill-gotten gains from her husband's schemes from the government. She later withdrew her plea, and then pleaded guilty to a newly filed misdemeanor tax crime. In 2005 she was released from a year-long prison sentence, and then had a year of supervised release.

In the end, Fastow received a lighter sentence than he otherwise might have because of his willingness to cooperate with investigators. In 2006, Fastow delivered an eight-and-one-half-day deposition in his role as plaintiff's witness. He helped to illuminate how Enron managed to get away with what it did, including detailing how many major banks were complicit in helping Enron manipulate its financials to help it look better to investors. In exchange for his deposition, Fastow's sentence was lowered to six years from ten for the fraud he perpetrated while COO at Enron.

The case against Fastow was largely based on information provided by Managing Director Michael Kopper, a key player in the establishment and operation of several of the off-balance-sheet partnerships and the first Enron executive to plead guilty to a crime. Kopper, a chief aide to Fastow, pleaded guilty to money laundering and wire fraud. He faced up to fifteen years in prison and agreed to surrender some $12 million he earned from his illegal dealings with the partnerships. However, Kopper only had to serve three years and one month of jail time because of the crucial role he played in providing prosecutors with information. After his high-powered days at Enron, Kopper got a job as a salaried grant writer for Legacy, a Houston-based clinic that provides services to those with HIV and other chronically ill patients.

Others charged in the Enron affair include Timothy Belden, Enron's former top energy trader, who pleaded guilty to one count of conspiring to commit wire fraud. He was sentenced to two years of court-supervised release and required to pay $2.1 million. Three British bankers, David Bermingham, Giles Darby, and Gary Mulgrew, were indicted in Houston on wire-fraud charges related to a deal at Enron. They were able to use secret investments to take $7.3 million in income that belonged to their employer, according to the Justice Department. The three, employed by the finance group Greenwich National Westminster Bank, were arrested in 2004 and extradited to America to face sentencing. They were sentenced to thirty-seven months in prison but were eventually sent back to Britain to serve out the remainder of their sentencing.

The Chief Executive Officer

Former CEO Jeffrey Skilling, generally perceived as Enron's mastermind, was the most difficult to prosecute. At the time of the trial, he was so sure he had committed no crime that he waived his right to self-incrimination and testified before Congress, saying, "I was not aware of any inappropriate financial arrangements." However, Jeffrey McMahon, who took over as Enron's president and COO in February 2002, told a congressional subcommittee that he had informed Skilling about the company's off-balance-sheet partnerships in 2000, when he was Enron's treasurer. McMahon said that Skilling had told him "he would remedy the situation."

Calling the Enron collapse a "run on the bank" and a "liquidity crisis," Skilling said that he did not understand how Enron went from where it was to bankruptcy so quickly. He also said that the off-balance-sheet partnerships were Fastow's creation. During the case, however, the judge dealt a blow to defendants Lay and Skilling when he told the jury that they could find the defendants guilty of consciously avoiding knowing about wrongdoing at the company. Many former Enron employees refused to testify because they were not guaranteed that their testimony would not be used against them at future trials to convict them. For this reason, many questions about the accounting fraud remained after the trial.

Skilling was found guilty and sentenced to twenty-four years in prison, which he has been serving in Colorado. Skilling maintains his innocence and has appealed his conviction. In 2008 a panel of judges sitting in New Orleans rejected his requests for overturning convictions of fraud, conspiracy, misrepresentation, and insider trading. However, the judges did grant Skilling one concession. The three-judge panel determined that the original judge had applied flawed sentencing guidelines in determining Skilling's sentence. Skilling will be resentenced, but the reduction in duration will likely be modest, probably fifteen to nineteen years in place of the original twenty-four. In the years since the trial, this concession constitutes the only part of the Enron case that has been overturned. The nineteen counts of criminal conviction still stand. As a result, Skilling has taken his appeal to the U.S. Supreme Court.

The Chair

Kenneth Lay became chair and CEO of the company that was to become Enron in 1986. A decade later, Lay promoted Jeffrey Skilling to president and chief operating officer, and then, as expected, Lay stepped down as CEO in 2001 to make way for Skilling. Lay remained as chair of the board. When Skilling resigned later that year, Lay resumed the role of CEO.

Lay, who held a doctorate in economics from the University of Houston, contended that he knew little of what was going on, even though he had participated in the board meetings that allowed the off-balance-sheet partnerships to be created. He said he believed the transactions were legal because attorneys and accountants approved them. Only months before the bankruptcy in 2001, he reassured employees and investors that all was well at Enron, based on strong wholesale sales and physical volume delivered through the marketing channel. He had already been informed that there were problems with some of the investments that could eventually cost Enron hundreds of millions of dollars. Although cash flow does not always follow sales, there was every reason to believe that Enron was still a company with strong potential. In 2002, on the advice of his attorney, Lay invoked his Fifth Amendment right not to answer questions that could be incriminating.

Ken Lay was expected to be charged with insider trading, and prosecutors investigated why Lay began selling about $80 million of his own stock beginning in late 2000, even while he encouraged employees to buy more shares of the company. It appears that Lay drew down his $4 million Enron credit line repeatedly and then repaid the company with Enron shares. These transactions, unlike usual stock sales, do not have to be reported to investors. Lay says that he sold the stock because of margin calls on loans he had secured with Enron stock and that he had no other source of liquidity.

Lay was convicted on nineteen counts of fraud, conspiracy, and insider trading. However, the verdict was thrown out in 2006 after Lay died of heart failure at his home in Colorado. The ruling protected some $43.5 million of Lay's estate that the prosecution had claimed Lay stole from Enron.

Vinson & Elkins

Enron was Houston law firm Vinson & Elkins' top client, accounting for about 7 percent of its $450 million revenue. Enron's general counsel and a number of members of Enron's legal department came from Vinson & Elkins. Vinson & Elkins seems to have dismissed Sherron Watkins's allegations of accounting fraud after making some inquiries, but this does not appear to leave it open to civil or criminal liability. Of greater concern are allegations that Vinson & Elkins helped structure some of Enron's special-purpose partnerships. Watkins, in her letter to CEO Ken Lay, indicated that the law firm had written opinion letters supporting the legality of the deals. In fact, Enron could not have done many of the transactions without such opinion letters. The firm did not admit liability, but agreed to pay $30 million to Enron to settle claims that Vinson & Elkins contributed to the firm's collapse.

Merrill Lynch

The brokerage and investment-banking firm Merrill Lynch, which was in the news for its high-profile collapse and subsequent acquisition by Bank of America in 2008, also faced scrutiny by federal prosecutors and the SEC for its role in Enron's 1999 sale of Nigerian barges. The sale allowed Enron to improperly record about $12 million in earnings and thereby meet its earnings goals at the end of 1999. Merrill Lynch allegedly bought the barges for $28 million, of which Enron financed $21 million. Fastow gave his word that Enron would buy Merrill Lynch's investment out in six months with a 15 percent guaranteed rate of return. Merrill Lynch went ahead with the deal despite an internal Merrill Lynch document that suggested that the transaction might be construed as aiding and abetting Enron's fraudulent manipulation of its income statement. Merrill Lynch denies that the transaction was a sham and said that it never knowingly helped Enron to falsify its financial reports.

There are also allegations that Merrill Lynch replaced a research analyst after his coverage of Enron displeased Enron executives. Enron reportedly threatened to exclude Merrill Lynch from a coming $750 million stock offering in retaliation. The replacement analyst is reported to have then upgraded his report on Enron's stock rating. Merrill Lynch maintains that it did nothing improper in its Enron business dealings. However, the firm agreed to pay $80 million to settle SEC charges related to the questionable Nigerian barge deal.

Arthur Andersen LLP

"Potential investors used Andersen's reports to judge Enron's financial soundness and future potential"

In its role as Enron's auditor, Arthur Andersen was responsible for ensuring the accuracy of Enron's financial statements and internal bookkeeping. Potential investors used Andersen's reports to judge Enron's financial soundness and future potential before they decided whether to invest, and current investors used those reports to decide if their funds should remain invested there. These investors expected that Andersen's certifications of accuracy and application of proper accounting procedures would be independent and without any conflict of interest. If Andersen's reports were in error, investors could be seriously misled.

However, Andersen's independence was called into question. The accounting firm was a major business partner of Enron, with more than one hundred employees dedicated to its account, and it sold about $50 million a year in consulting services to Enron. Some Andersen executives even accepted jobs with the energy trader. In March 2002, Andersen was found guilty of obstruction of justice for destroying Enron-related auditing documents during an SEC investigation of Enron. As a result, Anderson has been barred from performing audits.

It is still not clear why Andersen auditors failed to ask Enron to better explain its complex partnerships before certifying Enron's financial statements. Some observers believe that the large consulting fees Enron paid Andersen unduly influenced the company's decisions. An Andersen spokesperson said that the firm looked hard at all available information from Enron at the time; but shortly after speaking to Enron CEO Ken Lay, Vice President Sherron Watkins took her concerns to an Andersen audit partner, who reportedly conveyed her questions to senior Andersen management responsible for the Enron account. It is not clear what action, if any, Andersen took.

THE FALLOUT

Enron's demise caused tens of billions of dollars of investor losses, triggered a collapse of electricity-trading markets, and ushered in an era of accounting scandals that precipitated a global loss of confidence in corporate integrity. Now companies must defend legitimate but complicated financing arrangements. Legislation like Sarbanes-Oxley, passed in the wake of Enron, has placed more restriction on companies. On a more personal level, four thousand former Enron employees had to struggle to find jobs, and many retirees lost their entire retirement portfolios. One senior Enron executive committed suicide.

In 2003 Enron announced its intention to restructure and pay off its creditors. It was estimated that most creditors would receive between 14.4 cents and 18.3 cents for each dollar they were owed—more than most expected. Under the plan, creditors would receive about two-thirds of the amount in cash and the rest in equity in three new companies, none of which would carry the tainted Enron name. The three companies were CrossCountry Energy Corporation, Prisma Energy International Inc., and Portland General Electric.

CrossCountry Energy Corporation would retain Enron's interests in three North American natural gas pipelines. In 2004, Enron announced an agreement to sell CrossCountry Energy to CCE Holdings LLC for $2.45 billion. The money was to be used for debt repayment, and represented a substantial increase over a previous offer. Similarly, Prisma Energy International Inc., which took over Enron's nineteen international power and pipeline holdings, was sold to Ashmore Energy International Limited. The proceeds from the sale were given out to creditors through cash distributions. The third company, Portland General Electric (PGE), Oregon's largest utility, emerged from bankruptcy as an independent company through a private stock offering to Enron creditors.

All remaining assets not related to CrossCountry, Prisma, or Portland General were liquidated. Although Enron emerged from Chapter 11 bankruptcy protection in 2004, the company was wound down once the recovery plan was carried out. That year all of Enron's outstanding common stock and preferred stocks were cancelled. Each record holder of Enron Corporation stock on the day it was cancelled was allocated an uncertified, nontransferable interest in one of two trusts that held new shares of the Enron Corporation.

The Enron Creditors Recovery Corporation was formed to help Enron creditors. It states that its mission is "to reorganize and liquidate the remaining operations and assets of Enron following one of the largest and most complex bankruptcies in U.S. history." In the very unlikely event that the value of Enron's assets would exceed the amount of its allowed claims, distributions were to be made to the holders of these trust interests in the same order of priority of the stock they previously held. According to the Enron Creditors Recovery Corporation, over $128 million was distributed to creditors, which brings the total amount of recovery to $21.549 billion.

In addition to trying to pay back its jilted shareholders, Enron also had to pay California for fraudulent activities it committed against the state's citizens. The company was investigated in California for allegedly colluding with at least two other power sellers in 2000 to obtain excess profits by submitting false information to the manager of California's electricity grid. In 2005, Enron agreed to pay California $47 million for taking advantage of California consumers during an energy shortage. This serves to prove further that Enron's corporate culture was inherently flawed, with the company promoting profits at the expense of stakeholders.

LEARNING FROM ENRON

Enron was clearly the biggest business scandal of its time. Officials swore that such a disaster would never occur again and passed legislation like the Sarbanes-Oxley Act to prevent future business fraud. Yet, did the business world truly learn its lesson from Enron's collapse? The answer would be a resounding no, as the 2008–2009 financial crisis attested. The crisis made the Enron scandal look small in comparison and was the worst financial disaster since the Great Depression. Like the Enron scandal, the financial crisis largely stemmed from corporate misconduct. Corporations rewarded performance at all costs, even when employees cut ethical corners to achieve high performance. In the mortgage market, companies like Countrywide rewarded their sales force for making risky subprime loans, going so far as to approve loans that they know contained falsified information in order to make a quick profit. Other companies traded in risky financial instruments like credit default swaps (CDSs) when they knew that buyers did not have a clear understanding of the risks of such instruments. Although they promised to insure against default of these instruments, the companies did not have enough funds to cover the losses after the housing bubble burst.

The bankruptcy of Enron was nothing compared to how many companies and individuals were negatively affected by the financial crisis. The resulting crisis affected the entire world, bankrupting such established companies as Lehman Brothers and requiring government intervention in the amount of nearly $1 trillion in TARP (Troubled Asset Referendum Program) funds to salvage numerous financial firms. The U.S. government put forth $180 billion to rescue American International Group Inc. (AIG), and both Fannie Mae and Freddie Mac were placed in conservatorship of the Federal Housing Finance Industry. Merrill Lynch, who faced scrutiny during the Enron scandal, could not survive the crisis and was forced to sell to Bank of America. The 150-year-old company Lehman Brothers, which had survived the Great Depression, was forced to file for bankruptcy with $613 billion in debt. The losses from the crisis total in the hundreds of billions and probably will not be known for years to come.

> *“Like the Enron scandal, the financial crisis largely stemmed from corporate misconduct.”*

The misconduct of corporate officers like Ken Lay and Jeffrey Skilling has not disappeared in the ensuing years. Many of the failures during the financial crisis stemmed from the same types of crimes as those in the Enron debacle, and in many ways the scandals were a lot worse. Much like Ken Lay, Richard Fuld of Lehman Brothers has become the epitome of corruption in the eyes of the public. He was forced to testify before Congress as to why he received hundreds of millions of dollars in salary, bonuses, and stock options since 2000. He was also called to explain his part in the bankruptcy and was forced to defend himself against accusations that he misled stockholders, just days before the company filed for bankruptcy, into thinking that the company was doing well. Additionally, the crimes of Ken Lay and Jeffrey Skilling are overshadowed by the likes of Bernie Madoff, who operated a $65 billion Ponzi scheme that cheated many thousands out of their savings.

It is an unfortunate fact that the enormity of the Enron scandal did not hinder this misconduct. Despite legislation that was passed as a result of the Enron scandal, corporate corruption continued on a massive scale. Like Lay, many Wall Street CEOs attempted to portray their companies as doing well even as they were floundering. They relied on risky financial instruments and in some cases false financial reporting to make a quick profit and inflate earnings.

However, Enron does not have to be reduced to a mere page in a history book. Although it did not prevent future business misconduct, Enron still has lessons to teach us. Along with the business scandals of the financial crisis, Enron demonstrates that, first, regulatory bodies must be improved so as to better detect corporate misconduct. For instance, the Securities and Exchange Commission has not done its job in terms of detecting business fraud, even when warning signs were readily available. Second, the warnings of concerned employees and "whistle-blowers" like Sherron Watkins should be taken more seriously (employees had been informing lawmakers for years that Bernie Madoff was operating a Ponzi scheme but to no avail). Third, CEOs must have a better understanding of the financial instruments their companies are using, as well as a thorough knowledge of the inner workings of their companies (something that Ken Lay claimed he did not have). These conditions are crucial to preventing similar business fraud in the future.

CONCLUSION

Enron shows how an aggressive corporate culture that rewards high performance and gets rid of the "weak links" can backfire. Enron's culture encouraged fierce competition, not only among employees from rival firms, but also among Enron employees themselves. Such behavior creates a culture where loyalty and ethics are cast aside in exchange for high performance. The arrogant tactics of Jeffrey Skilling and the seeming ignorance of Lay as to what was going on in his company further contributed to an unhealthy corporate culture that encouraged cutting corners and falsifying information to inflate earnings.

The allegations surrounding Merrill Lynch and Arthur Andersen's involvement in the debacle demonstrate that rarely does any scandal of such magnitude involve only one company. Whether a company or regulatory body participates directly in a scandal or whether it refuses to act by looking the other way, such actions or inactions can result in further perpetuation of fraud. This was emphasized even more during the 2008–2009 financial crisis, where the misconduct of several major companies and the failure of monitoring efforts by regulatory bodies contributed to the worst financial crisis since the Great Depression. With the country in the midst of widespread corporate corruption, the story of Enron is once again at the forefront of people's minds.

The Enron scandal has become legendary. A mere four years after the scandal, in 2005, a movie was made about the collapse of Enron called "Enron: The Smartest Guys in the Room." To this day, Jeffrey Skilling continues to maintain his innocence, appealing his case as far as the Supreme Court. Enron's auditor, Arthur Andersen, faced some forty shareholder lawsuits claiming damages of more than $32 billion. In 2009 it agreed to pay $16 million to Enron creditors. Enron itself faced many civil actions, and a number of Enron executives faced federal investigations, criminal actions, and civil lawsuits. As for the giant tilted "E" logo so proudly displayed outside of corporate headquarters, it was auctioned off for $44,000.

QUESTIONS

1. How did the corporate culture of Enron contribute to its bankruptcy?
2. Did Enron's bankers, auditors, and attorneys contribute to Enron's demise? If so, what was their contribution?

3. What role did the chief financial officer play in creating the problems that led to Enron's financial problems?

SOURCES

Aldrick, Philip, "NatWest Three Return to UK," *Telegraph.co.uk*, November 7, 2008, http://www.telegraph.co.uk/news/worldnews/northamerica/usa/3394139/NatWest-Three-return-to-UK.html (accessed September 7, 2009);Associated Press, "Merrill Lynch Settles an Enron Lawsuit," *New York Times,* July 7, 2006, http://www.nytimes.com/2006/07/07/business/07enron.html?scp=3&sq=%22merrill%20lynch%22%20enron&st=cse (accessed September 7, 2009); Associated Press, "2 Enron Traders Avoid Prison Sentences," *New York Times,* February 15, 2007, http://www.nytimes.com/2007/02/15/business/15enron.html?ex=1329195600&en=0f87e8ca83a557ed&ei=50 90&partner=rssuserland&emc=rss (accessed September 7, 2009); Barrionuevo, Alexei, "Fastow Gets His Moment in the Sun," November 10, 2006, http://www.nytimes.com/2006/11/10/business/10fastow.html (accessed September 7, 2009); Barrionuevo, Alexei, Jonathan Weil, and John R. Wilke, "Enron's Fastow Charged with Fraud," *Wall Street Journal,* October 3, 2002, pp. A3–A4; Berger, Eric, "Report Details Enron's Deception," *Houston Chronicle,* March 6, 2003, pp. 1B, 11B; "British Bankers Indicted in Enron Case; Three Men Accused of Siphoning Off $7.3 Million Owed to Their Employer," HighBeam Research, *The Washington Post*, September 13, 2002, http://www.highbeam.com/doc/1P2-369257.html (accessed September 7, 2009); Chen, Christine Y., "When Good Firms Get Bad Chi," *Fortune,* November 11, 2002, p. 56; Eichenwald, Kurt, "Enron Founder, Awaiting Prison, Dies in Colorado," *New York Times,* July 6, 2006, http://www.nytimes.com/2006/07/06/business/06enron.html (accessed September 7, 2009); Elkind, Peter, and Bethany McLean, "Feds Move Up Enron Food Chain," *Fortune,* December 30, 2002, pp. 43–44; "Enron Announces Completed Sale of Prisma Energy International Inc," Enron Creditors Recovery Corp., September 7, 2006, http://www.enron.com/index.php?option=com_content&task=view&id=94&Itemid=34 (accessed September 7, 2009); "Enron Settles California Price-Gouging Claim," CBCNews.ca, July 15, 2005, http://www.cbc.ca/money/story/2005/07/15/enron-gouge050715.html (accessed September 7, 2009); Enron website, http://www.enron.com/ (accessed September 7, 2009); "Ex-Enron CFO Fastow Indicted on 78 Counts," *Los Angeles Times*, November 1, 2002, http://www.msnbc.com/news/828217.asp (accessed September 7, 2009); "FAQs," Enron Creditors Recovery Corp., http://www.enron.com/index.php?option=com_content&task=view&id=17&Itemid=27 (accessed September 7, 2009); Farrell, Greg, "Former Enron CFO Charged," *USA Today,* October 3, 2002, p. B1; Farrell, Greg, Edward Iwata, and Thor Valdmanis, "Prosecutors Are Far from Finished," *USA Today,* October 3, 2002, pp. 1B–2B; Felsenthal, Mark, and Lillia Zuill, "AIG Gets $150 Billion Government Bailout; Posts Huge Losses," Reuters, November 10, 2008, http://www.reuters.com/article/topNews/idUSTRE4A92FM20081110?feedType=RSS&feedName=topNews (accessed September 7, 2009); Ferrell, O. C., "Ethics," *BizEd,* May/June 2002, pp. 43–45; Ferrell, O. C. and Linda, *Examining Systemic Issues That Created Enron and the Latest Global Financial Industry Crisis* (2009), white paper; Ferrell, O. C. and Linda, "Understanding the Importance of Business Ethics in the 2008–2009 Financial Crisis," in Ferrell, Fraedrich, Ferrell, *Business Ethics,* updated 7th ed. (Boston: Houghton Mifflin, 2009); Fick, Jeffrey A., "Report: Merrill Replaced Enron Analyst," *USA Today,* July 30, 2002, p. B1; "Finger-Pointing Starts as Congress Examines Enron's Fast Collapse," *Investor's Business Daily,* February 8, 2002, p. A1; Fonda, Daren, "Enron: Picking over the Carcass," *Fortune,* December 30, 2002–January 6, 2003, p. 56; France, Mike, "One Big Client, One Big Hassle," *BusinessWeek,* January 28, 2002, pp. 38–39; Gruley, Bryan, and Rebecca Smith, "Keys to Success Left Kenneth Lay Open to Disaster," *Wall Street Journal,* April 26, 2002, pp. A1, A5; Hamburger, Tom, "Enron CEO Declines to Testify at Hearing," *Wall Street Journal,* December 12, 2001, p. B2; Kahn, Jeremy, "The Chief Freaked Out Officer," *Fortune,* December 9, 2002, pp. 197–198, 202; Kranhold, Kathryn, and Rebecca Smith, "Two Other Firms in Enron Scheme, Documents Say," *Wall Street Journal,* May 9, 2002, pp. C1, C12; McLean, Bethany, "Why Enron Went Bust," *Fortune,* December 24, 2001, pp. 58, 60–62, 66, 68; Morse, Jodie, and Amanda Bower, "The Party

Crasher," *Fortune,* December 30, 2002–January 6, 2003, pp. 53–56; Needles, Belverd E., Jr., and Marian Powers, "Accounting for Enron," *Houghton Mifflin's Guide to the Enron Crisis* (Boston: Houghton Mifflin, 2003), pp. 3–6; Norris, Floyd, "Ruling Could Open Door to New Trial in Enron Case," *New York Times,* January 6, 2009, http://www.nytimes.com/2009/01/07/business/07enron.html?scp=3&sq=skilling&st=nyt (accessed September 7, 2009); Ross, Brian, and Alice Gomstyn, "Lehman Brothers Boss Defends $484 Million in Salary, Bonus," ABC News, October 6, 2008, http://www.abcnews.go.com/Blotter/Story?id=5965360&page=1 (accessed September 7, 2009); Schulman, Miriam, "Enron: What Ever Happened to Going Down with the Ship?" Markkula Center for Applied Ethics, www.scu.edu/ethics/publications/ ethicalperspectives/schulman0302.html (accessed September 7, 2009); Sigismond, William, "The Enron Case from a Legal Perspective," *Houghton Mifflin's Guide to Enron,* pp. 11–13; Smith, Rebecca, and Kathryn Kranhold, "Enron Knew Portfolio's Value," *Wall Street Journal,* May 6, 2002, pp. C1, C20; Smith, Rebecca, and Mitchell Pacelle, "Enron Plans Return to Its Roots," *Wall Street Journal,* May 2, 2002, p. A1; Sorkin, Andrew Ross, "Ex-Enron Chief Skilling Appeals to Supreme Court," DealBook Blog, *New York Times,* March 12, 2009, http://dealbook.blogs.nytimes.com/2009/05/12/former-enron-chief-skilling-appeals-to-supreme-court/?scp=1-b&sq=skilling&st=nyt (accessed September 7, 2009); "Times Topics: Enron," *New York Times,* http://topics.nytimes.com/top/news/business/companies/enron/index.html?scp=1-spot&sq=Enron&st=cse (accessed September 7, 2009); Ulick, Jake, "Enron: A Year Later," CNN/Money, December 2, 2002, http://money.cnn.com/2002/11/26/news/companies/enron_anniversary/index.htm (accessed September 7, 2009); Weber, Joseph, "Can Andersen Survive?" *BusinessWeek,* January 28, 2002, pp. 39–40; Weidlich, Thomas, "Arthur Andersen Settles Enron Suit for $16 Million," Bloomberg.com, April 28, 2009, http://www.bloomberg.com/apps/news?pid=20601072&sid=avopmnT7eWjs (accessed September 7, 2009); Winthrop Corporation, "Epigraph," *Houghton Mifflin's Guide,* p. 1; Zellner, Wendy, "A Hero—and a Smoking-Gun Letter," *Business Week,* January 28, 2002, pp. 34–35.

CASE 13

BP (Beyond Petroleum) Focuses on Sustainability

Daryl Benson

BP, formerly British Petroleum and the Anglo-Persian Oil Company, has experienced a lot of ups and downs over its hundred-year history—from nearly bankrupting its founder William D'Arcy to becoming one of the world's largest energy companies. BP has also experienced its fair share of controversies regarding business practices, environmental damage, and hazards to workers. It and all other large energy companies have come under fire for being responsible for the release of huge amounts of greenhouse gasses into the atmosphere. BP, however, has attempted to turn a page in its history book toward a more environmentally-friendly future. The company has invested in renewable energy and has thrown large amounts of support behind ethics and compliance initiatives, even writing an expansive code of conduct for its 92,000 employees.

This case provides an opportunity to observe the efforts of BP to improve its image and manage decisions related to ethics and social responsibility. Before delving into recent issues that BP has faced, a brief history of BP is given to provide some background. Although BP has sought to establish itself as an ethically responsible company, certain disasters resulting from company negligence are detailed in this analysis to show that it has often failed at this goal in the past. In recent years, BP has realized the need to become more environmentally-friendly, being the first oil company to recognize the presence of global warming and to launch initiatives into producing cleaner forms of energy. In so doing, the company also hopes to educate others about how they can personally reduce their impact on the environment in the hopes of repositioning itself as an environmentally-responsible company.

This case was developed under the direction of O.C. Ferrell and Jennifer Jackson, with the editorial assistance of Jennifer Sawayda, University of New Mexico. It was adapted from a case by Eve Sieber and Lameck Lukanga, University of New Mexico. This case is meant for classroom discussion, and is not meant to illustrate either effective or ineffective handling of an administrative, ethical, or legal decision by management. All sources used for this case were obtained through publicly available material.

THE 100-YEAR HISTORY OF BP

BP was founded more than a century ago by William D'Arcy, a wealthy British gentleman who had invested all his savings in the quest for oil in the Middle East. While experts and scientists had encouraged D'Arcy to pursue the venture, after more than six years of drilling, both his patience and finances were running low. Finally, in 1908, the drillers reached almost 1,200 feet and a fountain of oil spewed out. After long years filled with disappointment, pain, and despair, the Anglo-Persian Oil Company, what would become BP, was born. The company quickly opened trade on the stock market, and D'Arcy, who had lost nearly his entire net worth, became rich.

A naptha field in Iran, formerly known as Persia, located around 130 miles from the mouth of the Persian Gulf, was the first place where the Anglo-Persian Oil Company established a refinery. (Naptha refers to any sort of petroleum product, in this case, the Anglo-Persian Oil Company was pumping crude oil.) George Reynolds, D'Arcy's head manager for all the miners, quickly discovered that navigating this rugged land was not going to be such an easy task. Simply moving equipment to the site had been a monumental task that took months. To facilitate transportation of the oil, BP started building a pipeline through the area, and many of the necessary supplies had to be shipped from the United States. In a time before paved roads, everything had to be hauled through the sand using manpower and mules. Because of the difficult mountainous terrain, the pipeline project took over two years to complete. The huge scope of the undertaking drew workers seeking to help build the largest refinery in the world. They came from nearby Arab countries and from far away India and China. The medical director for the project would eventually found a hospital in Abadan, originally created to serve BP employees, that would go on to become one of the two most important medical centers in the entire region.

"The twentieth century saw enormous growth in the oil industry, along with massive power shifts in the Middle East."

By 1914, BP was about to go bankrupt again. The company had a lot of oil but a shortage of people to sell the oil to. In 1914 the automobile had not become a mass-market product yet, and companies in the New World and Europe had first-mover advantages in the industrial oils market. An even worse problem was the strong smell of Persian oil, which eliminated it from the heating and kerosene lamp markets.

Winston Churchill, who was at the time British First Lord of the Admiralty, changed all that. He felt that the British navy, which was the envy of the world, needed a reliable and dedicated source of oil. Oil executives had been courting the navy for some years, but until Churchill, commanders had been reluctant to abandon coal. Churchill was adamant that only Anglo-Persian, because it was a British-owned company, could adequately protect British interests. Parliament overwhelmingly agreed, and soon was a major shareholder in the oil company. Thus began the debate over the repercussions of involving politics in the oil industry, a debate that only became louder throughout World War II, the Persian Gulf War, and the Iraq War.

The twentieth century saw enormous growth in the oil industry, along with massive power shifts in the Middle East. In 1969, Muammar al-Gaddafi led a coup in Libya, promptly demanding a tax increase on all oil exports. Gaddafi eventually nationalized BP's share of an oil operation in Libya. This move led other oil-rich countries in the Middle East, including Iran, Saudi Arabia, Abu Dhabi, and Qatar, to eventually nationalize. The effect on BP was massive—between 1975 and 1983, the oil production in the Middle East fell from 140 million to 500,000 barrels.

In order to survive, BP had to find new places to dig for oil. The Forties Field off the coast of Scotland, capable of producing 400,000 barrels of crude oil a day, and Prudhoe Bay in Alaska, where BP had tapped its largest oil field yet in 1969, were the two great hopes for BP's future at this time. However, transportation of the oil was again a problem. The remoteness of BP's best sites would challenge not only BP's engineering capabilities, but more importantly its commitment to the environment. The Forties Field pipeline would eventually become the largest deepwater pipeline ever constructed, a project that required special attention due to the harsh weather. The Trans-Alaska pipeline system would become the largest civil engineering project in North America, measuring nearly 746 miles long. The company performed extensive research to identify any potential environmental risks, making sure the pipeline included long above-water stretches to ensure that the warm oil transporting through it wouldn't melt the permafrost. BP also had to take steps to ensure that habitat disruption would be minimal. The company tried to assure concerned stakeholders that the environment was a serious matter to them, which they would address with an intense level of focus and commitment.

However, BP's actions have not always coincided with its words. The company's promises to act as a responsible environmental steward would be questioned as parts of BP shares were sold off, as competition in the energy industry began to stiffen, and as mergers started to occur.

QUESTIONS ABOUT BP'S ETHICAL CONDUCT

As one probes below the surface of BP's public façade, one finds numerous instances of questionable behavior within this multinational oil company. These questionable deeds include fraud, environmental crimes, deaths, and the endangering of habitats.

In March 2005, a huge explosion occurred at a BP-owned oil refinery in Texas that killed 15 employees and injured another 170 people. The company was found guilty by the Southern District of Texas for a one-count felony for violating the Clean Air Act and was ordered to pay \$50 million in criminal fines. The explosion was the result of a leak of hydrocarbon liquid and vapor, which then ignited. This specific unit had to be shut down for nearly a month in order to be repaired. BP admitted that it had ignored several procedures required by the Clean Air Act for ensuring mechanical integrity and a safe startup between 1999 until the explosion in 2005. The BP case was the first prosecution under a section of the Clean Air Act, which was created to help prevent injuries from such accidental leaks of explosive substances.

The company was also charged with violating the Clean Water Act when Alaskan oil pipelines leaked crude oil into the tundra and a frozen lake. The fines resulting from this infraction included \$12 million in criminal fines, \$4 million in payments to the National Fish and Wildlife Foundation, and \$4 million in criminal restitution to the state of Alaska. The leaks occurred in March and August of 2006, after BP failed to respond to numerous red flags. One of these flags was the dangerous corrosion of the pipes that went unchecked for more than a decade before the Clean Water Act violation. A contract worker discovered the first pipeline leak in March of 2006. This leak resulted in more than 200,000 gallons of crude oil spilling onto the fragile tundra and a nearby frozen lake and was the largest spill to ever occur on the North Slope. A second 1,000-gallon leak occurred shortly after the first, in August 2006. Although it was small, the second leak led to the shutdown of oil production in the east side of Prudhoe Bay until BP could guarantee that the pipelines were fit for use.

Regular routine cleaning of the pipes is simple and would have prevented the 2006 oil leaks in Alaska. Nevertheless, in October 2007, BP recorded yet another spill near Prudhoe Bay. This time it was 2,000 gallons of toxic methanol, a deicing agent, that spilled onto the tundra and killed many plants and animals.

In the Northern District of Illinois, BP was charged with conspiring to violate the Commodity Exchange Act and also to commit mail fraud and wire fraud. The fraud involved purchasing more than the available supply of TET propane, and then selling it to other market participants at a price inflated well above market value. This sort of market manipulation is not tolerated in the United States, and BP was forced to pay large fines. The company had to pay $100 million in criminal penalties, $25 million to the U.S. Postal Inspection Consumer Fraud Fund, and a restitution of $53 million. Additionally, BP had to pay a civil penalty of $125 million to the Commodity Futures Trading Commission. Furthermore, four former employees were indicted in February 2004 for conspiring to manipulate the propane market at an artificially high price. The estimated loss to consumers who paid over market value exceeded $53 million dollars. The violation resulted in a 20-count indictment by a federal grand jury in Chicago.

The legal, environmental, and ethical transgressions on the part of BP demonstrate clearly that the company has a history of disregarding the well-being of stakeholders. "The actions against BP, along with the criminal charges against the four former BP traders, reflect our continued efforts to ensure that companies and individuals that do not follow the law will face consequences for their actions," said Assistant Attorney General Alice S. Fisher of the Criminal Division. While purporting to be an ethical company, concerned with stakeholder well-being, BP's violations tell a different story.

"BP was the first global energy firm to publicly announce its recognition of the problem of climate change."

BP REPAIRS ITS IMAGE

BP has begun to work to repair its tattered image. The twenty-first century found stakeholders more wary of companies, especially after decades of repeated violations and misconduct on the part of the oil industry. Oil leaks, toxic emissions, dead animals, refinery fires, wars in the Middle East, rising gas prices, pollution, and dwindling supplies all have combined to paint a very ugly picture of the oil industry as a whole. A central topic of the debate over the future of the world's energy supply focuses on global warming and greenhouse gas emissions.

One way BP worked to repair its damaged image was by changing its name from British Petroleum to simply BP, and increasing alternative energy offerings in its product mix. John Browne, BP group chief executive proclaimed, "we are all citizens of one world, and we must take shared responsibility for its future and for its sustainable development." BP was the first global energy firm to publicly announce its recognition of the problem of climate change. Browne has publicly discussed BP's involvement in finding new sources of energy, and has stated that he believes in balancing the needs of development and environmental protection. While its primary product is still petroleum, BP accepts that global warming is human-made, and it has begun to seek alternative revenue streams in wind farms and other lower-emissions energy sources. The company invests around $1.4 billion, or 5 percent of its total capital investment, in renewable energy like wind, solar power, and biofuels.

BP also has worked hard to overcome its negligent image by focusing renewed efforts on areas, such as Alaska, where the company has received a lot of bad press. Every winter when the Alaskan tundra is icy and frozen, a team of BP specialists heads for the remote areas of the Alaska North slope oilfields. The specialists' purpose is to excavate gravel from the pads on which drilling rigs once stood. They also remove drill cuttings and other waste left behind by the original exploration teams. Most of the excavated gravel can be reused immediately or treated on-site. The remainder of the gravel is either processed for future use or is ground down before it is injected back into the ground. The specialists aim to do as much as possible to return the sites to their original tundra state. This includes selective replanting and reseeding of the area. The specialists are guided by scientists and engineers from BP's remediation management team. They have already completed approximately 40 percent of a clean-up and restoration exercise agreed upon by BP and the state of Alaska. The Sag Delta 1 site on the Beaufort Sea Coast and the Kuparuk 24-12-12 site by the Kuparak River are two examples of the sixteen sites already sanitized. The specialists will return on a regular basis until their job is complete. The estimated cost of BP's future efforts will be close to $250,000,000. Even with all that effort, ultimately, the final restoration is best left to nature, with native tundra species soon returning to cover any remaining evidence of human presence.

BP WORKS TO IMPROVE SUSTAINABILITY

To adapt in a changing world, BP launched its Alternative Energy business in 2005. While still a small part of its overall company at $1.4 billion in investments, BP sees "going green" as an increasingly important part of its business, which it will expand as it becomes more profitable to do so.

Wind

BP has over 500 megawatts (MW) of installed capacity, with 432 MW in operation. Starting in 2008, BP began full-scale commercial operation in conjunction with wind farms across the country, including Cedar Creek in Colorado, a 274–wind turbine outfit. BP's installed wind capacity has the potential to supply power to 6 million homes.

Solar

In order to affordably expand its solar capacity, BP signed agreements with numerous solar panel producers in Asia. BP has installed only 4 MW of solar panels in the United States, those going to Wal-Mart stores in California. It does 70 percent of its solar business in Europe where demand is higher. BP also has developed two of the largest solar power plants in the world in Spain, projects that will supply energy to up to a million homes. BP also supports the Solar Cities concept, which has brought more access to solar power to seven cities across Australia.

As BP has continued its worldwide efforts to reduce greenhouse gas emissions, it has introduced a new solar-driven pump system at the Moxa Gas Field site in Wyoming. Two kinds of pumps are located at each of the 460 wells: One pumps methanol, while the other circulates heated glycol to prevent the freezing of equipment, which is a recurring problem in the harsh fields of Wyoming. BP has installed 230 solar-driven methanol pumps to help reduce the amount of natural gas needed to run the site. BP estimates that by using these new solar pumps, it has reduced Moxa's annual natural gas needs by over 48 million cubic feet, which amounts to around $200,000 in savings. The new pumps also create a safer work environment, as they reduce the risk of gas cloud related hazards for the employees. BP has plans to install 460 additional solar-driven glycol pumps. By replacing all of the pumps, BP has the potential to completely eliminate the use of natural gas at the Moxa site, making the pumping system virtually greenhouse gas free.

Biofuels

Biofuels have received a lot of negative press for their contributions to diminished food supplies and increasing food prices, and for causing deforestation in places like the Philippines and Brazil where it has become increasingly profitable to plant biofuel stock like sugar cane and palm. However, BP sees biofuels as a significant part of its energy portfolio for the next two decades, until better alternative energy sources are perfected.

BP became the single largest foreign stockholder in a Brazilian bioethanol company when it purchased a 50 percent stake in Tropical Energia S.A. The company's facility in Goias state, Brazil, has a capacity of 115 million gallons of sugarcane bioethanol. BP has also been working with Dupont to develop biobutanol, a biofuel with higher energy content than bioethanol.

BP's push in the alternative energy sector prompted the creation of a special purpose entity (SPE) with Verenium Corporation, a leader in the development of cellulosic ethanol, a fuel that is still in its infancy but that many hope can be the future of biofuels. Both partners hope to speed the development of cellulosic ethanol, and to one day make it commercially viable. Cellulosic ethanol is a renewable fuel produced from grasses and nonedible plant parts, such as sugarcane waste (called bagasse), rice straw, switchgrass, and wood chips. Although at this point it is much more difficult and energy-intensive to produce than corn or sugarcane ethanol, many believe that, as the technology improves, cellulosic ethanol will provide such benefits as greater per-acre yields and lower environmental impact, and it will not affect commodity or food prices, since it uses only waste products. If all goes as planned, BP's and Verenium's strategic partnership will help stimulate the development, production, and consumption of cellulosic ethanol over other types of liquid fuels.

> *"BP sees biofuels as a significant part of its energy portfolio for the next two decades"*

Carbon Sequestration and Storage

Although it is a tremendously expensive undertaking, many experts believe that one of the best ways to control greenhouse gas emissions is through carbon sequestration and storage (CCS). CCS involves capturing greenhouse gas emissions from smokestacks and other sources of the pollutant and pumping the gasses deep underground to empty oil or gas fields or aquifers. BP has been researching CCS since 2000, and opened the Salah Gas Field in Algeria for experimentation in 2004. BP captures and stores up to 1 million tons of carbon dioxide per year at Salah, which is equivalent to removing 250,000 cars from the road. BP hopes to do the same thing at Hydrogen Energy, its joint venture with Rio Tinto to develop low-carbon-emissions power plants for Abu Dhabi and California. While questions remain about the long-term effectiveness of CCS (no one knows for sure if the CO_2 stays underground, or whether it eventually leaks out), many energy companies such as BP see it as a promising technology.

Other Energy-Saving Measures

Beyond alternative energy sources, BP is also looking to save energy through better planning and implementation of its many operations around the world. The BP Zhuhai (BPZ) PTA plant is setting an example by using more efficient forms of energy. This development of more efficient, cleaner energy and the reduction of CO_2 emissions is an increasing priority in China. Many companies in China still use heavy oil and coal for fuel. For the past four years, BPZ has worked to set new standards and make a greater contribution in this area. A sequence of heat recovery projects has allowed the plant to optimize the use of steam as a way to reduce liquefied petroleum gas (LPG) consumption significantly. This has greatly saved energy and reduced emissions. Since 2005, BPZ has reduced its CO_2 emissions by 35 percent and has reduced the use of LPG by 48 percent. Additionally, by reducing fuel consumption, BPZ also has reduced the road safety and operational risks associated with delivery and unloading of LPG. BPZ is recognized locally and regionally for its promotion of environmental values. It has set an environmental standard for other companies to follow. The company also is a prime example of how being green can be cost-efficient. It has achieved a net savings for BP worth approximately $7.6 million a year.

BP is also working in Algeria to help sustainability. The Algerian business unit of BP is striving to lessen groundwater and soil impacts from its operations. The company is doing this by incorporating liability prevention processes early in the process, even into the planning stages of operations. However, in a desert area, where sandstorms and other disastrous weather patterns are common, planning ahead and anticipating problems is not easy to do. The BP Algeria team, working in conjunction with the state oil company Sonatrach and Norway's Statoil, has established two primary environmental objectives: (1) to impact the environment as minimally as possible, and (2) to take actions swiftly to correct any potential liabilities from earlier operations. BP's Remediation Management Liability Prevention team supports the Algeria team and Sonatrach in identifying potential causes of soil and groundwater problems incurred at any point during BP's operations. Together, they have been able to identify problems by conducting a series of site visits, doing risk-analysis work, administering prevention assessment tool surveys, and identifying improvement opportunities in the area of operations. All parties involved have been able to synthesize their findings into a long-term plan for the management and prevention of environmental liabilities in Algeria.

BP REACHES STAKEHOLDERS WITH ITS SUSTAINABILITY PROGRAMS

In addition to its Alternative Energy program, BP also has implemented environmental awareness programs in Britain to help stakeholders understand the impacts of global warming and the importance of sustainability issues. BP is trying to help the environment by making people more aware of their carbon footprint. BP Educational Service (BPES) initiated the distribution of the Carbon Footprint Toolkit. It is an award-winning program designed to help high school students understand the effects of climate change and their own carbon footprint. Developed in conjunction with teachers and BP's experts, the toolkit enables students to examine their school's carbon footprint and to help develop carbon reduction plans for their schools. The Carbon Footprint Toolkit was originally developed as a response to teachers' demands that came out of a series of "green" workshops that BP held. Available free of charge to all high school students and their teachers, the Carbon Footprint Toolkit has been a successful initiative for BP. Available only in Britain, the kit is available in 80 percent of all British high schools.

The toolkit received a prestigious award for e-learning at the International Visual Communications Association (IVCA) awards in 2007. Follow-up research on the tool has shown that the toolkit has greatly helped to increase the profile of BPES and also has raised the level of trust and recognition for BP's education initiatives. In addition, the proportion of teachers surveyed who judged their students to be environmentally aware increased from 62 percent to 89 percent after using BPES resources.

THE CODE OF CONDUCT

To help deal with BP's growing reputation for ethical misconduct, BP's Ethics and Compliance team organized the creation, publication, and distribution of a company code of conduct in 2005. The code was distributed to BP employees around the globe and is also publicly available online at the BP website. Given the multinational nature of the BP business, the code seeks to unite its diverse employees behind a set of universal standards of behavior. The cross-functional team that drafted the code of conduct faced many major challenges, like how to agree upon and communicate consistent standards for all BP employees regardless of location, culture, and language. They had to devise a plan to make the code a one-stop reference and guide to individual behavior at BP. It would have to cover everything from health and safety to financial integrity. The code of conduct was the largest mass communications exercise ever attempted in BP.

Work began in 2004 with a large-scale benchmarking exercise. The ethics and compliance team, with the help of many external specialists, studied, in great detail, the codes of fifty-two other companies. Using the information collected from preliminary research, a team of senior regional, functional, and business segment leaders worked to develop the content of the BP code. A preliminary version of the code was tested in global workshops involving more than 450 BP employees from all levels of the company.

All BP employees must read the code. To facilitate understanding, it is translated into languages as diverse as Mandarin, German, Azeri, and Arabic. The company also holds awareness meetings to help employees understand the contents of the code. Perhaps the most important role of the code is that it put in writing, for the first time, BP's ethical and legal expectations. It gives clear guidelines for individuals covering five key areas: health, safety, security, and the environment; employees; business partners; government and communities; and company assets and financial integrity. The code is entitled "Our Commitment to Integrity," making the ethical intent of this document clear from the first page.

CONCLUSION

From the beginning, BP proved that it was able to overcome significant obstacles. It went from near bankruptcy to being one of the largest energy companies worldwide. BP has experienced a range of ethical issues, the most well-known stemming from the company's own negligence and misconduct. Yet, although BP has had a spotty past when it comes to integrity, the company has worked hard to overcome its negative image. It is not only investing in cleaner energy but also is trying to repair its image by reducing its environmental impact and cleaning up areas after it has used them. Some question whether BP's new socially responsible initiatives are a public relations ploy or a genuine attempt toward change. However, there is no question that BP's emphasis on environmental responsibility is having a positive impact to some extent.

From publishing a thorough code of conduct to investing in more renewable energy to being the first major oil company to admit that global warming is a threat to our future, BP has sought to establish itself at the forefront of ethical energy companies. The company realizes that being environmentally sustainable and ethically responsible not only is the right thing to do, but is also profitable. Good publicity and stakeholder goodwill can be powerful forces in helping companies maintain a competitive edge and thrive.

QUESTIONS

1. Based on the history of the company, why did BP get involved in so much questionable conduct?
2. Analyze BP's efforts to improve sustainability. Do you think they are sufficient, or does the company need to do more?
3. Do you believe the BP code of conduct and ethics initiatives will prevent future misconduct?

SOURCES

BP Sustainability Review, 2008, http://www.bp.com/liveassets/bp_internet/globalbp/STAGING/global_assets/e_s_assets/e_s_assets_2008/downloads/bp_sustainability_review_2008.pdf (accessed April 30, 2009); "British Petroleum to Pay More than $370 Million in Environmental Crimes, Fraud Cases," PR Newswire, http://www.prnewswire.com/cgi-bin/stories.pl?ACCT=104&STORY=/www/story/10-25-2007/0004690834&EDATE= (accessed April 30, 2009); Browne, John, "Breaking Ranks," *Stanford Business*, 1997, http://www.gsb.stanford.edu/community/bmag/sbsm0997/feature_ranks.html (accessed May 7, 2009); Frey, Darcey, "How Green Is BP?" *New York Times*, December 8, 2002, http://www.nytimes.com/2002/12/08/magazine/08BP.html?scp=3&sq=how%20green%20is%20BP&st=cse (accessed April 30, 2009); Gold, Russell, "BP Jumps into Next-Generation Biofuels with Plans to Build Florida Refinery," *Wall Street Journal*, February 19, 2009, p. B1, http://online.wsj.com/article/SB123500538913818241.html# (accessed April 30, 2009); "The History of BP," BP International website, http://www.bp.com/sectiongenericarticle.do?categoryId=2010123&contentId=7027817 (accessed April 30, 2009); Judd, Amy, "British Petroleum Ordered to Pay $180 Million in Settlement Case," Now Public.com, February 19, 2009, http://www.nowpublic.com/environment/british-petroleum-ordered-pay-180-million-settlement-case (accessed March 18, 2009); Kaskey, Jack, "BP, Dow Chemical Post Losses as Recession Cuts Demand," Bloomberg, February 3, 2009, http://www.bloomberg.com/apps/news?pid=20601102&sid=a2e75bA8i47k&refer=uk (accessed March 13, 2009); Mouawad, Jad, "Oil Giants Loath to Follow Obama's Green Lead," *New York Times*, April 7, 2009, http://www.nytimes.com/2009/04/08/business/energy-environment/08greenoil.html?fta=y (accessed April 30, 2009); Palast, Greg, "British Petroleum's 'Smart Pig,'" Greg Palast: Journalism and Film, August 9, 2006, http://www.gregpalast.com/british-petroleums-smart-pig/ (accessed April 30, 2009.

CASE 14

Tyco International: Leadership Crisis

On September 12, 2002, national television showcased Tyco International's former chief executive officer (CEO) L. Dennis Kozlowski and former chief financial officer (CFO) Mark H. Swartz in handcuffs after being arrested and charged with misappropriating more than $170 million from the company. They were also accused of stealing more than $430 million through fraudulent sales of Tyco stock and concealing the information from shareholders. The two executives were charged with more than thirty counts of misconduct, including grand larceny, enterprise corruption, and falsifying business records. Another executive, former general counsel Mark A. Belnick, was charged with concealing $14 million in personal loans. Months after the initial arrests, charges and lawsuits were still being filed—making the Tyco scandal one of the most notorious of the early 2000s.

This case begins with a brief history of Tyco, followed by an explanation of Tyco CEO L. Dennis Kozlowki's rise to power. As Kozlowki rose to become the second-highest-paid CEO, some red flags pointed toward the impending disaster. Most notably, Kozlowski's aggressive approach to business, his lavish lifestyle, his clashes with the former, more conservative CEO, and his ousting of employees who were critical of his decisions all acted as indicators of Kozlowki's unethical behavior. This analysis also shows how a decentralized corporate structure can make it difficult, even for the board of directors, to effectively monitor a firm's dealings and finances. Kozlowski's fall and the repercussions of his dirty dealings (financial penalties and jail time) are also detailed. Finally, an explanation of how Tyco survived the scandal is provided, along with safeguards the company has put into place to ensure that similar misconduct does not occur in the future.

This case was developed under the direction of John Fraedrich and Rob Boostrom. It was edited by Jennifer Jackson, Jennifer Sawayda, and Alexi Sherrill. This case is meant for classroom discussion, and is not meant to illustrate either effective or ineffective handling of an administrative, ethical, or legal decision by management. All sources used for this case were obtained through publicly available material.

TYCO'S HISTORY

Founded in 1960 by Arthur J. Rosenberg, Tyco began as an investment and holding company focused on solid-state science and energy conversion. It developed the first laser with a sustained beam for use in medical procedures. Rosenberg later shifted his focus to the commercial sector. In 1964, Tyco became a publicly traded company. It also began a series of rapid acquisitions—sixteen companies by 1968. The expansion continued through 1982, as the company sought to fill gaps in its development and distribution networks. Between 1973 and 1982, the firm grew from $34 million to $500 million in consolidated sales. In 1982, Tyco was reorganized into three business segments: Fire Protection, Electronics, and Packaging.

By 1986, Tyco had returned to a growth-through-acquisitions model and had restructured the company into four core segments: Electrical and Electronic Components, Healthcare and Specialty Products, Fire and Security Services, and Flow Control, which Tyco maintained through the 1990s. During this time, the company changed its name to Tyco International, in order to signal its global presence to the financial community. By the early 2000s, the firm had acquired more than thirty major companies, including well-known firms such as ADT, Raychem, and the CIT Group.

THE RISE OF DENNIS KOZLOWSKI

In 1975, armed with a degree in accounting, Dennis Kozlowski went to work for Tyco, following brief stints at SCM Corporation and Nashua Corporation. He soon found a friend and mentor in then CEO Joseph Gaziano. Kozlowski was impressed by Gaziano's lavish lifestyle—company jets, extravagant vacations, company cars, and country club memberships. However, Gaziano's reign ended abruptly in 1982 when he died of cancer. Gaziano was replaced by John F. Fort III, who differed sharply in management style. Where Gaziano had been extravagant, Fort was analytical and thrifty. His goal was to increase profits for shareholders and cut the extravagant spending characterizing Gaziano's tenure, and Wall Street responded positively to Tyco's new direction.

Kozlowski, who had thrived under Gaziano, was forced to adapt to the abrupt change in leadership. Adept at crunching numbers, Kozlowski focused on helping to achieve Fort's vision of putting shareholders first. He soon gained Fort's attention, and was promoted to president of Grinnell Fire Protection Systems Company, Tyco's largest division. At Grinnell, Kozlowski reduced overhead, eliminated 98 percent of paperwork, and revised compensation programs. Although he slashed managers' salaries, he also designed a bonus compensation package that gave them greater control over possible earnings. He publicly recognized both high and low achievers at a yearly banquet, giving awards to the best and calling attention to the lowest-producing units. Perhaps most importantly, Kozlowski systematically worked to acquire Grinnell's competitors. A *BusinessWeek* article described him as a "corporate tough guy, respected and feared in roughly equal measure."

Over the next few years, Kozlowski continued to rise up Tyco's corporate ladder. He became the company's president and later CFO. However, his aggressive approach concerned Fort, who wanted to slow the rate of acquisitions in Kozlowski's division. Kozlowski's largest acquisition was Wormald International, a $360 million global fire-protection concern. Integrating Wormald proved problematic, and Fort was reportedly unhappy with such a large purchase. Fort and Kozlowski also disagreed over rapid changes made to Grinnell. Kozlowski responded by lobbying to convince Tyco's board of directors that problems with Wormald were a "bump in the road" and that the firm should continue its strategy of acquiring profitable companies that met guidelines. The board sided with Kozlowski. In 1992, Fort resigned as CEO and later as chair of the board, although he remained a member of Tyco's board of directors until 2003.

KOZLOWSKI'S TYCO EMPIRE

After Fort's departure, Dennis Kozlowski, then 46, found himself CEO of Tyco International. With a new lifestyle—parties and multiple homes in Boca Raton, Nantucket, Beaver Creek, and New York City—and an aggressive management style, he appeared to be following in the footsteps of his mentor, former CEO Joseph Gaziano.

Kozlowski knew Tyco from the bottom up, and stated that he was determined to make it the greatest company of the next century. Among other things, he recognized that one of Tyco's major shortcomings was its reliance on cyclical industries, which tend to be very sensitive to economic ups and downs. He resolved to expand Tyco into noncyclical industries through even more acquisitions, such as the Kendall Company, a manufacturer of medical supplies that had declared bankruptcy two years earlier. Kozlowski quickly revived the business and doubled Tyco's earnings. Kendall became the core of Kozlowski's new Tyco Healthcare Group, which grew to become the second-largest producer of medical devices behind Johnson & Johnson. The board rewarded Kozlowski's performance by increasing his salary to $2.1 million and giving him shares of the company's stock.

> *"one of Tyco's major shortcomings was its reliance on cyclical industries"*

In 1997, Kozlowski acquired ADT Security Services, a British-owned company located in Bermuda. By structuring the deal as a "reverse takeover," wherein a public company is acquired by a private company so as to avoid the lengthy process of going public, Tyco acquired a global presence as well as ADT's Bermuda registration. Tyco was then able to create a network of offshore subsidiaries to shelter its foreign earnings from U.S. taxation.

Kozlowski also restructured Tyco by handpicking a few trusted individuals and placing them in key positions. One of these individuals was Mark Swartz, who was promoted from director of Mergers and Acquisitions to CFO. Swartz, who had a strong financial background as a former auditor for Deloitte & Touche and a reputation for being more approachable than Kozlowski, was aware of Kozlowski's business practices. Kozlowski also recruited Mark Belnick, a former litigator at Paul, Weiss, Rifkind, Garrison & Wharton, to become Tyco's general counsel.

By this time, Tyco's corporate governance system was comprised of Kozlowski and the firm's board of directors—including Joshua Berman, a vice president of Tyco; Mark Swartz, CFO; Lord Michael Ashcroft, a British dignitary who joined with the ADT merger; Richard S. Bodman, a venture capitalist; Stephen W. Foss, CEO of a textile concern; and Frank E. Walsh Jr., director of the board—among other high-profile members. The majority of members had served for ten years or more, and they were familiar with Kozlowski's management style. As directors, they were responsible for protecting Tyco's shareholders through disclosure of questionable situations or issues that might seem unethical or inappropriate. Despite this, after the arrests of Kozlowski and Swartz, investigations uncovered the following troubling relationships among the board's members:

- Richard Bodman invested $5 million for Kozlowski in a private stock fund managed by Bodman.

- Frank E. Walsh, Jr. received $20 million for helping to arrange the acquisition of CIT Group without the other board members' knowledge.
- Walsh also held controlling interest in two firms that received more than $3.5 million for leasing an aircraft and providing pilot services to Tyco between 1996 and 2002.
- Stephen Foss received $751,101 for supplying a Cessna Citation aircraft and pilot services.
- Lord Michael Ashcroft used $2.5 million in Tyco funds to purchase a home.

With his handpicked board in place, Kozlowski opened a Manhattan office overlooking Central Park, although the move was not broadcast to the public. For appearances, the firm maintained its humble Exeter, New Hampshire, office at which Kozlowski preferred to be interviewed. According to *BusinessWeek* magazine, he boasted to a guest, "We don't believe in perks, not even executive parking spots." However, the unpublicized Manhattan office became the firm's unofficial headquarters, and Kozlowski furnished it with every imaginable luxury, using Tyco funds to purchase and decorate apartments for key executives and employees.

Meanwhile, Jeanne Terrile, an analyst from Merrill Lynch who had Tyco as a client, was not impressed with Kozlowski's activities and Tyco's performance. Her job at Merrill Lynch was to make recommendations to investors on whether to buy, hold, or sell specific stocks. After Terrile wrote a negative review of Tyco's rapid acquisitions and mergers and refused to upgrade Merrill's position on Tyco's stock, Kozlowski met with David Komansky, the CEO of Merrill Lynch. Although the subject of the meeting was never confirmed, shortly thereafter Terrile was replaced by Phua Young and Merrill's recommendation for Tyco was upgraded to "buy" from "accumulate." Merrill Lynch continued as one of Tyco's top underwriters as well as one of its primary advisers for mergers and acquisitions.

Between 1997 and 2001, Tyco's revenues climbed 48.7 percent annually and its pretax operating margins increased to 22.1 percent. The pace of mergers and acquisitions escalated, assisted by Mark Swartz, Tyco's CFO. In February 2002, Tyco announced that it had spent over $8 billion on more than seven hundred acquisitions in the last three years. Some of the merged companies were dissatisfied with the arrangement. Kozlowski forced acquired companies to scale back sharply, eliminating any segments that were not profitable. The toll on workers in these companies was enormous. Tyco shareholders and directors, however, were thrilled with the company's performance, increasing Kozlowski's salary from $8 million in 1997 to $170 million in 1999, making him the second-highest-paid CEO in the United States at the time.

Between 1997 and 2002, Kozlowski's charismatic leadership style combined with the firm's decentralized corporate structure meant that few people, including members of the board of directors, accurately understood the firm's activities and finances. Tyco was organized into four distinct divisions—fire protection (53 percent); valves, pipes, and other flow-control devices (23 percent); electrical and electronic components (13 percent); and packaging materials (11 percent)—and there was little interaction between them. Each division's president reported directly to Kozlowski, who in turn reported to the board.

Those who dared to suggest that there were red flags at Tyco were shot down, including Jeanne Terrile at Merrill Lynch and David W. Tice, a short seller who questioned whether Tyco's use of large reserves in connection with its acquisitions was obscuring its financial results. A nonpublic investigation by the Securities and Exchange Commission (SEC) resulted only in Tyco amending its earnings per share (up 2 cents per share for the last quarter of 1999, and down 2 cents for the first quarter of 2000).

THE FALL OF DENNIS KOZLOWSKI AND OTHERS

In early 2002, Kozlowski announced Tyco's split of its four divisions into independent, publicly traded companies: Security and Electronics, Healthcare, Fire Protection and Flow Control, and Financial Services. Kozlowski stated, "I am extremely proud of Tyco's performance. We have built a great portfolio of businesses and over the five years ended September 30, 2001, we have delivered earnings per share growth at a compounded annual rate of over 40 percent and industry-leading operating profit margins in each of our businesses. During this same period, we have increased annual free cash flow from $240 million in 1996 to $4.8 billion in fiscal 2001. Nonetheless, even with this performance, Tyco is trading at a 2002 P/E multiple of 12.0x, a discount of almost 50% to the S&P 500."

Soon after, everything began to crumble. The board of directors learned that Frank Walsh (one of its members) had received a $20 million commission for his part in securing and aiding the CIT merger, without the knowledge of the rest of the board. Walsh was fined and later resigned. Troubled by the notion that Kozlowski had made a major payment without informing them, board members launched an investigation into whether other board members had earned such commissions. The probe uncovered numerous expense abuses.

Also in 2002, the New York State Bank Department observed large sums of money moving in and out of Tyco's accounts. What made this unusual was that the funds were being transferred into Kozlowski's personal accounts. Authorities discovered that Kozlowski had sought to avoid around $1 million in New York state import taxes. After purchasing around $14 million in rare artwork, Kozlowski had the invoices shipped to New Hampshire, although the paintings were actually destined for his apartment in Manhattan. To assist in perpetrating the fraud, Kozlowski instructed the shipping company to send empty boxes to New Hampshire along with the invoices. Kozlowski was caught in the act and ended up facing jail time and having to pay out over $100 million in restitutions and back taxes. Learning that he was about to be indicted for tax evasion, Kozlowski resigned as CEO on June 2, 2002. On June 3, he was arrested, but the scandal had barely begun.

In September of that year, Dennis Kozlowski and Mark Swartz, who also had resigned, were indicted on thirty-eight felony counts for allegedly stealing $170 million from Tyco and fraudulently selling an additional $430 million in stock options. Among other allegations, Kozlowski was accused of taking $242 million from a program intended to help Tyco employees buy company stock. Together with former legal counsel Mark Belnick, the three faced criminal charges and a civil complaint from the SEC. Kozlowski was also accused of granting $106 million to various employees through "loan forgiveness" and relocation programs. Swartz was also charged with falsifying documents in this loan program in the amount of $14 million. Kozlowski and Swartz were sentenced from eight and one-third years to twenty-five years in prison with the possibility of reducing the minimum by one-sixth due to good behavior and enrollment in prison programs. Belnick was charged with larceny and attempting to steer a federal investigation, as well as taking more than $26 million from Tyco. In 2006, he agreed to pay $100,000 in penalties to the SEC.

In addition, several former board members have been cited for conflict of interest. Frank Walsh pleaded guilty and agreed to repay $20 million plus an additional $2 million in court costs. Jerry Boggess, the president of Tyco Fire and Security Division, was fired and accused of creating a number of "bookkeeping issues" negatively impacting earnings of shareholders.

Richard Scalzo, the PriceWaterhouse auditor who signed off on Tyco's 2002 audit, was fired. Tyco's stock plunged from $60 per share in January 2002 to $18 per share in December 2002, and investors lost millions of dollars. Many of the firm's 260,000 employees were also shareholders and watched their savings dwindle. Tyco's retirees found that their savings and retirement plans, which were tied up in company shares, plummeted with the company's stock price.

In 2005, Kozlowski and Swartz both were found guilty on twenty-two of twenty-three counts of grand larceny, conspiracy, and falsifying business records and violating business law. The judge ordered both to pay $134 million to Tyco. Kozlowski was also ordered to pay a $70 million fine and Swartz a $35 million fine. Jail time for both appears to be a little less than seven years in a state facility. Both have appealed their sentences, but their sentences have so far been upheld.

REBUILDING AN EMPIRE

After Kozlowski's resignation, Edward Breen replaced him as CEO. The company filed suit against Dennis Kozlowski and Mark Swartz for more than $100 million. The SEC allows companies to sue insiders who profited by buying and selling company stock within a six-month period. Tyco stated, "To hold him accountable for his misconduct, we seek not only full payment for the funds he misappropriated but also punitive damages for the serious harm he did to Tyco and its shareholders."

Breen launched a review of the company's accounting and corporate governance practices to determine whether any other fraud had occurred. Although the probe uncovered no additional fraud, the firm announced that it would restate its 2002 financial results by $382.2 million. In a regulatory filing, Tyco's new management declared that the firm's previous management had "engaged in a pattern of aggressive accounting which, even when in accordance with Generally Accepted Accounting Principles, was intended to increase reported earnings above what they would have been if more conservative accounting had been employed." Although Tyco's investigations located no further fraud, over the next six months the company repeatedly restated its financial results and took accounting charges totaling more than $2 billion.

"The SEC allows companies to sue insiders who profited by buying and selling company stock"

To restore investors' faith, Tyco's new management team reorganized the company and recovered some of the funds allegedly taken by Kozlowski. At its annual meeting, shareholders elected a new board of directors, voted to make future executive severance agreements subject to shareholder approval, and voted to require the board chair to be an independent person rather than a Tyco CEO.

In 2006, Breen announced Tyco's split into three entities: Tyco Healthcare ($10 billion, 40,000 employees), one of the world's leading diversified health-care companies; Tyco Electronics ($12 billion, 88,000 employees), the world's largest passive electronic components manufacturer; and a combination of Tyco Fire & Security and Engineered Products & Services (TFS/TEPS) ($18 billion, 118,000 employees), a global business with leading positions in residential and commercial security, fire protection, and industrial products and services. Tyco has survived doomsday predictions, bringing in over $40 billion in revenue before the split, and preserving employee jobs and pensions. Tyco has worked hard to overcome its negative image.

In 2002, Eric Pillmore was hired as Vice President of Corporate Governance. His job was to transform Tyco from a model of poor governance to an exemplary leader of corporate governance done right. Pillmore installed a corporate ethics program, replacing 90% of headquarters staff. During his five years at Tyco, he helped to implement a dramatic corporate culture turnaround. Today Tyco's ethics program stands as a role model for how one can clean up corporate misconduct.

Tyco's efforts to rebuild its image have met with some success. In 2008, Tyco International was named Corporate Citizen of the Year by Catholic Charities for the company's work in helping the homeless in Mercer County, New Jersey. Kozlowski and company, however, have not recovered as well. Kozlowski and Swartz continue to appeal their convictions, most recently to the U.S. Supreme Court, but so far their efforts have been rebuffed.

CONCLUSION

The Tyco scandal offers major lessons for the business world, particularly in areas of corporate conduct. Above all, the story of Dennis Kozlowski shows what happens when too much company power is put into the hands of an individual—it can lead to a decentralized corporate structure that makes it difficult to detect misconduct. Tyco's story also reveals the decreasing tolerance that today's government and investors have for misconduct in any form, as even members of Tyco's board of directors faced consequences for their unethical behavior.

Tyco's survival proves that some companies can survive major ethical scandals if they take the correct courses of action. In response to the scandal, Tyco took actions that went beyond the bare minimum of what was needed. Although an investigation did not uncover additional fraud, the company still restated its financial results by hundreds of millions of dollars. It took measures to restore shareholder confidence by reorganizing the company and implementing safeguards to ensure greater objectivity on the part of the board of directors. As a result of its quick actions, the company has recovered significantly and has been praised by the public.

While the fortunes of Tyco International seem to be on the rebound, former CEO Dennis Kozlowski's fate remains in the hands of the law. After his sentencing in 2005 to twenty-five years in jail for grand larceny, securities fraud, other crimes, and for stealing \$137 million in unauthorized bonuses as well as selling \$410 million in inflated stock, Kozlowski remains adamant about his innocence. In an interview with Morley Safer for *60 Minutes*, Kozlowski claimed that jealous jurors sentenced him out of spite, not because he had done anything wrong. Kozlowski to this day feels that he was wrongly sentenced and claims to have no regrets over his dishonest behavior.

On an ironic note, Kozlowski did have the foresight to recognize the impending subprime mortgage disaster that came to a head in 2008. Perhaps this just shows that it takes a criminal to know others.

QUESTIONS

1. What role did Tyco's corporate culture play in the scandal?
2. How did Dennis Kozlowski have the opportunity to steal \$137 million in unauthorized bonuses?

3. Why is Kozlowski, now a prisoner for a long time, unrepentant about his conduct as CEO of Tyco?

SOURCES

Bandler, James, and Jerry Guidera, "Tyco Ex-CEO's Party for Wife Cost $2.1 Million, but Had Elvis," *Wall Street Journal,* September 17, 2002, p. A1; Bianco, Anthony, William Symonds, and Nanette Byrnes, "The Rise and Fall of Dennis Kozlowski," *BusinessWeek,* December 23, 2002, pp. 64–77; Bray, Chad, "Ex-Execs Kozlowski, Swartz Appeal to US Supreme Court," *Wall Street Journal,* April 14, 2009, http://online.wsj.com/article/BT-CO-20090414-711331.html (accessed April 28, 2009); Cohen, Laurie P., "Tyco Ex-Counsel Claims Auditors Knew of Loans," *Wall Street Journal,* October 22, 2002, http://online.wsj.com/article/SB103524176089398951.html?mod=googlewsj (accessed September 10, 2009); Cohen, Laurie P., and John Hechinger, "Tyco Suits Say Clandestine Pacts Led to Payments," *Wall Street Journal,* June 18, 2002, pp. A3, A10; Cohen, Laurie P., and Mark Maremont, "Tyco Ex-Director Faces Possible Criminal Charges," *Wall Street Journal,* September 9, 2002, pp. A3, A11; Cohen, Laurie P., and Mark Maremont, "Tyco Relocations to Florida Are Probed," *Wall Street Journal,* June 10, 2002, pp. A3, A6; "Corporate Scandals: Tyco, International," MSNBC, www.msnbc.com/news/corpscandal_front.asp?odm=C2ORB (accessed September 10, 2009); "Former Counsel for Tyco to Settle S.E.C. Charges," Reuters, May 3, 2006, via http://www.nytimes.com/2006/05/03/business/03tyco.html?_r=1&adxnnl=1&oref=slogin&adxnnlx=1214041391-Z+lUjZjI6TaIADXDvRXb8w (accessed September 10, 2009); Gaspaino, Charles, "Merrill Replaced Its Tyco Analyst After Meeting," *Wall Street Journal,* September 17, 2002, pp. C1, C13; Guidera, Jerry, "Veteran Tyco Director Steps Down," *Wall Street Journal,* November 12, 2002, p. A8; "History," Tyco International, http://tyco.com/wps/wcm/connect/tyco+who+we+are/Who+We+Are/History (accessed September 10, 2009); Lavelle, Louis, "Rebuilding Trust in Tyco," *BusinessWeek,* November 25, 2002, pp. 94–96; Lublin, Loann, and Jerry Guidera, "Tyco Board Criticized on Kozlowski," *Wall Street Journal,* June 7, 2002, p. A5; Maremont, Mark, "Tyco May Report $1.2 Billion in Fresh Accounting Problems," *Wall Street Journal,* April 30, 2003, http://online.wsj.com/article/SB105166908562976400.html?mod=googlewsj (accessed September 10, 2009); Maremont, Mark, "Tyco Seeks Hefty Repayments from Former Financial Officer," *Wall Street Journal,* October 7, 2002, p. A6; Maremont, Mark, and John Hechinger, "Tyco's Ex-CEO Invested in Fund Run by Director," *Wall Street Journal,* October 23, 2002, http://online.wsj.com/article/SB1035329530787240111.html?mod=googlewsj (accessed October 19, 2009); McCoy, Kevin, "Directors' Firms on Payroll at Tyco," *USA Today,* September 18, 2002, p. 1B; McCoy, Kevin, "Investigators Scrutinize $20M Tyco Fee," *USA Today,* September 16, 2002, p. 1B; McCoy, Kevin, "Tyco Acknowledges More Accounting Tricks," *USA Today,* December 31, 2002, p. 3B; Panter, Gary, "The Big Kozlowski," *Fortune,* November 18, 2002, pp. 123–126; "Prisoner Dennis Kozlowski: Still Unrepentant," *Sox First,* February 5, 2008, www.soxfirst.com/50226711/prisoner_dennis_kozlowski_still_unrepentant.php (accessed May 5, 2009); White, Ben, "Ex-Tyco Officers Sentenced: Pair Get Up to 25 Years in Prison, Must Pay Almost $240 Million," *Washington Post,* September 20, 2005, p. D01.

CASE 15

Mattel Responds to Ethical Challenges

Mattel, Inc. is a world leader in the design, manufacture, and marketing of family products. Well-known for toy brands such as Barbie, Fisher-Price, Disney, Hot Wheels, Matchbox, Tyco, Cabbage Patch Kids, and board games such as Scrabble, the company boasts nearly $6 billion in annual revenue. Headquartered in El Segundo, California, with offices in thirty-six countries, Mattel markets its products in more than one hundred and fifty nations.

HISTORY OF MATTEL, INC.

It all started in a California garage workshop when Ruth and Elliot Handler and Matt Matson founded Mattel in1945. The company started out making picture frames, but the founders soon recognized the profitability of the toy industry and switched their emphasis to toys. Mattel became a publicly owned company in 1960, with sales exceeding $100 million by 1965. Over the next forty years, Mattel went on to become the world's largest toy company in terms of revenue.

In spite of its overall success, Mattel has had its share of losses over its history. During the mid to late 1990s, Mattel lost millions to declining sales and bad business acquisitions. In January 1997, Jill Barad took over as Mattel's CEO. Barad's management style was characterized as strict and her tenure at the helm proved challenging for many employees. While Barad had been successful in building the Barbie brand to $2 billion by the end of the twentieth century, growth slowed in the early twenty-first. Declining sales at outlets such as Toys "R" Us marked the start of some difficulties for the retailer; Barad accepted responsibility for these problems and resigned in 2000.

Robert Eckert replaced Barad as CEO. Aiming to turn things around, Eckert sold unprofitable units and cut hundreds of jobs. In 2000, under Eckert, Mattel was granted

This case was prepared by Debbie Thorne, John Fraedrich, O.C. Ferrell, and Jennifer Jackson, with the editorial assistance of Jennifer Sawayda. This case is meant for classroom discussion, and is not meant to illustrate either effective or ineffective handling of an administrative, ethical, or legal decision by management. All sources used for this case were obtained through publicly available material and the Mattel website.

the highly sought-after licensing agreement for products related to the *Harry Potter* series of books and movies. The company continued to flourish and build its reputation, even earning the Corporate Responsibility Award from UNICEF in 2003. Mattel released its first Annual Corporate Responsibility Report the following year. By 2008 Mattel had fully realized a turnaround and was recognized as one of *Fortune* magazine's "100 Best Companies to Work For" and *Forbes* magazine's "100 Most Trustworthy U.S. Companies."

MATTEL'S CORE PRODUCTS

Barbie and American Girl

Among its many lines of popular toy products, Mattel is famous for owning top girls' brands. In 1959, Mattel introduced a product that would change its future forever: the Barbie doll. One of the founders, Ruth Handler, had noticed how her daughter loved playing with paper cutout dolls. She decided to create a doll based on an adult rather than on a baby. Barbie took off to become one of Mattel's critical product lines and the number-one girls' brand in the world. Since her introduction, Mattel has sold more than 1 billion Barbie dolls in more than 150 countries. The Barbie line today includes dolls, accessories, Barbie software, and a broad assortment of licensed products such as books, apparel, food, home furnishings, home electronics, and movies.

To supplement the Barbie line, in 1998 Mattel acquired a popular younger type of doll. Mattel announced it would pay $700 million to Pleasant Company for its high-end American Girl collection. American Girl dolls are sold with books about their lives, which take place during important periods of U.S. history. The American Girl brand includes several book series, accessories, clothing for dolls and girls, and a magazine that ranks in the top ten American children's magazines.

Hot Wheels

Hot Wheels roared into the toy world in 1968. More than forty years later, the brand is hotter than ever and includes high-end collectibles, NASCAR (National Association for Stock Car Auto Racing) and Formula One models for adults, high-performance cars, track sets, and play sets for children of all ages. The brand is connected with racing circuits worldwide. More than 15 million boys aged five to fifteen are avid collectors, each owning forty-one cars on average. Two Hot Wheels cars are sold every second of every day. The brand began with cars designed to run on a track and has evolved into a "lifestyle" brand with licensed Hot Wheels shirts, caps, lunch boxes, backpacks, and more. Together, Hot Wheels and Barbie generate 45 percent of Mattel's revenue and 65 percent of its profits.

Cabbage Patch Kids

Since the introduction of mass-produced Cabbage Patch Kids in 1982, more than 90 million dolls have been sold worldwide. In 1994, Mattel took over selling these beloved dolls after purchasing production rights from Hasbro. In 1996, Mattel created a new line of Cabbage Patch doll, called Snacktime Kids, which was expected to meet with immense success. The Snacktime Kids had moving mouths that enabled children to "feed" them plastic snacks. However, the product backfired. The toy had no on/off switch and reports of children getting their fingers or hair caught in the dolls' mouths surfaced during the

1996 holiday season. Mattel voluntarily pulled the dolls from store shelves by January 1997, and offered consumers a cash refund of $40 on returned dolls. The U.S. Consumer Product Safety Commission applauded Mattel's handling of the Snacktime Kids situation. Mattel effectively managed a situation that could easily have created bad publicity or a crisis situation. Mattel stopped producing Cabbage Patch Kids in 2000.

MATTEL'S COMMITMENT TO ETHICS AND SOCIAL RESPONSIBILITY

Mattel's core products and business environment create many ethical issues. Because the company's products are designed primarily for children, the company must be sensitive to social concerns about children's rights. It must also be aware that the international environment often complicates business transactions. Different legal systems and cultural expectations about business can create ethical conflicts. Finally, the use of technology may present ethical dilemmas, especially regarding consumer privacy. Mattel has recognized these potential issues and taken steps to strengthen its commitment to business ethics. The company also purports to take a stand on social responsibility, encouraging its employees and consumers to do the same.

> ***"Different legal systems and cultural expectations about business can create ethical conflicts."***

Privacy and Marketing Technology

One issue Mattel has tried to address repeatedly is that of privacy and online technology. Advances in technology have created special marketing issues for Mattel. The company recognizes that, because it markets to children, it must communicate with parents regarding its corporate marketing strategy. Mattel has taken steps to inform both children and adults about its philosophy regarding Internet-based marketing tools, such as the Hot Wheels website. This website contains a lengthy online privacy policy, part of which reads:

> *Mattel, Inc. and its family of companies ("Mattel") are committed to protecting your online privacy when visiting a website operated by us. We do not collect and keep any personal information online from you unless you volunteer it and you are 13 or older. We also do not collect and keep personal information online from children under the age of 13 without consent of a parent or legal guardian, except in limited circumstances authorized by law and described in this policy. (Mattel, Inc., Online Privacy Policy, http://www.hotwheels.com/policy.asp (accessed March 8, 2009)*

By assuring parents that their children's privacy will be respected, Mattel demonstrates that it takes its responsibility of marketing to children seriously.

Expectations of Mattel's Business Partners

Mattel, Inc. is also making a serious commitment to business ethics in its dealings with other industries. In late 1997, the company completed its first full ethics audit of each of its manufacturing sites as well as the facilities of its primary contractors. The audit revealed that the company was not using any child labor or forced labor, a problem plaguing other overseas manufacturers. However, several contractors were found to be in violation of

Mattel's safety and human rights standards and were asked to change their operations or risk losing Mattel's business. The company now conducts an independent monitoring council audit in manufacturing facilities every three years.

In an effort to continue its strong record on human rights and related ethical standards, Mattel instituted a code of conduct entitled Global Manufacturing Principles in 1997. One of these principles requires all Mattel-owned and contracted manufacturing facilities to favor business partners committed to ethical standards comparable with those of Mattel. Other principles relate to safety, wages, and adherence to local laws. Mattel's audits and subsequent code of conduct were designed as preventative, not punitive, measures. The company is dedicated to creating and encouraging responsible business practices throughout the world.

Mattel also claims to be committed to its workforce. As one company consultant noted, "Mattel is committed to improving the skill level of workers... [so that they] will experience increased opportunities and productivity." This statement reflects Mattel's concern for relationships between and with employees and business partners. The company's code is a signal to potential partners, customers, and other stakeholders that Mattel has made a commitment to fostering and upholding ethical values.

Legal and Ethical Business Practices

Mattel prefers to partner with businesses similarly committed to high ethical standards. At a minimum, partners must comply with the local and national laws of the countries in which they operate. In addition, all partners must respect the intellectual property of the company, and support Mattel in the protection of assets such as patents, trademarks, or copyrights. They are also responsible for product safety and quality, protecting the environment, customs, evaluation and monitoring, and compliance.

Mattel's business partners must have high standards for product safety and quality, adhering to practices that meet Mattel's safety and quality standards. In recent years, however, safety standards have been seriously violated, which will be discussed in more detail later. Also, because of the global nature of Mattel's business and its history of leadership in this area, the company insists that business partners strictly adhere to local and international customs laws. Partners must comply with all import and export regulations. To assist in compliance with standards, Mattel insists that all manufacturing facilities provide the following:

- Full access for on-site inspections by Mattel or parties designated by Mattel
- Full access to those records that will enable Mattel to determine compliance with its principles
- An annual statement of compliance with Mattel's Global Manufacturing Principles, signed by an officer of the manufacturer or manufacturing facility ("Mattel's Commitment to Ethics," *eBusiness Ethics*, http://www.e-businessethics.com/mattel9.htm (accessed May 8, 2009)

With the creation of the Mattel Independent Monitoring Council (MIMCO), Mattel became the first global consumer products company to apply such a system to facilities and core contractors worldwide. The company seeks to maintain an independent monitoring system that provides checks and balances to help ensure that standards are met.

If certain aspects of Mattel's manufacturing principles are not being met, Mattel will try to work with contractors to help them fix their problems. New partners will not be hired unless they meet Mattel's standards. If corrective action is advised but not taken, Mattel will terminate its relationship with the partner in question. Overall, Mattel is committed to both business success and ethical standards, and it recognizes that it is part of a continuous improvement process.

Mattel Children's Foundation

Mattel takes its social responsibilities very seriously. Through the Mattel Children's Foundation, established in 1978, the company promotes philanthropy and community involvement among its employees and makes charitable investments to better the lives of children in need. Funding priorities have included building a new Mattel Children's Hospital at the University of California, Los Angeles (UCLA), sustaining the Mattel Family Learning Program, and promoting giving among Mattel employees.

In November 1998, Mattel donated a multiyear, $25 million gift to the UCLA Children's Hospital. The gift was meant to support the existing hospital and provide for a new state-of-the-art facility. In honor of Mattel's donation, the hospital was renamed Mattel Children's Hospital at UCLA.

The Mattel Family Learning Program utilizes computer learning labs as a way to advance children's basic skills. Now numbering more than eighty throughout the United States, Hong Kong, Canada, and Mexico, the labs offer software and technology designed to help children with special needs or limited English proficiency.

> *Mattel does not tolerate discrimination.*

Mattel employees are also encouraged to participate in a wide range of volunteer activities, including Team Mattel, a program that allows Mattel employees to partner with local Special Olympics programs. Employees serving on boards of local nonprofit organizations or helping with ongoing nonprofit programs are eligible to apply for volunteer grants supporting their organizations. Mattel employees contributing to higher education or to nonprofit organizations serving children in need are eligible to have their personal donations matched dollar for dollar up to $5,000 annually.

International Manufacturing Principles

As a U.S.-based multinational company owning and operating facilities and contracting worldwide, Mattel's Global Manufacturing Principles reflects the company's needs to both conduct manufacturing responsibly and respect the cultural, ethical, and philosophical differences of the countries in which it operates. These principles set uniform standards across Mattel manufacturers and attempt to benefit both employees and consumers.

Mattel's principles cover issues such as wages, work hours, child labor, forced labor, discrimination, freedom of association, and working conditions. Workers must be paid at least minimum wage or a wage that meets local industry standards (whichever is greater). No one under the age of sixteen or the local age limit (whichever is higher) may be allowed to work for Mattel facilities. Mattel refuses to work with facilities that use forced or prison labor, or to use these types of labor itself. Additionally, Mattel does not tolerate discrimination. The company states that an individual should be hired and employed based on his or her ability—not on individual characteristics or beliefs. Mattel recognizes all employees' rights to choose to affiliate with organizations or associations without interference. Regarding working conditions, all Mattel facilities and its business partners must provide safe working environments for their employees.

OVERSEAS MANUFACTURING

Despite Mattel's best efforts, not all overseas manufacturers have faithfully adhered to its high standards. Mattel has come under scrutiny over its sale of unsafe products. In 2007, Mattel announced recalls of toys containing lead paint. The problem surfaced when a European retailer discovered lead paint on a toy. An estimated 10 million individual toys produced in China were affected. Mattel quickly stopped production at Lee Der, the company officially producing the recalled toys, after it was discovered that Lee Der had purchased lead-tainted paint to be used on the toys. Mattel blamed the fiasco on the manufacturers' desire to save money in the face of increasing prices. "In the last three or five years, you've seen labor prices more than double, raw material prices double or triple," CEO Eckert said in an interview, "and I think that there's a lot of pressure on guys that are working at the margin to try to save money."

The situation began when Early Light Industrial Co., a subcontractor for Mattel owned by Hong Kong toy tycoon Choi Chee Ming, subcontracted the painting of parts of *Cars* toys to another China-based vendor. The vendor, named Hong Li Da, decided to source paint from a nonauthorized third-party supplier—a violation of Mattel's requirement to use paint supplied directly by Early Light. The products were found to contain "impermissible levels of lead."

When it was announced that another of Early Light's subcontractors, Lee Der Industrial Company, used the same lead paint found on *Cars* products, China immediately suspended the company's export license. Afterward, Mattel pinpointed three paint suppliers working for Lee Der—Dongxin, Zhongxin, and Mingdai. This paint was used by Lee Der to produce Mattel's line of Fisher-Price products. It is said that Lee Der purchased the paint from Mingdai due to an intimate friendship between the two company's owners. In the latter part of 2007, Zhang Shuhong, operator of Lee Der, hung himself after paying his 5,000 staff members.

That same year, Mattel was forced to recall several more toys because of powerful magnets in the toys that could come loose and pose a choking hazard for young children. If more than one magnet is swallowed, the magnets can attract each other inside the child's stomach, causing potentially fatal complications. Over 21 million Mattel toys were recalled in all, and parents filed several lawsuits claiming that these Mattel products harmed their children.

At first, Mattel blamed Chinese subcontractors for the huge toys recalls; but the company later accepted a portion of the blame for the trouble, while maintaining that Chinese manufacturers were largely at fault. The Chinese viewed the situation quite differently. As reported by the state-run Xinhua news agency, the spokesperson for China's state Administration of Quality Supervision and Inspection and Quarantine (AQSIQ) said, "Mattel should improve its product design and supervision over product quality. Chinese original equipment manufacturers were doing the job just as importers requested, and the toys conformed to the U.S. regulations and standards at the time of the production." Mattel also faced criticism from many of its consumers, who believed Mattel was denying culpability by placing much of the blame on China. Mattel was later awarded the 2007 "Bad Product" Award by Consumers International.

How did this crisis occur under the watch of a company praised for its ethics and high safety standards? Although Mattel had investigated its contractors, it did not audit the entire supply chain, including subcontractors. This oversight left room for these violations to occur. Mattel has moved to enforce a rule that subcontractors cannot hire suppliers two or three tiers down. In a statement, Mattel claimed to have spent more than 50,000 hours investigating its vendors and testing its toys. Mattel also has announced a three-point plan that aims to tighten Mattel's control of production, discover and prevent the unauthorized use of subcontractors, and test the products itself rather than depending on contractors.

THE CHINESE GOVERNMENT'S REACTION

Chinese officials eventually did admit the government's failure to properly protect the public. The Chinese government is now promising to tighten supervision of exported products, but effective supervision is challenging in such a large country that is so burdened with corruption. In 2008, the Chinese government launched a four-month-long nationwide product quality campaign, offering intensive training courses to domestic toy manufacturers to help them brush up on their knowledge of international product standards and safety awareness. As a result of the crackdown, the state AQSIQ announced that it had revoked the licenses of more than 600 Chinese toy makers. Also in 2008, the State Administration for Commerce and Industry (SACI) released a report claiming that 87.5 percent of China's newly manufactured toys met quality requirements. Although this represents an improvement, the temptation to cut corners remains strong in a country that uses price, not quality, as its main competitive advantage. Where there is demand, some people will always try to turn a quick profit.

MATTEL VERSUS FORMER EMPLOYEE AND MGA

Since 2004, Mattel has been embroiled in a bitter intellectual property rights battle with former employee Carter Bryant and MGA Entertainment Inc. over rights to MGA's popular Bratz dolls. Carter Bryant, an on-again/off-again Mattel employee, designed the Bratz dolls and pitched them to MGA. A few months after the pitch, Bryant left Mattel to work at MGA, which began producing Bratz in 2001. In 2002, Mattel launched an investigation into whether Bryant had designed the Bratz dolls while employed with Mattel. After two years of investigation, Mattel sued Bryant. A year later MGA fired off a suit of its own, claiming that Mattel was creating Barbies with looks similar to those of Bratz in an effort to eliminate the competition. Mattel answered by expanding its own suit to include MGA and its CEO, Isaac Larian.

For decades, Barbie had reigned supreme on the doll market. However, Bratz dolls have given Barbie a run for her money. In 2005, four years after the brand's debut, Bratz sales were at $2 billion. At the same time, Barbie was suffering from declining sales. In 2008 Barbie's gross sales fell by 6 percent, although Bratz was not immune to sluggish sales either once consumers began to cut back on their spending during the 2008–2009 recession.

Much evidence appears to point toward Bryant having conceived of Bratz dolls while at Mattel. Four years after the initial suit was filed, Bryant settled with Mattel under an undisclosed set of terms. However, although some decisions were made, the battle between Mattel and MGA has continued. In July 2008, a jury deemed MGA and its CEO liable for what it termed "intentional interference" regarding Bryant's contract with Mattel. In August 2008, Mattel received damages in the range of $100 million. Although Mattel first requested damages of $1.8 billion, the company was pleased with the principle behind the victory.

In December 2008, Mattel appeared to win another victory when a California judge banned MGA from issuing or selling any more Bratz dolls. In the worst-case scenario, MGA will have to discontinue its line of Bratz dolls completely or hand Bratz over to Mattel. Some analysts, however, think this outcome is unlikely. Instead, they expect Mattel to work out a deal with MGA in which MGA can continue to sell Bratz dolls as long as Mattel shares in some of the profits. MGA plans to appeal the court ruling. Whatever the outcome, Mattel has managed to gain some control over Barbie's stiffest competition.

MATTEL LOOKS TOWARD THE FUTURE

Like all major companies, Mattel has weathered its share of storms. In recent years, the company has faced a series of difficult and potentially crippling challenges. During the wave of toy recalls, some analysts suggested that the company's reputation was battered beyond repair. Mattel, however, has refused to go quietly. Although the company admits to poorly handling recent affairs, it is attempting to rectify its mistakes and to prevent future mistakes as well. The company appears to be dedicated to shoring up its ethical defenses to protect both itself and its customers.

With the economic future of the United States uncertain, Mattel may be in for slow growth for some time to come. What is certain is Mattel's commitment to rebuilding its reputation as an ethical company. Mattel is hard at work restoring goodwill and faith in its brands, even as it continues to be plagued with residual distrust over the lead paint scandal. Reputations are hard won and easily lost, but Mattel appears to be steadfast in its commitment to corporate ethics and delivering quality products.

QUESTIONS

1. Do manufacturers of products for children have special obligations to consumers and society? If so, what are these responsibilities?
2. How effective has Mattel been at encouraging ethical and legal conduct by its manufacturers? What changes and additions would you make to the company's Global Manufacturing Principles?
3. To what extent was Mattel responsible for issues related to its production of toys in China? How might Mattel have avoided these issues?

SOURCES

"About Us: Philanthropy," Mattel, http://www.mattel.com/about-us/philanthropy/ (accessed September 8, 2009); American Girl, www.americangirl.com (accessed September 8, 2009); Bannon, Lisa, and Carlta Vitzhum,

"One-Toy-Fits-All: How Industry Learned to Love the Global Kid," *Wall Street Journal,* April 29, 2003, http://online.wsj.com/article/SB1051565784397990000.html?mod=googlewsj (accessed September 10, 2009); "Barbie," Mattel, http://www.mattel.com/our-toys/barbie.aspx (accessed September 7, 2009); Barboza, David, "Scandal and Suicide in China: A Dark Side of Toys," Iht.Com, August 23, 2007, http://www.iht.com/articles/2007/08/23/business/23suicide.php?page=1 (accessed September 8, 2009); Barboza, David, and Louise Story, "Toymaking in China, Mattel's Way," *New York Times,* July 26, 2007, http://www.nytimes.com/2007/07/26/business/26toy.html?pagewanted=1&_r=3&hp (accessed September 8, 2009); "Bratz Loses Battle of the Dolls," BBC News, December 5, 2008, http://news.bbc.co.uk/2/hi/business/7767270.stm (accessed September 8, 2009); Casey, Nicholas, "Mattel to Get Up to $100 Million in Bratz Case," *Wall Street Journal,* August 27, 2008, http://online.wsj.com/article/SB121978263398273857-email.html (accessed September 8, 2009); Casey, Nicholas, "Mattel Prevails Over MGA in Bratz-Doll Trial," *Wall Street Journal,* July 18, 2008, pp. B-18, B-19; Chen, Shu-Ching, "A Blow to Hong Kong's Toy King," Forbes.com, August 15, 2007, http://www.forbes.com/2007/08/15/mattel-china-choi-face-markets-cx_jc_0815autofacescan01.html (accessed September 8, 2009); "Children's Foundation," Mattel, http://www.mattel.com/about-us/philanthropy/childrenfoundation.aspx (accessed September 8, 2009); Duryea, Bill, "Barbie-holics: They're Devoted to the Doll," *St. Petersburg Times,* August 7, 1998; Hitti, Miranda, "9 Million Mattel Toys Recalled," WebMD, August 14, 2007, http://children.webmd.com/news/20070814/9_million_mattel_toys_recalled (accessed September 8, 2009); "Independent Monitoring Council Completes Audits of Mattel Manufacturing Facilities in Indonesia, Malaysia and Thailand," Mattel, press release, November 15, 2002, http://investor.shareholder.com/mattel/releasedetail.cfm?ReleaseID=95295 (accessed September 8, 2009); "International Bad Product Awards 2007," Consumers International, http://www.consumersinternational.org/Shared_ASP_Files/UploadedFiles/527739D3-1D7B-47AF-B85C-6FD25779149B_InternationalBadProductsAwards-pressbriefing.pdf (accessed September 8, 2009); "Investors and Media," Mattel, www.mattel.com/about_us/ (accessed September 8, 2009); Keating, Gina, "MGA 'Still Assessing' Impact of Bratz Ruling: CEO," Reuters, December 4, 2008, http://www.reuters.com/article/ousivMolt/idUSTRE4B405820081205 (accessed September 8, 2009); "Learning from Mattel," Tuck School of Business at Dartmouth, http://mba.tuck.dartmouth.edu/pdf/2002-1-0072.pdf (accessed September 8, 2009); "Mattel Annual Report 2008," http://www.shareholder.com/mattel/downloads/2007AR.pdf (accessed September 8, 2009); "Mattel Awarded $100M in Doll Lawsuit," *USA Today,* August 27, 2008, p. B-1; "Mattel CEO Jill Barad and a Toyshop That Doesn't Forget to Play," *New York Times,* October 11, 1998; "Mattel Children's Foundation Rewards Second Round of Domestic Grants to 34 Nonprofit Organizations," Mattel, December 7, 2005, http://investor.shareholder.com/mattel/releasedetail.cfm?ReleaseID=181309 (accessed September 8, 2009); "Mattel Continues to Lead the Toy Industry with Release of Its First Corporate Social Responsibility Report," October 12, 2004, http://www.shareholder.com/mattel/news/20041012-145079.cfm (accessed September 8, 2009); "Mattel History," Mattel, http://www.mattel.com/about-us/history/default.aspx (accessed September 8, 2009); Mattel, Hot Wheels website, www.hotwheels.com (accessed September 8, 2009); "Mattel, Inc., Launches Global Code of Conduct Intended to Improve Workplace, Workers' Standard of Living," *Canada NewsWire,* November 21, 1997; "Mattel, Inc., Online Privacy Policy," Mattel, www.hotwheels.com/policy.asp (accessed September 8, 2009); "Mattel Magnetic Toy Set Recall: Company Has History of Ignoring Product Safety Disclosure Laws. Did It Do So Again?," *Parker Waichman Alonso LLP,* September 4, 2007, http://www.yourlawyer.com/articles/read/13072 (accessed September 8, 2009); "Mattel Recalls Batman™ and One Piece™ Magnetic Action Figure Sets," CPSC, August 14, 2007, http://service.mattel.com/us/recall/J1944CPSC.pdf (accessed September 8, 2009); "Mattel to Sell Learning Company," Direct, October 2, 2000, http://directmag.com/news/marketing_mattel_sell_learning/ (accessed September 8, 2009); "Mattel and U.S. Consumer Product Safety Commission Announce Voluntary Refund Program for Cabbage Patch Kids Snacktime Kids Dolls," U.S. Consumer Product Safety Commission, Office of Information and Public Affairs, Release No. 97-055, January 6, 1997; Matzer, Marla, "Deals on Hot Wheels," *Los Angeles Times,* July 22, 1998; Olshin, Benjamin B., "China, Culture, and Product Recalls," S2R, August 20, 2007, http://www.s2r.biz/s2rpapers/papers-Chinese_Product.pdf (accessed September 8, 2009); "Product Recalls," Mattel Consumer Relations Answer Center, http://service.mattel.com/us/recall.asp (accessed September 8, 2009); Raisner, Jack A.,

"Using the 'Ethical Environment' Paradigm to Teach Business Ethics: The Case of the Maquiladoras," *Journal of Business Ethics,* 1997, http://www.springerlink.com/content/nv62636101163v07/fulltext.pdf (accessed May 10, 2008); Sellers, Patricia, "The 50 Most Powerful Women in American Business," *Fortune,* October 12, 1998; Spark, Laura S., "Chinese Product Scares Prompt US Fears," BBC News, July 10 2007, http://news.bbc.co.uk/2/hi/americas/6275758.stm (accessed September 8, 2009); "Third Toy Recall by Mattel in Five Weeks," *Business Standard,* September 6, 2006, http://www.business-standard.com/india/storypage.php?autono=297057 (accessed September 8, 2009); "Toymaker Mattel Bans Child Labor," *Denver Post,* November 21, 1998; "UCLA Children's Hospital Receives $25 Million Pledge from Mattel Inc.," November 12, 1998, http://investor.shareholder.com/mattel/releasedetail.cfm?ReleaseID=141937 (accessed September 8, 2009); "The United States Has Not Restricted Imports Under the China Safeguard," U.S. Government Accountability Office, September 2005, http://www.gao.gov/new.items/d051056.pdf (accessed September 8, 2009); White, Michael, "Barbie Will Lose Some Curves When Mattel Modernizes Icon," *Detroit News,* November 18, 1997.

CASE 16

PETCO Develops Successful Stakeholder Relationships

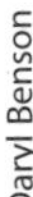

BACKGROUND AND HISTORY

PETCO Animal Supplies Inc., one of the nation's largest pet supply specialty retailers, boasts over 950 stores nationwide. Its pet-related products include food, supplies, grooming supplies, toys, novelty items, vitamins, small pets (excluding cats and dogs), and veterinary supplies. PETCO aims to offer its customers a complete assortment of pet-related products and services at competitive prices along with superior customer service on location and through its company website. While PETCO is one of the largest pet stores in the country today, it began as a much more specialized business. Walter Evan founded the company in 1965 under the name United Pharmacal Co (UPCO) as a mail-order veterinary-supply store. In 1976, UPCO opened its first bricks and mortar retail store in La Mesa, CA, selling quality pet and veterinary supplies at discounted prices directly to animal professionals and the public. In 1979, UPCO became PETCO. Today, the company's vision is to promote the well-being of companion animals and to support the human–animal bond. The company aims to provide a broad array of premium products, companion animals, and services along with a fun and exciting shopping experience with the help of its 22,000 employees.

PETCO stores offer a broad merchandise selection, convenient locations, and knowledgeable customer service. PETCO believes this combination makes its stores stand out and provides a competitive advantage. The principal store format is a 12,000- to 15,000-square-foot building, located near local neighborhood shopping destinations such as supermarkets, bookstores, coffee shops, and dry cleaners. Each store contains approximately 10,000 pet-related items and offers grooming, obedience training, veterinary services, and pet adoptions for cats and dogs in conjunction with local animal

This case was prepared by O. C. Ferrell, with the assistance of Jennifer Jackson and Jennifer Sawayda, The University of New Mexico. Melanie Drever and Alexi Sherrill assisted with the content and development of a previous edition of this case, which was prepared for classroom discussion rather than to illustrate either effective of ineffective handling of an administrative, ethical, or legal decision by management. All sources used for this case were obtained through publicly available material and the PETCO website.

welfare organizations. PETCO has long felt that its stores are well positioned, both in terms of product offerings and location, to benefit from favorable long-term demographic trends: a growing pet population and an increasing willingness to spend money on pets. However, the 2008–2009 recession has forced many pet owners to pare back their pet-related expenses. Nevertheless, PETCO's main competitor, PetSmart, has actually seen an increase in business since 2008, some of which appears to be at the expense of PETCO.

PETCO made history in 2006, becoming one of the largest public companies to be re-privatized. The company was purchased by private equity group Leonard Green & Partners and Texas Pacific Group for $1.8 billion. This is the second time these buyers have taken the firm private. Petco privatized in 2000, only to be taken public again in 2002. The company announced that the privatization would help it achieve its goals in an environment of tough competition and rising costs.

INDUSTRY

PETCO does business in a highly competitive industry where it is up against other major companies such as PetSmart and Wal-Mart. This competition may be categorized into three different segments: (1) supermarkets, warehouse clubs, and mass merchants; (2) specialty pet store chains; and (3) traditional pet stores and independent service providers. The principal competitive factors influencing PETCO are product selection and quality, convenient store locations, customer service, and price. PETCO believes it competes effectively within its various geographic areas. However, some of its competitors are much larger in terms of sales volume and have access to greater capital and management resources.

Over the past couple of decades, the pet food, supplies, and services industry has benefited from favorable demographic trends, including a steadily growing pet population. The U.S. pet population has now reached close to 400 million companion animals, with an estimated 63 percent of all U.S. households owning at least one pet and three-quarters of those households owning two or more pets. It is widely believed that the trend will continue, driven by an increasing number of children under 18 motivating the purchase of family pets and a growing number of empty nesters whose pets have become like replacement "children." Pet owners spend around $41.5 billion annually on their pets. Industry analysts have predicted that growth will continue into the future, despite the 2008–2009 economic recession. However, owners have become less likely to indulge in luxury items, focusing instead on high-quality necessities. This back-to-basics mentality has hurt PETCO and other major pet supply retailers, especially since discount giant Wal-Mart also offers pet products and services, sometimes at lower prices. Nevertheless, pet owners today are more likely to treat their pets as family members; this means that, even in tough economic times, many pet owners are prepared to spend considerable sums on pet products.

THE RISKS ASSOCIATED WITH THE PET INDUSTRY

Every industry carries with it unforeseen risks such as the chance that the public or a special interest group might uncover some questionable activity. Many times, critics and mass media, competitors, or simply skeptical stakeholders can blow problems out of proportion and can use the information to undermine a firm's reputation. Therefore, an ethical risk assessment is a critical component of most companies' ethics initiatives. A single negative incident can influence perceptions of a corporation's image, tarnishing its reputation and making recovery difficult. Particularly in the pet products industry, large groups such as PETA are always on the lookout for ethical fumbles.

Not all ethical concerns are of a company's making, and there are certainly those disgruntled antagonists who will distort the truth for their own self-interests. Since many people have strong emotional reactions to issues related to pets, assessing risk in this industry is especially important. For all companies selling pets, the question is not *if* there will be accusations, but rather can the companies—when accusations are made—respond rapidly enough to explain or correct questionable practices or to alter negative perceptions. The focus should be on a commitment to making appropriate ethical decisions and to constantly assessing and handling the risk of operating such a business.

PETCO claims to be committed to pets and to animals in general. However, that does not mean that PETCO has escaped criticism. Between 2000 and 2005, People for the Ethical Treatment of Animals (PETA) alleged cruelty and neglect to animals in PETCO's care and filed a complaint with the Securities and Exchange Commission (SEC). In particular, PETA was concerned about the sale of large birds; specifically, the fact that large birds were being denied the space to move around and to exercise. When kept as companions, large birds require a great deal of socialization and attention—at least eight hours a day—which PETCO was not providing them. Additionally, most parrots were dying from diseases such as obesity, high stress, and too little exercise. PETA alleged that about 70 percent of the parrots kept by PETCO were suffering from "miner's lung" disease (pneumoconiosis) due to living in dry, stuffy indoor environments.

> *"A single negative incident can influence perceptions of a corporation's image"*

On April 12, 2005, PETA and PETCO announced an agreement to advance animal welfare nationwide. PETA agreed to end its campaign against PETCO, including all references to "PETNO" and its "PETCOCruelty" website. PETCO agreed it would no longer sell large birds. It also agreed to continue working with shelter partners to assist in the adoption of homeless birds of all sizes as part of its "Think Adoption First" program. PETCO promised to make changes to be more sensitive to the needs of other animals as well. For example, the company began to separate rats and mice by gender to prevent breeding. Although PETCO was not required to respond to PETA, it did. This response to a special interest group indicates PETCO's desire to cooperate, to resolve issues and misunderstandings, and to improve operations.

In May 2004, PETCO paid nearly one million dollars to settle two precedent-setting California lawsuits involving the mistreatment of animals in PETCO stores located in five California counties. PETA had released undercover footage of North American Pet Distributor, Inc. (NAPD), supplier of at least 55 PETCO stores, engaging in extreme neglect. PETCO halted its business with NAPD immediately. This illustrates PETCO's ability to quickly respond to potentially negative situations that could adversely affect the company. Because of the risks involved with the pet industry, PETCO has a response system that rapidly deals with any supplier abuse of animals. When an organization such as PETCO has developed standards of conduct, it can more readily resolve any activities not in compliance with those standards.

Additional problems have plagued PETCO. In 2002, inspectors and customers found sick finches, a moldy dead turtle, dead birds, and a toad "cooked to death" at two San Francisco PETCO stores. The stores were also overcharging customers on sale items. In

2004 PETCO settled this case, agreeing to pay more than $900,000—most of which would be spent on new store scanners. PETCO also agreed to increase manager and employee training regarding the care of animals. The company again appeared willing to acknowledge and correct mistakes made by its employee, which is an inevitable issue in a corporation with 22,000 employees. PETCO's ability to expose and correct these issues indicates the effectiveness of its ethics program. Because many of its ethical dilemmas involved pets, PETCO sells only a limited number of small animals and no dogs and cats in an effort to reduce risk. Animal sales make up a small portion of the company's revenues, but avoiding risk in this way ensures PETCO keeps its customers and investors happy and also protects the animals in its care from abuse.

In 2007, the pet industry experienced a pet food recall crisis. The FDA discovered widespread melamine contamination in pet food imported from China, prompting large scale recalls. However, the problem was not discovered soon enough and many recalls were not issued in time to save a large number of pets from falling ill or dying. PETCO's response to these recalls, according to company press releases, was to promptly remove all tainted products from its shelves. The company continues to react quickly to any recall notices.

In the summer of 2008, the FDA asked U.S. Marshals to remove pet food products from a PETCO supply warehouse in Illinois due to unsanitary conditions. During two FDA inspections conducted in April and May, inspectors found the warehouse infested with rodents and birds. PETCO became a private company in 2006, and did not issue a response to this problem.

PETCO ETHICS PROGRAM

PETCO has a comprehensive code of ethics, emphasizing that animals always come first. It is critical for the success of PETCO that all employees adhere to the code and promote the health, well-being, and humane treatment of animals.

The code of ethics also addresses other stakeholders such as employees, customers, and businesses. It emphasizes that employees should treat customers with the utmost care and that they should respect customer privacy. PETCO also addresses its selling practices, advertising policies, pricing practices, and buying practices in the code of ethics. For example, it is against the code to promote one brand over another; associates are expected to interact honestly with customers and to clearly explain the purposes and benefits of all products and services. PETCO makes efforts to ensure that advertisements are clear and minimize misunderstandings, and that pricing decisions are made without influence from vendors, contractors, or competitors.

The matter of courtesy, dignity, and respect among associates is also taken seriously. The code of ethics addresses harassment, stating that any harassment complaint will be treated with confidentiality and appropriate corrective action will be taken. PETCO also addresses drug abuse, asset protection, and violence in the workplace. The company has implemented measures aimed to increase associate, vendor, and customer protection with the goal of providing everyone with a safe working environment.

PETCO associates are expected to avoid conflicts of interest, meaning that PETCO employees must not place themselves in situations in which they might be forced to choose between their own personal or financial interests and the interests of the company. Associates are encouraged to promptly relay potential conflicts of interest to management to determine whether a conflict actually exists. PETCO associates are also prohibited from accepting gifts or gratuities from vendors or potential vendors. Associates offered gifts are required to contact their supervisors or the PETCO Hotline for guidance and to ask vendors to refrain from future gift giving.

Associates who are looking for employment with suppliers, vendors, or others doing business with PETCO are expected to do it at their own discretion and use non-work time. Additionally, supervisors must be contacted. Associates and their immediate families may not invest in vendor companies without prior approval from PETCO's ethics committee. Employees are compelled to agree not to interfere with business by directly or indirectly soliciting the business of PETCO customers. Former associates are not allowed to encourage other associates to quit as well. Trade secrets and other proprietary information must also be kept confidential while employed with the company, as well as after.

"The PETCO Foundation supports the "Four Rs"—Reduce, Rescue, Rehabilitate, and Rejoice"

The code of ethics also addresses concerns such as workplace safety, wage laws, and reporting time worked. Neither political contributions nor payments to government personnel may come from PETCO funds. A section concerning managers and supervisors encourages them to act as role models. When dealing with the media, PETCO asks managers and supervisors to consult any parties involved to devise an appropriate media message.

The code of ethics also offers a chain of command to follow in the face of an ethical dilemma. If an associate suspects that he or she is being given false or misleading information, he or she is encouraged to phone the Code of Ethics Hotline or to consult a supervisor. The company also operates an internal ethics committee that oversees compliance and continually monitors related practices.

PETCO FOUNDATION FUNDRAISERS

In 1999 PETCO established the PETCO Foundation, allowing the company to directly promote charitable, educational, and other philanthropic activities of its choosing. The PETCO Foundation supports the "Four Rs"—Reduce, Rescue, Rehabilitate, and Rejoice—focusing on the welfare of companion animals and the importance of the human–animal bond. The PETCO Foundation is a non-profit organization that has raised more than $49 million since its inception. Through a combination of fundraisers, support has been offered to thousands of nonprofit grassroots animal welfare organizations. The foundation is also responsible for the donation of in-kind goods and services to worthwhile organizations with the same mission. Through an exclusive, long-term agreement with Petfinder.com, the foundation also supports over 10,000 additional animal welfare agencies.

The following organizations are a list of charities that PETCO supports. PETCO and these organizations share the common goal of improving the lives of the nation's pets.

Round Up Program

Every year, U.S. shelters euthanize between five and 10 million pets. Overpopulation due to unwanted animals sends millions of potential pets to shelters each year. In 2000, PETCO launched an annual "Spay Today" initiative addressing the issue of pet overpopulation. "Spay Today" funds come from customer donations; customers are encouraged to round up their purchases to the nearest dollar or to give more. Each PETCO store selects one or more spay/neuter-focused charitable partners and donates the funds to these organizations. In addition, 10 percent of all funds raised are donated to the Petfinder.com Foundation to assist its spay/neuter efforts. During 2007 the Round Up program raised over $10 million.

Think Adoption First

Launched in 2005, the Think Adoption First program combines the efforts of PETCO, the PETCO Foundation, and Petfinder.com to offer second chances to companion animals that have been sent to shelters after being rescued from abuse, neglect, or disaster. The program provides access to animals through its network of rescue groups and then works with these partners to make companion animals available for in-store adoption. The program has strengthened its relationship with Petfinder.com. Each year, the PETCO foundation works with over 5,700 local welfare partners to save over 200,000 animals. This program reinforces PETCO's commitment to both social responsibility and financial success.

Spring a Pet

The "Spring a Pet" fundraiser encourages pet lovers to donate $1, $5, $10, or $20 to animal welfare causes. Each PETCO store selects an animal welfare organization as recipient. In the past, the money has been used to provide veterinary care for homeless and abused animals and to fund outreach programs that help handicapped and disadvantaged individuals care for their companion animals. More than 900 PETCO stores collect donations. Pedigree also donated $1 for each Pedigree purchase of $10 or more. The event raised $1.95 million. Pedigree also funded the costs, saving the foundation about $35,000.

Tree of Hope

Customers visiting one of PETCO's 950 stores during the Christmas season can purchase card ornaments for $1, $5, $10, or $20. The foundation raised around $3 million during the 2008/2009 holiday season, despite the recession. PETCO also partnered with Iams in 2008 to run the Home 4 the Holidays adoption drive. Iams donated $1 for every bag of Iams pet food purchased along with about $110,000 in operating costs. Over 1.2 million animals were adopted.

The "Kind News" Program

The PETCO Foundation sponsors "Kind News," a program educating children about the proper humane treatment of companion animals and fellow human beings. It features training on taking care of pets, addresses pet-related issues, and provides information on all types of animals. It contains learning tools reinforcing the need for compassion and concern for all living things. The program is currently available in 1,000 elementary schools nationwide.

We are a Family Too

During the 2008–2009 economic recession, PETCO established the "We are a Family Too" fund. The company aims to aid families struggling to stay together with their pets while facing foreclosure, eviction, or a lack of funds. It also aims to help shelters deal with an increase in incoming animals. The program assists organizations already set up to deal with these issues by offering funding.

PETCO'S CHALLENGES AND ACCOMPLISHMENTS

While most companies focus specifically on customers, PETCO is also concerned about its impact on society. While providing quality products, information, and advice, it also addresses important issues related to animals in society. For example, foundation fundraising programs illustrate important contributions to society. "Kind News" is designed to educate children. PETCO, like any organization, experiences risk associated with doing business and has developed a comprehensive ethics program to manage relationships with stakeholders.

All retail organizations are subject to criticism and must work to maintain internal control and high ethical standards. PETCO accomplishes this through its ethics office and by developing an ethical corporate culture. PETCO's code of ethics is comprehensive, addressing risks related to human resources, conflicts of interests, and behavior in the workplace. Large organizations know that misconduct exists somewhere in their organizations; therefore, discovering, exposing, and addressing issues before they cause reputational damage is critical. For PETCO, the desire to do the right thing and to train all employees to make proper ethical decisions assures not only success in the marketplace but a significant contribution to society.

Despite an economic recession, PETCO continues to expand and to open new stores. As mentioned previously, its fundraisers continue to succeed as well. The company has begun offering low-cost clinics, such as one providing vaccinations, so that pet owners can afford to continue caring for their pets. In February 2009, the company hired its first Senior VP and Chief Marketing Officer, Elisabeth Charles. The gist of PETCO's reaction to the recession seems to be one of optimism, given the fact that analysts do predict a continued increase in pet owner spending.

QUESTIONS

1. How has PETCO's ethics and compliance program helped it to deal with ethical misconduct?
2. How do you think re-privatizing the company will help PETCO's performance? Or do you think it could hurt the company overall?
3. Should pet supply companies like PETCO be held responsible for the conditions at pet breeders and suppliers? How do you think exposés on poor breeder conditions have affected PETCO's reputation?

SOURCES

PETCO Code of Ethics, http://www.petco.com/assets/pdf/COE.pdf (accessed September 7, 2009); Lifestyle Trends Affect Pet Markets, *PET AGE*, January 2006, http://www.petage.com/News010607.asp (accessed September 7, 2009); CNN Money.com, *Fortune 500 2006*, http://money.cnn.com/magazines/fortune/fortune500/snapshots/2154.html (accessed September 7, 2009); Research and Markets, The Pet Market—Market Assessment 2007, http://

www.researchandmarkets.com/reports/c26485/ (accessed September 7, 2009); PETA and PETCO Announce Agreement, April 12, 2005, http://www.peta.org/feat/PETCOAgreement/default.asp (accessed September 7, 2009); PETCO's Bad Business Is Bad for Animals, PETA, http://www.peta.org/living/at-spring2003/comp2.html (accessed September 7, 2009); Say No to PETCO, http://www.thebeakretreat.com/images/flyersaynotopetco.pdf (accessed September 7, 2009); Pet Store Secrets: PETA Uncovers Shocking Back-Room Secrets, http://www.peta.org/living/at-summer2000/petco.html (accessed September 7, 2009); "PETCO Looks to the Web to Enhance Multi-Channel Marketing" *Internet Retailer,* January 16, 2006, http://www. internetretailer.com/internet/marketing-conference/08167-petco-looks-web-enhance-multi-channel-marketing.html (accessed September 7, 2009); "Just Say No! Petco—The Place Where Pets Die," http://www.kindplanet.org/petno.html (accessed September 7, 2009); Robert McMillan, "PETCO Settles Charge It Left Customer Data Exposed," Network World, November 17, 2004, http://www.networkworld.com/news/2004/1117petcosettl.html (accessed September 7, 2009); "PETCO Settles FTC Charges," *Federal Trade Commission.* November 17, 2004, http://www.ftc.gov/opa/2004/11/petco.htm (accessed September 7, 2009); Julie Schmidt, "Pet Bird Buyers Asking Sellers About Avian Flu," *USA Today*, November 28, 2005; "Pet Portion Control," *Prevention* 58, no. 2 (February 2006): 201; Michelle Higgins, "When the Dog's Hotel Is Better Than Yours," *The Wall Street Journal,* June 30, 2004, D1; "Animal Abuse Case Details: PETCO Lawsuit—Mistreating Animals San Diego, CA," Pet-Abuse.com, May 28, 2004, http://www.pet-abuse.com/cases/2373/CA/US (accessed September 7, 2009); Ilene Lelchuk, "San Francisco Alleges Cruelty at 2 PETCOs," Melissa Kaplan's Herp Care Collection, originally reported by the *San Francisco Chronicle,* June 19, 2002, http://www.anapsid.org/pettrade/petcocit2.html (accessed September 7, 2009); Melissa Kaplan, "PETCO settles Suit Alleging Abuse, Overcharging," Melissa Kaplan's Herp Care Collection, originally reported by *CBS News*, May 27, 2004, http://www.anapsid.org/pettrade/petcocit2.html (accessed September 7, 2009); Laura Bennett, "Pet Industry Trends for 2009," Small Business Trends, January 15, 2009, http://smallbiztrends.com/2009/01/pet-industry-trends-2009.html (accessed September 7, 2009); "Melamine Pet Food Recall 2007," U.S. Food and Drug Administration, Updated July 10, 2009, http://www.fda.gov/AnimalVeterinary/SafetyHealth/RecallsWithdrawals/ucm129575.htm (accessed September 7, 2009); "PETCO Pet Food Seized after Federal Warrant Issued," *The Los Angeles Times*, June 20, 2008, http://latimesblogs.latimes.com/unleashed/2008/06/petco-pet-food.html (accessed September 7, 2009); "Pet Statistics," ASPCA, www.aspca.org/about-us/faq/pet-statistics.html (accessed September 7, 2009); Lianne McLeod, "American Pet Ownership Statistics," About.com, http://exoticpets.about.com/cs/resourcesgeneral/a/petstates.htm (accessed September 7, 2009); "America's Largest Private Companies: #183 Petco Animal Supplies," Forbes.com, November 3, 2008, http://www.forbes.com/lists/2008/21/privates08_Petco-Animal-Supplies_UG5C.html (accessed September 7, 2009); Chris Noon, "Myers' Petco Goes Private Again," Forbes.com, July 14, 2006, http://www.forbes.com/2006/07/14/myers-petco-retail-cx_cn_0714autofacescan05.html (accessed September 7, 2009); Mike Robinson, "Marshals Seize Animal Food from PETCO Warehouse," *Houston Chronicle*, June 19, 2008, http://www.chron.com/disp/story.mpl/headline/nation/5847195.html (accessed September 7, 2009); "PETCO to Slash Number of Animals for Sale by 30 Percent After PETA Exposé of Shocking Conditions at Animal Breeding Mill," *Business Wire*, February 22, 2008, http://www.accessmylibrary.com/coms2/summary_0286-33939882_ITM (accessed September 7, 2009); Michael Souers, "What Makes PetSmart so Fetching," *BusinessWeek*, June 3, 2008, http://www.businessweek.com/investor/content/jun2008/pi2008062_164695.htm?chan=top+news_top+news+index_investing (accessed September 7, 2009).

CASE 17

Home Depot Implements Stakeholder Orientation

Daryl Benson

When Bernie Marcus and Arthur Blank opened the first Home Depot store in Atlanta in 1979, they forever changed the hardware and home-improvement retailing industry. Marcus and Blank envisioned huge warehouse-style stores stocked with an extensive selection of products offered at the lowest prices. Today, do-it-yourselfers and building contractors can browse from among 40,000 different products for the home and yard, from kitchen and bathroom fixtures to carpeting, lumber, paint, tools, and plant and landscaping items. If a product is not provided in one of the stores, Home Depot offers 250,000 products that can be special-ordered. Some Home Depot stores are open twenty-four hours a day, but customers can also order products online and pick them up from their local Home Depot stores or have them delivered. Additionally, the company offers free home-improvement clinics to teach customers how to tackle everyday projects like tiling a bathroom. For those customers who prefer not to "do it yourself," most stores offer installation services. Well-trained employees, recognizable by their orange aprons, are always on hand to help customers find just the right item or to demonstrate the proper use of a particular tool.

Currently, Home Depot employs more than 300,000 people and operates approximately 2,238 Home Depot stores, mostly in North America and Mexico. It also operates four wholly owned subsidiaries: Apex Supply Company, Georgia Lighting, Maintenance Warehouse, and National Blinds and Wallpaper. The company is the largest home-improvement retailer in the world (although revenue dropped from $81 billion to $65 billion annually during the 2008–2009 recession). Home Depot continues to do things on a grand scale, including putting its corporate muscle behind a tightly focused social responsibility agenda. Every week, 22 million customers visit Home Depot, which means that conflicts associated with providing services in a retail environment are inevitable.

This case was developed under the direction of O.C. Ferrell with the editorial assistance of Jennifer Jackson and Jennifer Sawayda. Melanie Drever helped to draft the previous edition. This case was prepared for classroom discussion, rather than to illustrate either effective or ineffective handling of an administrative, ethical, or legal decision by management. All sources used for this case were obtained through publicly available material and the Home Depot website.

MANAGING CUSTOMER RELATIONSHIPS

Since its inception, Home Depot has been focused on close customer relationships. Part of the company's competitive advantage has always been superior service. In 2006, John Costello was the chief marketing officer or, as he states, chief customer officer. Costello consolidated marketing and merchandising functions to help consumers achieve their goals in home-improvement projects more effectively and efficiently.

According to Costello, "Above all else, a brand is a promise. It says here's what you can expect if you do business with us. Our mission is to empower our customers to achieve the home or condo of their dreams." When Costello arrived in 2002, Home Depot's reputation was faltering. His plan called for overhauling the Home Depot website as well as integrating mass marketing and direct marketing with in-store experience. It was all integrated with the new Home Depot mantra: "You can do it. We can help." Teams of people from merchandising, marketing, visual merchandising, and operations attempted to provide the very best shopping experience at Home Depot. The philosophy was simple; Home Depot believed that customers should be able to read and understand why one ceiling fan is better than another, while associates (employees) should be able to offer installation and design advice.

In 2008, Frank Bifulco took over as new chief marketing officer and senior vice president. He took over at a tough time for Home Depot. Because of the 2008–2009 recession, consumers were spending less on their homes. As a result, Home Depot's new marketing strategy was to emphasize the store's everyday low prices, high product value, and quality energy-saving products. At the same time, the company cut back on special offers like discounts and promotions. According to Bifulco, the company's energy-saving devices are becoming popular as a way to offset fuel and heating costs, and the relationship between price and value is more important than ever. Home Depot's website is also receiving more traffic as fewer people drive to visit the store.

Despite Home Depot's proactive strategy to address customer issues, Home Depot has had to deal with negative publicity associated with customer-satisfaction measures published by outside sources. The University of Michigan's annual American Customer Satisfaction Index in 2006 showed Home Depot slipping to last place among major U.S. retailers. "This is not competitive and too low to be sustainable. It's very serious," wrote Claes Fornell, professor of business at the University of Michigan. Fornell believed that the drop in satisfaction was one reason why Home Depot's stock was stagnant.

On the other hand, Robert Nardelli, the Home Depot CEO during that time, said that the survey was a "sham." Nardelli pointed out that Fornell created his own ethical concerns when he shorted Home Depot stock before the survey came out (purchase options that would cause Fornell to profit from Home Depot's stock price decreasing). Fornell defended himself by saying that the trades were part of research into a correlation between companies' customer-satisfaction scores and stock price performance, but the University of Michigan banned the practice anyway, indicating concerns over moral problems with the practice.

Some former managers at Home Depot blamed the service issues on a culture that focused on military principles for execution. Under Nardelli, some employees feared being terminated unless they followed directions to a tee. Harris Interactive's 2005 Reputation Quotient survey ranked Home Depot number twelve among major companies and said that customers appreciated Home Depot's quality services. However, two years later it had lowered to number twenty-seven. Nardelli was ousted and replaced by Frank Blake in January 2007. The start of 2008 seemed more auspicious for Home Depot in terms of reputation, as it was listed as number six on *Fortune's* Most Admired Companies (still trailing behind Lowe's), up from 13 in 2006. Home Depot also bounced back up on the American Customer Satisfaction Index. Although it still trails behind Lowe's, Home Depot ranked 70 percent in 2008 (versus 5 percent at its lowest point).

A good example of a socially responsible activity meant to connect with customers is Home Depot's program to teach children skills related to home improvements. Home Depot provides a program called the Kids Workshop. The workshops are free, with how-to clinics designed for children ages five through twelve, available on the first Saturday of each month between 9 A.M. and noon at all Home Depot stores. Children, accompanied by an adult, use their skills to create objects that can be used in and around their homes or communities. Useful projects that kids can create include toolboxes, fire trucks, and mail organizers, as well as more educational projects such as building a window birdhouse, bughouse, or Declaration of Independence frame. Since 1997, more than 17.5 million projects have been built at Kids Workshops and more than 1 million children built their first toolbox at Home Depot. An average of 75 children attend Kids Workshops, while many stores have 200 kids who attend regularly. Home Depot also offers workshops specially designed for women and for people who have recently bought a new home. These workshops are all free of charge and open to the public.

ENVIRONMENTAL INITIATIVES

Cofounders Marcus and Blank nurtured a corporate culture that emphasized social responsibility, especially with regard to the company's impact on the natural environment. Home Depot began its environmental program on the twentieth anniversary of Earth Day in 1990 by adopting a set of Environmental Principles (see Table 1). These principles have since been adopted by the National Retail Hardware Association and Home Center Institute, which represents more than 46,000 retail hardware stores and home centers.

Guided by these environmental principles, Home Depot has initiated a number of programs to minimize the firm's—and its customers'—impact on the environment. In 1991, the retailer began using store and office supplies, advertising, signs, and shopping bags made with recycled-material content. It also established a process for evaluating the environmental claims made by suppliers. The following year, the firm launched a program to recycle wallboard shipping packaging, which became the industry's first "reverse distribution" program. In addition, it opened the first drive-thru recycling center in Duluth, Georgia, in 1993. In 1994, Home Depot became the first home-improvement retailer to offer wood products from tropical and temperate forests certified as "well-managed" by the Scientific Certification System's Forest Conservation Program. The company also began to replace wooden shipping pallets with reusable "slip sheets" to minimize waste and energy use and to reduce pressure on hardwood resources used to make wood pallets.

In 1999, Home Depot announced that it would endorse independent, third-party forest certification and wood from certified forests. The company joined the Certified Forests Products Council, a nonprofit organization that promotes responsible forest product buying practices and the sale of wood from Certified Well-Managed Forests. Yet environmentalists believed that the company was only interested in appearing environmentally-friendly and was not actually committed to the cause. Therefore, they

TABLE 1 Home Depot's Environmental Principles

The Home Depot acknowledges the importance of conservation. The following principles are Home Depot's response:
• We are committed to improving the environment by selling products that are manufactured, packaged and labeled in a responsible manner, that take the environment into consideration and that provide greater value to our customers.
• We will support efforts to provide accurate, informative product labeling of environmental marketing claims.
• We will strive to eliminate unnecessary packaging.
• We will recycle and encourage the use of materials and products with recycled content.
• We will conserve natural resources by using energy and water wisely and seek further opportunities to improve the resource efficiency of our stores.
• We will comply with environmental laws and will maintain programs and procedures to ensure compliance.
• We are committed to minimizing the environmental health and safety risk for our associates and our customers.
• We will train our employees to enhance understanding of environmental issues and policies and to promote excellence in job performance and all environmental matters.
• We will encourage our customers to become environmentally conscious shoppers.

Source: "The Home Depot Environmental Principles," Home Depot, http://corporate.homedepot.com/wps/portal/Environmental_Principles (accessed May 13, 2009. Reprinted by permission from The Home Depot Headquarters, Homer TLC.

picketed outside of stores in protest of Home Depot's practice of continuing to sell products made from wood harvested from old growth forests. Led by the Rainforest Action Network, environmentalists have picketed Home Depot and other home center stores for years in an effort to stop the destruction of old growth forests, of which less than 20 percent still survive. Later that year, during Home Depot's twentieth anniversary celebration, Arthur Blank announced that Home Depot would stop selling products made from wood harvested in environmentally sensitive areas.

To be "certified" by the Forest Stewardship Council (FSC), a supplier's wood products must be tracked from the forest, through manufacturing and distribution, to the customer. Harvesting, manufacturing, and distribution practices must ensure a balance of social, economic, and environmental factors. Blank challenged competitors to follow Home Depot's lead, and within two years several had met that challenge, including Lowe's, the number-two home-improvement retailer; Wickes, a lumber company; and Andersen Corporation, a window manufacturer. By 2003, Home Depot reported that it had reduced its purchases of Indonesian lauan, a tropical rainforest hardwood used in door components, by 70 percent, and it continued to increase its purchases of certified sustainable wood products. In addition to sustainable wood products, Home Depot offers compact fluorescent light bulbs (CFLs) in its stores and has even introduced an in-store recycling program for CFL bulbs. Customers can drop off their used bulbs in stores, and Home Depot works with an environmental management company to recycle the bulbs safely and responsibly.

Home Depot made cash and in-kind donations exceeding $50 million in 2008 and awarded $15.5 million in grant monies to housing development organizations. In 2002 the company founded the Home Depot Foundation, which provides additional resources to assist nonprofits in the United States and Canada. The Foundation awards grants to eligible nonprofits three times per year and partners with innovative nonprofits across the country that are working to increase awareness and successfully demonstrate the connection between housing, the urban forest, and the overall health and economic success of their communities. The company has established a carpooling program for more than three thousand employees in the Atlanta area, and remains the only North American home-improvement retailer with full-time staff dedicated to environmental issues.

These efforts have yielded many rewards in addition to improved relations with environmental stakeholders. Home Depot's environmental programs have earned the company an A on the Council on Economic Priorities Corporate Report Card, a Vision of America Award from Keep America Beautiful, and, along with Scientific Certification Systems and Collin Pine, a President's Council for Sustainable Development Award. The company was voted number five in *Fortune* magazine's "America's Most Admired Specialty Retailer" in 2008 and also has been recognized by the U.S. Environmental Protection Agency with its Energy Star Award for Excellence.

> ***"Home Depot's environmental programs have earned the company an A on the Council on Economic Priorities Corporate Report Card"***

Despite the fact that Home Depot has established better relations with some environmental activists, it has not placated all of them. In 2008, Home Depot came under controversy for doing business with two Chilean wood suppliers that supported the building of a dam in the Chilean region of Patagonia, a project that would cause irreparable harm to a fragile ecosystem. An environmental institution known as International Rivers demanded that Home Depot pull its contracts with the suppliers if they refused to abandon the dam project. However, Home Depot's environmental chief Ron Jarvis said that the two suppliers were obeying the 2003 agreement not to cut down endangered forests for tree farms. Since they were also not supplying Home Depot with wood products from native forests, Home Depot had no legitimate reason to cancel the contracts. Additionally, Jarvis maintained that the two Chilean suppliers were only minor players in the dam project and that the company's pull-out would not have much of an effect.

This raises the question of how much responsibility major companies have for the environment, particularly when the company itself is not directly doing harm. Is it fair for environmentalists to target companies simply because they are large? No matter how environmentally-friendly Home Depot attempts to portray itself, these are questions it will likely have to weigh constantly as it struggles to address its environmental stakeholders.

CORPORATE PHILANTHROPY

In addition to its environmental initiatives, Home Depot focuses corporate social responsibility efforts on disaster relief, affordable housing, and at-risk youth. In 2008 the company supported thousands of nonprofit organizations with over $50 million in contributions. The company also posts a Social Responsibility Report on its website, detailing its annual charitable contributions and the community programs in which it has become involved over the years.

Home Depot works with more than 350 affiliates of Habitat for Humanity, a nonprofit organization that constructs and repairs homes for qualified low-income families. In March 2008, Home Depot and Habitat for Humanity announced a five-year initiative to provide funding for creating at least 5,000 energy-efficient homes. The Home Depot Foundation will provide $30 million in support of this program. Home Depot also awards grants to housing projects throughout the nation. One of its grant programs, Affordable Housing Built Responsibly, was used to produce 12,223 homes in 2007.

Home Depot supports YouthBuildUSA, a nonprofit organization that provides training and skill development for young people. YouthBuildUSA gives students the opportunity to help rehabilitate housing for homeless and low-income families. Additionally, Home Depot supports other programs to help at-risk youth, such as Big Brothers/Big Sisters, KaBOOM!, and the National Center for Missing and Exploited Children. Home Depot believes that every child should have a safe and fun place to play. In 2007, Home Depot partnered with KaBOOM! to create 1,000 play spaces in only 1,000 days. Home Depot donated $25 million and 1 million volunteer hours in support of the program.

Home Depot has addressed the growing needs for relief from disasters such as hurricanes, tornadoes, and earthquakes. After the 9/11 terrorist attacks in 2001, the company set up three command centers with more than 200 associates to help coordinate relief supplies such as dust masks, gloves, batteries, and tools to victims and rescue workers. After Hurricanes Katrina, Rita, and Wilma, Home Depot, the Home Depot Foundation, their suppliers, and Home Depot's Homer Fund contributed $9.3 million in cash and materials to support recovery. Home Depot also donated $500,000 to support the tsunami relief efforts of the American Red Cross in Southeast Asia, and donated $300,000 to the American Red Cross for disaster relief for people who suffer from hurricanes. Separately, Home Depot's Homer Fund donated $500,000 to 650 associates who had suffered through Hurricane Gustav in 2008.

EMPLOYEE AND SUPPLIER RELATIONS

Home Depot encourages employees to become involved in the community through volunteer and civic activities. Home Depot, with more than 300,000 employees, provides about 2 million volunteer service hours each year. In 2005, Home Depot took part in the Corporate Month of Service. With the aid of the nonprofit Hands On Network, more than 40,000 volunteers from the Home Depot were able to help their communities log over 320,000 hours for thirteen hundred neighborhood projects. Home Depot continued to participate in Corporate Months of Service for the next two years.

Home Depot also strives to apply social responsibility to its employment practices, with the goal of assembling a diverse workforce that reflects the population of the markets it serves. However, in 1997 the company settled a class-action lawsuit brought by female employees who claimed they were paid less than male employees, awarded fewer pay raises, and promoted less often. The $87.5 million settlement represented one of the largest settlements of a gender discrimination lawsuit in U.S. history at the time. In announcing the settlement, the company emphasized that it was not admitting to wrongdoing and defended its record, saying it "provides opportunities for all of its associates to develop successful professional careers and is proud of its strong track record of having successful women involved in all areas of the company."

Since the lawsuit, Home Depot has worked to show that it appreciates workforce diversity and seeks to give all its associates an equal chance to be employed and advance in its stores. In 2005, Home Depot formed partnerships with the ASPIRA Association, Inc., the Hispanic Association of Colleges and Universities, and the National Council of La Raza to recruit Hispanic candidates for part-time and full-time positions. Additionally, in 2005, Home Depot became a major member of the American Association of Retired Persons' (AARP) Featured Retirement Program, which helps connect employees 50 years or older with companies that value their experience.

Home Depot also has a strong diversity supplier program. As members of the Women's Business Enterprise National Council and the National Minority Suppliers Development Council, Home Depot has come into contact and done business with a diverse range of suppliers, including many minority- and women-owned businesses. In 2005, the company became a founding member of The Resource Institute, whose mission is to help small minority- and women-owned businesses by providing them with resources and training. Home Depot's supplier diversity program has won it numerous recognitions. It ranked number nineteen on Diversity Business Top 50 Corporate Supplier Diversity Programs in 2006 and won Georgia's Minority Supplier Development Council Corporation of the Year award in 2008.

HOME DEPOT'S RESPONSE TO THE RECESSION

Home Depot's emphasis on expansion changed drastically in light of the 2008–2009 recession. CEO Frank Blake decided to halt expansion and focus on improving existing stores. Blake saw the warning signs of the impending crisis and began halting expansion in early 2007, reducing new store openings from around two a week to five a year, an enormous change from the company's decade of aggressive expansion. In early 2009, he shut down Home Depot's EXPO stores, which largely catered to the wealthier class, estimating that they would lose millions each year. The recession took a significant toll on Home Depot. While its 2007 revenue was over $80 billion, its revenue in 2009 fell to around $65 billion.

Home Depot's reaction to the crisis was swift and decisive. As the crisis worsened in September 2008, Home Depot managers transferred all extra cash to Home Depot headquarters, cut capital spending, and suspended a stock buy-back program in order to avoid losses and prevent having to borrow from the country's lenders. For the first time, Home Depot does not have to borrow money, but is instead paying all its expenses from its own revenue. This is a fiscally conservative strategy aimed at stemming future losses and reducing risk, yet it limits Home Depot's ability to grow and adapt quickly. Home Depot may need to develop new strategies in the future if revenues continue to fall.

Experts predict that if too many companies choose to cut back, the recession may in fact be prolonged. Additionally, Home Depot's tactic may put it at a disadvantage to competitors who choose the opposite approach. Lowe's, for instance, is continuing to expand, taking advantage of the recession's low costs of land and labor. Such an approach is risky, but may prove profitable once the recession ends. Essentially, Lowe's expansion could have one of two consequences: (1) overexpansion at a bad time might result in losses, or (2) its aggressive approach might pay off and make it an even more formidable foe for Home Depot to contend with. It remains to be seen whether Home Depot's cutbacks will keep it ahead of the competition once the recession ends.

A STRATEGIC COMMITMENT TO SOCIAL RESPONSIBILITY

Home Depot has strived to secure a socially responsible reputation with stakeholders. Although it received low scores in the past on customer surveys and the American Customer Satisfaction Index, it has worked hard to boost those scores back up. It has addressed environmentalist concerns by creating new standards and environmental principles to govern its relationship with its suppliers. Despite Home Depot's success, however, it does face challenges in the future. Though it remains the world's largest home retailer, its main competitor Lowe's is picking up the pace, and the recession has created an uncertain future for Home Depot. Still, Home Depot's philanthropic endeavors and its promotion of its low product prices and high value continue to make it a popular shopping destination for customers.

Knowing that stakeholders, especially customers, feel good about a company that actively commits resources to environmental and social issues, company executives believe that social responsibility can and should be a strategic component of Home Depot's business operations. The company should remain committed to its focused strategy of philanthropy, volunteerism, and environmental initiatives even during the recession. Customers' concerns over social responsibility and green products have not abated, at least in Home Depot's case. Home Depot's sales of green products are still going strong. Its commitment to social responsibility extends throughout the company, fueled by top-level support from the cofounders and reinforced by a corporate culture that places great value on playing a responsible role within the communities it serves.

QUESTIONS

1. On the basis of Home Depot's response to environmentalist issues, describe the attributes (power, legitimacy, urgency) of this stakeholder. Using the Reactive-Defensive-Accommodative-Proactive Scale in Chapter 2 (Table 2.6), assess the company's strategy and performance with environmental and employee stakeholders.
2. As a publicly traded corporation, how can Home Depot justify budgeting so much money for philanthropy? What areas other than the environment, disaster relief, affordable housing, and at-risk youth might be appropriate for strategic philanthropy by Home Depot?
3. Is Home Depot's recessionary strategy of eliminating debt and halting growth a wise one? What would you recommend to the CEO?

SOURCES

"America's Most Admired Companies," *Fortune,* http://money.cnn.com/magazines/fortune/mostadmired/2008/industries/11.html (accessed September 8, 2009); "Building a Home, Building a Community," The Home Depot Foundation, http://www.homedepotfoundation.org/ (accessed September 8, 2009); Carlton, Jim, "How Home

Depot and Activists Joined to Cut Logging Abuse," *Wall Street Journal*, September 26, 2000, p. A1; "CFL Recycling Program," Home Depot, http://www6.homedepot.com/ecooptions/index.html?MAINSECTION=cflrecycling (accessed September 8, 2009); "Corporate Financial Review," Home Depot, http://corporate.homedepot.com/en_US/Corporate/Public_Relations/Online_Press_Kit/Docs/Corp_Financial_Overview.pdf (accessed September 8, 2009); Daniels, Cora, "To Hire a Lumber Expert, Click Here," *Fortune*, April 3, 2000, pp. 267–270; Demaster, Sarah, "Use Proper Lumber, Demand Protesters," BNet, April 5, 1999, http://findarticles.com/p/articles/mi_moVCW/is_7_25/ai_54373184/ (accessed September 8, 2009); "Fourth Quarter, 2008," The American Customer Satisfaction Index, February 17, 2009, http://www.theacsi.org/index.php?option=com_content&task=view&id=190&Itemid=199 (accessed September 8, 2009); Grimsley, Kirstin Downey, "Home Depot Settles Gender Bias Lawsuit," *Washington Post,* September 20, 1997, p. D1; "Habitat for Humanity and the Home Depot Foundation Announce National Green Building Effort," Habitat for Humanity, March 20, 2008, http://www.habitat.org/newsroom/2008archive/03_21_08_Home_Depot.aspx (accessed September 8, 2009); HarrisInteractive, February 17–March 8, 2008, http://www.harrisinteractive.com/news/mediaaccess/2008/HI_BSC_REPORT_AnnualRQ_USASummary07-08.pdf (accessed September 8, 2009); Heher, Ashley M., "Home Depot Reports Loss of $54M, but Beats Estimates," *USA Today*, February 24, 2009, http://www.usatoday.com/money/companies/earnings/2009- 02-24-home-depot_N.htm (accessed September 8, 2009); "Home Depot Announces Commitment to Stop Selling Old Growth Wood; Announcement Validates Two-Year Grassroots Environmental Campaign," *Common Dreams Newswire*, August 26, 1999, http://www.commondreams.org/pressreleases/august99/082699c.htm (accessed September 8, 2009); "The Home Depot to Celebrate 25th Anniversary with Month of Service," PR Newswire, http://www.prnewswire.com/cgi-bin/stories.pl?ACCT=105&STORY=/www/story/09-23-2004/0002257339 (accessed September 8, 2009); "Home Depot CEO Nardelli Quits," MSNBC, January 3, 2007, http://www.msnbc.msn.com/id/16451112/ (accessed March September 8, 2009); "The Home Depot Donates $300,000 to American Red Cross for Hurricane Relief and Preparation Efforts," Home Depot, September 2, 2008, http://www.homedepotfoundation.org/redcross08.pdf (accessed September 8, 2009); "The Home Depot and The Environment," http://corporate.homedepot.com/wps/portal/Environmental_Principles (accessed September 8, 2009); "The Home Depot Launches Environmental Wood Purchasing Policy," PR Newswire, August 26, 1999, http://www.prnewswire.com/cgi-bin/stories.pl?ACCT=104&STORY=/www/story/08-26-1999/0001010227&EDATE= (accessed September 8, 2009); "Home Depot Retools Timber Policy," *Memphis Business Journal,* January 2, 2003, www.bizjournals.com/memphis/stories/2002/12/30/daily12.html (accessed September 8, 2009); "Home Depot Vs. Lowe's," CNBC, August 26, 2008, http://www.cnbc.com/id/26406040/?__source=aol|headline|quote|text|&par=aol (accessed September 8, 2009); Jackson, Susan, and Tim Smart, "Mom and Pop Fight Back," *BusinessWeek,* April 14, 1997, p. 46; Jacobs, Karen, "Home Depot Pushes Low Prices, Energy Savings," Reuters, September 10, 2008, http://www.reuters.com/article/ousiv/idUSN1051947020080910 (accessed September 8, 2009); Lloyd, Mary Ellen, "Home Improvement Spending Remains Tight," *Wall Street Journal*, May 6, 2009, http://online.wsj.com/article/SB124162405957992133.html (accessed September 8, 2009); McGregor, Jena, "Home Depot Sheds Units," *BusinessWeek*, January 26, 2009, http://www.businessweek.com/bwdaily/dnflash/content/jan2009/db20090126_454995.htm (accessed September 8, 2009); "Message from the Supplier Diversity Director," Home Depot, http://corporate.homedepot.com/wps/portal/SupplierDiversity (accessed September 8, 2009); "Our History," Home Depot, http://corporate.homedepot.com/wps/portal/!ut/p/c1/04_SB8K8xLLM9MSSzPy8xBz9CPoos3gDdwNHHotDU1M3g1APRoN31xBjAwgAykfC5H1MzNoMzDycDANMYdIGBHT7eeTnpuoX5EaUAwDOvP5h/dl2/d1/L2dJQSEvUUt3QS9ZQnB3LzZfMEcwQUw5TDQ3RjA2SEIxUEY5MDAwMDAwMDA!/ (accessed September 8, 2009); "Our Mission and Outreach Efforts," Home Depot, http://corporate.homedepot.com/wps/portal/!ut/p/c1/04_SB8K8xLLM9MSSzPy8xBz9CPoos3gDdwNHHosfE3M3AzMPJ8MAfzcDKADKR2LKmxrD5fHr9vPIzo3VL8iNKAcAC4X4Kg!!/dl2/d1/L2dJQSEvUUt3QS9ZQnB3LzZfMEcwQUw5TDQ3RjA2SEIxUFBGMDAwMDAwMDA!/ (accessed September 8, 2009); Pettit, Dixie, "Home Depot Volunteers Give Youth Club a Facelift," *Ramona Sentinel,* November 12, 2008, http://www.ramonasentinel.com/article.cfm?articleID=18278 (accessed September 8, 2009); PR Newswire, "The Home Depot Forms Unprecedented Partnership with Four Leading

National Hispanic Organizations," Hispanic Business.com, February 15, 2005, http://www.hispanicbusiness.com/news/newsbyid.asp?idx=20997&page=1&cat=&more= (accessed September 8, 2009); "Profiles in Leadership: 2008 ENERGY STAR Award Winners," Energy Star, http://www.energystar.gov/ia/partners/pt_awards/2008_profiles_in_leadership.pdf (accessed September 8, 2009); Ramos, Rachel Tobin, "Home Depot in Middle of Patagonian Dam Debate," International Rivers, May 18, 2008, http://internationalrivers.org/en/node/2828 (accessed September 8, 2009); "Renovating Home Depot," *BusinessWeek,* March 6, 2006, http://www.businessweek.com/print/magazine/content/06_10/b3974001.htm?chan=gl (accessed September 8, 2009); Scelfo, Julie, "The Meltdown in Home Furnishings," *New York Times,* January 28, 2009, http://www.nytimes.com/2009/01/29/garden/29industry.html (accessed September 8, 2009); "2008 Annual Report," Home Depot, http://www.homedepotar.com/ (accessed September 8, 2009); Uchitelle, Louis, "Home Depot Girds for Continued Weakness," *New York Times,* May 18, 2009, http://www.nytimes.com/2009/05/19/business/19depot.html (accessed September 8, 2009); "United We Can—Take on Challenges, Shape Careers and Improve Communities," Home Depot, https://careers.homedepot.com/cg/content.do?p=/united (accessed May 21, 2009); "We Build Community: Team Depot," Home Depot, http://corporate.homedepot.com/wps/portal/!ut/p/c1/04_SB8K8xLLM9MSSzPy8xBz9CPo0s3gDdwNHHosfE3M3AzMPJ8MALxcDKADKR2LKmxrD5fHr9vPIz03VL8iNKAcAbzcnOw!!/dl2/d1/L2dJQSEvUUt3QS9ZQnB3LzZfMEcwQUw5TDQ3RjA2SEIxUE1EMDAwMDAwMDA!/ (accessed March 12, 2009); "What We Do," The Home Depot Foundation, http://www.homedepotfoundation.org/what.html (accessed September 8, 2009); "World's Most Admired Companies: Home Depot," *Fortune,* http://money.cnn.com/magazines/fortune/globalmostadmired/2008/snapshots/2968.html (accessed September 8, 2009); Zimmerman, Ann, "Home Depot Spanish Site Is Shuttered," *Wall Street Journal,* May 2, 2009, http://online.wsj.com/article/SB124122625291179435.html (accessed September 8, 2009).

CASE 18

New Belgium Brewing: Ethical and Environmental Responsibility

Daryl Benson

Although most of the companies frequently cited as examples of ethical and socially responsible firms are large corporations, it is the social responsibility initiatives of small businesses that often have the greatest impact on local communities and neighborhoods. These businesses create jobs and provide goods and services for customers in smaller markets that larger corporations often are not interested in serving. Moreover, they also contribute money, resources, and volunteer time to local causes. Their owners often serve as community and neighborhood leaders, and many choose to apply their skills and some of the fruits of their success to tackling local problems and issues that benefit everyone in the community. Managers and employees become role models for ethical and socially responsible actions. One such small business is the New Belgium Brewing Company, Inc., based in Fort Collins, Colorado.

HISTORY OF THE NEW BELGIUM BREWING COMPANY

The idea for the New Belgium Brewing Company began with a bicycling trip through Belgium. Belgium is arguably the home of some of the world's finest ales, some of which have been brewed for centuries in that country's monasteries. As Jeff Lebesch, an American electrical engineer, cruised around that country on his fat-tired mountain bike, he wondered if he could produce such high-quality beers back home in Colorado. After acquiring the special strain of yeast used to brew Belgian-style ales, Lebesch returned home and began to experiment in his Colorado basement. When his beers earned thumbs up from friends, Lebesch decided to market them.

This case was developed under the direction of O.C. Ferrell and Jennifer Jackson. Jennifer Sawayda, Nikole Haiar, and Melanie Drever provided editorial assistance. We appreciate the input and assistance of Greg Owsley, New Belgium Brewing, in developing this case. This case was prepared for classroom discussion, rather than to illustrate either effective or ineffective handling of an administrative, ethical, or legal decision by management. All sources used for this case were obtained through publicly available material and the New Belgium website.

The New Belgium Brewing Company (NBB) opened for business in 1991 as a tiny basement operation in Lebesch's home in Fort Collins. Lebesch's wife, Kim Jordan, became the firm's marketing director. They named their first brew Fat Tire Amber Ale in honor of Lebesch's bike ride through Belgium. New Belgium beers quickly developed a small but devoted customer base, first in Fort Collins and then throughout Colorado. The brewery soon outgrew the couple's basement and moved into an old railroad depot before settling into its present custom-built facility in 1995. The brewery includes an automated brew house, two quality assurance labs, and numerous technological innovations for which New Belgium has become nationally recognized as a "paradigm of environmental efficiencies."

Today, New Belgium Brewing Company offers a variety of permanent and seasonal ales and pilsners. The company's standard line includes Sunshine Wheat, Blue Paddle, Abbey, Mothership Wit, 1554, Trippel, and the original Fat Tire Amber Ale, still the firm's best-seller. Some customers even refer to the company as the Fat Tire Brewery. The brewery also markets four types of specialty beers on a seasonal basis. Seasonal ales include Frambozen, released at Thanksgiving, Skinny Dip, released during the summer, 2° for winter, and Mighty Arrow for spring. The firm has started a Lips of Faith program, where small batch brews like La Folie, Biere de Mars, and Abbey Grand Cru are created for internal celebrations or landmark events. In addition, New Belgium is working in collaboration (or collabeeration) with Elysian Brewing Company, in which each company will be able to use the other's brewhouses though they are still independent businesses. Through this, they hope to create better efficiency and experimentation along with taking collaborative strides in the future of American beer making. One collabeeration beer resulting from this partnership is Trippel IPA.

Until 2005, NBB's most effective form of advertising was customers' word of mouth. Indeed, before New Belgium beers were widely distributed throughout Colorado, one liquor store owner in Telluride is purported to have offered people gas money if they would stop by and pick up New Belgium beer on their way through Ft. Collins. Although New Belgium beers are distributed in less than half of the United States, the brewery receives numerous e-mails and phone calls every day inquiring when its beers will be available elsewhere.

Although still a small brewery when compared to companies like its in-state rival Coors, NBB has consistently experienced strong growth and has become the third-largest "craft" brewery in the nation with 2007 sales of $96 million. Sales for its Fat Time brand were up 39 percent in 2009 over the year before. This was the largest increase in sales for any craft brewer in the nation. It now has its own blog, MySpace, and Facebook pages. The plant is currently capable of producing 700 bottles of beer a minute, and they are developing a capacity for canned beer of 50 to 60 per minute. In 2008, they were in twenty states from the Pacific coast to the Midwest and looking to release products in five more states in 2009 (see Figure 1). This growth has been driven by beer connoisseurs who appreciate the high quality of NBB's products as well as what the company stands for. When NBB began distribution in Minnesota, it was so popular that a liquor store had to open early and make other accommodations for the large number of customers. The store sold 400 cases of "Fat Tire" in the first hour it was open. The brewery is now the ninth largest of any kind in the country.

With expanding distribution, however, the brewery has recognized a need to increase its opportunities for reaching its far-flung customers. It consulted with Dr. Douglas Holt, an Oxford professor and cultural branding expert. After studying the young company, Holt, together with Marketing Director Greg Owsley, drafted a 70-page "manifesto"

FIGURE 1 New Belgium's Distribution Territories

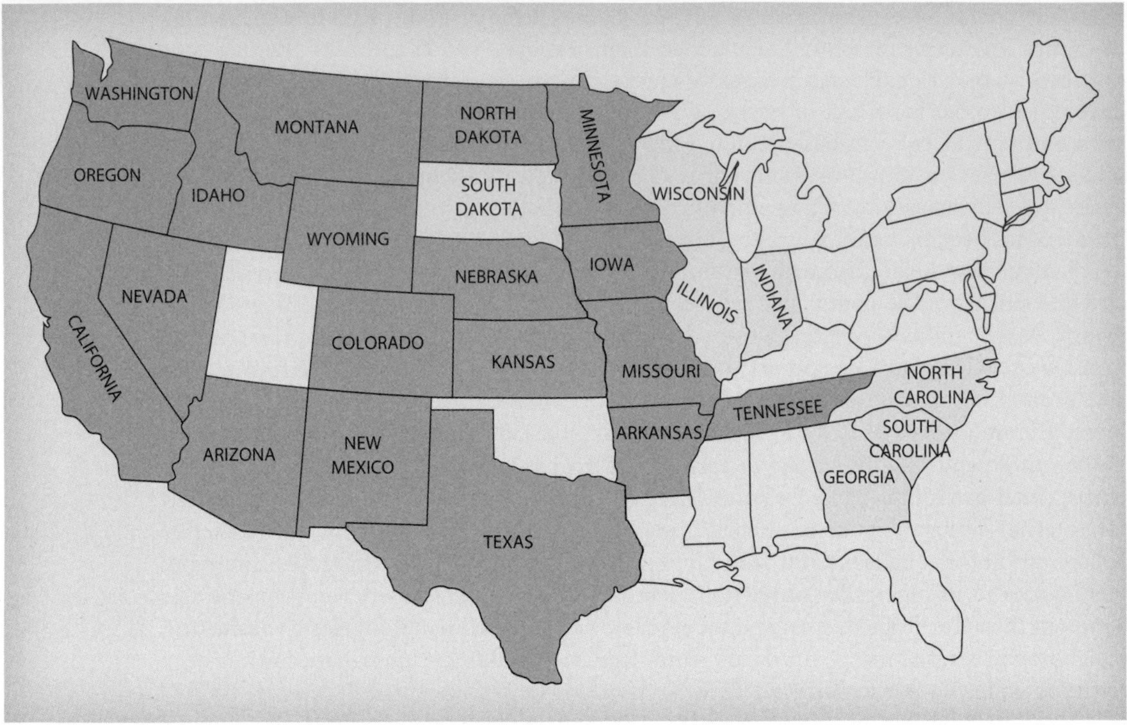

Source: Information obtained from http://www.newbelgium.com/faq.

describing the brand's attributes, character, cultural relevancy, and promise. In particular, Holt identified in New Belgium an ethos of pursuing creative activities simply for the joy of doing them well and in harmony with the natural environment.

With the brand thus defined, New Belgium went in search of an advertising agency to help communicate that brand identity; it soon found Amalgamated, an equally young, independent New York advertising agency. Amalgamated created a $10 million advertising campaign for New Belgium that targets high-end beer drinkers, men ages 25 to 44, and highlights the brewery's image as being down-to-earth. The grainy ads focus on a man, Charles the Tinkerer, rebuilding a cruiser bike out of used parts and then riding it along pastoral country roads. Shot around Hotchkiss and Paonia, Colorado, the producers were going for a spontaneous, easygoing vibe. The product appears in just five seconds of each ad between the tag lines, "Follow Your Folly . . . Ours Is Beer." At first, New Belgium thought that "Folly" carried too much of a negative connotation, but department support encouraged the company to keep the line. With nostalgic music playing in the background, the ads have helped position the growing brand as whimsical, thoughtful, and reflective. In addition to the ad campaign, the company has maintained its strategy of promotion through event sponsorships.

NEW BELGIUM ETHICAL CULTURE

According to Greg Owsley, director of marketing for New Belgium Brewing, there is a fundamental focus on the ethical culture of the brand. Although consumer suspicion of business is on fully raised eyebrows, those in good standing—as opposed to those trading on hype—are eyed with iconic-like adoration. From this off polarization comes a new paradigm in which businesses that fully embrace citizenship in the communities they serve can forge enduring bonds with customers.

Meanwhile, these are precarious times for businesses that choose to ignore consumers who look at brands from an ethical perspective. More than ever before, what the brand says and what the company does must be synchronized. NBB believes that as the mandate for corporate social responsibility gains momentum beyond the courtroom to the far more powerful marketplace, any current and future manager of business must realize that business ethics are not so much about the installation of compliance codes and standards as they are about the spirit in which they are integrated. Thus, the modern-day brand steward—usually the most externally focused member of the business management team—must prepare to be the internal champion of the bottom-line necessity for ethical, values-driven company behavior.

At New Belgium, a synergy of brand and values occurred naturally as the firm's ethical culture (in the form of core values and beliefs) was in place long before NBB had a marketing department. Back in early 1991, New Belgium was just a home-brewed business plan of Jeff Lesbesch, an electrical engineer, and his social worker wife, Kim Jordan. Before they signed any business paperwork, the two took a hike into Rocky Mountain National Park. Armed with a pen and a notebook, they took their first stab at what the fledgling company's core purpose would be. If they were going forward with this venture, what were their aspirations beyond profitability? What was the real root cause of their dream? What they wrote down that spring day, give or take a little wordsmithing, are the core values and beliefs that you can read on the NBB website today.

More importantly, ask just about any New Belgium worker, and she or he can list for you many, if not all, of these shared values and can inform you about which are the most personally poignant. For NBB, branding strategies are as rooted in its company values as in other business practices.

NEW BELGIUM'S PURPOSE AND CORE BELIEFS

New Belgium's dedication to quality, the environment, and its employees and customers is expressed in its mission statement: "To operate a profitable brewery which makes our love and talent manifest." The company's stated core values and beliefs about its role as an environmentally concerned and socially responsible brewer include the following:

- Producing world-class beers
- Promoting beer culture and the responsible enjoyment of beer
- Continuous, innovative quality and efficiency improvements
- Transcending customers' expectations
- Environmental stewardship: minimizing resource consumption, maximizing energy efficiency, and recycling
- Kindling social, environmental, and cultural change as a business role model
- Cultivating potential: through learning, participative management, and the pursuit of opportunities
- Balancing the myriad needs of the company, staff, and their families

- Committing ourselves to authentic relationships, communications, and promises
- Having Fun

Employees believe that these statements help communicate to customers and other stakeholders what New Belgium, as a company, is about. These simple values developed nineteen years ago are just as meaningful to the company and its customers today as they were then, even though the company has experienced much growth.

EMPLOYEE CONCERNS

Recognizing employees' roles in the company's success, New Belgium provides many generous benefits for its 320 employees. In addition to the usual paid health and dental insurance and retirement plans, employees get a free lunch every other week as well as a free massage once a year, and they can bring their children and dogs to work. Employees who stay with the company for five years earn an all-expenses-paid trip to Belgium to "study beer culture." Perhaps most importantly, employees can also earn stock in the privately-held corporation, which grants them a vote in company decisions. Employees currently own about 32 percent of company stock. Open-book management also allows employees to see the financial costs and performance of the company.

> *New Belgium is considered to be the number-one place to work by* Outside Online.

New Belgium also wishes to get its employees involved not only in the company, but in sustainability efforts as well. To help their own sustainability efforts, employees are given a cruiser bike after one year's employment so they can ride to work instead of drive. The NBB sales force is provided with Toyota Prius hybrids. A recycling center on-site is provided for employees to recycle their old items. Additionally, each summer New Belgium hosts the Tour de Fat, where employees can dress in costumes and lead locals on a bike tour. Other company perks include inexpensive yoga classes, free beer at quitting time, and a climbing wall. Due to its desire to create a pleasant worker atmosphere, New Belgium is considered to be the number-one place to work by *Outside Online*.

SUSTAINABILITY CONCERNS

New Belgium's marketing strategy involves linking the quality of its products, as well as its brand, with the company's philosophy toward affecting the planet. From leading-edge environmental gadgets and high-tech industry advancements to employee-ownership programs and a strong belief in giving back to the community, New Belgium demonstrates its desire to create a living, learning community.

NBB strives for cost-efficient, energy-saving alternatives for conducting its business and reducing its impact on the environment. In staying true to the company's core values and beliefs, the brewery's employee-owners unanimously agreed to invest in a wind turbine, making New Belgium the first fully wind-powered brewery in the United States. Since the switch from coal power, New Belgium has been able to reduce its CO_2 emissions by 1,800 metric tons per year. The company further reduces its energy use by employing a steam condenser that captures and reuses the hot water that boils the barley and hops in the production process to start the next brew. The steam is redirected to heat the floor tiles and de-ice the loading docks in cold weather. NBB also purchased a brew kettle, the second of its kind installed in the nation, which heats wort sheets instead of the whole kettle at once. This kettle heating method conserves energy more than standard kettles do. Another way that NBB conserves energy is by using "sun tubes," which provide natural daytime lighting throughout the brew house all year long. Finally, the brewery uses a complex system to capture its waste water and extract methane from it. This can contribute up to 15 percent of the brewery's power needs while reducing the strain on the local municipal water treatment facility.

New Belgium takes pride in reducing waste through recycling and creative reuse strategies. The company strives to recycle as many supplies as possible, including cardboard boxes, keg caps, office materials, and the amber glass used in bottling. The brewery stores spent barley and hop grains in an on-premise silo and invites local farmers to pick up the grains, free of charge, to feed their pigs. Going further down the road to producing products for the food chain, NBB is working with partners to take the same bacteria that create methane from NBB waste water and convert them into a harvestable, high-protein fish food. NBB even encourages its employees to reduce air pollution by using alternative transportation like the cruiser bikes the company provides for employees after a year of company employment.

New Belgium has been a long-time participant in green building techniques. With each expansion of the facility, it has incorporated new technologies and learned a few lessons along the way. In 2002, NBB agreed to participate in the U.S. Green Building Council's Leadership in Energy and Environment Design for Existing Buildings (LEED-EB) pilot program. From sun tubes and daylighting throughout the facility to reusing heat in the brew house, NBB continues to search for new ways to close loops and conserve resources.

Reduce, Reuse, Recycle—the three Rs of being an environmental steward—are taken seriously at NBB. The company's reuse program includes heat for the brewing process, cleaning chemicals, water, and much more. Recycling at New Belgium takes on many forms, from turning "waste" products into something new and useful (like spent grain to cattle feed), to supporting the recycling market in creative ways (like turning their keg caps into table surfaces). The company also buys recycled products whenever possible, from paper to office furniture. The graph in Figure 2 depicts New Belgium's 2008 recycling efforts.

To measure its efforts in the area of the first "R," reduction, New Belgium has created its own Life-cycle Assessment that helps the company to account for the energy flows of its products' lifecycles in order to see how much energy has been reduced. Its numerous reduction efforts, including everything from motion sensors on the lights throughout the building to induction fans that pull in cool winter air to chill the beer, offset New Belgium's energy needs and are the cornerstone to being environmentally efficient.

Finally, NBB has begun changing its product line-up to include an organic beer. This beer is really a microcosm of the company—it is a wit (white) beer, which is a traditional Belgian style of unfiltered wheat beer with orange and coriander flavors. This new organic beer coincides with New Belgium's environmental initiatives, as making it from organic ingredients poses less of a threat to the environment.

New Belgium has made significant achievements in the area of sustainability, particularly compared to other companies in the industry. For one, New Belgium uses only 4 gallons of water to make 1 gallon of beer, which is 20 percent less than most other companies in the industry. New Belgium was able to recycle 73 percent of its waste in 2007,

FIGURE 2 Recycling at New Belgium

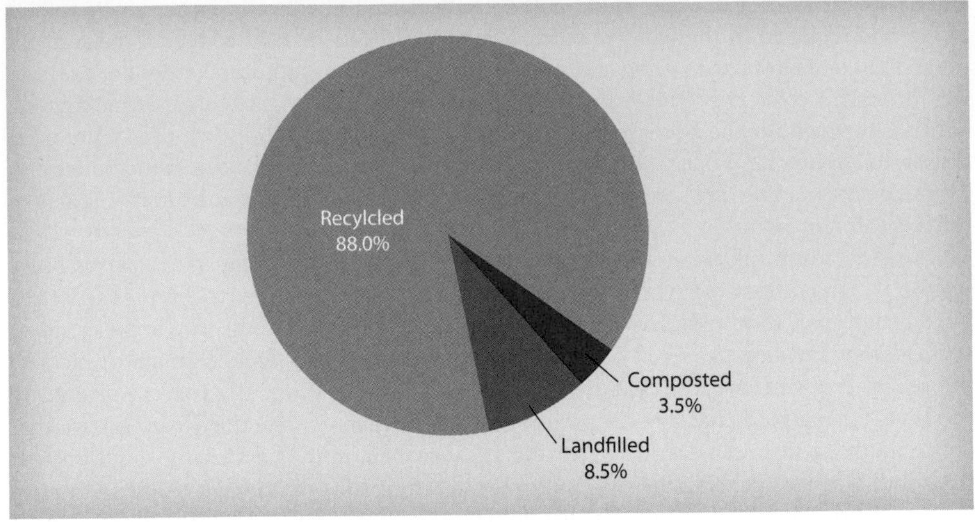

Source: Information obtained from http://www.newbelgium.com/blog/post/waste-not-want-not (accessed September 11,

and today 100 percent of its electricity comes from renewables. Despite these achievements, New Belgium has no intention of halting its sustainability efforts. It hopes to reduce the amount of water used to make beer by 10 percent through better production processes and to decrease its carbon footprint by 25 percent per barrel of its Fat Tire Beer by 2015.

SOCIAL CONCERNS

Beyond its use of environmental-friendly technologies and innovations, New Belgium Brewing Company strives to improve communities and enhance people's lives through corporate giving, event sponsorship, and philanthropic involvement.

Since its inception, NBB has donated more than $2.9 million to philanthropic causes. For every barrel of beer sold the prior year, NBB donates $1 to philanthropic causes within their distribution territory. The donations are divided between states in proportion to their percentage of overall sales. This is the company's way of staying local and giving back to the communities that support and purchase NBB products. In 2006, Arkansas, Arizona, California, Colorado, Idaho, Kansas, Missouri, Montana, Nebraska, Nevada, New Mexico, Oregon, Texas, Washington, and Wyoming all received funding. In 2008, NBB donated $490,000 in funds for philanthropic causes. It also participates in One Percent For The Planet, a philanthropic network to which NBB donates 1 percent of its profits.

Funding decisions are made by New Belgium's philanthropy committee, which is comprised of employees throughout the brewery including owners, employee-owners, area leaders, and production workers. New Belgium looks for nonprofit organizations that demonstrate creativity, diversity, and an innovative approach to their mission and objectives. The philanthropy committee also looks for groups that involve the community to reach their goals.

Additionally, NBB maintains a community bulletin board in its facility where it posts an array of community involvement activities and proposals. This community board allows tourists and employees to see the different ways they can help out the community, and it gives nonprofit organizations a chance to make their needs known. Organizations can even apply for grants through the New Belgium Brewing Company website, which has a link designated for this purpose. In 2009, the company hoped to award grants in the areas of water stewardship, sensible transportation and bike advocacy, sustainable agriculture, and youth environmental education.

NBB also sponsors a number of events, with a special focus on those that involve "human-powered" sports that cause minimal damage to the natural environment. Through event sponsorships, such as the Tour de Fat, NBB supports various environmental, social, and cycling nonprofit organizations. In the Tour de Fat, one participant hands over his or her car keys and vehicle title in exchange for an NBB commuter bike and trailer. The participant is then filmed for the world to see as he or she promotes sustainable transportation over driving. In addition, New Belgium has been supporting the National Multiple Sclerosis Society. NBB has helped by donating jerseys and by partnering with another organization to create a team for Pedal the Plains 2009. The team, known as Bike MS, will ride for a weekend to raise donations for the society. NBB also sponsored the Ride the Rockies bike tour, which donated the proceeds from beer sales to local nonprofit groups. The money raised from this annual event funds local projects, such as improving parks and bike trails. In the course of one year, New Belgium can be found at anywhere from 150 to 200 festivals and events across fifteen western states.

ORGANIZATIONAL SUCCESS

New Belgium Brewing Company's efforts to live up to its own high standards have paid off with numerous awards and a very loyal following. It was one of three winners of *Business Ethics* magazine's Business Ethics Awards for its "dedication to environmental excellence in every part of its innovative brewing process." Kim Jordan and Jeff Lebesch were named the recipients of the Rocky Mountain Region Entrepreneur of the Year Award for manufacturing, and NBB was listed in the *Wall Street Journal* as one of the fifteen best small workplaces. The company has also captured the award for best mid-sized brewing company of the year and best mid-sized brewmaster at the Great American Beer Festival. New Belgium has taken home medals for three different brews, Abbey Belgian Style Ale, Blue Paddle Pilsner, and LaFolie specialty ale. Additionally, the exemplary leadership of CEO Kim Lebesch was recognized as she won *ColoradoBiz* magazine's 2008 CEO of the year and was invited to meet then presidential-elect Barack Obama.

According to David Edgar, director of the Institute for Brewing Studies, "They've created a very positive image for their company in the beer-consuming public with smart decision making." Although some members of society do not believe that a company whose major product is alcohol can be socially responsible, New Belgium has set out to prove that for those who make a choice to drink responsibly, the company can do everything possible to contribute to society. Its efforts to promote beer culture and the connoisseurship of beer have even led it to design a special "Worthy Glass," the shape of which is intended to retain foam, show off color, enhance visual presentation, and release aroma. New Belgium Brewing Company also promotes the responsible appreciation of beer through its participation in and support of the culinary arts. For instance, it frequently hosts New Belgium Beer Dinners, in which every course of the meal is served with a complementary culinary treat.

According to Greg Owsley, director of marketing, although the Fat Tire brand has a bloodline straight from the enterprise's ethical beliefs and practices, the firm's work is not done. The company must continually reexamine ethical, social, and environmental responsibilities. In 2004, New Belgium received the Environmental Protection Agency's regional Environmental Achievement Award. It was both an honor and a motivator for the company to continue its socially responsible goals. After all, there are still many ways for NBB to improve as a corporate citizen. For example, the manufacturing process is a fair distance from being zero waste or emission free. Although all electric power comes from renewable sources, the plant is still heated in part by using natural gas. Additionally, there will always be a need for more public dialog on avoiding alcohol abuse.

Practically speaking, the company has a never-ending to-do list. NBB must acknowledge that as its annual sales increase, the challenges for the brand to remain on a human scale and to continue to be culturally authentic will increase too. How to boldly grow the brand while maintaining its humble feel has always been a challenge. Additionally, reducing waste to an even greater extent will take lots of work on behalf of both managers and employees, creating the need for a collaborative process that will require the dedication of both parties toward sustainability.

Every six-pack of New Belgium Beer displays the phrase, "In this box is our labor of love. We feel incredibly lucky to be creating something fine that enhances people's lives." Although Jeff Lebesch has "semi-retired" from the company to focus on other interests, the founders of New Belgium hope this statement captures the spirit of the company. According to employee Dave Kemp, NBB's environmental concern and social responsibility give it a competitive advantage because consumers want to believe in and feel good about the products they purchase. NBB's most important asset is its image—a corporate brand that stands for quality, responsibility, and concern for society. Defining itself as more than just a beer company, the brewer also sees itself as a caring organization that is concerned with all stakeholders, including the community, sustainability, and employees.

QUESTIONS

1. What environmental issues does the New Belgium Brewing Company work to address? How has NBB taken a strategic approach to addressing these issues? Why do you think the company has chosen to focus on environmental issues?
2. Are New Belgium's social initiatives indicative of strategic philanthropy? Why or why not?
3. Some segments of society vigorously contend that companies that sell alcoholic beverages and tobacco products cannot be socially responsible organizations because of the nature of their primary products. Do you believe that New Belgium Brewing Company's actions and initiatives are indicative of an ethical and socially responsible corporation? Why or why not?

SOURCES

Arnold, Katie, "Where to Apply Now," *Outside Online*, May 2008, http://outside.away.com/outside/culture/200805/best-companies-1.html (accessed September 8, 2009); Asmus, Peter, "Goodbye Coal, Hello Wind," *Business*

Ethics 13 (July/August 1999): 10–11.; Baun, Robert, "What's in a Name? Ask the Makers of Fat Tire," *[Fort Collins] Coloradoan*, October 8, 2000, pp. E1, E3; "The Carbon Footprint of a 6-Pack of Fat Tire Amber Ale," New Belgium Brewing Blog, August 18, 2008, http://www.newbelgium.com/blog/post/carbon-footprint-6-pack-fat-tire-amber-ale (accessed September 8, 2009); "Collabeeration," New Belgium, http://www.newbelgium.com/beerline/collabeeration (accessed September 8, 2009); Deter, Stevi, "Fat Tire Amber Ale," The Net Net, www.thenetnet.com/reviews/fat.html (accessed September 8, 2009); Dwyer, Robert F., and John F. Tanner Jr., *Business Marketing* (Boston: Irwin McGraw-Hill, 1999), p. 104; Fera, Rae Ann, "Small Shops, Big Moves," *'boards*, January 1, 2005, http://www.boardsmag.com/articles/magazine/20050101/smallshops.html?__b=yes (accessed September 9, 2009); "Four Businesses Honored with Prestigious International Award for Outstanding Marketplace Ethics," Better Business Bureau, press release, September 23, 2002, http://www.bbb.org/us/article/four-businesses-honored-with-prestigious-international-award-for-outstanding-marketplace-ethics-193 (accessed September 9, 2009); "GABF 2000 Awards," Reelbear.com, http://www.realbeer.com/edu/gabf/gabf2000.php (accessed September 9, 2009); Gordon, Julie, "Lebesch Balances Interests in Business, Community," *Coloradoan*, February 26, 2003; Haiar, Nikole, "New Belgium Brewing Company Tour" November 20, 2000; Hawkins, Del I., Roger J. Best, and Kenneth A. Concy, *Consumer Behavior: Building Marketing Strategy*, 8th ed. (Boston: Irwin McGraw-Hill, 2001); Kemp, David, "Tour Connoisseur," New Belgium Brewing Company, personal interview by Nikole Haiar, November 21, 2000; "Lips of Faith," New Belgium, http://www.newbelgium.com/beerline/lips-of-faith (accessed September 8, 2009); "New Belgium Brewing," MySpace, http://www.myspace.com/follyyourfolly (accessed September 8, 2009); "New Belgium Brewing Blog," New Belgium, http://www.newbelgium.com/blog/post/2008-sustainability-nonreport (accessed September 8, 2009); New Belgium Brewing Company, Ft. Collins, CO, www.newbelgium.com (accessed September 8, 2009); "New Belgium Brewing to Cut CO_2 Emissions by 25% Per Barrel," *Environmental Leader*, January 20, 2009, http://www.environmentalleader.com/2009/01/20/new-belgium-brewing-to-cut- co2-emissions-by-25-per-barrel/ (accessed September 8, 2009); "New Belgium Brewing Wins Ethics Award," *Denver Business Journal*, January 2, 2003, http://denver.bizjournals.com/denver/stories/2002/12/30/daily21.html (accessed September 8, 2009); Owsley, Greg, "The Necessity for Aligning Brand with Corporate Ethics," in Sheb L. True, Linda Ferrell, and O. C. Ferrell, *Fulfilling Our Obligation, Perspectives on Teaching Business Ethics* (Kennesaw State University Press, 2005), pp. 128–132; Raabe, Steve, "New Belgium Brewing Turns to Cans," denverpost.com, May 15, 2008, http://www.denverpost.com/ci_9262005 (accessed September 8, 2009); "Recession-Proof Brewing," *Colorado Biz*, September 2009, pp. 62–64; Reuteman, Rob, "REUTEMAN: Colorado Rides on Fat Tire to Beer Heights," *Rocky Mountain News*, November 24, 2007, http://www.rockymountainnews.com/news/2007/nov/24/reuteman-colorado-rides-on-fat-tire-to-beer/ (accessed September 9, 2009); Simpson, Bryan, *New Belgium Brewing: Brand Building Through Advertising and Public Relations*, http://e-businessethics.com/NewBelgiumCases/newbelgiumbrewing.pdf (accessed September 8, 2009); "South Dakota—Bike MS: Pedal the Plains 2009," *National Multiple Sclerosis Society*, http://main.nationalmssociety.org/site/TR?pg=team&fr_id=10070&team_id=171995 (accessed September 9, 2009); "Sponsorship," New Belgium, http://www.newbelgium.com/sponsorship (accessed September 9, 2009); Spors, Kelly K., "Top Small Workplaces 2008," *Wall Street Journal*, February 22, 2009, http://online.wsj.com/article/SB122347733961315417.html (accessed September 8, 2009); "Sustainability," New Belgium website, http://www.newbelgium.com/sustainability.php (accessed September 8, 2009); "A Tour of the New Belgium Brewery—Act One," LiveGreen blog, April 9, 2007, http://www.livegreensd.com/2007/04/tour-of-new-belgium-brewery-act-one.html (accessed September 9, 2009); "Trade Your Car for a Bike," New Belgium, http://www.newbelgium.com/trade (accessed September 8, 2009); Tuttle, Andrea, *Ride the Rockies*, June 15–21, 2008, http://www.postnewsads.com/interactivekit/uploads/rtr/RideTheRockies.pdf (accessed September 9, 2009); "2007 Sustainability Report," New Belgium, http://www.newbelgium.com/files/shared/07Sus tainabilityReportlow.pdf (accessed September 8, 2009).

Chapter 1

1. "New US Consumer Survey Shows High Distrust of Financial Services Companies," *Business Wire,* January 20, 2009, http://findarticles.com/p/articles/mi_m0EIN/is_2009_Jan_20/ai_n31202849/ (accessed May 27, 2009).
2. "New National Poll: Nearly 40 Percent of 'Ethically Prepared' Teens Believe Lying, Cheating, or Violence Necessary to Succeed," Junior Achievement/Deloitte Teen Ethics Survey, http://www.ja.org/files/polls/2008-JA-Deloitte-Teen-Ethics-Survey-Data.pdf (accessed January 13, 2009).
3. "Teens Respect Good Business Ethics," *USA Today,* December 12, 2005, B1.
4. Marianne Jennings, "An Ethical Breach by Any Other Name," *Financial Engineering News,* January/February 2006.
5. Paul W. Taylor, *Principles of Ethics: An Introduction to Ethics,* 2nd ed. (Encino, CA: Dickenson, 1975), 1.
6. Adapted and reproduced from *The American Heritage Dictionary of the English Language,* 4th ed. Copyright © 2002 by Houghton Mifflin Company.
7. Wroe Alderson, *Dynamic Marketing Behavior* (Homewood, IL: Irwin, 1965), 320.
8. Ethics Resource Center, *2005 National Business Ethics Survey: How Employees Perceive Ethics at Work* (Washington, DC: Ethics Resource Center, 2005), 4, 28, 29.
9. Heather Timmons and Bettina Wassener, "Satyam Chief Admits Huge Fraud," http://www.nytimes.com/2009/01/08/business/worldbusiness/08satyam.html (accessed January 13, 2009).
10. Mark Dolliver, "Corporate Reputation Hits a New Low," April 28, 2009, http://www.adweek.com/aw/content_display/data-center/research/e3i0dac803b1646d6af9cc89a12ad823619 (accessed May 27, 2009).
11. "Ex-Goldman Associate Is Sentenced in Insider Trading Case," *New York Times,* January 13, 2009, http://dealbook.blogs.nytimes.com/2008/01/03/ex-goldman-associate-is-sentenced-in-insider-trading-case/ (accessed January 13, 2009).
12. "PWC Accounting Firm Reaches $97 Million Settlement with Ohio in AIG Case," *Insurance Journal,* http://www.insurancejournal.com/news/national/2008/10/06/94335.htm (accessed January 14, 2009).
13. "In Wake of Stevens Case Dismissal, Alaska Republicans Call for Special Election," http://www.foxnews.com/politics/2009/04/02/wake-stevens-case-dismissal-alaska-republicans-special-election/ (accessed May 27, 2009).
14. John Lyman, "Who Is Scooter Libby? The Guy Behind the Guy," *Center for American Progress* (October 28, 2005).
15. Leonard Cassuto, "Big Trouble in the World of 'Big Physics'," Salon, September 16, 2002, http://dir.salon.com/story/tech/feature/2002/09/16/physics/index.html (accessed August 4, 2009).
16. Nicholas Wade and Choe Sang-Hun, "Researcher Faked Evidence of Human Cloning, Koreans Report," *The New York Times,* January 10, 2006, http://www.nytimes.com/2006/01/10/science/10clone.html?_r=1 (accessed August 4, 2009).
17. Dylan Hernandez, "Dodgers' Manny Ramirez suspended 50 games after failing drug test," May 8, 2009, http://www.latimes.com/sports/la-sp-manny-ramirez8-2009may08,0,7402416,print.story (accessed June 3, 2009).
18. "Caraco Pharmaceutical Laboratories, Lfd. Announces a Nationwide Voluntary Recall of All Lots of Digoxin Tablets Due to Size," FDA Product Recall, March 31, 2009, http://www.hipusa.com/downloads/digoxinrecall2009.pdf (accessed May 27, 2009).
19. Archie B. Carroll and Ann K. Buchholtz, *Business and Society: Ethics and Stakeholder Management* (Cincinnati: South-Western, 2006), 452–455.
20. Alan R. Yuspeh, "Development of Corporate Compliance Programs: Lessons Learned from the DII Experience," in *Corporate Crime in America: Strengthening the "Good Citizenship" Corporation* (Washington, DC: U.S. Sentencing Commission, 1995), 71–79.
21. Eleanor Hill, "Coordinating Enforcement Under the Department of Defense Voluntary Disclosure Program," in *Corporate Crime in America: Strengthening the "Good Citizenship" Corporation* (Washington, DC: U.S. Sentencing Commission, 1995), 287–294.
22. "Huffing and Puffing in Washington: Can Clinton's Plan Curb Teen Smoking?" *Consumer Reports* 60 (1995): 637.
23. Arthur Levitt, with Paula Dwyer, *Take on the Street* (New York: Pantheon Books, 2002).
24. Hill, "Coordinating Enforcement."
25. Richard P. Conaboy, "Corporate Crime in America: Strengthening the Good Citizen Corporation," in *Corporate Crime in America: Strengthening the "Good Citizenship" Corporation* (Washington, DC: U.S. Sentencing Commission, 1995), 1–2.
26. *United States Code Service* (Lawyers' Edition), 18 U.S.C.S. Appendix, Sentencing Guidelines for the United States Courts (Rochester, NY: Lawyers Cooperative Publishing, 1995), sec. 8A.1.
27. Steve Stecklow and Diya Gullapalli, "SEC Sues Reserve's Bent and Son," *Wall Street Journal,* May 6, 2009, http://online.wsj.com/article/SB124154900090988321.html (accessed May 5, 2009).
28. "WorldCom CEO Slaps Arthur Andersen," CNN, July 8, 2002, www.cnn.com.
29. "Fraud Inc.," CNN/Money, http://money.cnn.com/news/specials/corruption/ (accessed February 5, 2002); "SEC Formalizes

Investigation into Halliburton Accounting," *Wall Street Journal* online, December 20, 2002, http://online.wsj.com.
30. World Economic Forum, "Trust in Governments, Corporations and Global Institutions" December 15, 2005, http://www2.weforum.org/site/homepublic.nsf/Content/Full+Survey_+Trust+in+Governments,+Corporations+and+Global+Institutions+Continues+to+Decline.html (accessed August 4, 2009).
31. "Corporate Reform Bill Passed," CNN, July 25, 2002, www.cnn.com.
32. KPMG Forensic Integrity Survey 2008-2009, http://www.kpmg.com.br/publicacoes/forensic/Integrity_Survey_2008_2009.pdf (accessed June 3, 2009).
33. Masamitsu Sakurai, "Environmental Commitments in Global Business," *Ethisphere,* May 13, 2009, http://ethisphere.com/environmental-commitments-in-global-business/ (accessed May 27, 2009).
34. Bernard J. Jaworski and Ajay K. Kohli, "Market Orientation: Antecedents and Consequences," *Journal of Marketing* 57 (1993): 53–70.
35. Ethics Resource Center, *2000 National Business Ethics Survey: How Employees Perceive Ethics as Work* (Washington, DC: Ethics Resource Center, 2000), 67.
36. Wal-Mart Sustainability Progress Report, 2008, http://walmartstores.com/Sustainability/7951.aspx; Wal-Mart Stores, Inc., http://walmartstores.com (accessed June 2, 2009).
37. Terry W. Loe, "The Role of Ethical Culture in Developing Trust, Market Orientation and Commitment to Quality" (PhD diss., University of Memphis, 1996).
38. Ethics Resource Center, *2000 National Business Ethics Survey,* 5.
39. John Galvin, "The New Business Ethics," SmartBusinessMag.com, June 2000, 99.
40. "How Ethics Influence Future Profitability—Wal-Mart's Way," May 20, 2009, http://www.insideretailing.com.au/Default.aspx?articleId=5395&articleType=ArticleView&tabid=53 (accessed June 3, 2009).
41. "Biz Deans Talk—Business Management Education Blog," January 2, 2009, http://www.deanstalk.net/deanstalk/2009/01/warren-buffetts.html (accessed May 27, 2009).
42. "Investors Prefer Ethics over High Return," *USA Today,* January 16, 2006, B1.
43. Patagonia, Zumer, http://www.zumer.com/companies/show/18 (accessed May 27, 2009.)
44. "Trend Watch," *Business Ethics,* March/April 2000, 8.
45. Marjorie Kelly, "Holy Grail Found. Absolute, Definitive Proof That Responsible Companies Perform Better Financially," *Business Ethics,* Winter 2004.
46. "Google's Corporate Culture," http://www.google.com/intl/en/corporate/culture.html (accessed May 27, 2009).
47. O. C. Ferrell, Isabelle Maignan, and Terry W. Loe, "The Relationship Between Corporate Citizenship and Competitive Advantage," in *Rights, Relationships, and Responsibilities,* ed. O. C. Ferrell, Lou Pelton, and Sheb L. True (Kennesaw, GA: Kennesaw State University, 2003).
48. Annual Report 2008, Green Mountain Coffee, http://www.greenmountaincoffee.com/gmcrcontent/GMCR-ANNUAL-REPORT-2008.pdf (accessed June 2, 2009).
49. Galvin, "The New Business Ethics."
50. Chung Hua-Shen and Yuan Change, "Ambition Versus Conscience, Does Corporate Social Responsibility Pay Off? The Application of Matching Methods," *Journal of Business Ethics,* (2009) 88: 133–153.

Chapter 2

1. Vikas Anand, Blake E. Ashforth, and Mahendra Joshi, "Business as Usual: The Acceptance and Perpetuation of Corruption in Organizations," *Academy of Management Executive* 18, no. 2 (2004): 39–53.
2. Debbie Thorne, O. C. Ferrell, and Linda Ferrell, *Business and Society* (Boston: Houghton Mifflin, 2003), 64–65.
3. Stephanie Simon and Julie Jargon, "PETA Ads to Target McDonald's," *The Wall Street Journal,* May 1, 2009, http://online.wsj.com/article/SB124112986550474853.html (accessed June 2, 2009).
4. Lynn Brewer, Robert Chandler, and O. C. Ferrell, "Managing Risks for Corporate Integrity: How to Survive an Ethical Misconduct Disaster," (Mason OH: Texere/Thomson, 2006), 11.
5. Roger Parloff, "Wall Street: It's Payback Time," *Fortune,* January 19, 2009, 61.
6. Press Release, "JP Morgan Chase Completes Bear Stearns Acquisition," http://www.bearstearns.com/includes/pdfs/PressRelease_BSC_31May08.pdf (accessed August 4, 2009).
7. Ji Lee, "The End," *Conde Nast Portfolio,* December 9, 2008, 116–117.
8. David Enrich, "Citigroup Is Halting Some Payouts," *The Wall Street Journal,* June 2, 2009, http://online.wsj.com/article/SB124391159480975333.html (accessed June 11, 2009).
9. Brewer, Chandler, and Ferrell, "Managing Risks for Corporate Integrity," 11.
10. Adapted from Isabelle Maignan, O. C. Ferrell, and Linda Ferrell, "A Stakeholder Model for Implementing Social Responsibility in Marketing," *European Journal of Marketing* 39 (2005): 956–977.
11. Ibid.
12. Ibid.
13. Thorne, Ferrell, and Ferrell, *Business and Society.*
14. Isabelle Maignan and O. C. Ferrell, "Corporate Social Responsibility: Toward a Marketing Conceptualization," *Journal of the Academy of Marketing Science* 32 (2004): 3–19.
15. Ibid.
16. Ibid.
17. Roger Bate, "China's Bad Medicine," *The Wall Street Journal,* May 5, 2009, http://online.wsj.com/article/SB124146383501884323.html (accessed June 10, 2009).
18. Maignan and Ferrell, "Corporate Social Responsibility."
19. G. A. Steiner and J. F. Steiner, *Business, Government, and Society* (New York: Random House, 1988).
20. Milton Friedman, "Social Responsibility of Business Is to Increase Its Profits," *New York Times Magazine,* September 13, 1970, 122–126.
21. "Business Leaders, Politicians and Academics Dub Corporate Irresponsibility 'An Attack on America from Within,'" *Business Wire,* November 7, 2002, via America Online.
22. Adam Smith, *The Theory of Moral Sentiments,* Vol. 2. (New York: Prometheus, 2000).
23. Theodore Levitt, *The Marketing Imagination* (New York: Free Press, 1983).
24. Norman Bowie, "Empowering People as an End for Business," in *People in Corporations: Ethical Responsibilities and Corporate Effectiveness,* ed. Georges Enderle, Brenda Almond, and Antonio Argandona (Dordrecht, Netherlands: Kluwer Academic Press, 1990), 105–112.
25. Herman Miller, www.hermanmiller.com; level, http://levelcertified.org/ (accessed June 2, 2009).
26. Press Release, "PNC Commits $28 Million to National City Communities for 2009," PNC Media Room, November 12, 2008, http://pnc.mediaroom.com/index.php?s=43&item=595 (accessed August 4, 2009).
27. Paige Brady, "Walking the Walk," Whole Foods Market Blog, April 23, 2009, http://blog.wholefoodsmarket.com/2009/04/walking-the-walk/ (accessed August 4, 2009).
28. Ibid.

29. Steve Quinn, "Wal-Mart Green with Energy," *[Fort Collins] Coloradoan*, July 24, 2005, E1–E2.
30. ISO Standards Catalogue, http://www.iso.org/iso/iso_catalogue.htm (accessed June 2, 2009).
31. Anne Carey and Keith Simmons, "USA Leads in Wind Power," American Wind Energy Association and the Global Wind Energy Council, printed in *USA Today*, February 17, 2009, p. A1.
32. Tobias Webb, James Rose, and Peter Davis, "ISO 26000 Indicates Immaturity: If Corporate Responsibility Is to Be Effective, Prominence Has to Be Given to Both Quantitative and Qualitative Analyses," *Ethical Corporation* (December 2005): 9.
33. Archie B. Carroll, "The Pyramid of Corporate Social Responsibility: Toward the Moral Management of Organizational Stakeholders," *Business Horizons* 34 (1991): 42.
34. Isabelle Maignan, O. C. Ferrell, and G. Tomas M. Hult, "Corporate Citizenship: Cultural Antecedents and Business Benefits," *Journal of the Academy of Marketing Science* 27 (1999): 457.
35. Gallup Daily Tracking, http://www.gallup.com/poll/us.aspx?CSTS=pollnav&to=POLL-US-News (accessed June 2, 2009).
36. *Dodge v. Ford Motor Co.*, 204 Mich.459, 179 N.W. 668, 3 A.L.R. 413 (1919).
37. "The Moral Hazards of Managing Other People's Money," *The Wall Street Journal*, April 29, 2009, http://online.wsj.com/article/SB124087477951861329.html (accessed June 2, 2009).
38. Alfred Marcus and Sheryl Kaiser, "Managing Beyond Compliance: The Ethical and Legal Dimensions of Corporate Responsibility," *North Coast Publishers*, 2006, 79.
39. Joann S. Lublin, "Corporate Directors' Group Gives Repair Plan to Boards," *The Wall Street Journal*, March 24, 2009, http://online.wsj.com/article/SB123784649341118187.html (accessed June 11, 2009).
40. Phil Mattingly, "AIG Chief Goes Off Script, Says Employees Will Return Some of Bonus Money," " CQ Politics, March 18, 2009, http://www.cqpolitics.com/wmspage.cfm?docID=news-000003077969 (accessed August 4, 2009).
41. Ben W. Heineman, Jr., "Are You a Good Corporate Citizen?" *Wall Street Journal*, June 28, 2005, B2.
42. Phred Dvorak, "Poor Year Doesn't Stop CEO Bonuses," *The Wall Street Journal*, March 18, 2009, http://online.wsj.com/article/SB123698866439126029.html (accessed June 11, 2009).
43. Darryl Reed, "Corporate Governance Reforms in Developing Countries," *Journal of Business Ethics* 37 (2002): 223–247.
44. Bryan W. Husted and Carlos Serrano, "Corporate Governance in Mexico," *Journal of Business Ethics* 37 (2002): 337–348.
45. Maria Maher and Thomas Anderson, *Corporate Governance: Effects on Firm Performance and Economic Growth* (Paris: Organisation for Economic Co-operation and Development, 1999).
46. A. Demb and F. F. Neubauer, *The Corporate Board: Confronting the Paradoxes* (Oxford, Eng.: Oxford University Press, 1992).
47. Maher and Anderson, *Corporate Governance.*
48. Organisation for Economic Co-operation and Development, *The OECD Principles of Corporate-Governance* (Paris: Organisation for Economic Co-operation and Development, 1999).
49. Louis Lavelle, "The Best and Worst Boards," *BusinessWeek*, October 7, 2002, 104–114.
50. Damian Paletta, Maya Jackson Randall, and Michael R. Crittenden, "Geithner Calls for Tougher Standards on Risk," *The Wall Street Journal*, March 25, 2009, http://online.wsj.com/article/SB123807231255147603.html (accessed June 11, 2009).
51. Melvin A. Eisenberg, "Corporate Governance: The Board of Directors and Internal Control," *Cordoza Law Review* 19 (1997): 237.
52. S. Trevis Certo, Catherine Dalton, Dan Dalton, and Richard Lester, "Boards of Directors' Self-Interest: Expanding for Pay in Corporate Acquisitions?" *The Journal of Business Ethics* 77, no. 2 (January 2008): 219–230.
53. Geoffrey Colvin, "CEO Knockdown," *Fortune*, April 4, 2005.
54. David Weidner, "Changing the Dynamic of Shareholder Influence," *The Wall Street Journal*, June 4, 2009, http://online.wsj.com/article/SB124406195031882459.html (accessed June 11, 2009).
55. Saks Shareholders Call for Annual Director Election," Reuters, http://www.reuters.com/article/ousiv/idUSTRE5525DZ20090603 (accessed June 3, 2009).
56. Amy Borrus, "Should Directors Be Nervous," *BusinessWeek* online, March 6, 2006 http://www.businessweek.com/magazine/content/06_10/b3974062.htm (accessed August 4, 2009).
57. John A. Byrne, with Louis Lavelle, Nanette Byrnes, Marcia Vickers, and Amy Borrus, "How to Fix Corporate Governance," *BusinessWeek*, May 6, 2002, 69–78.
58. "How Business Rates: By the Numbers," *BusinessWeek*, September 11, 2000, 148–149.
59. Michael R Crittenden and Patrick Yoest, "AIG's Liddy Asks Employees to Give Back Bonuses," *The Wall Street Journal*, March 18, 2009, http://online.wsj.com/article/SB123738312138170487.html (accessed June 11, 2009).
60. "2009 Executive PayWatch," AFL-CIO, http://www.aflcio.org/corporatewatch/paywatch/ (accessed June 3, 2009).
61. Sarah Anderson, John Cavanagh, Ralph Estes, Chuck Collins, and Chris Hartman, *A Decade of Executive Excess: The 1990s Sixth Annual Executive*. Boston: United for a Fair Economy, 1999, online, June 30, 2006, http://www.faireconomy.org/press_room/1999/a_decade_of_executive_excess_the_1990s (accessed August 4, 2009).Louis Lavelle, "CEO Pay, The More Things Change…," *BusinessWeek*, October 16, 2000, 106–108.
62. Kara Scanell, "SEC Ready to Require More Pay Disclosures," *The Wall Street Journal*, June 3, 2009, http://online.wsj.com/article/SB124397831899078781.html (accessed June 11, 2009).
63. Gary Strauss, "America's Corporate Meltdown," *USA Today*, June 27, 2002, 1A, 2A.
64. Li-Chiu Chi, "Do transparency and performance predict firm performance? Evidence from the Taiwan Market," *Expert Systems with Applications*, Vol 36, Issue 8, October 2009, http://www.sciencedirect.com/science?_ob=ArticleURL&_udi=B6V03-4VTVPW4-1&_user=10&_rdoc=1&_fmt=&_orig=search&_sort=d&_docanchor=&view=c&_acct=C000050221&_version=1&_urlVersion=0&_userid=10&md5=3b7a30dbefb291c4c56f3a5f3a62d859 (accessed August 5, 2009).
65. Marjorie Kelly, "Business Ethics 100 Best Corporate Citizens 2005," *Business Ethics* (Spring 2005): 20–25.
66. "Obesity Issue Looms Large," Washington Wire, *Wall Street Journal* online, March 3, 2006, http://blogs.wsj.com/washwire/2006/03/03/obesity-issue-looms-large/ (accessed August 4, 2009).
67. "Six in Ten Say Family Put Off Medical Care Due to Cost," MarketWatch, April 23, 2009, http://www.marketwatch.com/story/six-ten-say-family-put?dist=msr_8 (accessed June 3, 2009).
68. "Corporate Social Responsibility at Starbucks," http://www.starbucks.com/aboutus/csr.asp (accessed March 21, 2006).
69. Stephanie Armour, "Maryland First to OK 'Wal-Mart Bill' Law Requires More Health Care Spending," *USA Today*, January 13, 2006, B1.
70. Kris Hudson, "Wal-Mart to Offer Improved Health-Care Benefits," *Wall Street Journal*, February 24, 2006, A2.
71. "Oil Watchdog: Running Scared on Hot Fuel," Consumer Watchdog, April 27, 2009, http://www.oilwatchdog.org/articles/?storyId=26724 (accessed June 3, 2009).

Chapter 3

1. Kevin Duffy, "Beazer Homes, SEC Reach Settlement on Earnings," AJC Media Solutions, September 24, 2008, http://www.ajc.com/ee/content/business/stories/2008/09/24/beazer_homes_settlement.html?cxntlid=inform_sr (accessed June 4, 2009).
2. Deborah Solomon and Mark Maremont "Bankers Face Strict New Pay Cap," *The Wall Street Journal*, February 14–15, 2009, p. A1, A10.
3. Eric H. Beversluis, "Is There No Such Thing as Business Ethics?," *Journal of Business Ethics* 6 (1987): 81–88. Reprinted by permission of Kluwer Academic Publishers, Dordrecht, Holland.
4. Carolyn Said, "Ellison Hones His 'Art of War' Tactics," *San Francisco Chronicle*, June 10, 2003, A1.
5. Michael Liedtke, "Oracle CEO to Pay $122M to Settle Lawsuit," Associated Press, *Washington Post* online, November 22, 2005, via http://www.accessmylibrary.com/coms2/summary_0286-12061795_ITM (accessed August 5, 2009).
6. Beversluis, "Is There No Such Thing as Business Ethics?" 82.
7. Vernon R. Loucks, Jr., "A CEO Looks at Ethics," *Business Horizons* 30 (1987): 4
8. Press Release, "As Labor Day Nears, Workplace Bullying Institute Finds Half of Working Americans Affected by Workplace Bullying," Zogby International, August 30, 2007, http://www.zogby.com/search/ReadNews.cfm?ID=1353 (accessed August 5, 2009).
9. Lisa Broadt, "Proposed Laws Could Send Firms to Court for 'Abusive' Behavior'", *Washington Business Journal*, http://www.bizjournals.com/washington/stories/2008/09/29/smallb8.html (accessed February 2, 2009).
10. David Whelan, "Only the Paranoid Resurge," *Forbes*, April 10, 2006, 42–44.
11. Charles Forelle, "EU Plans Fresh Strike on Microsoft," *The Wall Street Journal*, May 30, 2009, http://online.wsj.com/article/SB124362706194767281.html (accessed June 4, 2009).
12. Duff Wilson, "Harvard Medical School in Ethics Quandary," *The New York Times*, March 2, 2009, http://www.nytimes.com/2009/03/03/business/03medschool.html?scp=3&sq=harvard%20medical&st=cse (accessed June 4, 2009).
13. "Panel Seeks Fuller Disclosure of Drug Company Payments," *Forbes*, April 27, 2009, http://www.forbes.com/feeds/hscout/2009/04/28/hscout626501.html (accessed June 4, 2009).
14. "The Company We Keep: Why Physicians Should Refuse to See Pharmaceutical Representatives," *Annals of Family Medicine* 3, no. 1 (2005): 82–85.
15. "GAO Document B-295402," Lockheed Martin Corporation, February 18, 2005, http://www.gao.gov/decisions/bidpro/295402.htm (accessed August 5, 2009).
16. John Byrne, "Fall from Grace," *BusinessWeek*, August 12, 2002, 50–56.
17. Dionne Searcey, "U.S. Cracks Down on Corporate Bribes," *The Wall Street Journal*, May 26, 2009, http://online.wsj.com/article/SB124329477230952689.html (accessed June 4, 2009).
18. Ira Winkler, *Corporate Espionage: What It Is, Why It's Happening in Your Company, What You Must Do About It* (New York: Prima, 1997); Ira Winkler, *Spies Among Us: How to Stop the Spies, Terrorists, Hackers, and Criminals You Don't Even Know You Encounter Every Day* (Indianapolis: Wiley, 2005); Kevin D. Mitnick and William L. Simon, *The Art of Intrusion: The Real Stories Behind the Exploits of Hackers, Intruders and Deceivers* (Indianapolis: Wiley, 2005).
19. William M Bulkeley, "Suit Alleges Internet Espionage," *The Wall Street Journal*, February 2, 2009, http://online.wsj.com/article/SB123353995726038063.html (accessed June 11, 2009).
20. "About Equal Employment Opportunity," U.S. Equal Employment Opportunity Commission, http://www.eeoc.gov/abouteeo/index.html (accessed August 5, 2009).
21. Bureau of the Census, *Statistical Abstract of the United States*, 2001 (Washington, DC: Government Printing Office, 2002), 17.
22. John C. Hendrickson, "EEOC Charges Sidley & Austin with Age Discrimination," Equal Employment Opportunity Commission, January 13, 2005, http://www.eeoc.gov/press/1-13-05.html (accessed August 5, 2009).
23. "Lockheed Martin to Pay $773,000 to Settle Age Discrimination Lawsuit," Occupational Health & Safety, April 8, 2008, http://ohsonline.com/articles/2008/04/lockheed-martin-to-pay-773000-to-settle-age-discrimination-lawsuit.aspx (accessed June 3, 2009).
24. Sue Shellenberger, "Work and Family," *Wall Street Journal*, May 23, 2001, B1.
25. "What Is Affirmative Action?" HR Content Library, October 12, 2001, http://www.hrnext.com/content/view.cfm?articles_id=2007&subs_id=32 (accessed August 5, 2009).
26. "What Affirmative Action Is (and What It Is Not)," National Partnership for Women & Families, http://www.nationalpartnership.org/site/DocServer/AffirmativeActionFacts.pdf?docID=861 (accessed August 5, 2009).
27. Ibid
28. Ibid
29. Debbie Thorne McAlister, O. C. Ferrell, and Linda Ferrell, *Business and Society: A Strategic Approach to Social Responsibility*, 2nd ed. (Boston: Houghton Mifflin, 2008), 165-166.
30. Joe Millman, "Delayed Recognition; Arab Americans Haven't Put Much Effort into Advancing Their Rights as a Minority. Until Relatively Recently, That Is." *Wall Street Journal*, November 14, 2005, R8.
31. See http://www.eeoc.gov/stats/harass.html for EEOC statistics.
32. Paula N. Rubin, "Civil Rights and Criminal Justice: Primer on Sexual Harassment Series: NIJ Research in Action," October 1995, http://www.ncjrs.org/txtfiles/harass.txt (accessed August 5, 2009).
33. Steve Stecklow, "Sexual-Harassment Cases Plague U.N.," *The Wall Street Journal*, May 21, 2009, http://online.wsj.com/article/SB124233350385520879.html (accessed June 11, 2009).
34. *Zabkowicz v. West Bend Co.*, 589 F. Supp. 780, 784, 35 EPD Par.34, 766 (E.D. Wis.1984)
35. Iddo Landau, "The Law and Sexual Harassment," *Business Ethics Quarterly* 15, no. 2 (2005): 531–536.
36. "Enhancements and Justice: Problems in Determining the Requirements of Justice in a Genetically Transformed Society," *Kennedy Institute Ethics Journal* 15, no. 1 (2005): 3–38.
37. "EEOC Litigation Settlements, June 2004" The U.S. Employment Opportunity Commission, October 5, 2004, http://www.eeoc.gov/litigation/settlements/settlement06-04.html (accessed August 5, 2009).
38. Alex Frangos, "Timber Backs a New 'Green' Standard," *The Wall Street Journal*, March 29, 2006, p. B6.
39. Ibid
40. Russell Gold and Ian Talley, "Exxon CEO Advocates Emissions Tax," *The Wall Street Journal*, January 9, 2009, http://online.wsj.com/article/SB123146091530566335.html (accessed June 4, 2009).
41. William T. Neese, O. C. Ferrell, and Linda Ferrell, "An Analysis of Mail and Wire Fraud Cases Related to Marketing Communication: Implications for Corporate Citizenship," *Journal of Business Research* (2005), 58, p. 910-918
42. "Snapshot," *USA Today*, October 3, 2002, A1.
43. Donna Kardos, "KPMG Is Sued Over New Century," *The Wall Street Journal*, April 2, 2009, http://online.wsj.com/article/SB123860415462378767.*html* (accessed June 11, 2009).
44. Matt Kranz, "More Earnings Restatements on Way," *USA Today*, October 25, 2002, 3B.

45. Tess Stynes, "WellCare Swings to Loss on Legal Costs, Investment Charges," *The Wall Street Journal,* May 11, 2009, http://online.wsj.com/article/SB124204184849506371.html (accessed June 11, 2009).
46. Cassell Bryan-Low, "Accounting Firms Face Backlash over the Tax Shelters They Sold," *Wall Street Journal* online, February 7, 2003, http://online.wsj.com/article/SB1044568358985594893.html?mod=googlewsj (accessed August 5, 2009)
47. Press release, "Court Bars Global Marketing Group From Payment Processing," Federal Trade Commission, February 18, 2009, http://www.ftc.gov/opa/2009/02/gmg.shtm (accessed June 11, 2009).
48. *Gillette Co. v. Wilkinson Sword, Inc.,* 89-CV-3586, 1991 U.S. Dist. Lexis 21006, *6 (S.D.N.Y. January 9, 1991).
49. *Am. Council of Certified Podiatric Physicians & Surgeons v. Am. Bd. of Podiatric Surgery, Inc.,* 185 F.3d 606, 616 (6th Cir. 1999); *Johnson & Johnson-Merck Consumer Pharms. Co. v. Rhone-Poulenc Rorer Pharms., Inc.,* 19 F.3d 125, 129–30 (3d Cir. 1994); *Coca-Cola Co. v. Tropicana Prods., Inc.,* 690 F.2d 312, 317 (2d Cir. 1982).
50. Jeff Bater, "FTC Says Companies Falsely Claim Cellphone Patches Provide Protection," *Wall Street Journal* online, February 21, 2002, http://online.wsj.com/article/SB101423360415658320.html?mod=googlewsj (accessed August 5, 2009).
51. Archie B. Carroll, *Business and Society: Ethics and Stakeholder Management* (Cincinnati: South-Western, 1989), 228–230.
52. "Netgear Settles Suit over Speed Claims," *Wall Street Journal,* November 28, 2005, C5.
53. "AT&T Settles Lawsuit Against Reseller Accused of Slamming," *Business Wire,* via America Online, May 26, 1998.
54. "Newsletter; Federal Trade Commission Report: ID Theft #1 Complaint," February 2005, http://www.machine-solution.com/_Article+FTC+ID+Theft.html (accessed August 5, 2009).
55. Keith B. Anderson, "Consumer Fraud in the United States: The Second FTC Survey," The Federal Exchange Commission, October 2007, http://www2.ftc.gov/opa/2007/10/fraud.pdf (accessed August 5, 2009).
56. Kathy Grannis, "Troubled Economy Increases Shoplifting Rates, According to National Retail Security Survey," National Retail Federation, June 16, 2009, http://www.nrf.com/modules.php?name=News&op=viewlive&sp_id=746 (accessed August 5, 2009).
57. Liz Rappaport, "Case Opens New Front on Insider Trading," *The Wall Street Journal,* May 6, 2009, http://online.wsj.com/article/SB124153448113387615.html (accessed June 11, 2009).
58. Tami Luhbu, "Countrywide's Mozilo Accused of Fraud," *CNN Money,* June 4, 2009, http://money.cnn.com/2009/06/04/news/economy/mozilo_fraud_charges/index.htm (accessed June 11, 2009).
59. Anna Wilde Mathews, "Copyrights on Web Content Are Backed," *Wall Street Journal,* October 27, 2000, B10.
60. "Today's Briefing," *Commercial Appeal,* November 15, 2000, C1.
61. Roger Bate, "China's Bad Medicine," *The Wall Street Journal,* May 5, 2009, http://online.wsj.com/article/SB124146383501884323.html (accessed August 5, 2009); "Chinese Intellectual Property Violations," Idea Buyer, http://www.ideabuyer.com/news/chinese-intellectual-property-violations/ (accessed August 5, 2009).
62. Deli Yang, Mahmut Sonmez, Derek Bosworth, and Gerald Fryzell, "Global Software Piracy: Searching for Further Explanations," *Journal of Business Ethics,* September 2008.
63. "Cryptography Policy," the Electronic Protection Information Center, //www.epic.org/crypto/ (accessed August 5, 2009).
64. Nora J. Rifon, Robert LaRose, and Sejung Marina Choi, "Your Privacy Is Sealed: Effects of Web Privacy Seals on Trust and Personal Disclosures," *Journal of Consumer Affairs* 39, no. 2 (2002): 339–362.
65. Steven Ward, Kate Bridges, and Bill Chitty, "Do Incentives Matter? An Examination of On-line Privacy Concerns and Willingness to Provide Personal and Financial Information," *Journal of Marketing Communications* 11, no. 1 (2005): 21–40.
66. "2005 Electronic Monitoring and Surveillance Survey: Many Companies Monitoring, Recording, Videotaping—and Firing—Employees," *New York Times,* May 18, 2005, via http://www.amanet.org/press/amanews/ems05.htm (accessed August 5, 2009).
67. Mans Hulden, "Amid widening privacy investigation, Finnish police arrest Sonera executive," Associated Press, November 22, 2002, via http://www.highbeam.com/doc/1P1-69756506.html (accessed August 5, 2009).
68. Tamar Lewin, "Chevron Settles Sexual Harassment Charges," *The New York Times,* February 22, 1995, http://www.nytimes.com/1995/02/22/us/chevron-settles-sexual-harassment-charges.html (accessed August 5, 2009).
69. John Galvin, "The New Business Ethics," SmartBusinessMag.com (June 2000): 97.
70. "Ethical Issues in the Employer–Employee Relationship," *Society of Financial Service Professionals,* via https://www.iema.net/news/envnews?startnum=1901&cids[]=230&aid=1753 (accessed August 5, 2009); Mitch Wagner, "Google's Pixie Dust," *InformationWeek,* issue 1061 (2005): 98.
71. Stephenie Steitzer, "Commercial Web Sites Cut Back on Collections of Personal Data," *Wall Street Journal,* March 28, 2002, http://online.wsj.com/article/SB1017247161553469240.html?mod=googlewsj (accessed August 5, 2009).
72. Christopher Conkey, "FTC Goes After Firm That Installs Spyware Secretly," *Wall Street Journal,* October 6, 2005, D4.
73. Eve M. Caudill and Patrick E. Murphy, "Consumer Online Privacy: Legal and Ethical Issues," *Journal of Public Policy & Marketing* 19 (2000): 7.
74. Galvin, "The New Business Ethics," 98.
75. Steitzer, "Commercial Web Sites Cut Back on Collections of Personal Data."

Chapter 4

1. "Corporate Information: Corporate Culture," Google, http://www.google.com/corporate/culture.html, (accessed June 4, 2009).
2. Alistair Barr, "IRS Tries to Force UBS to Reveal US Tax Dodgers," Market Watch, February 19, 2009, http://www.marketwatch.com/story/ubs-kept-52000-secret-bank-accounts?print=true&dist=printMidSection (accessed June 4, 2009).
3. "Targeting Illegal Tax Shelters," Democratic Leadership Council, July 30, 2008, http://www.dlc.org/ndol_ci.cfm?kaid=139&subid=900082&contentid=252601 (accessed January 14, 2009).
4. Kara Scannell, "Assured of SEC's Survival, Schapiro Now Fights to Keep Regulatory Teeth," *The Wall Street Journal,* June 11, 2009, http://online.wsj.com/article/SB124468047175204449.html (accessed June 12, 2009).
5. Loretta Chao and Sky Canaves, "Legality of China Web Filter Is Challenged," *The Wall Street Journal,* June 15, 2009, http://online.wsj.com/article/SB124482083845410171.html?mod=googlenews_wsj (accessed June 12, 2009).
6. Gregory T. Gundlach, "Price Predation: Legal -Limits and Antitrust Considerations," *Journal of Public Policy & Marketing* 14 (1995): 278.
7. David Goldman, "Obama Vows Antitrust Crackdown," *CNN Money,* May 11, 2009, http://money.cnn.com/2009/05/11/news/economy/antitrust/index.htm (accessed June 12, 2009).
8. Steve Lohr, "High-Tech Antitrust Cases: The Road Ahead," *The New York Times,* May 13, 2009, http://bits.blogs.nytimes.com/2009/05/13/high-tech-antitrust-the-road-ahead/?scp=1&sq=high-tech%20antitrust&st=cse (accessed June 12, 2009).

9. "10 Ways to Combat Corporate Espionage," Data Destruction News, http://www.imakenews.com/accushred/e_article001225805.cfm?x=bdtNVCP,bbGvRs5c,w (accessed August 5, 2009).
10. "Baseball's Antitrust Exemption: Q&A," ESPN, December 5, 2001, http://sports.espn.go.com/espn/print?id=1290707&type=story (accessed June 4, 2009).
11. "A Child Shall Lead the Way: Marketing to Youths," *Credit Union Executive,* May–June 1993, 6–8.
12. Julia Angwin, "How to Keep Kids Safe Online," *The Wall Street Journal,* January 22, 2009, http://online.wsj.com/article/SB123238632055894993.html (accessed June 12, 2009).
13. Jennifer Levitz, "Laws Take on Financial Scams Against Seniors," *The Wall Street Journal,* May 19, 2009, http://online.wsj.com/article/SB124269210323932723.html (accessed June 12, 2009).
14. "Women's Earnings as a Percentage of Men's 1951–2007," U.S. Women's Bureau and the National Info Please, http://www.infoplease.com/ipa/A0193820.html (accessed August 5, 2009).
15. Joan Lowy, "Airline Industry Changes Raise Safety Issues," *USA Today,* May 16, 2009, http://www.usatoday.com/news/nation/2009-05-16-airline-pilots_N.htm (accessed August 5, 2009).
16. "United Nations General Assembly Report," http://www.un.org/documents/ga/res/42/ares42-187.htm (accessed June 4, 2009).
17. "Consumer Interest in Environmental Purchasing Not Eclipsed by Poor Economy," Cone 2009 Environmental Survey, http://www.coneinc.com/content2032 (accessed June 12, 2009).
18. "Smackdown: GE, Siemens Duel Over Who's Greener," *The Wall Street Journal,* May 28, 2009, http://blogs.wsj.com/environmentalcapital/2009/05/28/smackdown-ge-siemens-duel-over-whos-greener/ (accessed June 12, 2009).
19. Ibid.
20. Michael Arndt, Wendy Zellner, and Peter Coy, "Too Much Corporate Power," *BusinessWeek,* September 11, 2000, 149.
21. Marilyn Adams, "U.S. Keeps Wary Eye on Cruise Ships for More Pollution," *USA Today,* November 8, 2002, http://www.usatoday.com/travel/news/2004-05-05-norway-pollution_x.htm (accessed August 5, 2009).
22. "Electronics Recycling is Making Gains, Says EPA," *PC World,* January 8, 2009, http://www.pcworld.com/businesscenter/article/156721/article.html?tk=nl_bnxnws (accessed June 12, 2009).
23. Sarah Lynch, "Schapiro: More Oversight Needed for Credit-Rating Firms," *The Wall Street Examiner,* April 15, 2009, http://forums.wallstreetexaminer.com/index.php?showtopic=807630 (accessed June 12, 2009).
24. Mike Spector and Shelly Banjo, "Pay at Nonprofits Gets a Closer Look," *The Wall Street Journal,* March 27, 2009, http://online.wsj.com/article/SB123811160845153093.html (accessed June 12, 2009).
25. Penelope Patsuris, "The Corporate Scandal Sheet," *Forbes* online, August 26, 2002, www.forbes.com/home/2002/07/25/accountingtracker.html (accessed August 5, 2009).
26. Nelson D. Schwartz, "The Looting of Kmart, Part 2," *Fortune,* February 17, 2003, 30; Elliot Blair Smith, "Probe: Former Kmart CEO 'Grossly Derelict,'" *USA Today,* January 27, 2003, B1.
27. David McHugh, "Business Wants to Restore Public Trust," America Online, January 28, 2003.
28. Amy Borrus, "Learning to Love Sarbanes–Oxley," *BusinessWeek,* November 21, 2005, 126–128.
29. Stephen Taub, "SEC:1,300 'Whistles' Blown Each Day" CFO.com, August 3, 2004, http://www.cfo.com/article.cfm/3015607 (accessed March 15, 2006).
30. Julie Homer, "Overblown (In the Wake of Sarbanes–Oxley, Some Serious Misconceptions Have Arisen About What Blowing the Whistle Actually Means)," *CFO Magazine,* October 1, 2003, http://www.cfo.com/article.cfm/3010513/c_2984349/?f=archives (accessed August 5, 2009).
31. "Foley Study Reveals Continued High Cost of Being Public," Foley & Lardner LLP, August 2, 2007, http://www.foley.com/news/news_detail.aspx?newsid=3074 (accessed June 12, 2009).
32. "Sarbanes–Oxley Act Improves Investor Confidence, But at a Cost," *CPA Journal,* October 2005, http://www.nysscpa.org/cpajournal/2005/1005/perspectives/p19.htm (accessed March 16, 2006).
33. Tricia Bisoux, "The Sarbanes–Oxley Effect," *BizEd,* July/August 2005, 24–29.
34. Ibid.
35. "Sarbox and the Constitution," *The Wall Street Journal,* May 20, 2009, http://online.wsj.com/article/SB124268754900032175.html (accessed June 12, 2009).
36. James C. Hyatt, "Birth of the Ethics Industry," *Business Ethics* (Summer 2005): 20–27.
37. Amy Borrus, "Learning to Love Sarbanes- Oxley," *BusinessWeek,* November 21, 2005, 126–128.
38. Win Swenson, "The Organizational Guidelines' 'Carrot and Stick' Philosophy, and Their Focus on 'Effective' Compliance," in *Corporate Crime in America: Strengthening the "Good Citizenship"-Corporation* (Washington, DC: U.S. Sentencing Commission, 1995), 17–26.
39. *United States Code Service* (Lawyers' Edition), 18 U.S.C.S. Appendix, Sentencing Guidelines for the United States Courts (Rochester, NY: Lawyers Cooperative Publishing, 1995), sec. 8A.1.
40. O. C Ferrell and Linda Ferrell, "Current Developments in Managing Organizational Ethics and Compliance Initiatives," University of Wyoming, white paper, Bill Daniels Business Ethics Initiative 2006.
41. Ibid.
42. Lynn Brewer, "Capitalizing on the Value of Integrity: An Integrated Model to Standardize the Measure of Non-financial Performance as an Assessment of Corporate Integrity," in *Managing Risks for Corporate Integrity. How to Survive an Ethical Misconduct Disaster,* ed. Lynn Brewer, Robert Chandler, and O. C. Ferrell (Mason, OH: Thomson/Texere, 2006), 233-277.
43. "Balanced, Active Lifestyles," McDonald's, http://www.mcdonalds.com/usa/good/balanced__active_lifestyles.html (accessed August 5, 2009).
44. Ingrid Murro Botero, "Charitable Giving Has 4 Big Benefits," *Business Journal of Phoenix* online, January 1, 1999, www.bizjournals.com/phoenix/stories/1999/01/04/smallb3.html (accessed August 5, 2009).
45. 2007 Corporate Citizen Report, Wells Fargo, https://www.wellsfargo.com/downloads/pdf/about/csr/reports/wf2007corporate_citizenship.pdf (accessed June 4, 2009).
46. "Walmart Foundation Fact Sheet," http://walmartstores.com/FactsNews/FactSheets/#CharitableGiving (accessed June 4, 2009).
47. "Wal-Mart Giving," Walmartfacts.com, http://www.walmartfacts.com/community/walmart-foundation.aspx (accessed March 17, 2006).
48. Steve Hilton, "Bisto: Altogether now, 'Aah…,'" *Ethical Corporation,* December 2005, 50.
49. "How We're Helping," Home Depot, http://corporate.homedepot.com/wps/portal/!ut/p/c1/04_SB8K8xLLM9MSSzPy8xBz9CP0os3gDdwNHH0sfE3M3AzMPJ8OAEBcDKADKR2LKmxrD5fHr9vPIz03VL8iNKAcAJzsP4g!!/dl2/d1/L2dJQSEvUUt3QS9ZQnB3LzZfMEcwQUw5TDQ3RjA2SEIxUEs5MDAwMDAwMDA!/ (accessed June 12, 2009).
50. Swenson, "The Organizational Guidelines' 'Carrot and Stick' Philosophy."

Chapter 5

1. Thomas M. Jones, "Ethical Decision Making by Individuals in Organizations: An Issue-Contingent Model," *Academy of*

Management Review 16 (February 1991): 366–395; O. C. Ferrell and Larry G. Gresham, "A Contingency Framework for Understanding Ethical Decision Making in Marketing," *Journal of Marketing* 49 (Summer 1985): 87–96; O. C. Ferrell, Larry G. Gresham, and John Fraedrich, "A Synthesis of Ethical Decision Models for Marketing," *Journal of Macromarketing* 9 (Fall 1989): 55–64; Shelby D. Hunt and Scott Vitell, "A General Theory of Marketing Ethics," *Journal of Macromarketing* 6 (Spring 1986): 5–16; William A. Kahn, "Toward an Agenda for Business Ethics Research," *Academy of Management Review* 15 (April 1990): 311–328; Linda K. Trevino, "Ethical Decision Making in Organizations: A Person-Situation Interactionist Model," *Academy of Management Review* 11 (March 1986): 601–617.

2. Jones, "Ethical Decision Making," 367, 372.
3. Donald P. Robin, R. Eric Reidenbach, and P. J. Forrest, "The Perceived Importance of an Ethical Issue as an Influence on the Ethical Decision-Making of Ad Managers," *Journal of Business Research* 35 (January 1996): 17.
4. Jack Beatty, "The Enron Ponzi Scheme," *The Atlantic Monthly,* March 13, 2002, http://www.theatlantic.com/doc/200203u/pp2002-03-13 (accessed August 17, 2009).
5. Roselie McDevitt and Joan Van Hise, "Influences in Ethical Dilemmas of Increasing Intensity," *Journal of Business Ethics* 40 (October 2002): 261–274.
6. Anusorn Singhapakdi, Scott J. Vitell, and George R. Franke, "Antecedents, Consequences, and Mediating Effects of Perceived Moral Intensity and Personal Moral Philosophies," *Journal of the Academy of Marketing Science* 27 (Winter 1999): 19.
7. Ibid.
8. Ibid.
9. Ibid., 17.
10. Steven A. Holmes, "Fannie Mae Eases Credit to Aid Mortgage Lending," *New York Times,* September 30, 1999, http://www.nytimes.com/1999/09/30/business/fannie-mae-eases-credit-to-aid-mortgage-lending.html (accessed April 7, 2009).
11. Reuters, "Fannie Mae, Freddie Mac Subprime Restrictions Ease," *CNBC,* September 19, 2007,. http://www.cnbc.com/id/20869608/ (accessed April 8, 2009).
12. T. W. Loe, L. Ferrell, and P. Mansfield, "A Review of Empirical Studies Assessing Ethical Decision-Making in Business," *Journal of Business Ethics* 25 (2000): 185–204.
13. Steven Kaplan, Kurt Pany, Janet Samuels, and Jian Zhang, "An Examination of the Association Between Gender and Reporting Intentions for Fraudulent Financial Reporting Intentions for Fraudulent Financial Reporting," *Journal of Business Ethics* 87, No. 1 (June 2009): 15–30.
14. Michael J. O'Fallon, and Kenneth D. Butterfield, "A Review of the Empirical Ethical Decision-Making Literature: 1996–2003," *Journal of Business Ethics* 59 (July 2005): 375–413; P. M. J. Christie, J. I. G. Kwon, P. A. Stoeberl, and R. Baumhart, "A Cross-Cultural Comparison of Ethical Attitudes of Business Managers: India, Korea and the United States," *Journal of Business Ethics* 46 (September 2003): 263–287; G. Fleischman and S. Valentine, "Professionals' Tax Liability and Ethical Evaluations in an Equitable Relief Innocent Spouse Case," *Journal of Business Ethics* 42 (January 2003): 27–44; A. Singhapakdi, K. Karande, C. P. Rao, and S. J. Vitell, "How Important Are Ethics and Social Responsibility? A Multinational Study of Marketing Professionals," *European Journal of Marketing* 35 (2001): 133–152.
15. R. W. Armstrong, "The Relationship Between Culture and Perception of Ethical Problems in International Marketing," *Journal of Business Ethics* 15 (November 1996): 1199–1208; J. Cherry, M. Lee, and C. S. Chien, "A Cross-Cultural Application of a Theoretical Model of Business Ethics: Bridging the Gap Between Theory and Data," *Journal of Business Ethics* 44 (June 2003): 359–376; B. Kracher, A. Chatterjee, and A. R. Lundquist, "Factors Related to the Cognitive Moral Development of Business Students and Business Professionals in India and the United States: Nationality, Education, Sex and Gender," *Journal of Business Ethics* 35 (February 2002): 255–268.
16. J. M. Larkin, "The Ability of Internal Auditors to Identify Ethical Dilemmas," *Journal of Business Ethics* 23 (February 2000): 401–409; D. Peterson, A. Rhoads, and B. C. Vaught, "Ethical Beliefs of Business Professionals: A Study of Gender, Age and External Factors," *Journal of Business Ethics* 31 (June 2001): 225–232; M. A. Razzaque and T. P. Hwee, "Ethics and Purchasing Dilemma: A Singaporean View," *Journal of Business Ethics* 35 (February 2002): 307–326.
17. J. Cherry and J. Fraedrich, "An Empirical Investigation of Locus of Control and the Structure of Moral Reasoning: Examining the Ethical Decision-Making Processes of Sales Managers," *Journal of Personal Selling and Sales Management* 20 (Summer 2000): 173–188; M. C. Reiss and K. Mitra, "The Effects of Individual Difference Factors on the Acceptability of Ethical and Unethical Workplace Behaviors," *Journal of Business Ethics* 17 (October 1998): 1581–1593.
18. O. C. Ferrell and Linda Ferrell, "Role of Ethical Leadership in Organizational Performance," *Journal of Management Systems* 13 (2001): 64–78.
19. James Weber and Julie E. Seger, "Influences upon Organizational Ethical Subclimates: A Replication Study of a Single Firm at Two Points in Time," *Journal of Business Ethics* 41 (November 2002): 69–84.
20. Sean Valentine, Lynn Godkin, and Margaret Lucero, "Ethical Context, Organizational Commitment, and Person-Organization Fit," *Journal of Business Ethics* 41 (December 2002): 349–360.
21. Bruce H. Drake, Mark Meckler, and Debra Stephens, "Transitional Ethics: Responsibilities of Supervisors for Supporting Employee Development," *Journal of Business Ethics* 38 (June 2002): 141–155.
22. Ferrell and Gresham, "A Contingency Framework," 87–96.
23. R. C. Ford and W. D. Richardson, "Ethical Decision-Making: A Review of the Empirical Literature," *Journal of Business Ethics* 13 (March 1994): 205–221; Loe, Ferrell, and Mansfield, "A Review of Empirical Studies."
24. National Business Ethics Survey, *How Employees Perceive Ethics at Work* (Washington, DC: Ethics Resource Center, 2000), 30.
25. "Employee Theft Solutions," *The Shulman Center,* http://www.employeetheftsolutions.com/ (accessed January 14, 2009).
26. Niraj Sheth, Jackie Range, and Geeta Anand, "Corporate Scandal Shakes India," *Wall Street Journal,* January 8, 2009, http://online.wsj.com/article/SB123131072970260401.html (accessed January 9, 2009).
27. National Business Ethics Survey, 30.
28. R. Eric Reidenbach and Donald P. Robin, *Ethics and Profits* (Englewood Cliffs, NJ: Prentice-Hall, 1989), 92.
29. "Small Virtues: Entrepreneurs Are More Ethical," *BusinessWeek* online, March 8, 2000, www.businessweek.com/smallbiz/0003/ib3670029.htm?scriptFramed (accessed August 17, 2009).
30. Constance E. Bagley, "The Ethical Leader's Decision Tree," *Harvard Business Review,* January–February 2003, 18.
31. Choe San-hun, "Samsung Chairman Resigns," *The New York Times,* April 23, 2008, http://www.nytimes.com/2008/04/23/business/worldbusiness/23samsung.html?scp=1&sq=samsung%20lee&st=cse (accessed June 5, 2009); "About Samsung," http://www.samsung.com/us/aboutsamsung/index.html (accessed June 5, 2009).
32. Daniel J. Brass, Kenneth D. Butterfield, and Bruce C. Skaggs, "Relationship and Unethical Behavior: A Social Science Perspective," *Academy of Management Review* 23 (January 1998): 14–31.
33. Andrew Kupfor, "Mike Armstrong's AT&T: Will the Pieces Come Together?" *Fortune,* April 26, 1999, 89.

34. From *Managing Risks for Corporate Integrity: How to Survive an Ethical Misconduct Disaster,* 1st edition, by Brewer, Chandler, and Ferrell. Copyright © 2006. Reprinted with permission of South-Western, a division of Thomson Learning: www.thomsonrights.com. Fax 800 730-2215.
35. J. M. Burns, *Leadership* (New York: Harper & Row, 1985).
36. Royston Greenwood, Roy Suddaby, and C. R. Hinings, "Theorizing Change: The Role of Professional Associations in the Transformation of Institutionalized Fields," *Academy of Management Journal* 45 (January 2002): 58–80.
37. Eric Pillmore, "How Tyco International Remade its Corporate Governance," speech at Wharton Business School, September 2006.
38. Stephen R. Covey, *The 7 Habits of Highly Effective People* (New York: Simon & Schuster, 1989).
39. Archie B. Carroll, "Ethical Leadership: From Moral Managers to Moral Leaders," in *Rights, Relationships and Responsibilities,* Vol. 1, ed. O. C. Ferrell, Sheb True, and Lou Pelton (Kennesaw, GA: Kennesaw State University, 2003), 7–17.
40. Andy Serwer, "Wal-Mart: Bruised in Bentonville," *Fortune* online, April 4, 2005, http://money.cnn.com/magazines/fortune/fortune_archive/2005/04/18/8257005/index.htm (accessed August 17, 2009).
41. Thomas I. White, "Character Development and Business Ethics Education," in *Rights, Relationships and Responsibilities,* Vol. 1, ed. O. C. Ferrell, Sheb True, and Lou Pelton (Kennesaw, GA: Kennesaw State University, 2003), 137–166.
42. Carroll, "Ethical Leadership," 11.
43. Keith H. Hammonds, "Harry Kraemer's Moment of Truth," *Fast Company* online, December 19, 2007, www.fastcompany.com/online/64/kraemer.html (accessed August 17, 2009).
44. Carroll, "Ethical Leadership," 11.
45. "About Herman Miller: Awards and Recognition," http://www.hermanmiller.com/About-Us/About-Herman-Miller/Awards-and-Recognition (accessed August 17, 2009); Press Release, "Herman Miller, Inc. Again Recognized Among '100 Best Companies to Work For' in America, Herman Miller, Inc., January 23, 2009, http://www.hermanmiller.com/DotCom/jsp/aboutUs/newsDetail.jsp?navId=194&topicId=49&newsId=662 (accessed August 17, 2009); Press Release, "Herman Miller, Inc. Celebrates 20 Years as Industry Leader in *Fortune's* 'Most Admired' Companies Survey," March 7, 2008, http://www.hermanmiller.com/DotCom/jsp/aboutUs/newsDetail.jsp?navId=194&topicId=49&newsId=591 (accessed August 17, 2009).
46. Carroll, "Ethical Leadership," 12.
47. About Xerox, http://www.xerox.com/go/xrx/portal/STServlet?projectID=ST_About_Xerox&pageID=Landing&Xcntry=USA&Xlang=en_US (accessed June 5, 2009).
48. Nanette Burns and Roger O. Crockett, "Ursula Burns: An Historic Succession at Xerox," *Businessweek,* May 28, 2009, http://www.businessweek.com/magazine/content/09_23/b4134018712853.htm (June 5, 2009).
49. Supplier Diversity Program, Xerox, http://www.xerox.com/about-xerox/citizenship/supplier-diversity/enus.html (accessed June 5, 2009).
50. Brent Smith, Michael W. Grojean, Christian Resick, and Marcus Dickson, "Leaders, Values and Organizational Climate: Examining Leadership Strategies for Establishing an Organizational Climate Regarding Ethics," *Journal of Business Ethics,* as reported at "Research @ Rice: Lessons from Enron—Ethical Conduct Begins at the Top," Rice University, June 15, 2005, www.explore.rice.edu/explore/NewsBot.asp?MODE=VIEW&ID=7478&SnID=878108660 (accessed August 17, 2009).
51. "Our Core Values," Whole Foods, http://www.wholefoodsmarket.com/company/corevalues.php (accessed June 5, 2009).
52. Herb Baum and Tammy Kling, "Book Review: The Transparent Leader," in *Leadership Now,* http://www.leadershipnow.com/leadershop/0060565470.html (accessed August 17, 2009).
53. Waste Management Earns Top Honors in Global Ranking of Ethical Firms," *Houston Business Journal,* June 4, 2008, http://www.bizjournals.com/houston/stories/2008/06/02/daily27.html (accessed June 5, 2009).
54. 2008 Sustainability Report, Waste Management, http://www.wm.com/wm/WM_2008_ExecSummary_SRR.pdf (accessed June 5, 2009).

Chapter 6

1. James R. Rest, *Moral Development Advances in Research and Theory* (New York: Praeger, 1986), 1.
2. "Business Leaders, Politicians and Academics Dub Corporate Irresponsibility 'An Attack on America from Within,'" *Business Wire,* November 7, 2002, via Find Articles, http://findarticles.com/p/articles/mi_m0EIN/is_2002_Nov_7/ai_94631434/ (accessed August 19, 2009). A.C. Ahuvia, If Money Doesn't Make Us Happy, Why Do We Act As If It Does?, *Journal of Economic Psychology* 29 (2008): 491–507.
3. Abhijit Biswas, Jane W. Licata, Daryl McKee, Chris Pullig, and Christopher Daughtridge, "The Recycling Cycle: An Empirical Examination of Consumer Waste Recycling and Recycling Shopping Behaviors," *Journal of Public Policy & Marketing* 19 (2000): 93.
4. Miguel Bastons, "The Role of Virtues in the Framing of Decisions," *Journal of Business Ethics* (2008): 395.
5. "Court Says Businesses Liable for Harassing on the Job," *Commercial Appeal,* June 27, 1998, A1.
6. Richard Brandt, *Ethical Theory* (Englewood Cliffs, NJ: Prentice-Hall, 1959), 253–254.
7. J. J. C. Smart and B. Williams, *Utilitarianism: For and Against* (Cambridge, UK: Cambridge University Press, 1973), 4.
8. C. E. Harris, Jr., *Applying Moral Theories* (Belmont, CA: Wadsworth, 1986), 127–128.
9. Gordon Fairclough, "Tainting of Milk Is Open Secret in China," *Wall Street Journal,* November 3, 2008, http://online.wsj.com/article/SB122567367498791713.html (accessed August 18, 2009).
10. Immanuel Kant, "Fundamental Principles of the Metaphysics of Morals," in *Problems of Moral Philosophy: An Introduction,* 2nd ed., ed. Paul W. Taylor (Encino, CA: Dickenson, 1972), 229.
11. Example adapted from Harris, *Applying Moral Theories,* 128–129.
12. Gerald F. Cavanaugh, Dennis J. Moberg, and Manuel Velasquez, "The Ethics of Organizational Politics," *Academy of Management Review* 6 (1981): 363–374; U.S. Bill of Rights, http://www.law.cornell.edu/constitution/constitution.billofrights.html (accessed August 18, 2009).
13. Marie Brenner, "The Man Who Knew Too Much," *Vanity Fair,* May 1996, available at http://www.jeffreywigand.com/vanityfair.php (accessed August 18, 2009).
14. Norman E. Bowie and Thomas W. Dunfee, "Confronting Morality in Markets," *Journal of Business Ethics* 38 (2002): 381–393.
15. Kant, "Fundamental Principles," 229.
16. Thomas E. Weber, "To Opt In or Opt Out: That Is the Question When Mulling Privacy," *Wall Street Journal,* October 23, 2000, B1.
17. GNews, "Hoover High School from MTV's 'Two-a-Days' in Major Controversy," July 18, 2007, http://gnewsworld.com/HooverHighSchool (accessed June 15, 2009).
18. C. R. Bateman, J. P Fraedrich, and R. Iyer, "The Integration and Testing of the Janus-Headed Model Within Marketing," *Journal of Business Research* 56 (2003): 587–596; J. B. DeConinck and W. F. Lewis, "The Influence of Deontological and Teleological

Considerations and Ethical Culture on Sales Managers' Intentions to Reward or Punish Sales Force Behavior," *Journal of Business Ethics* 16 (1997): 497–506; J. Kujala, "A Multidimensional Approach to Finnish Managers' Moral Decision-Making," *Journal of Business Ethics* 34 (2001): 231–254; K. C. Rallapalli, S. J. Vitell, and J. H. Barnes, "The Influence of Norms on Ethical Judgments and Intentions: An Empirical Study of Marketing Professionals," *Journal of Business Research* 43 (1998): 157–168; M. Shapeero, H. C. Koh, and L. N. Killough, "Underreporting and Premature Sign-Off in Public Accounting," *Managerial Auditing Journal* 18 (2003): 478–489.

19. William K. Frankena, *Ethics* (Englewood Cliffs: Prentice-Hall, 1963).
20. R. E. Reidenbach and D. P. Robin, "Toward the Development of a Multidimensional Scale for Improving Evaluations of Business Ethics," *Journal of Business Ethics* 9, no. 8 (1980): 639–653.
21. Patrick E. Murphy and Gene R. Laczniak, "Emerging Ethical Issues Facing Marketing Researchers," *Marketing Research* 4, no. 2 (1992): 6–11.
22. T. K. Bass and Barnett G. Brown, "Religiosity, Ethical Ideology, and Intentions to Report a Peer's Wrongdoing," *Journal of Business Ethics* 15, no. 11 (1996): 1161–1174; R. Z. Elias, "Determinants of Earnings Management Ethics Among Accountants," *Journal of Business Ethics* 40, no. 1 (2002): 33–45; Y. Kim, "Ethical Standards and Ideology Among Korean Public Relations Practitioners," *Journal of Business Ethics* 42, no. 3 (2003): 209–223; E. Sivadas, S. B. Kleiser, J. Kellaris, and R. Dahlstrom, "Moral Philosophy, Ethical Evaluations, and Sales Manager Hiring Intentions," *Journal of Personal Selling & Sales Management* 23, no. 1 (2003): 7–21.
23. Manuel G. Velasquez, *Business Ethics Concepts and Cases,* 4th ed. (Upper Saddle River, NJ: Prentice-Hall, 1998), 132–133.
24. Ibid.
25. Adapted from Robert C. Solomon, "Victims of Circumstances? A Defense of Virtue Ethics in Business," *Business Ethics Quarterly* 13, no. 1 (2003): 43–62.
26. Ian Maitland, "Virtuous Markets: The Market as School of the Virtues," *Business Ethics Quarterly* (January 1997): 97.
27. Ibid.
28. Stefanie E. Naumann and Nathan Bennett, "A Case for Procedural Justice Climate: Development and Test of a Multilevel Model," *Academy of Management Journal* 43 (2000): 881–889.
29. Joel Brockner, "Making Sense of Procedural Fairness: How High Procedural Fairness Can Reduce or Heighten the Influence of Outcome Favorability," *Academy of Management Review* 27 (2002): 58–76.
30. "Wainwright Bank and Trust Company Award for Social Justice Inside and Out," *Business Ethics* (November/December 1998): 11.
31. John Fraedrich and O. C. Ferrell, "Cognitive Consistency of Marketing Managers in Ethical Situations," *Journal of the Academy of Marketing Science* 20 (1992): 245–252.
32. Manuel Velasquez, Claire Andre, Thomas Shanks, S. J., and Michael J. Meyer, "Thinking Ethically: A Framework for Moral Decision Making," *Issues in Ethics* (Winter 1996): 2–5.
33. Lawrence Kohlberg, "Stage and Sequence: The Cognitive Developmental Approach to Socialization," in *Handbook of Socialization Theory and Research,* ed. D. A. Goslin (Chicago: Rand McNally, 1969), 347–480.
34. Adapted from Kohlberg, "Stage and Sequence."
35. Clare M. Pennino, "Is Decision Style Related to Moral Development Among Managers in the U.S.?" *Journal of Business Ethics* 41 (2002): 337–347.
36. A. K. M. Au and D. S. N. Wong, "The Impact of Guanxi on the Ethical Decision-Making Process of Auditors—An Exploratory Study on Chinese CPA's in Hong Kong," *Journal of Business Ethics* 28, no. 1 (2000): 87–93; D. P Robin, G. Gordon, C. Jordan, and E. Reidenback, "The Empirical Performance of Cognitive Moral Development in Predicating Behavioral Intent," *Business Ethics Quarterly* 6, no. 4 (1996): 493–515; M. Shapeero, H. C. Koh, and L. N. Killough, "Underreporting and Premature Sign-Off in Public Accounting," *Managerial Auditing Journal* 18, no. 6 (1996): 478–489; N. Uddin and P. R. Gillett, "The Effects of Moral Reasoning and Self-Monitoring on CFO Intentions to Report Fraudulently on Financial Statements," *Journal of Business Ethics* 40, no. 1 (2002): 15–32.
37. David O. Friedrichs, *Trusted Criminals, White Collar Crime in Contemporary Society* (Belmont, CA: Wadsworth, 1996).
38. Jason Szep, "Recession Leads to Surge in Online Crime: U.S. Report," Canada.com, March 30, 2009, http://www.canada.com/news/Recession+leads+surge+online+crime+report/1445008/story.html (accessed June 15, 2009).
39. "FBI Turns to Fraud After Focus on Terror," IOL, February 14, 2009, http://www.iol.co.za/?set_id=1&click_id=3&art_id=nw20090214102435228C386891 (accessed August 18, 2009).
40. Stephen Bernard, "SEC Charges Texas Financier With 'Massive Fraud'," ABC News, February 17, 2009, http://abcnews.go.com/Business/wireStory?id=6896169 (accessed August 18, 2009).
41. "Blagojevich Arrested on Federal Charges," Chicago Breaking News, December 9, 2008, http://www.chicagobreakingnews.com/2008/12/source-feds-take-gov-blagojevich-into-custody.html (accessed August 18, 2009).
42. Diana B. Henriques and Jack Healy, "Madoff Goes to Jail After Guilty Pleas," *The New York Times,* March 12, 2009, http://www.nytimes.com/2009/03/13/business/13madoff.html?hp (accessed March 12, 2009).
43. H. J. Eysenck, "Personality and Crime: Where Do We Stand?" *Psychology, Crime & Law* 2, no. 3 (1996): 143–152; Shelley Johnson Listwan, *Personality and Criminal Behavior: Reconsidering the Individual,* University of Cincinnati, Division of Criminal Justice, 2001, http://criminaljustice.cech.uc.edu/docs/dissertations/ShelleyJohnson.pdf (accessed August 18, 2009).
44. J. M. Rayburn and L. G. Rayburn, "Relationship Between Machiavellianism and Type A Personality and Ethical-Orientation," *Journal of Business Ethics* 15, no. 11 (1996): 1209–1219.
45. Quoted in Marjorie Kelly, "The Ethics Revolution," *Business Ethics* (Summer 2005): 6.
46. O. C. Ferrell and Larry G. Gresham, "A Contingency Framework for Understanding Ethical Decision Making in Marketing," *Journal of Marketing* 49 (2002): 261–274.
47. Thomas I. White, "Character Development and Business Ethics Education," in *Fulfilling Our Obligation: Perspectives on Teaching Business Ethics*, ed. Sheb L. True, Linda Ferrell, and O. C. Ferrell (Kennesaw, GA: Kennesaw State University Press, 2005), 165.
48. Ibid., 165–166.

Chapter 7

1. J. W. Lorsch, "Managing Culture: The Invisible Barrier to Strategic Change," *California Management Review* 28 (1986): 95–109.
2. "Transforming Our Culture: The Values for Success," Mutual of Omaha, http://www.careerlink.org/emp/mut/corp.htm (accessed February 19, 2003).
3. Richard L. Daft, *Organizational Theory and Design* (Cincinnati: South-Western, 2007).
4. Stanley M. Davis, quoted in Alyse Lynn Booth, "Who Are We?" *Public Relations Journal* (July 1985): 13–18.
5. SWAMEDIA, Southwest Airlines Story Leads, http://www.swamedia.com/ (accessed May 28, 2009).

6. William Clay Ford, Jr., "A Message from the Chairman," Ford Motor Company, http://www.ford.com/en/ourCompany/corporateCitizenship/ourLearningJourney/message (accessed February 19, 2003); "GM and Ford: Roadmaps for Recovery," *BusinessWeek* online, March 14, 2006, http://www.businessweek.com/print/investor/content/mar2006/pi20060314_416862.htm (accessed March 30, 2006).
7. Bill Vlasic and Nick Bunkley, "Ford Seeks to Eliminate $10.4 Billion of its Debt," *The New York Times,* March 4, 2009, http://www.nytimes.com/2009/03/05/business/economy/05ford.html?_r=1&pagewanted=print (accessed May 29, 2009).
8. Abstracted from "Enhancing Compliance with Sarbanes-Oxley 404," Quantisoft, http://www.quantisoft.com/Industries/Ethics.htm (accessed June 8, 2009).
9. Taras Vasyl, Julie Rowney, and Piers Steel, "Half a Century of Measuring Culture: Approaches, Challenges, Limitations, and Suggestions Based on the Analysis of 121 Instruments for Quantifying Culture," white paper, 2008, Haskayne School of Business/University of Calgary, 2500 University Drive N.W., Calgary, Alberta, T2N 1N4, Canada, (403) 220-6074, taras@ucalgary.ca, http://www.ucalgary.ca/˜taras/_private/Half_a_Century_of_Measuring_Culture.pdf (accessed June 8, 2009).
10. Ibid.
11. Geert Hofstede, Bram Neuijen, Denise Daval Ohayv; and Geert Sanders, "Measuring Organizational Cultures: A Qualitative and Quantitative Study across Twenty Cases," *Administrative Science Quarterly* 35, no. 2 (1990): 286–316.
12. N. K. Sethia and M. A. Von Glinow, "Arriving at Four Cultures by Managing the Reward System," in *Gaining Control of the Corporate Culture* (San Francisco: Jossey-Bass, 1985), 409.
13. "United Parcel Service, Inc: Company Report," http://moneycentral.msn.com/companyreport?Symbol=UPS (accessed May 30, 2009).
14. "Brown Deeply Rooted in Going Green: Some of the Many Ways UPS Conserves," http://compass.ups.com/features/article.aspx?id=1891&srch_pos=1&srch_phr=Compressed+%22natural+gas%22+Vehicles (accessed May 30, 2009).
15. "The Boston Consulting Group Leaps to Number Three on FORTUNE's '100 Best Companies to Work For," January 22, 2009, http://www.bcg.com/about_bcg/media_center/press_releases.jsp?id=2825&yearpub (accessed May 30, 2009).
16. Peter Lattman, "Boeing's Top Lawyer Spotlights Company's Ethical Lapses," January 31, 2006, http://blogs.wsj.com/law/2006/01/31/boeings-top-lawyer-rips-into-his-company/ (accessed March 31, 2006).
17. Susan M. Heathfield "Five Tips for Effective Employee Recognition," http://humanresources.about.com/od/rewardrecognition/a/recognition_tip.htm (accessed June 4, 2009).
18. Christopher Lawton, "Judge Sanctions Gateway for Destroying Evidence," *Wall Street Journal,* March 31, 2006, A3.
19. Isabelle Maignan, O. C. Ferrell, and Thomas Hult, "Corporate Citizenship, Cultural Antecedents and Business Benefit," *Journal of the Academy of Marketing Science* 27 (1999): 455–469.
20. R. Eric Reidenbach and Donald P. Robin, *Ethics and Profits* (Englewood Cliffs, NJ: Prentice-Hall, 1989), 92.
21. Paul Lindow and Jill Race, "Beyond Traditional Audit Techniques," *Journal of Accountancy Online*, July 2002, http://www.journalofaccountancy.com/Issues/2002/Jul/BeyondTraditionalAuditTechniques.htm (accessed August 19, 2009).
22. S.C. Johnson Company, "We Offer an Innovative Environment" and "Our Philosophy," http://www.scjohnson.com/careers/car_aie.asp and http://www.scjohnson.com/family/fam_com_phi.asp (accessed June 4, 2009).
23. E. Sutherland and D. R. Cressey, *Principles of Criminology,* 8th ed. (Chicago: Lippincott, 1970), 114.
24. O. C. Ferrell and Larry G. Gresham, "A Contingency Framework for Understanding Ethical Decision Making in Marketing," *Journal of Marketing* 49 (1985): 90–91.
25. Walter Cunningham, "Get the Shuttle Back Up In the Air!" May 16, 2003, http://www.waltercunningham.com/op_ed_051603.htm (accessed August 19, 2009).
26. "Ethics and Nonprofits," *Stanford Social Innovation Review* (Summer 2009), http://www.ssireview.org/articles/entry/ethics_and_nonprofits (accessed June 4, 2009).
27. Matthew Goldstein, "Ex-Employees at Heart of Stanford Financial Probe," *BusinessWeek,* February 13, 2009, http://www.businessweek.com/bwdaily/dnflash/content/feb2009/db20090213_848258.htm (accessed June 9, 2009).
28. Thomas S. Mulligan, "Whistle Blower Recounts Enron Tale," *Los Angeles Times,* March 16, 2006, via http://www.whistleblowers.org/storage/whistleblowers/documents/whistle_blower_-_la_times.pdf (accessed August 19, 2009).
29. John W. Schoen, "Split CEO-Chairman Job, Says Panel," MSNBC.com, January 9, 2003, http://www.msnbc.com/news/857171.asp (accessed June 27, 2006).
30. Michael Barbaro, "Wal-Mart Says Official Misused Company Funds," *The Washington Post,* July 15, 2005, http://www.washingtonpost.com/wp-dyn/content/article/2005/07/14/AR2005071402055.html (accessed August 19, 2009).
31. "Making Your Whistleblower Case Succeed: Basic Workings of Whistleblower Complaints," http://www.jameshoyer.com/practice_qui_tam.html?se= Overture (accessed April 5, 2006).
32. Paula Dwyer and Dan Carney, with Amy Borrus, Lorraine Woellert, and Christopher Palmeri, "Year of the Whistleblower," *BusinessWeek,* December 16, 2002, 106–110.
33. Paula J. Desio (2009) "Federal Whistleblower Rights Increase Under the Stimulus Law," *Ethics Today,* February 18, 2009, http://www.ethics.org/ethics-today/0209/policy-report3.asp (accessed June 4, 2009).
34. Darren Dahl, "Learning to Love Whistleblowers," *Inc.*, March 2006, p. 21–23.
35. Jeff Benedict, *The Mormon Way of Doing Business: Leadership and Success Through Faith and Family,* (Warner Business Books, 2007), p. 22.
36. John R. P. French and Bertram Ravin, "The Bases of Social Power," in *Group Dynamics: Research and Theory,* ed. Dorwin Cartwright (Evanston, IL: Row, Peterson, 1962), 607–623.
37. The Welch Way, "The Case for 20-70-10, http://www.welchway.com/Principles/Differentiation/The-Case-for-20-70-10.aspx (accessed June 4, 2009).
38. Frank Reynolds, "Ex-Worldcom CFO Gets Five Years for Role in $11 B Fraud," Findlaw, August 19, 2005, http://news.findlaw.com/andrews/bf/cod/20050819/20050819sullivan.html (accessed August 20, 2009).
39. "Valuing Corporate Social Responsibility: McKinsey Survey Results," February 2009, http://www.mckinseyquarterly.com/Surveys/Valuing_corporate_social_responsibility_McKinsey_Global_Survey_Results_2309 (accessed August 20, 2009); Julie Hutchinson, "BYOB: Bring Your Own Bag," *Rocky Mountain News,* April 18, 2008, http://www.rockymountainnews.com/news/2008/apr/18/byob-bring-your-own-bag/ (accessed August 20, 2009).
40. "What Employees Want," April 2, 2008, http://www.managesmarter.com/msg/content_display/training/e3i34cf9af7da51e4a7eb30cd7c0b9b01fa?imw=Y (accessed June 5, 2009).
41. Clayton Alderfer, *Existence, Relatedness, and Growth* (New York: Free Press, 1972), 42–44.

42. Elaine Engeler, "UN: Forced Laborers Losing $21 Billion a Year," *The San Francisco Chronicle,* May 12, 2009, http://www.sfgate.com/cgi-bin/article.cgi?f=/n/a/2009/05/12/international/i052329D45.DTL (accessed August 20, 2009).
43. Stanley Holmes, "Cleaning Up Boeing," *BusinessWeek* online, March 13, 2006, http://www.businessweek.com/print/magazine/content/06_11/b3975088.htm?chan=gl (accessed April 6, 2006).
44. Spencer Ante, "They're Hiring in Techland," *BusinessWeek* online, January 23, 2006, http://www.businessweek.com/print/technology/content/jan2006/tc20060123_960426.htm (accessed April 6, 2006).
45. Corporate Governance-Board Committees, Texas Instruments, http://www.ti.com/corp/docs/csr/corpgov/bcmembership.shtml (accessed June 5, 2009); "Texas Instruments and the TI Foundation Committed to United Way," http://www.ti.com/corp/docs/csr/factsheets/unitedWay.shtml (accessed June 5, 2009.)
46. Joseph A. Belizzi and Ronald W. Hasty, "Supervising Unethical Sales Force Behavior: How Strong Is the Tendency to Treat Top Sales Performers Leniently?" *Journal of Business Ethics* 43 (2003): 337–351.
47. John Fraedrich and O. C. Ferrell, "Cognitive Consistency of Marketing Managers in Ethical Situations," *Journal of the Academy of Marketing Science* 20 (1992): 243–252.
48. "Helping Reduce Underage Tobacco Use," Phillip Morris, http://www.philipmorrisusa.com/en/cms/Responsibility/Helping_Reduce_Underage_Tobacco_Use/default.aspx?src=top_nav (accessed August 20, 2009).
49. Matthew Kirdahy, "Smoke and Mirrors," *Forbes*, November 1, 2006, http://www.forbes.com/2006/10/31/smoking-altria-lorillard-biz-bizhealth-cx_mk_1101smoking.html (accessed August 20, 2009).

Chapter 8

1. Bob Lewis, "Survival Guide: The Moral Compass- -Corporations Aren't Moral Agents, Creating Interesting Dilemmas for Business Leaders," *InfoWorld,* March 11, 2002, via http://www.findarticles.com (accessed June 8, 2009).
2. "The 100 Best Corporate Citizens," March 6, 2009, http://www.forbes.com/2009/03/05/best-corporate-citizens-leadership-citizenship-ranking.html (accessed June 8, 2009).
3. Indra Nooyi, "Business Has a Job to Do: Rebuild Trust," April 22, 2009, http://www.money.cnn.tv/2009/04/19/news/companies/nooyi.fortune/index.htm (accessed June 8, 2009).
4. Linda K. Trevino and Stuart Youngblood, "Bad Apples in Bad Barrels: Causal Analysis of Ethical Decision Making Behavior," *Journal of Applied Psychology* 75 (1990): 378–385.
5. Roger Parloff, "Wall Street: It's Payback Time," *Fortune,* January 19, 2009, 69.
6. Trevino and Youngblood, "Bad Apples in Bad Barrels."
7. "AmericaEconomia Annual Survey Reveals Ethical Behavior of Businesses and Executives in Latin America," AmericaEconomia, December 19, 2002, via http://www.prnewswire.com.
8. Constance E. Bagley, "The Ethical Leader's Decision Tree," *Harvard Business Review* (February 2003): 18–19.
9. "Wall Street's Entitlement Culture Hard to Shake," January 23, 2009, http://www.msnbc.msn.com/id/28817800/ (accessed June 8, 2009).
10. "Forensic Leadership Message," KPMG Forensic Ethics Survey 2008–2009, http://www.kpmg.com/SiteCollectionDocuments/Integrity-Survey-2008-2009.pdf (accessed June 17, 2009).
11. "Conducting Ourselves Ethically and Transparently," http://www.merck.com/corporate-responsibility/business-ethics-transparency/approach.html (accessed June 8, 2009).
12. "Special Report: The OCEO 2005 Benchmarking Study Key Findings," http://www.oceg.org/Details/18594 (accessed June 9, 2009).
13. "How Am I Doing?" *Business Ethics* (Fall 2005): 11.
14. KPMG Forensic Integrity Survey 2008–2009, http://www.kpmg.com/SiteCollectionDocuments/Integrity-Survey-2008-2009.pdf (accessed June 8, 2009).
15. *National Business Ethics Survey 2007: An Inside View of Private Sector Ethics,* Ethics Resource Center, 2007, 18.
16. Mark S. Schwartz, "A Code of Ethics for Corporate Code of Ethics," *Journal of Business Ethics* 41 (2002): 37.
17. Ibid.
18. "ASCE: Code of Ethics," http://www.asce.org/inside/codeofethics.cfm (accessed June 8, 2009); "Engineers Commit to Ending Corruption," http://www.asce.org/pressroom/news/display_press.cfm?uid=2789, (accessed June 8, 2009).
19. *National Business Ethics Survey 2007*, 39.
20. "USSC Commissioner John Steer Joins with Compliance and Ethics Executives from Leading U.S. Companies to Address Key Compliance, Business Conduct and Governance Issues," *Society for Corporate Compliance and Ethics,* PR Newswire, October 31, 2005.
21. "ECOA Sponsoring Partner Member L'Oreal Sponsors the First Law and Business Ethics Masters Degree," October 6, 2008, http://www.csrwire.com/press/press_release/19336-ECOA-Sponsoring-Partner-member-L-Oreal-Sponsors-the-first-Law-and-Business-Ethics-Masters-Degree (accessed June 9, 2009).
22. Jim Nortz "Compliance and Ethics Officers: A Survival Guide for the Economic Downturn," March 10, 2009, http://www.corporatecomplianceinsights.com/2009/compliance-and-ethics-officers-surviving-economic-downturn (accessed June 9, 2009).
23. Anne M. Simmons "Want to Avoid Unpleasant Compliance Surprises? Embrace a Strong Whistle-Blowing Policy," January 8, 2009, http://ethisphere.com/want-to-avoid-unpleasant-compliance-surprises-embrace-a-strong-whistle-blowing-policy/ (accessed June 9, 2009).
24. "Combat Fraud of Almost $1 Trillion," April 17, 2009, http://ethicaladvocate.blogspot.com/2009_04_01_archive.html (accessed June 9, 2009).
25. Sven Erik Holmes, "The Road to a Model Ethics and Compliance Program," May 13, 2009, http://ethisphere.com/the-road-to-a-model-ethics-and-compliance-program (accessed August 20, 2009).
26. Linda Ferrell and O.C. Ferrell, *Ethical Business* (DK Essential Managers Series, May 4, 2009), 1–72.
27. "Key TI Ethics Publications," http://www.ti.com/corp/docs/csr/corpgov/ethics/publication.shtml (accessed June 10, 2009).
28. Debbie Thorne LeClair and Linda Ferrell, "Innovation in Experiential Business Ethics Training," *Journal of Business Ethics* 23 (2000): 313–322.
29. Press release, "Top Corporate Ethics Officers Tell Conference Board that More Ethics Scandals are Ahead" The Conference Board, June 17, 2002, via Highbeam, http://www.highbeam.com/doc/1G1-87469997.html (accessed August 20, 2009).
30. Ibid.
31. David Slovin, "The Case for Anonymous Hotlines," *Risk & Insurance,* April 15, 2007, via FindArticles, http://findarticles.com/p/articles/mi_m0BJK/is_5_18/ai_n27221119/ (accessed August 20, 2009).
32. Mael Kaptein, "Guidelines for the Development of an Ethics Safety Net," *Journal of Business Ethics* 41 (2002): 217.
33. *National Business Ethics Survey 2007*, 6.
34. Curt S. Jordan, "Lessons in Organizational Compliance: A Survey of Government-Imposed Compliance Programs," *Preventive Law Reporter* (Winter 1994): 7.
35. Lori T. Martens and Kristen Day, "Five Common Mistakes in Designing and Implementing a Business Ethics Program," *Business and Society Review* 104 (1999): 163–170.

36. Anne C. Mulkern, "Auditors Smelled Trouble," *Denver Post*, October 2, 2002, A1.

Chapter 9

1. John Rosthorn, "Business Ethics Auditing—More Than a Stakeholder's Toy," *Journal of Business Ethics* 27 (2000): 9–19.
2. Debbie Thorne, O. C. Ferrell, and Linda Ferrell, *Business and Society: A Strategic Approach to Corporate Citizenship*, 3rd Edition (Boston: Houghton Mifflin, 2008).
3. Rosthorn, "Business Ethics Auditing."
4. BP Sustainability Review 2008, http://www.bp.com/liveassets/bp_internet/globalbp/STAGING/global_assets/e_s_assets/e_s_assets_2008/downloads/bp_sustainability_review_2008.pdf (accessed June 11, 2009).
5. "Accountability," Business for Social Responsibility, http://www.bsr.org/BSRResources/WhitePaperDetail.cfm?DocumentID=259 (accessed February 13, 2003).
6. Frank Reynolds, "Earnings Announcement Caused 25 Percent Stock Drop, Suit Says," November 26, 2008, http://news.findlaw.com/andrews/bf/cod/20081126/20081126_cadence.html (accessed June 11, 2009).
7. Kevin J. Sobnosky, "The Value-Added Benefits of Environmental Auditing," *Environmental Quality Management* 9 (1999): 25–32.
8. "Accountability," Business for Social Responsibility.
9. Trey Buchholz, "Auditing Social Responsibility Reports: The Application of Financial Auditing Standards," Colorado State University, professional paper, November 28, 2000, 3.
10. "Accountability," Business for Social Responsibility.
11. Fortune's World's Most Admired Companies, February 27, 2009, http://money.cnn.com/magazines/fortune/mostadmired/2009/index.html (accessed June 11, 2009).
12. "100 Most Influential People in Business Ethics 2008," December 31, 2008, http://ethisphere.com/100-most-influential-people-in-business-ethics-2008/ (accessed June 11, 2009).
13. John Pearce, *Measuring Social Wealth* (London: New Economics Foundation, 1996) as reported in Warren Dow and Roy Crowe, *What Social Auditing Can Do for Voluntary Organizations* (Vancouver, Canada: Volunteer Vancouver, July 1999), 8.
14. Colin Barr, "Obama Talks Tough on CEO Pay," February 4, 2009, http://money.cnn.com/2009/02/04/news/obama.exec.pay.fortune/index.htm (accessed June 11, 2009).
15. "The Effect of Published Reports of Unethical Conduct on Stock Prices," reported in "Business Ethics," Business for Social Responsibility, http://www.bsr.org/BSRResources/WhitePaperDetail.cfm?DocumentID=270 (accessed March 5, 2003).
16. Penelope Patsuris, "The Corporate Accounting Scandal Sheet," *Forbes* online, August 26, 2002, www.forbes.com/2002/07/25/accountingtracker.html (accessed September 3, 2009).
17. "Managing American Competitiveness," PricewaterhouseCoopers, http://www.pwc.com/extweb/pwcpublications.nsf/docid/B3C7B78DCB0AF4E285257583005001A7 (accessed June 12, 2009).
18. Lynn Brewer, Robert Chandler, and O. C. Ferrell, *Managing Risks for Corporate Integrity: How to Survive and Ethical Misconduct Disaster* (Mason, Ohio: Thompson Higher Education), 49–50.
19. The methodology in this section was adapted from Thorne, Ferrell, and Ferrell, *Business and Society*.
20. "Accountability," Business for Social Responsibility.
21. Ethics Resource Center, "Mission and Values," http://www.ethics.org/page/erc-mission-and-values (accessed September 3, 2009).
22. "Verification," Business for Social Responsibility, http://www.bsr.org/BSRResources/White PaperDetail.cfm?DocumentID=440 (accessed February 13, 2003).
23. "Ethical Statement," Social Audit, SocialAudit.org, http://www.socialaudit.org/pages/ethical.htm (accessed March 4, 2003).
24. "Our Five Core Values," Franklin Energy, http://www.franklinenergy.com/corevalues.html (accessed January 14, 2009).
25. "Verification," Business for Social Responsibility.
26. "Audit and Evaluation," Open Compliance and Ethics Group, http://www.oceg.org/view/15839 (accessed September 3, 2009).
27. "Ethical Statement," Social Audit.
28. "About Us: The Environment," National Grid, https://www.nationalgridus.com/niagaramohawk/about_us/environment.asp (accessed June 17, 2009).
29. "Verification," Business for Social Responsibility.
30. Green Mountain Coffee, http://www.greenmountaincoffee.com (accessed June 11, 2009).
31. Buchholz, "Auditing Social Responsibility Reports," 15.
32. Willem Landman, Johann Mouton, and Khanyisa Nevhutalu, "Chris Hani Baragwanath Hospital Ethics Audit," Ethics Institute of South Africa, 2001, http://ethicssa.intoweb.co.za/UserFiles/ethicssa.intoweb.co.za//CHBHFinalReport.pdf (accessed September 3, 2009).
33. "Verification," Business for Social Responsibility.
34. "Introduction to Corporate Social Responsibility," Business for Social Responsibility, http;//www.bsr.org/BSRResources/WhitePaperDetail.cfm?Document ID=138 (accessed March 5, 2003).
35. Landman, Mouton, and Nevhutalu, "Chris Hani Baragwanath Hospital Ethics Audit."
36. "Introduction to Corporate Social Responsibility," Business for Social Responsibility.
37. Liz Gunnison, "The Best and Worst CEOs Ever," *Condé Nast Portfolio*, May 9, 2009, p. 44.
38. "Accountability," Business for Social Responsibility.
39. Ibid.
40. Ethics and Compliance Officer Association, http://www.theecoa.org (accessed June 18, 2009).
41. "Verification," Business for Social Responsibility.
42. Ibid.
43. "Environment and Sustainability," BP, http://www.bp.com/subsection.do?categoryId=6932&contentId=7050724 (accessed June 18, 2009).
44. Nicole Dando and Tracey Swift, "From Methods to Ideologies," *Journal of Corporate Citizenship*, December 2002, via http://goliath.ecnext.com/coms2/gi_0199-1001798/From-methods-to-ideologies-closing.html (accessed September 3, 2009), 81.
45. Buchholz, "Auditing Social Responsibility Reports," 16–18.
46. Ibid., 19–20.
47. "Accountability," Business for Social Responsibility.
48. Buchholz, "Auditing Social Responsibility Reports," 19–20.
49. Mouton, "Chris Hani Baragwanath Hospital Ethics Audit."
50. "OCEG 2005 Benchmarking Study Key Findings," Open Compliance Ethics Group, http://www.oceg.org/Details/18594 (accessed September 3, 2009).
51. International Corporate Responsibility Survey, 2008, KPMG, http://www.kpmg.com/SiteCollectionDocuments/International-corporate-responsibility-survey-2008_v2.pdf (accessed June 17, 2009), 28.
52. International Corporate Responsibility Survey, 2008, KPMG, http://www.kpmg.com/SiteCollectionDocuments/International-corporate-responsibility-survey-2008_v2.pdf (accessed June 17, 2009).
53. Buchholz, "Auditing Social Responsibility Reports," 1.
54. Sandra Waddock and Neil Smith, "Corporate Responsibility Audits: Doing Well by Doing Good," *Sloan Management Review* 41 (2000): 75–83.

55. Buchholz, "Auditing Social Responsibility Reports," 1.
56. Waddock and Smith, "Corporate Responsibility Audits."
57. J. C. Collins and J. I. Porras, *Built to Last: Successful Habits of Visionary Companies* (New York: HarperCollins, 1997).
58. Waddock and Smith, "Corporate Responsibility Audits."

Chapter 10

1. Alan K. Reichert, Marion S. Webb, and Edward G. Thomas, "Corporate Support for Ethical and Environmental Policies: A Financial Management Perspective," *Journal of Business Ethics* 25 (2000): 54.
2. "What Happens when Countries Go Bankrupt?" *TimeTurk: English,* November 5, 2008, http://en.timeturk.com/What-Happens-when-Countries-Go-Bankrupt-10871-haberi.html (accessed June 13, 2009).
3. Alan S. Blinder, *Keynesian Economics,* Library of Economics and Liberty, http://www.econlib.org/library/Enc/KeynesianEconomics.html (accessed June 1, 2009).
4. Robert L. Formaini, "Milton Friedman—Economist as Public Intellectual," *Economic Insights,* 7, no. 2 (2002), Federal Reserve Bank of Dallas, http://www.dallasfed.org/research/ei/ei0202.html (accessed June 5, 2009).
5. E. Roy Wientraub, "Neoclassical Economics," Library of Economics and Liberty, http://www.econlib.org/library/Enc1/NeoclassicalEconomics.html (accessed June 22, 2009).
6. "North Dakota Executive Pleads Guilty to Nine Counts of Tax Fraud on Eve of Trial," May 29, 2009, http://www.usdoj.gov/opa/pr/2009/May/09-tax-533.html (accessed June 1, 2009).
7. Richard Whitely, "U.S. Capitalism: A Tarnished Model?" *The Academy of Management Perspectives* (May 2009): 11–22.
8. Thayer Watkins, "The Economy and the Economic History of Sweden," San José State University Department of Economics, http://www.sjsu.edu/faculty/watkins/sweden.htm (accessed June 22, 2009).
9. Tarun Khana, "Learning from Economic Experiments in China and India," *The Academy of Management Perspectives* (May 2009): 36–43.
10. Timothy M. Devinney, "Is the Socially Responsible Corporation a Myth? The Good, the Bad, and the Ugly of Corporate Social Responsibility," *The Academy of Management Perspectives* (May 2009): 44–56.
11. John (Jack) Ruhe and Monle Lee, "Teaching Ethics in International Business Courses: The Impacts of Religions," *Journal Of Teaching In International Business,* 19, no. 4 (2008); Andrew Wilson, editor, *World Scripture: A Comparative Anthology of Sacred Texts,* A project of the international religious foundation (Paragon House: New York, 1995), ISBN: 1-55778-723-9.
12. "Global Roundup," *International Business Ethics Review* (Spring/Summer 2005): 17.
13. The Principles for Responsible Management Education, http://www.unprme.org/the-6-principles/index.php (accessed June 22, 2009); The United Nations Global Compact, http://www.unglobalcompact.org/ (accessed June 22, 2009).
14. Neil King, Jr., "WTO Panel Rules Against Law on U.S. Punitive Import Duties," *Wall Street Journal,* June 18, 2002, A2.
15. Emad Mekay, "Trade: U.S. Defies WTO Ruling on Duties," Inter Press Service, http://www.ipsnews.net/interna.asp?idnews=25307 (accessed June 22, 2009).
16. Dionne Searcey, "U.S. Cracks Down on Corporate Bribes," *The Wall Street Journal,* May 26, 2009, http://online.wsj.com/article/SB124329477230952689.html (accessed June 22, 2009).
17. "Blow the Whistle—No Wait: Ethics Hotlines May Be Illegal in Europe," *Business Ethics* (Fall 2005): 10.
18. Ethics Office News, Xerox, http://www.xerox.com/about-xerox/citizenship/ethics/enus.html (accessed June 21, 2009).
19. "Court Rules Against Part of Wal-Mart Code," Blog. WakeupWalMart.com, http://blog.wakeupwalmart.com/ufcw/2005/06/court_rules_aga.html, accessed June 22, 2009.
20. Anup Shah, "Consumption and Consumerism," *Global Issues,* September 3, 2008,. http://www.globalissues.org/issue/235/consumption-and-consumerism (accessed June 22, 2009).
21. Keith Bradsher, "China Losing Taste for Debt From U.S." *The New York Times,* January 7, 2009, http://www.nytimes.com/2009/01/08/business/worldbusiness/08yuan.html (accessed June 22, 2009).
22. Karen Stein, "Understanding Consumption and Environmental Change in China: A Cross-national Comparison of Consumer Patterns," *Human Ecology Review*; 16, no. 1 (Summer 2009): 41–49.
23. Louisa Lim. "In China, A Roaring Debate Over Hummer," National Public Radio, All Things Considered, June 9, 2009, http://www.npr.org/templates/story/story.php?storyId=105168900 (accessed June 22, 2009).
24. Bay Fang and Thomas Omestad, "Spending Spree," *U.S. News & World Report,* 140 no. 16 (May 1, 2006).
25. "China Mobile Internet Marketplace to Reach CNY 14.88 bn," TMC News, June 18, 2009, http://www.tmcnet.com/usubmit/2009/06/18/4232826.htm (accessed June 21, 2009).
26. Eric Bellman, "New Indian Middle Class Gets Caught In the Whirlwind of Revolving Credit," *The Wall Street Journal,* October 28, 2008, http://online.wsj.com/article/SB122515009213974167.html (accessed June 22, 2009).
27. Subhash Agrawal, "India's Premature Exuberance," *The Wall Street Journal,* June 16, 2009, http://online.wsj.com/article/SB124513568534118169.html (accessed June 22, 2009).
28. Maryam Niamir Fuller, KEYNOTE SPEECH: The Global Social and Ethical Context of Sustainable Land Management, UNDP/GEF Pub, September 4, 2007, http://www.energyandenvironment.undp.org/undp/index.cfm?DocumentID=6445&module=Library&page=Document (accessed June 20, 2009).
29. "How Much of the World's Resource Consumption Occurs in Rich Countries?" Earth Trends, http://earthtrends.wri.org/updates/node/236 (accessed June 22, 2009); "The Global Sustainability Challenge," http://www.globalsustainabilitychallenge.com/ (accessed September 4, 2009).
30. Matt Villano, "Office Space: Career Couch; The Separation of Church and Job," *The New York Times,* February 5, 2006, http://query.nytimes.com/gst/fullpage.html?res=9C0CE7D8163EF936A35751C0A9609C8B63 (accessed June 22, 2009).
31. "Global Trade Union Rights Situation Worsening," 2009 ITUC Annual Survey of Trade Union Rights Violations, http://survey09.ituc-csi.org/ (June 22, 2009).
32. David Barboza, "McDonald's in China Agrees to Unions," *The New York Times,* April 10, 2007, http://query.nytimes.com/gst/fullpage.html?res=9D00E6DC153FF933A25757C0A9619C8B63&n=Top/Reference/Times%20Topics/Subjects/F/Fringe%20Benefits (accessed June 16, 2009).
33. David G. Savage, "AT&T Wins Court Case Over Maternity Leave," *Los Angeles Times,* May 19, 2009, http://articles.latimes.com/2009/may/19/nation/na-court-pregnancy19 (accessed June 22, 2009).
34. Bob Sullivan, "La Difference' Is Stark in EU, U.S. Privacy Laws" MSNBC.com, October 19, 2006, http://www.msnbc.msn.com/id/15221111/ (accessed June 22, 2009).
35. Loretta Chao, "China Squeezes PC Makers," *The Wall Street Journal,* June 8, 2009, http://online.wsj.com/article/SB124440211524192081.html (accessed June 8, 2009).
36. Anup Shah, "Health Issues," *Global Issues,* October 27, 2008, http://www.globalissues.org/issue/587/health-issues (accessed June 22, 2009).

37. Jeff Aronson, "Dying For Drugs," *British Medical Journal*, May 3, 2003, http://www.pubmedcentral.nih.gov/articlerender.fcgi?artid=1125906 (accessed June 22, 2009).
38. Robert Pear, "Obama Push to Cut Health Costs Faces Tough Odds," *The New York Times*, May 12, 2009, http://www.nytimes.com/2009/05/12/us/politics/12health.html (accessed September 4, 2009); John McCormick and Bruce Japsen, "Obama Tells AMA US Health-Care Costs Are a 'Ticking Time Bomb'," *The Chicago Tribune*, June 15, 2009, http://www.commondreams.org/headline/2009/06/15-9 (accessed June 20, 2009).
39. Reed Abelson, "While the U.S. Spends Heavily on Health Care, a Study Faults the Quality," *The New York Times*, July 17, 2008, http://www.nytimes.com/2008/07/17/business/17health.html?scp=2&sq=U.S.%20Healthcare&st=cse (accessed June 20, 2009).
40. "Germany: Development of the Health Care System,". Country Database, http://www.country-data.com/cgi-bin/query/r-4924.html (accessed June 20, 2009).
41. Dan Butterfield, "China's 'Sticky Floor' Gender Pay Differences," *The McKinsey Quarterly*. May 15, 2009, http://www.mckinseyquarterly.com/Chinas_sticky_floor_2354 (accessed September 4, 2009).
42. Don Wells, "Global Unions—Challenging Transnational Capital through Cross-Border Campaigns," edited by Kate Bronfenbrenner, *British Journal of Industrial Relations* 47, no. 2 (June 2009): 448–451.
43. Jonathon Weisman and Joann S. Lublin, "Obama Lays Out Limits on Executive Pay," *The Wall Street Journal*, February 17, 2009, http://online.wsj.com/article/SB123375514020647787.html (accessed June 21, 2009).
44. Deborah Solomon and Mark Maremont, "Bankers Face Strict New Pay Cap," *The Wall Street Journal*, February 14, 2009, http://online.wsj.com/article/SB123457165806186405.html (accessed June 21, 2009).
45. Joann S. Lublin, "More Directors Are Cutting Their Own Pay," *The Wall Street Journal*, March 16, 2009, http://online.wsj.com/article/SB123698734278425765.html (accessed June 21, 2009).
46. "China Orders Finance Executives to Cut Pay," AOL News Australia, April 09, 2009, http://www.aol.com.au/news/story/China-orders-finance-executives-to-cut-pay/1900051/index.html (accessed June 21, 2009).
47. *A Global Alliance Against Forced Labour: Global Report Under the Follow-Up to the ILO Declaration on Fundamental Principles and Rights at Work 2005*, Yale Global Online, http://www.yaleglobal.yale.edu/pdfs/globalalliance.pdf (accessed June 20, 2009).
48. Marka Hansen and Thomas Harkin, "Gap's Message On Child Labor," *WWD: Women's Wear Daily*, June 2, 2008, 195(124): 18.
49. Stora Enso's 2008 Sustainability Report to Shareholders, http://www.storaenso.com/media-centre/publications/sustainability-report/Documents/Sustainabilty%20Performance%202008.pdf (accessed June 20, 2009).
50. Remarks by U.S. Treasury Secretary Henry M. Paulson, Jr. on the U.S., the World Economy and Markets before the Chatham House, Press Room: U.S. Department of Treasury, HP-1064, June 2, 2008, http://www.treas.gov/press/releases/hp1064.htm (accessed June 21, 2009).
51. "Global Roundup," *International Business Ethics Review* (Spring/Summer 2005): 17.
52. "'One World, One Forest'; The World Trade Organization," American Lands Alliance, http://www.americanlands.org/forestweb/world.htm (accessed March 7, 2003).
53. Paul Burnham Finney, "The Perils of Bribery Meet the Open Palm," *New York Times*, May 17, 2005, Global Policy Forum, http://www.globalpolicy.org/nations/launder/general/2005/0517bribery.htm (accessed June 22, 2009).
54. John W. Miller, "WTO Details Rising Protectionism, Pushes Countries to Reverse Course," *The Wall Street Journal*, March 26, 2009, http://online.wsj.com/article/SB123808014186248481.html (accessed June 21, 2009).
55. Peter Waldman, "Unocal to Face Trial over Link to Forced Labor," *The Wall Street Journal*, June 13, 2002, B1, B3.
56. "Ethics in the Global Market," Texas Instruments, http://www.ti.com/corp/docs/company/citizen/ethics/market.shtml (accessed June 21, 2009).
57. Business for Social Responsibility, http://www.bsr.org (accessed June 21, 2009).
58. Mauro F. Guillén and Esteban García-Canal, "The American Model of the Multinational Firm and the "New" Multinationals From Emerging Economies," *The Academy of Management Perspectives* (May 2009): 23–25.

INDEX

Page numbers followed by a "t" or "f" indicate that the entry is included in a table or figure.

B

C

G

H

I

J

Q

R

S